The Social Reality
of Ethnic America

Wingning Pang

THE SOCIAL REALITY OF ETHNIC AMERICA

EDITED AND WITH INTRODUCTIONS BY

Rudolph Gomez
General Editor
University of Texas, El Paso

Clement Cottingham, Jr.
University of Pennsylvania

Russell Endo
University of Colorado, Boulder

Kathleen Jackson
University of Washington

D. C. HEATH AND COMPANY

Lexington, Massachusetts Toronto London

1974

Copyright © *1974 by D. C. Heath and Company.*

Published simultaneously in Canada.

Printed in the United States of America.

International Standard Book Number: 0-669-84111-0

Library of Congress Catalog Card Number: 73-10653

PREFACE

The literature on the subject of ethnic groups in the United States has grown in almost geometric progression over the past decade. Why then, contribute another volume to that growth? It is our judgment that so much has been written on the subject in the past ten years that students who wish *to begin their* study of ethnic groups in America are hard pressed to know where to begin.

The purpose of this book is to identify four of the major ethnic groups found in the United States today and to present an overview of their activities in such a way that the student will be able to perceive the configuration of each group as it is revealed by its size, its attitudes, its grievances, its activities, and its leaderships.

Hopefully, the student will be able to use the book not only to obtain basic information about each of these groups but also to make comparisons among and between the groups. Such analyses should be helpful in formulating tentative conclusions and generalizations about ethnic groups in the United States. Whether such formulations will stand the test of subsequent empirical inquiry is for each individual reader to determine. If this book serves as a stimulus for readers to delve further into the more specialized literature available for each group, then it will have served a most worthwhile purpose.

The format of the book is such that it may be used in a general liberal arts context as well as in more specialized departmental or interdisciplinary programs. Our hope is that the interdisciplinary nature of the articles is broad enough to be useful to students already majoring in a discipline as well as to students who are looking about for a discipline in which to major.

Each of the editors owes intellectual and scholarly debts to a variety of teachers, scholars, and researchers who have assisted in influencing their own intellectual development and behavior. We thank each of those collectively rather than singly for fear of leaving out some deserving of inclusion. We do, however, wish to thank Barbara Hamelburg, editor at D. C. Heath and Company, for her support and encouragement. Ken Dolbeare of the University of Washington also deserves special thanks for his initial and continuing support of the project.

RUDOLPH GOMEZ
CLEMENT COTTINGHAM, JR.
RUSSELL ENDO
KATHLEEN JACKSON

CONTENTS

INTRODUCTION

RUDOLPH GOMEZ

It is estimated that there are at least eight major constellations of ethnic or racial minority groups living in the United States today.[1] Seven of the eight are readily identifiable by physical characteristics which set them apart from the dominant white majority of Americans whose appearances are considered to be the "normal" ones. The one characteristic that black, Indian, Japanese, Chinese, Filipino, Puerto Rican, and Mexican minorities share is that their appearance alone is sufficient to call attention to their "different-ness."

It is the theme of this book that that "different-ness" in appearance has led to discriminatory treatment of racial and ethnic minorities by dominant white majorities. A bare outline of this theme was formulated by two anthropologists who interpreted data gathered for a UNESCO study on world minorities. They found:

> (1) Minorities are *subordinate segments* of complex state societies; (2) minorities have special physical or cultural traits which are held in *low esteem* by the dominant segments of the society; (3) minorities are self-conscious units bound together by the special traits which their members share and by the *special disabilities* which these bring; (4) membership in a minority is transmitted by a rule of descent which is capable of affiliating succeeding generations even in the absence of readily apparent physical or cultural traits. . . .[2]

More documentation of our theme is to be found in the selections that make up the body of this book.

The intent of the editors of this collection of readings was to inform beginning students about a particular ethnic group as it appeared in the literature of most of the social sciences. Thus, articles prepared by sociologists, psychologists, political scientists, and anthropologists are to be found here.

Each collection of articles was prepared by a social scientist who is a member of, and/or professionally associated with, the minority group being considered. The fact that the editors represent different academic disciplines accounts, in part, for the variety of articles collected. Also responsible for some of the variety is the fact that the state of knowledge about ethnic groups varies considerably in the existing literature. Thus the Afro-American editor had the difficult problem of selecting a representative collection from a rich and extensive literature in contrast to the Mexican-American editor who tried to present a total picture although some of the most recent articles on political activism were not available for reprinting. Nevertheless, each editor sought to offer beginning students a comprehensive account of the ethnic group of his concern and interest.

The four specific minority groups were chosen because they are the oldest and most populous; they represent four different introductions to the white culture—slavery, conquest, immigration, and annexation; and their amply documented experiences provide a means for comparing the treatment by the dominant society. Although we acknowledge that a finding, conclusion, or generalization about one ethnic group in the United States is not necessarily transferable and applicable to another, we do argue that some observations may be applicable to or symptomatic of the relationship between dominant groupings and all, or most, minority ethnic groups in the United States. To illustrate, we believe that the problems faced by Mexican Americans due to language barriers also apply to other Spanish-speaking groups such as Puerto Ricans and Cubans. And, probably, the problems encountered by Japanese Americans will be familiar to other Asian-originated groups. The point is not that the four groups selected for treatment here are more "significant" than those excluded. It is that, in the United States, each minority that can be identified easily—by skin color, shape of eyes, or some other physical characteristic—has undergone similar experiences; and, thus, what can be said about one group's experiences is applicable to other groups as well.

In order to test the assertion that the groups to be discussed here—the Afro-American, American Indian, Japanese-American, and Mexican-American —can represent the other ethnic minorities to be found in the United States, we must answer the following question: What similarities in experience have been shared by all ethnic minority groups in the United States?

PREJUDICE AND DISCRIMINATION

The most common experience shared by members of identifiable ethnic minorities in the United States has been the prejudice and discrimination directed towards them by members of the dominant white majority. If there are any who still doubt the existence of racial prejudice and discrimination in the United States—particularly after living through the 1960's—they are encouraged to read on below and to consult such standard works as Theodore Becker and Vernon Murray's *Government Lawlessness in America* [3] and Richard Hofstadter and Michael Wallace's *American Violence: A Documentary History*.[4] The fact that members of the four ethnic groups studied here have shared the experience of racial prejudice and discrimination endows them with a view of American government, culture, society, and economy that is distinct from the view held by members of the dominant majority. For members of these groups, government is not an ally to be trusted or turned to in times of trouble—too often in the past government has been an ally of those who have practiced racial discrimination. In addition to acting as ally to those who practiced racial discrimination, the American government has, in the past, itself practiced racism either directly or indirectly. Evidence of governmental racism can be seen as early as Article I, Section 2 of the Constitution, which reads, in part: ". . . Representatives and direct Taxes shall be apportioned among the several states . . . according to their respective numbers . . . and *excluding Indians* not taxed, [and] *three fifths of all other Persons*. . . ." [5]

To support the argument that a policy of racism has been openly supported by state and national governments in America, we have only to recall the legal slavery of blacks until the Civil War, or consider what amounts to their illegal slavery today by practices—which these governments seem unable, or unwilling to eliminate—that perpetuate racism in, for example, suburban housing [6] and public education financing systems.[7] Wartime-inspired racism shunted thousands of loyal Japanese Americans into concentration-like "relocation centers"—an action the Supreme Court found constitutional for "security reasons" during World War II.[8] The forced removal of Indian tribal groups from their homelands and the restriction of these sovereign nations to reservations chosen by the federal government represents the manner in which the dominant society sought to isolate Indians and to eradicate their traditional cultures. Finally, it is argued that Mexican Americans are in fact a conquered people held in bondage by practices condoned by the state governments of Texas, New Mexico, Arizona, California, and Colorado.[9]

The fact that the American government has latterly sought to eliminate the scourge of racial prejudice and discrimination does not gainsay the tremendous damage done the system by its earlier racism or condoning of racism. Enactment of significant civil rights legislation in the mid-1960's by the national government has not yet undone the damage done the system by its acquiescence in the Supreme Court's 1896 decision in *Plessy v. Ferguson*,[10] which permitted the practice of racial segregation in American life. The upshot of this sort of governmental "flip-flopping" on the matter of racial prejudice and discrimination in America has been that members of ethnic minority groups are not disposed to put a great deal of trust in government in most matters of public life—experience has made them most wary of governmental promises and actions. Indeed one is tempted to suggest that members of most ethnic minorities in the United States would agree with a statement made recently by Vine Deloria, Jr., when he wrote: "We need a new policy by Congress acknowledging our right to live in peace, free from arbitrary harassment. . . . What we need is a cultural leave-us-alone agreement in spirit and in fact." [11]

POLITICALLY SANCTIONED RACISM— TREATIES AND DISHONOR

A second common experience—shared by members of the American Indian, Mexican-American, and, to a lesser extent, Japanese-American groups— is the manner in which the American government has manipulated treaties to the disadvantage of ethnic minority groups. Professors Jackson and Gomez cite how treaties have been formulated and *breached* to the disadvantage of the American Indians and Mexicans, while Professor Endo describes how an agreement with the Japanese government was formulated and scrupulously administered to prevent the further continued immigration of Japanese nationals to the United States.

Vine Deloria, Jr., contends that the American government has breached every treaty or agreement concluded with the Indian tribes.[12] He makes his point dramatically, and with understated irony, when he notes that:

> After Lyndon B. Johnson had been elected he came before the American people with his message on Vietnam. The import of the message was that America had to keep her commitments in southeast Asia or the world would lose faith in the promises of our country.
>
> Some years back Richard Nixon warned the American people that Russia was bad because she had not kept any treaty or agreement signed with her. . . .
>
> Indian people laugh themselves sick when they hear these statements. America has yet to keep one Indian treaty or agreement despite the fact that the United States government signed over *four hundred such treaties and agreements* with Indian tribes. It would take Russia another century to make and break as many treaties as the United States has already violated.[13]

Gomez notes that the Treaty of Guadalupe Hidalgo concluded by the United States and Mexico in 1848, after the war with Mexico, has been breached countless times.[14] Article nine of the treaty guaranteed to Mexicans residing in the territories ceded to the United States by Mexico all the rights and privileges of citizens of the United States. Presumably those rights were passed on to the descendants of the people living at the time the treaty was formulated. Yet Mexican Americans in the Southwest have not been permitted the rights of American citizens, but rather have been treated as racial inferiors, stripped of their property rights, and abused, even systematically murdered, without justice or redress.[15]

Finally, Professor Endo mentions the Gentlemen's Agreement of 1907–

1908. This agreement was a response to the desire of many Californians to end Japanese immigration into "their" state. The immediate cause of the executive agreement was an order passed by the San Francisco Board of Education in 1906, requiring all Asian-American pupils to attend a public school specially set aside for them. However, the order was directed specifically at the Japanese since the Chinese already attended a segregated school. The Japanese government regarded the order as an insult and as a suggestion of their racial inferiority.[16] The major provision of the Agreement was that the Japanese government agreed to stop issuing passports only to laborers heading for the mainland United States. This was a significant step but it did not exclude: laborers headed for Hawaiian plantations, laborers who had already been in the United States, and significantly, the brides, wives, parents, and children of laborers already in the United States. The Japanese capitalized on these loopholes, and between the 1908 Agreement and the immigration closure of 1924, 10,000 immigrants per year entered the United States, many of them the so-called picture brides. While the provisions of the Agreement were being negotiated the San Francisco School Board rescinded its school order.[17]

The experience that American Indians, Japanese Americans, and Mexican Americans have had with the United States and its treaties is one that places doubt on the sincerity and honor of the American government. Clearly that experience suggests to members of ethnic minorities that the "word" of the government is not to be taken seriously—if at all.

VIOLENCE

A third experience shared by ethnic minority groups in the United States is the violence directed towards them by the dominant majorities. Historically, state and national governments have done little to bring to justice those guilty of this violence, and have thus further undermined their own credibility with the ethnic minorities.

A book recently published on the subject of American violence reveals a history of racially induced violence dating back to 1712. In that instance, a "number of blacks along with some Indians, planned to revolt against their enslavement. . . . They managed to kill nine whites. . . . The slaves fled, but most were captured. . . . Of the . . . eighteen who were tried, some were hanged, some were tortured, some burned to death. One sentence read that the rebel was to be burned with a slow fire that he may continue in torment for eight or ten hours. . . ."[18] Professor Cottingham, in his introduction to the section on Afro-Americans, notes that racially inspired violence against blacks has continued through the ghetto riots of 1967.

The Indian wars of the nineteenth century were not manifestations of the excesses of unbridled territorial aspirations but of a deep-seated expression of cultural superiority. The degree of violence perpetrated against Indians extended well beyond the battlefield and beyond the conventions of civilized warfare. The Cheyenne Massacre of 1864 saw a contingent of the Colorado militia, under the command of Colonel J. M. Chivington, "slaughter and mutilate perhaps as many as 450 [Indian] men, women, and children. . . . Chivington later remarked that the children had to be killed because 'nits make lice.' "[19] And on December 29, 1890, 200 to 250 disarmed Indians were killed at Wounded Knee, South Dakota, by the troops of the Seventh Cavalry (General Custer's old command) under the command of Colonel James W. Forsyth.[20] Forsyth was relieved of his command, by General Nelson A. Miles, for his part in the massacre. "But Forsyth was restored by the Secretary of War, who blamed the incident entirely on the Indians, and eighteen soldiers received Congressional Medals of Honor. The massacre marked the psychic as well as physical crushing of the Sioux, the end of the Indian wars, and the completion of the white man's conquest of the Indians." [21]

Professor Endo notes the institutional violence that took place in World War II against the Japanese Americans when they were placed in relocation centers and suffered loss of property and civil rights—not to mention status and dignity as well. Professor Gomez notes in his introduction to the section on Mexican Americans that from 500 to 5,000 Mexicans were killed in the Rio Grande valley of Texas between the years 1908 and 1925; and he quotes Stan Steiner, who wrote:

> In the early 1920's the [Texas] Rangers "executed from 100 to 300 known Mexican residents of the border towns, without trials or formal charges. . . ." President Venustiano Carranza of Mexico offered evidence documenting the murder and lynching of 114 "Mexican citizens" who were "mistakenly" killed in the Rio Grande valley.[22]

It may be that physical violence toward members of ethnic minority groups is on the wane in the United States—it is much too soon to tell. The potential for racial violence will continue on into the foreseeable future or as long as there are racially associated problems such as busing to achieve racial balance in the schools, segregated housing in the inner cities and suburbs, and inadequate employment opportunities for members of ethnic minorities. Perhaps the most we can hope for is that such violence be contained in time and space to isolated occurrences and that it becomes increasingly rarer; for humans, of what ever group, seem to have an inherent intolerance for that which is "different."

THE STRUGGLE FOR SELF-DETERMINATION

Frustration of the desire for political, cultural, social, and economic self-determination is another common experience shared by ethnic minority groups. This desire for self-determination probably goes back to the time these groups first experienced the inequities of life in the new world. Certainly the first slave rebellions of the eighteenth century were motivated by the desire of the slaves to free themselves from a life in which their only role was that of showing obedience to the wishes and whims of their legal masters. The Indian wars are a melancholy chronicle of a people trying to live a life free from the strictures imposed by a self-appointed "superior" civilization. And, until just recently, Mexican Americans in the Southwest who did not "knuckle-under" to those in power paid for their temerity with their rights, their property, and often with their lives.[23]

Although we have not, of course, exhausted the shared experiences of ethnic minorities in the United States, we have demonstrated above that each group has been victimized by mindless racial discrimination and prejudice; each has experienced violence from the dominant portions of the society; each has known the bitter experience of government being used against it; and each has struggled, and continues to struggle, to surmount the disadvantages forced upon it by the social, cultural, economic, and political systems in America.

The organizational development of each ethnic group studied here is traced through its various stages, and each editor establishes several important findings. These readings show, first, that political activities occupied each group's leadership as early as the nineteenth century; that the failure of their attempts to achieve political self-determination was due to the fact that the barriers were virtually insurmountable; and that the only meaningful expression of protest seemed to be riots or other violent activity because legal avenues within the system were blocked. Gomez traces such a development for the Mexican Americans as does Cottingham. Endo and Jackson provide the same sort of history for their groups, but they do not go back as far in time as do the other two.

Secondly, the diversity of each group's leadership is revealed. None of the groups studied in this volume can be adjudged as possessing a unity of views on what the proximate goals of the group are or on how best to achieve them. Each is subdivided into factions pursuing various ends through a variety of tactics. Each group contains both militant factions and conventional types of political organizations. Each group contains a surprising number of members who are apolitical and seek only to make personal adjustments to their condition through their own private efforts. In this regard the ethnic groups can be said to be a mirror image of the larger society, which is composed, for the most part, of privately oriented persons.

LONG-TERM GOALS AND POLITICAL STRATEGIES

Finally, these selections establish that the long-term goal sought by each group is actualization of the rights contained in the Constitution of the United States. That is, the groups represented here want the Fourteenth Amendment interpreted and administered—by governments and individuals —in such a way that their members will not have to keep shouting that all they want are the rights accorded them by *their* Constitution.[24] Racial characteristics may identify members of ethnic minority groups in the United States as different, but each is as much an American citizen as is the most conventional-appearing white, Anglo-Saxon, Protestant, Mayflower-descendant to be found in the upper reaches of Boston's Brahmin society. And, in essence, that is what the current foment about ethnic groups is concerned with in the United States. Ethnic group members want to be accorded—by governments, private enterprise, and private individuals—the dignity and freedom to be different without sanctions from the dominant society. The possibility that they may never receive such treatment does not, however, curb their desire for it.

DIFFERENCES AMONG ETHNIC GROUPS

Just as there are similarities between the ethnic groups covered here, there are differences between them—they are not, however, as apparent as the similarities. The reader, by a careful comparison of the articles offered here, may detect those differences—some of which are noted below.

One of Dr. Cottingham's major themes is that blacks are pursuing greater allocations of resources by utilizing *conventional* politics. This tactic cannot be said to be one relied upon as heavily by the Indians nor the Mexican Americans. Another difference is the degree of electoral success gained by blacks and not remotely approached by the three other groups. Professor Cottingham emphasizes the various sociopolitical and cultural changes that have occurred in the historical transformation of blacks from a rural, agrarian to an urban, industrial population. Despite the current differences and greater internal social differentiation, blacks have nevertheless attained some degree of shared political goals. Cottingham suggests, through the readings, that despite increased political representation, however, black political influence is by no means sufficient to overcome the massive effects of racial stigmatization, discrimination, and concentration in unskilled occupational roles.

Paradoxically, Cottingham suggests that the recent uneven socioeconomic gains of some of the blacks, while significant, are unlikely to compensate for the historical disadvantages of being a stigmatized and economically dependent minority. Consequently, the partial, uneven black urban adaptation will probably continue to be a source of political demands and transitional strains in the next decade.

Attainment of higher education by the Japanese Americans marks still another area in which there are differences. For reasons that apparently did not apply to the Japanese, the black, Indian, and Mexican groups have not attained a relatively high (as a group) level of education. But this too is changing. Members of the last three groups are increasingly attending colleges and universities, with the blacks attending, proportionately, in greater numbers than the Indians or Mexican Americans.

The differences that remain are differences of degree. Professor Jackson, for example, notes the heterogeneity of the Indian tribes, the high infant mortality rate of American Indians, and the high levels of unemployment. Each of the groups, save possibly the Japanese American, can argue that they too suffer the identical problems and handicaps.

When the similarities and differences of each of the groups discussed are viewed, they offer vivid testimony to the hardships experienced by nonwhite minority groups living in a white society. But just as we can perceive the hardships, so too we can see grounds for optimism and hope. For each of the groups discussed has embarked on a course called "self-determination," and each is fighting to attain the same status in all walks of life that is currently enjoyed by the heretofore-dominant white majorities.

THE READINGS

It was mentioned earlier that the editors who collaborated in putting this book together are from different disciplines and orientations. Despite the differences, however, an attempt was made to select articles that would either examine a particular activity of a group or offer an overview of the group's range of concerns.

Clement Cottingham, Jr., chose the first approach in writing about black Americans. His was an extremely difficult task, given the voluminous literature on the subject. Since there is wide general knowledge of the subject, Professor Cottingham focused on the area of political activity. The articles he selected nicely demonstrate that black politics is concerned with obtaining sufficient political influence to alter the "current distribution of political roles and resources" of blacks in the United States.

Professor Cottingham is Assistant Professor of Political Science at the University of Pennsylvania. He received his Ph.D. from the University of California, Berkeley in 1969. In 1967–1968 he was on a fellowship from the Foreign Area Fellowship Program, which permitted him to study comparative politics in Senegal, Gambia, Paris, and London. His publications include articles carried in the *Berkeley Journal of Sociology*, the *Canadian Journal of African Studies*, and the *Harvard Journal of Negro Affairs*, as well as several chapters in forthcoming books.

Professor Kathleen Jackson seeks to accomplish three objectives in her section: (1) to provide an introduction to the past and current status of Native Americans in American society; (2) to provide some insights into the meaning of American democracy through the experience of one of the least privileged groups; and (3) to provide some explanations for why the conditions exist as they do and what the group is trying to do about them, given the institutional barriers which present themselves.

Dr. Jackson was awarded her Ph.D. degree in 1971 from the University of Oregon. Her doctoral dissertation was titled "A Study of Changes in Authority Relations Between American Indians and Government." She was a recipient of a Ford Dissertation Fellowship in Ethnic Studies in 1970–1971, and is the author of *The Politics of School-Community Relations* (University of Oregon, 1971) and "The Role of Voluntary Associations in the Development of the Rural Community" appearing in the *International Review of Community Development*. She is currently an Assistant Professor in the Department of Health Services in the School of Public Health and Community Medicine of the University of Washington (Seattle).

The collection of articles on the Japanese Americans was compiled by Professor Russell Endo. He points out that Japanese Americans, while becoming middle-class, have continued to experience racial discrimination. He notes that their successes are limited to a few dimensions and that the group possesses strong desires for cultural identity and community development. He argues that the successes Japanese Americans have scored mask some severe problems and minimize some of the cultural costs experienced by the group.

Professor Endo is Assistant Professor of Sociology at the University of Colorado. He will receive his Ph.D. from the University of Washington early in 1974. He has engaged in considerable research on Japanese-American and black communities and in the areas of stratification and urban sociology. His publications include *Perspectives on Black America* (co-author) and articles on ethnic studies, ethnic communities, evaluation research, and community intervention and institutional change.

Rudolph Gomez edited the Mexican-American portion of the book. He is Professor and Chairman of the Department of Political Science at The University of Texas at El Paso. He received his Ph.D. from the University of Colorado in 1963. He was the recipient of a Woodrow Wilson Fellowship in 1959–1960. He was a Fulbright-Hayes Visiting Professor of Political Science at the Catholic University of Peru in Lima in 1967. His publications include *The Peruvian Administrative System, The Changing Mexican Americans, Colorado Government and Politics* (co-author), and articles on political activity and behavior in the American West.

NOTES

1. CHARLES F. MARDEN and GLADYS MEYER, *Minorities in American Society,* 3rd ed. (New York: American Book, 1968), p. 7.
2. As cited in *ibid.,* p. 23. Emphasis added.
3. THEODORE L. BECKER and VERNON G. MURRAY, Eds., *Government Lawlessness in America* (New York: Oxford University Press, 1971).
4. RICHARD HOFSTADTER and MICHAEL WALLACE, Eds., *American Violence: A Documentary History* (New York: Random House, First Vintage Edition, 1971).
5. The phrase "other Persons" refers to black slaves. Emphasis added.
6. MARK R. ARNOLD, "Decision Nears on Whether to Force People to Integrate in Suburbia," *The National Observer* (February 8, 1971), p. 1.

7. "School Districts: Why They Are Inherently Unequal," *The New York Times*, September 5, 1971.

8. *Korematsu v. United States*, 323 U.S. 214.

9. RODOLFO ACUÑA, *Occupied America: The Chicano's Struggle Toward Liberation* (San Francisco: Canfield Press, 1972), *passim*.

10. *Plessy v. Ferguson*, 163 U.S. 537.

11. VINE DELORIA, JR., *Custer Died for Your Sins: An Indian Manifesto* (New York: Macmillan, Avon Edition, 1971), p. 34.

12. *Ibid.*, p. 35.

13. *Ibid.*, emphasis added.

14. See p. 320.

15. See p. 321.

16. THOMAS A. BAILEY, *A Diplomatic History of the American People*, 6th ed. (New York: Appleton-Century-Crofts, 1958), pp. 520–23.

17. ROGER DANIELS, *The Politics of Prejudice* (Berkeley and Los Angeles: University of California Press, 1962), pp. 31–45.

18. HOFSTADTER and WALLACE, *op. cit.*, p. 187.

19. *Ibid.*, p. 274.

20. *Ibid.*, p. 279.

21. *Ibid.*

22. STAN STEINER, *La Raza: The Mexican Americans* (New York: Harper & Row, Colophon Edition, 1970), p. 360.

23. See p. 321.

24. Section I of the Fourteenth Amendment contains the key passage of concern to ethnic group members. It reads: "All persons born or naturalized in the United States, and subject to the jurisdiction thereof, are citizens of the United States and of the State wherein they reside. No State shall make or enforce any law which shall abridge the privileges or immunities of citizens of the United States; nor shall any State deprive any person of life, liberty, or property, without due process of law; nor deny any person within its jurisdiction the equal protection of the laws."

PART I

BLACKS IN TRANSITION: AN OVERVIEW OF AFRO-AMERICANS

CLEMENT COTTINGHAM, JR.

A decade of dramatic conflict between racially distinct groups in contemporary American society, particularly between whites and blacks, has modified intergroup relations. These changes represent the cumulative outcome of the civil rights movement, black urban riots, confrontations, and political discontent during the past decade. The results are evident in the new black cultural trends, the rise of black politics, and the recent acceleration of black socioeconomic progress. The results are also evident in current racial assumptions, the wide range of racially tinged issues, and in the more racially oriented political style among many urban blacks. The pursuit of new values and the reversal, or at least modification, of traditional assumptions about the psychological costs of an integrated society, have raised uncertainty among many blacks concerning the appropriate objectives and means for achieving racial equality. The intensity and scope of these recent changes in intergroup relations have perhaps shattered, if not the castelike structure, at least the under-

NOTE: This article was supported through research funds provided by the National Science Foundation. NSF-G1-29939. Nevertheless, the views expressed here are entirely my own.

1

pinnings of American racial stratification. The Afro-Americans' rapidly changing socioeconomic status, political perceptions, and deepening racial consciousness, plus their central position as the largest racial minority, have made them the primary example of a minority in transition.

BLACK URBANIZATION

Among the many long-term factors that have contributed to this transition, black urbanization is perhaps among the most important. Throughout the twentieth century, a variety of push and pull factors have stimulated the large-scale black movement out of the rural South and into the industrial North. Since their arrival in the United States in 1619, most blacks have resided in the South. In the late 1800's, however, blacks began to migrate from the rural South. In 1910, for example, there was no city with as many as 100,000 blacks.[1] But black migration to the industrializing North rapidly increased during the first quarter of this century. With the outbreak of World War I, industrial demand for black labor increased so significantly that by 1920 there were 6 cities with black populations numbering more than 100,000. In the rural South, most blacks obtained their livelihood as agricultural laborers, farmers, planters, servants, waiters, and launderers and laundresses [2]; in the North, however, though they at first filled mainly unskilled occupations, they later, with the outbreak of World War I, entered industrial occupations.[3]

Although restricted employment opportunities, the 1890's depression, the boll weevil, and the gradual mechanization of Southern agriculture, among others, were certainly important stimuli to black outmigration, the steady expansion of employment opportunities in the industrial North was, perhaps, equally as important.[4] Congressional passage of the Immigration Control Act of 1914 reduced European immigration and provided additional incentives to black migration. Between 1910 and 1920, approximately 414,000 blacks migrated from the South; in addition, high rates of black urbanization continued during the depression years of the 1930's. In all, between 1910 and 1940, approximately 1.55 million blacks migrated northward. This level of black movement out of the South has remained high over the last three decades: between 1940 and 1970, the South lost about 1,500,000 blacks in each decade as blacks moved to the North and West in search of industrial opportunities. Table 1 illustrates the present distribution of blacks by region and inside and outside metropolitan areas.

Thus, in 1970, 53 per cent of the black population still resided in the South. Although black migration out of the South has continued, the population gain from the rate of natural increase has still been greater than the population lost through migration.[5] Nevertheless, urbanization has transformed the status of blacks: most blacks now reside in metropolitan areas and more than 54 per cent reside in central cities. In addition, the black population is predominately employed in industrial and service occupations. Today, the black population is more highly urbanized than the white and the black urban population is both younger and growing more rapidly than the white population.

The growth of the black urban population has been accompanied by certain correlates such as residential segregation. Racial prejudice often compelled blacks to reside in specifically separated urban areas. In 1912, for example, Louisville, Kentucky enacted the first housing segregation law, though informal patterns of residential segregation existed in Boston as early as 1860.[6]

According to Franklin, "The law provided that blocks containing a majority of whites were designated as white blocks; and those with a majority of Negroes were Negro blocks."[7] Although not always imposed through legal means, this pattern of black residential segregation now exists in New York,

TABLE 1. Per Cent Distribution of the Negro Population, Inside and Outside Metropolitan Areas, for Regions: 1960 and 1970

Region	Number (millions)	Total	Metropolitan [a]				Non-metro-politan
			Total	Inside Central Cities	Outside Central Cities	
Northeast: 1960	3.0	100	96	77	19	4
1970	4.3	100	96	78	19	4
North Central: 1960	3.4	100	93	81	12	7
1970	4.6	100	94	81	13	6
South: 1960	11.3	100	50	36	14	50
1970	12.0	100	56	41	15	44
West: 1960	1.1	100	94	68	26	6
1970	1.7	100	95	66	30	5

[a] Includes Middlesex and Somerset counties in New Jersey.
SOURCE: U.S. Bureau of the Census, Current Population Reports, Series P-23, No. 42, *The Social and Economic Status of the Black Population in the United States*, 1971.

Philadelphia, Chicago, and other northern cities.[8] Ironically, while recent surveys indicate that a significant increase in white acceptance of racial integration in public schools and transportation facilities since 1942, white attitudes towards residential integration have evolved much more slowly.[9] As the Taeubers have pointed out,[10] "Increasing racial residential segregation was evident in most large cities in the United States between 1940 and 1950, while during the 1950's southern cities continued to increase in segregation and northern cities generally registered modest declines." Whereas during the nineteenth century, the cities had considerable racial, ethnic, and class heterogeneity and "integration" within their boundaries, black residential segregation has gradually increased since 1920 to such an extent that several cities are now predominately black: Newark, New Jersey; Gary, Indiana; Washington, D.C.; Compton, California; among others. Other cities, such as Detroit, New Orleans, Baltimore, Cleveland, St. Louis, Philadelphia, and Chicago may soon have black majorities according to some estimates.[11] Not surprisingly, the modification in the racial composition of the northern industrial cities has been accompanied by important shifts in black political and cultural attitudes.[12] Table 2 shows the urban places with the highest proportion of blacks.

Black urbanization created the physical and social conditions supporting a range of cultural, social, and political changes in the black community. First, large-scale black urbanization has transformed the racial issue from a regional problem into a national problem in which an array of racially tinged issues and conflicts, such as black concern with the quality of urban education, the quest for quality housing, increased employment opportunities, and the eventual "integration" of blacks into American society, have increasingly become, since the 1960's, a central focus of national concern. Second, urbanization has been accompanied by increased social and political tensions within the black urban communities regarding the appropriate tactics (confrontation versus peaceful petition) and objectives (integration versus some form of racial autonomy) for attaining racial equality in a white dominated society. Thus, the movement of blacks out of the rural South and into the urban North and out of agriculture and into industry has resulted in new social and political formulations on a variety of issues of immediate concern to black Americans.

THE BLACK URBAN COMMUNITY

Afro-American social history during this period of black resettlement has been accompanied by racial stigmatization, racial riots, and trade union conflicts, all of which have influenced black urban adaptation. During the first quarter of this century, for example, racial riots occurred frequently: East St. Louis in 1917, Chicago in 1919, and Tulsa in 1919. These incidents were sparked by working-class whites who attacked blacks, causing numerous deaths and extensive urban destruction. In the typical scenario a racial incident, putatively involving a black male assault upon a white female, was followed by rampant rumors, circulated informally or in a local press. Whites reacted to such incidents by resorting to mob rampages in which numerous blacks were killed, beaten, or terrorized as occurred in the Atlanta riot in 1906, in the South Springfield, Ohio riots of 1904 and 1906, and later in the Springfield, Illinois riots of August 1908. The importance of these riots lies not only in the pattern of interracial conflicts, but also in what they reveal about the social mechanisms utilized to establish a racially stratified social order in the early years of the twentieth century as the black urban population was rapidly increasing.

Blacks responded to such incidents by forming several national protest organizations. In 1905, for example, W. E. B. DuBois, the famous black historian and sociologist, convened a black leadership conference in Niagara

TABLE 2. Thirty Places with the Highest Proportion of Negroes, by Rank: 1970, 1960, and 1950

| | | 1970 | | | | | |
| | | Negro | | | Popula-tion 18 years and Over— Per Cent Negro | 1960, Per Cent Negro | 1950, Per Cent Negro |
Rank	City and State	Per Cent of Total	Number	Total Popula-tion			
1	Willowbrook, Calif. (U)	82.3	23,616	28,705	81.5	(X)	(X)
2	Westmont, Calif. (U)	80.6	23,635	29,310	74.5	(X)	(X)
3	Washington, D.C.	71.1	537,712	756,510	65.0	53.9	35.0
4	Compton, Calif.	71.0	55,781	78,611	65.0	39.4	4.5
5	East St. Louis, Ill.	69.1	48,368	69,996	62.7	44.5	33.5
6	East Cleveland, Ohio	58.6	23,196	39,600	49.9	2.1	0.2
7	Florence-Graham, Calif. (U)	56.0	24,031	42,895	55.7	44.9	(X)
8	Highland Park, Mich.	55.3	19,609	35,444	71.2	20.9	8.4
9	Petersburg, Va.	55.2	19,914	36,103	51.0	47.2	42.2
10	Newark, N.J.	54.2	207,458	382,417	48.0	34.1	17.1
11	East Orange, N.J.	53.1	40,099	75,471	46.4	24.9	11.4
12	Gary, Ind.	52.8	92,695	175,415	48.2	38.8	29.3
13	Bessemer, Ala.	52.2	17,442	33,428	47.1	57.4	60.7
14	Greenville, Miss.	52.0	20,619	39,648	47.7	48.6	59.3
15	Atlanta, Ga.	51.3	255,051	496,973	45.9	38.3	36.6
16	Prichard, Ala.	50.5	21,005	41,578	45.9	47.1	33.5
17	Augusta, Ga.	49.9	29,861	59,864	44.5	45.0	41.0
18	Selma, Ala.	49.7	13,606	27,379	45.3	49.2	55.2
19	Vicksburg, Miss.	49.3	12,568	25,478	45.2	46.4	48.8
20	Ft. Pierce, Fla.	48.5	14,422	29,721	41.3	46.9	40.4
21	Goldsboro, N.C.	48.1	12,896	26,810	43.7	41.2	44.9
22	Baltimore, Md.	46.4	420,210	905,759	40.8	34.7	23.7
23	Charleston, S.C.	45.2	30,251	66,945	38.4	50.8	44.0
24	Chester, Pa.	45.2	25,469	56,331	39.7	33.3	20.9
25	New Orleans, La.	45.0	267,308	593,471	39.0	37.2	31.9
26	Savannah, Ga.	44.9	53,111	118,349	40.1	35.5	40.4
27	Inkster, Mich.	44.5	17,189	38,595	43.5	34.5	53.7
28	Atlantic City, N.J.	43.7	20,937	47,859	37.5	36.2	27.2
29	Detroit, Mich.	43.7	660,428	1,511,482	38.9	28.9	16.2
30	Wilmington, Del.	43.6	35,072	80,386	35.9	26.0	15.6

NOTE: Thirty places were selected from places with a total population of 25,000 or more and Negro population of at elast 10,000. Rank is according to per cent Negro in 1970.

(X) Not applicable.

(U) Denotes unincorporated place.

SOURCE: U.S. Bureau of the Census, Current Population Reports, Series P-23, No. 42, *The Social and Economic Status of the Black Population in the United States, 1971.*

Falls, Canada. DuBois represented an early strain of black militant, integrationist thought, which sought full citizenship, expanded economic opportunities, improved education and housing facilities, and equal justice in the rigid, racially segregated society of his time. Subsequently, shocked liberal Northern whites as well as blacks met in 1909 to discuss the formation of the National Association for the Advancement of Colored People (NAACP). Formed in 1910, the NAACP's philosophy was based, in DuBois's words, upon the "*claim* that racial differences between white and black in the United States offer no essential barrier to the races living together on terms of mutual respect and helpfulness." [13] The NAACP lost little time in preparing litigations. In 1910, it sought the removal of the Grandfather clause in Oklahoma's state constitution, which in 1915 the Supreme Court ruled unconstitutional. Although generally perceived in its early years as a militant racial organization, the NAACP, in effect, followed the style of other moderate, progressive movements; it pursued integrationist aims, emphasized legal reforms, and appealed to white elites.[14] In short, while the large-scale black migration represented the beginning of black integration into the urban industrial economy, the NAACP inaugurated the movement for black integration into the American political and social structure.

The NAACP, however, did not immediately exert a dominant influence over blacks. Black and white political and social attitudes in this period were instead significantly influenced by the accommodationist philosophy of Booker Taliaferro Washington, the leading black spokesman and educator of the period. Washington became famous in 1895 as *the* national black leader for his Atlanta compromise, in which he urged that "In all things that are purely social we can be as separate as the fingers, yet one as the hand in all things essential to mutual progress." He urged blacks to remain in the South, to avoid politics and racial protest, and, instead, to develop economic self-help and industrial education. He felt that slavery had so weakened blacks that economic power would be necessary before blacks could be integrated into American society. Washington's views were, of course, welcomed by whites and brought him considerable acclaim. He dined at the White House in 1901, and gained extensive financial support from southern whites and northern philanthropists. Although Washington today stands as a symbol of a self-effacing, white-appointed black leader, his ideology of racial accommodation had a considerable effect at the time upon black political style and upon the small black mulatto elite.[15] DuBois repeatedly criticized Washington's version of black capitalism or, as he called it, his businessmen's solution to racial problems in the United States: Commenting on Washington's Atlanta Compromise of 1895, DuBois wrote "Since that time four states have disfranchised Negroes, dozens of cities and towns have separated the races on street cars, 1,250 Negroes have been publicly lynched without trial, and serious race riots have taken place in nearly every southern state and several northern states. . . ." [16] Despite these criticisms of his "do for self" program Washington greatly influenced the patron-client style of black politics in the first quarter of the twentieth century, and modified elements can even be found in Garveyism.

A second strain of black political thought also emerged in the first quarter of the twentieth century. This perspective, rooted in a positive, ethnic evaluation of black culture, found its fullest expression in Marcus Garvey's Jamaica founded nationalist movement, The Universal Negro Improvement Association (UNIA), whose purpose was to unite "all the Negro peoples of the world into one great body to establish a country and government absolutely their own." [17] Garveyism, as it came to be called, represented black Zionism and drew a favorable response from frustrated southern migrants during his speaking engagements in the black urban ghettos in 1916 and 1917. A magnetic speaker and masterful political agitator, Garvey aroused the intense opposition of the black middle class, but captured the imagination of the downtrodden black urban masses. As his movement grew, he created several institutions: the Black Cross Navigation and Trading Company, the Black Star Lines, the Negro Factories Corporation, the African Legion, among others. Most importantly, Garvey had his greatest impact upon the black masses in the ideological sphere: for example, when DuBois critically described him as "a little, fat black man, ugly but with intelligent eyes and a big head," [18] Garvey repeatedly used this denigrating description to confirm his racial pride and to assert that the greatest enemy of blacks was not whites, but the light skinned mulatto elite. Though Garvey's efforts to create black institutions ultimately proved abortive, he did validate black self-esteem; indeed, the residual effects of his movement are still evident in contemporary black nationalism. Garvey's UNIA reached its peak in 1923, when, with an alleged membership of 500,000, he was convicted on dubious charges of fraud. Following his legal difficulties, his black middle-class enemies attacked him unrelentingly, demanding his immediate imprisonment or deportation. Finally, his appeal to higher courts refused, he entered the Atlanta penitentiary in February 1925. Thereafter his movement fragmented and all but collapsed.

The rise of Garvey's movement and the advent of the NAACP reveal deep, persistent political and social cleavages within the black population: integration, then as now, had come to be viewed by many blacks as the rejection of black culture and as an escape from the black community; for many blacks, it now apparently no longer means inclusion into the mainstream of American society but, in effect, the permanent imposition of white domination. As an ideal, separatism retains at least a certain symbolic appeal among some segments of the black population; yet most blacks also view it as totally politically and economically unrealistic as a possible black option. Thus the rise of the black urban population in the first three decades of the twentieth century produced enduring fundamental racial issues confronting Afro-Americans: those of integration in some form versus separation in some form. The appropriate role of cultural nationalism; the relationship between Afro-Americans, West Indians, and Africans; the quest for black capitalism as an instrument of racial, political, and economic equality; and the relationship between black elites and black masses,[19] were all issues raised in the first quarter of this century. Political cleavages on racial issues within the black population largely derive from the different reactions to racial conflict: in short, while the middle-class black integrationist responds to racial adversity by stressing black-white similarities, the working class or intellectual black separatist responds by emphasizing and validating black-white cultural dissimilarities.

CIVIL RIGHTS

The decline of Garveyism during the late 1920's and 1930's was accompanied by a similar decline in black nationalism until the gradual rise of black nationalism in the late fifties and sixties. More recently black nationalism has taken a somewhat different form under the auspices of the Nation of Islam, better known as the Black Muslims. In a sense, the Muslims are a lineal descendant of Garveyism in that they share a basic nationalist racial ideology, separatist aspirations, extensive institutional forms, and appeal to recent southern migrants. But its religious ideology, discipline, and organizational development have been to some extent more successful largely because of the more rigorous recruitment criteria, organizational distinctivness, and discipline generally required of black Muslims. Under the leadership of Elijah Muhammad and the late Malcolm X, the Muslims gradually developed an organization that is now said to number 100,000 members and to possess extensive financial resources, despite constraints upon the Muslims' growth because of their peculiar blend of Islamic religious doctrine and black cultural nationalism. The significance of the Black Muslims lies primarily in their relative success in recruiting thousands of urban blacks, the deep transformation that it produces among members, and its explicit, conscious rejection of the larger white society.

Meanwhile, the NAACP had initiated several legal suits which modified significantly constraints upon black political participation. In *Nixon v. Herdon* (1927) the Supreme Court declared a Texas statute excluding blacks from Democratic primaries null and void. In *Nixon v. Condon* (1935) the high Court nullified another Texas law giving the Democratic party executive committee the right to fix party membership criteria. Other cases, such as *Smith v. Allwright* (1944), are similar indications of the NAACP's successful efforts, despite periodic setbacks, to eradicate legal constraints upon black political participation. Other legal suits against racial discrimination in admissions to law schools and graduate schools had also gone a long way toward undermining the "separate but equal" rule instituted by the Supreme Court in *Plessy v. Ferguson* in 1896; yet, the final blow to de jure racial segregation occurred in 1954, when the Supreme Court in *Brown v. Board of Education of Topeka* ruled that racially separate public schools were not equal. The NAACP's legal actions have clearly resulted in the overturn of court decisions constraining black political rights and black participation—in juries, transportation, parks, municipal golf courses—as well as the elimination of racially motivated residential zoning and restrictive covenants. Its repeated success in the judiciary area, in fact, remains a persuasive illustration of the effectiveness of political strength and careful preparation in securing the social and political rights of blacks.

Black political influence within the Democratic party also grew during the 1940's. Under Roosevelt, blacks were appointed to the Federal government as advisors in several executive departments. Blacks also benefited from the expanded social service activities. The Civilian Conservation Corps, the Works Project Administration, and the National Youth Administration provided employment or temporary employment for thousands of blacks. Similar gains were registered under the Truman administration. In 1946, for example, Truman appointed the President's Committee on Civil Rights, which later presented numerous recommendations for eliminating racial segregation. Thus, there was a gradual assault upon institutional racism and a gradual weakening of racial segregation during the 1940's. The pace of racial desegregation quickened during the 1950's under the auspices of aggressive civil rights organizations.

Another major influence upon black social history over the last two decades has been the biracial civil rights movement. In 1942, James Farmer, who formed the Congress of Racial Equality or CORE, introduced new techniques into the struggle for racial equality: direct, nonviolent social action to develop a more comprehensive approach to racial issues. An interracial organization, CORE conducted sit-ins, lie-ins, and freedom rides aimed at eradicating racial discrimination in restaurants, schools, employment, and transportation facilities. Martin Luther King, Jr., the prominent black minister and Nobel prize winner, used similar techniques in the 1953 boycott of racially segregated buses in Montgomery, Alabama. The techniques of militant, nonviolent, direct action soon spread to other southern cities. In 1960, black students in Greensboro, North Carolina launched a sit-in at a lunch counter. The Student Non-Violent Coordinating Committee, SNCC, actively conducted voter registration campaigns in Mississippi and Alabama among poor rural blacks. In these two states, in particular, civil rights workers frequently encountered massive white resistance, even resulting in the murder of civil rights workers and prominent civil rights leaders.

In 1963, the civil rights movement began to change as white extremists exerted violent resistance. In part, the changes were related to a modification in the social basis of the civil rights movement; in 1963, urban blacks participated more actively in civil rights demonstrations in Selma, Alabama. The scale of the civil rights movement also changed when supporters marched on Washington in August 1963. Prior to this, President John F. Kennedy had proclaimed his support for black civil rights in his June 19, 1963 message to Congress when he submitted a comprehensive civil rights bill. The bill sought to outlaw racial segregation in places of public accommodation, to eliminate racial discrimination in employment, to ensure unhindered suffrage to blacks, and to end racial discrimination in housing. The civil rights legislation encountered delays; but was eventually passed, thanks to President Johnson's strong support. The Voting Rights Act, in July 1964; The Public Accommodations Act of 1965; and the Housing Act of 1968 were later passed, thus terminating legalized racial discrimination. At the same time, the civil rights movement had spread to northern cities, where it faced surprising resistance.

This resistance became manifest at a time of rising discontent in the black ghettos of Watts, Los Angeles, Newark, Detroit, Harlem, and other northern cities, where, after 1964, intense urban riots began to erupt. During the first nine months of 1967, for example, there were 104 riots in 23 cities, resulting in large numbers being killed and ·in much property destruction. The riots continued during the rest of 1967 and 1968 and were followed by black student confrontations on college campuses during 1969 and 1970.[20] The new pattern of racial confrontation and political protest reflected the breakdown of the biracial civil rights coalition and the advent of the Black Power movement. In the course of these events, the pattern of racial conflict and the civil rights ideology movement were being redefined. Blacks were no longer moving psychologically towards whites, but against them; young whites were no longer as active in the civil rights movement; and the exploitative, colonial character of black-white relations stimulated new perceptions as well as radical black demands for further changes in the American social order. The new conception of racial equality was, therefore, no longer based on middle-class faith in the American ideology, but on the contrary, upon the bitter, raw experience of urban ghetto blacks.

A major cleavage among contemporary blacks focuses centrally upon the perceived subordination of blacks to white political interests. Militant blacks, younger blacks, and others argue passionately that blacks should alter this political dependence. What is normally referred to as black separatism, Black Power, or black nationalism, signifies nothing more than an attempt to formulate a viable basis for national and local black participation by blacks. Black Power represents an expressive symbolism that structured the new attitudes, values, and group consciousness which surfaced in the wake of the civil rights conflicts and black rebellions in the late sixties. As a potential ideology, it ignited black politics, which presumed the commonality of the black interests, values, and culture among Afro-Americans. A common historical origin, a common historical oppression, common needs, and a common racial and political subordination could lead, it is argued, to a common black political organization. Two basic factors would be necessary to spawn black power: first, blacks must have the political space or territory to organize their common interests. The social and economic differentiation of blacks from whites in large cities has apparently provided one of the requisite conditions. Second, black attitudes would have to shift from vaguely defined political interests and be focused around more specific programmatic goals. In this way, Black Power has functioned as a conversion mechanism for the formation of a more coherent black coalition.

CULTURE AND COMMUNITY

Formal and informal devices that contribute to black residential segregation also reinforce distinct aspects of urban black culture or ways of perceiving reality. This culture has evolved mainly out of the black folk traditions originally developed in the rural South. Although slavery completely eradicated African social and political institutions among black Americans, the oral traditions and aesthetic perceptions of African cultures have persisted through Afro-American oral traditions and music. Despite the fact that Afro-American cuture basically derives from ancient African forms—most notably in religion, music, and some aspects of life style—contemporary black urban culture has been forged out of the separate black American leisure-time activities, life styles, family values, and religious traditions. While black ghetto residents share, with other Americans, the fundamental values of American culture, their distinctive life style, racial separation, and oral traditions have infused urban blacks with perceptions and idioms that may be imitated but not entirely duplicated in the larger white society. To analyze black culture, it is necessary to evaluate those cultural elements that are more or less unique to blacks.

The growth of the black urban population awakened new cultural expression and experimentation in literature and poetry, which crystallized in the Harlem Renaissance of the 1920's. This literature, in particular, heralded the emergence of a new racial identity among urban blacks: its major themes included the rejection of racial accommodation and oppression, a demand for social and economic equality; and was characterized by the intense efforts of the small, black, urban intellectual elite of this period to actualize or define the new urban black racial consciousness and identity. Some of the most striking characteristics of this urban culture found expression in urban music, formed out of the complex social life styles, institutions, and socialization experiences of the expanding black urban ghetto. Traditionally, the most classical elements of black culture have been expressed in black music: slave songs, plantation songs, the blues, spirituals, and jazz express the poetry of black culture. The "St. Louis Blues" and the creative literature of the Harlem Renaissance all express the dynamics of black urban life in the 1920's and early 1930's. New musical forms also accompanied the growth of the black urban population during the post-World War I period as black music and the general mood, themes, and experiences of black urban life became professionalized as urban entertainment. According to Imamu Amiri Baraka, the prominent black poet, playwright, and student of black music—formerly known as LeRoi Jones—urban blues resulted from a fusion of the southern black migrant's older country and class traditions of black music with the "new learning" (the adjustment to the conflicts and strangeness of the city) of the North.[21] The urban music that grew out of this fusion of tradition and urban context was harder, crueler, more stoical and hopeless than the folk music of the rural South. Sidran has recently argued that black music derives its innovative qualities and uniqueness from the oral traditions of black culture and that, in fact, music is a basic socializing mechanism and supportive element of black social structure.[22]

Another distinctive component of black culture centers around the idealistic ritual drama of the black church. Despite the immoral accommodation of white Christianity to slavery and racial discrimination, blacks could legitimately claim that some elements of Christian theology provided succor for a marginal and oppressed people, if not in this world, at least in the next. The emphasis of black church life is one in which dramatic style or verve dominates performance. Out of the crucible of religious emotional expression, blacks infused their church life with the content of their emotional experiences, and, in this way, found the church an indispensable mechanism for sustaining social and cultural community life; for developing early black community leadership; and, later, for developing broader social services. Moreover, whatever one may think of the persistent organizational deficiencies or periodic lapses of the "black" church as a spokesman for socioeconomic change in the black community, it performs substantial sociological functions especially in providing leadership in an otherwise frequently leaderless community. The church within the black community has, in effect, provided the black "preacher" with political skills, oratory, status, esteem, and other leadership attributes. As such, it has been a major source of black leadership among southern blacks, as in the civil rights movement. In recent years, this leadership function has in many instances provided black politicians with a political model and style, having solid appeal among the black urban masses. Further, the socioeconomic activities of black leaders such as the Rev. Jesse Jackson in Chicago, the Rev. Leon Sullivan in Philadelphia, and the Rev. Albert Cleaque in Detroit suggest that, with the growth of the black urban community, the black "preacher's" role is expanding beyond the church and into the economic sphere. In short, the black church, though it is not a uniquely black cultural expression, represents a central mechanism for sustaining and organizing the cultural and social life of the black community.

Although this synopsis obviously does not exhaust the many cultural features and styles to be found within the black community context, it does point out some of the most salient features. It should also be noted that various strata of the black population partake of black culture in different degrees. Even among those whose life remains almost entirely situated in the black urban ghetto, variations in life style and culture, according to age, sex, class, or other forms of social differentiation can be found. Nor are all blacks equally active participants in church organizations. In other words, a broad range of cultural variations exist within the black subculture, which, in turn, of course, is influenced by external socioeconomic pressures of the larger society and culture, as well as the internal dynamics and experiences of the black urban community. Thus, black culture contains many distorting adaptive elements. In recent years, the growing activities of the black theatre in New York, Cleveland, Newark, and to a lesser extent Chicago, and the vibrant interest in black poetry, as well as the emergence of "black" movies, is indicative of the extensive mechanisms now involved in black cultural expression. The accelerated growth of the black urban population has thus provided new incentives and support for an increased range of black cultural activities.

In summary, while black culture shares fundamental values with the larger American culture, it possesses unique features which express the particular needs, purposes, and emotional life of the black urban community. In form, black culture is most unique in its musical and oral innovations, which derive from the persistence of the southern folk tradition. By and large, these cultural forms express the inner emotional life of blacks. Most, yet not all, blacks share elements of black culture—which is probably most widely shared among urban blacks, particularly the working and lower class blacks who remain the principal carriers of black southern folk and musical traditions. This culture exhibits its most dynamic and purest forms in situations where blacks remain relatively separate from whites; that is, the cultural building process among blacks occurs in large residential locations where blacks "relate" not to whites, but to one another. Both the size of the black minority and its growing residential segregation in black urban ghettos has enabled blacks to develop more extensive institutional mechanisms of cultural expression. Consequently, some aspects of black culture, especially its musical expressions, have been assimilated into the larger American society, and indeed, into parts of Europe and Africa as well.

The transitional character of the black urban population is also reflected in recent socioeconomic status changes. Accentuating the positive, Wattenberg and Scammon contend in a recent article that on the whole blacks have made remarkable progress in the past decade and that, in fact, a majority of blacks have now entered the "middle class." [23] This contention is based on a partial analysis of the 1970 census and other statistics which attempt to demonstrate (a) that while white family incomes increased by 69 per cent over the past decade, income for black families increased 99.6 per cent; (b) and that the percentage of black families earning more than $10,000 grew from 13 per cent in 1961 to 31 per cent in 1971. In addition to increases in black family income, Wattenberg and Scammon report that unemployment rates for married black men, 20 years and over, dropped by 53 per cent between 1962 and 1972, compared to the unemployment rate for whites of similar status and age. Blacks also registered significant gains in the skilled craftsmen categories, in median years of schooling for blacks, aged 25–29, and in the percentage of blacks enrolled in college. The Wattenberg and Scammon analysis concentrates in large part upon the younger, more stable black families, emphasizing that these categories of the black population have indeed recorded, as other studies have reported, significant socioeconomic gains in the past decade.

Nevertheless, the Wattenberg and Scammon data also reveal persistent signs of disintegration among other significant segments of the black population. For example, black female-headed households climbed from 22.4 per cent of all black families in 1960 to 30.1 per cent in 1972. Consequently, nearly a third of all black families are now headed by females; and, in 1971, more than 54 per cent of these families were living below the official poverty level. Moreover, the incidence of black, female-headed families among the poor has increased substantially in recent years. As Wattenberg and Scammon report, "by 1971 six in ten black families in poverty were female headed. As male-headed families exited from the poverty class, female-headed families entered it in growing numbers." Although some blacks have apparently improved their socioeconomic status over the past decade, the socioeconomic status of many others declined both relatively and absolutely.

Though Wattenberg and Scammon have heralded the overall progress of blacks during the past decade as "revolutionary," many blacks are perhaps likely to be less sanguine about such ambiguous trends and the increasing black residential segregation in job-declining urban areas. Though the growth of the black urban population raises the specter of black-majority cities, the cities no longer provide the same mobility opportunities or political influence they conveyed upon past minorities. Indeed, the late arrival of southern black migrants in the cities has coincided with and stimulated the departure of middle-class whites from the cities to the outer urban fringe, depriving the city of much-needed fiscal resources. As the *Report of the National Advisory Commission on Civil Disorders* noted in 1968: "Since World War II especially, America's urban-industrial society has matured; unskilled labor is far less essential than before, and blue-collar jobs of all kinds are decreasing in number and importance as a source of new employment." [24] In other words, manufacturing firms are now rapidly exiting to predominantly white suburbs: these firms might have supplied additional jobs for unskilled blacks, to replace the growing managerial, technical, urban industrial employment opportunities for which most unskilled urban black workers are at present inadequately equipped.[25] Blacks thus lack the broad access to a dynamic urban-industrial economy which in an earlier era provided increasing income; expanding employment opportunities; more modern life styles; and, generally, higher socioeconomic status for poor white, urban immigrants.

Despite recent gains in socioeconomic mobility among some middle-class blacks, there are legitimate doubts about whether working-class blacks will share in these gains. Indeed, a recent study of black labor and the political economy of racism by Harold M. Baron presents persuasive evidence that urban industrialists recruited the new black urbanites into a secondary labor market during the first quarter of the twentieth century.[26] Since then, the urban black working force has been largely relegated to a subordinate labor position involving the most unpleasant labor tasks, lower earnings, slower promotions, and cyclically induced layoffs. Black political awareness of and discontent with the dual labor market, dual housing market, and dual educational system—which systematically and severely constrain black socioeconomic opportunities—has become increasingly manifest in the widespread black fears about their survival in an accelerated technologically oriented economy. This survival component of black political thought,[27] extended into the political sphere, generates political demands which exert special pressures upon black politicians. In their efforts to respond to these issues, black political leaders must operate in a crisis atmosphere which infuses black politics with a distinctive content.

READINGS

This brief overview provides an introduction to the recent migration, history, and culture of Afro-Americans, and a background for the selected readings. The first reading, "The New Negro," by Nathan Huggins, traces the cultural expressions, militancy, and search for definition that appears in the writings of the Harlem Renaissance figures during the 1920's. Nathan Irvin Huggins is Professor of History at Columbia University. He formerly taught at California State College at Long Beach, Lake Forest College in Illinois, the University of Massachusetts in Boston, and the University of California at Berkeley. He is also the author of *Protestants Against Poverty* and, most recently, co-editor of *Key Issues in the Afro-American Experience*.

The second reading, "Political Change in the Negro Ghetto," by Martin Kilson, provides an overview of the political and sociological changes in the community structures and political styles that emerged among urban blacks during the first part of the twentieth century. His second article, "Politics of Black Ethnicity," focuses on more contemporary changes in black political resources, such as the rise of black militancy, the mass-oriented black political style, leadership differentiation, and enlarged political leadership group, which have, in turn, contributed to increased black political representation at the federal, state, and local government levels. Martin Kilson is Professor of Government at Harvard University and has written widely on both African and Afro-American politics.

The third reading, "Minority Group Psychology: Implications for Social Action," by Alvin F. Poussaint, outlines the negative effects of white racism upon black self-esteem and the various stages of black adaptation to it. Alvin F. Poussaint, is Associate Professor of Psychiatry and Associate Dean of Students at the Harvard Medical School. He has contributed numerous articles which have appeared in *The New York Times Magazine*, *The Black Scholar*, *The Journal of Pediatrics*, and *The Journal of Psychiatry*. The next article, "The Myth of Coalition," by Stokely Carmichael and Charles V. Hamilton, defines the conditions for independent black coalitions and points up the severe limitations of biracial coalition politics. Stokely Carmichael is a former civil rights activist and Pan-African nationalist, who has recently returned from Guinea after several years of study with the late Kwame Nkrumah, the former President of Ghana. Charles V. Hamilton is Professor of Political Science at Columbia University. His most recent book, *The Black Preacher in America*, was published in 1972. The final article, "The Election of Blacks to City

Councils: . . . ," by John Kramer, reports on the growth of black representation in several major cities in the late 1960's. John Kramer is Professor of
Sociology and Director of the Project for Suburban Studies at the State University of New York, Brockport. He is the recent editor of *North American
Suburbs: Politics, Diversity, and Change,* which appeared in 1972.

NOTES

1. For an overview of black history, see JOHN HOPE FRANKLIN, "A Brief History
   of the Negro in the United States," in John P. Davis, Ed., *The American Negro Reference Book* (Englewood Cliffs, N. J.: Prentice-Hall, 1966), pp. 1–95.
2. W. E. B. DuBOIS, "The Negro Race in the United States of America," reprinted
   from *Papers on Inter-Racial Problems Communicated to the First Universal Races
   Congress* (London: King & Son, 1911).
3. J. D. ABERBACH and J. L. WALKER, *Race and the City* (Boston: Little, Brown),
   pp. 7–12.
4. REYNOLDS FARLEY, "The Urbanization of Negroes in the United States," *Journal
   of Social History* 1 (Spring 1968), pp. 241–58.
5. *Ibid.*
6. LEO F. SCHNORE and PETER R. KNIGHTS, "Boston in the Ante-Bellum
   Period," in Stephan Thernstrom and Richard Sennett, Eds., *Nineteenth-Century
   Cities* (New Haven and London: Yale University Press, 1969), pp. 247–57.
7. FRANKLIN, *loc cit.*
8. NATHAN KANTROWITZ, "Ethnic and Racial Segregation in the New York
   Metropolis, 1960," *American Journal of Sociology* 74 (May 1969), pp. 685–95.
9. For an overview of recent public opinion surveys on racial attitudes, see THOMAS
   F. PETTIGREW, "Attitudes on Race and Housing: A Social-Psychological View,"
   in Amos H. Hawley and Vincent R. Rock, Eds., *Segregation in Residential Areas*
   (Washington: National Academy of Sciences, 1973), pp. 21–81. Also see HUBERT
   HYMAN and PAUL B. SHEATSLEY, "Attitudes Towards Desegregation," *Scientific America* 211 (July 1964), pp. 16–23.
10. KARL E. TAEUBER and ALMA F. TAEUBER, "The Negro As an Immigrant
    Group: Recent Trends in Racial and Ethnic Segregation in Chicago," *American
    Journal of Sociology* 69 (January 1969), p. 378.
11. H. PAUL FRIESEMA, "Black Control of Central Cities: The Hollow Prize,"
    Journal of the American Institute of Planners 35 (March 1969), pp. 75–79.
12. See PETTIGREW, *op. cit.*
13. See DuBOIS, *op. cit.*
14. ROBERT ASH, *Social Movements in America* (Chicago: Markham Publishing, 1972),
    pp. 183–90.
15. See LARRY CUBAN, "A Strategy for Racial Peace: Negro Leadership in Cleveland,
    1900–1919," *Phylon* (third quarter), pp. 299–311. Also see AUGUST MEIER,
    "Booker T. Washington and the Negro Press," *Journal of Negro History* 38 (January
    1953), pp. 67–90.

16. See DuBOIS, *op cit.*, p. 363.

17. ROBERT H. BRISBANE, *The Black Vanguard* (Valley Forge: Judson Press, 1970), p. 83.

18. *Ibid.*

19. ASH, *loc cit.*

20. See MARVIN E. WOLFGANG and BERNARD COHEN, *Crime and Race* (New York: Institute of Human Relations Press, 1970), pp. 57–65.

21. See LEROI JONES, "Blues, Jazz, and the Negro," in John P. Davis, Ed., *The American Negro Reference Book* (Englewood Cliffs, N. J.: Prentice-Hall, 1966), pp. 759–65.

22. BEN SIDRAN, *Black Talk* (New York: Holt, Rinehart & Winston, 1971), p. xiii.

23. BEN J. WATTENBERG and RICHARD M. SCAMMON, "Black Progress and Liberal Rhetoric," *Commentary* 45 (April 1973), pp. 35–44.

24. *Report of the National Advisory Commission on Civil Disorders* (New York: Bantam Books, 1968), pp. 278–82.

25. For reports on the migration of industrial jobs to the urban fringe, see *U.S. Commission on Civil Rights*, St. Louis, Missouri, January 14–17, 1970, pp. 454–55.

26. HAROLD M. BARON, "The Demand for Black Labor: Historical Notes on the Political Economy of Racism," *Radical America* 5:2 (March-April 1971).

27. SAMUEL F. YETTE, *The Choice* (New York: G. P. Putnam's Sons, 1971).

The New Negro

Nathan I. Huggins

. . . The black man's metamorphosis was assumed by everyone, and thought-
ful people knew that the change would have a profound effect not only on the
American Negro but on American culture and, indeed, the multicolored world
itself. Alain Locke, a dapper, gentle, nut-brown man, a Rhodes Scholar, and
professor of philosophy at Howard University saw no limit to the transformation. He brought together a varied group of essays, stories, poems, and pictures
in *The New Negro* (1925), all searching to define what was assumed to be a
grand cultural flux. Locke's editing of and contribution to this volume and his
energetic championing of the intellectual achievement of Negroes in the
1920's made him the father of the New Negro and the so-called Harlem
Renaissance.

Locke insisted that a change in the Negro had occurred far beyond the
measurement of the sociologist. The appearance of the New Negro seemed
sudden and shocking only because the Old Negro had long since been a
shadow and fiction, perpetuated in white minds through sentimentalism and
reaction. The Negro, because he had found it paid, helped perpetuate this
fiction through protective social mimicry. "So for generations in the mind of
America, the Negro has been more of a formula than a human being—a something to be argued about, condemned or defended, to be 'kept down,' or 'in
his place,' or 'helped up,' to be worried with or worried over, harassed or
patronized, a social bogey or a social burden." Even the Negro intellectual
tended to see himself as a social problem, Locke argued. He had to make his
appeal in the face of the unjust stereotype of his enemies and the equally
questionable stereotypes of his friends. In neither case could he see himself
as he really was. "His shadow, so to speak, was more real to him than his personality." But a renewed sense of self-respect was forcing the Negro to look
at himself afresh, to reject the stereotypes and clichés, and to insist on integrity of race and personality.

As Locke saw it, the traditional and fictional view of the Negro had been
made embarrassingly obsolete by the changes in the realities of Negro life.
The migration that had pulled the Negro out of the South, putting him in
the Midwest and East, had made him an urban and industrial man. Only the
most obtuse and sentimental could continue to find "aunties," "uncles,"
"mammies," Uncle Toms, and Samboes, in modern city life.

The city made a difference, in Locke's mind, because it forced the Negro

SOURCE: From *Harlem Renaissance* by Nathan Irvin Huggins. Copyright © 1971 by Oxford
University Press, Inc. Reprinted by permission. (Footnotes omitted.)

from the simple to the complex life, from rural homogeneity to urban pluralism; he was forced to see himself in broad and sophisticated terms. Harlem
was a perfect example. Not only was it the "largest Negro community in the
world," but it brought together black men of the most diverse backgrounds
and interests. There were Africans and West Indians as well as Negroes from
the south and north of the United States. There were city men, town men,
and village men; "the peasant, the student, the business man, the professional
man, artist, poet, musician, adventurer and worker, preacher and criminal,
exploiter and social outcast. Each group has come with its own separate motives and for its own special ends, but their greatest experience has been the
finding of one another." This shared experience, Locke held, was race-building.
Until that moment, he insisted, the Negro had been a race more in name
than in fact, "more in sentiment than in experience." What had defined them
as a race was a common condition and a common problem. What was needed
to make a race, however, was a common consciousness and a life in common.
Life in the city, life in Harlem, would satisfy that need. "In Harlem," he
wrote, "Negro life is seizing upon its first chances for group expression and
self-determination. It is—or promises at least to be—a race capital." Harlem
was for the New Negro what Dublin was to the New Ireland, Prague to the
New Czechoslovakia, and Belgrade to the New Yugoslavia.

Race-building, according to Locke, was forcing the Negro to reject old
assumptions and old images. If the white man had erred in his defining the
Negro in order to justify his treatment of him, the Negro too often had found
his treatment an excuse for his condition. The new social sciences were taking
a hard look at the realities, and the intelligent Negro would welcome the hard-
eyed scientific evaluation in place of the soft and crippling judgment of the
philanthropist. All racial groups had to be weaned from some dependency, and
the Negro was no exception. Locke argued that the Negro's time had come to
free himself from the patronizing and distant philanthropy of sentimental
white society. The New Negro's race consciousness and racial cooperation were
clear indications that his time had come to be a race, to be free and self-
assertive. While expressed in racial and collective terms, Locke's view of the
New Negro was strikingly familiar, an iteration of very traditional values of
self-sufficiency and self-help, as American as the Puritans and the "self-
reliance" of Ralph Waldo Emerson. Whatever else he was then, as Locke
explained him, the New Negro was an assertion of America.

So, Alain Locke believed that the profound changes in the American Negro
had to do with the freeing of himself from the fictions of his past and the
rediscovery of himself. He had to put away the protective coloring of the
mimicking minstrel and find himself as he really was. And thus the new militancy was a self-assertion as well as an assertion of the validity of the race. The
Negro was in the process of telling himself and the world that he was worthy,
had a rich culture, and could make contributions of value. And as Locke saw
it, this new consciousness would be auspicious in two special ways. It made
the New Negro the "advance-guard of the African peoples in their contact

with the Twentieth Century civilization," and it also provided "the sense of a mission of rehabilitating the race in world esteem. . . ." He thus incorporated in his thinking the American sense of mission, a strange variation on the "white man's burden."

The New Negro's task was to discover and define his culture and his contribution to what had been thought a white civilization. In Locke's words, the Negro "now becomes a conscious contributor and lays aside the status of a beneficiary and ward for that of a collaborator and participant in American civilization." Thus, the considerable talents of the Negro could be released from the "arid fields of controversy and debate to the productive fields of creative expression." So it was to be through a cultural awakening that the Negro was to express himself. Locke could not promise that the race would win the long-desired end of material progress, but the enrichment of life through art and letters would be an ample achievement. What is more, the Negro would be a people rather than a problem. Echoing the words of Van Wyck Brooks, who ten years earlier had searched to find value in white American culture, Alain Locke announced the New Negro as the race's "spiritual Coming of Age."

It was no mere coincidence that both Alain Locke and Van Wyck Brooks saw crisis in terms of cultural maturity. Americans have been consistently perplexed as to what culture is, what is distinctively American culture, and what of value America has contributed to Western civilization. Concern over the thinness of American culture forced many intellectuals to give continued backward glances to Europe. Sometimes the American's consciousness of Europe was ridiculed, as in the probing satire of Mark Twain, sometimes it was marked by a fascination with its richness, sophistication, and corruption, as with Henry James. Always, it seemed culture was something alien to the fresh and rough American; always something learned, attained, achieved, never the natural gift of one's soil, one's land, one's blood.

Malcolm Cowley has made this point very well in *Exile's Return*. In its early pages Cowley explains why a group of young intellectuals around World War I felt no sense of value in their own experience and past. All of their education, as Cowley remembers, pointed them toward some other place than home. They were trained out of their regional dialects and into a colorless, school-learned Ameri-English which all of their teachers had dutifully acquired. The stuff of imagination, art, and literature was never pulled from the mysteries of their own country and the experiences of their own people. Rather, they were asked to dream of medieval European castles and English country life. It was as if the things that they could touch and see were unworthy of art and culture. Then, they were drawn to eastern colleges; fitting-rooms of culture, as Cowley remembers. Culture to the educated American had nothing to do with folk roots—one's past or one's life—rather, it was clothes that one could wear after a long process of divestment of the familial, the regional, the natural. Thus Cowley makes most understandable the feeling of uprootedness and alienation of the generation of young men who were in college, or had just finished college, around World War I. Set adrift from a past without meaning or value, or so their education had trained them to believe, they went searching for some roots in European civilization grafting themselves on to the only culture America had taught them to respect.

If anything, this alienation was more accentuated among Negro intellectuals. There had been little in the public schools or the colleges to give them a sense of their cultural past or the distinctiveness of their people. The black boy or girl who went to mixed northern schools and to white colleges could have expected little. But even the segregated southern schools provided little of their own past besides the names of heroines and heroes: Harriet Tubman, Sojourner Truth, Frederick Douglass, and of course Booker T. Washington. The fact that the line back to the past was snarled where enslavement and migration from Africa had begun made the racial past hazy, distant, and impossible to know. But even the more recent history of the Afro-American, that which could be touched and measured, seemed to provide little of the stuff for race-building. A society weaned on self-reliance and individual freedom could find little to honor in servitude, no matter how enforced. The shame that black men felt about their past was a measure of how much they had drunk up the values of the white American world around them. So they were left with the few names that had survived of the men and women who had defied oppression, achieved success in white men's terms, and who stood thus as proof that the past would not enslave blacks forever.

Shame of the past made the Negro reject much of the reality of his people's condition. In the mad rush from slavery, inferiority, and oppression into citizenship and manhood, much was garbled and confused. Those things reminiscent of the former condition—unskilled and field labor, enthusiastic religion—were to be denied. The professions (medicine, dentistry, law, the ministry, teaching, and undertaking) and business were to be embraced. One was to join the more sober Protestant denominations. It was not simply a matter of achievement or social mobility, these attainments were bench-marks measuring the distance a black man or woman had traveled from his past of chains. They were symbols which connoted to the Negro freedom and manhood. And they were not just in a few men's minds; they were built into those institutions, most of all the schools, charged with the impress of social values.

Of course, white schools transmitted "American culture," an ethnic cultural blandness—America was made up of many different peoples, but they were all the same. When the black child was well treated in such schools— not made to feel shame for his blackness—he was taught that he was like everyone else; a truth that his experience surely belied. And while Negro schools had many virtues in teaching the child that he had worth, they taught him also that he should be like white men, not like himself, and surely not like his father. It did not matter whether the teacher followed W. E. B. DuBois's philosophy of the "talented tenth" or Booker T. Washington's even more condescending notion that the Negro should prove himself acceptable as a citizen in white men's terms.

The point is not that teachers and schools were misguided or pernicious. White and black teachers gave many a young Negro his first feeling of genuine, personal worth. Rather, despite their best intended efforts they could not give to the black child a rich, dense, and mysterious sense of a past like that of traditional cultures. It was not merely that the ingredients were difficult to pull out of the American Negro's history, and that the sophistication and beauty of African cultures were not yet understood, but that the experience of American institutions worked against it. The object of American public schools was to make their charges American; which meant a rounding off of points of difference. Oriental and Jewish children were able to retain the gift of their past through special schools. But Negro children were swept into the cultural blender with other Americans, pulled into the vortex of Anglo-Saxon norms. Having no known culture to deny, the Negro was doubly damned. For when he discovered the emptiness and soulessness of the bland amalgam, or when he saw that the ultimate truth of the lie was that you had to be white, he had no place to return to. Adrift, his "shadow, so to speak, was more real to him than his personality."

Like white children, black children were taught that the speech of their fathers was not proper English speech. They were encouraged to leave behind their dialects and regional and ethnic idioms. The tales that they had heard the old folks tell were not the stuff of culture; they would read Jane Austen and Thackeray and dream of English romance. Nor were the special rhythms of their speech suitable for poetry when Keats and Shelley were the models. In time, they could learn to accept the spirituals, with their decorum and simple majesty, but never the more spirited gospel songs and surely not the profane blues. Culture was something distant and alien—generally English— to be studied, and, as Cowley remembers, fitted on like a suit of clothes. Negroes in provincial communities were introduced into Western culture by their churches. Vocal ensembles toured these towns, as well as soloists like Roland Hayes and Marian Anderson. Church members would sell tickets to a performance which would include the standard tour repertory with some spirituals. Local talent would be given a chance to perform, and there was always an elocutionist who would read from classical English literature. One would not have been surprised to find Browning Societies here and there in black communities. Of course, the experience of the people had been there all along. The folk wisdom that had sustained Afro-Americans through their most devastating trials persisted. The music in the language, the distinctive folk imagery, the drama of religion, the essential delight in music remained. In a very vital and real way, that folk culture and tradition was undergoing the genuine alchemy of art. Work songs, gospels, and hollers were being trans- formed into blues, ragtime, and jazz. But, strangely, although black intel- lectuals were quick to acknowledge the contribution of black music to

American culture—the only distinctive American contribution as it was often put—they were rarely willing to claim it was *serious* music of high culture. And while many Harlem intellectuals enjoyed the music of the cabarets, none were prepared to give someone like Jelly Roll Morton the serious attention he deserved. Jazz was infectious entertainment and not an ingredient of high civilization. So, provincialism pulled the black intellectual—like his white American brother—away from the culture of his experience into the culture of his learning.

Since culture was not something that could be taken for granted, the announcement of its attainment by both white and black Americans seemed natural enough. The vogue of the New Negro, then, had all of the character of a public relations promotion. The Negro had to be "sold" to the public in terms they could understand. Not the least important target in the campaign was the Negro himself; he had to be convinced of his worth. It is important to understand this, because much of the art and letters that was the substance on which the New Negro was built and which made up the so-called Harlem Renaissance was serving this promotional end. Understanding this gives added meaning to the prose and poetry that were produced, and helps us appreciate their problems as art. Alain Locke and the others were correct in saying that there was a New Negro: an artistic self-consciousness of the Negro's human and cultural worth, the sense of an urgent need for self-assertion and militancy, and the belief in a culturally enriched past in America and Africa; these themes were real enough in the works of Negroes of talent. It was not merely Locke's imagination, although like an anxious parent he nurtured every suspicion of talent as if it were the bloom of genius. If the American context forced it to be artificial and contrived, it should not be thought Alain Locke's fault.

There is, however, a problem which promotions such as Van Wyck Brooks's New American and Alain Locke's New Negro share. It is in the metaphor itself. For whatever promise the new man has for the future, his name and the necessity for his creation imply some inadequacy in the past. Like the New Year's resolution or the "turning over a new leaf," the debut of the New Negro announced a dissatisfaction with the Old Negro. And since the New/ Old dichotomy is a mere convenience of mind—Afro-Americans were really the same people all along—the so-called Old Negro was merely carried within the bosom of the New as a kind of self-doubt, perhaps self-hate. How can one take up the promotion of race (or nationality) through art without exposing this doubt? How can one say that Negroes are worthy and civilized and new men without at the same time acknowledging doubt and denial? Even the best of the poems of the Harlem Renaissance carried the burden of self-consciousness of oppression and black limitation. . . .

Political Change in the Negro Ghetto, 1900-1940's

Martin Kilson

The term "political change" or "development" has many meanings, depending upon the context of one's usage; but when referring to the kinds of political adjustments characteristic of modernizing social systems, it means what
S. N. Eisenstadt has called the spread or dispersal of power—that is, the
easing of ordinary people's access to the institutions of authority, decision
making, command, and administration in a social system.[1] After the spread
of power from the few to the many, political change takes on additional
features: it becomes a matter of the growth of political structures like interest
groups, parties, and movements which in turn are used to politicize hitherto
politically inert strata and relationships.

Thus conceived, political change is modern in at least three senses: it is
associated most frequently with the industrial, urban civilization which
evolved out of the nineteenth century; the individual is assumed to be a subject of the political process; and a person's achieved status rather than his
socially ascribed or inherited status increasingly determines his relationship to
authority and power.[2]

In the past century, the pattern of political modernization has varied greatly
among nations and between groups, classes, and regions within nations. For
black Americans, political modernization since the 1870's has been characterized by marked variation and disparity between blacks and whites in the
acquisition of effective political attributes. With the end of Reconstruction,
which was coincident with the rise of urban America, the Negro, resident
mostly in the South, was coercively (albeit through laws) and violently deprived of formal political rights.[3] This loss of political rights contributed to
the massive migration of blacks out of the South that began in the first
decade of the twentieth century, though in itself the loss of political rights
was not always enough to induce migration.

The important consequence of this migration was the endowment of thousands of Negroes with the political rights they were forcibly denied in the
post-Reconstruction South. Had migration not been feasible for Negroes in
this period, doubtless the acquisition of basic political rights and thus the
primary stages of political modernization would have been delayed for another half-century. The white leadership of the South had the political will to

SOURCE: From *Key Issues in the Afro-American Experience*, Volume II, by Nathan I.
Huggins, *et al.* Copyright © 1971 by Harcourt Brace Jovanovich, Inc. Reprinted by
permission.

effect such a delay, and, alas, the connivance of the North was hardly unthinkable. The Supreme Court upheld the segregation of schools in the South (and outside it) in 1893, Congress refused to use its legislative powers to protect and extend the Negro's civil rights either in the South or outside it, and city and state governments outside the South seldom used their authority and power either to cultivate the Negro's rights or to extend them.

In addition to the acquisition of formal political rights, migration afforded blacks their first intensive experience of urbanization. The significance of urbanization to the political modernization of Negroes cannot be overemphasized: it afforded them the quality of social organization and institutional differentiation or specialization without which effective political development is impossible. As W. E. B. DuBois, one of the first systematic observers of the urban Negro, recognized, there is a strong correlation between the social and institutional differentiation available to Negroes in cities and their political modernization.[4]

The initial urban experience of rural or peasant blacks was disorienting because of their pervasive social disorganization. Yet, as the late E. Franklin Frazier was the first to perceive, such disorganization was the price urban Negroes had to pay for a more effective social system.[5] Only through urbanization could a black working class skilled in and adapted to modern industry emerge. Only in cities, despite their special stress and strain, was a differentiated Negro elite available, capable of coping with a range of leadership functions more demanding than those typical of the Negro elite in the South.[6] Political modernization is, after all, a matter of highly differentiated strata and institutions sustaining political articulation and order beyond parochial settings (ethnic, religious, regional) in order to provide public services.

The urbanization of the Negro from 1900 onward was not, of course, simply any urbanization. It was a particular form of city dwelling; it occurred in a historically specific place and time. Of all the variables governing Negro city dwelling outside the South, preeminent were those associated with white racism. No other major American immigrant community—Irish, Jews, Italians —faced such systematic and hateful restrictions upon its urban adaptation as did the Negro.[7] W. Lloyd Warner, the distinguished sociologist of mainstream America, discovered this in Yankee City: "The caste barrier or color line, rigid and unrelenting, has cut off this small group [blacks—0.48 per cent of the population] from the general life of the community." [8] The Lynds discovered a comparable situation in their study of a typical American community, the city of Muncie, Indiana (35,000 population in 1920):

> The sense of racial separation appears in widely diverse groups. At a meeting of school principals held at the Y.M.C.A. to arrange for interschool basketball games, one of the Y.M.C.A. secretaries said that any school having a Negro on its team could not play in the Y.M.C.A. building, but would have to play in the high school. . . . The secretary of the Trades Council has tried to persuade the Molders' Union to take in Negro molders, but they have

consistently refused. One is struck by the absence of Negroes at a place like the large tabernacle built for a community revival. They appear to keep very much to themselves, and Klan agitation has emphasized this tendency.[9]

What W. Lloyd Warner called the separation of blacks "from the general life of the community" is central to grasping the dynamics of Negro political modernization in the years 1900–1940. Whatever the general life of a modern community is, surely politics is a salient feature, for politics is the process through which services and benefits are allocated among competing sectors of society. Thus restrictions by whites on the Negroes' social adaptation to cities jeopardized the political capacity of the group; it made city blacks victims of the whims and caprice of white politicians, political machines, and bureaucracies, few of which were notable for exemplary political behavior.[10]

In the reaction of white city politicians and officeholders lay the key to Afro-American political modernization. Where white politicians surmounted, relatively speaking, the normal tendency of whites to restrict Negro access to the general life of a city, the Afro-American urban community proved nearly as capable as its white ethnic counterparts at acquiring the attributes and habits conducive to political modernization. This situation, however, obtained only in rare instances—most markedly in Chicago from 1915 onward.[11] The usual situation for black city dwellers outside the South was one where white politicians, consciously or not, followed restrictive and coercive patterns toward blacks. Herbert Gans, placing this situation in historical context, remarks that white ethnic immigrants "came into a society in which the Negro was already discriminated against":

> In fact, had it not been for discrimination, the North might well have recruited Southern Negroes after the Civil War. . . . [But] once the immigrants came they were able to take jobs away from Negroes, even pushing them out of the few urban occupations they had dominated, for example, catering and barbering. . . . The immigrants and their descendants who controlled the [political] machines were anti-Negro and gerrymandered ghetto neighborhoods so that they would not have to share their power with Negroes.[12]

Moreover, the coercive and regulatory agencies of cities—especially police—facilitated the exclusion of blacks from effective social and political participation. As Myrdal remarked some thirty years ago:

> In most Northern communities Negroes are more likely than whites to be arrested under any suspicious circumstances. They are more likely to be accorded discourteous or brutal treatment at the hands of the police than are whites. The rate of killing of Negroes by the police is high in many Northern cities. . . . The attitudes of the police will sometimes be found among the most important items considered in local Negro politics in the North.[13]

Confronted, then, with pervasive and mean restrictions upon their access to the social system of American cities outside the South, the Negroes' adaptation to the political structure of cities necessarily took unique form during the period 1900–1940. Inevitably, the patterns of Negro political adaptation to cities were not nearly as conducive to the long-run political modernization of blacks as were the modes of adaptation available to white immigrant groups like the Irish, Poles, Jews, and Italians.

CLIENTAGE POLITICS

One of the patterns of Negro political adaptation to cities in the formative years 1900–1940 may be described as clientage politics, or patron-client politics.[14] This rather primary pattern of Negro politics, widespread in the years of Negro urbanization (1900–1920), entailed a small group of blacks who fashioned personalized links with influential whites, becoming clients of the whites for a variety of sociopolitical purposes. Some students of this period of Negro history see clientage politics as conterminous with Negro politics in general.[15] In fact, it was nothing of the sort: it was almost exclusively the political method of the Negro middle class—a bourgeois affair. The black bourgeoisie ideologically portrayed clientage politics as "race politics," presumably beneficial to all blacks, though in reality it was of benefit more to the elites than to the urban Negro masses.[16]

The prestige available to the elites within the urban Negro ghetto enabled them to enter clientage relations with influential whites. Though within the Negro subsystem the prestige of elites (clergymen, doctors, teachers, clerks, foremen, gamblers) was circumscribed by a variety of cleavages (class, color-caste, sectional), this prestige had enough credibility to be converted into political influence. Clientage politics was the first means for realizing this influence in both Northern and Southern cities, and in the late nineteenth century both Negro clients and white patrons seized it.[17]

Politically, white support lent substance to the bid for leadership by the prestigious elements in the Negro ghetto in the formative period of black urbanization. It enabled the Negro client leadership to obtain positions in community and government institutions reasonably commensurate with their leadership-claimant status. It permitted the Negro client leadership to control or at least influence some part of the political process that allocated services to the Negro urban subsystem, especially welfare and settlement services. In a word, white support of Negro claimants for leadership of urban blacks in the period 1900–1920 helped legitimate this black leadership: it enabled it to appear in the eyes of the lower-class Negroes as the agent of the political "payoff," or benefits, that accrued to the Negro subsystem. Thus in Minneapolis in the late 1920's (Negro population 6,000 out of 400,000) the clientage political pattern provided much of the welfare and community settlement services available to the Negro lower classes.[18]

On the client's side of the typical white-black clientage relationship there is often much more leeway in the client's mode of reciprocation than is usually recognized. The political forms of client reciprocation often occur outside the presence of specified white patrons. In these situations the reciprocating behavior of black client elites becomes part of a discrete leadership pattern: the black client elites structure their leadership role in a manner presumed to be acceptable to white patrons.

Data illustrating this type of leadership among urban Negroes were reported by Frank U. Quillin in his invaluable study of Negro political adaptation in Ohio cities before World War I. One situation described by Quillin involved a collective effort by urban Negro client leaders to alleviate discord between blacks and whites:

> A colored photographer, a man far above the average of his race, said that there was no question but that the ordinary negroes in Columbus merit the ill opinion of all decent people for the manner in which they live. They are generally to be found living in miserable hovels, or in big "rat-and-fire-trap tenements," where every Sunday, especially, they get intoxicated, hold dog, cat, and chicken fights, play the banjo, dance cakewalks, and in other ways make the day hideous for their neighbors. . . . My informant said that, while this is true for the average negroes of the city, it applies especially to the new negroes that have lately come up from the South. A dozen colored women of the better class went to these negroes a short time ago and tried to do a little missionary work among them. They were received with insults on all sides, and were called "the white folks' niggers." A pastor of the leading colored church of the city and one of the best known colored preachers of Ohio, confirmed the above statements . . . and told me that these negroes were going about the streets dirty and half-clothed, with but an undergarment for a shirt, and that often open in front. They were used to doing this in the South, and they never thought of being tidy, and did not realize that they were making themselves and their race offensive to the white people. He said that he, and other ministers, had of late appealed to them to better these conditions.[19]

The second situation reported by Quillin illustrates how an individual Negro client, quite without direct inducement from a white patron, performs a client leadership function:

> One other great complaint made by the white people against the negroes, aside from their shiftlessness and stealing, was that they had a strong desire to antagonize the whites in all possible ways, especially in public places. Their actions on street cars were condemned by all whites, and by the better class of blacks. . . . The following incident told by the colored photographer already referred to will illustrate this matter quite fully. He was on a streetcar one evening when a negro, fresh from his work in the steel mill, with his filthy working clothes on, boarded the car and, although there was no room, crowded into a seat by the side of a white woman, elegantly dressed. When the colored photographer remonstrated with him for his action, he turned and said, "I'm no d——d white man's nigger like you. I have a right here, and I am going to take it." The conductor came along and put him off the car, the colored photographer giving the conductor his name as a witness if needed.[20]

In other cities there prevailed a form of clientage politics which entailed a political arrangement that made appointive political and civic posts the main means of exchange from white patrons to black clients. This pattern of urban white-black clientage politics was particularly developed in the first two decades of the twentieth century in New Haven,[21] Philadelphia,[22] Cincinnati,[23] Baltimore,[24] and New York.[25] The appointive posts exchanged by white patrons in return for political mediation of black-white interactions by Negro clients were occasionally of little specific political import but of high social value—for example, appointment to the board of a YMCA or some other community agency financed largely by influential whites, like the Charity Organization Society in Baltimore in the early 1900's.[26] But other appointive posts were of very much political relevance. These included appointment to school boards, tax boards, police posts, post office positions, and teaching posts.

By World War I this particular form of clientage politics was well developed in the larger cities. Moreover, it became a stimulus to a qualitative transformation of clientage politics, which took the form of the political institutionalization of cliques and interest groups within the Negro subsystem. The reasons for this superseding of typical clientage politics by a more politically articulate pattern of Negro political adaptation to cities were many. One reason, central to the nature of black-white clientage politics, was the well-nigh universal failure of clientage politics to guarantee the furtherance of Negro group interests when issues or policies germane to those interests were under political consideration.[27]

INTEREST GROUP ARTICULATION: THE CONTEXT

In addition to clientage politics, another pattern of Negro political adaptation to cities in the years 1900–1940 was the institutionalization of cliques and interest groups, otherwise called interest group articulation. This was essentially a matter of groups like doctors, lawyers, grocers, gamblers, and long-standing clusters of influential persons (cliques) advancing their own needs and, by extension, presumably those of Negroes generally through specialized political organization. The effort to institutionalize cliques and interest groups necessarily encroached upon and transformed typical clientage politics. For one thing, the failure of clientage politics to facilitate the political modernization of the Negro community as a subsystem stimulated the growth of interest group articulation. Second, and most important, from 1915 onward the sheer growth in number, scale, and range of socioeconomic differentiation of the Negro urban community rendered clientage politics short-lived, or at least insufficient.

The period 1915–1930 witnessed unprecedented demographic change in Negro urbanization. As shown in Tables 1 and 2, the population movement was northerly (including the Midwest) and westerly, toward the cities and away from the farms. The force of the pull of the cities on Negro population

TABLE 1.   Negro Urban and Rural Populations by Region, 1900–1930

Region	1900	1910	1920	1930
South				
Urban	1,365,000	1,854,000	2,251,000	2,966,000
Rural	6,558,000	6,661,000	6,661,000	6,395,000
North and West				
Urban	637,600	830,000	1,309,000	2,228,000
Rural	274,000	248,000	242,000	302,000
Total				
Urban	2,002,000	2,684,000	3,560,000	5,194,000
Rural	6,832,000	6,909,000	6,903,000	6,697,000

SOURCE: From T. J. Woofter, "The Status of Racial and Ethnic Groups," p. 567, in *Recent Social Trends in the United States* by Wesley Mitchell et al. Copyright 1933. Used with permission of McGraw-Hill Book Company.

TABLE 2.   Increase in Negro and White Populations in Selected Northern Cities, 1910–1920

City	Negro Population 1910–1920		Increase in Negro Population, 1910–1920	Percentage of Increase in Negro Population, 1910–1920	Percentage of Increase in White Population, 1910–1920
Detroit	5,741	40,838	35,097	611.3	107.0
Cleveland	8,448	34,451	26,003	307.8	38.1
Chicago	44,103	109,458	65,355	148.2	21.0
New York	91,709	152,467	60,758	66.3	16.9
Indianapolis	21,816	34,678	12,862	59.0	31.9
Philadelphia	84,459	134,229	49,770	58.9	15.4
St. Louis	43,960	69,854	25,894	58.9	9.4
Cincinnati	19,639	30,079	10,440	53.2	7.9
Pittsburgh	25,623	37,725	12,102	47.2	8.3

SOURCE: *Negroes in the United States, 1920–1932* (Washington, D.C.: Bureau of the Census, 1935), p. 55, Table 10.

in the North is seen in the fact that in 1920, of the 198,483 Negroes in New York State, 75 per cent lived in New York City; three cities in Ohio (Cleveland, Columbus, and Cincinnati) accounted for 46 per cent of all blacks in Ohio, though these cities claimed only 22 per cent of Ohio's population; and Philadelphia had 47 per cent of all Negroes in Pennsylvania and, combined with Pittsburgh, claimed 60 per cent of all Negroes in the state, though these two cities accounted for only 28 per cent of Pennsylvania's population.

TABLE 3.   Occupations Among Negroes, 1890–1930

Occupation	1890 Number	Per Cent	1900 Number	Per Cent	1910 Number	Per Cent	1920 Number	Per Cent	1930 Number	Per Cent
Agriculture	1,757,403	57.2	2,143,176	53.7	2,893,674	55.7	2,178,888	44.4	2,150,000	43.9
Domestic Service	963,080	31.3	1,324,160	33.2	1,099,715	21.2	1,064,590	22.7	1,000,000	20.4
Commerce and Transportation	145,717	4.7	209,154	5.2	425,043	8.2	540,451	11.2	575,000	11.8
Industry	172,970	5.6	275,149	6.9	692,506	13.6	960,039	19.9	1,060,039	21.7
Professions	34,184	1.1	47,491	1.0	68,898	1.3	80,183	1.7	107,833	2.2

SOURCE: Monroe N. Work, *Negro Year Book: An Annual Encyclopedia of the Negro, 1931–1932* (Tuskegee, Ala.: Tuskegee Institute Press, 1932), p. 347.

The sociological differentiation of the Negro in the years 1910–1930 was no less notable than the population change. The period saw a sharp transition of Negroes out of agriculture and into manufacturing, industry, commerce, and transportation. As shown in Table 3, marked growth of the Negro middle class and professional strata also occurred in the years 1900–1930, expanding the supply and differentiating the types of leadership.

These social and economic changes qualitatively altered the range and depth of the modern social system of the Negro ghetto outside the South in the years between the two world wars. World War I was central to these changes: it elaborated the complexity of urban life in the Negro ghetto and multiplied the interactions between the Negro urban subsystem and the dominant white social system. Moreover, the latter change spawned profound political by-products, for, alas, the war's multiplication of black-white interactions occurred before new political methods or agencies for mediating black-white relations were available. Thus discord and conflict frequently characterized black-white (particularly lower-class and working-class white) interactions during and immediately following World War I and often resulted in veritable warfare in the form of white-initiated riots.[28]

INTEREST GROUP ARTICULATION: SOME CASES

In the war-related context of increased black-white urban interaction, clientage politics, the dominant pattern of Negro political adaptation to cities in the period 1900–1920, began to give way to, or at least to coexist with, another pattern of Negro political adaptation which I call the institutionalization of cliques and interest groups. As a type of Negro political adaptation to cities, interest group articulation had one feature in common with clientage politics: both required influential white patrons as a major political resource enabling the Negro community, or rather special interests thereof, to derive benefits from the political process. Furthermore, the previous ex-

perience of clientage politics—lasting usually fifteen or twenty years, and
nearly thirty years in some cities, such as Oberlin, Ohio—imprinted itself
on the urban Negro leadership style, often irrespective of ideological cleavages
within the Negro leadership, like radical-conservative or nationalist-integra-
tionist.[29] This suggests a tendency among black leadership groups to depend
excessively or uncreatively upon white allies or patrons, thereby short-circuiting
the process of political modernization within the Negro urban subsystem.[30]

In initiating Negro interest group articulation in the years 1915–1930 the
politically assertive individuals among the organized white-collar and professional Negroes proceeded along a variety of political paths. In some instances
an established profession, whose members had usually been involved in clientage politics, moved to institutionalize its political potential, first through
professional organization and then through national and local articulation as
a political interest or pressure group. Thus in 1924 about 2,000 Negro lawyers
formed the National Bar Association. Under the leadership of politically
assertive personalities like Raymond Pace Alexander, a Philadelphia lawyer
who became a major political figure in that city, the association quickly institutionalized Negro lawyers as an interest group. Addressing the National Bar
Association in 1931, Alexander exhorted the black lawyers: "The political
future of our race should intimately concern the Negro lawyer, if he hopes to
meet the problems . . . which retard the development of his people and his
own development." [31] Alexander proceeded to make clear that the new political cohesion of Negro lawyers meant the demise of clientage politics. "We are
forced by circumstances," he declared, "to adopt the position that we shall
cast our ballot, not by virtue of traditional allegiance, not because the Republican Party was the party of Lincoln, but shall vote for the man—for the party
that offers opportunities to the men and women of color to participate in the
affairs of government by appointing to public positions of responsibility and
credit and by endorsing and supporting Negro men and women to high elective or appointive offices." [32]

The foregoing mode of interest group formation was pursued by other elements of the Negro professional strata. The large number of Negro social
welfare workers, including a small group of professional sociologists, who
formed the National Urban League in 1916 were part of the institutionalization of interest groups, as were the intellectuals—writers, teachers, orators,
journalists, critics—who had founded the National Association for the Advancement of Colored People (NAACP) six years earlier in 1910. The Negro
social workers who rallied around the Urban League and the intellectuals
who raised the banner of the NAACP had, like Negro lawyers prior to the
establishment of the National Bar Association, experienced mostly clientage
politics.[33]

In time the last two interest groups politically outdistanced others like
the National Bar Association. For example, the NAACP and the Urban
League, utilizing clientage relations with powerful whites for their finances and
for access to powerful national figures, forged national structures underpinned

by local urban chapters, which afforded them a range of pressure politics at the federal and state levels unavailable to Negro groups with little national organization, like the National Bar Association. In fact, the NAACP and the Urban League specialized in national pressure politics, one crucial conse-quence of which was the integration into the national political arena of Negro urban voluntary associations (churches, mutual benefit societies, economic cooperatives) upon which branches of the NAACP and the Urban League rested.[34]

Still other modes of interest group articulation prevailed in the years 1915–1930. Of particular interest is the political movement based on the aggrega-tion of voluntary associations. In this situation, a skillful and often charis-matic leader first maximizes the politicization of his own voluntary association and then, having secured this initial base, branches out, penetrating first ideologically and then organizationally other nonpoliticized voluntary associa-tions. The penetration or aggregation process was pursued by a highly politi-cized voluntary agency of the leader, and invariably ideology (usually racialist or black nationalist) proved the most important political resource.

Thus in the late 1930's the Reverend Adam Clayton Powell, Jr., formed precisely this type of political instrument, the Greater New York Coordinat-ing Committee, with which he politicized a segment of the Harlem ghetto, especially the newly emerging middle class and the upwardly mobile skilled workers (usually a part of the lower middle class among Negroes).[35] Basing the Coordinating Committee initially on his own church, the Abyssinian Bap-tist Church in Harlem, Powell elaborated it to include a broad spectrum of Harlem's middle-class and lower-middle-class voluntary associations, align-ing them often in sharp opposition to the established black bourgeoisie, who relied heavily upon and benefited from clientage politics. Powell's Coordin-ating Committee made explicit use of a black racialist or black nationalist ideology, often attacking the black bourgeoisie as an enemy of Negro advance-ment.

Along with similar organizations in other urban ghettos outside the South, the Coordinating Committee pioneered militant actions, like boycotts and picketing for jobs for middle-class and skilled working-class blacks. Of even more important long-run political significance, Powell transformed the Greater New York Coordinating Committee into a veritable political machine. In this new guise, often the terminal development of the process of aggregating in-terest groups, Adam Clayton Powell's political machine, exploiting the dis-array of Tammany Hall's organization in Harlem and aided by redistricting, successfully elected Powell in 1944 to the House of Representatives.[36] This made Powell the first Negro from the East to be elected to Congress.

Numerous other instances of interest group articulation occurred, of course, during the 1920's and 1930's, and in most of these the result was increased quality and scale in Negro political adaptation to cities. It should be noted, however, that one type of interest group articulation in this period contributed less to the quality of political institutional adaptation than to the ideological techniques underlying such adaptation. This was particularly true of the interest group politics of the Universal Negro Improvement Association, otherwise known as the Garvey movement, which reached maturity in the mid-1920's and continued into relatively inactive old age in the 1930's.

The Garvey movement pursued far less political activity through established political processes, like machine politics, city, state, and congressional elections, than the other interest groups that gained political articulation in the 1920's and 1930's. It seldom utilized its organization for the political growth of the Negro urban subsystem. Rather, the Garvey movement, largely dominated by the petty bourgeoisie and for this reason perhaps wary of political overextension, was obsessed with economic policies like the "Buy Black" movement and considered politics secondary.[37] Only occasionally did a branch of the Garvey movement assist Negro candidates for elective office or otherwise enter normal urban politics, and in such instances it did so without the support of the Garvey movement as a whole.[38]

The nearest Garvey himself came to formulating a practical view of politics for his movement was at their 1923 annual convention. He declared to his followers at the convention that "it is toward things political that the Universal Negro Improvement Association is now to turn its attention." But, alas, Garvey's notion of the uses of politics was bizarre. Rather than use political pressure to accomplish the possible, Garvey exhorted his followers to seek the impossible—mass migration to Africa. It was reported of the 1923 convention that Garvey "urged his followers to register and vote, claiming that in such a position they could demand a place in Africa, and the 7,000 enthusiasts cheered their leader's words." [39]

Yet the Garvey movement radicalized the style of Negro political adaptation to cities in the interwar era: it pioneered the ideological manipulation of the historical experience of Negroes as material for sharpening the Negro's perception of his status in white society, and it proposed solutions, after a fashion, exclusive of white society. Accordingly, at the fourth annual convention of the Universal Negro Improvement Association in New York in 1924, Garvey laid down a formulation of the ideological politicization of urban blacks that has yet to spend itself: "We've got to teach the American Negro blackness," he remarked. "Give them black ideals, black industry, black United States of Africa and black religion." [40]

Thus was born modern urban black nationalism or ideological militancy, the primary function of which has been, since the 1920's, twofold: first, to politicize and radicalize apathetic lower-class Negroes, turning thousands into predictable nationalist followers; second, to create black nationalist leadership out of the lower-middle-class or newly emergent middle-class Negroes.[41] What rendered the lower-middle-class black artisans, paraprofessionals, petty businessmen (tailors, shoemakers, grocers, semi-educated, or "jack-leg," clergymen [42]) especially prone to politicization through black nationalist ideology was their special marginal status. They experienced not merely white caste dominance but the added rub of the peculiar status dominance within the

Negro social system, controlled by a black bourgeoisie highly acculturated to white patterns.[43]

It should be reiterated that the growth of interest group articulation in the urban ghetto in the years between the world wars occurred not in place of but along with and supplementary to clientage politics. However, politically institutionalized interest groups, whether limited to cities (as most were) or operating on a national or federal level (as did the NAACP), constituted a more inclusive political process for the urban ghetto. This growth involved a greater variety of political groups and needs and a more demanding or specialized political organization than clientage politics. It therefore served wider segments of the urban ghetto. In this sense, then, the growth of interest group articulation in the 1920's and 1930's did indeed supersede clientage politics as the dominant mode of Negro political adaptation. Yet clientage politics persisted within the emergent interest group system of urban Negro politics and remains relevant to it today. It also persisted within the third major mode of Negro political adaptation to cities in the years 1900–1940, namely, machine politics.

MACHINE POLITICS: THE RISE OF MODERN NEGRO POLITICAL BEHAVIOR

The political adaptation of Negroes to cities by way of machine politics encompassed both formative and mature stages. Save where political machines interacted formally with the Negro urban subsystem, the formative stage for black urban communities was decidedly different and longer lasting than the formative stage for white immigrant communities. The mature stage seldom was experienced by Negro urban communities in the years 1900–1940, for maturity means the systematic inclusion of a given ethnic area or community into the dominant pattern of machine or boss rule in a given city. Such inclusion of the black urban area was extremely rare in those years, the notable exception being Chicago from 1915 onward.

The formative stage of the relationship between urban Negroes and machine politics differed from that of the relationship of white immigrants and the machine primarily in regard to the goals sought by city machines. For white immigrants the city machines sought, with few exceptions, to include the disparate ethnic turfs.[44] But for the Negro the machine lacked precisely this purpose or goal. Rather, in the years 1900–1940 the goal of white-dominated city machines toward Negroes was to neutralize and thus minimize the political clout of the Negro urban community and not infrequently even to distort that community's social and political modernization.

The goals of neutralization and distortion of the political position of the Negro urban community emanated largely from the racist perspective of the American social system. These goals appeared only occasionally in the relationship of city machines to white immigrant groups [45] but frequently in city machines' interaction with Negroes. Thus the patterns or ideology of white racism explain the extent and intensity of city machines' policy of neutralizing and distorting the political capability of the Negro urban subsystem in the years 1900–1940.

Usually an influential Negro—a professional, businessman, small bureaucrat, gambler, or underworld figure—was singled out by city machines and cast as agent of the application of what can be called neoclientage politics to the Negro urban community in the years 1900–1940. Thus in East St. Louis, Illinois, from around 1910 onward, Dr. Le Roy Bundy, a Negro dentist, functioned as the agent of a neoclientage political linkage between the Negro community and East St. Louis Republican machine politics.[46] A similar relationship was forged between the Negro subsystem and the Republican machine in New York City from 1908 onward. In this case a professional Negro politician of the small bureaucrat variety, Charles W. Anderson, effected neoclientage control of the Negro voters in New York City by the Republican party. Anderson held a succession of typical jobs provided by the Republican machine—largely appointments in federal agencies located in New York, like the Internal Revenue Service—and thus was beholden to the machine for his existence.[47]

From 1910 to 1940 the function of Negro neoclientage machine politicians like Anderson was to guarantee the Negro vote for Republicans and when necessary discourage Negro voting altogether rather than allow Negro voting power to grow and diversify, as did the Italian vote in New Haven,[48] the Irish vote in Philadelphia,[49] and the Jewish vote in New York,[50] among others. However, Anderson's counterparts in other cities were less reputable figures than he. They were prone to play their neoclientage role in machine politics in ways starkly dysfunctional to Negro political modernization.

In Baltimore, Philadelphia, Buffalo, and elsewhere many of the Negro leaders in neoclientage machine politics were gamblers, successful hustlers, flophouse keepers, and occupants of other antisocial roles. From the 1900's to the 1920's one of the worst uses of such Negro leaders in the neoclientage linkage of Negroes to machine politics was to be found in Philadelphia, though a politically functional linkage of blacks to white machine politics later evolved. DuBois, who had a keen sociological eye for politically dysfunctional relationships in the Negro urban community, observed in Philadelphia at the turn of the twentieth century the consequences of using Negroes of questionable occupation as leaders in machine politics:

> Next to this direct purchase of votes, one of the chief and most pernicious forms of bribery among the lowest classes is through the establishment of political clubs, which abound in the Fourth, Fifth, Seventh and Eighth Wards, and are not uncommon elsewhere. A political club is a band of eight or twelve men who rent a club house with money furnished them by the boss, and support themselves partially in the same way. The club is often named after some politician—one of the most notorious gambling halls of the Seventh Ward is named after a United States Senator—and the business of the club is to see that its precinct is carried for the proper candidate, to get

"jobs" for some of its "boys," to keep others from arrest and to secure bail and discharge for those arrested. Such clubs become the centre of gambling, drunkenness, prostitution and crime. Every night there are no less than fifteen of these clubs in the Seventh Ward where open gambling goes on, to which almost any one can gain admittance if properly introduced; nearly every day some redhanded criminal finds refuge here from the law. Prostitutes are in easy reach of these places and sometimes enter them. Liquor is furnished to "members" at all times and the restrictions on membership are slight. The leader of each club is boss of his district; he knows the people, knows the ward boss, knows the police; so long as the loafers and gamblers under him do not arouse the public too much he sees that they are not molested. If they are arrested, it does not mean much save in grave cases. Men openly boast on the street that they can get bail for any amount. And certainly they appear to have powerful friends at the Public Buildings.[51]

What disturbed DuBois about this political pattern was that machine politics, utilizing neoclientage ties, was articulated into the fiercely pathological social structure characteristic of lower-class Negro urban life throughout the twentieth century. He knew, or believed he knew, that effective institutional development, both social and political, for lower-class Negroes was impossible under this type of relationship to city political machines. He was correct in this belief, for perhaps no other factor has so marred and distorted Negro political adaptation to cities in this century as the way in which machine politics, by means of neoclientage ties, reinforced the structural pathologies of lower-class urban Negro life.[52]

No doubt on balance neoclientage machine politics was a better relationship for the Negro urban community to the wider city politic than the alternatives of typical clientage politics and interest group politics or no relationship at all. For all its limitations and its distorting implications for Negro sociopolitical modernization, the neoclientage linkage of Negroes to machine politics from early in the 1900's to the 1930's provided several new political opportunities to blacks. Above all, it established, after a fashion, the principle of institutionalized interaction between the Negro urban community and the formal white power structure—a principle that white immigrant groups took virtually for granted.[53] The establishment of this principle was, after all, basic to the transformation of the Negro urban community into a viable subsystem of the wider urban polity.

A NEGRO MACHINE IN CHICAGO, 1915–1940's

No detailed study of the special case of Chicago in the Negro's relationship to machine politics will be offered here, but the salient features of that relationship must be grasped if one wants an adequate understanding of the Negro experience with machine politics.[54] Perhaps basic to the Negro's success at having his ethnic turf in Chicago included fully in the city-wide machine organization was the keen competition between the Democratic and

Republican parties for city office, as well as the internal divisions between city and state factions within the Republican party.[55] Unlike Philadelphia, Baltimore, and New York, where Republicans (Philadelphia) or Democrats (Baltimore and New York) had a veritable built-in majority, no such situation prevailed in Chicago. Both parties had to work hard for victory in Chicago, and when victory came the margin was small. A number of ethnic communities provided the margin of victory, and among them was the Negro community, 4 per cent of Chicago's population in 1920 and nearly 7 per cent in 1930.

For Negroes to help supply the margin of victory in keenly contested elections like those that occurred in Chicago between the two world wars required certain facilitating situations. One was the presence of white politicians—in fact just one major white politician was all that was needed— reasonably indifferent to matters of race regarding supporters. Another was a group of Negro politicians who would not rest satisfied with limited co-optation as the defining feature of their relationship to machine politics, but rather sought within the Negro area the full-fledged control of the machine that their Irish, Jewish, Italian, and other ethnic political counterparts possessed within the boundaries of their areas.[56]

Both these situations prevailed in Chicago in the years between the two world wars. William Hale ("Big Bill") Thompson was the white politician who exhibited relative color blindness in his dealings with the Chicago Negro, particularly after his first bid (1915) to become the mayoral candidate of the faction-ridden Republican party was markedly enhanced, if not clinched, by Negro support in the largely Negro second ward. Thus the results of the city-wide Republican primary for mayor in 1915 were 87,333 for Thompson, 84,825 for Olson, and 4,283 for Hey. The Republican vote in the second ward was 8,633 for Thompson, 1,870 for Olson, and 47 for Hey.[57] This pattern prevailed in the four primaries in which Thompson was a candidate for mayor; Negroes in the second ward gave him over 80 per cent of their votes. And, as Harold Gosnell has pointed out, the same held for elections:

> Upon a number of occasions the pluralities received in the districts inhabited largely by Negroes have been decisive. Without these pluralities Thompson could not have defeated his Democratic opponents in the mayoralty elections of 1919 and 1927. In the latter year, when Thompson ran against Mayor Dever, he received 91.2 per cent of the vote cast in the Second Ward.[58]

Thompson's mode of organizing Negroes in Chicago in order to guarantee their support was even more important to the eventual inclusion of blacks in Chicago machine politics than the voting pattern. Negro votes in the interwar years had been crucial in elections in Philadelphia, St. Louis, and Cleveland but had never resulted in Negro inclusion in the political machines. Unlike those in any other major city in this period, the Republican leaders in Chicago cultivated the independent-minded Negro middle-class leaders rather than those Negro political leaders inclined to neoclientage linkages with white power structures. Equally important, the Negro leaders who organized Big Bill Thompson's Negro support insisted upon something other than neoclientage ties to the Chicago machine.[59] In fact, Chicago seems to have had a larger group of Negro middle-class politicians of this persuasion than other cities and in general probably had a more professionally and socially differentiated Negro elite than any other major city, including New York.[60]

Furthermore, the highly differentiated elite possessed a number of men who were very political-minded and perceived the many uses of politics. The two men most important in integrating the Negro community of Chicago into Thompson's machine were of this persuasion—namely, Edward Wright and Oscar De Priest. They were also, unlike their predecessors in Chicago's Negro leadership, self-made men, and politics was basic to their rise to professional status. Edward Wright worked in the late nineteenth and early twentieth centuries as a porter, clerk, and bookkeeper, among other jobs, and he had a preference for government jobs; he studied law in his spare time and qualified for the bar in 1892. In the same year he was elected Cook County Commissioner, his first public office in Illinois; he was the third Negro from Chicago to hold the post. Early in his political career, Wright displayed the qualities that determined the choice he made in relationship to the Thompson machine—qualities Harold Gosnell has vividly described:

> Commissioner Wright's activities on the county board showed him to be shrewd, forceful, and highly race conscious. Shortly after his election he deliberately held up the appropriation for the office of State's Attorney Charles S. Deneen in order to secure the appointment of a colored man as assistant state's attorney. When Deneen was informed as to why his appropriation was delayed, he is alleged to have said: "I want you to understand, Mr. Wright, that I am all powerful in this office." To this Wright replied: "Yes, and I am county commissioner." A few days later Ferdinand L. Barnett became the first colored assistant state's attorney for Cook County and Deneen's appropriation was passed.[61]

De Priest, like Wright, was self-made. He began as a house painter and interior decorator in the late nineteenth century and in 1904 gained election to the Cook County Board. In 1907 he entered real estate, utilizing his political relationships, and soon amassed a sizable fortune. His bid for major office came in 1915 when he stood as Republican candidate for city council in the second ward, following a brilliantly executed grass-roots campaign for the nomination.[62]

The special type of leadership offered by Wright and De Priest and the men who became their intimates and co-workers, in combination with Big Bill Thompson's particular attributes, produced the first machine-type political adaptation of a major Negro urban community. The details of the Negro subdivision of the Chicago machine from the 1920's to the 1940's will not detain us.[63] But the qualitative features of the Negro submachine, so to speak, must be mentioned. The available evidence indicates that the Negro subdivision of the Chicago machine from the 1920's to the 1940's was like subdivisions in other cities. By the late 1920's, the ward, district, and precinct heads were Negro, unlike the case in Philadelphia. The Negro submachine had one leader—Wright—appointed by Big Bill Thompson to a $100-a-day post as lawyer to the State Traction Commission in 1919; in 1923 the governor appointed him to the Illinois Commerce Commission, a $7,000-a-year post. Oscar De Priest was nominated and elected to Congress in 1926, being the first Negro to achieve that distinction in this century, and another Negro, Democrat Arthur Mitchell, succeeded De Priest. A variety of responsible and key posts went to members of the Negro elite who backed the Wright-De Priest machine. Concerning these officeholders, Ralph Bunche, one of the keenest observers of Negro urban politics in the interwar era, remarked:

> These men are all entrusted with responsible positions. In illustration, in the office of the corporation counsel, a Negro, as assistant corporation counsel and trial lawyer in property damage litigation, represents the city in suits mounting to millions of dollars yearly. There are approximately twenty Negro investigators in the various legal departments. Additional appointments in the many city departments, as teachers, clerks, police, etc., run into the hundreds.[64]

Other data support Bunche's observations: Negroes in Chicago, 6.9 per cent of the population, held 25 per cent of some 11,888 postal service jobs in 1930 and 6.4 per cent of city civil service jobs in 1932. Moreover, these data show reasonable Negro representation in the white-collar and professional ranks of both city civil service and postal service jobs.[65]

The Chicago pattern persisted, moreover, through World War II and the postwar era.[66] Yet when profound crisis, characterized by widespread black nationalist militancy and lower-class aggression on white institutions through riots, engulfed the Negro urban subsystem in the early 1960's, the relatively successful Chicago pattern of adaptation of Negroes to cities through machine politics proved nearly as fragile as the neoclientage patterns that persisted in Philadelphia and elsewhere. This was due largely to the fact that the demands upon government and politics emanating from the postwar urban Negro were simply beyond any solution available to cities, Chicago or any other.[67]

POLITICAL CHANGE AND DIFFERENTIATION AMONG NEGROES

This study has described the political status of the Negro in the first half of the twentieth century in terms of the modes of political adaptation available to blacks in white-dominated cities. The delineated modes of adaptation were not merely a function of white power; they were also an outgrowth of the evolution of the Negro urban community as a subsystem and of variations within that system, which differ from city to city. Moreover, as a given urban

Negro community progresses from one mode of adaptation to another there are a number of measures of the impact of such change: election behavior, patterns of racial discord, rates of violence, Negro occupational mobility as affected by politics. Election behavior as a measure of the impact of modes of Negro adaptation to cities has a utility the other measures lack: it conveys cleavages among the members of a community that derive from the community's particular mode of adaptation.

Electoral data from 1900 to the early 1930's reveal little differentiation within the Negro community as a result of the patterns of political adaptation then evolving. Neither the mode of typical clientage political adaptation nor that of interest group articulation produced a major change in Negro electoral behavior. The attachment to the Republican party persisted throughout the evolution of those patterns of Negro adaptation to cities.

It was not until some variant of machine politics characterized the adaptation of Negroes to cities that a sizable degree of differentiation in Negro voting became apparent. For the most part, city machines did not significantly affect wide segments of blacks in cities until the mid-1920's, and some voting data suggest that it was in this period that the Negro vote began to discard the deep-seated attachment to the Republican party. Thus data in Table 4 show that Negroes were more decidedly Republican than any other ethnic group in Chicago in 1924 but by 1928 exhibited a disaffection with Republicans which continued into 1932, the start of the New Deal.

TABLE 4. Presidential Voting of Ethnic Groups in Chicago, 1924–1932

Year		Percentage of Democratic Vote	Percentage of Republican Vote	Percentage of Third Party Vote
1924	German	18	52	30
	Jewish	37	43	20
	Polish	51	37	12
	Negro	5	91	4
1928	German	45	55	
	Jewish	78	22	
	Polish	83	17	
	Negro	29	71	
1932	German	59	41	
	Jewish	85	15	
	Polish	85	15	
	Negro	30	70	

SOURCE: From *The Politics of Provincialism: The Democratic Party in Transition, 1918–1932,* by David Burner. Copyright © 1965, 1968 by David Burner. Reprinted by permission of Alfred A. Knopf, Inc.

Only in New York City does the evidence show a majority of Negroes breaking with the Republican party in 1932 in order to support Franklin D. Roosevelt's Democratic candidacy for President.[68] In the other industrial cities, a small movement of Negroes toward the Democratic party was recorded: for example, in Detroit, where 19.5 per cent of the Negro vote had been Democratic in 1930, 36.7 per cent was Democratic in 1932.[69] But on the whole, in large industrial cities the Negro vote in 1932 remained overwhelmingly Republican. For example, in the four largely Negro wards of Cleveland where the Democrats had received 30 per cent of the vote in 1928, only 24 per cent was theirs in 1932 (although in other industrial cities the Democrats advanced on the previous vote of 1928).[70] Only in 1936 did the Democrats outstrip the Republicans in the Negro wards of industrial cities like Detroit and Cincinnati. The Democrats gained 63.5 per cent of the Negro vote in the former and 65.1 per cent in the latter. In Gary, Indiana, another industrial city, the predominantly Negro fifth ward voted Democratic by a margin of 2 to 1, whereas in 1932 the Negro vote was 85 per cent Republican.[71]

In most cities from 1932 onward the impact of the Depression greatly influenced the voting of the lower class among both Negroes and whites.[72] One gauge of this may be seen in the fact that in many cities lower-class Negroes moved more sharply toward the Democrats than did middle-class Negroes. But still it would seem that city machines also influenced the Negro shift toward the Democrats which commenced somewhat tentatively in 1932 but was distinctly apparent by 1936.

For example, in both Detroit and Cincinnati the Republicans had negatively utilized neoclientage links with the Negro community.[73] The Democrats, on the other hand, cultivated the independent tendencies among the Negro elites of Detroit and Cincinnati in the 1920's, thereby providing the Negro subsystem more effective relations to the political machines. This policy of accommodating new changes in the urban ghetto won the Democrats in those cities no small political notice among blacks; and when combined with the relief and welfare policies of the Democratic administration from 1934 onward,[74] the Negro shift to the Democratic party in most major cities was hardly surprising. Moreover, this shift has persisted for over thirty years, and today the Negro is more strongly Democratic than any other ethnic group—a voting pattern the reverse of Negro political behavior at the dawn of Negro political modernization in the early 1900's.

It should be noted, finally, that in the post-World War II era there has been a drastic diminution of the efficacy of political machines for the upwardly mobile white ethnic groups. But there is no reason to expect this development to apply equally to urban blacks. Barring any substitute arrangement for performing the political functions heretofore performed by political machines for groups lacking effective political modernity, there is no reason whatever to expect a major decline in the efficacy of political machines to the urban Negro.[75] Just as the Negro was late in commencing the process of political modernization compared to white ethnic groups, it can be expected that blacks will be late in realizing this process and that thus they will require the services of political machines (with sizable Negro leadership) for at least a generation beyond the period machine politics lose their efficacy for white ethnic groups.

I say this, moreover, despite the fact that I am critical of the historical role of ethnicity (the political manipulation of ethnic variables) in modern American institutions. A number of notable American scholars have virtually —and most unfortunately—deified the ethnic factor in American history.[76] But no critical observer of the key problems of power and participation in American society can ignore the dysfunctional, as well as morally or intellectually indecent, attributes of ethnicity.

Surely, in the form of white racism toward blacks since the end of Reconstruction, ethnicity can be evaluated as nothing other than a deadly force: an albatross, or worse, around the neck of American society. Today ethnicity, in the hands of a new set of Negro leaders—bent like their Irish, Polish, Jewish, Italian historical counterparts on the ethnic redress of differentials between subordinate and superordinate groups—might well lead to profound political crisis at many levels of the American political system. If this should come to pass, the apologists, both black and white, for the historical pattern of ethnic manipulation—which too often resembles ethnic madness—must share a major responsibility.

NOTES

1. S. N. EISENSTADT, "Modernization and Conditions of Sustained Growth," *World Politics* (July 1964), pp. 576–94.
2. For the application of this concept of political change, see MARTIN KILSON, *Political Change in a West African State* (Cambridge, Mass.: Harvard University Press, 1966).
3. Cf. PAUL LEWISON, *Race, Class and Party: A History of Negro Suffrage and White Politics in the South* (New York: Grosset & Dunlap, 1932), and C. VANN WOODWARD, *The Strange Career of Jim Crow*, rev. ed. (New York: Oxford University Press, 1966).
4. W. E. B. DuBOIS, *The Philadelphia Negro: A Social Study* (Philadelphia: University of Pennsylvania Press, 1899), pp. 233–34.
5. Cf. E. FRANKLIN FRAZIER, *The Negro Family in Chicago* (Chicago: University of Chicago Press, 1932).
6. On the Negro elite strata and their leadership roles in the South, see HORTENSE POWDERMAKER, *After Freedom: A Cultural Study in the Deep South* (New York: Viking Press, 1939), and ALLISON DAVIS et al., *Deep South* (Chicago: University of Chicago Press, 1941).
7. See ROBERT WEAVER's classic account of barriers to Negro urban adaptation,

The Negro Ghetto (New York: Harcourt, 1948). For a viewpoint that differentiates little, if at all, between the adjustment barriers of blacks and white ethnics, see OSCAR HANDLIN, *The Newcomers* (Cambridge, Mass.: Harvard University Press, 1959).

8. W. LLOYD WARNER and PAUL S. LUNT, *The Social Life of a Modern Community* (New Haven, Conn.: Yale University Press, 1941), p. 217.

9. ROBERT S. and HELEN M. LYND, *Middletown: A Study in Modern American Culture* (New York: Harcourt, 1929), p. 479. Cf. FRANK U. QUILLIN, *The Color Line in Ohio: A History of Race Prejudice in a Typical Northern State* (Ann Arbor, Mich.: George Wahr, 1913), pp. 125–65.

10. See the classic account of the ways of political machines by HAROLD F. GOSNELL, *Machine Politics: Chicago Model* (Chicago: University of Chicago Press, 1937). See also HAROLD ZINK, *City Bosses in the United States: A Study of Twenty Municipal Bosses* (Durham, N.C.: Duke University Press, 1930).

 On the notion of victimization as the outcome of white barriers to Negro urban adaptation, see ST. CLAIR DRAKE, "The Social and Economic Status of the Negro in the United States," *Daedalus* 95 (Fall 1965), pp. 771–73.

11. See RALPH J. BUNCHE, "The Negro in Chicago Politics," *National Municipal Review* 17 (May 1928), pp. 261–64.

12. HERBERT J. GANS, "The Ghetto Rebellions and Urban Class Conflict," in Robert Connery, Ed., *Urban Riots: Violence and Social Change* (New York: Random House, 1969), pp. 52–53.

13. GUNNAR MYRDAL, *An American Dilemma* (New York: Harper, 1944), p. 527. On the role of police in facilitating violent acts (especially riots) of the white lower and working classes against Negroes in cities outside the South, see ROBERT FOGEL-SON, "Violence as Protest," in Connery, *Urban Riots*, pp. 28–30. See also GILBERT OSOFSKY, "Race Riot 1900: A Study of Ethnic Violence," *Journal of Negro Education* 32 (Winter 1963), pp. 16–24.

14. On the nature of clientage political ties as a form of political linkage, see M. G. SMITH, *The Economy of Hausa Communities of Zaria* (London: Colonial Social Science Research Council, 1955).

15. See, for example, LESLIE H. FISHEL, JR., "The Negro in Northern Politics, 1870–1900," *Mississippi Valley Historical Review* 42 (December 1955), pp. 466–89.

16. Cf. AUGUST MEIER, "Negro Class Structure and Ideology in the Age of Booker T. Washington," *Phylon* (Fall 1963), pp. 258–66.

 Professor Meier's work on ideologies of Negro elites at the turn of the twentieth century is seminal, and his larger study should be consulted: *Negro Thought in America, 1880–1915* (Ann Arbor, Mich.: University of Michigan Press, 1963). For an analysis of the ideas of Negro elites in the 1920's and 1930's, Ralph Bunche's studies are the best. See RALPH J. BUNCHE, "The Programs of Organizations Devoted to the Improvement of the Status of the American Negro," *Journal of Negro Education* 9 (July 1939), pp. 539–50.

17. On clientage politics among Negroes in the urban South, see the excellent material on Atlanta, Georgia, in FLOYD HUNTER, *Community Power Structure* (Chapel Hill: University of North Carolina Press, 1953).

18. ETHEL R. WILLIAMS, "Minneapolis Builds a Social Settlement," *Opportunity: Journal of Negro Life* 8 (August 1930), pp. 236–37.

19. QUILLIN, *The Color Line in Ohio*, pp. 150–51.

20. *Ibid.*, p. 152.

21. ROBERT AUSTIN WARNER, *New Haven Negroes: A Social History* (New Haven, Conn.: Yale University Press, 1940), chap. 9.

22. DuBOIS, *The Philadelphia Negro*.

23. WENDELL P. DABNEY, *Cincinnati's Colored Citizens: Historical, Sociological and Biographical* (Cincinnati: Dabney Publishing, 1926), pp. 116–29.

24. HENRY BAIN, "Five Kinds of Politics: A Historical and Comparative Study of the Making of Legislators in Five Maryland Constituencies," vol. 2 (Ph.D. diss., Harvard University, 1970).

25. GILBERT OSOFSKY, *Harlem: The Making of a Ghetto* (New York: Harper, 1963), chaps. 4, 11.

26. See HELEN B. PENDLETON, "Negro Dependence in Baltimore," *Charities* 15:1 (October 1905), pp. 50–58.

27. See AARON WILDAVSKY's study of Oberlin, Ohio, *Leadership in a Small Town* (Totawa, N.J.: Bedminister Press, 1964), pp. 41–47.

28. See the Chicago Commission on Race Relations' incisive analysis of the impact of World War I on the Negro ghetto and expanding black-white interaction in Chicago, *The Negro in Chicago: A Study of Race Relations and a Race Riot* (Chicago: University of Chicago Press, 1922). This study was written largely by CHARLES S. JOHNSON, then head of the research division of the Urban League.

29. On the sway of the patron-client ethos among early black nationalists, see EDMUND CRONON, *Black Moses: The Story of Marcus Garvey and the Universal Negro Improvement Association* (Madison: University of Wisconsin Press, 1962), especially Chapters 4 and 5, dealing with the Garvey movement's economic ties with whites. For the patron-client element in the relations of radical and race-conscious Negro intellectuals with whites in the 1920's and 1930's, see LANGSTON HUGHES, *The Big Sea: An Autobiography* (New York: Alfred A. Knopf, 1940), especially Parts 2 and 3. See also HAROLD CRUSE, *The Crisis of the Negro Intellectual* (New York: Random House, 1967). For current black militants' ties to white allies or patrons, including the most politically aggressive groups, like the Black Panther Party, see MARTIN KILSON, "The New Black Intellectuals," *Dissent* 16:4 (July-August 1969), pp. 309–10, and "Political Sociology of Black Militancy," in Seymour Martin Lipset and S. M. Miller, Eds., *Poverty, Stratification and Politics* (forthcoming). It may be noted, *en passant*, that much of the current outward show of bitterness by middle-class Negro militants toward whites—especially liberal whites—is no doubt a function of the inability of Negro political and interest groups, whatever their ideological proclivity, to dispense with white allies and thus to discard the context of the patron-client ethos.

30. I intend to develop this thesis more fully in a forthcoming book, *Politics in Black America: Crisis and Change in the Negro Ghetto* (New York: St. Martin's Press, forthcoming).

31. RAYMOND PACE ALEXANDER, "The Negro Lawyer," *Opportunity: Journal of Negro Life* 9 (September 1931), p. 271.

32. ALEXANDER, "The Negro Lawyer," p. 271. For a more radical contemporary view of the need to politicize Negro professional groups, see LOREN MILLER, "The Flight of the Negro Professional Man," *Opportunity: Journal of Negro Life* 9 (August 1931), pp. 239–41.

33. DuBOIS' autobiography is informative on the clientage politics experienced by the Negro intellectuals who helped found the NAACP. See W. E. B. DuBOIS, *Dusk of Dawn: An Essay Toward an Autobiography of a Race Concept* (New York: Harcourt,

1940). No better source exists on the clientage political ties of Negro social workers and community organizers than the National Urban League's now defunct monthly organ, *Opportunity: Journal of Negro Life*, which was published between 1923 and 1948.

34. There is yet no good study of the role of the NAACP and the Urban League in politicizing the infrastructure of voluntary associations in the Negro ghetto from World War I onward. But see RALPH J. BUNCHE's writings on the political role of the NAACP and the Urban League, referred to by MYRDAL in *An American Dilemma*, pp. 819–42.

35. This account is based on ADAM CLAYTON POWELL, JR., *Marching Blacks: An Interpretive History of the Rise of the Black Common Man* (New York: Dial Press, 1945), pp. 95–103.

36. See JAMES Q. WILSON, *Negro Politics: The Search for Leadership* (Glencoe, Ill.: Free Press, 1960), pp. 35–36. See also Wilson's incisive analysis of Powell in "Two Negro Politicians: An Interpretation," *Midwest Journal of Political Science* 4:1 (1960).

37. Cf. CRONON, *Black Moses*.

38. See HAROLD GOSNELL, *Negro Politicians: The Rise of Negro Politics in Chicago* (Chicago: University of Chicago Press, 1935), p. 113. The Chicago branch of the movement aided the primary campaign of a Negro candidate in the first ward, largely Negro, in 1924, and the candidate considered the support of some value.

39. *Opportunity: Journal of Negro Life* 1 (November 1923), p. 348.

40. Quoted in *Opportunity: Journal of Negro Life* 2 (September 1924), p. 284.

41. The special role of black nationalism in the politicization of the Negro lower middle class or emergent middle class awaits serious study. E. FRANKLIN FRAZIER was one of the first to perceive this relationship. See his article "The Garvey Movement," *Opportunity: Journal of Negro Life* 4 (November 1926), pp. 346–48. Furthermore, the Garvey movement still awaits serious and sophisticated political analysis. The political role of the Garvey movement is shrouded in black nationalist wishful thinking and mythology (e.g., membership figures of one to two million are surely mythological, the figure 85,000 preferred by DuBois in the 1920's being nearer the mark), and purportedly serious accounts of the Garvey movement have not avoided the myths. A step toward demythologizing the study of black nationalism and a method of historical analysis are provided in THEODORE DRAPER, *The Rediscovery of Black Nationalism* (New York: Viking Press, 1970).

42. For one of the few studies of one group among this poltically important segment of the Negro lower middle class, see IRA DE AUGUSTINE REID, "Let Us Prey!" *Opportunity: Journal of Negro Life* 4 (September 1926), pp. 274–76. This petty middle class and the infinite variety of charlatans it spawned need serious study.

43. Cf. E. FRANKLIN FRAZIER, *Black Bourgeoisie* (Glencoe, Ill.: Free Press, 1956).

44. Cf., for example, OSCAR HANDLIN, *The Uprooted* (Boston: Atlantic-Little, Brown, 1951). See also LAWRENCE H. FUCHS, Ed., *American Ethnic Politics* (New York: Harper, 1968).

45. See, for example, DAYTON DAVID McKEAN, *The Boss: The Hague Machine in Action* (Boston: Houghton Mifflin, 1940).

46. The best account of Bundy's neoclientage role in East St. Louis is in ELLIOTT M. RUDWICK, *Race Riot at East St. Louis, July 2, 1917* (Carbondale: Southern Illinois University Press, 1964), pp. 174–96.

47. The best account of Charles Anderson's neoclientage role in New York City politics in the first two decades of the twentieth century is OSOFSKY, *Harlem*, pp. 161–78.

48. RAYMOND E. WOLFINGER, "The Development and Persistence of Ethnic Voting," *American Political Science Review* 59 (December 1965). See also ROBERT DAHL, *Who Governs? Democracy and Power in an American City* (New Haven, Conn.: Yale University Press, 1961).

49. J. T. SALTER, *Boss Rule: Portraits in City Politics* (New York: Whittlesey House, 1935), pp. 73–207.

50. DAVID BURNER, *The Politics of Provincialism: The Democratic Party in Transition, 1918–1932* (New York: Alfred A. Knopf, 1968), pp. 239 ff. Burner provides excellent data illustrative of diversity in the voting of Jews, Italians, and other white groups in New York and other cities as compared to the uniformity of the Negro vote for the Republican party. For evidence of a greater political clout and larger payoff due to diversification of an ethnic group's voting, see THEODORE LOWI, *At the Pleasure of the Mayor: Patronage and Power in New York City, 1898–1958* (Glencoe, Ill.: Free Press, 1964), pp. 29–46.

51. DuBOIS, *The Philadelphia Negro*, pp. 378–79.

52. There is precious little material on this important subject, and serious study of it is wanting; but see ST. CLAIR DRAKE and HORACE R. CAYTON, *Black Metropolis: A Study of Negro Life in a Northern City* (New York: Harcourt, 1945), pp. 576 ff.

53. For a case study of the almost natural accession of white immigrants to machine politics and an equally natural succession in time to executive control of the machine, see ELMER E. CORNWALL, "Party Absorption of Ethnic Groups," *Social Forces* 38 (March 1960), pp. 205–10.

54. Fortunately, there are both limited and detailed studies of Negro politics in Chicago, the best being the classic account by HAROLD GOSNELL, *Negro Politicians* (1935), and the more recent study by WILSON, *Negro Politics* (1960). One should also consult ALLAN H. SPEAR, *Black Chicago: The Making of a Negro Ghetto, 1890–1920* (New York: New York University Press, 1967); and DRAKE and CAYTON, *Black Metropolis* (1945).

55. Cf. GOSNELL, *Negro Politicians*, chaps. 3. 4.

56. On ethnic control of subdivisions of city machines, see GOSNELL, *Machine Politics*.

57. GOSNELL, *Negro Politicians*, p. 41.

58. *Ibid.*, p. 47.

59. See RALPH J. BUNCHE, "The Thompson-Negro Alliance," *Opportunity: Journal of Negro Life* 7 (March 1929), pp. 78–80.

60. Cf. SPEAR, *Black Chicago*, chaps. 3, 4.

61. GOSNELL, *Negro Politicians*, pp. 154–55.

62. *Ibid.*, pp. 170–71.

63. *Ibid.*

64. BUNCHE, "The Thompson-Negro Alliance," p. 79. See also BUNCHE, "The Negro in Chicago Politics," pp. 263–64.

65. For comparative data on Philadelphia, showing a much weaker pattern of payoff from participation in city politics, see JOHN H. STRANGE, "The Negro in Philadelphia Politics, 1963–1965" (Ph.D. diss., Princeton University, 1966), chap. 3.

66. See WILSON, *Negro Politics*.

67. Cf. EDWARD C. BANFIELD, *The Unheavenly City: The Nature and Future of Our Urban Crisis* (Boston: Atlantic-Little, Brown, 1970).

68. See BURNER, *The Politics of Provincialism*, p. 237.

69. EDWARD H. LITCHFIELD, "A Case Study of Negro Political Behavior in Detroit," *Public Opinion Quarterly* 5 (June 1941), p. 271.

70. HENRY LEE MOON, *Balance of Power: The Negro Vote* (New York: Doubleday, 1948), p. 18.

71. See RICHARD J. MEISTER, "The Black Man in the City: Gary, Indiana, 1906–1940" (Paper delivered at the Annual Conference of the Association for the Study of Negro Life and History, 1969).

72. See HAROLD GOSNELL, *Grass Roots Politics: National Voting Behavior of Typical States* (Washington, D.C.: American Council on Public Affairs, 1942).

73. See DABNEY, *Cincinnati's Colored Citizens*, pp. 122–23.

74. For comparative data on the incidence of relief among Negroes in several cities, see E. FRANKLIN FRAZIER, "Some Effects of the Depression on the Negro in Northern Cities," *Science and Society: A Marxian Quarterly* 2:4 (Fall 1938), pp. 491–94. See also ROBERT WEAVER, "The New Deal and the Negro," *Opportunity: Journal of Negro Life* 8 (July 1935), pp. 200–202.

75. I develop this issue more adequately in *Politics in Black America*.

76. For a recent example of this kind of scholarship, see ANDREW N. GREELEY, "Turning Off 'The People': The War and White Ethnic Groups," *New Republic* 163 (27 June 1970), pp. 14–16.

Minority Group Psychology: Implications for Social Action

Alvin F. Poussaint, M.D.

Much has been written about the black man's psychic reactions to being a member of an oppressed minority in a white man's land. The position of the Negro is unique among minority groups in America because he alone bears the scars of a slave heritage and wears the indelible mark of oppression, his black skin. It is impossible to discuss in this short paper all the aspects and implications of the Negro's psychological adaptation to white racism. Therefore, in view of the national crisis in race relations and the black rebellions taking place in our cities, I would like to focus on what I consider those key aspects of the psychology of black Americans having special relevance for the formulation of programmatic solutions to the urban crisis.

HISTORICAL BACKGROUND

The system of slavery in its original form and as its remnants exist today had three dramatic consequences for the black man's psyche. It generated in him (1) self-hatred and negative self-esteem, (2) suppressed aggression and rage, and (3) dependency and nonassertiveness. Although these manifestations are analytically distinguishable, they are, of course, not discrete phenomena, being interdependent and interrelated on many different levels. Thus, while we will deal with each in turn, a consideration of one necessarily involves reference to the others. (It should be understood that we are here dealing in generalities and that any individual could of course respond differently from what we see as predominant trends.)

Let us briefly look at the genesis and initial consequences of racism and examine Negroes' responses to it.

The castration of Afro-Americans and the resulting problems of negative self-image, suppressed aggression, and dependency started more than 350 years ago when black men, women, and children were wrenched from their

SOURCE: From *Thinking About Cities: New Perspectives on Urban Problems*, Anthony Pascal, Ed. Copyright © 1970 by Dickenson Publishing Co., Inc. Reprinted by permission.

Work on this topic was originally commissioned by the Center for Policy Studies, University of Chicago. The author presented a paper with similar title at the Center's Conference on Short Term Measures to Avert Urban Violence in November 1967.

native Africa, stripped bare both physically and psychologically, and placed in an alien white land. They thus came to occupy the most degraded of human conditions, that of a slave—a piece of property, a nonperson. Families were broken: black men were emasculated and black women were systematically exploited sexually and otherwise vilely degraded. The plantation system implanted and fostered the growth of a helplessness and subserviency in the minds of Negroes that made them dependent upon the good will and paternalism of the white man.[1] The more acquiescent the slave was, the more he was rewarded within the plantation culture. This practice forced the suppression of felt retaliatory rage and aggression in black men and women. Those who bowed and scraped for the white boss and denied their aggressive feelings were promoted to "house nigger" and "good nigger." Thus, within this system, it became a virtue for the black man to be docile and nonassertive. "Uncle Toms" are exemplars of these conditioned virtues. In order to retain the most menial of jobs and keep from starving, black people quickly learned such servile responses as "Yassuh, Massa." Thus, from the days of slavery to the present, passivity (and the resultant dependency) became a necessary survival technique.

By 1863, when slavery was abolished, the Afro-American had been stripped of his culture and left an oppressed black man in a hostile white man's world. He had, furthermore, learned to repress his aggression, behave subserviently, and view himself as an inferior. These things had been inculcated under the duress of slavery. All of these teachings were, however, reinforced after "freedom" when Jim Crow was born in the late 1800's and early 1900's. In the days following Reconstruction the systematized racist and sometimes psychotic propaganda of the white man, haranguing about the inferiority of the Negro, increased in intensity. He was disenfranchised, terrorized, mutilated, and lynched. The black man became every unacceptable, pernicious idea and impulse that the white man's psyche wished to project, that is, the Negro was an animal, violent, murderous, with ravaging sexual impulses. The intensity of the white man's psychological need that the Negro be shaped in the image of this projected mental sickness was such as to inspire the whole Jim Crow system of organized discrimination, segregation, and exclusion of Negroes from society.

In the resulting color caste system, white supremacists constructed an entire "racial etiquette" constantly to remind Negroes that they are only castrated humans. In their daily lives, Negroes are called "girl" and "boy" by whites. In the South, in particular, they are addressed by their first name by whites no matter how lowly that white person is. Negroes in turn are, however, expected to use courtesy titles such as Mr., Mrs., or Miss when addressing whites. White racists through the centuries have perpetrated violence on those blacks who demonstrate aggressiveness or insubordination. To be an "uppity nigger" was considered by white supremacists one of the gravest violations of the racial etiquette. Negro mothers learned to instruct their two- and three-year-old children to "behave" and say " 'yes sir and no sir' when the white man talks to you." Similarly, various forms of religious worship in the Negro community have fostered passivity in blacks and encouraged them to look to an afterlife for eventual salvation and happiness. Negroes have even been taught that they must love their oppressor and that it is "sinful" to hate or show appropriate anger.

In addition to demanding nonaggression and subservience, whites also inculcated in the Negro self-hatred and low self-esteem. They made certain that any wares allotted to the Negro were inferior. The Caucasian American socialized the black man to internalize and believe the many deprecating things that were said about him. They encouraged and rewarded behavior and attitudes in Negroes that substantiated these indicting stereotypes. Thus black men were happy-go-lucky and were laughed at by whites. Negroes were lazy, stupid, and irresponsible, and whites bemoaned this, but "put up with it" in a good-natured "noblesse oblige" fashion. Our mass media vigorously reinforced these images with such characters as Amos and Andy, Stepin Fetchit, and Beulah. In this way many Negroes were conditioned to believe, "Yes, I am inferior."

Not only were black men taught that black was evil and that Negroes were "no-good," they were also continually brainwashed into believing that only "white is right." This psychological feat was accomplished by allowing light-skinned Negroes with straight hair to elevate themselves in society above darker Negroes. As this happened, the whites suggested, and Negroes came to believe, that such blacks were better because they had much white blood. Thus, for the darker Negroes, their lack of social and economic success and their deprived conditions came to be associated with their Negroid qualities. Consequently Negroes exhibited profound shame in the vestiges of their African identity and sought to hide or deny these. Without the positive history of their former African culture and its achievements to raise their self-esteem, and with the achievements of both the white men and the "whiter Negroes" staring them in the face, black men sought to be white. They revered Caucasian characteristics—pale skins, straight hair, aquiline features—and despised their own curly hair, broad noses, and full lips.

The most tragic, yet predictable, part of all of this structuring is that the Negro has come to form his self-image and self-concept on the basis of what white racists have prescribed; therefore, black men and women learn quickly to hate themselves and each other because they are black.

These, then, are the broad historical outlines of certain aspects of the black man's situation in the United States, those related to his socialization in an oppressive system and having consequences for his psychological development. We have briefly discussed those patterned and institutionalized stimuli present over the years in black-white interaction which gave rise in the Negro to such learned habits of response as self-hatred and negative self-esteem, suppressed rage, and subserviency. In the following sections some of the more critical dynamics and manifestations of these characteristics are discussed, with special emphasis on those having implications for social action planning.

NEGRO SELF-IMAGE

Although the Negro's self-concept is affected by factors associated with poverty and low economic class status, blackness in itself has consequences for ego development not inherent in lower-class membership. The black person develops in a color caste system and usually acquires the negative self-esteem that is the natural outcome of membership in the lowest stratum of such a system. Through contact with such institutionalized symbols of caste inferiority as segregated schools, neighborhoods, and jobs and more indirect negative indicators such as the reactions of his own family, he gradually becomes aware of the social and psychological implications of his racial membership. He is likely to see himself as an object of scorn and disparagement, unwelcome in a white high caste society and unworthy of love and affection. The young Negro child learns very early in life to despise himself and to reject those like himself. From that time on, his entire personality and style of interaction with his environment became molded and shaped in a warped, self-hating, and self-denigrating way.

Sometimes this self-hatred can take on very subtle manifestations. For instance, competition, which may bring success, may also bring failure. Thus the efforts that may bring success to a black man are often not made even when the opportunity exists. There are, no doubt, two reasons for this failure to act: First, the anxiety that accompanies growth and change is avoided if a new failure is not risked; therefore, a try is not made. Second, the steady state of failure represented by nonachievement (and defined by someone other than yourself) rather than by an unsuccessful trial, is what many Negroes have come to know and expect, and so they feel safer (less psychologically discomforted) with the more familiar. Furthermore it has often meant survival to black men to deny the possession of brains, thoughts, and feelings, thus making it difficult to move from a position of passivity to one of activity and to acknowledge heretofore forbidden feelings and behavior as now safe, legitimate, and acceptable.

It is all too frequent that Negroes with ability, intelligence, and talent do not aspire to the full extent of their potential. Being unused to occupying positions of prestige and responsibility, many Afro-Americans have lower aspirations than their talents and abilities warrant. They tend to shy away from competition, particularly with white people, and often feel insecure even when their abilities and success have been acknowledged. In fact, at least one study has demonstrated that, even when Negroes are given objective evidence of their equal intellectual ability in an interracial situation, they typically continue to feel inadequate and to react submissively.[2] This lack of aggressiveness may also account at least in part for Negroes' below par achievement in school. Negro girls, however, who are not as threatening to whites and therefore not as systematically crushed as Negro boys, have been found to exceed Negro boys in achievement at all grade levels through college.[3] Thus their low aspirations and achievement may be attributable not only to their own feelings of inferiority, but also to a learned inability to be normally aggressive. Many psychiatrists feel that self-denigration in Negroes is associated primarily with the more general castration of the black man by white society. Some even believe that the self-hatred should be viewed as rage turned inward, rather than as primarily their shame in being black and their desire to be white. Let us look further at this relationship of rage to self-hatred.

SELF-HATRED AND RAGE

Even if a Negro does not start out with self-hatred feelings, these can develop from compromising with a suppressive society. A Negro with all the self-love and self-confidence in the world cannot express legitimate feelings of anger or rage in a system that is brutally and unstintingly suppressive of self-assertion; therefore, after a while, even a confident Negro would have to hate himself for biting his tongue and not expressing himself in an appropriate way. Even though talking back to a white man, in the South for example, may mean his life and keeping quiet is the most sensible self-preservatory response, a person has to hate not only the person who forces him to be silent, but also *himself* for acquiescing and compromising his integrity. This is the self-hatred that comes from a feeling of helplessness and powerlessness in the face of overwhelming oppression. The whole system of southern legal justice has been designed—and still functions—to inflict severe and inequitable penalties on Negroes showing even minor aggression toward whites. Negroes who dare to show their anger at whites are usually punished out of proportion to their "crime." Even in the North, blacks who are "too outspoken" about racial injustices often lose their jobs or are not promoted to higher positions because they are considered "unreasonable" or "too sensitive." It is significant that the civil rights movement had to adopt passive resistance and nonviolence in order to win acceptance by white America. But, alas, even here, there was too much "aggression" shown by Negroes. Whites recoiled and accused civil rights groups of "provoking violence" by peaceful protest.

These responses are, of course, related to tendencies to be dependent and subservient. The inability of Negroes to be self-assertive has fostered a dependency which has had devastating consequences for the social behavior and psychic responses of Negroes. It has been found, for instance, that Negroes are less likely to go into business or entrepreneurial ventures.[4] This is the result, no doubt, of their trained incapacity to be assertive, assertiveness being essential to the entrepreneurial spirit. For example, a Negro may be afraid to make a decision without checking with a white man, or being assured of white approval.

The demands of being unwillingly subservient, unwillingly self-denigrating, and unwillingly nonaggressive are psychically extremely taxing. Frustration and anger are the obvious by-products of the requirement to be less than a man, less than human. Thus we come to an obvious question: What does the black man do with his anger and aggression?

DEALING WITH ANGER AND AGGRESSION

The simplest method for dealing with rage is to suppress it and substitute an opposing emotional attitude—compliance, docility, or a "loving attitude." Sometimes anger can be denied completely and replaced by a compensatory happy-go-lucky disposition, flippancy or—an attitude extremely popular among Negroes—"being cool." Another way for aggression to be channeled is through competitive sports, music, or dancing. These are the few activities white society has traditionally opened to Negroes. Another acceptable means of channeling rage is to identify with the oppressor and put all of one's energy into striving to be like him. A third means for the oppressed to give expression to their feelings is to emphathize or identify with someone objectively like themselves (black), who for one reason or another is free to express appropriate rage directly at the oppressor. Malcolm X and Adam Clayton Powell served this function. Still another technique for dealing with anger is to replace it with a type of chronic resentment and stubbornness toward white people, interpreted as a "chip on the shoulder." Trying to control rage in this way frequently shows itself in a general irritability and always has the potential of becoming explosive. Thus, the spreading wave of riots in Negro ghettos may be seen as outbursts of suppressed rage. Although these riots are contained in the ghetto, the hatred is usually directed at those whom the rioters see as controlling and oppressing them economically, psychologically, and physically—store owners and policemen.

Sometimes suppressed emotions will be expressed in such psychosomatic symptoms as headaches, low back pain, and diarrhea. Rage is also directed inward in such deviations as alcoholism, drug addiction, and excessive gambling, and also in the tendency of Negroes to distrust and hate other blacks more than they do their white oppressors. In psychiatric practice it is a generally accepted principle that a chronic repressed rage will eventually lead to a low self-esteem, depression, emotional dullness, and apathy.

It appears now as if more and more Negroes are freeing themselves of suppressed rage through greater outspoken release of pent-up emotions. Perhaps this is an indication that self-love is beginning to outbalance self-hate in the black man's soul. The old passivity is fading and being replaced by a drive to undo centuries of powerlessness, helplessness, and dependency under American racism.

APPROACHES TO THE PROBLEM

If we believe that self-hatred, suppressed rage, nonassertiveness, and dependency are at the core of many of the black man's social and psychological difficulties, what can American society do to remove some of these scars from the black psyche? What programs in the black community itself will foster a positive self-image, channel rage, and encourage constructive self-assertion?

The answers to these questions are obviously not simple ones and perhaps they will require a serious examination of the basic value system of American society. But some answers are suggested by a consideration of the consequences of the two major philosophies underlying social action programs designed to change the position of the Negro in the United States. There are, first, those whose aims are integration of the black man into society, and second, those who aim to improve the position of the black man in society, but do not emphasize his integration into it. Let us first look at the integrationist orientation.

INTEGRATION AND ASSIMILATION

The civil rights gains in the past decade, and especially in the 1960's, have done much to modify the negative self-concepts of Afro-Americans. The civil rights movement itself has brought a new sense of dignity and respect to those blacks most severely deprived by poverty and oppression in the rural South and northern ghetto. One factor that may have been significant in improving the self-image of the masses of Negroes was that black men were leading this struggle, rather than white men. This fact in itself probably made Negroes, through the process of identification, take more pride in their group and feel less helpless, for they could see black men, through *their* efforts, knowing more and bringing about positive changes in their environment. The feeling of "fate control," that is, that one can have "control" over social forces rather than be a victim of them, is crucial to one's feelings of ego-strength and self-esteem. Thus, the movement brought to the Negro a new sense of power in a country dominated by a resistant white majority. The movement also acted to channel the expressions of assertiveness among Negroes even if this expression came mainly through nonviolent protest. Beyond these achievements, however, civil rights leaders at that time tended to see total integration of the black and white races as the final step in destroying the Negro's negative self-esteem and dependency on white authority.

Now we have seen emerge in segments of the civil rights movement a disenchantment with the social and psychological consequences of American "integration." This disenchantment arises, at least in part, from the fact that integration has moved at a snail's pace and has been marked by white resistance and tokenism. The Negro has found himself in the demeaning and uncomfortable position of asking and demanding that the white man let him into *his* schools, *his* restaurants, *his* theaters, even though he knows that the white man does not want him. In both the South and the North, many Afro-Americans have resented the indignity of constantly being in the position of begging for acceptance into the white man's institutions. Such a posture placed blacks in the same old dependent relationship to the white man as when he asked for and expected food and protection from the slave master. Negroes have become further demoralized upon seeing that the recent civil rights laws did not effectively change this pattern of relationships with whites. It immediately became apparent that integration, especially in schools, was not to be integration in a real sense at all, but merely token placement of Negro children, that is, "one-way integration." Negro parents in the South and North, for example, rarely speak of sending their children to the "integrated school": they say, "My child is going to the *white* school." In the overwhelming majority of instances, no white children are "integrated" into Negro schools. Since integration is only a one-way street that Negroes travel to a white institution, then inherent in the situation itself is the implied inferiority of the black man and the fact that *he* must seek out whites to better his position, the implication that only the Negro can benefit and learn, that he has nothing to offer whites and they have nothing to learn from him. Thus an already negative self-image is reinforced.

Parents who fear psychological harm to their children are not anxious to send them to "integrated" schools. Some of the college aged young people in the movement stated frankly that they find this type of integration personally degrading and do not want to go to any school where they have to be "accepted by white racists." It must be remembered that black people are seeking not only social and economic help but psychological salvation. The Negro is not only demanding equal rights but is desperately searching for *inner* emancipation and escape from the chronic effects of white racism upon his psyche. In this search for peace, many young blacks (even on our college campuses) feel a need to insulate themselves from the subtle expressions of racism they experience in their daily encounters with whites. In this context the growth of black organizations on campuses takes on a significance notably different from the one of "racist separatism" often imputed by the press. Perhaps this isolation serves to protect them from feelings of self-consciousness which they experience in the presence of whites. Such uncomfortable feelings prevent them from feeling relaxed and thus "being themselves."

Since the number of Negroes at any white school is token, particular hardships are created for these individuals. They immediately find themselves surrounded by children who are generally the products of white racist homes. In this situation, since all children want to belong, the Negro must become an expert at "being liked and accepted." In such a social setting, if the self-esteem of the black student grows, it is likely to be not so much from feelings of comfort and satisfaction in being Negro as it is from his own conditioned beliefs that "white is right" and that he has succeeded in a white world; thus he is either a successful pioneer or a martyr.

Those people who offer assimilation as a solution must examine what they are asking Negroes to do. Many Negroes, including segments of both the old civil rights movement and nationalists, are beginning to fear that "token integration" may augment the identity problems of the Negro. Such integration as has existed in the North has not substantially helped to solve the Negro's identity problems. Assimilation by definition takes place into and according to the larger societal (white) model of culture and behavior. Thus, if Negroes are to assimilate, it is they who must give up their black identity and subculture to be comfortably integrated. Many Negroes who seek complete assimilation thus become preoccupied with proving to white people that they are just like all other human beings, that is, white, and worthy of being assimilated. At the same time they express their willingness to give up all elements of their black identity. This in itself means to them that they are giving up something of inferior or negative value to gain something of greater value: a white identity.

In seeking acceptance among whites, many Afro-Americans expend a great deal of internal energy trying to prove that they are all right; but this effort is vain and fruitless because personal acceptability must be repeatedly proven to each new group of whites. Thus, before a Negro can be an individual he must first prove that he is a human. The Negro groups' vigorous pursuit of middle-class status symbols is frequently an overdetermined attempt to demonstrate to the white man, as well as to themselves, that they can be successful, worthwhile human beings. White America, however, has lumped all Negroes together into one collective group. Hence, there can be no individual freedom for any one Negro until there is group freedom for all.

That an individual can achieve individual status only through changing his group's status, is, however, an idea foreign to American thought. The Negro, like other Americans, has accepted the belief (descended from the tenets of the Protestant ethic) that individuals succeed or fail solely as a result of their individual efforts. Thus, an individual's worth is assessed solely on the basis of his merits: he is accepted or rejected because of what he is as an individual. The acceptance by the Negro of this idea of individual merit has worked to his detriment, for it has operated to sustain a delusion in the face of a contradicting reality. It would perhaps be more realistic for black people to develop and orient themselves in terms of overcoming barriers to them as a group. Only then will acceptance or rejection as *individuals* follow. Achievement of this group freedom, however, requires undoing racial self-hatred, expending greater group assertiveness for social and political action, and adopting a positive and proud stance toward themselves and others.

Those individuals and organizations who reject the integration philosophy for improving the position of Negroes in American society focus on the achievement of group freedom, maintaining that only through strength as a group can black men win human dignity and power. Among these advocates would be those who are committed to the philosophy of "black power" or "black consciousness."

BLACK CONSCIOUSNESS OR BLACK POWER

As we mentioned, an important issue in the emancipation of black people is self-determination and fate control. Black consciousness movement supporters argue that as long as Negroes are powerless politically and do not have a degree of control over their own communities, they will remain psychological beggars in a white man's house. For instance, they ask, why shouldn't the black community have the final word about the type of policemen that are permitted in their community? Why should a white man downtown be able to send white racist police who shout or think "nigger" into the black community to "enforce the law"? Why, they reason, can't black communities have some degree of autonomy in governing their community, particularly since white-controlled urban governments have vested interests in protecting the majority white interests? Who is watching out for black interests? Following the same line of reasoning, black consciousness supporters maintain that local groups should have some say in deciding who will teach in their schools, who will run local welfare departments, in short, who will control their local institutions. To many blacks this does not represent "separatism"; it is simply democracy. The next question, however, is whether or not all-black institutions can provide Negroes with a more stable, positive sense of identity and self-esteem.

It is known that such groups and individuals as the Black Muslims and Malcolm X have frequently had many positive and constructive effects on members of the black community. This group has brought greater self-reliance and dignity to hard-core, untouchable segments of the Negro community. The Muslims were once the one major Negro group (now there are others of the black power orientation) that called for separation of the races and black self-sufficiency as an alternative approach to the remedy of the black man's problems of negative identity and self-esteem. Observers generally agree that the Muslims were quite effective in rehabilitating many antisocial and criminal types by fostering in them a positive self-image and pride in their blackness. This group also afforded blacks a channel for expressing their rage at the "white devils." The significant fact is that the Muslims were able to alleviate much of the individual Negro's self-hatred without holding up or espousing integration or "full acceptance" of the black man into American white society.

Other black consciousness groups have instilled pride and esteem in Negroes by emphasizing Negro history and achievements. Programs based on this philosophy can build Negro self-confidence and self-assertion by calling upon black men to think and do for themselves. They may also provide the stimulus for more independent thought and grass-roots problem solving and lead to the development of community leadership. Such programs seem to have the potential for undoing much of the black man's self-hatred and emasculation, and these are the feelings that, in part, lead to behavior destructive of self and others. Finally, such "race consciousness" programs can constructively channel the Negro frustrations and anger that now lead to destructive violence and riots.

The question must be raised, however, whether all-black programs will in some ways lead to more identity and self-esteem problems for the Negro since such groups would always exist within a surrounding dominant white culture and would run the risk of being considered inferior. Can you really build a sense of community and pride in the ghettos when these neighborhoods carry the stigma of forced segregation by and from the white community? Can people develop a pride in a neighborhood made up of dilapidated housing usually in the most dismal part of our cities? Definitive answers to these questions cannot yet be given. We would suggest, however, that if Negroes were truly *equals* in the larger society, a black subculture could exist much in the same way that America has subcultures of other national and racial groups such as the Jews, Irish, Chinese, and so on. That is, if community derives from choice and is among people who feel common bonds, it can be a more salutary situation for blacks than if people of disparate interests, abilities, and needs are forced together in a ghetto solely on the basis of a common skin color.

News dispatches make it clear that, despite the drive for racial integration, it is being vigorously resisted by the white population, particularly in the area of housing; therefore, we can expect to have isolated, predominantly black communities for a long time to come. Black power advocates hold that the potentiality of these communities cannot be ignored while integration is awaited. They insist on building strong black-based institutions now. Whether these can become positive communities founded on common interests and supported by pride—or will remain run-down ghettos that are encampments of human misery—remains to be seen. But the answer rests with both blacks and whites: whether blacks will support this development, and whether whites will allow the movement to proceed without insuperable harassment.

IMPLICATIONS FOR SOCIAL CHANGE

We have discussed in the preceding pages the psychological predispositions that have been generated in the Negro by virtue of his position and relationship in the American social system. We have also given some attention to the consequences of these psychic orientations and the programs and philosophies that have arisen to attempt to change them. It remains for us to suggest what we see as the implications of all this.

Since the black man's need for a sense of self-worth, self-assertion, and independence cannot be met through token integration and since assimilation appears to be a remote possibility, it seems logical that both black and white men must turn to the development and rehabilitation of Negro communities. In this endeavor, however, it is crucial that as much responsibility as possible be placed in the hands of black men, since self-development and self-determination lead to a greater sense of self-worth and power.

The white establishment can help to alleviate those problems that afflict black Americans by undoing white supremacy and the oppression of colored peoples. In doing so, white people will have to give up some share of their control and power over black communities. At the same time the white community must earnestly struggle for open housing so that Negroes can have a *free choice* about where they will live. With a choice, the many Negroes who choose to live among blacks will know that they have exercised their free will rather than that they have acquiesced to powers forcing them into a box.

In our cities, white officials can help to build the status of black communities by making them centers of business and cultural attraction for *all* the people. Why not have major theaters, museums, and trade centers located in black communities as part of a general rehabilitation program for the ghettos? There are many other small ways in which the black ghettos could be made part of the mainstream of our urban centers. Even though much has been said in the past decades about the urgent need for jobs, decent housing, and quality education and training programs, very little has been done to implement these ideas. The society is now paying with urban disorder and riots for this chronic neglect in alleviating some of these basic problems.

The availability of jobs is especially crucial for the black man in his struggle for dignity. Not only do jobs give men a sense of importance and self-worth, but they may also be a channel for the appropriate release of aggression. As in sublimation and displacement they may allow black men to express the assertiveness that has been so long dammed up. It is also obvious that if we are to do something to stabilize the Negro family we must begin by providing secure jobs for the black man. Men without work cannot fulfill their role and responsibility as husbands and fathers. The entire welfare system must be remodeled so that it will encourage the growth and independence of its recipients. These are only a few of the many social and economic programs that can be developed to alleviate these deplorable human conditions.

It becomes obvious after this long discussion of the psychology of a minority group that this subject cuts across broad social, economic, and political areas. The subject and its implications for social change cannot be considered in isolation. In order to relieve the psychic problems of Negroes that now manifest themselves in self-hatred, suppressed aggression, nonassertiveness, and dependence, we must address ourselves to the many ramifications of white racism in America.

The President's Commission on Civil Disorders has already made important recommendations for taking a decisive step in solving some of these problems; however, this arduous task requires the creative minds, brave spirits, and imaginative plans of all Americans who are sincerely concerned with the future of this country.

NOTES

1. The present welfare system is in many ways analogous to this system in that it perpetuates this psychological dependency.
2. I. KATZ and L. BENJAMIN, "Effects of White Authoritarianism in Bi-racial Work Groups," *J. Abnormal and Soc. Psych.* 61 (1960), p. 448.
3. T. F. PETTIGREW, *A Profile of the Negro American* (Princeton: D. Van Nostrand Co., 1964).
4. N. GLAZER and D. P. MOYNIHAN, *Beyond the Melting Pot* (Cambridge: Massachusetts Institute of Technology Press, 1963).

The Myth of Coalition

Stokely Carmichael and
Charles V. Hamilton

There is a strongly held view in this society that the best—indeed, perhaps the only—way for black people to win their political and economic rights is by forming coalitions with liberal, labor, church and other kinds of sympathetic organizations or forces, including the "liberal left" wing of the Democratic Party. With such allies, they could influence national legislation and national social patterns; racism could thus be ended. This school sees the "Black Power Movement" as basically separatist and unwilling to enter alliances. Bayard Rustin, a major spokesman for the coalition doctrine, has written:

> Southern Negroes, despite exhortations from SNCC to organize themselves into a Black Panther Party, are going to stay in the Democratic party—to them it is the party of progress, the New Deal, the New Frontier, and the Great Society—and they are right to stay.[1]

Aside from the fact that the name of the Lowndes County Freedom Party . . . is not the "Black Panther Party," SNCC has often stated that it does not oppose the formation of political coalitions per se; obviously they are necessary in a pluralistic society. But coalitions with whom? On what terms? And for what objectives? All too frequently, coalitions involving black people have been only at the leadership level; dictated by terms set by others; and for objectives not calculated to bring major improvement in the lives of the black masses.

. . . We propose to reexamine some of the assumptions of the coalition school, and to comment on some instances of supposed alliance between black people and other groups. In the process of this treatment, it should become clear that the advocates of Black Power do not eschew coalitions; rather, we want to establish the grounds on which we feel political coalitions can be viable.

The coalitionists proceed on what we can identify as three myths or major fallacies. First, that in the context of present-day America, the interests of black people are identical with the interests of certain liberal, labor and other reform groups. Those groups accept the legitimacy of the basic values and institutions of the society, and fundamentally are not interested in a major

SOURCE: From *Black Power*, by Stokely Carmichael and Charles V. Hamilton. Copyright © 1967 by Stokely Carmichael and Charles V. Hamilton. Reprinted by permission of Random House, Inc.

reorientation of the society. Many adherents to the current coalition doctrine recognize this but nevertheless would have black people coalesce with such groups. The assumption—which is a myth—is this: what is good for America is automatically good for black people. The *second myth* is the fallacious assumption that a viable coalition can be effected between the politically and economically secure and the politically and economically insecure. *The third myth* assumes that political coalitions are or can be sustained on a moral, friendly, sentimental basis; by appeals to conscience. We will examine each of these three notions separately.

The major mistake made by exponents of the coalition theory is that they advocate alliances with groups which have never had as their central goal the necessarily total revamping of the society. At bottom, those groups accept the American system and want only—if at all—to make peripheral, marginal reforms in it. Such reforms are inadequate to rid the society of racism.

Here we come . . . to an important point . . . : the overriding sense of superiority that pervades white America. "Liberals," no less than others, are subjected and subject to it; the white liberal must view the racial scene through a drastically different lens from the black man's. Killian and Grigg were correct when they said in *Racial Crisis in America*:

> . . . most white Americans, even those white leaders who attempt to communicate and cooperate with their Negro counterparts, do not see racial inequality in the same way that the Negro does. The white person, no matter how liberal he may be, exists in the cocoon of a white-dominated society. Living in a white residential area, sending his children to white schools, moving in exclusively white social circles, he must exert a special effort to expose himself to the actual conditions under which large numbers of Negroes live. Even when such exposure occurs, his perception is likely to be superficial and distorted. The substandard house may be overshadowed in his eyes by the television aerial or the automobile outside the house. Even more important, he does not perceive the subjective inequalities inherent in the system of segregation because he does not experience them daily as a Negro does. Simply stated, the white American lives almost all of his life in a white world. The Negro American lives a large part of his life in a white world also, but in a world in which he is stigmatized.[2]

Our point is that no matter how "liberal" a white person might be, he cannot ultimately escape the overpowering influence—on himself and on black people—of his whiteness in a racist society.

Liberal whites often say that they are tired of being told "you can't understand what it is to be black." They claim to recognize and acknowledge this. Yet the same liberals will often turn around and tell black people that they should ally themselves with those who can't understand, who share a sense of superiority based on whiteness. The fact is that most of these "allies" neither look upon the blacks as co-equal partners nor do they perceive the goals as any but the adoption of certain Western norms and values.

Professor Milton M. Gordon, in his book, *Assimilation in American Life*, has called those values "Anglo-conformity" (p. 88). Such a view assumes the "desirability of maintaining English institutions (as modified by the American Revolution), the English language, and English-oriented cultural patterns as dominant and standard in American life." Perhaps one holding these views is not a racist in the strict sense of our original definition, but the end result of his attitude is to sustain racism. As Gordon says:

> The non-racist Anglo-conformists presumably are either convinced of the *cultural* superiority of Anglo-Saxon institutions as developed in the United States, or believe simply that regardless of superiority or inferiority, since English culture has constituted the dominant framework for the development of American institutions, newcomers should expect to adjust accordingly.[3]

We do not believe it possible to form meaningful coalitions unless both or all parties are not only willing but believe it absolutely necessary to challenge Anglo-conformity and other prevailing norms and institutions. Most liberal groups with which we are familiar are not so willing at this time. If that is the case, then the coalition is doomed to frustration and failure.

The Anglo-conformity position assumes that what is good for America—whites—is good for black people. We reject this. The Democratic Party makes the same claim. But the political and social rights of black people have been and always will be negotiable and expendable the moment they conflict with the interests of their "allies." A clear example of this can be found in the city of Chicago, where Mayor Daley's Democratic "coalition" machine depends on black support and unfortunately black people vote consistently for that machine. Note the results, as described by Banfield and Wilson in *City Politics*:

> The civic projects that Mayor Daley inaugurated in Chicago—street cleaning, street lighting, road building, a new airport, and a convention hall, for example—were shrewdly chosen. They were highly visible; they benefited the county as well as the city; for the most part they were noncontroversial; they did not require much increase in taxes; and they created many moderately paying jobs that politicians could dispense as patronage. *The mayor's program conspicuously neglected the goals of militant Negroes*, demands for the enforcement of the building code, and (until there was a dramatic exposé) complaints about police inefficiency and corruption. *These things were all controversial, and, perhaps most important, would have no immediate, visible result; either they would benefit those central-city voters whose loyalty could be counted upon anyway or else* (as in the case of police reform)* they threatened to hurt the machine in a vital spot [author's italics].[4]

As long as the black people of Chicago—and the same can be said of cities throughout the country—remain politically dependent on the Democratic machine, their interests will be secondary to that machine.

Organized labor is another example of a potential ally who has never deemed it essential to question the society's basic values and institutions. The earliest advocates of unionism believed in the doctrine of *laissez faire*. The labor organizers of the American Federation of Labor (AFL) did not want the government to become involved in labor's problems, and probably for good reason. The government then—in the 1870's and 1880's—was antilabor, promanagement. It soon became clear that political power would be necessary to accomplish some of the goals of organized labor, especially the goals of the railroad unions. The AFL pursued that power and eventually won it, but generally remained tied to the values and principles of the society as it was. They simply wanted in; the route lay through collective bargaining and the right to strike. The unions set their sights on immediate bread-and-butter issues, to the exclusion of broader goals.

With the founding and development of mass industrial unionism under the Congress of Industrial Organizations (CIO), we began to see a slight change in overall union orientation. The CIO was interested in a wider variety of issues—foreign trade, interest rates, even civil rights issues to an extent—but it too never seriously questioned the racist basis of the society. In *Politics, Parties and Pressure Groups*, Professor V. O. Key, Jr. has concluded: ". . . on the fundamental question of the character of the economic system, the dominant labor ideology did not challenge the established order." [5] Professor Selig Perlman wrote: ". . . it is a labor movement upholding capitalism, not only in practice, but in principle as well." [6] Organized labor, so often pushed as a potential ally by the coalition theorists, illustrates the pitfalls of the first myth; as we shall see later . . . its history also debunks the second myth.

Yet another source of potential alliance frequently cited by the exponents of coalitions is the liberal-reform movement, especially at the local political level. But the various reform-politics groups—particularly in New York, Chicago and California—frequently are not tuned in to the primary goals of black people. They establish their own goals and then demand that black people identify with them. When black leaders begin to articulate goals in the interest of black people first, the reformers tend, more often than not, to term this "racist" and to drop off. Reformers push such "good government" programs as would result in posts being filled by professional, middle-class people. Wilson stated in *The Amateur Democrat*, "Blue-ribbon candidates would be selected, not only for the important, highly visible posts at the top of the ticket, but also for the less visible posts at the bottom." [7] Black people who have participated in local reform politics—especially in Chicago—have come from the upper-middle class. Reformers generally reject the political practice of ticket balancing, which means that they tend to be "color blind" and wish to select candidates only on the basis of qualifications, of merit. In itself this would not be bad, but their conception of a "qualified" person is usually one who fits the white middle-class mold. Seldom, if ever, does one hear of the reformers advocating representation by grass-roots leaders from the ghettos: these are hardly "blue-ribbon" types. Again, when reformers push for elections at large as opposed to election by district, they do not increase black political power. "Blue-ribbon" candidates, government by technical experts, elections at large— all these common innovations of reformers do little for black people.

Francis Carney concludes from his study of California's liberal-reform Democratic clubs that although those groups were usually strong on civil rights, they were nonetheless essentially middle-class oriented.[8] This could only perpetuate a paternalistic, colonial relationship—doing for the blacks. Thus, even when the reformers are bent on making significant changes in the system, the question must be asked if that change is consistent with the views and interests of black people—as perceived by those people.

Frequently, we have seen that a staunch, militant stand taken by black leaders has frightened away the reformers. The latter could not understand the former's militancy. "Amateur Democrats (reformers) are passionately committed to a militant stand on civil rights, but they shy away from militant Negro organizations because they find them 'too race-conscious,'"[9] says Wilson in *The Amateur Democrat*, citing as one example the Independent Voters of Illinois, who felt they could not go along with the desire of some black members to take a very strong, pro-civil rights and anti-Daley position. The liberal-reform politicians have not been able fully to accept the necessity of black people speaking forcefully and for themselves. This is one of the greatest points of tension between these two sets of groups today; this difference must be resolved before viable coalitions can be formed between the two.

To sum up our rejection of the first myth: . . . the political and economic institutions of this society must be completely revised if the political and economic status of black people is to be improved. We do not see how those same institutions can be utilized—through the mechanism of coalescing with some of them—to bring about that revision. We do not see how black people can form effective coalitions with groups which are not willing to question and condemn the racist institutions which exploit black people; which do not perceive the need for, and will not work for, basic change. Black people cannot afford to assume that what is good for white America is automatically good for black people.

The second myth we want to deal with is the assumption that a politically and economically secure group can collaborate with a politically and economically insecure group. Our contention is that such an alliance is based on very shaky grounds. By definition, the goals of the respective parties are different.

Black people are often told that they should seek to form coalitions after the fashion of those formed with so-called Radical Agrarians—later Populists—in the latter part of the nineteenth century. In 1886, the Colored Farmers' Alliance and Cooperative Union was formed, interestingly enough, by a white Baptist minister in Texas. The platform of this group was similar to that of the already existing Northern and Southern Farmers' Alliances, which were white. But upon closer examination, one could see substantial differences in interests and goals. The black group favored a Congressional bill (The Lodge Federal Elections Bill) which aimed to guarantee the voting rights of Southern black people; the white group opposed it. In 1889, a group of black farmers in North Carolina accused the Southern Alliance of setting low wages and influencing the state legislature to pass discriminatory laws. Two years later, the Colored Alliance called for a strike of black cotton pickers. Professors August Meier and Elliot Rudwick ask a number of questions about these two groups, in *From Plantation to Ghetto*:

> Under what circumstances did Negroes join and to what extent, if any, was participation encouraged (or even demanded) by white employers who were members of the Southern Alliance? . . . Is it possible that the Colored Alliance was something like a company union, disintegrating only when it became evident that the Negro tenant farmers refused to follow the dictates of their white employers? . . . And how was it that the Alliance men and Populists were later so easily led into extreme anti-Negro actions? In spite of various gestures to obtain Negro support, attitudes such as those exhibited in North Carolina and on the Lodge Bill would argue that whatever interracial solidarity existed was not firmly rooted.[10]

The fact is that the white group was relatively more secure than the black group. As C. Vann Woodward writes in *Tom Watson, Agrarian Rebel*, "It is undoubtedly true that the Populist ideology was dominantly that of the landowning farmer, who was, in many cases, the exploiter of landless tenant labor." [11] It is difficult to perceive the basis on which the two could coalesce and create a meaningful alliance for the landless, insecure group. It is no surprise, then, to learn of the antiblack actions mentioned above and to realize that the relation of blacks to Populists was not the harmonious arrangement some people today would have us believe.

It is true that black people in St. Louis and Kansas backed the Populists in the election of 1892, and North Carolina blacks supported them in 1896. But it is also true that the Populists in South Carolina, under the leadership of "Pitchfork" Ben Tillman, race-baited the black man. In some places —like Georgia—the Populists "fused" with the lily-white wing of the Republican Party, not with the so-called black-and-tan wing.

Or take the case of Tom Watson. This Populist from Georgia was at one time a staunch advocate of a united front between Negro and white farmers. In 1892, he wrote: "You are kept apart that you may be separately fleeced of your earnings. You are made to hate each other because upon that hatred is rested the keystone of the arch of financial despotism which enslaves you both. You are deceived and blinded that you may not see how this race antagonism perpetuates a monetary system which beggars both." [12]

But this is the same Tom Watson who, only a few years later and because the *political* tide was flowing against such an alliance, did a complete turnabout. At that time, Democrats were disfranchising black people in state after state. But, as John Hope Franklin recorded in *From Slavery to Freedom*, "Where the Populists were unable to control the Negro vote, as in Georgia in 1894, they believed that the Democrats had never completely disfranchised the Negroes because their votes were needed if the Democrats were to stay in power. This belief led the defeated and disappointed Tom Watson to support a constitutional amendment excluding the Negro from the franchise—a complete reversal of his position in denouncing South Carolina for adopting such an amendment in 1895." [13]

Watson was willing to ally with white candidates who were anti-Democratic-machine Democrats. With the black vote eliminated, the Populists stood to hold the balance of power between warring factions of the Democratic Party. Again C. Vann Woodward spells it out in his book, *Tom Watson, Agrarian Rebel*:

> He [Watson] . . . pledged his support, and the support of the Populists, to any anti-machine, Democratic candidate running upon a suitable platform that included a pledge to "a change in our Constitution which will perpetuate white supremacy in Georgia."
> How Watson managed to reconcile his radical democratic doctrine with a proposal to disfranchise a million citizens of his native state is not quite clear.
> "The white people dare not revolt so long as they can be intimidated by the fear of the Negro vote," he explained. Once the "bugaboo of Negro domination" was removed, however, "every white man would act according to his own conscience and judgment in deciding how he shall vote." With these words, Watson abandoned his old dream of uniting both races against the enemy, and took his first step toward the opposite extreme in racial views.[14]

At all times, the Populists and Watson emerge as politically motivated. The history of the period tells us that the whites—whether Populists, Republicans or Democrats—always had their own interests in mind. The black man was little more than a political football, to be tossed and kicked around at the convenience of others whose position was more secure.

We can learn the same lesson from the politics of the city of Atlanta, Georgia today. It is generally recognized that the black vote there is crucial to the election of a mayor. This was true in the case of William B. Hartsfield, and it is no less true for the present mayor, Ivan Allen, Jr. The coalition which dominates Atlanta politics has been described thus by Professor Edward Banfield in *Big City Politics*:

> The alliance between the business-led white middle class and the Negro is the main fact of local politics and government; only within the limits that it allows can anything be done, and much of what is done is for the purpose of holding it together.[15]

Mayor Hartsfield put together a "three-legged stool" as a base of power. The business power structure, together with the "good government"-minded middle class that takes its lead from that power structure is one leg. The Atlanta press is another. The third leg is the black community. But something is wrong with this stool. In the first place, of course, the third leg is a hollow one. The black community of Atlanta is dominated by a black power structure of . . . "leaders" . . . concerned primarily with protecting their own vested interests and their supposed influence with the white power structure, unresponsive to and unrepresentative of the black masses. But even this privileged group is economically and politically insecure by comparison with the other two forces with whom they have coalesced. Note this description by Banfield:

> Three associations of businessmen, *the leadership of which overlaps greatly*, play important parts in civic affairs. The Chamber of Commerce launches ideas which are often taken up as official city policy, and it is always much involved in efforts to get bond issues approved. The Central Atlanta Association is particularly concerned with the downtown business district and has taken the lead in efforts to improve expressways, mass transit, and urban renewal. Its weekly newsletter is widely read and respected. *The Uptown Association is a vehicle used by banks and other property owners to maintain a boundary line against expansion of the Negro district. To achieve this purpose it supports nonresidential urban renewal projects* [author's italics].[16]

Atlanta's substantial black bourgeoisie cannot compete with that line-up.

The political and economic interests causing the white leaders to enter the coalition are clear. So is the fact that those interests are often diametrically opposed to the interests of black people. We need only look at what the black man has received for his faithful support of politically and economically secure "alliance partners." Banfield puts it succinctly: "Hartsfield gave the Negro practically nothing in return for his vote" (p. 30). That vote, in 1957, was nine-tenths of the 20,000 votes cast by black people.

In 1963, a group of civic leaders from the black community of Southeast Atlanta documented the injustices suffered by that community's 60,000 black people. The lengthy list of grievances included faults in the sewerage system, sidewalks needed, streets which should be paved, deficient bus service and traffic control, substandard housing areas, inadequate parks and recreation facilities, continuing school segregation and inadequate black schools. Their report stated:

> Atlanta city officials have striven to create an image of Atlanta as a rapidly growing, modern, progressive city where all citizens can live in decent, healthful surroundings. This image is a blatant lie so long as the city provides no health clinics for its citizens but relies entirely upon inadequate county facilities. It is a lie so long as these health clinics are segregated and the city takes no action to end this segregation. Because of segregation, only

one of the four health clinics in the South side area is available to over 60,000 Negroes. This clinic . . . is small, its equipment inadequate and outdated, and its service dangerously slow due to general overcrowding.

In 1962, the city employed 5,663 workers, 1,647 of them black, but only 200 of those did other than menial work. The document lists 22 departments in which, of 175 equipment operators in the Construction Department, not one was black. The city did not even make a pretense of belief in "getting ahead by burning the midnight oil": there was only one public library in the community, a single room with 12,000 volumes (mostly children's books) for 60,000 people.[17]

This is what "coalition politics" won for the black citizens of one sizeable community. Nor had the situation in Atlanta's ghettos improved much by 1966. When a so-called riot broke out in the Summerhill community, local civic groups pointed out that they had deplored conditions and called the area "ripe for riot" many months earlier.

Black people must ultimately come to realize that such coalitions, such alliances have *not* been in their interest. They are "allying" with forces clearly not consistent with the long-term progress of blacks; in fact, the whites enter the alliance in many cases precisely to impede that progress.

Labor unions also illustrate very clearly the treacherous nature of coalitions between the economically secure and insecure. From the passage of the Wagner Act in 1935 (which gave unions the right to organize and bargain collectively), unions have been consolidating their position, winning economic victories for their members, and generally developing along with the growing prosperity of the country. What about black workers during this time? Their status has been one of steady deterioration rather than progress. It is common knowledge that the craft unions of AFL (printers, plumbers, bricklayers, electrical workers) have deliberately excluded black workers over the years. These unions have taken care of their own—their white own. Meanwhile, the unemployment rate of black workers has increased, doubling, in some cases, that of white workers. The unions themselves were not always innocent bystanders to this development:

> . . . The war has been over twenty years now, and instead of more Negroes joining labor unions, fewer are doing so; for the Negro, increased unionization has in too many instances meant decreased job opportunity. . . .
>
> When the International Brotherhood of Electrical Workers became the collective bargaining agent at the Bauer Electric Company in Hartford, Connecticut in the late forties, the union demanded and got the removal of all Negro electricians from their jobs. The excuse was advanced that, since their union contract specified "whites only," they could not and would not change this to provide continued employment for the Negroes who were at the plant before the union was recognized. Similar cases can be found in the Boilermakers' Union and the International Association of Machinists at the Boeing Aircraft Company in Seattle.[18]

And so, precisely *because* of union recognition, black workers *lost* their jobs.

The situation became so bad that in 1959 black workers in the AFL-CIO, under the leadership of A. Philip Randolph, organized the Negro American Labor Council (NALC). Some black workers, at least, finally accepted the reality that they had to have their own black representatives if their demands were to be made—not to mention being met. The larger body did not particularly welcome the formation of this group. Randolph told the NAACP convention in June 1960 in St. Paul, Minnesota that "a gulf of misunderstanding" seemed to be widening between the black community and the labor community. He further stated: "It is unfortunate that some of our liberal friends, along with some of the leaders of labor, even yet do not comprehend the nature, scope, depth, and challenge of this civil rights revolution which is surging forward in the House of Labor. They elect to view with alarm practically any and all criticisms of the AFL-CIO because of racial discrimination." [19]

It has become clear to many black leaders that organized labor operates from a different set of premises and with a different list of priorities, and that the status of black workers does not occupy a high position on that list. In fact, they are highly expendable, as in the political arena. Note the following observation:

> . . . the split has even deeper causes. It arises out of the Negro's declaration of independence from white leadership and white direction in the civil rights fight—the Negro view today is that the whites, in labor or in other fields, are unreliable race campaigners when the chips are down, and that only the Negro can carry through to race victories.
>
> "Negro trade unionists and workers must bear their own cross for their own liberation. They must make their own crisis decisions bearing upon their life, labor, and liberty," Randolph told the NAACP. [20]

The Negro American Labor Council itself, however, suggests that such realizations may not be sufficient. It is our position that a viable group cannot be organized *within* a larger association. The subgroup will have to acquiesce to the goals and demands of the parent; it can only serve as a conscience-pricker—because it has no independent base of power from which to operate. Coalition between the strong and the weak ultimately leads only to perpetuation of the hierarchical status: superordinance and subordinance.

It is also important to note that the craft unions of the AFL were born and consolidating their positions at the same time that this country was beginning to expand imperialistically in Latin America and in the Philippines. Such expansion increased the economic security of white union workers here. Thus organized labor has participated in the exploitation of colored peoples abroad and of black workers at home. Black people today are beginning to assert themselves at a time when the old colonial markets are vanishing; former African and Asian colonies are fighting for the right to control their own natural resources, free from exploitation by Western and American capitalism. With whom will economically secure, organized labor cast its lot—with the big businesses of exploitation or with the insecure poor colored peoples? This question gives additional significance—a double layer of meaning—to the struggle of black workers here. The answer, unfortunately, seems clear enough.

We cannot see, then, how black people, who are massively insecure both politically and economically, can coalesce with those whose position is secure—particularly when the latter's security is based on the perpetuation of the existing political and economic structure.

The third myth proceeds from the premise that political coalitions can be sustained on a moral, friendly or sentimental basis, or on appeals to conscience. We view this as a myth because we believe that political relations are based on self-interest: benefits to be gained and losses to be avoided. For the most part, man's politics is determined by his evaluation of material good and evil. Politics results from a conflict of interests, not of consciences.

We frequently hear of the great moral value of the pressure by various church groups to bring about passage of the Civil Rights Laws of 1964 and 1965. There is no question that significant numbers of clergy and lay groups participated in the successful lobbying of those bills, but we should be careful not to overemphasize the value of this. To begin with, many of those religious groups were available only until the bills were passed; their sustained moral force is not on hand for the all-important process of ensuring federal implementation of these laws, particularly with respect to the appointment of more federal voting registrars and the setting of guidelines for school desegregation.

It should also be pointed out that many of those same people did not feel so morally obliged when the issues struck closer to home—in the North, with housing, as an example. They could be morally self-righteous about passing a law to desegregate southern lunch counters or even a law guaranteeing southern black people the right to vote. But laws against employment and housing discrimination—which would affect the North as much as the South—are something else again. After all, ministers—North and South—are often forced out of their pulpits if they speak or act too forcefully in favor of civil rights. Their parishioners do not lose sleep at night worrying about the oppressed status of black Americans; they are not morally torn inside themselves. As Silberman said, they simply do not want their peace disrupted and their businesses hurt.

We do not want to belabor the church in particular; what we have said applies to all the other "allies" of black people. Furthermore, we do not seek to condemn these groups for being what they are so much as we seek to emphasize a fact of life: they are unreliable allies when a conflict of interest arises. Morality and sentiment cannot weather such conflicts, and black people must realize this. No group should go into an alliance or a coalition relying on the "good will" of the ally. If the ally chooses to withdraw that "good will," he can do so usually without the other being able to impose sanctions upon him of any kind.

Thus we reject the last myth. In doing so, we would reemphasize a point. . . . Some believe that there is a conflict between the so-called American Creed and American practices. The Creed is supposed to contain considerations of equality and liberty, at least certainly equal opportunity, and justice. The fact is, of course, that these are simply words which were *not even originally intended* to have applicability to black people: Article I of the Constitution affirms that the black man is three-fifths of a person.[21] The fact is that people live their daily lives making practical day-to-day decisions about their jobs, homes, children. And in a profit-oriented, materialistic society, there is little time to reflect on creeds, especially if it could mean more job competition, "lower property values," and the "daughter marrying a Negro." There is no "American dilemma," no moral hang-up, and black people should not base decisions on the assumption that a dilemma exists. It may be useful to articulate such assumptions in order to embarrass, to create international pressure, to educate. But they cannot form the basis for viable coalitions.

What, then, are the grounds for viable coalitions?

Before one begins to talk coalition, one should establish clearly the premises on which that coalition will be based. All parties to the coalition must perceive a *mutually* beneficial goal based on the conception of *each* party of his *own* self-interest. One party must not blindly assume that what is good for one is automatically—without question—good for the other. Black people must first ask themselves what is good for *them*, and then they can determine if the "liberal" is willing to coalesce. They must recognize that institutions and political organizations have no consciences outside their own special interests.

Secondly, there is a clear need for genuine power bases before black people can enter into coalitions. Civil rights leaders who, in the past or at present, rely essentially on "national sentiment" to obtain passage of civil rights legislation reveal the fact that they are operating from a powerless base. They must appeal to the conscience, the good graces of the society; they are, as noted earlier, cast in a beggar's role, hoping to strike a responsive chord. It is very significant that the two oldest civil rights organizations, the National Association for the Advancement of Colored People and the Urban League, have constitutions which specifically prohibit partisan political activity. (The Congress of Racial Equality once did, but it changed that clause when it changed its orientation in favor of Black Power.) This is perfectly understandable in terms of the strategy and goals of the older organizations, the concept of the civil rights movement as a kind of liaison between the powerful white community and the dependent black community. The dependent status of the black community apparently was unimportant since, if the movement proved successful, that community was going to blend into the white society anyway. No pretense was made of organizing and developing institutions of community power within the black community. No attempt was made to create any base of organized political strength; such activity was even prohibited, in the cases mentioned above. All problems would be solved by forming coalitions with labor, churches, reform clubs, and especially liberal Democrats.

. . . It should . . . be clear that the building of an independent force is necessary; that Black Power is necessary. If we do not learn from history, we are doomed to repeat it, and that is precisely the lesson of the Reconstruction era. Black people were allowed to register, to vote and to participate in politics, because it was to the advantage of powerful white "allies" to permit this. But at all times such advances flowed from white decisions. That era of black participation in politics was ended by another set of white decisions. There was no powerful independent political base in the southern black community to challenge the curtailment of political rights. At this point in the struggle, black people have no assurance—save a kind of idiot optimism and faith in a society whose history is one of racism—that if it became necessary, even the painfully limited gains thrown to the civil rights movement by the Congress would not be revoked as soon as a shift in political sentiments occurs. (A vivid example of this emerged in 1967 with Congressional moves to undercut and eviscerate the school desegregation provisions of the 1964 Civil Rights Act.) We must build that assurance and build it on solid ground.

We also recognize the potential for limited, short-term coalitions on relatively minor issues. But we must note that such approaches seldom come to terms with the roots of institutional racism. In fact, one might well argue that such coalitions on subordinate issues are, in the long run, harmful. They could lead whites and blacks into thinking either that their long-term interests do *not* conflict when in fact they do, or that such lesser issues are the *only* issues which can be solved. With these limitations in mind, and a spirit of caution, black people can approach possibilities of coalition for specific goals.

Viable coalitions therefore stem from four preconditions: (a) the recognition by the parties involved of their respective self-interests; (b) the mutual belief that each party stands to benefit in terms of that self-interest from allying with the other or others; (c) the acceptance of the fact that each party has its own independent base of power and does not depend for ultimate decision making on a force outside itself; and (d) the realization that the coalition deals with specific and identifiable—as opposed to general and vague—goals.

The heart of the matter lies in this admonition from Machiavelli, writing in *The Prince:*

> And here it should be noted that a prince ought never to make common cause with one more powerful than himself to injure another, unless necessity forces him to it. . . . for if he wins you rest in his power, and princes must avoid as much as possible being under the will and pleasure of others.[22]

Machiavelli recognized that "necessity" might at times force the weaker to ally with the stronger. Our view is that those who advocate Black Power should work to minimize that necessity. It is crystal clear that such alliances can seldom, if ever, be meaningful to the weaker partner. They cannot offer the optimum conditions of a political *modus operandi*. Therefore, if and when such alliances are unavoidable, we must not be sanguine about the possibility of their leading to ultimate, substantial benefit for the weaker force.

Let black people organize themselves *first*, define their interests and goals, and then see what kinds of allies are available. Let any ghetto group contemplating coalition be so tightly organized, so strong, that—in the words of Saul Alinsky—it is an "indigestible body" which cannot be absorbed or swallowed up.[23] The advocates of Black Power are not opposed to coalitions *per se*. But we are *not* interested in coalitions based on myths. To the extent to which black people can form *viable* coalitions will the end results of those alliances be lasting and meaningful. There will be clearer understanding of what is sought; there will be greater impetus on all sides to deliver, because there will be *mutual* respect of the power of the other to reward or punish; there will be much less likelihood of leaders selling out their followers. Black Power therefore has no connotation of "go it alone." Black Power simply says: enter coalitions only *after* you are able to "stand on your own." Black Power seeks to correct the approach to dependency, to remove that dependency, and to establish a viable psychological, political and social base upon which the black community can function to meet its needs.

At the beginning of our discussion of Black Power, we said that black people must redefine themselves, state new values and goals. The same holds true for white people of good will; they too need to redefine themselves and their role.

Some people see the advocates of Black Power as concerned with ridding the civil rights struggle of white people. This has been untrue from the beginning. There is a definite, much-needed role whites can play. This role can best be examined on three different, yet interrelated, levels: educative, organizational, supportive. Given the pervasive nature of racism in the society and the extent to which attitudes of white superiority and black inferiority have become embedded, it is very necessary that white people begin to disabuse themselves of such notions. Black people, as we stated earlier, will lead the challenge to old values and norms, but whites who recognize the need must also work in this sphere. Whites have access to groups in the society never reached by black people. They must get within those groups and help perform this essential educative function.

One of the most disturbing things about almost all white supporters has been that they are reluctant to go into their own communities—which is where the racism exists—and work to get rid of it. We are not now speaking of whites who have worked to get black people "accepted," on an individual basis, by the white society. Of these there have been many; their efforts are undoubtedly well-intended and individually helpful. But too often those efforts are geared to the same false premises as integration; too often the society in which they seek acceptance of a few black people can afford to make the gesture. We are speaking, rather, of those whites who see the need for basic change and have hooked up with the black liberation movement because it seemed the most promising agent of such change. Yet they often admonish black people to be nonviolent. They should preach nonviolence in the white community. Where possible, they might also educate other white people to the need for Black Power. The range is great, with much depending on the white person's own class background and environment.

On a broader scale, there is the very important function of working to reorient this society's attitudes and policies toward African and Asian countries. Across the country, smug white communities show a poverty of awareness, a poverty of humanity, indeed, a poverty of ability to act in a civilized manner toward non-Anglo human beings. The white middle-class suburbs need "freedom schools" as badly as the black communities. Anglo-conformity is a dead weight on their necks too. All this is an educative role crying to be performed by those whites so inclined.

The organizational role is next. It is hoped that eventually there will be a coalition of poor blacks and poor whites. This is the only coalition which seems acceptable to us, and we see such a coalition as the major internal instrument of change in the American society. It is purely academic today to talk about bringing poor blacks and poor whites together, but the task of creating a poor-white power block dedicated to the goals of a free, open society—not one based on racism and subordination—must be attempted. The main responsibility for this task falls upon whites. Black and white can work together in the white community where possible; it is not possible, however, to go into a poor southern town and talk about "integration," or even desegregation. Poor white people are becoming more hostile—not less—toward black people, partly because they see the nation's attention focused on black poverty and few, if any, people coming to them.

Only whites can mobilize and organize those communities along the lines necessary and possible for effective alliances with the black communities. This job cannot be left to the existing institutions and agencies, because those structures, for the most part, are reflections of institutional racism. If the job is to be done, there must be new forms created. Thus, the political modernization process must involve the white community as well as the black.

It is our position that black organizations should be black-led and essentially black-staffed, with policy being made by black people. White people can and do play very important supportive roles in those organizations. Where they come with specific skills and techniques, they will be evaluated in those terms. All too frequently, however, many young, middle-class, white Americans, like some sort of Pepsi generation, have wanted to "come alive" through the black community and black groups. They have wanted to be where the action is—and the action has been in those places. They have sought refuge among blacks from a sterile, meaningless, irrelevant life in middle-class America. They have been unable to deal with the stifling, racist, parochial, split-level mentality of their parents, teachers, preachers and friends. Many have come seeing "no difference in color," they have come "color blind." But at this time and in this land, color *is* a factor and we should not overlook or deny this. The black organizations do not need this kind of idealism, which borders on paternalism. White people working in SNCC have understood this. There are white lawyers who defend black civil rights workers in court, and white activists who support indigenous black movements across the country. Their function is not to lead or to set policy or to attempt to define black people to black people. Their role is supportive.

Ultimately, the gains of our struggle will be meaningful only when consolidated by viable coalitions between blacks and whites who accept each other as co-equal partners and who identify their goals as politically and economically similar. At this stage, given the nature of the society, distinct roles must be played. The charge that this approach is "antiwhite" remains as inaccurate as almost all the other public commentary on Black Power. There is nothing new about this; whenever black people have moved toward genuinely independent action, the society has distorted their intentions or damned their performance. . . .

NOTES

1. BAYARD RUSTIN, "Black Power and Coalition Politics," *Commentary* (September 1966).
2. LEWIS KILLIAN and CHARLES GRIGG, *Racial Crisis in America* (Englewood Cliffs, N.J.: Prentice-Hall, 1964), p. 73.
3. MILTON M. GORDON, *Assimilation in American Life* (New York: Oxford University Press, 1964), pp. 88, 103–104.
4. EDWARD C. BANFIELD and JAMES Q. WILSON, *City Politics* (Cambridge: Harvard University Press, 1963), pp. 31–32, 35, 124.
5. V. O. KEY, JR., *Politics, Parties and Pressure Groups* (New York: Thomas Y. Crowell).
6. SELIG PERLMAN, "The Basic Philosophy of the American Labor Movement," *Annals of the American Academy of Political and Social Science* 274 (1951), pp. 57–63.
7. JAMES Q. WILSON, *The Amateur Democrat* (Chicago: University of Chicago Press, 1962), p. 128.

8. FRANCIS CARNEY, *The Rise of the Democratic Clubs in California*, Eagleton Institute Cases in Practical Politics (New York: McGraw-Hill, 1959).

9. WILSON, *op. cit.*, p. 285.

10. AUGUST MEIER and ELLIOT RUDWICK, *From Plantation to Ghetto* (New York: Hill and Wang, 1970), pp. 158–59.

11. C. VANN WOODWARD, *Tom Watson, Agrarian Rebel* (New York: Oxford University Press, 1963), p. 18.

12. TOM WATSON, "Negro Question in the South," Arena 6 (1892), p. 548.

13. JOHN HOPE FRANKLIN, *From Slavery to Freedom* (New York: Alfred A. Knopf, 1967), p. 218.

14. WOODWARD, *op cit.*, pp. 371–72.

15. EDWARD C. BANFIELD, *Big City Politics* (New York: Random House, 1965), p. 35.

16. *Ibid.*, pp. 31–32.

17. "The City Must Provide. South Atlanta: The Forgotten Community," Atlanta Civic Council, 1963.

18. MYRNA BAIN, "Organized Labor and the Negro Worker," *National Review* (June 4, 1963), p. 455.

19. "Labor-Negro Division Widens," *Business Week* (July 9, 1960), p. 79.

20. BAIN, "Organized Labor and the Negro Worker."

21. "Representatives and direct Taxes shall be apportioned among the several States which may be included within this Union, according to their respective Numbers, which shall be determined by adding to the whole Number of free Persons, including those bound to Service for a Term of Years, and excluding Indians not taxed, three-fifths of all other Persons. "

22. NICCOLÒ MACHIAVELLI, *The Prince and the Discourses* (New York: Random House, 1950), p. 84.

23. SAUL ALINSKY speaking at the 1967 Legal Defense Fund Convocation in New York City, May 18, 1967.

Politics of Black Ethnicity

Martin Kilson

POLITICAL SOCIOLOGY OF RACISM

For the first half-century after slavery was abolished in the United States, the Negro lived mainly in the rural South and, save for a brief 10–15 years of Reconstruction, he had no rights of political participation. During this same period, the major white non-Protestant ethnic groups were crowding into the cities of the East, North, and Midwest, and by the end of the nineteenth century they had laid the basis for mastering the politics of the emerging urban society.[1] But the Negro did not enter urban society in significant numbers until World War I, and so for nearly 40 years, roughly from the early 1880's to 1915, the typical black had neither political rights (stripped from him by the white racist rule in the post-Reconstruction South) nor access to the social system of urban America.

The cities were becoming the center of sociopolitical influence, and the Negro's belated migration from the South to the cities of the East, North, and Midwest meant that his institutional capability for handling modern urban life was much weaker than that of the white ethnic urban groups which had preceded him by 40 years. In fact, their lead in settling in the cities amounted to more than 40 years; for although black migration from the South began in earnest around 1910–1915, in the succeeding 50 years more than half of the Negro population remained in the South. (See Table 1.)

In the first 60 years of this century, only a minority of the black population, though an increasing minority (e.g., 10 per cent in 1910, 23 per cent in 1930, 32 per cent in 1950, 40 per cent in 1960), had any opportunity at all to experience modern political life.[2] However, the political experience of this urbanized black minority obviously was part of the kind of political life that was to dominate twentieth-century America. Therefore this black urban sector has been and remains crucial in shaping both current and future Negro politics. What, then, was the experience of this critical urban minority of the Negro population that resided outside the South from 1910 to the post-World War II era?

Of primary importance was that the migration from the South brought hundreds of thousands of Negroes at least some of the political rights they had so long been denied. Without this migration, they doubtless would not have obtained these primary political rights far beyond the 1960's, when they were secured, at least in the written law. Ruling elites in the South certainly

SOURCE: From "Black Politics: A New Power," by Martin Kilson. Copyright © *Dissent* Magazine. Reprinted by permission.

TABLE 1. Per Cent Distribution of the Population Region—1950, 1960, and 1966

Region	Negro Population 1950	1960	1966
United States	100	100	100
South	68	60	55
North	28	34	37
Northeast	13	16	17
North-central	15	18	20
West	4	6	8

SOURCE: *Report of the National Advisory Commission on Civil Disorders* (Washington, D.C., 1968).

were both willing and able to sustain Negro political subservience to the end of this century, and the connivance of the North, Midwest, and West cannot be discounted.[3] Fortunately, the measure of political freedom available to blacks in other parts of the country was sufficient to allow an attack on white authoritarianism in the South.

Urbanization provided blacks with the social organization and institutional differentiation that is necessary for effective political power.[4] Essentially, political modernization is a matter of highly differentiated strata and institutions that will sustain political articulation beyond parochial settings (ethnic, religious, regional, economic, etc.) in order to provide public and civil services.

But black urbanization was a *particular* form of city-dwelling.

Negro city-dwelling in this century was stifled by that cluster of norms or customs characterized by the term white racism. W. Lloyd Warner, the sociologist of main-stream America, discovered this in Yankee City: "The caste barrier or color line, rigid and unrelenting, has cut off this small group [of blacks—0.48 per cent of the population] from the general life of the community."[5] As Warner knew well, whatever the general life of a modern community is, surely politics is a salient feature: for politics is, after all, the process through which services and benefits are allocated among competing sectors of society. The restrictions imposed by whites upon blacks necessarily jeopardize the latter's capacity for political adaptation to life in the cities: blacks were victims of the whims and caprices of white politicians, bureaucrats, and party machines, few of which were notable for exemplary political manners even in dealings with whites.[6]

From World War I onward, the coercive regulatory agencies of the cities combined with party and machine organizations to exclude the Negro from an effective political role. Not that the black city-dwellers were ignored by white-controlled city politics; their numbers alone argued against total indifference. (See Table 2.) Rather, white city machines, with the notable exception of Chicago,[7] simply dealt halfheartedly with the problem of the

TABLE 2. Number and Percentage of Negroes in Selected Northern Cities,
1910–1940

	Number of Negroes				Per Cent Negroes in Population			
	1910	1920	1930	1940	1910	1920	1930	1940
New York	91,709	152,467	327,706	458,444	1.9	2.7	4.7	6.1
Chicago	44,103	109,458	233,903	277,731	2	4.1	6.9	8.2
Philadelphia	84,459	134,229	219,599	250,880	5.5	7.4	11.3	13
Detroit	5,741	40,838	120,066	149,119	1.2	4.1	7.7	9.2
St. Louis	43,960	69,854	93,580	108,765	6.4	9	11.4	13.3
Cleveland	8,448	34,451	71,899	84,504	1.5	4.3	8	9.6
Pittsburgh	25,623	37,725	54,983	62,216	4.8	6.4	8.2	9.9
Cincinnati	19,639	30,079	47,818	55,593	5.4	7.5	10.6	12.2
Indianapolis	21,816	34,678	43,967	51,142	9.3	11	12.1	13.2
Los Angeles	7,599	15,579	38,894	63,774	2.4	2.7	3.1	4.2
Newark	9,475	16,977	38,880	45,760	2.7	4.1	8.8	10.6
Gary	383	5,299	17,922	20,394	2.3	9.6	17.8	18.3
Dayton	4,842	9,025	17,077	20,273	4.2	5.9	8.5	9.6
Youngstown	1,936	6,662	14,552	14,615	2.4	5	8.6	8.7

SOURCE: *United States Census Reports.*

political inclusion of black ethnic groups on terms comparable to that of white
ethnic groups. Even more, special acts of city machines from World War I
onward sought to truncate top Negro political development: "The immigrants
and their descendants who controlled the [political] machines were anti-
Negro," remarked Herbert Gans, "and gerrymandered ghetto neighborhoods
so that they would not have to share their power with Negroes." [8] The coercive power of city machines related to the urban black in ways that demoralized him. As Gunnar Myrdal observed some 30 years ago:

> In most Northern communities, Negroes are more likely than whites to be
> arrested under any suspicious circumstances. They are more likely to be ac-
> corded discourteous or brutal treatment at the hands of the police than are
> whites. The rate of killing of Negroes by the police is high in many Northern
> cities. . . . The attitudes of the police will sometimes be found among the
> most important items considered in local Negro politics in the North.[9]

In summary, the rigid and inhuman restrictions placed upon the Negro's
access to the modern social system of American cities distorted and truncated
his political development in the past 60 years. No other American immigrant
group faced comparable barriers to political modernization.[10] It was precisely

the white immigrants' reasonably, though not fully, caste-free interaction with the city power structures that enabled them to shape their social institutions.[11]

ETHNICITY AND THE NEGRO POLITICAL SUBSYSTEM

Surely an interplay of politics and social structure similar to that of white ethnic groups was required for effective and modern politicization of Negroes. As it happened, however, much less than this occurred. The violence and militancy typical of contemporary urban Negro politics stem directly from this situation. So do the current endeavors of two kinds of black leadership to utilize black ethnicity as an instrument for political efficacy in the black ghetto. One kind of leadership is highly ideological, articulating militancy and black ethnicity as a matter of willed belief; the other is pragmatic, though not without a world view, articulating militancy and black ethnicity as a matter of political necessity. In the latter, militancy and ethnicity are wedded to established city politics, much in the manner of white ethnic late-nineteenth-century and early-twentieth-century politicians. The goal is to facilitate the Negro community's vertical political structure, and to surmount the horizontal class cleavages. This was never realized through other forms of politics available to urban Negroes in this century—not through the second-class version of machine politics available to urban blacks (which I have characterized elsewhere as neoclientage machine politics [12]) and not through civil rights or protest politics.

The limited relationship between the urban Negro and the white-controlled city machine, from World War I through World War II, deprived the blacks of a primary mode of political development that had been available to white immigrant groups—*the politicization of ethnicity*. This means simply to use ethnic patterns and prejudices as the primary basis for interest-group and political formations, and to build upon these to integrate a given ethnic community into the wider politics of the city and the nation.[13] To the extent that a given ethnic community was successful in so organizing itself, it could claim a share of city-based rewards and, through congressional and presidential politics, of Federal Government rewards.[14] To fall outside or be only partially integrated into this process, since World War I, was necessarily to be without a basis for sociopolitical power.

The urban Negro thus was either outside or only partially linked to this politicization of ethnicity through city machines, and his political actions have borne the mark of this experience ever since. Thus, the Negro lower or popular strata (that is, the working class, the marginal working class, and the chronically unemployed class) have been, until the past decade, deprived of participatory incentives, an experience that had motivated the white ethnic lower strata's political development.[15] This, in turn, has produced a Negro urban lower strata that by the 1960's ranked low in all salient indices of modern political life: low political skill and knowledge, a high sense of powerlessness and estrangement from institutionalized processes, and low participation. Second, the city machines' relative neglect of the black ghetto in the years 1915–1960 deprived the Negro elites (the black middle and upper classes) of the opportunity and incentives to give political leadership. Whereas the city machines' full-fledged inclusion of white ethnic communities provided a powerful stimulus to the Irish, Italian, Jewish, Polish, and other ethnic bourgeoisies to participate in the political organization (and thus control) of their ethnic lower strata,[16] the black bourgeoisie, for the most part, was indeed not induced to use its institutions to politicize the black lower strata in order to bring their votes to the service of party machines. Only in Chicago did this pattern of political relationship between the black bourgeoisie and the black lower strata evolve between the two World Wars. In Chicago, contrary to the pattern of other cities, the white politicians—especially Republicans—accepted the full-fledged inclusion of the black ethnic turf on terms comparable to those applied to the white ethnic turfs.[17] In other cities, however, the Negro elites, denied full-fledged inclusion in machine politics, turned to civil rights or protest politics.

Civil rights politics was largely a middle-class affair: from 1915 to the 1950's the leadership and membership were mainly middle class, and the large Negro lower strata had little political relationship to civil rights politics. This meant that the politics pursued by Negro elites in most cities never produced a vertical integration of the elites with the Negro lower strata. In short, the civil rights politics, which the neglect of city machines caused Negro elites in most cities to adopt, had a class and status bias that prevented the black ghetto from taking on the attributes of an ethnic political subsystem—that is, an articulate and politically cohesive group within the structure of the city machine.

Only with the rise of a politically cultivated black ethnicity in the past decade has the Negro ghetto acquired the features of a politically institutionalized ethnic community. But this belated politicization of black ethnicity exhibits features that were uncommon in the development of white ethnic communities at an earlier period. One such feature is sharp conflict with the American political system as such, at all levels—city, state, and federal. This conflict takes the form either of popular-based urban riots, commencing in 1964 and initiated largely by lower-strata blacks, or the intensive cultivation of antiwhite perspectives among blacks. Both of these conflict-laden tendencies are directed toward the wider political mobilization of the ghetto and for the growth of Negro political capability. Of course, none of this can be realized without leadership, and two leadership strata now vie for the main role in the politicization of black ethnicity: one is of lower-strata background and so has a special claim to having spearheaded the militant style now common to much of Negro leadership; the other is middle class, though a good portion of this second leadership group is first-generation middle class, and this segment is currently leading the bid of the black bourgeoisie to seize a dominant role in the emerging politics of black ethnicity.

LEADERSHIP AND BLACK ETHNICITY:
LOWER-STRATA MILITANTS

Although the riots initiated by lower-strata Negroes in the mid-1960's stimulated the rise of militant political leaders, it was the federal government's War on Poverty that enabled these leaders to institutionalize their politics. In 1965–1970 the government allocated nearly $5 billion under the 1964 Economic Opportunity Act to a community action program, which led to the formation of more than 2,000 so-called community action organizations. These organizations were quickly politicized by lower-strata black militants throughout the 1960's and became their primary political structure.

The federal government did not intend, of course, to transform the community action organizations into militant political instruments. The government's purpose was rather to provide the Negro lower strata with an opportunity to develop basic administrative and executive skills, a goal some observers claim was realized, though I doubt it.[18]

However, federal agencies administering the War on Poverty could not adequately control either what was done at the city level with the resources of community action organizations or the composition of these bodies. In this way the lower-strata militant leaders converted the War on Poverty's action organizations from social service agencies into instruments for politicizing (and radicalizing) such heretofore inarticulate Negro lower-strata groups as welfare mothers, gangs, school dropouts, semiskilled workers, etc.

Yet little of this politicization of the lower strata represented a long-run political gain. It is, after all, one thing to use community action organizations to attract adherents to ideas of black nationalist militancy and incite a demonstration by welfare mothers; it is another matter altogether to use community action agencies to encourage welfare mothers to register to vote, to participate in precinct and ward committee elections and activities, to evaluate candidates and issues, etc. Clearly this latter form of politicization in cities would be of more lasting political value than the rather ad hoc politicization used by lower-strata black militants.

The lower-strata militant leaders pursue a policy of short-run rather than long-run politicization of the ghetto because they are accustomed in general to short-run behavior. The turn of these militant leaders to politics after the riots of the mid-1960's was less a matter of wanting to provide leadership than of utilizing their new status in order to derive benefits on a scale unavailable to them in their previous "hustling" roles such as pimp, narcotics pusher, small holdup man, numbers writer, and others. A previous experience with hustling, which is common to some lower-strata militant leaders, has also influenced their political style. For just as their hustling roles afforded them a certain celebrity status—virtually that of "culture heroes" [19]—their concern with such ad hoc political action as confrontations with officials provides them both publicity and celebration. The Black Panther leaders have taken this style to its extreme; but they have contributed little to the durable politicization of the Negro lower strata, since they prefer short-run tactics linked to violent rhetoric and symbolism, and sometimes to violence itself.[20]

It appears, then, that the lower-strata militant leaders lack the habits, values, and skills required for a durable politicization of the Negro population. Though they have become an important force in the new politics of urban black ethnicity, *they have proved incapable of institutionalizing this politics.* Their main contribution is rather different: they stamp the politics of black ethnicity with a lower-class style, which means that the experiences and problems of the Negro lower strata (marginal working class and lower class) rather than the black bourgeoisie have a determining role in the politics of black ethnicity.

One cannot overstate the significance of this. For one thing, it signifies the profoundly important difference between the earlier civil rights politics and the new politics of black ethnicity. And to the extent that middle-class and upper-strata Negroes participate in the politics of black ethnicity, they must do so at least partly in terms of the lower-class criteria that legitimate this politics. Thus middle-class politicians participating in the politics of black ethnicity now articulate needs, demands, and policies that touch more on problems of lower-strata than of middle- and upper-strata blacks. In making this shift in the style of political articulation, middle-class leaders allow the lower strata a leverage that has existed never before. In short, by stamping the politics of black ethnicity with a lower-class style, the lower-strata militants have, largely unwittingly, effected a veritable revolution in the structure of Negro politics. For the first time in this century, black politics possesses a style and an ideological structure that facilitate vertical political linkages among the various strata in the black ethnic turf.

Now there is need for a leadership with the skill and political sophistication necessary to institutionalize these vertical political linkages, and thereby to maximize the political power of the Negro ethnic sector on a scale comparable to that realized earlier by other ethnic groups.

LEADERSHIP AND BLACK ETHNICITY: NEW MIDDLE-CLASS POLITICIANS

The leadership needed for this difficult task is in fact available. This leadership draws upon the Negro working class, a stratum in the urban black ghetto that since World War I has made numerous attempts to facilitate a ghetto-wide leadership, but with little success,[21] partly because of the working class's inability to provide enough of its sons with higher education.

In the past 20 years, however, this weakness of the Negro working class has been significantly overcome, and this, along with the marked growth of the Negro middle class, constitutes the most striking sociological change in contemporary Negro society.[22] This new leadership comes out of the post-World War II college-educated generation of the Negro working class. It represents the black working-class segment that rejects lower-class life styles and cultivates instead upwardly mobile or middle-class aspirations, occasionally marries upward when opportunity allows, purchases a home, has some savings, and above all inspires sons and daughters to pursue higher education.[23]

This new leadership is exemplified at its best by recently successful politicians like Richard Hatcher, son of a steel worker and first Negro mayor of Gary, Indiana; Thomas Atkins, son of a working-class clergyman, and the first Negro city councilman in Boston in over 30 years; Shirley Chisholm, daughter of an artisan and the first Negro woman to be elected to Congress, representing a new district in Bedford-Stuyvesant, New York City. Others in this category include Carl Stokes, first Negro mayor in Cleveland; Louis Stokes, first Negro congressman from Cleveland; Kenneth Gibson, first Negro mayor in Newark. The political resources marshalled by this new group of Negro politicians—the first generation in their families to gain a college education—equip it to begin the task of institutionalizing the politics of black ethnicity. *What are these political resources?*

First, personal attributes. Primary among these is higher education, which affords the new leaders not only skills (e.g., Gibson is an engineer; Atkins, Hatcher, and Stokes are lawyers), but a grasp of institutional dynamics in American society—a grasp unavailable to the lower-strata militant leaders.

Second, their background within the lower strata of the black community. This gives them a certain perception of and empathy with the special material and psychological needs of the black lower strata and thus, perhaps, a capacity to articulate these needs in a manner reasonably satisfactory to wide segments of the lower strata. Though these new politicians may not perform this role as convincingly as the lower-strata militants, they will certainly be more acceptable than the established middle-class Negro leaders. The fact that new middle-class politicians like Richard Hatcher are only recently removed from the Negro lower strata strengthens their position in this regard. Some have fathers, mothers, siblings, and kin still residing in working-class quarters and can readily point to this as evidence of their ties to the black masses.

Third, the rapid growth in the past decade of Negro population in the inner city, together with the emigration of whites to city fringes, is also to be counted as a resource. (The rates of Negro concentration in the inner city since the 1950's and of white emigration to the city fringe and suburbs are shown in Table 3; Table 4 shows the percentage growth of Negroes in the 30 largest cities in the 1950's to 1960's.) It is projected that within the next 15 years the population of some 11 major cities will become nearly 50 per cent Negro. Included among these cities are Baltimore (1972), Gary (1973), Cleveland (1975), St. Louis (1978), Detroit (1979), Philadelphia (1981), Oakland (1973), and Chicago (1984).

TABLE 3. Population Change by Location, Inside and Outside Metro-
          politan Areas, 1950–1966 (numbers in millions)

	Population					
	Negro			White		
	1950	*1960*	*1966*	*1950*	*1960*	*1966*
United States	15.0	18.8	21.5	135.2	158.8	170.8
Metropolitan areas	8.4	12.2	14.8	80.3	99.7	109.0
Central cities	6.5	9.7	12.1	45.5	47.7	46.4
Urban fringe	1.9	2.5	2.7	34.8	52.0	62.5
Small cities, town and rural	6.7	6.7	6.7	54.8	59.2	61.8

SOURCE: *Report of the National Advisory Commission on Civil Disorders* (Washington, D.C., 1968).

Fourth and last, the federal government's recognition, since the riots of the 1960's, of the city's problems as a national priority is another and in a way the most crucial political resource available to the emergent middle-class Negro politicians. This recognition, though already acted on by both Democratic and Republican administrations through the War on Poverty, the Model Cities project, and new welfare legislation, still awaits substantial action.

INSTITUTIONALIZING A POLITICS OF BLACK ETHNICITY

Negro politicians, the main agents of the political institutionalization of black ethnicity, are more numerous today than they were at any period in this century. There are now about 1,500 elected Negro politicians or officials, 62 per cent of them outside the South, representing overwhelmingly city constituencies. They are located in 41 of the 50 states, and include, among others, 12 congressmen, 168 state legislators, 48 mayors, 575 other city officials, 362 school board members, and 114 judges and magistrates. It is noteworthy that Negro communities in the populous industrial states claim a major share of these congressmen and state legislators, and several of these black mayors head industrial cities. Thus two congressmen (Shirley Chisholm and Charles Rangel) represent Negroes in New York City, two (Charles Diggs and John Conyers) Negroes in Detroit, one (Louis Stokes) Negroes in Cleveland, one (Robert Nix) Negroes in Philadelphia, two (Ralph Metcalfe and George Collins) Negroes in Chicago, and one (Parren Mitchell) Negroes in Baltimore. Illinois, New York, and Ohio have 14, 12, and 13 Negro state legislators respectively, and the proportion of Negro legislators in Ohio is larger than the Negro share of population. Only in Detroit and Gary do Negroes have a majority of city councilmen, and in Pittsburgh the percentage of Negro councilmen is larger than the Negro percentage in Pittsburgh's population.

TABLE 4. Percentage of Negroes in Each of the Thirty Largest Cities, 1950, 1960, and Estimated 1965

New York, N.Y.	10	14	18
Chicago, Ill.	14	23	28
Los Angeles, Calif.	9	14	17
Philadelphia, Pa.	18	26	31
Detroit, Mich.	16	29	34
Baltimore, Md.	21	35	38
Houston, Tex.	24	23	23
Cleveland, Ohio	16	29	34
Washington, D.C.	35	54	66
St. Louis, Mo.	18	29	36
Milwaukee, Wisc.	3	8	11
San Francisco, Calif.	6	10	12
Boston, Mass.	5	9	13
Dallas, Tex.	13	19	21
New Orleans, La.	32	37	41
Pittsburgh, Pa.	12	17	20
San Antonio, Tex.	7	7	8
San Diego, Calif.	5	6	7
Seattle, Wash.	3	5	7
Buffalo, N.Y.	6	13	17
Cincinnati, Ohio	16	22	24
Memphis, Tenn.	37	37	40
Denver, Colo.	4	6	9
Atlanta, Ga.	37	38	44
Minneapolis, Minn.	1	2	4
Indianapolis, Ind.	15	21	23
Kansas City, Mo.	12	18	22
Columbus, Ohio	12	16	18
Phoenix, Ariz.	5	5	5
Newark, N.J.	17	34	47

SOURCE: *Report of the National Advisory Commission on Civil Disorders* (Washington, D.C., 1968).

As Negroes are more concentrated in cities than any other ethnic group, the city is now more than ever the main arena for institutionalizing the politics of black ethnicity. The political infrastructure necessary to realize the long-run goals of this politics begins in cities and evolves outward, either directly through congressmen to the federal government, or indirectly through county, city, and state offices.

Increasingly, mayors and city councilmen spend more time seeking federal revenues. This is particularly true for Negro mayors and city councilmen because their primary constituency, the black population, has more poor, unskilled, and semiskilled persons than any other community. This means that resources required to alter these people's lives can no longer be found in the cities but must be acquired from the federal government.

In fact, the resources that ultimately enabled the Irish, Italian, Polish, Jewish, and other whites to consolidate their power and improve their conditions also came not from the cities but from the federal government. Without this intervention it is doubtful that the large lower strata of poor, unskilled, and semiskilled persons in the white ethnic groups of 50 years ago would have largely been transformed into skilled workers and homeowners.

Federal government intervention in city politics is required if this politics is to serve Negroes as a means of social change. But before this can happen, the black city population, like its white ethnic counterparts, must make its contribution to the political forces that make possible such federal government intervention. For it was the ability of political leaders of white ethnic groups to mobilize the votes in their communities than enabled the Democratic party to dominate the presidency in the era 1932–1960. The same is now required of the new Negro politicians.

The Negro mayors and city councilmen are in the front line of this development. For a variety of reasons, mayors and city councilmen, more so than congressmen, have in the popular mind been symbolic of the political growth and success of ethnic groups. In cities where the chances to elect Negro mayors and councilmen are good, the problems facing the effective mobilization of Negro votes and some white support are for the most part still unsolved.

This was apparent in rather stark fashion in the mayoralty election in the City of East St. Louis in 1967—a city in which some 84,000 Negroes comprise 60 per cent of the total population and somewhat over 50 per cent of the voters. Although a Negro had stood for the city office of commissioner (four commissioners and a mayor constitute executive government in East St. Louis) and won as a machine candidate, no black had contested the mayoralty before 1967. But a Negro stood as mayor in 1967, and at the head of an all-black ticket contesting all executive posts; he was confronted by an incumbent ticket, all but one, white. Moreover, East St. Louis like other cities experienced some black militancy in the 1960's, including a small riot, and the head of the Negro ticket, Elmo Bush, an educational administrator, conducted the campaign in militant style, which included a visit to the city by Stokely Carmichael whose address at a mass rally included the remark: "Let me tell you, baby, when we got 52 per cent of the voters in a city, we own that city— lock, stock, and barrel." [24]

The election results were the opposite of Carmichael's projection. The incumbent mayor polled 71 per cent of the votes and none of the four incumbent commissioners less than 60 per cent; Elmo Bush, the Negro mayoral candidate, got 29 per cent and his running mates 20–26 per cent. What is more, the incumbent mayor won 88 per cent of the votes in white precincts, compared to 12 per cent for the Negro candidate; and in the black precincts, where some 59 per cent of all votes were cast, the incumbent white gained 60 per cent against the Negro candidate's 40 per cent. The incumbent commissioners received no less than 52 per cent of the votes in the black precincts, while none of the commissioners on the all-black ticket received more than 35 per cent. Of special interest was that the incumbent Negro commissioner on the incumbent mayor's ticket, E. Saverson, polled the largest vote of all candidates in the black precincts; and though he received only 46 per cent of the votes in white precincts, a return much below his white running mates, no candidate on the all-black ticket received more than 12 per cent of the votes in white precincts.

It is clear from the foregoing that the all-black ticket in the 1967 East St. Louis mayoralty race was defeated by the weight of the city machine. The racial edge claimed by the all-black ticket was of little moment in face of a well-organized and disciplined party machine. The machine's only Negro candidate, E. Saverson, longtime leader of the city's Negro Democratic organization, brilliantly exhibited the machine's strength. Moreover, the black militant rhetoric of the candidates on the all-black ticket was far from persuasive to the voters in the East St. Louis ghetto. Though they had no illusions about the white city machine, they understood that from it they did or could derive concrete gains in the form of jobs.

The hold of this kind of machine patronage over the Negro vote in East St. Louis, as in many other cities, was aided by the fact that in 1964 some 33 per cent of the city's Negro males were unemployed, and 52 per cent of those Negroes holding jobs earned less than $3,000. Clearly anything the city machine did to aid employment and income in East St. Louis would have an important political effect on the Negro vote.

Other Negro candidates for city offices, who are unable to see the political limitations of black militant rhetoric, have failed in the past five years and will continue to fail until they learn that the rhetoric of blackness, though of some value in the political mobilization of the ghetto, is no substitute for viable political *organization*. Candidacies which in the past five years have recognized the limitations of this rhetoric, and have based their campaigns upon sound organization, have registered major victories.

This situation characterized the victory of Richard Hatcher in the 1967 mayoralty election in Gary, Indiana. As in East St. Louis, Negroes were by 1967 slightly over 50 per cent of the population. Also as in East St. Louis, the Democratic city machine was well-organized in the ghetto. However, unlike the all-black ticket in East St. Louis, Hatcher did not rely simply upon militant rhetoric. Instead, he organized a grass-roots campaign—a united front of Negro organizations—which endeavored to overcome the Democratic machine's foothold in the ghetto. He also recognized the need for allies in the white precincts. But since the corrupt Democratic machine opposed him even after he won the primary, his main instrument turned out to be the local press, which though not supporting Hatcher still did not oppose him, thereby allowing some whites to appraise him on the basis of his merit and the issues of his campaign.[25] As a result, Hatcher won by a narrow margin, and though

91 per cent of Hatcher's votes came from black precincts, 17 per cent came from white ones. It is clear that the 6,762 white votes Hatcher gained were indispensable to his victory.

Another successful Negro candidacy for mayor of a major city occurred in Cleveland where in 1965 Negroes were 34 per cent of the city's 800,000 population. Carl Stokes, typical of the black middle-class politicians, made his first bid for mayor in 1965, unsuccessfully, but stood again in 1967, winning the Democratic primary in a three-sided race with 52 per cent of the votes. Like Hatcher in Gary, Stokes recognized the need to confront the Democratic machine, again basically racist in its response to a Negro's candidacy, with a competitive organization in the ghetto. This was achieved by Stokes's campaign, getting 96 per cent of the votes in black precincts, with 74 per cent of the Negro electorate participating. Equally significant was his showing in white precincts: he polled 17,000 white votes, a figure that represents nearly his margin of victory—18,736. In the November 1967 mayoralty election where Stokes confronted the Republican candidate Seth C. Taft, Stokes's campaign organization repeated its primary victory. Stokes polled 94 per cent of the votes in black precincts and one-fifth of the white votes, which amounted to the balance of victory. The key to the white votes was a brilliantly executed alliance with liberal white Protestants and a scattering of white ethnic supporters, reinforced by the endorsement of Cleveland's most powerful newspaper, the *Cleveland Plain Dealer*.

THE FUTURE

The pattern of politically cultivating black ethnicity in order to consolidate Negro voting power and to discipline the black vote in favor of one candidate can be expected to persist through the 1970's and into the succeeding decades. Additional electoral victories employing this method were registered in 1970 in the mayoralty campaign of Negro candidate Kenneth Gibson in Newark, New Jersey, where blacks are one-half of the population, and in the congressional campaign of Parren Mitchell in Baltimore. In both cases a disciplined use of the black militant style forged vertical linkages among groups within the Negro ghetto, allowing these campaigns to surmount the divisions of the Negro community. But both candidacies combined, as they must, the politics of black ethnicity by alliances with liberal sectors of the white population, and in both instances the white voters provided the margin of victory. These alliances will persist and gain in sophistication as the politics of black ethnicity matures, though some vigilance will be necessary to combat the simplistic and erroneous notion of black-white coalitions as tantamount to a zero-sum game, which was first enunciated by Stokely Carmichael and Charles Hamilton in their book *Black Power: The Politics of Liberation in America* (New York: Random House, 1967).[26]

Gaining white voters was central to Mitchell's campaign, for his congressional district was composed of only 40 per cent blacks and 60 per cent whites

(40 per cent Jews and 20 per cent WASPS). Mitchell's forces made a black-white alliance that was based on two (largely Protestant) New Politics groups and two Jewish-Negro integrated organizations, backed by liberal labor leaders. These alliances were successful and Parren Mitchell's election as the first Negro congressman from Maryland was assured; so was the election of the first Negro city district attorney, Milton Allen, and the election of the state legislature of 16 Negroes among the 55 legislators representing Baltimore. Furthermore, white liberals gained over 20 of the additional city seats in the state legislature, which enables the Negro and white liberal legislators to be a decisive force if they nurture their alliance.[27]

It would seem, curiously, that a long-run problem for the new middle-class black politicians is less their capacity to forge and maintain alliances with enough whites to ensure victory than the maintenance of discipline within the politics of black ethnicity. Now in its formative period, this politics has yet to encounter major internal conflicts. Two developments will help keep such conflicts at bay: one, the co-optation of lower-class militants by the new black middle-class politicians; two, adequate aid to cities by the federal government.

As for the lower-strata militants' place in the politics of black ethnicity, they will be of little positive value if they persist in a political style emphasizing short-run and merely symbolic political gains. If, however, the lower-strata militants grasp the long-run needs of Negro political development, they will redefine their role in a manner conducive to a division of political tasks between themselves and the middle-class politicians. This division of political roles in the leadership of the ghetto will entail the lower-strata militants' acquiring political roles as local (ward, district, precinct) organizers, while the middle-class politicians would hold the executive political roles. The lower-strata militant leaders would apply their skills to the task of linking the middle-class politicians with the Negro lower classes, rather like the ward and precinct organizers in the traditional city machine.[28] Also like the traditional ward, district, and precinct party workers, the lower-strata militants who enter this political relationship with middle-class black politicians will be put on city payrolls as patronage workers, which will guarantee them support during the intervals between elections. And the more talented among these transformed lower-strata militants would surely have opportunity to rise to executive roles. Finally, lower-strata militants such as the Black Panthers could—if they come to reject violence—perform the important task of keeping the middle-class politicians informed of the changing needs and interests among the black lower strata, and could thus be a major factor in ensuring the political accountability of the politicians, something few American ethnic groups ever succeeded in maintaining.

As for possible conflicts over the rewards required by the emergent black ethnic politics, clearly these can be derived in adequate measure only from or through the federal government. No other level of government today has the tax power necessary to secure the revenues required to upgrade the Negro's low skills, health care, home ownership, educational facilities, etc. But this depends upon what kind of regime controls the federal government, whether Republican or Democratic. Unless the latter can regain power in Washington and hold it for another 20 years, it is unlikely that the rewards needed for the politics of black ethnicity will be forthcoming. But if rewards are forthcoming from the federal government, there is little doubt that the politics of black ethnicity will mature in coming decades; it will acquire a degree of institutionalization comparable to the development of ethnic-centered politics among white ethnic groups at an earlier period.

NOTES

1. See CHARLES MERRIAM, *The American Party System* (New York, 1924).
2. Negroes did not acquire effective voting rights in the South until the Federal Voting Act of 1965.
3. See RAYFORD W. LOGAN, *The Negro in American Life and Thought: The Nadir 1877–1901* (New York, 1954).
4. W. E. B. DuBOIS, *The Philadelphia Negro: A Social Study* (Philadelphia, 1899), pp. 233–34, *passim*. DuBois, one of the first systematic observers of the urban Negro, recognized over 70 years ago that there is a strong correlation between the institutional differentiation available to city-dwelling blacks and their political modernization.
5. W. LLOYD WARNER and PAUL S. LUNT, *The Social Life of a Modern Community* (New Haven, 1941), p. 217, *passim*. The Lynds discovered a similar situation in their study of a typical American community, the small-sized city of Muncie, Indiana (35,000 population) in the 1920's. So did Frank Quillin, who surveyed Negro status in several cities of Ohio before World War I. See ROBERT S. LYND and HELEN M. LYND, *Middletown* (New York, 1929); FRANK U. QUILLIN, *The Color Line in Ohio* (Ann Arbor, 1913).
6. See, e.g., DAYTON DAVID McKEAN, *The Boss: The Hague Machine in Action* (Boston, 1940).
7. Cf. HAROLD F. GOSNELL, *Negro Politicians: The Rise of Negro Politics in Chicago* (Chicago, 1935).
8. HERBERT J. GANS, "The Ghetto Rebellions and Urban Class Conflict," in Robert Connery, Ed., *Urban Riots* (New York, 1969), pp. 52–53.
9. GUNNAR MYRDAL, *An American Dilemma* (New York, 1944), p. 527, *passim*.
10. Cf. OSCAR HANDLIN, *The Uprooted* (Boston, 1951), chaps. 7–8; also LAWRENCE H. FUCHS, Ed., *American Ethnic Politics* (New York, 1968).
11. Cf. ROBERT K. MERTON, *Social Theory and Social Structure* (Glencoe, 1949).
12. MARTIN KILSON, "Political Change in the Negro Ghetto, 1900–1940," in Nathan Huggins, Martin Kilson, Daniel Fox, Eds., *Key Issues in the Afro-American Experience* (New York, 1971), pp. 167–92.
13. See, e.g., HAROLD GOSNELL, *Machine Politics: Chicago Model* (Chicago, 1937).
14. For a study of city-based rewards stemming from the politicization of ethnicity, see

THEODORE LOWI, *At The Pleasure of The Mayor: Patronage and Power In New York City 1898–1958* (London, 1964). Since the 1930's the federal government has become the major source of the politically inspired benefits called patronage for ethnic groups that contribute to congressional and presidential victories.

15. It is often forgotten how crucial city (and county) party machines were in providing the white ethnic lower strata with viable political organization. Neither interest nor pressure groups such as trade unions or lesser political forms of voluntary associations equalled city machines in this regard. Indeed, interest groups like trade unions and veterans' organizations realized their more effective politicization through city machines. Moreover, the majority of white ethnics in the working class and marginal working class, not to mention those who were lower class, never gained trade-union membership anyway, which meant that they could rely only on party machines or paramachine organizations for their politicization. On the central role of city (and county) machines in politicizing white ethnic lower strata, see GOSNELL, *Machine Politics*, chaps. 1–4. On role of party machines in politicizing interest groups that serve the lower strata, see MARTIN MEYERSON and EDWARD BANFIELD, *Politics, Planning, and the Public Interest* (Glencoe, 1955). See also J. DAVID GREENSTONE, *Labor in American Politics* (New York, 1969).

16. HAROLD ZINK, *City Bosses in the United States: A Study of Twenty Municipal Bosses* (Durham, 1930).

17. See GOSNELL, *Negro Politicians.*

18. See SAR A. LEVITAN, "The Community Action Program," *The Annals of the American Academy of Political and Social Science* (September 1969), p. 67.

19. See MALCOLM X (with Alex Haley), *Autobiography of Malcolm X* (New York, 1966).

20. See MARTIN KILSON, "The 'Put-On' of Black Panther Rhetoric: On the Function of Polemical Excess," *Encounter* (April 1971), pp. 57–58.

21. See STERLING D. SPERO and ABRAM L. HARRIS, *The Black Worker: The Negro and the Labor Movement* (New York, 1931), chaps. 6 and 20, which deal with the role of independent Negro unions, especially among Pullman workers, from World War I to 1930. See also JAMES W. FORD, *The Negro and the Democratic Front* (New York, 1938). This study, written by the leading Negro Communist in the 1930's, covers the efforts of the Communist party to manipulate the Negro working class into a ghetto-wide leadership role.

22. For example, in 1955 only 9 per cent of Negro families had income of $7,000 or more, compared to 31 per cent of white families; but in 1967 nearly 39 per cent of Negro families fell into this income category, compared to 55 per cent of white families. Educationally, 50 per cent of Negro males over 25 years of age completed high school by 1967 (compared to 73 per cent of white males) while in 1960 only 36 per cent of Negro males at 25 years of age had completed high school (compared to 63 per cent of white males at 25 years of age). See Bureau of Census, *Social and Economic Conditions of Negroes in the United States* (Washington, 1967).

23. An area of major neglect in the sociology of the urban Negro is the study of the life-style and social structure of the working-class Negro. For example, a classic description of a ghetto like DRAKE's and CAYTON's *Black Metropolis* has virtually nothing to say about the working class, compared to the marginal lower class, and the term "working class" is not even in the book's index. An earlier study does have some data on homeowning tendency among the Negro working class; see THOMAS WOOFTER, Ed., *Negro Problems in Cities* (New York, 1928), pp. 106–111, *passim.*

24. *Metro-East Journal* (April 3, 1967).
25. See EDWARD GREER, "The 'Liberation' of Gary, Indiana," *Trans-action* (January 1971), pp. 30–39.
26. For an excellent antidote to the Carmichael-Hamilton view of coalition politics, see BAYARD RUSTIN, " 'Black Power' and Coalition Politics," *Commentary* (September 1966), pp. 35–40.
27. See PATRICK J. McCAFFREY, "Black and White in Baltimore," *The Nation* (December 21, 1970), pp. 652–53.
28. See, e.g., J. T. SALTER, *Boss Rule: Portraits in City Politics* (New York, 1935).

The Election of Blacks to City Councils
A 1970 Status Report and a Prolegomenon

John Kramer

In the next decade, as in the last, change is likely to be the central fact of urban black politics. During the 1970's events are almost certain to challenge the accuracy of many of the traditional axioms which now underpin discussions of the subject. As examples, center cities' changing racial mixes and rising black political consciousness offer prospects for greater, perhaps approaching equitable, levels of black representation in urban government and a more active and politically sophisticated black electorate. As James Q. Wilson (1965: preface) has written: "any book on Negroes, particularly on their politics, ought to be published in a loose-leaf binder, so that it can be corrected and updated on a monthly basis." Students of black urban politics, in their efforts merely to keep abreast of ongoing events in the nation's diverse urban settings, must digest large, multidimensional masses of data which accrete almost daily, and certainly with each municipal election.

This paper deals with a largely unstudied aspect of black *elective* politics, a crucial portion of the total black urban political thrust. It focuses upon the election of black city councilmen in 12 of the country's major cities. The paper has two purposes. First, it is the outgrowth of a research project. It summarizes cogent data about councilmanic elections in the late 1960's and, in that sense, is a status report about black councilmanic representatives at the beginning of the 1970's. Second, and more significantly, it is intended as a prolegomenon. Few attempts are made to generalize from that data. Instead, the text and tables contain implicit and explicit suggestions for further research. The overriding aim of the paper is to indicate the growing heuristic utility of black councilmanic politics as a focus for intensive investigation.

BLACKS AND CITY COUNCILS

City councils in the United States vary enormously in election prescriptions, operations, and prerogatives (see Adrian and Press, 1968: ch. 10). Any

NOTE: The research project upon which this paper is based was supported by the State University of New York Research Foundation.

SOURCE: From "The Election of Blacks to City Councils: A 1970 Status Report and a Prolegomenon" by John Kramer. Reprinted from *Journal of Black Studies*, Volume 1, Number 4 (June 1971), pp. 443–76, by permission of the publisher, Sage Publications, Inc.

generalizations about city councils must be tenuous. As a general rule, councils today are less prestigious and powerful than they were before being tethered by reformers in the early days of this century. Nevertheless, without exception, they retain at least a residue of legislative authority, especially over municipal financing, and this makes them latent, if not functioning, agencies for assisting blacks in their struggle for social equality.

Although a black was elected to Cleveland's Council as early as 1909 (Cuban, 1967: 301), the first black councilman of note was Oscar DePriest. Later the first black Congressman since Reconstruction, DePriest was elected to Chicago's Board of Aldermen in 1915 (Gosnell, 1967: 170–172) from the predominantly black Second Ward on the Near South Side.[1] The first 60 years of the century, however, did not see any great number of black councilmen. Across the country, black council representation ranged from none to token. As evidence, not until 1957, 1963, and 1967 respectively were the first blacks elected to councils of Detroit, Los Angeles, and San Francisco. Banfield and Wilson (1963: 293) and Wilson (1966: 435) have used the paucity of black councilmen to illustrate the underrepresentation of blacks in city government.

In the latter years of the 1960's, the number of black councilmen increased dramatically. No claim can be made that blacks anywhere are proportionately represented, but in most cities with sizable black populations there now are at least several blacks in council seats. Nor can it be assumed that all black councilmen, as is sometimes suggested by militant rhetoric, behave totally in their own political self-interest, thereby ignoring the crushing needs of their constituents. With numbers, political variety and diverse motivations have been introduced. The heterogeneity of black councilmen, the localized nature of councilmanic politics, and the potential role of councils in bringing about positive change, combine to make black councilmen, and the political milieu in which they function, a subject worthy of intensive study. At the very least, studies with this focus offer potential for discovering and assessing some of the sure-to-come changes in urban black politics during the 1970's and beyond.

METHODOLOGY

The aims of the research project upon which this paper is based were to develop social and political information about black councilmen and about unsuccessful black candidates for council posts, and to collect data about the issues and voting patterns in council campaigns involving black participants. Geographically, the study was limited to those 12 U.S. cities, outside the South, with 1960 nonwhite populations of 100,000 or more. These ranged from New York, with a 1960 nonwhite census of 1,141,322, to Pittsburgh, with 101,739—figures for this are taken from the 1968 *Statistical Abstract of the United States*. In these cities, it was felt, black councilmanic politics would be most highly developed. Temporally, the project concentrated upon the last municipal election (or sets of elections) held in the 12 cities during the 1960's.

Regardless of the contestants' races, councilmanic politics in most cities tends to be quasi-subterranean. Election campaigns usually are badly eclipsed by races for higher city and state offices held on the same dates. Moreover, the daily press in most cities gives these elections, as well as day-to-day council proceedings, little space in its news columns. As a result of the almost covert nature of the subject, data had to be collected from a wide array of sources. The Leagues of Women Voters in the 12 cities were especially helpful. So, too, were the Boards of Election. Current and back issues of daily newspapers and of the cities' black press were combed for information. Some of the local political parties supplied material, as did Clerks of the City Councils and the local Urban Leagues in some of the cities. In New York, the Citizen's League was of major assistance. Finally, a number of councilmen and unsuccessful council candidates, both white and black, responded to mail and phone requests for specific information.[2]

Table 1 contains the essential city council election arrangements for the 12 cities included in the study.

OVERVIEW

Prior to the final municipal elections in the 1960's, a total of 43 blacks held council seats in the 12 cities studied. As a result of these elections, the number of black councilmen increased by 10, to a total of 53. The city-by-city data are shown in Table 2.

The largest single gain occurred in Chicago, where three additional blacks were elected, bringing that city's number of black councilmen to ten. In six other cities the number of black councilmen increased by one or two, and in four cities the number remained unchanged. Only in Cincinnati, of the cities studied, did the number of black councilmen decrease. Cincinnati's electorate failed to return one of that city's three black incumbents.

DISTRICT-BASED ELECTIONS

Eight of the twelve cities elect all or part of their councils by district. There is great variation in the size of these electoral units. The districts in New York, Philadelphia, Los Angeles, and Baltimore are relatively large; they are composed of clusters of wards. The districts in Chicago, Cleveland, St. Louis, and Newark are comparatively small. Each is conterminous with a single ward's boundaries.[3]

Observers of urban politics long have been aware that chances for minority representation on city councils are greater in district, and particularly in small district, elections than they are in at-large formats. As shown in Table 2, 43 of the 53 black councilmen elected during the late 1960's were the products of district balloting. Of the 43 black councilmen from districts, 32 were elected in the four cities with single-ward units. Further, as shown in Table 3, eight of the ten council seats *gained* by blacks in the late 1960's were the result of district elections.

TABLE 1. City Council Election Arrangements for the Twelve Selected Cities

City	Number of Councilmen	Elected at-Large	Elected from Districts	Length of Term (Years)	Partisan (P) or Nonpartisan (NP) Elections	Primary (Pr) or Runoff (R) Election Systems
Baltimore	19	1[a]	18	4	P	Pr
Chicago	50	0	50	4	P[d]	R
Cincinnati	9	9	0	2	P[d]	General election only
Cleveland	33	0	33	2	P[d]	R
Detroit	9	9	0	4	NP	Pr
Los Angeles	15	0	15	4[c]	NP	R
New York	38	11[ab]	27	4	P	Pr
Newark	9	4	5	4	NP	R
Philadelphia	17	7	10	4	P	Pr
Pittsburgh	9	9	0	4[c]	P	Pr
San Francisco	11	11	0	4[c]	NP	General election only
St. Louis	28	1[a]	0	4[c]	P	Pr

a. Includes Council President, elected from city at large specifically for that post.

b. Two New York Councilmen are elected at large from within each of the city's five boroughs. Only the Council President faces the total city electorate.

c. Terms are staggered, so that approximately half expire every two years.

d. Party affiliations do not appear on the ballot but, in practice, they are well publicized and the elections, in fact, are partisan.

SOURCE: Leagues of Women Voters

TABLE 2. Number of Black Councilmen in the Twelve Selected Cities Before and After Last Elections (or Sets of Elections) in 1960's

City	Before (district-at-large)	Dates of Elections	After (district-at-large)	Gains or Losses
Baltimore	2 (2–0)	November '67	4 (4–0)	+2
Chicago	7 (7–N/A)	February-April '67	10 (10–N/A)	+3
Cincinnati	3 (N/A–3)	November '69	2 (N/A–2)	−1
Cleveland	11 (11–N/A)	November '69	12 (12–N/A)	+1
Detroit	2 (N/A–2)	November '69	3 (N/A–3)	+1
Los Angeles	3 (3–N/A)	April-May '67 April-May '69	3 (3–N/A)	—
New York	2 (2–0)	November '69	2 (2–0)	—
Newark	1 (1–0)	May-June '66 September '68[a] June '69[a]	3 (2–1)	+2
Philadelphia	2 (1–1)	November '67	3 (2–1)	+1
Pittsburgh	1 (N/A–1)	November '67 November '69	2 (N/A–2)	+1
San Francisco	1 (N/A–1)	November '67 November '69	1 (N/A–1)	—[b]
St. Louis	8 (8–0)	April '67 April '69	8 (8–0)	—
	43 (35–8)		53 (43–10)	+10 (8–2)

a. Dates of special elections, held to fill vacancies, which resulted in quantitative changes in Newark's black representation.

b. The black incumbent had been appointed in 1966. He was elected in 1967, marking the first time a black achieved election to city-wide office in San Francisco.

TABLE 3. Racial Composition of District Elections for Council
(Last Elections in 1960's)

		Intraracial Contests		Interracial Contests	
City	District Seats	White/ White	Black/ Black	White/ Black	Black/ White
Baltimore	18	11	3*a	3	1*
Cleveland	33	21	11	2	1*
Chicago	50	39	8*	1	2**
Los Angeles	15	12	3	0	0
New York	27	24	2	1	0
Newark b	5	3	1	1	0
	1	0	0	1	0
	1	0	0	0	1*
Philadelphia	10	7	2*	1	0
St. Louis c	28	20	8	0	0
Total	188d	137	38***	10	5*****

a. Each asterisk denotes a seat gained by blacks.

b. The three rows represent, respectively, Newark's regular election in 1966 and special election held in 1968 and 1969.

c. Composite totals for St. Louis elections of 1967 and 1969.

d. There are 186 district seats in the twelve cities. The two special elections in Newark account for the total of 188 shown in the table.

For purposes of preliminary analysis, Table 3 divides the 188 district-based council elections in the late 1960's into four racially focused categories. The first designation in each category reflects the race of the victorious candidate. The second indicates the presence or absence of a significant primary or general election challenger of the "other" race. Hence white/white and black/black elections involved racially homogeneous contests. White/black and black/white elections were those in which interracial contests were held.[4] Of particular interest are the councilmanic contests in Cleveland, Chicago, Baltimore, and Newark.

Cleveland

One often-made allegation is that white council incumbents linger in racially changing districts long after blacks have become the population majority. Unfortunately, the absence of precise population data between censuses makes it difficult to undertake definitive tests of the charge. In Cleveland, however, a special census was taken in 1965, allowing at least an approximate test of the proposition.

The racial compositions (indicated by percentage of black) in Cleveland's mixed and predominantly black wards are shown in Table 4. Also in the table are the racial characteristics of the wards' 1969 council elections. Each of the ten largely black wards (over 75 per cent black) experienced black/black council races. No whites contested for council seats. In the city's eight racially mixed wards (20–60 per cent black), two blacks were elected to council and two other black candidates made significant challenges against whites.

TABLE 4. 1969 Councilmanic Elections in Cleveland's Mixed and Black Wards

	Ward	*1965* *Per Cent* *Black*	*Racial Categorization* *of 1967 Elections*
Mixed wards	16	56.6	White/Black
	19	25.3	White/White
	21	61.1	White/Black
	23	20.3	White/White
	28	28.5	Black/White
	29	24.4	White/White
	30	51.7	Black/Black
	31	21.8	White/White
Black wards	10	91.3	Black/Black
	11	91.8	Black/Black
	12	82.7	Black/Black
	13	75.2	Black/Black
	17	99.0	Black/Black[a]
	18	89.3	Black/Black
	20	91.0	Black/Black
	24	92.6	Black/Black
	25	90.9	Black/Black
	27	85.7	Black/Black

a. Ward 17 incumbent black councilman Charles Carr, leader of the Democratic Caucus in the Council, had no opposition.

SOURCE for racial percentages: Jeffrey Hadden, Louis Masotti, Victor Thiessen. The Making of the Negro Mayors 1967, in James D. Barber, Ed., *Readings in Citizen Politics*, (Chicago: Markham Publishing Co., 1969), p. 178.

The circumstances behind three of Cleveland's mixed-ward elections deserve brief elaboration. Each would make an excellent individual subject for in-depth study.

In the rapidly changing East Side Twenty-Eighth Ward, estimated to be approximately 60 per cent black in 1969, a black Republican, Paul Haggard, defeated the white Democratic incumbent Charles L. Flynn. Haggard was 33 years old; Flynn was 61. But Flynn had been appointed to council in August of 1968, to fill the remainder of an unexpired term and, thus, was not the classic well-entrenched white political veteran. Nor was Haggard the stereotype black insurgent. Stressing the need for additional police protection in the ward, along with a generally conservative political philosophy, Haggard campaigned as a strong cross-party supporter of black Mayor Carl Stokes. In an extremely close run-off contest, Haggard won by a mere 20 votes (3,827 to 3,807 for Flynn).

Cleveland's Twenty-First Ward presents an even more heuristically suggestive election story. In the late 1960's, Cleveland's Democratic Party was badly factionalized: Mayor Stokes headed one branch and Council President James Stanton another. The Twenty-First Ward, in 1969, was perhaps 80 per cent black. Its white incumbent, Edward Katalinas, sought a fifth term against a strong black challenger, State Senator Larry Smith. Katalinas had never been known as a strong advocate of his black constituents. On the other hand, Katalinas sided with Stokes in his political battles with Stanton and, indeed, was one of the Mayor's strongest allies in the party's strident infighting. The Mayor entered Ward Twenty-One on a number of occasions, to campaign for the white incumbent. On September 24, Stokes was quoted by the *Plain Dealer:* "This is a changing ward. But merely because a ward is changing color should it change its councilman too? I do not think so." Despite its overwhelmingly black electorate, Ward Twenty-One handily returned Katalinas to council, by a vote of 2,520 to 1,218 for Smith.

Cleveland's Thirtieth Ward lies at the city's southeastern extremity. While its population is more than half black, many of the blacks in the ward are middle-class escapees from the ghettos of Cleveland's inner city. During Mayor Stokes' first term, he proposed the creation of a 277-unit public housing project to occupy 51 acres in the ward. The black incumbent councilman from the district, Clarence R. Thompson, objected vehemently to the plan. In the 1969 elections, Thompson was opposed by John E. Barnes, also black and actively supported by Stokes. After a bitter campaign, Thompson was reelected by 63 votes (4,943–4,880).

Baltimore

In a departure from the usual one district/one councilman format, the city of Baltimore is divided into six councilmanic districts, and each elects three councilmen from the district as a whole. Thus each Baltimore citizen has three councilmanic representatives. A nineteenth councilman, the council president, is elected at-large from the total city.

Baltimore's Second District, despite a black population estimated to be 55 per cent in 1967, never had elected a black councilman. During the September 1967 primaries, 25 individuals, the majority of them black, contested for three Democratic spaces on the district's November general election ballot. The primary victors were Robert Douglass, a relatively militant black, and two white conservatives, one an incumbent, who on their previous records were generally considered unsympathetic to blacks. The Republican Party, which had not elected a Baltimore councilman since 1939, slated three black candidates. One of them, Walter Lively, a young, well-known, and extremely outspoken civil rights advocate, was accorded a modest chance of election.

The campaign was intricate and especially bitter. Douglass sought votes independently of his two white Democratic running mates. Then, on election eve, handbills were circulated in the *white* sections of the district calling upon voters to vote "black power" and for Walter Lively in particular, who purportedly stood for "more welfare, forced open-housing, forced school busing, disarming the police, and state-paid rent, telephones, and electric bills" (*Baltimore News-American*, 1967). The final results showed the three Democrats winning handily, with Douglass leading the ticket. The two white Democrats made surprisingly strong showings. Lively claimed, and not without justification, that the fraudulent handbills had aroused the white electorate to vote against him.

The election in Baltimore's more heavily black Fourth District was quiet by comparison. Of significance, however, was the primary defeat of black three-term incumbent Walter T. Dixon, 73-year-old member of the James H. Pollack organization. Pollack, a white political "boss" of the old school, long had controlled Fourth Ward politics, judiciously mixing white and black council slates (see Fleming, 1960). In the November general election, the Fourth Ward voters elected three non-Pollack Negro Democrats, thereby giving Baltimore a total of four black councilmen, two more than ever previously.

Chicago

After Chicago's municipal elections of 1967, the number of black councilmen rose from seven to ten. The retirement of long-time white councilmen in two predominantly black wards (the West Side Twenty-Ninth and the South Side Eighth) paved the way for two black additions. In the Twenty-Ninth, the Democratic organization (synonymous with Major Richard Daley) nominated a black undertaker, Robert Biggs, who was elected with only token opposition. In the Eighth, however, the organization's black candidate was defeated by a black independent, William Cousins. Once an Assistant State's Attorney, Cousins had broken from his former political base, the Illinois Republican Party, when Barry Goldwater was nominated for President in 1964.

The third black addition in Chicago resulted from a complex black/white contest in the city's far South Side Twenty-First Ward. There a black organization candidate (William Frost) easily unseated a white Republican incumbent. The Twenty-First Ward election featured the appearance of such black celebrities as author Lerone Bennett and entertainer Oscar Brown, Jr. ("Mr. Kicks") campaigning on behalf of independent and avowedly anti-organization black candidate Augustus (Gus) Savage. Savage originally was ruled off the ballot because of improper nominating petitions, was reinstated by court order approximately three weeks before the election, and finished a distant third.

Of the seven seats held by blacks prior to the 1967 elections, three changed hands (two in 1967 and the other in a special election held in 1969). One election, in the Seventeenth Ward, was a routine affair in which one organization black succeeded another. The other two involved the defeat of organization blacks by black independents. A. A. (Sammy) Rayner, in the South Side Sixth Ward, defeated organization incumbent Robert Miller in 1967. Then, in a special election in March of 1969, held to fill a vacancy in the Second Ward, Fred Hubbard, an anti-organization social worker, defeated organization-backed Lawrence C. Woods, an administrative aide to black Congressman William Dawson. As a result of the regular 1967 elections, and the special election of 1969, not only did the total number of blacks in Chicago's city council increase, but three anti-organization blacks (Cousins, Rayner, and Hubbard) acceded to office.

One other Chicago councilmanic election deserves mention. The city's Sixteenth Ward, on the South Side, is approximately 80 per cent black and the site of numerous public housing projects. For 22 years, the councilman for the Sixteenth was Paul Sheridan, a white power-figure in the Democratic organization. Upon his death in 1965 he was succeeded in office by his son, Paul Sheridan, Jr. In 1967, the younger Sheridan was opposed by an articulate black female attorney, Mrs. Anna Langford, who drew the support of many of Chicago's civil rights organizations. Mrs. Langford was defeated badly (6,369–2,752) in the city's only white/black councilmanic election of that year. According to various observers in Chicago, many blacks in the Sixteenth were reluctant to elect an anti-organization councilman, of whatever race, for fear of losing vital services administered by the city to the projects.

Newark

As can be determined easily by accounts in the public press, the racial and political situations in Newark are so fluid that descriptions of that city's elective politics are badly outdated before reaching print. Rival independent black organizations, as well as a number of white "law and order" groups, plan to wage energetic campaigns for mayoralty and councilmanic candidates in the 1970 municipal elections. The following account of councilmanic elections in the 1960's, therefore, can be viewed only as background for the comprehension of ongoing events. Of necessity, because the Newark district and at-large council elections were linked with one another in the 1960's, both will be discussed here.

Since adopting its present city charter in 1954, Newark has elected five councilmen from geographically designated wards (Central, North, South, East, and West) and four from the city at-large. One black councilman, Irvine Turner, of the city's badly deteriorated Central Ward, was first elected with the adoption of the 1954 charter and has been returned to office by overwhelming majorities ever since (see Pomper, 1966, for an analysis of the voting patterns in Newark's 1962 municipal elections). Until April of 1966,

Turner was Newark's lone black council representative. But in that year's municipal election another black, Calvin West, was elected at-large.

West barely achieved election. In a race for four seats, West finished fourth in a fifteen-man field. He led all candidates in the Central Ward, was second in the racially changing South Ward, but finished far down the list of fifteen in the city's three predominantly white wards. In fact, West's overall vote of 20,201 exceeded that for the fifth-place finisher (a white) by less than 1,500. Under Newark's complicated election procedure, West was spared a run-off (which almost certainly would have meant defeat) only because the two top vote getters (whites) received overwhelming support in the city's white ethnic districts. Newark's election code prescribes that the third- and fourth-place finishers are elected to office, without a run-off, if the top two candidates pull one-eighth of the total vote each. West, formerly a clerk in the city's office of Civil Defense, joined Turner as a strong councilmanic ally of Newark's Democratic Mayor, Hugh Addonizio.

In January of 1968, Newark's Council appointed a third black political ally of Addonizio, Leon Ewing, to fill an unexpired at-large term until a special election could be held. Ewing had run seventh in the 1966 regular at-large election in which West had become Newark's first at-large councilman. Again, in the special election of November 1968, Ewing failed to achieve election, this time finishing third in a race for two seats. Newark's black councilmanic representation was thereby reduced again to two.

Ewing trailed the white second-place finisher by 78 votes, and in the process collected 24,862 ballots, the highest citywide vote total ever obtained by a black. The election was marked by the activity of a coalition of militant black organizations (the Committee for a United Newark), spearheaded by playwright LeRoi Jones. The coalition at first refused to support Ewing but later grudgingly adopted him as one of its candidates. According to various students of Newark politics, the coalition's support for Ewing cut into his vote in white districts and among middle-class blacks as well. Almost half of Ewing's votes came from the South Ward, about to boil over in political revolt. After the election, Ewing charged that black extremists had interfered with *his* campaign workers, preventing them from passing out literature at the polls. Demanding a recount, Ewing warned Newark's blacks to be aware of "collusion, trickery, and double-dealing within their own race" (*Newark Evening News*, 1968).

Early in 1969, the black political unrest in Newark's South Ward began building to a climax. A successful recall petition was initiated against incumbent councilman Leo Bernstein, and a special election was called for June of that year. Formerly a Jewish residential area, the South Ward by 1969 was estimated to be approximately 80 per cent black. Bernstein had served since 1962 and long had been accused of indifference toward his black constituents. In 1966 he narrowly defeated an energetic black opponent in an especially bitter reelection campaign. Perhaps his greatest fault was political insensitivity. For example, campaigning to hold his seat in the special election, Bernstein advocated the extensive use of police dogs for crime control in the ward. Victorious in the special election was the Reverend Horace P. Sharper, a leader in the recall movement, an outspoken advocate of black political power, and a vocal critic of Mayor Addonizio. Sharper handily defeated Ewing, Bernstein, and Mrs. Jennie Lemons, a third black in the race. Thus, at the end of 1969, Newark's nine-man council contained three blacks —one an independent, and two allied with the incumbent mayor.[5]

Other District Elections

New York. Space limitations prevent more than brief notations about district races in other cities. New York City's Council districts are so arranged as to preclude more than two black incumbents (one from Harlem and one from the Bedford-Stuyvesant section of Brooklyn).[6] In the 1969 Harlem race (the Fifth District of Manhattan), Liberal Party candidate Charles Taylor, an ally of mayoralty winner John Lindsay, upset the militant and well-publicized civil rights activist Jesse Gray, who had won the Democratic primary. Taylor and Gray contested for the seat of retiring incumbent J. Raymond Jones, once the leader of New York's Tammany organization and probably the most powerful black political figure in the city's history. New York's lone white/ black contest occurred in Manhattan's racially and economically heterogenous East Side Forth District, which begins at Fifty-Ninth Street, encompasses the luxury apartments lining the East River, and extends northward through East Harlem. A black woman, Mrs. Hilda Stokely, waged an energetic campaign in the Democratic primary, but was defeated easily by a white candidate.

Philadelphia. The gain of one black seat in Philadelphia came about through the two-to-one election victory of Democrat Charles Durham over a black Republican opponent in that city's heavily black Third District (in West Philadelphia). The district's seat was vacated by a white Democrat who did not seek reelection. Philadelphia's white/black councilmanic campaign (Table 3) occurred in the Eighth District (Germantown), where black attorney Joseph Coleman entered the Democratic primary with substantial backing from the city's decaying Democratic organization. The Eighth District is changing racially, but remains predominantly white. Coleman finished a poor third. Mention should be made, too, of the entrance of a pair of Black Panther Party candidates into two special councilmanic elections (in predominantly white districts) in November of 1969. The Panthers' vote totals were 252 and 215, out of approximately 40,000 votes cast in each of the districts.

Los Angeles. During the early 1960's Los Angeles was the scene of spirited attempts by blacks to elect their first representative to council (see Patterson, 1969). By 1969, three blacks were entrenched in office (Gilbert W. Lindsay, Billy Mills, and unsuccessful 1969 mayoralty candidate Thomas Bradley). In their campaigns for reelection, Lindsay (1969) and Bradley (1967) ran unopposed, and Mills (1967) had only token opposition.

St. Louis. On the surface, St. Louis' black councilmanic politics is relatively placid: there were no interracial contests in either the 1967 or 1969 elections, and black incumbents were routinely returned to their seats. The situation is especially deserving of intensive study, however, as the eight black councilmen were variously allied with separate segments of the city's factionalized Democratic party. Of note, too, in St. Louis is the extremely weak showing of black Republican candidates for council, despite the lack of Democratic cohesion. The best showing by a black Republican councilmanic candidate in either 1967 or 1969 occurred in the latter year, in the city's Fifth Ward. There, Republican Sidney Davis received 575 votes, losing by better than a three-to-one margin to his Democratic opponent.

AT-LARGE ELECTIONS

With the exception of those in New York City, candidates for at-large council seats in the 12 cities studied must face citywide electorates (see Table 1, note b). Thus, until cities have black population majorities which actually vote in proportion to their numbers, black at-large councilmanic candidates will face many of the same racially oriented difficulties now experienced by black candidates for mayor. The at-large campaign problems of blacks are well known (see Wilson, 1965: ch. 1). Basically, blacks in at-large elections must receive solid black support while gathering sizable numbers of white votes as well. This dilemma, according to students of such contests, forces blacks into relatively conservative stances on issues. Furthermore, because campaigns are not limited by district boundaries, at-large races tend to be time-consuming and expensive. Organization support, endorsements, or a name well known to the voters (often achieved by virtue of being an incumbent), are invaluable assets.

As shown in Table 5, after the last municipal elections of the 1960's, ten blacks were serving in at-large seats in the twelve cities studied. This represented a gain of two black at-large councilmen. Of particular interest were the contests in Detroit, Cincinnati, and Pittsburgh.

Detroit

Salaries for councilmen in Detroit are the highest for the 12 cities ($17,500 per year plus various expenses). At the same time, Detroit places the fewest barriers to getting on the primary ballot. All a prospective candidate need do is pay a $100 filing fee, and even that is refunded if the individual secures more than half the votes gained by the lowest qualifier for the general election. In addition, council elections are nonpartisan. The result, in the primary, is a bewildering array of names. In September of 1969, 118 candidates contested for 18 spots on the November general election ballot.

Prior to the 1969 elections, two blacks held seats in Detroit's nine-man council. One, the Reverend Nicholas Hood, a more than moderate civil rights exponent, had been elected in 1965. The other, Robert Tindal, former

TABLE 5.　At-Large Council Races (Last Elections in 1960's)

City[a]	Dates of Elections	Seats to be Filled	Total Number of Candidates in General Election[b]	Approximate Number of Black Candidates	Placement Position of Blacks (asterisk indicates elected)	Black Gains or Losses
Cincinnati	November '69	9	19	4	2*,5*,17,19	−1
Detroit	November '69	9	18	6	2*,5*,9*,15,17,18	+1
Newark	April-May '66	4	15	5	4*,7,8,11,12	+1
	September '68	2	13	2	3,4	(−1)[c]
Philadelphia	November '67	7	21	6	3*,8,15,16,17,19	—
Pittsburgh	November '67	4	8	2	3*,8	—
	November '69	5	10	2	5*,8	+1
San Francisco	November '67	6	44	2	5*,39	—
	November '69	5	16	1[d]	16	—
Total		51	164	30	(Ten blacks elected)	+2

a. Table does not include figures for New York City's at-large elections. The ten at-large councilmen in New York are elected at-large within the five boroughs (two from each) and, hence, the New York data are not comparable to those from the other cities. In November of 1969, there were no blacks among the significant candidates for any of the New York at-large seats.

b. Detroit, Philadelphia, and Pittsburgh have primaries which are not shown in the table. In Detroit, in 1969, 118 candidates (of whom approximately 17 were black) contested for the 18 positions on the general election ballot.

c. In Newark's special election of September 1968, a black incumbent finished third, in a race for two seats, and thus was voted out of office. This individual, however, had been appointed barely six months before the special election and, hence, did not serve in Newark's council before the last set of municipal elections. His appointment, and defeat, serve to cancel each other in the computation of the number of blacks serving before and after the elections.

d. The only black candidate in San Francisco's 1969 councilmanic elections was ruled off the ballot for filing improper nominating petitions. Nevertheless, he received a scattering of write-in votes.

Executive Secretary of Detroit's NAACP, had been elected in a vacancy-filling contest held in 1968. In the September 1969 primary, Hood finished second and Tindal third. Four other blacks also finished in the top eighteen, thereby gaining places for the general election.

Although Detroit's 1969 population was estimated at approximately 40 per cent black, blacks in that year actually made up only about 25 per cent of the registered voters. The problem of overcoming a three-fourths' white majority was diminished, however, by the composition of the 1969 mayoralty race. The leading white conservative candidate was defeated in the primary, creating a general election contest between "liberal" white Roman Gribbs and a black aspirant, Richard Austin. Gribbs narrowly defeated Austin, but the combination of racially mixed, pro-civil rights mayoralty candidates produced a heavy liberal turnout. As a result, Hood and Tindal were reelected easily (finished second and fifth respectively), and a third black, Ernest Browne, finished a successful ninth in the eighteen-man field. Indeed, where Detroit's council previously contained a 5–4 conservative majority, liberals took a 6–3 lead (including the three blacks in the liberal column) after the 1969 election.

Browne received 192,203 votes, a bare 2,306 more than the tenth-place finisher, a conservative and former councilwoman. Before election, Browne was an analyst in the city's Budget Bureau. He had started his career in the city's Health Department in 1947, rising in that time, in his own words, "from rats to litter." Browne was aided by a number of significant endorsements: among them, the United Auto Workers, the *Detroit News*, Civic Searchlight (a nonprofit "good government" organization), and black incumbents Hood and Tindal.

Cincinnati

Cincinnati is the only city of the 12 to show a *decrease* in the number of black councilmen after 1969. As was true with the gain in Detroit, the loss in Cincinnati was, at least in part, related to the broader political context in the city.

Cincinnati's local political milieu is a function of three active parties; the Democratic, the Republican, and the Charter. The last originated in the 1920's to push for reorganization in city government (Straetz, 1958). Although the city's "third" party today, it retains considerable strength. By city charter, Cincinnati's Council elects one of its members as mayor and, in addition, names a city manager. Since 1957, control of Cincinnati's Council and, hence, of Cincinnati itself, has been in Republican hands.

Prior to the 1969 elections, each of the three parties had a black councilmanic representative. Myron Bush, a Charterite, was first elected in 1965 and was reelected in 1967. William J. Chenault, a Democrat, was named by the Republican administration in 1968 to fill a vacant seat. And Arthur Reid, a Republican attorney, also was named in 1968 to fill a vacancy. Thus, of the three blacks, only one actually had been elected to office.[7]

Midway through 1969, the Democrats and Charterites joined forces for the express purpose of overthrowing Republican rule. The Democrat-Charterite coalition and the Republicans each named nine-man slates for council. Bush and Chenault were on the former ticket, Reid on the latter. A nineteenth candidate, Robert C. Weaver, the fourth black in the race, ran as an independent.[8] The Democrat-Charterites, in their joint effort, succeeded only in reducing the Republican council majority by one, from a 6–3 Republican advantage to 5–4. Bush finished a successful third and Chenault achieved election by finishing eighth. Reid was the only Republican incumbent to be defeated, coming in seventeenth. Weaver trailed the nineteen-man field.

Reid's defeat is probably owed to a mixture of political as well as racial factors. First, as perhaps the least-known Republican incumbent, Reid was not helped by the Republican party-in-power strategy of waging a relatively quiet campaign. Second, the underdog Democrat-Charterites made energetic appeals for votes in black neighborhoods. Bush and Chenault, while advocating support for Reid as a show of black strength, also spoke vehemently against the effects of 12 years of Republican rule in Cincinnati. Third, in contrast to Bush and Chenault, Reid failed to get such influential endorsements as those of the *Cincinnati Inquirer*, the AFL-CIO Labor Council's Committee on Political Education (COPE), or the nonpartisan Independent Voters of Ohio (IVO). Finally, even though parties run slates, Cincinnati municipal election ballots do not actually indicate the party affiliation of council candidates, and voters cannot pull a straight party lever. Hence, on purely mechanical grounds, Reid doubtless failed to get as many Republican straight-ticket votes as he might have obtained elsewhere.

Pittsburgh

In Pittsburgh, the gain of one black councilman in 1969 is directly attributable to the decision of the Democratic organization to increase black councilmanic representation. Virtually a one-party city, Pittsburgh's Council, in 1970, had been entirely Democratic for over thirty years. Regular Democratic candidates are selected by the Allegheny County Democratic Policy Committee, made up of a coterie of high-ranking party officials. The organization's city council candidates routinely win the primaries held in May, and then easily defeat their Republican opponents in November.

Until 1969, the Democrats accorded blacks one council seat. Occasionally, independent blacks would attempt to gain additional seats by running in the Democratic primary, but they seldom made more than token showings.[9] The Republican Party ordinarily included one black on its ticket, but in a city with a more than two-to-one Democratic registration majority, this was little more than a gesture.

Organization control over city council elections never was more evident than in 1969. In the May primary the organization's mayoralty candidate was dealt a stunning defeat by Democratic insurgent and then city councilman Peter Flaherty. Nevertheless, in the primary, the organization's five council nominees all easily survived the mayoralty upset. Included on the organiza-

tion slate was George Shields, intended as the party's second black councilman. Louis Mason, the black incumbent, had been elected in 1967 to a
four-year term.

Campaigning in the general election, Flaherty disassociated himself from
the organization candidates for council. He advised his supporters that he
was "not running with a slate" and to "look them all [Republicans as well as
Democrats] over" (*Pittsburgh Press*, 1969a). For its part, the organization,
dispirited with a maverick at the head of the Democratic ticket, gave its
council candidates only limited support. Indeed, at one point, a Republican
council candidate only half facetiously asked the city's Democratic Chairman
for the names of his "faceless" opponents, so that he could mount a campaign against them (*Pittsburgh Press*, 1969b).

Flaherty achieved an overwhelming two-to-one victory. The quintet of
relatively anonymous Democratic council aspirants, supposedly cut adrift by
the reformist mayoralty winner, also swept into office by approximately two-
to-one margins. Shields proved to be the poorest vote getter of the five,
polling approximately 10,000 votes less than the leading council candidate,
but he outdistanced his nearest Republican rival by nearly 40,000 ballots.

Other At-Large Elections

Philadelphia. Philadelphia's black councilman-at-large is Edgar Campbell.
Politically allied with Democratic Mayor James J. Tate, Campbell was elected
to his first term in 1967. In effect, Campbell took over the traditionally black
at-large seat made vacant by the death earlier that year of Reverend Marshall
Shepard. Campbell finished third in a field of 21. Philadelphia's election procedures are such that the minority party is guaranteed at least two at-large
seats of the seven. Five Democrats, including Campbell, were elected. Finishing third among the Republicans, and missing election by approximately
500 votes (he received over 320,000) was a black disc jockey, George Woods
("The Man With The Goods").

San Francisco. San Francisco's at-large council politics is even more chaotic
than that in Detroit. As occurs in the latter city, candidates run without party
labels, and there are only minimal impediments to getting on the ballot.
Moreover, in San Francisco, there is no primary. The whole field runs in
November, with the top five or six (in alternate biannual elections) gaining
election. Terry Francois, a black attorney, was appointed to the San Francisco Council in 1966 to fill a vacancy. He then ran a strong race in 1967,
finishing fifth, in a field of 44, and became the first black to win a citywide
election in that city. Francois, by militant standards, is a black conservative.
In 1969, he authored an article for the September *Reader's Digest* entitled
"A Black Man Looks at Black Racism," in which he openly criticized
black extremists.

Surprisingly, despite the ease with which one can get on the San Francisco
ballot, few blacks have chosen to run for council. In the most recent election, in 1969, only one black sought a place. Wilfred T. Ussery, a National

Director of CORE, and of militant persuasion, submitted a nominating petition with only fifty valid signatures out of the required sixty. Since he filed one day before the September 11 deadline, he had no time to submit additional names. Ruled off the ballot, Ussery immediately announced his intention of forming an independent political organization to create, in San Francisco, a black political movement free of white influence.

New York. Blacks in New York, too, seldom appear as at-large council candidates. One small factor in this phenomenon may be the relative unimportance of the council vis-a-vis the city's Board of Estimate. Made up of the mayor, the comptroller, the president of the city council, and the five elected borough presidents, the Board of Estimate in New York assumes many of the prerogatives over municipal finance granted councils in other cities. The Democratic Party customarily reserves the position of Manhattan borough president for a black. In 1969, the black incumbent, Percy Sutton, was easily reelected.

CITY COUNCIL PRESIDENCIES

City council presidencies (or their equivalents), in nine of the twelve cities, are filled by the councils themselves, electing one of their members through in-house proceedings. In New York, St. Louis, and Baltimore, the positions of city council president are separate elective offices, contested on citywide bases. During the last elections of the 1960's, black candidates sought each of these council presidencies, and each contest displayed marked racially oriented voting.

Harlem State Assemblyman Charles Rangel contested for the presidency of the New York Council in the June 1969 Democratic primary. He finished last in a field of six, but he carried the eight predominantly black assembly districts in the city.[10] Rangel's total vote exceeded 70,000, slightly less than half the ballots cast for the primary winner, white incumbent Francis X. Smith.

Councilman Joseph Clark, of St. Louis' predominantly black Fourth Ward, ran for that city's council presidency in the June 1969 Democratic primary. Finishing fourth in a field of six, Clark carried five of the eight St. Louis wards represented by black councilmen, and finished second in the other three. His total vote of over 15,000 was approximately half that of the primary victor, Democratic organization candidate Sorkis Webbe. Webbe, in turn, carried by narrow margins the three black wards not won by Clark.

State Senator Clarence Mitchell finished second in a field of three in Baltimore's June 1967 Democratic primary. Although he carried every black precinct in the city, Mitchell's vote of approximately 33,000 was only one-third that of the white organization candidate. Baltimore's Republican Party slated another black, Horace Ashby, as its candidate for city council president. Ashby easily won the Republican primary and then, along with the total Republican ticket, was snowed under in the general election. Of some interest is the fact that Ashby, making a modest inroad into the black vote, obtained 3,000 more ballots in the general election than the white Republican candidate for mayor.

Of course, blacks need not be elected president to hold important posts in city councils. The following is only a partial list of blacks holding at least nominally significant council positions at the close of the 1960's. St. Louis' Laurence Woodson was vice-president of that city's council, selected for the post by his Democratic council peers. Myron Bush was chairman of the Cincinnati Council's Employment and Human Resources Committee. Cleveland's Charles Carr held the position of majority leader of the council for ten years, until his resignation in October of 1969.[11] Carr retained his post as chairman of the council's powerful Finance Committee. And Terry Francois, in San Francisco, was chairman of the Fire, Safety, and Police Committee which, in addition to its more trenchant responsibilities, evaluates the propriety of the city's topless and bottomless dancers.

PARTY AFFILIATION

Without detailed studies of decision making within the 12 separate councils, it is impossible to test the real "strength" of blacks in these legislative bodies. However, some idea of at least *potential* black strength, in a collective sense, can be gained by noting the degree to which blacks compose various councilmanic partisan blocs. Data for the eight cities with readily ascertainable partisan divisions are shown in Table 6. These data, of course, ignore the very real issue of intraparty factionalization.

In none of the councils, after the last election of the 1960's, did blacks compose a majority of the party in power. Nor, in any city, would the defection of all black votes in the council have prevented the majority party from achieving a plurality. Nevertheless, most black councilmen (34 of 43 in the 8 cities shown in Table 6) are members of the councils' controlling partisan blocs. One should not ignore the patronage and other advantages of majority party membership even though, in the case of black councilmen, the parameters of this advantage need to be established by empirical research.

SUGGESTIONS FOR FURTHER RESEARCH

The data about black councilmen presented in this paper are not designed to form the foundation for new and definitive generalizations about urban Negro politics. They are, as previously mentioned, intended to provide a preliminary description of the state of affairs at the beginning of the 1970's and, of more consequence, they should be viewed as suggestive of further research. Readers are encouraged to develop their own avenues of inquiry from the rudimentary and descriptive material presented in the text and tables.

What follows is only a minimal list of subtopics and questions which might be investigated.

TABLE 6.   Partisan Composition of City Councils and the Party Affiliations
of Black Councilmen
(After the Last Elections in the 1960's)

City	Dates of Last Elections	Total Council	Blacks in Council	
			Number	Percentage
Baltimore	November '67	Dem. 19	Dem. 4 (21)[a]	
		‾19	‾4 (21)[b]	
Chicago	February-April '67	Dem. 37	Dem. 7 (19)	
	April '68[c]	Rep. 7	Rep. 0	
	April '69[c]	Ind. 6	Ind. 3 (50)	
		‾50	‾10 (20)	
Cleveland	November '69	Dem. 27	Dem. 9 (33)	
		Rep. 6	Rep. 3 (50)	
		‾33	‾12 (36)	
Cincinnati	November '69	Rep. 5	Rep. 0	
		Dem. Charter 4	Dem. Charter 2 (50)	
		‾9	‾2 (22)	
New York	November '69	Dem. 30	Dem. 1 (3)	
		Rep. 4	Rep. 0	
		Liberal 4	Liberal 1 (25)	
		‾38	‾2 (5)	
Philadelphia	November '67	Dem. 13	Dem. 3 (23)	
		Rep. 4	Rep. 0	
		‾17	‾3 (18)	
Pittsburgh	November '67	Dem. 9	Dem. 2 (22)	
	November '69	‾9	‾2 (22)	
St. Louis	April '67	Dem. 23	Dem. 8 (30)	
	April '69	Rep. 6	Rep. 0	
		‾29	‾8 (28)	

a. Black percentage of partisan bloc.
b. Black percentage of total council.
c. Two special elections in Chicago, in April 1968 and 1969, did not change the number of blacks in that city's council but they did alter the council's partisan composition.

1. Councilmanic elections provide excellent vehicles for the study of racially motivated voting. As 1970 census data is made available, it should be possible to investigate the quantitative aspects of city council elections occurring early in the decade. For example, one question which immediately

occurs: at what point in the transition from white to black is a changing ward likely to elect a black councilman?

2. Quantitative voting studies, of course, are of only limited value unless they are linked with information about the relevant campaign issues. If, for the moment, we trichotomize city wards into white, black, and changing, can separate patterns of issues in councilmanic campaigns be discovered in the three types? One researchable phenomenon, which promises to increase in frequency, is black versus black councilmanic races in predominantly black districts. Heretofore, black political cleavage has been muffled by the perceived need to maintain a united front against whites. As councilmanic contests *between* blacks grow in number, the opportunity is afforded to explore ideological and other differences within the urban black electorate.

3. Studies of black campaigns for at-large council seats also offer distinct possibilities for research. For example, as the black populations of cities increase, and in some instances as blacks become the majority of the population and at least a *potential* majority of the electorate, will black at-large candidates find more success with militant, rather than conservative, political appeals?

4. Most of the material in this paper has dealt with elections. The rising incidence of black councilmen, however, offers an opportunity to investigate another dimension of the issue. How do black councilmen, district and at-large, conduct themselves once in office? What are the relationships between black councilmen and the prevailing political organizations in the city? To what extent are black councilmen involved in the making of meaningful decisions, and in what directions do they exert their influence (for a series of relevant case studies see Banfield, 1961)? And how, if at all, do the political fiefs carved out by black district-based councilmen differ from those traditionally constructed by whites?

5. The growing number of black councilmen also provides a chance for insight into the question of political recruitment among blacks. Who, in the social and political sense, are the blacks who achieve these relatively prominent positions? Who are their active supporters? Furthermore, what are the career mobility patterns of black councilmen after election? Are councilmanic posts for blacks viewed as terminal political positions? Are they seen essentially as stepping-stones to higher office? Or are they valued for the tangible and intangible rewards they can bring to an individual's other occupational endeavors? Associated with this general issue is the question of self-contained black political organizations. As these agencies grow in strength and begin to name serious candidates for council races, will their nominees differ significantly, on whatever dimensions, from black political independents or from those blacks slated by the standard political parties?

6. Finally, a quasi-heretical suggestion. Despite the growing importance of the black vote, and a corollary increase in the number of black public officials, the power in most cities for the foreseeable future is likely to rest with declining, yet ubiquitous, old-line political organizations. Black councilmen,

then, can readily be placed into two oversimplified categories; those tied to the controlling organizations, and those opposed. Black organization politicians long have been castigated as Uncle Toms or worse. It would be instructive to study, by means of rigorous empirical research, the extent and quality of governmental services which flow to the districts of black organization councilmen, as contrasted to the services rendered districts represented by the growing number of black councilmen outside the "Establishment." Further, if the districts of organization councilmen fare better, as might be expected, on what grounds will the anti-organization black incumbents campaign for reelection? Wilson has observed that blacks without tangible rewards to offer their constituents often resort to racial ideology as a substitute (Wilson, 1965: 34). Does the advent of councilmanic "outsiders," therefore, promise to increase the level of racially oriented political invective in the nation's already traumatized cities?

NOTES

1. For simplicity, the term councilman is used throughout this paper, although in some cities the appelations "supervisor" or "alderman" are colloquially substituted.
2. Because of the politically sensitive nature of the material solicited, many of the individual respondents requested anonymity. In order to honor these requests, it was decided to include no direct quotations in the paper (other than those taken from newspapers) and to cite none of the respondents, even those who did not expressly ask that their names be withheld.
3. Between censuses, voter registration is probably the most meaningful device for cross-city comparisons of district size. For example, Cleveland's 33 wards ranged from 3,922 to 16,327 registered voters at the time of the 1969 municipal election. Los Angeles, by contrast, requires that each of its councilmanic districts contain approximately 15 per cent of the city's nearly 1,200,000 registered voters. By city charter, Los Angeles redistricts every four years. In any particular election, councilmanic districts containing over 100,000 registered voters are not uncommon.
4. The first designation presented no placement problems; only the race of the general election winners had to be ascertained. The second posed serious difficulties. Council races, particularly in primary contests, sometimes involve both black and white candidates with no organized support and no practical chance of winning. The essential question was: where blacks or whites entered council contests in which a member of the other race achieved victory, at what point could the contest actually be considered interracial?

   After some fruitless attempts to apply a single criterion (placement position in the election; or some other like it), it finally was decided to utilize an ad hoc scheme. Each contest, including the primary (where held), was examined separately. If an unsuccessful candidate of the other race was supported by a party or by an organization, or if he was mentioned as a "serious" candidate by the daily or black press or by an informant, or if all candidates of the other race collectively received as much as 10 per cent of the total vote (in either the primary or the general election), the contest was considered interracial.

5. On December 17, 1969, Mayor Addonizio, incumbent black councilmen West and Turner, and seven other past and present Newark public officials were indicted by a Federal Grand Jury on charges including extortion and income tax evasion.

6. Proposals are made periodically to reduce the size of New York's Council districts, or to rearrange their boundaries, so as to increase the number of minority-group councilmen. While blacks in New York are drastically underrepresented, the city's nearly 1,000,000 Puerto Rican-Americans were entirely without representation in the city council elected in 1969. Two Puerto Ricans served in the 1965–1969 Council. One, Carlos Rios (Democrat, at-large, Manhattan) failed to obtain enough signatures to get on the June primary ballot for reelection. The other, Robert Lebron (Tenth District, Bronx) was opposed in the Democratic primary by another candidate of Puerto Rican background. The two split the Puerto Rican vote, enabling a white non-Spanish candidate to achieve nomination.

7. During the late 1940's and early 1950's, two blacks regularly were elected to Cincinnati's Council. The vote-getting ability of one, Theodore Berry, and the possibility that he might become mayor under the then existing "proportional representation" election system, precipitated changes in the city's election procedures.

8. The owner of a clothing store, Weaver had finished last in a field of 22 in 1967. During the 1969 campaign, he paraded like Diogenes through Cincinnati's city hall carrying a 94-cent gas lantern and failing, by his own account, to find an honest man.

9. Perhaps the best primary showing by a nonorganization black occurred in 1967. The Reverend James J. (Jimmy Joe) Robinson, in the 1940's the first black to play as a starter on the University of Pittsburgh football team, finished fifth behind the four organization candidates. With over 23,000 votes, Robinson trailed the fourth party regular by 10,000.

10. Four Harlem assembly districts in Manhattan, three Bedford-Stuyvesant and South Williamsburg districts in Brooklyn, and the Springfield Gardens district in Queens. New York's 68 assembly districts are customarily regarded as the basic voting units in the city, and voting returns, even for municipal elections, are often analyzed in those terms.

11. Carr had held the post since 1960. He resigned, reportedly, because of the untenable man-in-the-middle nature of the position in the political feud between Mayor Stokes and Council President James Stanton.

BIBLIOGRAPHY

ADRIAN, C. R., and C. PRESS (1968) *Governing Urban America.* New York: McGraw-Hill.

Baltimore News-American (1967) November 8.

BANFIELD, E. C., (1961) *Political Influence.* New York: Free Press.

———, and J. Q. WILSON (1963) *City Politics.* New York: Vintage.

CUBAN, L. (1967) "A strategy for racial peace: Negro leadership in Cleveland, 1900–1919." *Phylon* (third quarter), pp. 299–311.

FLEMING, G. J. (1960) An All-Negro Ticket in Baltimore. New York: McGraw-Hill.

GOSNELL, H. F. (1967) Negro Politicians: The Rise of Negro Politics in Chicago. Chicago: University of Chicago Press.

Newark Evening News (1968) November 7.

PATTERSON, B. C. (1969) "Political action of Negroes in Los Angeles: a case study in the attainment of concilmanic representation." Phylon (second quarter), pp. 170–183.

Pittsburgh Press (1969a) October 10.

———— (1969b) September 28, September 25.

POMPER, G. (1966) "Ethnic and group voting in nonpartisan municipal elections." Public Opinion Q. (Spring), pp. 79–97.

STRAETZ, R. A. (1958) PR Politics in Cincinnati. New York: New York University Press.

WILSON, J. Q. (1966) "The Negro in American politics: the present." In J. Davis, Ed., The American Negro Reference Book. Englewood Cliffs, N.J.: Prentice-Hall, pp. 424–448.

———— (1965) Negro Politics: The Search for Leadership. New York: Free Press.

PART II

INTRODUCTION TO
THE AMERICAN INDIANS

KATHLEEN O'BRIEN JACKSON

Despite volumes of material available about Indian people of the United States, the contemporary social, economic, and political situation of the diverse people collectively categorized as Native Americans or Indians is not well known or understood by non-Indian society. More is known about the Indian as an historic curiosity—as a romanticized and stereotyped character in the drama of the settlement of the American frontier—than as a member of a small, but enduring ethnic minority with unique claims upon the American conscience. Contrary to some misconceptions, Indians are not "wards" of the government but are full citizens with special rights derived from their tribal status as former sovereign nations and as original inhabitants of the land mass now known as the fifty states. Descendants of the first Americans have a heritage of conquest; a process that spanned four centuries and involved brutal suppression, cultural extermination, and coercive assimilation. That over three hundred distinct Indian tribal groups survived with much of their cultures intact is indeed remarkable. The Indian experience as a minority must be understood in terms of its historical origin, for the past has much relevance to the current situation and future role of Indians in American society.

HISTORICAL BACKGROUND

Prior to the invasion of the New World by European adventurers, there were no "Indians." The name was attached to the inhabitants encountered by Columbus when he reached the land that he mistakenly thought was the East Indies. The diversity of people populating the Americas was vast, ranging from the highly structured civilizations of Central America to the small, nomadic bands of people in the arctic and plains areas. Their languages, religions, and cultural traditions were centuries old and had developed quite independently from the Greco-Roman, Judeo-Christian civilization of Western Europe.

The primary impact of the European exploration of the Western Hemisphere was to disrupt and change the ways of life of the people who lived there. The Europeans were motivated by territorial expansionism and a search for wealth. Since the people they encountered were viewed as obstacles to these objectives and their culture was considered inferior to that of the Europeans, expedient means were used to separate the indigenous people from their land and resources. Some of the invaders sought to convert Indians to Christianity and to "civilize" them according to European norms. Others sought to engage the Indians as allies in power struggles over land for settlements and over furs and other valuable resources. Still others sought to exterminate the Indian "savages" or to isolate them from further contact. The introduction of guns and liquor, the spread of exotic diseases, warfare, and the forced removal of Indians from their homelands weakened and decimated the Indian population. Although Indians resisted these pressures, the superior technology and large numbers of the immigrants made the outcome of the conflict inevitable. One historian has characterized the process of conquest in the following way:

> The European conquest of the Americas had been termed one of the darkest chapters of human history, for the conquerors demanded and won authority over the lives, territories, religious beliefs, ways of life, and means of existence of every native group with which they came in contact. No one will ever know how many Indians or how many tribes were enslaved, tortured, debauched, and killed. No one can ever reckon the dimensions of the human tragedy that cost, in addition to lives, the loss of homes, dignity, cultural institutions, standards of security, material and intellectual accomplishments, and liberty and freedom to millions upon millions of people. The stain is made all the darker by the realization that the conflict was forced upon those who suffered; the aggressors were the whites, the scenes of tragedy the very homelands of the victims.[1]

In the area that is now the United States, the process of nation building involved a century of almost continual warfare between Indians and whites over the acquisition of land. Although the Europeans had seized Indian land, they had also set the precedent of treaty making by recognizing tribes as sovereign powers with basic rights to the land they occupied. This practice was continued after the American Revolution by the new American government in an attempt to establish peace with Indians who had been allies of the British. Between the time of the American Revolution and 1871, the United States government negotiated over four hundred treaties with various Indian tribes.

Treaties were the main instrument used to legitimize the colonists' claims to territory, but were also a means of inducing Indians to abandon their tribal ways of life and become "civilized." In the early stages of treaty making, the Indians were in a relatively strong position vis-à-vis the colonists and the main provisions entailed the formal cession of Indian lands in return for money and promises by the federal government to recognize Indian rights to occupy other territory. Some of the later treaties also included provisions for Indian education, agricultural equipment, and other services. In some cases, special hunting and fishing rights were guaranteed by treaties. Increased population pressures of the expanding colonies made these agreements short-lived, however, and conflicts erupted over violation of treaty rights by whites.

Not all treaty negotiations were honorable proceedings, as Indians were typically in a defeated position as a result of warfare and thus unable to bargain for favorable terms. Signers of treaties on behalf of the tribes were frequently not recognized as legitimate representatives by other tribal members. Nor were some of the provisions of the treaties fully understood by both parties, particularly regarding the restriction of Indians from land they had ceded. Indians and whites had very different concepts of land. For the Indians, land was integrally related to a basic philosophy about the relation of man to nature and was used by all tribal members in common. The white man viewed land as a commodity to be bought and sold, owned and used, exploited for economic purposes and controlled for political ends under the system of private property.

The practice of treaty making with the Indians raised basic issues about the legal status of Indians. Treaties were contracted with the same validity as treaties negotiated with foreign nations and thus recognized tribes as sovereign political entities. As disputes arose over the interpretation of Indian rights under treaty provisions, however, the United States Supreme Court ruled that while Indian tribes retained some attributes of sovereignty, they were more analogous to domestic dependent nations than to foreign nations.[2] According to constitutional provisions, the federal government had exclusive rights to regulate affairs with Indians. Eventually, a role of federal guardianship evolved by the creation of a special administrative agency to deal exclusively with Indian affairs. It is significant to note that this Office of Indian Affairs, later known as the Bureau of Indian Affairs (BIA), was originally part of the War Department inasmuch as Indians were viewed primarily as a military problem.

Although the basis for federal administration of Indian Affairs had its roots in constitutional clauses pertaining to Indians, and in interpretations of treaty provisions, the scope and direction of government involvement in tribal life reflected the basic attitude of whites towards Indian culture. It was clear from the practice of removing Indians from lands adjacent to white settlements and later confining them to reservations that Americans were not interested in coexistence with Indians as equals. Further, it was clear that traditional tribal organization was not valued by the whites, as it was common practice to relocate tribes in geographic areas radically different from their homelands and to combine separate tribal groups—often rival groups—on one reservation. White intolerance was displayed through efforts to "civilize" Indians by banning tribal religious and ceremonial practices, by imposing white hair styles and clothing styles, by taking Indian children away from home for education, and by converting Indians to a private-property system of farming.

By the end of the nineteenth century, Indian communities were managed by federal agents with extraordinary powers over all aspects of Indian life. All decisions relating to land use, employment, allocation of money, education, and even movement to and from the reservation were made by the resident agent. This had the effect of seriously undermining leadership arising from within the tribe and fostered a relationship of total dependency of Indians upon the government. Under this system, the Indian population diminished as they lived in abject poverty, their land base was eroded by the allotment or parceling of individual tracts of land to individuals, their culture was suppressed, and an atmosphere of despondency prevailed.[3]

During the 1920's, social reformers became interested in the plight of American Indians. Efforts to assimilate Indians by educating them in white schools and by making them into farmers had failed. Even though Indians had been declared citizens in 1924, it was clear that they were not treated as though they had equal rights. An investigation of conditions among Indian communities, contained in the Meriam Survey Report, led to a shift in federal policy towards Indians. In 1934, Congress passed the Wheeler-Howard Act, better known as the Indian Reorganization Act, as a means of remedying some of the worst conditions. Although integration was still an ultimate objective, tribal self-government was encouraged as a means of restoring leadership within Indian communities and reviving Indian culture. Tribal land was placed in trust status as a means of maintaining reservations. Under the previous system of alloting land to individual tribal members, two-thirds of all land originally held by Indians had been lost. By placing land in trust status, it was exempt from taxation and could not be sold or leased without prior approval of the Bureau of Indian Affairs, which was designated as administrator for the trusteeship. Improvements in medical and educational facilities and an upgrading in services provided Indians by the Bureau of Indian Affairs were also provided by the Act.

Even though the Indian Reorganization Act marked a major improvement for many tribes in terms of their ability to resume management of their own lives, significant power was still retained by federal agents, particularly in the area of finances. It took some time for many Indian communities to adjust to this new policy after so many years of total control by outsiders. Bans on the exercise of Indian religion were lifted and tribes were allowed to rebuild community institutions and reestablish traditional authority roles. However, the Bureau of Indian Affairs was frequently an obstacle to Indian control of their communities through its paternalistic approach towards its clientele.

By the early 1950's, criticism of the federal role in Indian affairs renewed and another change in policy occurred. House Concurrent Resolution 108 was passed advocating the severance of federal ties to Indians and the liquidation of the Bureau of Indian Affairs. This policy, known as termination, had the objective of abolishing special recognition of Indian tribes as political entities with special claims upon the federal government. As was typical of federal policy decisions involving Indians, the people directly affected were not consulted even though termination was opposed by Indians and their advocates.

Considerable controversy surrounded the termination policy throughout the 1950's and 1960's. Indians viewed termination as a coercive form of assimilation and as another landgrab by whites. The termination of the Klamath reservation in Oregon and the Menominee reservation in Wisconsin exemplified the negative aspects of termination. Neither group was prepared to be integrated into the health and other social service sector. As a result, new hardships were perpetrated and the overall conditions of life were not improved for these tribes.

Termination had yet a broader impact in the area of federal Indian relations. It shifted the emphasis from developing programs and resources to strengthen reservations as viable communities to relocating Indians in urban environments. The participation of Indians in World War II and the employment of Indians in war industries had started a trend of migration of young Indians away from the reservation. Nevertheless, many Indians chose to remain on reservations and to retain distinct cultural traditions. Termination was viewed by this latter group as a threat to the way of life they valued.

Another by-product of termination was the passage of Public Law 280 which gave state governments the unilateral right to assume jurisdiction over civil and criminal matters on Indian reservations. Prior to passage of this law, tribal courts and law enforcement authorities had legal jurisdiction over Indians residing upon reservations, with the exception of ten crimes under federal jurisdiction. Public Law 280 impinged upon tribal authority derived from the special legal status of tribes as quasi-sovereign entities. It also reversed the intent of the Indian Reorganization Act to strengthen tribal institutions and raised the issue of discriminatory law enforcement.

A turning point in the relationship between Indians and the federal government occurred in 1961. In that year, a convention of Indian leaders formulated a Declaration of Indian Purpose expressing their views on past federal policy and proposing recommendations for a new role of Indians in determining their own destinies. Concurrently, a task force headed by Secretary of the Interior Stewart Udall reported a study of reservation conditions that concluded that the threat of termination had produced an environment of confusion and uncertainty which impeded the development of Indian communities. Self-sufficiency, full participation of Indians in American life, the development of Indian resources, and equal rights for Indians were defined as new policy objectives. Understandably, many Indians were cynical about the real meaning of these themes, given their past experience with vacillating attitudes of political authorities towards Indians.

During the 1960's there were a number of investigations into various aspects of Indian life. One of the most important dealt with the complex issue of the legal status of the Indians as both citizens and members of quasi-independent tribal groups. The Subcommittee on Constitutional Rights of the Senate Committee on the Judiciary conducted numerous hearings to determine Indians' civil rights in relation to federal law, tribal authority, administrative regulations, and state law.[4] The hearings documented numerous circumstances in which the rights of Indians as citizens were violated. Discrimination in housing, employment, and schools; restrictive voting practices; denial of state welfare and other social benefits; discriminatory law enforcement; and denial of equal protection under the law by state governments were documented by the hearings. The administration of justice under tribal courts at times also resulted in a denial of procedural and substantive rights guaranteed citizens by the Constitution. As a result of these findings, a special Indian Rights Section was included in the Civil Rights Bill of 1968. In essence, it explicitly extended the Bill of Rights to Indians subject to tribal courts and provided that state governments could no longer assume legal jurisdiction over reservations without tribal consent. While seen by its supporters as a landmark piece of legislation in securing equal citizenship rights for American Indians, it was not universally welcomed by Indian communities. Some tribes felt it constituted an infringement upon their legal codes of justice and presented severe burdens by stipulating a revision of their legal systems to conform to Anglo-Saxon norms.

CURRENT SITUATION

Today, there are fewer than a million people classified as American Indians or Alaskan Natives by the U.S. Census of the population. Although population statistics for Indians are notably unreliable, Table 1 indicates trends in Indian population since 1900. While it is generally acknowledged that there has been an increase in Indian people since the all-time low at the turn of the century, the data presented does not reflect an absolute rate of growth, as procedures for collecting population figures have changed the manner in which ethnic identity is reported.[5]

The majority of Indians are concentrated in the states of Arizona, New Mexico, North Dakota, South Dakota, Oklahoma, New York, North Carolina,

TABLE 1. U.S. Indian Population: 1900–1970

Year	Population	Year	Population
1900	237,196	1940	345,252
1910	276,927	1950	357,499
1920	244,437	1960	523,591
1930	343,352	1970	792,730

SOURCE: From U.S. Department of Commerce, Bureau of the Census, *1970 U.S. Census of the Population: United States General Summary*, Table 48.

Alaska, and California. For the last two decades, there has been a steady migration of Indian people from reservations and rural areas to cities for employment and educational opportunities. Census reports from 1970 indicate that almost one half of the Indian population is located in urban areas. The remainder of the population is either located in rural areas or on reservations. In 1969, there were 244 federal and state Indian reservations located in thirty states. Indian residents on these reservations range from less than 5 people on some California Rancherias to 119,546 people living on the 13-million-acre Navajo Reservation in Arizona and New Mexico.[6] Reservations vary a great deal with regard to history, culture, resources, government, and community facilities.

The diversity among Indian groups makes it hazardous to draw conclusions about the overall socioeconomic status of Indians. However, it is apparent that by most indices of health, housing, education, or employment, American Indians are considerably more disadvantaged than non-Indians. On the average, Indians die at younger ages than non-Indians: the average age of death for Indians is 44 years compared with 64 for the population as a whole.[7] Accidents and diseases, many of them virtually eliminated in the wider population, are the main causes of Indian deaths and physical impairments. Indian mortality rates for all causes are disproportionately higher than for other people and this has retarded population growth even though Indian birth rates are more than double that of the United States population as a whole.

Since 1956, an Indian division of the U.S. Public Health Service has been responsible for providing health care to reservation Indians.[8] Although there have been marked improvements, there are still many serious health problems afflicting American Indians. Health conditions are related to other deficiencies as indicated by the 1970 edition of *Indian Health Trends and Services*:

> . . . The inferior health status of Indians and Alaskan Natives results from their impoverished socioeconomic status, limited education, poor and crowded housing, inadequate nutrition, lack of basic sanitary facilities, unsafe water supplies, gross unsanitary practices, and emotional problems inherent in a transitional culture.

American Indian reservations have been referred to as pockets of under-development in the midst of the most affluent nation in the world. Indeed, conditions of chronic unemployment and poverty prevail on most reservations, although there are a few exceptions. According to a survey conducted in 1969, unemployment rates on the ten largest Indian reservations ranged from a low of 23 per cent to a high of 52 per cent.[9]

Tribal economies are dependent upon the existence of productive resources as well as the ability to attract industrial development. Although some reservations have abundant forest and mineral resources, the Indian owners often receive only minimal returns because these resources are frequently exploited by non-Indians who have leased rights to use the land at very low fees. The geographic isolation of many reservations from large population centers and the lack of sufficient tribal capital to attract outside industries have impeded economic development. Even in cases where commercial enterprises are located in reservations, it is frequently the case that Indian employees remain in nonmanagerial positions or the type of employment is not suited for the characteristics of the population.

The educational system is the major agent for socializing children into the norms of American society. The education provided for American Indians has been termed "a national tragedy." The average educational level for all Indians under federal supervision was 5 school years, and 27 per cent of the adult population was illiterate as of 1969.[10] Most Indian students attend public schools, although boarding schools operated by the Bureau of Indian Affairs still enroll about 30 per cent of the school age children. Until recently, the opportunity for higher education was virtually nonexistent for most Indians. Some progress is evident by the fact that Indian enrollment in colleges and universities had quadrupled in the last ten years.

A rather consistent pattern of Indian students' performance is evident in all schools—repetition of grades, low attendance rates, and high dropout rates. Research indicates that Indian children progress at a rate comparable to that of other children until around the fourth to seventh grades when a marked decline in school achievement takes place.[11] This phenomenon has been linked to a basic conflict between the cultural norms and values learned by Indian students at home and those prevailing in the Anglo, middle-class educational system. Distorted and derogatory treatment of Indians in textbooks, exposure to insensitive and ill-prepared teachers, and a failure of the curriculum to incorporate linguistic and cultural courses have further contributed to the barriers encountered by Indian children. For many years, Indian leaders have demanded greater control over school policy in order to reverse this trend, and have already demonstrated the success of an Indian-oriented curriculum at the Rough Rock School in Arizona.

Most of the basic health, educational, employment, and environmental problems which typify Indian life on reservations are also prevalent among urban Indians. It is difficult to estimate the magnitude of the problems of urban Indians, for this subpopulation tends to be quite mobile, not concentrated in particular geographic areas, and generally combined with the non-white population in statistical data. From information that is available, however, it is evident that cities are frequently alien and insecure places for Indians. A basic orientation to the complexities of city life such as transportation, shopping, and housing facilities is often lacking. Employment agencies attempting to place Indians report their clients frequently lack suitable clothing for seeking employment, find it difficult to communicate with potential employers, and find application blanks and rigid time schedules frustrating.[12] Further, median incomes for urban Indians are lower than comparable groups due to their employment in low-skill work and discrimination by employers.[13]

The socioeconomic problems of urban Indians are further compounded by an apparent lack of information about community services available to them as well as a reluctance to deal with social service agencies. Very few Indians or others sensitive to the particular needs of Indians are employed in administrative positions by agencies with an Indian clientele. Misconceptions about services provided to Indians by the Bureau of Indian Affairs often results in inadequate referrals for housing, health care, or welfare benefits. As far as the Bureau of Indian Affairs is concerned, urban Indians are assimilated into the general population and are no longer eligible for the services the Bureau provides to reservation Indians.

POLITICAL ISSUES AND POLITICAL ACTIVISM

During the last five years, increased national attention has been directed towards the situation of American Indians. In large part, this is due to events such as the widely publicized invasion and occupation of Alcatraz by Indians in 1969, and the "Trail of Broken Treaties" to Washington, D.C.—which culminated in the seizure of the office of the Bureau of Indian Affairs shortly before the 1972 presidential election, and the occupation of the site of the Wounded Knee Massacre in South Dakota in 1973. Although these events represent only one dimension of the political activity engaged in by American Indians, their primary significance lies in the needs, frustrations, and demands that are made visible by these actions.

The main issues of Indian politics arise from the historical origins described earlier—the special relationship between Indians and government and federal administrative practices. Four interlocking issues may be defined as the core of Indian politics:

1. Self-determination.
2. The role of the Bureau of Indian Affairs.
3. Services for nonreservation Indians.
4. Protection of treaty rights.

Self-determination is the most basic demand of Indians because it entails the recognition by non-Indian society, and the federal government in particular, that Indians have a right to exercise control over their own destinies. As outlined by Indian leaders, self-determination means the direct participation of recognized Indian leaders in all levels of decisions that affect the future of Indian communities. It is not generally meant to include the severance of the special legal relationship between Indians and the federal government, but rather to secure a maximum of assistance for self-help with a minimum of interference. Subsumed under this issue are concerns for community development and the upgrading of the quality of life for Indians.

Given the objective of self-determination, the future role of the Bureau of Indian Affairs is of utmost importance to Indian communities. Traditionally, the BIA has adopted a managerial role of extensive control over tribal affairs rather than a role of advocacy for their clientele or a service-oriented approach. Indians have long been critical of the quality of BIA personnel and the insensitivity of the agency to their needs and desires. The fact that the BIA is a subagency of the Department of the Interior has raised issues of conflict of interest and inappropriate placement within the federal structure.[14] As currently organized, the BIA must compete with more powerful land and recreation agencies for appropriations. There have been numerous instances in which projects initiated by one of the other Interior agencies have adversely affected Indian lands and resources. Furthermore, the basic orientation of the Department of the Interior is towards natural resources rather than social services such as schools, employment, and housing. For these reasons, Indians have proposed the restructuring of the BIA as a cabinet-level office which incorporates full participation of Indians in all stages of operation and is accountable to Indian people. Its function would be to provide better services suited to the unique needs of Indians while recognizing tribal sovereignty in the management of local affairs.

Not all Indians come under the jurisdiction of the Bureau of Indian Affairs. There are many enclaves of tribal communities throughout the United States that are seeking federal recognition so that they may be eligible for the extension of financial assistance and services. Many of these groups are eastern tribes which were never given reservations or lost their lands many years ago but maintained strong ethnic identity. There are also the relatively large numbers of urban Indians who are excluded from special federal assistance even though they are still enrolled as tribal members and often remain in active contact with the reservation. It has been the assumption that these groups need only temporary services at the most until they integrate into the mainstream. Indian centers in the major cities have provided ample evidence of the need for special services for urban Indians on a continuing basis.

Demands for recognition of a special status for nonreservation Indians in turn relates back to the fundamental basis for the federal services that arise from treaty obligations and other legal commitments to the ancestors of contemporary Indians. Indians view treaties as binding contracts not to be lightly dismissed only because they are several decades old. The failure of government to meet these responsibilities has resulted in deep frustration, disillusionment, and distrust of political authorities. It is significant that one of the proposals presented by activists involved in the Wounded Knee confrontation to White House representatives was the creation of a special Treaty Commission to enforce existing treaty provisions.

The protection of Indian rights to land, water, and fishing areas promised by treaties is an emotion-laden issue, as these rights have been linked to the basic survival of tribal communities. Population pressures, illegal actions by state governments, conflicts with resource agencies, and outright violations of treaty provisions have not only impinged upon Indian rights, but have posed threats to the vital supply of resources such as water. In some cases, legal redress is available to tribes through the Indian Claims Commission, a body created in 1946 to review and adjudicate grievances of Indians arising out of losses resulting from mistakes, frauds, negligence, or duress on the part of government. However, this body has limited jurisdiction and is empowered to grant monetary settlements only. Other claims must proceed through litigation in courts of law or seek a special act of Congress to restore lost land or rights. Small tribes with minimal resources are at an obvious disadvantage in securing protection of their treaty rights.

Demands for self-determination for Indian communities, for a more responsive role of the BIA, for improved services and programs for all Indians regardless of place of residence, and for protection of treaty provisions have taken many forms. In recent years, political activism by Indians has run the gamut from participation in the major political parties to demonstrations in the streets. There have been lobbying activities and there have been violent confrontations with police. There have been workshops and conferences with government officials, and there have been armed occupations of government offices and other sites chosen for their symbolic significance.

It cannot be said that there is a unified American Indian political movement, for there are a multitude of organizations claiming Indian membership with markedly different political strategies. There is, however, a recognition of basic "Indian" issues and a concern, on the part of Indian leadership, for a unified approach to confronting common problems. Where coalitions with non-Indian groups have occurred, these have tended to be focused upon particular issues rather than enduring alliances.

There are a number of factors which help to explain the barriers to Indian unity and the fragmentation of political resources. Indian political activity has historically revolved around tribal concerns, and these concerns have in turn been influenced by the resources and leadership of each particular group. The limited amount of appropriations from federal sources available for Indian purposes and the process by which they are distributed among tribes has a built-in element of competition among groups. Furthermore, the dependency of reservation tribes upon federal funds has generated a fear that appropriations will be cut if Indians antagonize officials in the Interior Department or in the House and Senate Committees on Interior and Insular Affairs. These factors help to explain why reservation groups frequently withhold support from demonstrations and other activities generated by urban Indians. It is likewise difficult for nonreservation groups to identify with some of the issues that concern reservations, such as taxation and revolving capital funds.

Philosophical differences about strategies for affecting change for Indian communities have been a further divisive element. Some Indian leaders have publically denounced demonstration and militant protests as not in keeping with "the Indian way." Counter-critics have pointed to the slowness of change using traditional channels for exercising political pressure. Both sides to the controversy can claim some successes and have even aligned on key issues. One of the most widely acclaimed mobilizations of all-Indian support occurred in the case of the Taos Pueblos of New Mexico. For 64 years, this group sought to regain possession of land with religious significance that had been expropriated for use as a national forest. They had successfully presented their case before the Indian Claims Commission and had been offered a sizable sum of money as compensation. The Taos refused the money and persistently presented their case to Congress and the media until finally, in 1970, the land was awarded to them by an Act of Congress. This case involved support from virtually all tribes and Indian organizations as well as from non-Indians.

Apart from difficulties in achieving an overall strategy for dealing with issues of concern to Indians, political awareness and communication among tribal groups have increased. Regional organizations to consolidate strength in seeking solutions to mutual problems have been formed with positive results in some parts of the country. Representation of urban and other nonreservation Indians in national Indian organizations has broadened their scope of activities. Indians with professional and technical expertise have convened to pool their resources in attacking problems of concern to many tribal groups. Finally, Indian newspapers and journals such as *Wassaja, The Sentinel*, and *The Indian Historian* serve to inform Indians about impending legislation, court rulings, and other actions that affect Indians as well as to suggest means of exercising political influence.

INDIANS AND OTHER AMERICANS

The experiences of American Indians as a minority differ from other groups in two important respects. First, the native Americans have a tradition of tribal identity which includes the basic right of self-government. The fact that tribal sovereignty was both recognized by the federal government and yet suppressed by means of bureaucratic control demonstrates an important paradox of our democratic political system. As Felix Cohen, an expert on Indian law, once observed:

Like the miner's canary, the Indian marks the shifts from fresh air to poison gas in our political atmosphere; and our treatment of Indians, even more than our treatment of other minorities, reflects the rise and fall of our democratic faith.[15]

Second, no other minority may so clearly trace the deprivations and injustices of their condition directly to the highest level of federal administration. Indians have not been victims of "benign neglect" but rather products of a form of paternalism predicated on a lack of tolerance or respect for cultural differences. Over a century ago, Alexis de Tocqueville warned of a tyranny of the majority arising out of the conformity he saw associated with the emphasis on egalitarianism in American democracy. Indeed, equality alone is not the main issue to be resolved about the role of Indians in American society; rather it is the possibility of coexistence of diverse cultures without the suppression of the minority by the majority.

It is, unfortunately, too easy to dwell upon the problems and negative experiences of American Indians as a minority. There is another side of Indian life—derived from the rich cultural heritage of Indian art, poetry, literature, music, and religion—that is enduring and dynamic.[16] It is within these media that non-Indians may begin to appreciate the meaning of "Indianness."

THE READINGS

The first selection in the readings is taken directly from testimony presented before the House of Representatives by the governor of the San Felipe Pueblo. It presents a convincing case against legislation requiring that the Pueblo judicial system be reconstituted to conform to the Anglo-Saxon system of jurisprudence. It is a statement blending an historical perspective on the ancient traditions of the San Felipe Pueblo with the issue of tribal sovereignty that remains at the heart of Indian concerns.

The steady erosion and exploitation of reservation lands in the past, combined with increasing pressures on Indian lands by the continual expansion of population centers, have increased the necessity of Indians to act to protect their own interests. The second reading is a position paper prepared by the National Congress of American Indians, the broadest based and largest Indian organization. It clearly demonstrates Indian concerns about the pressures entailed in the development process for Indians to change their ways of life and adapt to the industrial ethic. It capsulizes the essential differences between Indians and other groups striving for self-determination and stresses the importance of white society listening to the Indian point of view.

The third reading presents a summary of the basic issues involved in the protection of Indian water rights. There is a twofold significance to the selection. First, it concerns a matter that directly threatens the survival of Indian reservations in the southwest portion of the United States. The diversion of water from Indian lands to other population centers is creating critical water shortages that may produce a new kind of termination of Indian reservations and is thus one of the greatest fears of Indians. Secondly, as is so well outlined by the summary, federal encroachment on Indian water rights demonstrates a basic conflict of interest entailed in the current system of federal administration of Indian Affairs. It further evokes the moral and legal obligations of the federal government to honor solemn promises and commitments made to Indians and which must not be considered irrelevant only because they were made many years ago.

Most non-Indians probably associate Indian life as synonymous with reservation life. However, as indicated earlier in this introduction, substantial numbers of Indians have migrated to urban areas in the last two decades, yet retain an Indian identity. The fourth selection chronicles the personal experiences of some Indians who followed the path to the "cement prairies."

A great number of Indian groups lost virtually all of their land during the time when reservations were subdivided into individual allotments. In western Washington, there are numerous small tribes with only remnants of their former land holding but who maintain communal ties and have preserved traditional ways of life. Three of these tribes, the Muckleshoots, the Puyallups, and the Nisquallys have been engaged in a long-standing struggle with state authorities over fishing rights guaranteed by treaties over one hundred years ago. At various stages, this struggle has entailed fish-in demonstrations, which have received national publicity; clashes on the rivers with armed state game wardens and law enforcement officials; attacks by white vigilantes upon Indian fishermen; and the posting of armed Indian guards to protect men and equipment.

The fifth selection is taken from a study of the Indian fishing rights controversy by members of the American Friends Service Committee. The authors argue that the fundamental issue between Indians and their opponents is an attitudinal one having to do with white intolerance towards difference. This issue is obscured by the emphasis upon conservation concerns by opponents of Indian fishing rights. Powerful commercial and sports fishing interests have actively opposed fishing practices of Indians which do not comply with regulations set by the state government. The case raises a peculiar dilemma for American democracy, revolving around the extension of "special" privileges to a group that has paid so dearly with its lives and lands.

The two final selections deal with the politicization of American Indians. In ways dramatic and visible to non-Indian society, Indians operating from urban bases have captured the attention of the press and nation by "invasion" and occupation of federally owned property. The "take over" of Alcatraz Island at Thanksgiving, 1969, and subsequent occupation for almost two years set the precedent for this type of activity. In at least one case in California, the effort was met with success, that is, eventually land was turned over to Indians for their use.

The proclamation to the "Great White Father" was issued by the invaders of Alcatraz Island explaining the intent of their action. Variations of this document, obviously patterned after the rhetoric of treaties, were used in subsequent occupations of federal lands.

The selection on Indian activism was written by Vine Deloria, Jr., one of the best-known contemporary Indian authors. His first two books, *Custer Died for Your Sins* and *We Talk, You Listen*, attacked many of the predominant myths cultivated by non-Indian society, and forcefully presented issues of concern to the Indian community. A lawyer by profession and a former Executive Director of the National Congress of American Indians, Deloria has written extensively about Indian affairs and has been an active political participant.

NOTES

1. ALVIN M. JOSEPHY, JR., *The Indian Heritage of America* (New York: Bantam Books, 1969), p. 277.
2. *Cherokee Nation v. Georgia*, 30 U.S. (5 Pet.) 1 (1831).
3. MERIAM LEWIS et al., *The Problem of Indian Administration* (Baltimore: Johns Hopkins Press, 1928).
4. "Constitutional Rights of The American Indian," Summary Report of Hearings and Investigations by the Subcommittee on Constitutional Rights of the Committee on the Judiciary, Committee Print, 89th Congress, 2d Session, 1966.
5. Prior to the 1960 and 1970 census, race and color classifications were obtained by observation rather than by self-enumeration, which tended to undercount people of quarter or half Indian ethnicity.
6. U.S. Department of Commerce, Economic Development Administration, *Federal and State Indian Reservations: An EDA Handbook* (Washington, D.C.: U.S. Government Printing Office, 1971).
7. HELEN W. JOHNSON, *Rural Indian Americans in Poverty* (Washington, D.C.: Department of Agriculture, Economic Research Service, 1969).
8. See ROBERT L. KANE and ROSALIE A. KANE, *Federal Health Care (with Reservations)* (New York: Springer Publishing Company, 1972), for a discussion of this aspect of reservation life.
9. *EDA Handbook*.
10. "Indian Education: A National Tragedy—A National Challenge," 1969 Report made by the Special Subcommittee on Indian Education of the Senate Committee on Labor and Public Welfare, Special Report No. 91-501, 91st Congress, 1st Session, 1969.
11. HENRY L. SASLOW and MAY J. HARROVER, "Research on Psychological Adjustment of Indian Youth," *American Journal of Psychiatry* 125 (August 1968), pp. 224–31.
12. See the League of Women Voters of Minneapolis with the Assistance of the Training Center for Community Programs, *Indians in Minneapolis* (Minneapolis: League of

Women Voters, April 1968), for an agency point of view and the excellent novel by
N. SCOTT MOMADAY, *House Made of Dawn* (New York: Harper & Row, 1968),
for an Indian perspective on urban life.

13. ALAN L. SORKIN, "Some Aspects of American Indian Migration," *Social Forces*
(December 1969), pp. 243–51.

14. See ALVIN JOSEPHY, JR., "The American Indian and the Bureau of Indian Affairs—
1969, A Study with Recommendations," in *Hearings on the Education of Indian
Children*, 90th Congress, 1st Session, Part II, Appendix, pp. 1421–59.

15. FELIX COHEN, *Yale Law Journal* (February 1953).

16. For example, see JOHN G. NEIHARDT, *Black Elk Speaks* (Lincoln: University of
Nebraska Press, 1961); FRANK WATERS, *The Man Who Killed the Deer* (New
York: Simon and Schuster, 1970); HAL BORLAND, *When the Legends Die* (Phila-
delphia: Lippincott, 1963); and SHIRLEY HILL WITT and STAN STEINER, Eds.,
The Way: An Anthology of American Indian Literature (New York: Random House,
Vintage Books, 1972).

BIBLIOGRAPHY

BROPHY, WILLIAM A., and SOPHIE D. ABERLE. *The Indian: America's Unfinished
Business*. Report of the Commission of the Rights, Liberties and Responsibilities of the
American Indian. Norman, Oklahoma: University of Oklahoma Press, 1968.

CAHN, EDGAR S., Ed. *Our Brother's Keeper: The Indian in White America*, Washington,
D.C.: New Community Press, Inc., 1969.

COLLIER, JOHN. *Indians of the Americas*. New York: North American Library, 1961.

Council on Interracial Books for Children. *Chronicles of American Indian Protest*. Greenwich, Conn.: Fawcett Publishing, 1971.

DELORIA, VINE, JR. *Custer Died for Your Sins*. London: Macmillan, 1969.

———. *Of Utmost Good Faith*. San Francisco: Straight Arrow Books, 1971.

———. *We Talk, You Listen*. New York: Macmillan, 1969.

FEY, HAROLD E., and D'ARCY McNICKLE. *Indians and Other Americans*. New York:
Harper & Row, 1969.

FORBES, JACK D. *The Indian in America's Past*. Englewood Cliffs, N. J.: Prentice-Hall,
1964.

HAGAN, WILLIAM T. *American Indians*. Chicago: University of Chicago Press, 1961.

HOUGH, HENRY W. *The Development of Indian Resources*. Denver: World Press,
1967.

The Indian Historian. Published by the American Indian Historical Society Quarterly.

JOSEPHY, ALVIN M., JR. *The Indian Heritage of America*. New York: Bantam Books,
1969.

———. *Red Power: The American Indians' Fight for Freedom*. New York: American
Heritage Press, 1971.

LEVINE, STUART, and NANCY OESTREICH LURIE. *The American Indian Today*.
Baltimore: Penguin Books, 1970.

LEVITAN, SAR A., and BARBARA HETRICK. *Big Brother's Indian Programs—with Reservations*. New York: McGraw-Hill, 1970.

OSWALT, WENDELL H. *This Land Was Theirs*. New York: Wiley, 1966.

SLOTKIN, JAMES S. *The Peyote Religion: A Study in Indian-White Relations*. New York: Free Press, 1956.

SPICER, EDWARD H. *A Short History of the Indians of the United States*. New York: Van Nostrand Reinhold, 1969.

UNDERHILL, RUTH M. *Red Man's America*. Chicago: University of Chicago Press, 1953, 1971.

U.S. Department of the Interior: Bureau of Indian Affairs. *Indian Record*. Published monthly.

WILSON, EDMUND. *Apologies to the Iroquois*. New York: Random House, 1959, 1960.

FILMS

"Treaties Made, Treaties Broken," New York: McGraw-Hill.

"As Long as the Rivers Run," Survival of American Indians Association Inc., P.O. Box 719, Tacoma, Washington, 98401

History of San Felipe Pueblo People

Governor Sanchez

In response to the Ervin (Senate) Bill 1843, the Tribal Officials with the Tribal Council of San Felipe Pueblo wish to be recorded as having reviewed and considered the Ervin Bill. Though it proposes to establish rights for individual Indians in their relationship with their Indian tribes and for other purposes, the Council finds the Bill most intruding on what was theirs in the beginning. The free sovereign exercise of self-government was theirs, shaped and given to them intangibly by the Spirit. Specifically, said the Council, should Titles I and II of Bill 1843 become law the Federal Government will empower and arm the Secretary of the Interior with another lethal weapon to push the so-called "Model Code of Justice" down the Indians' throat. Wherein a final holocaust of Titles I and II of the Congressional Act will result in the alienation of the democratic tradition of the Indians to exercise its sovereign government now practiced by the Indian tribes everywhere. It is for this reason the Tribal Officials with its Council of the sovereign Pueblo of San Felipe, situated in the sovereign State of New Mexico, has decided to review the history of its people as a method of counterattacking the composite pending legislation herein specifically mentioned, and to share this review with its fellow tribesmen and with the United States Congress, hoping to clarify its reasons and desires to remain free from further inundation with premature legislations the Congress of the United States may think to pass for the benefit of the so-called "American Indians." It is the Council's earnest desire to retain the sovereignty of self-government for the sake of heritage, and to preserve other basic values of Indian heritage while making slow but continual adjustment, though sometimes superficial, to the economic and political demands of the whiteman society.

Thus the Council solemnly began its recollection of the ancient ancestors, those of the great great grandfathers, great grandfathers, and grandfathers of long ago, first, as people of spiritual beliefs, and secondly, as people of material contributors to the new continent. For the Indians had in the beginning what the world has finally and irretrievably lost, and we have it yet as it is, "a way of life." The Council in telling the spiritual legend of the ancient people remember them telling of the fortunes of the spirit world, the egress

SOURCE: From "History of San Felipe Pueblo People" in Hearings Before the Subcommittee on Indian Affairs of the Committee on Interior and Insular Affairs, House of Representatives, 90th Congress, 2d Session on H.S. 15419 and Related Bills to Establish Rights for Individuals in Their Relations with Indian Tribes and for Other Purposes, March 28, 1968.

136

or emergence into the world, and the ingress or returning to the hereafter, whence we came. They remember too, that the emergence into the world was a great act of the Spirit for it came about with reverence and love for what was left behind in the spirit world, and of fear and respect for what was found above, on earth and in the sky. So it came to reality long ago that all life came forth from the womb of the earth, said the Council.

With them came the Spirit, and the Spirit guided the ancient people through all sorts of arduous tasks of everyday life. Age after age the Spirit, the guardian and leader of the Pueblo Indians, took the ancient people across this great continent southward, until they came to settle temporarily in the places of today's National Parks and National Monuments. Everything they planted was harvested and was eaten along the route. Maybe to preserve the human race from total annihilation of any attack which may befall them, the Spirit caused the people to migrate in groups in separate directions from these places of historic settlements. He continued to guide each group on their trek until he brought them to a region where they can readily be safe and begin their tribal settlement.

So said the Council. This was how it came about that the ancestral people of San Felipe Pueblo were guided into the region of the valley of Rio del Norte where they were eventually settled for sometime by the Spirit on the west bank of the Rio Grande River atop the black mesa north of the present San Felipe Pueblo. Their first settlement was in the proximity northeast of the present main bridge over the Rio Grande River and southwest of te-me-teh, a lonely hill standing on the northeast side of where the railroad track transverses the Tonque arroyo. Because of the imminent dangers of disasters they were gradually moved west across the Rio Grande River and to the top of the black mesa. Here as well as on the east side, and throughout the entire region of pueblo settlement, the Spirit began to give final instructions to the people. They were reminded of the past trials and dangers they had endured; the sorrows and joys they experienced together; the unity they showed each other at working and living together in a community, and the necessity of planting and farming crops for survival. The ancient people remembered these experiences well and began to show great concern. Now the Spirit was telling of another plan, he pointed out indigenous plants that grew wild and abundantly which the people can use as food; teaching the people to respect and obey the laws of nature and the orders of its chief, the Cacique. The Cacique, said the Spirit, will guide you henceforth, and as the head of the tribe he will be concerned with your spiritual lives as well as with your government when the need for it arises. With these revelations, the Spirit empowered the Cacique with spiritual properties and with jurisdictional powers by which to make laws and govern his people. Hitherto, said the Spirit, it is the only way you and your children can live and give protection to each other. Thus, the plan was revealed to the ancient people and it was truly a way of life and living.

However, the people were not without dangers. They were warned of the dangers to come as more people inhabit the new continent. Here again, the Spirit reminded her people of their past experiences of building dwelling places in fortress style. "This you must do," said the Spirit. Then before secluding, the Spirit promised the people protection from the dangers of war when the time was near. Perhaps then sometimes between the first and the second settlement in the region of Rio del Norte marks the beginning of the famous legend of the Pueblo people about the twin boys known to them as Masewi and Oyoyewi. They were the young gods of war who protected their people by killing their enemies, and when not at war, they attended to prayers asking the Great Spirit to grant them courage and valor with which to guide their people towards peaceful settlement. Some Councilmen remember the twins as more than gods of war, they were also more or less explorers of the nature, constantly seeking out better land for cultivation and for permanent settlement. This is true in the case of San Felipe people where they gave credit to the twin boys for having made the final move of the ancestral people from the top of the black mesa to the present location of the Pueblo down in the valley of Rio del Norte as the Spanish had named the Rio Grande River.

From the time the Spirit had secluded, the people have lived everafter under the guidance of the Cacique, and obeyed his orders for they all knew he was empowered by the Spirit. Everything went according to the prophesy of the Great Spirit. Wars were encountered courageously under the leadership of Masewi and Oyoyewi, and the preparation for better livelihood were made under the leadership of the Cacique. However, as the population increased and civilization took roots many problems begin to burden the Cacique. Naturally, more and more this took the attention of the Cacique away from his primary duties of devotion to prayers for spiritual livelihood of his people. Constant prompting of the Spirit to exercise the power vested in him, the Cacique began on a plan to formulate a sovereign government by which his people can be governed. Calling upon the assistance of the Great Spirit, for he did no important act without the ritual, he began to work on a momentous plan for his people and his community. The work, said the Council, had to first meet with the criterion of the Spirit. This being done, the Cacique felt encouraged to call forth the first office, the War Chiefs. Having honorably guided their people through war and having had the blessings of the Spirit, the Cacique felt honored to assign this Office to the twin boys, Masewi and Oyoyewi, to handle the traditional ceremonial activities as well as assisting the Cacique in related matters of religious beliefs of the people of the community. Creating the first Office he then searched his mind solemnly for other offices, upon which he then called chronologically the second and third offices respectively.

Fortunately, for the people, about this time into our world entered a new breed of people from another world. These new people called themselves Spaniards. And in keeping with the forecast of the Great Spirit these new people also suggested and contributed to the newest positions in our hierarchy of government. The second Office, ta-pooph, or the Governors, were assigned to a couple of honorable men of the community (to head the Office, and) to handle civic and temporal affairs of the people. The third Office, pe-scar-lee or the Fiscales, were assigned the Office in a similar manner to a couple of honorable men to coordinate Christian church activities, and to assist the Padres in achieving its assigned missions.

Having established each Office chronologically for his people he blessed and empowered each Office, and enjoined each Office to serve the people of the community henceforth honorably; and to exercise the power of authority judiciously on the problems and on the people of the community. Justice, in the mind of the Cacique, must at all times be attuned to the dictates of the Spirit. Then the Cacique said, "Those persons who shall serve in the Offices will become members of the tribal council for a lifetime, unless duly retired by the Cacique for reasons of acts contrary to the design of justice of the government." With these words he empowered the tribal council to function as advisory and approving body in the internal and civic affairs of the tribal government with some authority to make settlements when the Officers of the Government are reluctant to go at it alone. In a similar manner, with the judicial matters of the tribe the Tribal Council functions as a jury in the tribal courts, and has the authority to make a final decision on the case making it relative to the Governor and the rest of the head tribal officials. The power to convene the councilmen rested with the Governor of San Felipe Pueblo. Through the centuries then, prior to the discovery by the whiteman, the ancient people of San Felipe operated under this system of government, and all took part in the functionings of the tribal government. All this took place long ago said the Council, for they themselves do not know how long ago it was. There were no records kept by the ancestors and everything depended on the mind or memory.

Today the setup of the tribal government of San Felipe Pueblo is still the same and its function, in nature, is similar to the olden times except with minor changes made by the people where feasible. Simply, then, this sparsely constitutes the history of the San Felipe Pueblo and its people, and most assuredly of the other Pueblos in general. One then can see at this point that the idea of sovereignty and self-government are deep rooted in the history of the Pueblo people.

Perhaps at this point it is appropriate to turn to some recorded histories of today which has depicted the noble side of the American Indian and which the Congress of the United States and the American public may have sparse knowledge of the aborigines. When the European or the Spaniards, who called them savages, discovered the Pueblo people in the 16th century they were quite amazed to find a distinct and in some respects highly developed civilization. The simple human decency and the amenities of daily life, and the disciplines of its government were observed in them in the relationship between man and man, and between man and his God. As the Council had remembered in the opening paragraphs of this review, the ancient people were material contributors to this continent. The changes that these people worked into the lives of the "white pioneers" were far more impressive and less destructive than any changes the white teachers have yet brought to the Indian life. In the realm of the intangible the Indian gave more. The orderliness of the political ideas of young America owed much to the Indian democratic tradition. On many occasions Thomas Jefferson recognized this debt by making numerous references to the freedom and democracy of the Indian society when he said: ". . . had achieved the maximum degree of order with the minimum degree of coercion." Felix Cohen, the late noted scholar and Indian legal authority, remarked: "Those accustomed to the histories of the conqueror will hardly be convinced, though example be piled on example, that American democracy, freedom, and tolerance are more American than European, and have deep aboriginal roots in our land." The habit of treating chiefs as servants of the people instead of Masters, the insistence that the community must respect the diversity of men and their dreams, all these things were part of the Indian way of life before 1492.

The Council recalls at this point a recognition of credence given the Pueblo Indians, first, by the Spanish Government then next by the Mexican and the United States Governments respectively, "that the Indians' right to self-government is not a right derived from these Caucasian Governments, but a right which they held prior and maintained subsequent to the discovery of this continent." Since this discovery said the Council, the Indians did not ask for recognition, but it came forward spontaneously because of the respect and understanding the conqueror and the whiteman had for Indians' primacy of self-government. Upon this a covenant was made respectively by the Spanish, Mexican, and United States Governments to recognize the sovereignty of government of the Pueblo Indians by bringing the Canes of the Country's King or President to each Pueblo Government as a symbol of the solemn covenant and recognition. The Spanish kingdom in the 16th century and then the United States Government under the administration of President Abraham Lincoln in 1863 gave its recognition of the Pueblo Indian Governments. Today the Governor of San Felipe Pueblo uses these Canes as a symbol of authority of the Governor. Now this covenant is about to be amissed by Titles I and II of the Senate Bill 1843.

At this point one may well ask: "Of what relevance is this buried legacy to the present and future?" First, there is still much that the Indian can contribute to America's cultural enrichment. Second, recognition by legislators, administrators, and the American public of the true nature of our Indian heritage has great importance in freeing the Indian from a haughty and stupidly silly stereotype. It also may diminish the persistent themes of pity, superiority, and the whiteman's burden, which have been twisted into vicious weapons of legislations against Indian culture. Third, the respect for different cultures may bring about a reasoned and humane policy which will fulfill Indian desires to achieve a higher living standard and still maintain his ethnic identity. Fourth, the Indian needs of stability and rights to their government should be left to the tribes to rectify through their unique aspects of the Indians' membership in special political bodies, or tribes, which largely take the place that states and municipalities occupy for other American citizens.

What then does the American Indian want of the United States Congress? Certainly, their dependency on and control by, the Federal Government is much greater since 1848 because of the tacit and implicit trusteeship relationship between the United States Government and the Indian Tribes. Since then too, the Indian has sacrificed many of its youth in the whiteman's wars so as to have a free Nation of discriminating views, and today continues to sacrifice its youth in the commitments of the great "White Father" to wars of foreign Nations. How is it then the American Indian is involved in these wars? Certainly it is not for want of war, nor for greed of wealth, nor for fear of disgrace, but of respect to fellowman and to its Nation under one God that the Indian took up the challenge so that we may all enjoy the freedom, liberty, and justice for all together. With these point of views the American Indian wants to be given justice of being involved in making his own plan of change and be given greater voice on all and any legislation to be proposed in committee or the Congress affecting both his Reservation and his freedom of self-government. Perhaps then the type of Indian's needs of real liberal system of justice can best be summed up in the view of the 1958 congressional proposal establishing a technical assistance program modeled after the so-called Point Four Program of Foreign Aid. The pertinent section of that proposal reads: "It is declared to be the sense of Congress . . . that Indian culture and identity shall not be restricted or destroyed; that technical guidance and financial assistance shall be made available; that the request for such assistance shall come from the Indians, after each Indian group has studied itself in terms of its own needs. . . ." Unfortunately the proposal dies in committee. Such a legislation of this calibre is most urgently needed for the Indian Reservations, and in the final analysis would achieve the liberal justice so much desired for the American Indian.

In summary then, the Ervin Senate Bill 1843 is well intended, but the Council of San Felipe Pueblo is not ready to implement such a proposal because it is premature in nature that no voice of the Indian tribes was involved to determine whether state criminal and civil laws should apply on their reservations. That rights of Indians to self-government are inherent in their backgrounds and should not be coerced to be alienated from the long history of democratic practice of their traditions. Finally, in view of the Indian history, it is self-evident that life, liberty, and right to sovereign government was the forethought of the ancient people to which we give whole hearty support to earnestly ask for understanding of our desire to preserve our Indian heritage, in any shape or form, for here lies the true foundation of America's history. In conclusion then, we the Tribal Council of the Sovereign Pueblo of San Felipe solemnly decline to accept Tiles I and II of the Senate Bill 1843 in its present form, and respectfully refuse to alienate our people, and ourselves, from the sovereign government, to wit, of San Felipe Pueblo.

Economic Development of the American Indian and His Lands

National Congress of American Indians

The National Congress of American Indians (NCAI) is the only private, national Indian-directed organization limiting its voting power membership to Indian tribes and individuals. Serving as the speaking voice of the American Indian people, we include within our membership 105 Indian tribes, representing over 350,000 American Indians, and we provide services which reach even more of the Indian population.

NCAI has pledged itself to an economic development policy which contains the following principles:

1. Self-determination by the Indian people in their quest for social and economic equality.

2. Protection of Indian tribal and individual ownership of Indian lands and resources, and maintenance of tax-exempt status for income derived from such lands, and for the lands themselves.

3. Maximum development of the human and natural resources of Indians with the assistance of the BIA and all other federal agencies offering programs and services designed to relieve conditions of poverty among all Americans.

We have spoken out often on this matter of Indian self-determination with respect to the matters affecting the lives and destiny of Indians, and there has been much lipservice, but little real substance, given to this concept by the officials of the government.

Far too often, we have found the Congress voting on Indian matters with little knowledge of our views, and with no sensitivity to, or understanding of, them. We cannot contend more strongly that Congress cannot legislate or otherwise establish a successful program of Indian economic development without significant Indian input, or without recognition that success in the final analysis will depend, not on what the Congress thinks is good for the Indians, but what the Indian thinks is good for himself.

SOURCE: From "Economic Development of the American Indian and His Lands," Position Paper of the National Congress of American Indians in *Toward Economic Development for Native American Communities*, A Compendium of Papers Submitted to the Subcommittee on Economy in Government of the Joint Economic Committee, 91st Congress, 1st Session, Joint Committee Print. Part II: Development Programs and Plans.

For over 100 years, it has been the policy of the U.S. Government to assist the American Indian to become economically self-sufficient. In large measure, as the statistics which follow will reveal, this policy has been a failure. At the root of this failure is the fact that the Indian's goals and cultural attitudes have largely been ignored in the perpetuation of this policy. It has never occurred to the majority of those pronouncing this policy that many Indians may not want to swim in a mainstream they largely regard as polluted and that they should be free to refuse; or that there might exist an Indian culture, which not only rejects the materialistic value system of the White Man, but has positive values in terms of brotherhood, and preservation of one's environment, from which the White Man could learn, if he were willing to listen.

Let us dispel another frequently made, yet erroneous assumption; that there is a close analogy to be drawn between the economic problems of Indians and those of other minority groups, and that, therefore, the same solutions will apply. To be sure, Indians bear the same mantle of alienation borne by other minorities: this is a product of rejection and discrimination against them by the dominant culture on the one hand, and denigration by the country's educational system of minority group status and values on the other; so that, for perhaps one-third of the country's Indians, the urban Indians who have attempted to make it in the main economy, and frequently are found, as President Nixon has said, "confined to hopeless city reservations of despair," the problems are similar, if not identical, to those of other minority groups in urban ghettos. But, for the remainder, the two-thirds of the American Indians living on reservations, attempting to retain their cultural identity, the problems of economic development are substantially different. These differences arise not only out of the cultural heritage that we have mentioned; and the unique attachment to the land that it has created, but out of the trust relationship of the Indian to the federal government, and the tax-exempt, restricted status of Indian land, which many people would hastily forget was bought and paid for by the cession of close to 2 billion acres of Indian-owned land to the federal government.

All too often, second class status in the dominant culture has been the sole alternative offered to starvation on the reservation. NCAI believes that a successful economic development program must, on the one hand, provide for the Indian who desires to leave the reservation and enter into the general economy, a fair-fighting chance and equal opportunity for success, while, on the other hand providing the opportunity for the reservation economy to develop, in ways compatible with its own cultural values, to a point where it is capable of self-support at a level which will provide an equitable share of the bounty of our homeland—the world's richest nation.

Let us look for a moment at what the late Senator Robert F. Kennedy called "the cold statistics which illuminate a national tragedy and a national disgrace":

The average Indian income is $1,500 annually, which is 74 per cent below the national average; his unemployment rate hovers around 50 per cent, which is ten times the national average, and on some reservations reaches 70–80 per cent. The average American Indian's life expectancy is 10 years less than the national average.

Even more startling were the observations of author Stan Steiner, in his recently published book, *The New Indians*, in which he related statistics from a 1962–63 government study of employment among tribal Indians. The statistics have not changed much. Let us look at them:

> . . . on the plains of the Dakotas, the Pine Ridge Sioux had 2,175 of 3,400 tribal adults unemployed (yearly family income was $105); the Rosebud Sioux has 1,720 of 2,996 unemployed (yearly family income, $1,000— though the tribe, 4 years later, estimated $600 was more accurate); the Standing Rock Sioux had 500 of 880 heads of households unemployed (yearly family income, $190). . . .
>
> To the north, on the Blackfeet Reservation of Montana, the "Permanent unemployment" rate was 72.5 per cent. The yearly tribal income was "less than $500 per family."
>
> Down in Mississippi, on the Choctaw Reservation, of 1,225 adults there were 1,055 jobless. Unemployment rate: 86.1 per cent.
>
> Where the tranquil and ancient Pueblos of New Mexico stood, seemingly impervious to the economic winds, there were 10,699 jobless out of 13,711. Unemployment among these, perhaps the oldest of the country's inhabitants, was 77 per cent. The Hopis, too, those idyllic "peaceful people," had a less than idyllic unemployment rate of 71.7 per cent.
>
> In the Pueblo de Acoma, the "City in the Sky," unemployment stood at 89.6 per cent.
>
> In the mythology of the oil-rich Indians so credulously huzzahed by television comedians and popular legends, none are supposedly wealthier than the Oklahoma tribes. And yet, the Five Civilized Tribes reported an annual unemployment rate of 55 per cent, and an annual income per family, including the fabled oil-lease payments, that came to little more than $1,200. . . .
>
> Of 19,000 adult Indians in eastern Oklahoma, between the ages of 18 and 55, an estimated 10,000, or 52.6 per cent, were unemployed; of the 10,000 jobless adult Indians, well over half received no unemployment insurance, or any other welfare assistance—whatsoever.
>
> So it went from tribe to tribe. Unemployment rates from 40 to 80 per cent; incomes from $105 to $1,200.
>
> These are statistics neither new nor surprising. However, the mixture of the old poverty and the new Indians who have seen the material riches of the outside world, and who are angered and impatient, has created an explosive situation. "If something isn't done, the young men may go to violence. . . ."

At its 1968 25th Annual Convention NCAI made it clear that:

> The social and economic conditions of many Indian people when compared to that of the general population, almost defy comprehension. Adult Indians living on reservations are, as a group, only half as well educated as

other citizens, their life expectancy is one-third less, and their average annual income two-thirds less. Nine out of 10 of their homes are comparatively unfit for human habitation and their unemployment rate is several times above the national average.

It is time that these critical problems were faced and programs funded which will overcome them, without exacting a price so high that the status quo is preferable.

Although many significant proposals have been placed in the congressional hopper which would, perhaps, improve the economic situation of the Indian, few of these have the support of the Indians. Members of Congress have often been frustrated by what appears to them to be the ultraconservatism of the Indians. And, to some extent, the Indian is afraid of change—chiefly because proposals for change emanating from Congress have, regardless of the language in which they were couched, usually been schemes to liberate the Indian from his land, and because the Indian desires to design his own program for change.

Linked to the preservation of Indian land rights is the whole question of termination. Nothing has been more threatening to long-range tribal planning than the hovering specter of termination. On the one hand, the federal government has talked of itself as a partner available to work with the Indians in economic expansion and future development; on the other hand, the Congressional policy of termination has lingered like a death sentence under constant appeal by the Indian for commutation.

To be sure, the Omnibus Bill of the last session, reintroduced as separate bills H.R. 6717, 6718, 6719, and 6720 in this session, was rejected by Indians in part because of objections to the way it was presented. But the real objections were and remain substantive:

For example, the proposed "Indian Financing Act" offers the Indian an important new source of credit, not unlike a Small Business Administration for Indians, but on an unacceptable condition that the tribes be authorized to mortgage trust land, or any other land to which the tribe has title, subject to foreclosure.

This is no solution to the difficult problem of finding a way to broaden the sources of available credit for Indians *without* requiring tribal assets to be subject to foreclosure. Under such legislation, the Indian would be worse off than he is now. For he is compelled to risk everything, with a high chance of failure, for a limited possibility of success.

The same bill contains authorization much sought after for tribes to issue tax-exempt bonds: but limits such issuance to industrial or commercial purposes while only non-tax-exempt bonds may be issued to provide entertainment, recreation or civic facilities, transportation facilities, or to supply electric energy, gas, water, or sewage disposal or other utility services to the tribe. NCAI sees no valid reason for this distinction. The authority to issue tax-exempt bonds would be a valuable stimulant to capitalization of these desperate needs of the Indian community, for it offers an easy way to bring in outside capital, at relatively low cost to the tribe. But this proposal has individual merits, and should be considered apart from the loan fund.

In large measure, the past eight years have shown a great stride forward by American Indians in attaining a greater degree of self-government and economic independence. But, the extent of progress and programs has reached only a small number of Indian tribes. Generally, those tribes that have had the funds to employ adequate legal counsel, and that have had a significant income for use in program planning, have been able to move forward with programs funded by a variety of government agencies.

As of December 31, 1968, there were 150 industrial and commercial enterprises established on or near reservations as a result of Indian industrial development programs; of these 140, or 93 per cent, had been established since the beginning of 1962.

At the present time these enterprises have created approximately 10,000 new jobs, of which only 4,700 are held by Indians. If industrial development seems like a panacea to the problem of the reservation Indians, we remind you that in 1962 there were 10,699 unemployed Pueblos alone; and in 1968, there were approximately 45,000 Indians in the 14-to-21 age bracket.

For the industrial enterprises now in existence, it is projected that eventually these will provide a total of 15,000 jobs of which, it is hoped, 65 per cent will be held by Indians. Twice, or even three times, this number of jobs will not solve the problem. And, at the same time that jobs are created, Indians must be trained for employability.

There are approximately 600,000 Indians living in the United States, and in recent years the Indian population has been increasing faster than among any other minority group. The Indian labor force numbers approximately 100,000 with the unemployment rate hovering around 50 per cent, more than 10 times the national average. "Industrial development of reservations," has often meant economic exploitation of cheap Indian labor for the benefit of white capitalists, leaving in its wake sociological disaster. We should point out further that some reservations have frequently been unable to share in the expanded opportunities for community and economic development which have been provided in recent years. Not only do they lack the wherewithal to make their needs known, but they are frequently unable to meet matching fund requirements, or other strings, which limit development.

Among our other activities, NCAI has undertaken a program to assist the tribes which have not been able to begin programs on their reservations, with the hope that, in short order, they will be able to generate sufficient income as tribal bodies to plan and carry out their own programs and attain greater measures of self-sufficiency and self-government. Note, however, that our purpose is to strengthen tribes, not weaken them, as Congress so frequently has tried to do.

In general, the Indians who have been overlooked are in small federal tribes or eastern nonfederal surviving groups. We do not believe that because Congress denies these Indians federal recognition, they cease to be Indians.

From our contact with these groups over the past several years, we believe that, with some technical and financial assistance, these groups can be placed on the road to total self-sufficiency. Indeed, they could be made totally independent in some cases with the financial assistance and expanded reservation or group programs to fit their immediate needs.

On the other hand, there are a number of instances of tribes so disconsolate, and dejected, and with such a feeling of general helplessness, that they must first be convinced that effort is worth making. It is a mistake to assume, as Congress frequently has, that progress will be easy of attainment, and that results must show up immediately if a project is to be continued. The very uncertainty of congressional appropriations, and vacillation in federal programing has bred distrust among the Indians, and led to the failure of some potentially viable programs.

In years when there is a change of administration, these feelings necessarily multiply.

It has too often been the fate of Indian groups that government agencies have tried to create "showcases" of gigantic programs of employment on reservations, when the need has been much simpler and more basic. We believe that the "shotgun" approach to community development has not paid off in the past, and we have no reason to anticipate sudden success in the future for this type of operation.

We have initiated a program of national scope funded by a Ford Foundation grant to zero in on the problems of small tribes and nonfederal surviving groups to work on the basic problems of the Indian community, as viewed by that community. Our orientation is directed to total community involvement and development, with primary emphasis on one simple goal—increase of tribal income and subsequent development of tribal assets with that increased income.

We are continually finding that there are specific legal, economic, administrative, and social problems that are hampering smaller tribes and particular Indian groups, which never come to the fore until we actually have contact with the Indian community concerned. If these groups are to make any significant progress in the years to come, someone must bring them into the picture of national economic and social development in the very near future. We believe this can be done, without sacrificing tribal values. Indeed, in most instances, it can be done only tribally.

NCAI, among its other goals, hopes to serve as a central clearinghouse operation, in economic planning and development among American Indians, supporting the efforts of member tribes to develop viable economic programs with technical advice and funding, by being a central agency with capabilities in these dimensions. As our staffing on separate projects increases, our capacity to play this role increases.

Our overall economic program evolves from three factors: First, the staff capabilities and funding of the organization, and its relationship with Indian leadership; second, the limited number of people in the Indian community familiar with the private enterprise money concept and economy, and the many intricate mechanisms it requires in economic planning; third, the shortage of socioeconomic data on the American Indians, which is generally regarded as a prerequisite base from which to establish sound and sensible economic design. Although the Bureau of Indian Affairs has been in the business, nominally at least, for many years, of economic development on Indian reservations, the Bureau itself has developed no meaningful and reliable statistics to serve this need. We are hopeful that the newly funded Office of Minority Business Enterprises in the Department of Commerce, through its Rural Division, will begin to amass and supply this data.

Because it is in the interest of efficiency and economic progress to maximize both the coordination of federal interagency resources and Indian organization resources for economic development, we are in the process of expanding the scope and capacity of the NCAI Fund to make it the focal point and repository of nongovernmental funds allocated to assist the American Indian in the development and implementation of economic plans. We have thus been in a position to monitor grants to other smaller Indian organizations serving special needs. But the Indian community cannot meet its economic needs by itself; at best, we can hope to provide seed money or matching funds. The bulk of this effort must of necessity come from the federal government.

In both 1968 and 1969, NCAI has cosponsored two National Economic Development Conferences for 31 selected Indian Reservations, which were attended by representatives of major firms in the private sector. This program is funded by a separate grant from the Office of Economic Opportunity. The major aim of these conferences was to help tribes attract industry into locations within communities, in accord with the economic plans of such communities. The conferences also serve to give a major boost to the economic plans which have been endorsed or funded by NCAI.

In addition to the economic programs we have described, NCAI is involved in community planning activities among its constituent groups. We believe that no economic plan can succeed which takes into account merely the economic and industrial implications of a proposed activity, without considering the sociological implications as well—that is, the impact which the development of such a plan will have on the tribe itself. Too often in the past, such consequences have been heedlessly disregarded.

Where such implications are not considered, what may be a successful economic venture for a visiting industrialist, can turn into a sociological disaster for the tribe.

NCAI also provides technical assistance, in such diverse forms as interpreting the regulations of the BIA for tribes who do not understand them; helping tribes receive certificates of eligibility for EDA or OEO programs; providing legal research assistance with respect to federal Indian laws applicable to particular situations; providing practical assistance on the familiar problems of land consolidations, Law and Order Codes, program develop-

ment—land leasing—credit unions, and other tribal enterprises; supporting
and assisting the creation and maintenance of intertribal ventures to attack
regional problems; and providing a referral service between tribes and appropriate private, state and federal agencies, which can provide assistance
with particular problems.

Our approach is to define specific areas of concern in community development, designating Indian groups eligible to receive assistance from the program. Tribal groups are asked to define and clarify immediate problems and
long-range goals. Technical and financial assistance is available only until the
group has reached the point where it has sufficient resources to begin programing and funding by itself. Then, program support ceases, thereby cancel-
ing out dependency upon the program for continued survival.

Financial assistance for accelerated community development consists of
grants for capital improvements to enable tribes to overhaul community
facilities and to provide matching grants "in kind" for programs; to assist
unorganized communities to plan basic community organization; to enable
Indian groups to employ professional service people in particular cases of
need, as, for incorporation of enterprises, formation of credit unions, establishment of leasing programs, or writing of tribal constitutions; and, for
travel by tribal representatives to enable them to follow up on program applications, where necessary.

One priority area is the number of small tribes whose members are, for
the most part employed, but the tribe as a governing body is too poor to
begin a program of housing on a community basis; so, nothing is done. With
some assistance in developing a housing program, and formulation of a plan
to establish either a credit union or a tribal tax on the members, such a tribe
could create housing for its people, with the program generating enough mo-
mentum to set up a basic community development program for the future.
Once the program is undertaken, counselling and financial assistance can be
provided to assist the tribe in building a basic tribal income to cover such
future services as the members require. Such a tribe would then be, for all
predictable purposes, self-sufficient.

Having waited in vain for Congress to approve a federal government endorsed, chartered and underwritten all-Indian Development Corporation, in
accord with the recommendations of the Striner Report, NCAI has just obtained a substantial grant from EDA to study the feasibility of, and assuming
a feasible method is found, to establish a National Indian Development Organization. Although the terms of the proposal require an organization to be
established within existing law (if feasible), we will undoubtedly be seeking
congressional assistance to strengthen the significance of this organization.
We see this as potentially the single most significant development in the field
of Indian economic development. The need for a financial institution which
can accommodate the unique requirements of the Indian for credit and other
needs is quite apparent. To the extent that such an organization can be developed in the private sector under Indian direction, we think it will be the

most useful. Some sort of federal subsidization may well be needed, at least in the early stages, to make the organization feasible, and to that extent, we will turn to Congress for support.

In closing, we would like to remind you of the words President John F. Kennedy used in his inaugural address: "If a free society cannot help the many who are poor, it cannot save the few who are rich."

Federal Encroachment on Indian Water Rights and the Impairment of Reservation Development

William H. Veeder

SUMMARY

1. American Indian reservations in the western United States contain invaluable natural resources. These include the land of which they are comprised, minerals, forests, lakes, streams and other sources of water which arise upon, border, traverse, or underlie the reservations.

2. Economic development of the western reservations is inseparable from Indian rights to the use of water, which in turn are the most valuable of all natural resources in the arid and semiarid regions. Those rights are the catalyst for all economic development. Without them the Reservations are virtually uninhabitable, the soil remains untilled, the minerals remain in place, and poverty is pervasive.

3. Since time immemorial the Indians' water resources were inextricably a part of their way of life; indeed, a prime feature of their sustenance. Highly sophisticated irrigation systems were developed along the Gila River by the Pimas and Maricopas. Menominees harvested their wild rice, used the streams for travel, fishing and hunting. The Mohaves, Quechans, and other Colorado River Indians depended on the stream's annual Nile-like floods to irrigate their crops. The Yakimas lived upon and traded salmon taken from the Columbia, as did the Northern Paiutes—the fisheaters—who took the famous Labanton cutthroat trout from the Truckee River and Pyramid Lake—their species destroyed by the Bureau of Reclamation.

4. The Indian *Winters Doctrine Rights* to the use of water in the streams or lakes which arise upon, border, traverse, or underlie their reservations, have been accorded by the Supreme Court and other courts a prior, para-

SOURCE: From "Federal Encroachment on Indian Water Rights and the Impairment of Reservation Development," by William H. Veeder, in *Toward Economic Development for Native American Communities*, A Compendium of Papers Submitted to the Joint Economic Committee, 91st Congress, 1st Session, Joint Committee Print. Part II: Development Programs and Plans.

NOTE: William Veeder is a Water Conservation and Utilization Specialist employed by the Bureau of Indian Affairs. In 1971, he was the only non Indian invited to the second convocation of Indian Scholars. He has won the respect of Indians and the censure of the BIA by his advocacy of Indian rights.

mount, and superior status on the streams for the present and future economic development of the western reservations.

5. By the Constitution of the United States there was created a relationship between the nation and the American Indians of transcendent dignity. That relationship of great dignity had its genesis in the policies adhered to by the European sovereigns who colonized this continent and it was firmly established during the harsh and bitter years of the Revolutionary War and the years which were to ensue prior to and including the adoption of the Constitution.

6. It has been declared that the relationship existing between the American Indians and the nation "resembles that of a ward to his guardian"—a trust relationship with all of the express and implied obligations stemming from it. Only the uninformed ascribe to that trust a demeaning connotation in regard to the American Indians.

7. Great stress must be applied to the nature of the Indian trust property, including Indian rights to the use of water.

(a) It is *private property*, legal title to which is held by the United States in trust for the American Indians as beneficial holders of equitable title.

(b) Indian property is *not public property* as is the other property of the nation.

8. Plenary power and responsibility under the Commerce Clause of the Constitution reside with the Congress to effectuate the trust relationship between the United States and the American Indians.

9. Congress is likewise invested by the Constitution with plenary power over the "public lands," all other lands, all rights to the use of water, title to which resides in the nation. These lands and rights to the use of water are to be administered for the nation as a whole. It is imperative that the nature of the right, title, interests, and obligations of the nation in regard to these properties held in trust for the nation as a whole be sharply distinguished from the lands and rights to the use of water of the American Indians.

10. Congress in the exercise of its plenary power over the nation's lands and rights to the use of water has invested the Department of the Interior with broad authority to administer, develop, sell, dispose of, and otherwise to take all required action respecting those lands and rights to the use of water. Agencies within the Department of the Interior carrying out the will of Congress in regard to those properties held for the public as a whole include but are not limited to: The Bureau of Reclamation, Bureau of Land Management, National Park Service, Bureau of Outdoor Recreation, and the agencies generally responsible for the propagation and protection of fish and wildlife.

11. Administrators, engineers, scientists, within the Department of the Interior, all acting within the scope of the authority vested in the Secretary of the Interior, are:

(a) Charged with the responsibility of fulfilling the nation's trust status in regard to the Indian lands and rights to the use of water, which, as stated, are private in character, to be administered solely for the benefit of the Indians;

(b) Charged with the responsibility of administering lands and rights to the use of water claimed in connection with reclamation projects, administration of grazing districts, and other land uses requiring the exercise of rights to the use of water; fish and wildlife projects; recreational areas; and other activities, all of which require rights in the streams.

12. (a) Lawyers in the Department of the Interior directly responsible to the Solicitor, in whom resides the obligation of performing the "legal" work for that department; all of the agencies of it, including the Bureau of Indian Affairs, Indians and Indian Tribes, are constantly confronted with the sharp conflicts of interests between the Indian land and rights to the use of water, and the numerous other agencies referred to that likewise make claims to those waters and contest the rights and claims of the Indians to them;

(b) Lawyers in the Department of Justice directly responsible to the Attorney General, the nation's chief law officer, have the responsibility:

(1) To defend, protect, preserve, and have adjudicated, title to the lands of the Indians and their rights to the use of water, and otherwise to act as lawyers for the trustee obligated to perform with the fullest degree of loyalty to the Indians;

(2) To proceed as an adversary against the Indian claims for the seizure of their lands and rights to the use of water, seeking to limit or otherwise defeat the claims of the Indians predicated upon the laws which other attorneys of the Justice Department are required effectively to espouse and advocate on behalf of the Indians;

(3) To perform legal services in regard to lands and rights to the use of water in streams and other water sources where the Indian rights are in conflict with claims of other agencies of the United States.

13. Both the administrators of the Department of the Interior and the lawyers of both Interior and Justice owe the highest degree of ethical, moral, loyal, and equitable performance of their trust obligations to the American Indians. They are charged, moreover—as professionals—with the highest degree of care, skill and diligence in executing their broad assignments for the protection, preservation, administration and legal duties respecting Indian trust properties including, but not limited to, the invaluable Indian *Winters Doctrine Rights* to the use of water.

14. Conflicting responsibilities, obligations, interests, claims, legal theories— indeed, philosophies—oftentimes prevent the Interior and Justice Department administrators, planners, engineers and lawyers from fulfilling the trust obligation [which the nation owes] to the American Indians in regard to natural resources, particularly in the complex and contentious field of Indian rights to the use of water in the arid and semiarid regions of western United States. Failure by those departments, agencies and personnel to fulfill the nation's

obligation to protect and preserve Indian rights to the use of water includes, but most assuredly is not limited to: (a) Lack of knowledge of the existence, or the nature, measure, and extent of those rights to the use of both surface and ground waters—refusal to recognize Indian rights are private rights to be administered separate, apart, and independent of the "public rights" of the nation as a whole in identically the same manner as other private rights are protected and preserved; (b) lack of timely action to preserve, protect, conserve, and administer those rights; (c) inability or reluctance at the decisional level to insist upon recognition and preservation of Indian rights to the use of water when to do so would prevent the construction—and/or administration in the manner desired—of a reclamation or other project conflicting with the Indians for water, the supply of which is insufficient; (d) attempted subordination, relinquishment, or conveyance of Indian rights to the use of water which are in conflict with other claims, federal, state, or local; (e) failure to assert rights, interests and priorities of the Indians on a stream or project when to do so would limit the interests of non-Indians; (f) opening reservations to non-Indian occupancy with the seizure of Indian land and rights to the use of water, with or without the payment of just compensation; (g) the imposition of servitudes, easements, and illegal occupancy or use of Indian lands and rights to the use of water.

15. Economic development of the American Indian reservations in western United States, due largely to conflicting interests within the Interior and Justice Departments, or vacillating policies—a natural consequence of conflicting interests, responsibilities, and obligations within the federal establishment—has been (a) prevented by the abridgment of loss of Indian rights to the use of water; (b) intentionally prevented in whole or in part, or deferred in whole or in part, by the refusal to permit development of Indian lands with rights to the use of water.

16. Irreparable damage to the American Indians in western United States has ensued by reason of the consequences flowing from the conflicts described above. The Indians have suffered from extreme poverty, with the attendant ills of malnutrition, high infant mortality rate, reduced life expectancy, disease, and the shattering loss of human dignity which stems from poverty and deprivation of the necessities of life.

CONCLUSION

Economic development of the American Indian reservations in western United States will continue to be prevented or severely curtailed in the absence of drastic changes in the laws and policies which would eliminate conflicting rights, responsibilities, and obligations which presently exist among the several agencies of the national government, all as reviewed in the accompanying memorandum and the summary set forth above.

RECOMMENDATION

Congress should enact legislation which would place in an agency independent from the Department of the Interior and the Department of Justice the full responsibility for the protection, preservation, administration, development, adjudication, determination, and control, including but not limited to all legal services required in connection with them, of the lands and rights to the use of water of the American Indian reservations in western United States.

In furtherance of economic development of the American Indian reservations in western United States it is imperative that there be undertaken an inventory of all of the Indian rights to the use of water in the streams and other sources of water arising upon, bordering upon, traversing, or underlying their lands. This inventory should be undertaken with the objective of ascertaining, to the extent possible, the existence, character, and measure of the rights as they relate to the present and future development of the reservations. It is equally important to determine the highest and best use which can be made of these invaluable rights to the use of water and to chronicle those rights as they relate to each water source, indicating the highest and best present use to which they may be applied. They should likewise be evaluated from the standpoint of their maximum potential in the future by reason of the fact that those rights must be exercised in perpetuity and in contemplation of the ever-changing environment of western United States with its increasing population and water demands. . . .

The Cement Prairies

Stan Steiner

In Billings, Montana, there is a hill. In Sioux it is called Place of Many Sorrows. There a child dies every week. A wife dies too young. A man he is old and sad at 30, and the sick are too many. The dead songs are singed there till a tall man runs from his shack, from all his family, and he drinks not to hear. Now he sits, drunk so much he cannot talk, and too sad to not sing the same hard songs. He cannot go away. There is no place to go. These men, these people, are Indians who have sold their land.

The unlettered Indian had written his anguish on the back of an unused government form. He had not signed his name. He had mailed his outcry to the Denver *Post*, which sent a reporter, Robert W. Fenwick, to find the Dantesque inferno—the Place of Many Sorrows. Fenwick found not one but several.

One of these, known as "Hill 57," in Great Falls, Montana, was typical of the rest:

"It's an Indian village of shocking filth, poverty and degradation. Its outstanding features are the frail huts, the battered hulks of automobiles, the ever-present outhouses, a hand-pump which is the sole water supply for the entire community, and an almost unbelievable sea of junk resembling a city rubbish disposal," Fenwick wrote.

"Now, the Indian sits on the White Man neck," the nameless Indian had written, "and the White Man is saddened because of this. We are both sad because only grief has come to both of us because of sale [of Indian land]. Soon, if this goes on, all Indians must come to town.

"What town want one more Place of Many Sorrows? Who will fight this thing? What man is so brave? Now something must be done. Who will do it?"

One young Sioux in San Francisco, who was shown a copy of the pathetic letter, scoffed at it. "Man, I think that letter is a put-on," he said. "For one thing that's not how a Sioux thinks. There's no Sioux I know of who would say, 'He cannot go away. There is no place to go.' He can go home to his reservation any time. If he can crawl, they'll take him home. For another thing living in towns, lousy as it may be, doesn't scare us into writing gibberish. Man, we been doing the towns ever since Sitting Bull laid down the tools of his trade on the Little Big Horn and joined the touring Wild West Show of Buffalo Bill.

SOURCE: "The Cement Prairies" from *The New Indians* by Stan Steiner. Copyright © 1968 by Stan Steiner. Reprinted by permission of Harper & Row, Publishers, Inc.

156

"Every town has a hellhole like that. Every town in the West has its 'native quarter,'" the San Francisco Sioux said. "That's not the problem. You see, living in the city is your problem, really. We just come visiting to make a little money. Our problem is making it."

Interestingly enough, when the Denver *Post* reporter searched Billings, Montana, asked everywhere, he could not find the Place of Many Sorrows.

Are the city Indians invisible?

The tribal Indians are unquestionably coming to town. Half of the Indians in the country may be city Indians, Vine Deloria, Jr., has estimated. There are a quarter of a million living in the metropolitan areas alone, thought Mel Thom. And the San Francisco Indian Center publication *The American Indian*, has reported that the Indian adults living "off-reservation"—estimated at 198,000—outnumbered those "on-reservation"; for many job-seeking parents left their children at home with grandparents.

One decade ago, The *Harvard Law Review* estimated that "about 100,000 Indians [reside] in American cities and towns" ("American Indians: People Without a Future," by Ralph Nader, May 10, 1956). Even if the statistic was a reasonably inaccurate guess, the urban population of tribesmen has doubled within ten years.

But the city Indians have always been invisible statistics. The U.S. Census Bureau counts Indians only when they so identify themselves, or are identifiable. And the city Indians often "pass" as whites, when it is economically necessary, or socially desirable. Those who don't "pass" have been usually counted as "nonwhite"—a nearly invisible shade, it seems, when they happen to be Indians.

The statistics of the Bureau of Indian Affairs have been as equalitarianly invisible, for the Bureau's concern has traditionally been the reservation Indian, and the cajoling of him to leave the reservation. Once he goes, however, the Bureau no longer counts him.

So the city Indian has been an invisible man. He has not even become a statistic.

"Chicago does not realize they have a 'reservation of Indians' right in their own backyard," commented an official of the American Indian Center on the near North Side. "There are better than ten thousand Indians representing seventy tribes in Chicago." Half of these are wedged into a few-block area between the Puerto Rican ghetto and the luxury apartment houses on the Lake Shore Drive.

"We don't riot," said Nathan Bird, one of the Chicago Indian leaders, "so no one knows we're here."

Brooklyn, New York, Cleveland, Detroit, St. Louis, Minneapolis, Omaha, Denver, Phoenix, Los Angeles, San Francisco, and Seattle all have their own "native quarters" of Indians. Many of these have more than ten thousand tribal residents. And in the smaller cities of the Rocky Mountains, the Plains, and the Southwest, there are repetitious "Hill 57's." "The Cement Prairies" was what some of the city Indians nicknamed these homeless homes away from home.

In a tongue-in-the-throat article entitled "The Indian in Suburbia," *The American Indian* offered its own tourist guide to tribesmen coming to town:

> When an Indian family first comes to Oakland, or San Francisco, they will find thousands of cement streets running in every direction.
>
> On these streets will be tens of thousands of automobiles. These automobiles are filled with people who are trying to kill each other off with these steel monsters as fast as the white man killed off the Buffalo.
>
> To find his way around in this cement prairie, the white man uses a map, and so must the Indian.
>
> All of the houses have numbers and some of the streets are called by numbers. Some streets have other names, and in many cases streets are not called streets but avenues, places, boulevards and freeways. Freeways are the most dangerous and no one walks on them, and sometimes it is even hard to drive on them. . . .

"This may sound confusing to some of our people on reservations who have never been to California," laconically commented *The American Indian*, "but, it is." In the words of Calvin O'John:

> A dirt road begins at the highway
> And ends at our front yard.
> I walk on dirt roads,
> But never will I walk on highways.

And yet they come, in bemused bewilderment, and in growing migrations.

In the eyes of an Indian what does the city look like? He has seen villages and he has seen towns. Nowhere has he seen one million people, five million, living in houses like great tombstones, row upon row, and running about like little mechanical ants, to and fro, on streets full of cars like plagues of grasshoppers. He has lived most of his life without a sidewalk, without a subway, without a superhighway, and often without a supermarket.

He has lived beside the still waters.

Living in the city is then not something he can adjust to with a street map, an orientation course, and a job. It is beyond his imagination, beyond his emotion.

Within a few miles of the metropolitan areas of Los Angeles and New York City more human beings live than in the more than one million square miles of all the states of the western mountains and plains and deserts, where most of the tribal Indians come from.

So the tribesmen come into the metropolis with its glass and steel office buildings, where the twentieth century is on perpetual display like a living museum piece.

How exotic are the artifacts of the urban civilization! Its rituals of folk-rock chants, commercial ceremonials, and automobile worship were fascinating.

The tribal Indians come with the curiosity of tourists. It is like visiting a circus in a foreign country.

Richard McKenzie, a young Sioux who lived in San Francisco for several years—successfully—and was a leader of the Indian Center in that city, cast a dubious eye on this citifying of the tribesmen. "The reservation Indian has not been prepared to make his way in the city of 1860's—much less the demanding fast-paced and cold-blooded city of 1960's," he said.

Life in the city whetted the Indian's curiosity, McKenzie said, but he faced a "hopeless situation." Most of the Indians he met were lost. "The simplest facts of life in the city were new to them: gearing your entire day by a clock, when to go to work, when to eat lunch. They don't even understand where you board a bus, how to pay, and how to open and close the doors.

"Because they have been sent from the reservation with the lack of training, information, and money," he said, they would be victims of "the hardships and loneliness of the disillusioned Indian in the city."

Why then, if the city Indian faces a "hopeless situation," do more and more rural Indians come to the cities?

"Lots of the younger kids want to leave the reservation and get a job," said Mary Lou Payne, a Cherokee girl who made the journey to the city herself. "It's not that they really want to get away from the reservation, but that they want to have an income. Everyone is encouraged to go away. To leave. To become a working American. To join the 'rat race,' really. What they call the 'mainstream.'"

The exodus has been not wholly voluntary. "It reflects a policy the Bureau of Indian Affairs has had and still has: to get the Indians off the reservation," Mary Lou Payne said.

"Relocation" is the term given this trek. It was instituted by Commissioner of Indian Affairs Dillon Myer, who . . . was director of the Relocation Centers where Japanese-Americans were imprisoned during World War II. Thus, the term had a disquieting connotation to young Indians, many of whom had fought in that war. Nonetheless, tens of thousands of tribal Indians have been "relocated" since the early 1950's.

Vice President Hubert Humphrey has written optimistically about the "Relocation" Program: It is aimed at "encouraging Indians to move off the less promising reservations and into industrial centers where work opportunities are more plentiful. . . . A package program—vocational training and job placement, with all expenses paid for trainee and family—has lured 50,000 Indians into successful urban living."

The former Commissioner of Indian Affairs, Philleo Nash, who guided the program during the administration of the late President John F. Kennedy, was more cautious and less optimistic: "Relocation by itself solves nothing," Nash said. ". . . As long as relocation was merely a program to transport people from one pocket of poverty to another, little was accomplished. Not everyone likes city living—not everyone is suited to it. To combat poverty successfully will require programs that relate people to jobs wherever they choose to live."

Some of the relocated Indians were even more skeptical. The Sioux Richard McKenzie said that when a reservation Indian arrived in San Francisco he was referred by the Relocation Office to "the few boarding houses available to Indians under the Bureau program [that were] usually ill-run, often short on food, and in bad districts—especially for girls."

The jobs that the Bureau found for "the usually unskilled Indians" were often with "fly-by-night outfits who enjoy getting as much labor as possible from their workers, while paying them as little as possible," McKenzie said. Since the Indians did not know union rules, many were working up to twelve hours a day without overtime pay. When "the pitifully small cash given him to make the trip" ran out, the relocated Indian was often penniless and lost.

His own family, McKenzie said, had housed and fed "many Indians who were in dire need, but somehow did not qualify for aid from any [welfare] agency."

"Mr. Indian," said the irate Sioux, "your 'Green Pastures' in the city will be even worse than what you have now at home. Sending Indians [to the city] on a sink or swim basis is the way to guarantee most will sink."

"It was shameful," Mary Lou Payne said, "to force rural Indians into urban ghettos. It's no answer to poverty to dump these people into the cities. They are so unprepared for city life, paying bills every month, going to work every day, that they filter out to the very bottom of society.

"This shipping out of unprepared people is just shameful. It doesn't work out. They just go back to what they did before. Which is pick up odd jobs. But doing it in the cities."

Vice President Hubert Humphrey sounded an official note of concern: "Most of them [those Indians who go on their own] have never held jobs of any duration and are almost totally unequipped for industrial work. They seek to escape from poverty on the reservation without realizing that they may be making another and worse trap for themselves. Unless we take measures to help this group, we will find new ghettos being established in our cities and towns, new slum children growing up, a new breed of unemployed unemployables, taxing our welfare services."

Measures had to be taken immediately. . . .

Relocation had become a fancy word for "dumping the rural poor into the ghettos," said Mel Thom. The idea of urbanizing and integrating the tribal Indian was forgotten, momentarily, and practical reality was recognized by changing the name of the Bureau of Indian Affairs, Branch of Relocation, to Branch of Employment Assistance.

The Vocational Education Act for Indians was intensified when Congress increased the appropriation from $12 to $15 million. Under this act, originally part of the Relocation Program, tribal Indians were job-trained and paid to leave their reservations. Yet, in the first ten years of its operation, but thirteen thousand of the tens of thousands of Indians who went to the cities benefited from its largess. "Usually Indians must leave the reservation to take advantage of it," *Eyapaha*, the Rosebud Sioux newspaper, complained.

Mary Lou Payne was less polite: "I have gripes about the on-the-job training programs. On the Cherokee Reservation back home we have two factories. One of them is a stitching plant, they make bed clothing; and the other is a bobby pin factory. They run the Indian kids through the training courses, the government picks up part of their salary while they're training, and then when they're through training, the company employs them for a month, or two months, and drops them, and hires another crew for training.

"How many jobs are there on the Cherokee Reservation where they can go and make stitched bed clothing? It's so impractical. They should be trained to become plumbers, carpenters, electricians, television repairmen."

Joe Maday, a young Chippewa boy on the Bad River Reservation in Wisconsin, had just come home from an on-the-job-training project, two thousand miles from his home.

He sat in his father's gas station, on a muddy river flat, near the wild-rice fields of his tribe on Lake Superior. He reminisced and he cursed the government for sending him to Seattle.

"Couldn't they send me to Milwaukee?" the boy said. He had gone wide-eyed and eager to see the country, on a $130-a-month government allowance, paying $90 a month for boarding-house rent. "Who could live on what was left? That rent for a dormitory-type room," he said. But it was exciting, anyway, being with Indians from a dozen tribes he had never heard of. "It was like a big powwow all the time. It didn't ever stop."

What did he learn? "Nothing!" he shrugged. "They wanted to teach me mechanic. But I didn't want to work as a mechanic way out there. So far away from home. And mechanics are a dime a dozen around here. So I come back. I'm going to learn electronics this time. If there's a job around here, I rather stay. But maybe I will go away. There's no work here. No one stays."

In spite of the newer urban-orientation course that had been started the tribal Indians still seemed disoriented by city life. So it was decided to urban-orientate them twice. Upon their arrival in the cities, the Bureau of Indian Affairs began to offer them a secondary education course in the rituals and customs of urban living.

Dr. Sophie D. Aberle and the late William A. Brophy, in *The Indian: America's Unfinished Business*, described one of these advanced courses:

"Orientation courses for Eskimos and reservation Indians unfamiliar with the manners and customs of life outside their villages have been started in Seattle, Washington. The three-week course is based on the assumption that the quickest way for students to adjust to modern life is to let them use up-to-date conveniences. . . .

"The training center is, therefore, located in a modern motel. Seven furnished apartments are rented for the trainees and their families. . . . All accommodations have carpeted floors, draperies, an all-electric kitchen, private bath, and living rooms.

"It is too early to evaluate the results of the orientation or prevocational training courses," the authors wrote. "However, methods of teaching have been developed and are being studied by psychologists, psychiatrists, linguists, and other specialists, so that improvements are being constantly made."

When oriented the Indians were moved out of the all-electric kitchens and the wall-to-wall-carpeted motel suites into the nearest ghetto. The transition was jarring. "One Indian woman in Cleveland didn't know how to light a gas stove," Mary Lou Payne related, "and a welfare worker who visited her walked in and found this woman standing in the middle of her kitchen and throwing matches into the oven."

In the ghetto of Puerto Rican Harlem, the Barrio of Nueva York, lives a very different sort of city Indian. Her name is Princess Wa Wa Chaw— Mrs. Bonita Nuñez.

She was one of the earliest of the city Indians in New York, and she is now one of the oldest. In the cluttered memories of her rooms, high in a municipal housing project, are stacks of boxes full of history: souvenirs of the days when she danced with Isadora Duncan; her painting of Joe Gould, the Greenwich Village poet and eccentric; invitations to the White House; mementos of the vaudeville stage; books on the mysteries of the occult; and news stories of tours and arrests in the Indian-rights fight of fifty years ago.

"When I came here I was one of the first," the old woman said. "I 'came out' [off the reservation] so long ago. I lived on the Lower East Side for some time. The Jews from Europe had never seen an Indian before. There was quite a commotion. But we became good friends. Sometimes I don't know who has had it worse—the Jews or the Indians.

"The Negroes talk about discrimination. In those days there was worse discrimination in the cities against Indians. 'Savages' they called us then."

The old woman is very old, how old she would not say. She was born a Rincon Indian, in California, and was adopted by a white family at birth. "It was before the earthquake in San Francisco," was all she would say. She was on the stage at the age of ten. She lived all her life in the world of the white man. She knew no other life.

"Oh, I had friends everywhere. I could sing and act and dance and paint. I was not afraid," she recalled. "But you see I am still an Indian. Should the Indians be afraid of the city? No, the 'mainstream' should not frighten us. I am an existentialist," the old woman said.

Huddled under a shawl, in her modern apartment in the New York City housing project, she looked out on the defaced walls of the cold slums below her window and thought of one day long ago.

"One day I was walking down the street when a lady stopped me. She looked me in the eye. Then she hit me in the face. 'Go back where you came from! You foreigner!' she shouted. She was Italian, I think. But I was a brown Indian, you see." She sighed: "I am aware that [we] can become victims of the 'lonely people.'"

Who are these "lonely people"?

The "lonely people" are, of course, "the lonely crowd." It is the remoteness and coldness and self-interest of the harassed urban populace that has created the "cold-blooded city" of Richard McKenzie's image. And it is this that is so strange to the tribal Indian.

"*That lonesome path that leads to Nowhere is taking me away from this lonesome place*" was the lament of the Plains Indian boy Calvin O'John, who had come to a very different city, in a very different era. He too had felt the cold hand of the "lonely people." So did his fellow student at the Santa Fe Institute of American Indian Arts, Donna Whitewing, who thought of the city as a "blank cold wall":

> Against a blank cold wall
> room enough for many flowers
> to grow and bloom.
> Feel the heart hesitate
> as flowers and buds
> wilt and die with pain.

Where was the warmth and love of the kinship family? In the impersonal and cold efficiency of the city there is no such human touch. The "lonely people" do not touch one another.

Donna Whitewing wrote:

> The essence of death
> is the untouched sense
> of being felt.

Loyal Shegonee, another of the young city Indians, poignantly cried out: "Where are my friends? What is there to do? Would someone, anyone, please come and talk to me?" He heard, the young man said, "the deafening tick-tick of the clock." He felt "the dark room crowding its silence upon me."

"Oh God," he cried out. "Someone, please come and talk to me!"

Who in the city talks to strangers? The "lonely people" prefer to talk to their machinery; for didn't they say "the medium is the message"? Kathryn Polacca, a Navajo teacher who has been to many cities, said: "Your people have so many ways of communication: IBM machines, telephones, newspapers, telegraphs, radios, and television. In the Navajo ways the most important communication is still person to person. This is the way we solve many of our problems. This is the way we enjoy life." The Indian way of talking and living, she said, was based on human values, not on mechanical or monetary values.

Unlike so many newcomers to the cities the tribal Indians "are not with it," Mel Thom said. "He doesn't think of making money. He just wants to make a living and live." That is why, though there are an estimated twenty thousand Indians in the environs of San Francisco, and perhaps thirty thousand in Los Angeles, Thom said he knew of only two or three Indian-owned establishments in either city. One was a bar.

"Money! Money! Money! That is all the white man thinks of when it comes to the Indian," said a Pomo Indian of California. "The only thing they see is money. For me a heartbeat is enough."

On the icy tundra of far northwest Alaska in an Eskimo village, where the silence of centuries was being broken by a plant of Kennecott Copper, there came the quiet voice of William Hensley. He is a young Eskimo of Kotzebue, who graduated from George Washington University in Washington, D.C., and who has become the executive director of the Northwest Alaska Native Association, the vice president of the statewide Native Federation, and a member of the state legislature.

For all the vast distances that separate them, the young Eskimo's words might have been those of one of the new Indians: "I would rather be a poverty-stricken Eskimo way up in the North than a wealthy white man in your cities," Hensley said. "Many of our villages are just as they were hundreds of years ago. Very, very slow moving, fairly primitive way of living. I'm not saying it's a bad life; in fact, I think it's a good life. I would prefer for my people not to have to live in the cities that I have seen throughout the country.

"There isn't any comparison. And this is one of the things that native people are thinking about life in the larger, urban society. Many of them don't want to become part of this mainstream of yours.

"Last summer I was up in Point Hope, one of the oldest villages. I was staying with the head of the village. There had just been some mass crime—of a white man in Texas killing a half dozen or more people. And the head of the village said to me, 'If this is civilization, I don't want any part of it.'"

A Chippewa youth, Ronald Head, who has worked in Texas, has similar trepidations: "Come and join the Great Society, they say. I don't know if I want to join. What for? To be killed by a white man in a University tower, in a 'seat of learning'?"

It was not the violence that these Indians feared. Guns and shooting do not frighten them. The urban man lives in terror of a hunting rifle on the ordered, policed, shattering quiet of the city street; the Indian does not. Hunting is a household commonplace to Indian youth. Rather it was the inhumanity of the mass killings that frightened the Indians. The cold-blooded way in which urban man would kill strangers to him for no emotional reason, with no feelings.

"Why do they kill like that?" an Oklahoma Cherokee, who regularly went home to hunt, asked. "I would not shoot deer that way."

Those Indians who chose to stay in the "cold-blooded city" had to protect themselves—politically, economically, and culturally. They were often abandoned by the federal bureaus, with little knowledge of the city agencies, left on their own, uncomfortable with urban life, separated from their tribes, and something had to be done for them, by themselves. The invisible city Indian had to become visible.

Where Indians have come, they have built Indian centers. The men and women from tribes throughout the country, with different cultures and different languages, would get together and establish a meeting place where they could meet relatives and tribesmen, reminisce about life back at home, discuss the frustrations of city life, and help and protect themselves. The Indian center might be a tiny, dreary storefront, or an elaborate and well-equipped community hall. But, whatever it looked like, it was run by and financed by tribal Indians, for tribal Indians.

Powwows in the city? A nostalgic attempt to transplant tribal life to the cement prairie? These Indian centers are not governmental or social-work-sponsored, not tribal nor intertribal. In coming to these community halls the Indians come as Indians, not representing their tribes. The city Indians have created something new and independent and yet Indian. They speak of the "Indian language"—"Let's talk Indian," they say; though there is, of course, no such language—and seek to preserve their "Indian traditions," and they dance in powwows, doing "Indian dances," and they fight for their "Indian rights."

In doing these things they are not only building an Indian urban community, but are building an Indian consciousness that is no longer tribal, but is extratribal. It too is an embryo of Indian nationalism.

Chicago's Indian Center, one of the oldest and largest of these urban, extratribal groups, is typical in its goals of most. Its aim is to help tribesmen in becoming "a functioning part of the social fabric of the city," while "sustaining cultural values perhaps uniquely their own."

The Indians of Chicago are seeking, in other words, to become urban citizens outwardly, but to remain Indians inwardly. And these Indians wish to do this not by urbanizing the tribal life, nor by tribalizing the urban life, but by combining both. Fascinating are the combinations. Rock 'n' roll and tribal dances. Potlatch dinners and auto-mechanic classes.

In the San Francisco Indian Center within an ordinary week there was: Tuesday—Indian dancing; Wednesday—ladies' sewing club, Indian arts and crafts, girls' ping-pong and boys' pool tournaments; Thursday—council meeting on job, housing, and welfare problems; Friday—modern ballet class and a powwow (singers and dancers were "paid with gas money"); Saturday—children's health clinic and rock 'n' roll dance (music by The Enchanters).

And on Sunday there was a movie entitled *The Exiles.*

These programs are run with a tribal communality: "Our Center is operated by Indians for all Indians in the Bay Area. All help is voluntary. Everyone just comes and does whatever they think has to be done for improvement. There is no one sponsoring the organization. Indians work here not for profit, but to contribute their time for a preservation of our disintegrating culture and heritage."

In a similar spirit of tribalism the American Indian Center in Chicago declared: "The Center is an achievement of their own [the Indians'], and not something provided for Indians by others. . . . The Center is not a sort of missionary outpost of the urban majority. It is a grass-roots effort."

Yearly the Chicago Indian Center provides services for thousands of tribesmen, but since its members have "never been wealthy people" it is in a perpetual state of near bankruptcy. The Welfare Council of Chicago, to which it is affiliated, suggested that the comfortably endowed and well-known Hull House take over the administration of the Indian Center. Its financial problems would be solved, and it would benefit from professional social work management.

The Chicago Indian Center voted down the beneficent offer, to the surprise of the city fathers. It was like voting not to accept a congressional appropriation.

Nathan Bird, an Indian woodworker, who was on the board of directors of the Indian Center, tried to explain: "The Hull-House is a fine place. We have nothing against it. We were afraid that we would lose our identity if they took us over. It always happens. It would not longer be an Indian Center. The whites would take us over and tell us what to do. It was a bribe. We could use the money. We won't sell our Indian rights for money.

"That's what happens on the reservations," Mr. Bird said. "The government is always taking things over to 'help us.' We don't want that kind of 'help.' We didn't come all the way to Chicago for some more of that."

City Indians, because they are on their own—neither protected nor restricted by the Bureau of Indian Affairs—tend to be more independent and more outspoken. In Minneapolis the city Indians twice in two years picketed the Bureau's area office. Picketing, in itself, had been unknown to tribal movements; tribesmen would sooner take up a rifle in defense of their treaty rights than take up a picket sign. It was "un-Indian," the elders said.

But the Urban American Indian Protest Committee of the Twin Cities had no such fears. It was organized by two younger Indians, Mary Thunder and George Mitchell. On its first picket line it mustered 35 city Indians, who carried signs demanding that the government begin programs to help them. It had none, they said, and they demanded assistance in getting housing, jobs, and education; referral services for medical and legal care; and practical urban orientation programs.

The "Bureau employees shut the window," said Gerald Vizenor, one of the protest committee youth—in shock, perhaps. However, the area director, Glenn Landbloom, proclaimed: "My door is always open," and invited the picketing Indians to come up and talk. None came.

"The Indians replied that the door had been open for more than a hundred years," Vizenor said. "Talk is what the Indians did *not* want to do. They were protesting to change policy, not to cultivate conversation."

One-third of the Minnesota Indians now live in the Twin Cities. There are more urban tribesmen than there are Indians on any reservation in the state. Yet, Vizenor said, "The Bureau has no programs directed to their needs. What is the Bureau doing with its growing budget to serve a decreasing reservation Indian population? If assimilation is the Bureau policy then it seems logical that the Bureau should offer some referral and urban assistance to Indians moving from the poor rural reservation areas to the Twin Cities."

The area director, Landbloom, explained that the Bureau served only Indians "on or adjacent to Indian trust lands." He was not clear how near "adjacent" meant, but he thought the Twin Cities were not really an Indian reservation.

Gerald Vizenor was jovial in spite of the rebuff: "Another picket is planned. Many Indians felt so good about the last one that there are plans for a group three times as large with moccasin games and dancing, if the Bureau doesn't come across with some proposals for adequate programs for urban Indians."

The invisibility of the city Indian belongs to the past. He is becoming visible. He may have been lost in the city; but the longer he has stayed the more he has begun to feel it is the city that is lost—not he. When the city Indian began to build urban tribal communities he discovered the Indian way of life filled the lonely void of "the cement prairies." And he began to wonder if "the lonely crowd" might learn neighborliness from him.

"The very values the Indian represents may contribute to the improvement of our frantic cities," said Richard McKenzie. He thought the values of tribal humanism might "make the cities more human." And one young Pueblo Indian in the Chicago Indian Center said: "Instead of giving Indians these urban-orientation courses, maybe they ought to give Chicagoans human-orientation courses."

Has the "alienation" of the city Indian been too convenient and self-comforting a concept? It has been used by non-Indians to define the feelings of the Indian, but it has described the effect and not the cause. It has placed the onus on the Indian for his failure to conform to urban life and for his return home to the reservation. But, at a time when the disappearance of communities and the demise of neighborhoods are troubling city planners, the communal feeling of the city Indian has something to be said for it.

If the "alienation" of urban life becomes too overwhelming, the city Indian returns to his tribal community, and home to the reservation many had gone.

"The return to the reservations," former Commissioner of Indian Affairs Philleo Nash, estimated, "was about as frequent as the permanent relocation." Mary Lou Payne thought it even greater: "On this relocation the return home is fantastic. I bet it is 60 per cent and up who return to the reservations." Richard McKenzie said it was his experience that 90 per cent returned home as soon as there were jobs on the reservations.

A young girl of the Laguna Pueblo, Pat Pacheco, who returned to her pueblo from college, where she had studied psychology, said: "It's almost impossible to adjust to the outside world, and many of our people are coming back from Cleveland, Chicago, and Los Angeles, because they can work here now."

Not only are the relocated Indians beginning to go home, the *Wall Street Journal* observed, but "there's evidence Indians aren't moving off reservations as readily as a short while ago."

Into the Indian Center of San Francisco, up the shabby stairs, one day walked an unknown tribesman. He was welcomed, as every Indian was, a tall man, with a tight face and puzzled eyes. The man was a newcomer; perhaps he had just arrived from the reservation, and was ill at ease.

The stranger was something more, however. He was a relocation officer of the government who had been sent from the reservation to see how the tribal Indians were being urbanized.

"He was told we took a rather dim view of the program," a San Francisco Indian recalled. "I pinned him down about the lack of adequate orientation on the reservation. And he said they did indeed tell people about buses, housing, and so forth. I told him that John Glenn could tell me in six orientation lessons how to fly a space ship and I wouldn't know a thing about it if I got in one."

That broke up the official meeting. "Last three hours of our visit were spent talking about hunting, fishing, and wide-open spaces on the reservation. The cheaper cost of living and better life in general back home," the relocated Indian said. "Naturally, many of the things the relocation officer said, and many of the things he saw, will never be included in his written report to Washington, D.C., or for that matter in his verbal report to his superintendent on the reservation.

"One wonders, after seeing relocation at the other end, if he will not be more reluctant about sending Indian people out. Will the relocation officer relocate himself?" The city Indian laughed.

The most unusual tale of relocation-in-reverse, however, occurred in Los Angeles. In that multiplicity of the Angels lived a group of Cherokees. Some of the families were well established and some were well to do. They were all Los Angeles boosters; for they had done well enough and lived quite happily.

Yet the hills of eastern Oklahoma of the Cherokee Nation haunted them. "Twelve years ago a group of Indians, many of us children, or grandchildren, of Oklahomans, decided to 'put down a fire' in California," said Dr. John Harris Jeffries, a lawyer and chiropractic doctor who was a leader of these Los Angeles Cherokees. He explained that to "put down a fire," in the Cherokee tradition, meant just that. A ceremonial ground was prepared and a fireplace dug in the earth. There the fire was lighted for religious rituals. There a stomping ground for religious dances was established around the fire.

In the city of Los Angeles, the Western Keetoowah Society was founded. The Keetoowah Society is the nativist religious group of the Cherokees. Its traditional worship, with masks and robes and rites, was not only sacred, but in the urban frenzy was an island of the Indian spirit. Though the city Cherokees were separated by miles of freeways, they held regular religious ceremonies and prayers. In the kinship families they kept their matriarchal clans intact. The old customs of the tribe were practiced, and the children given Cherokee names in the traditional way.

One of the Western Keetoowah Society of Los Angeles members was a lawyer. One was an insurance salesman. One was the owner of an electrical firm. One was a professional golfer. One was a professional artist. One was a surveyor. One was a doctor. One was a computer analyst. And yet—business

suits off, ties loosened, brief cases left in the foyers of the suburban houses—
they were traditionalist Indians.

"Suddenly we began to think about coming home," Dr. Jeffries said. "I
don't know with whom the idea originated. We knew we wanted to get out of
the rat race in Los Angeles. There just wasn't any discussion about where we
should go. It was Tahlequah."

And so to Tahlequah, Oklahoma, the old capital of the Cherokee Nation,
the families began to come. In the beginning just seven families moved. Then
four more came. Soon forty of the Cherokees had come. Dr. Jeffries expected
that in all one hundred and fifty would come home.

"It was home instantly," he said. "No one has mentioned moving back."
Somehow it was as though they had never left.

The coals of the sacred fires that they had "put down" in Los Angeles were
unearthed. In their cars the coals were carefully carried halfway across the
continent, once more to be buried, but this time in the earth of their Cherokee
homeland. Once more, the fires would flame.

Toward Cooperation and Dignity

American Friends Service Committee

CONSERVATION, INDIANS, AND ALLOCATION

Beyond any doubt, continuation of the salmon and steelhead resource requires the vigorous and coordinated application of conservation principles and practice. All share the responsibility—users of the rivers, users of the land through which the rivers flow, all categories of fishermen, the various local, state, federal, and international agencies which are responsible for control of land and river use, and the citizenries to which these agencies are accountable. The mere listing of interests indicates part of the complexity of the task, for no one agency controls more than a comparatively small portion of the total.

Indians share the responsibility as users of the fish—perhaps no group has a greater interest in the outcome. Although the non-Indian community, including both the state and the Bureau of Indian Affairs, has looked upon Indian fishing as something which would soon disappear as Indians became farmers or industrial workers and "entered the mainstream," nothing of the sort has happened. Fishing by Indians of the Pacific Northwest, including the Muckleshoots, Puyallups, and Nisquallys, has continued as one of the most important aspects of their life, important in both economic and nonmaterial ways.

The economic value is obvious—for many Indians fishing is their only effective income-producing skill, whether the fish are caught for personal use or for sale to provide other necessities. A great many people believe that the Indians' only reason for insisting on their treaty rights to fish is the economic advantage. The values, however, are more than economic. People already poor do not deliberately risk expensive equipment and their own imprisonment solely for the hope of financial gain. Fishing is their life in a much more profound sense than simply making a living.

Traditionally, life on the sea and the rivers dominated the economy, art, religion, and social life of the Northwest Coast Indians. Though patterns have changed, to many modern Indians the meaning of the inherited tradition is so strong that their determination to hold it for themselves, to use it, to insist on fishing even in defiance of official interference and legal actions, continues in spite of all the pressures to change. The intensity of feeling has led some

SOURCE: From *Uncommon Controversy: Fishing Rights of the Muckleshoot, Puyallup and Nisqually Indians*, by the American Friends Service Committee. Copyright © 1970 by the University of Washington Press. Reprinted by permission of the University of Washington Press.

Indians to apply the term "cultural genocide" to the attacks on their fishing. Fishing remains the center, in a sense the soul, of the Indian time-continuity and of the feeling of relationship to the environment. The fact of fishing as a fundamental aspect of personal and group relationship to what is important in existence is as real for many Indians today as it was for the treaty signers, and for those before them.

This sense of the spiritual, essential nature of fishing has not been understood by non-Indians, or even perceived by them. It is surely part of the reason that Indian tenacity in insisting on holding to their own fishing, their "treaty rights," has been so perplexing to most outsiders.

Another factor in the perplexity has been the complete confidence of the white people and the white agencies in the superiority of their own outlook and ways. That confidence was also the root of the agencies' inability, from Stevens on, to see what was already at hand—a ready-made fishery, capable of extended development and indefinite continuation for the support of the Indian people, to the benefit of both themselves and others. The same unexamined confidence also brought about the insistence upon imposing inappropriate and irrelevant non-Indian patterns, demanding the remodeling of the Indians. To this day, if an Indian man's occupation is given as "fisherman" it is frequently taken as indicative of backwardness and lesser competence.

Therefore no real planning assistance has ever been given to the Indian fisheries. Except for approving tribal regulatory codes, the federal government has virtually ignored them. Until 1962 it offered no technical advice or assistance to tribes either for setting up suitable regulations or for developmental programs. It did not attempt to obtain, or to make it possible for tribes to obtain, biolgoical and other information about Indian rivers and the runs in them. Only in the last few years has it provided educational assistance for some young Indians to become fish biologists or fisheries technicians.[1]

The state of Washington has never taken Indian fisheries into consideration in fisheries planning, except as they affect other fisheries. In one way or another, by legal definition, licensing, regulation of gear, and agreement, the state has allocated the salmon and steelhead between commercial and sport fishermen and between different types of commercial fishermen. It has accommodated to Indian fisheries from time to time, sometimes with good will and sometimes as a result of court action, and sometimes simply as a *modus vivendi*; but it has never planned for the allocation of salmon or steelhead to the Indian fisheries as a legitimite part of the total fisheries. It has never looked at the Indian fisheries as a component of an integrated fisheries program. The Indian catch has been seen primarily as a nuisance or a threat, and generally as an impingement on those regarded as the approriate users. The efforts of the state to come to agreements with Indians have been principally designed to assure fish to the sport and commercial fishermen.[2]

The Indian fisheries have in a real sense survived and developed in isolation. Indians have not had access to the growing body of knowledge about the anadromous fish, nor have they had the opportunity to contribute their own knowledge. They have not been brought into any kind of overall decision-making, by either state or federal governments, with respect to managing the fisheries. Their authority to regulate their members' fishing at sites outside reservation boundaries has generally not been supported. They have been expected by state agencies to accept decision and controls made for the state's view of needs, and based on the attitude that the Indian fishery as a distinct fishery is a troublesome anachronism. Indians have in effect been denied the right of responsible participation.

Their isolation is increasingly less tenable. Whatever the effect of the Indian fisheries on other fisheries or of others on them—and they all reciprocally affect each other—the fisheries of both Indian and non-Indian are inexorably affected by the changes in the physical environment of the region. Before white men came to the Northwest Coast, Indian tradition and practice took into account salmon propagation needs, and the fish continued in ample supply. Today the question of salmon and steelhead survival remains moot. The ending of all Indian fishing, perhaps of all fishing, would not appreciably affect the outcome. The salmon will not survive unless enough of their world survives for them to live.

The environmental changes to which every serious discussion of salmon depletion points as the fundamental cause of the decline, and as the basic continuing threat, were not brought about by Indians. They came with the industrial and commercial activities of white men and with the growth of population. Neither have Indian fishing practices changed as much in kind or degree as those of the non-Indians. Indians have not been in a position to control or remedy the major changes affecting the fish.

The state, attempting to establish its own "unified control," has endeavored to regulate Indian off-reservation fishing. Because a net in a river can block it—though less efficiently than a dam for real estate development or power—the attack has been based on conservation: Indians endanger the "seed stock for the future." The argument ignores the fact that all salmon, including the alevins waiting to emerge from the gravel which may be taken for a logging road, are "seed stock." It ignores the effects of sportsmen's fishing on the same rivers, with different gear but in far greater numbers. It ignores the environmental damage which has destroyed more salmon than the most controversial Indian fishing. It ignores the kind of concern the Muckleshoots, Puyallups, and Nisquallys have expressed about the condition of their rivers, and it ignores the fisheries programs developed by the Quinaults and Makahs. An argument basically so fallacious could not have been used to such effect if the Indian fisheries had not already been regarded as being not actually legitimate fisheries.

Including the Indian fisheries in overall planning, which requires consideration of the share to be allocated to them, would provide a basis for settling the disputes. Allocation of the fish among the various fisheries has been carried out as a function of the state. Allocation to a particular fishery is based on its recognition as legitimate. In the state's general position of antagonism to the Indian fisheries and its attempt to ignore the on-reservation fisheries, it is left without a logical basis for discussion or agreement with the tribes; and any steps it takes from this position the tribes are certain to rebuff. Recognition of the Indian fisheries' place in the total fisheries and their inclusion in allocation would allow consideration of them as distinct fisheries whether on or off reservation.

It would also make active participation by Indians both possible and necessary.

Allocating a share to the Indian fisheries, however, presumes their legitimacy. Legally, legitimacy seems to be well established. The question about it exists in people's minds. What is the reason?

THE ISSUE: DIFFERENCE, NOT CONSERVATION

However real and serious the problems of conservation, they are not the basis of this controversy. The real issue is the attitude of the whole society toward difference.

The Indians look at fishing and fishing rights differently, and they fish in different ways. Difference is nearly intolerable in a society which expects conformity in behavior and outlook—one which tends to equate equal treatment with identical treatment, acceptable behavior with conforming behavior, integration with assimilation. The Indians' right to fish in different ways and under different rules is felt by many non-Indians to be completely inappropriate, and the connection of fishing rights with identity to be nonsense. Hostility rises from the threat presented by the differences, not from danger to the fish. Efforts to control Indian fishing have been rationalized around conservation, but they have recognized neither the pervasive importance of environmental changes nor the questions of humanness.

Indians, on the receiving end, see the matter more clearly than do non-Indians. Although they may not express it in so many words, they are well aware that the aim is to get rid of them as Indians. The expression "treaty rights" becomes emotion-laden and, like "conservation" on the other side, may sometimes arouse feeling more than promote thought. The terms become shibboleths, and the arguments go past each other. But the fact remains that for many Indians survival as Indians requires the survival of Indian fishing; the end of Indian fishing would be a great step toward extinction as Indians.

The problems of conservation have actually been obscured by the fishing rights controversy. The attention of all—the public, the conservation agencies, the Indian tribes—has been diverted from basic problems of environment to the quarrel over the right of certain Indians to fish at certain places. The controversy has rendered impossible the orderly regulation of their own off-reservation fishing by these three small tribes. It has contributed nothing toward working out a suitable integration of Indian fishing with other fishing. On the contrary, it has fanned fears and antagonisms which may make this much more difficult. The state's attack on "Indian fishing" is viewed by many,

Indians and others, as meaning that state officials desire control of fishing on the reservations as well as off, and regard such control as the proper ultimate outcome.

The Muckleshoots, Nisquallys, and Puyallups—and most other Indian groups in the state of Washington—face significant problems in mustering resources for communicating their views of fishing with those having different styles of thinking, and in resisting the pressures that would submerge them. None of these groups have adequate funds for legal representation in their disputes with the state agencies. Neither do they have the political power of the other fishing interests, especially the sport fishermen. Within Indian groups, differences over strategy in meeting the threats have produced divisions which have impeded efforts at rational fisheries development. Some of the extreme reactions have further hampered communication both among Indians and between Indians and others, and have rendered the Indians' planning more difficult. A tremendous amount of the resources and energy which could have been directed toward development of the fish has been spent instead on defense of the very right to an Indian fishery.

News stories in the mass media both illustrate the problem of attitude toward differences and contribute to it through their public impact. The message frequently is: "Indian fishing is destroying the salmon and steelhead." Important distinctions have been made between off- and on-reservation fishing, different reservations, different practices, and different fishermen. "Hundred-year-old treaties" are described directly or by implication as outdated and inappropriate. The concern of the state and the sportsmen for preservation of the fish runs is emphasized. The massive problems of controlling the fish environment are touched only in passing.

One of the effects of the publicity attending the fishing rights dispute has been to induce a further sense of separation on the part of the Indians. What has been the effect on the attitudes about Indians on the part of others, the largely non-Indian public? The portrayal of Indians as irresponsible and unreasonable in their fishing practices must have strengthened existing stereotypes, without conveying a sense of legitimate disagreement.

What responsibility do public officials and mass media have in presenting complex issues to the public? The information is bound to be equally complex. Sometimes that released to the mass media has been simplified to the point of distortion, and apparently selected to support the view that Indian off-reservation fishing, not very clearly distinguished from on-reservation fishing, is the principal danger to fish runs in many of the rivers. Few readers are likely to question the statements of experts; nor will it even occur to them that there might be a question. Few have knowledge enough to evaluate and put into perspective specific statements made by game and fisheries department representatives about "Indian fishing."

The *Annual Reports* and other papers of the Department of Fisheries show their concern about all the elements of conservation and their continuing efforts to control conditions detrimental to the fish. Their *Ten-Year Plan* . . .

could not have stated more plainly the seriousness of the threats from the environment. However, the publicity campaign has been directed against Indian fishing. "Conservation," with its connotations of reasonableness, cooperation, and progress, has been given a narrow definition and made the summation of intolerance toward certain differences.

Indians, insisting on their right to unique tribal existence, including fishing, are asserting the right to a freedom of choice—asking to *stay out* of certain aspects of American society. Whether intentionally or not, they are challenging the claim that the society believes in freedom of choice, and are providing the opportunity for the society to conserve, to its own enrichment, a certain human viewpoint and set of values. Both the fish and the particular people are part of the country's patrimony, part of its diverse wealth. The loss of either as a by-product of change would be an irredeemable impoverishment.

NOTES

1. A few Indians have expressed the opinion that these courses were really intended to get the young men into non-Indian fisheries work.
2. The new Squaxin agreement seems to be based on the idea that at the present time a separate Indian fishery can be tolerated at that place and still allow adequate escapement.

Proclamation: To the Great White Father and All His People

The American Indian Center of San Francisco

We, the native Americans, re-claim the land known as Alcatraz Island in the name of all American Indians by right of discovery.

We wish to be fair and honorable in our dealings with the Caucasian inhabitants of this land, and hereby offer the following treaty:

We will purchase said Alcatraz Island for twenty-four dollars (24) in glass beads and red cloth, a precedent set by the white man's purchase of a similar island about 300 years ago. We know that $24 in trade goods for these 16 acres is more than was paid when Manhattan Island was sold, but we know that land values have risen over the years. Our offer of $1.24 per acre is greater than the 47¢ per acre the white men are now paying the California Indians for their land.

We will give to the inhabitants of this island a portion of the land for their own to be held in trust by the American Indian Affairs and by the bureau of Caucasian Affairs to hold in perpetuity—for as long as the sun shall rise and the rivers go down to the sea. We will further guide the inhabitants in the proper way of living. We will offer them our religion, our education, our life-ways, in order to help them achieve our level of civilization and thus raise them and all their white brothers up from their savage and unhappy state. We offer this treaty in good faith and wish to be fair and honorable in our dealings with all white men. . . .

We feel that this so-called Alcatraz Island is more than suitable for an Indian Reservation, as determined by the white man's own standards. By this we mean that this place resembles most Indian reservations in that:

1. It is isolated from modern facilities, and without adequate means of transportation.

2. It has no fresh running water.

3. It has inadequate sanitation facilities.

4. There are no oil or mineral rights.

5. There is no industry and so unemployment is very great.

SOURCE: From "Proclamation: To the Great White Father and All His People," by Indians of All Tribes. Reprinted from the *Journal of American Indian Education* 9:2 (January 1970), pp. 16–18, by permission of the publisher.

6. There are no health care facilities.

7. The soil is rocky and nonproductive; and the land does not support game.

8. There are no educational facilities.

9. The population has always exceeded the land base.

10. The population has always been held as prisoners and kept dependent upon others.

Further, it would be fitting and symbolic that ships from all over the world, entering the Golden Gate, would first see Indian land, and thus be reminded of the true history of this nation. This tiny island would be a symbol of the great lands once ruled by free and noble Indians.

USE TO BE MADE OF ALCATRAZ ISLAND

What use will we make of this land? Since the San Francisco Indian Center burned down, there is no place for Indians to assemble and carry on tribal life here in the white man's city. Therefore, we plan to develop on this island several Indian institutions:

1. A center for native American studies will be developed which will train our young people in the best of our native arts and works as well as educate them to the skills and knowledge relevant to improve the lives and spirits of all Indian peoples. Attached to this center will be travelling universities, managed by Indians, which will go to the Indian Reservations, learning those necessary and relevant materials now about.

2. An American Indian spiritual center which will practice our ancient tribal religious and sacred healing ceremonies. Our cultural arts will be featured and our young people trained in music, dance, and healing rituals.

3. An Indian center of ecology which will train and support our young people in scientific research and practice to restore our lands and waters to their pure and natural state. We will work to de-pollute the air and water of the Bay Area. We will seek to restore fish and animal life to the area and to revitalize sea life which has been threatened by the white man's ways. We will set up facilities to desalt sea water for human benefit.

4. A great Indian training school will be developed to teach our peoples how to make a living in the world, improve our standards of living, and to end hunger and unemployment among all our people. This training school will include a center for Indian arts and crafts, and an Indian restaurant serving native foods, which will restore Indian culinary arts. This center will display Indian arts and offer Indian foods to the public, so that all may know of the beauty and spirit of the traditional Indian ways.

5. Some of the present buildings will be taken over to develop an American Indian Museum, which will depict our native foods and other cultural contributions we have given to the world. Another part of the museum will

present some of the things the white man has given to the Indians in return for the land and life he took: disease, alcohol, poverty and cultural decimation (as symbolized by old tin cans, barbed wire, rubber tires, plastic containers, etc.). Part of the museum will remain a dungeon to symbolize both those Indian captives who were incarcerated for challenging white authority, and those who were imprisoned on reservations. The museum will show the noble and the tragic events of Indian history, including the broken treaties, the documentary of the Trail of Tears, the Massacre of Wounded Knee, as well as the victory over Yellow Hair Custer and his army.

In the name of all Indians, therefore, we re-claim this island for our Indian nations. For all these reasons, we feel this claim is just and proper, and that this land should rightfully be granted to us for as long as the rivers shall run and the sun shall shine.

                                        Signed,

                                        Indians of All Tribes
                                        November, 1969
                                        San Francisco, California

The Rise of Indian Activism

Vine Deloria, Jr.

As the civil rights movement turned from integration to the development of Black Power in 1966, a corresponding shift in emphasis was made in the Indian community. Formerly people had depended upon the tribal councils to initiate movements and generate issues. The tradition had been set during the previous decade when tribal councils led the fight against the termination policy. And in many instances city-dwelling Indians and young people waited for the tribes to define vital issues before they became active in pushing for reform.

As early as 1963, however, the climate began to change. In that year, the National Indian Youth Council, a group of younger college-trained Indians who had organized following the Chicago conference of 1961, led a demonstration in the northwest in an effort to highlight the problem of Indian treaty fishing rights. Marlon Brando offered his support to the movement and the Indians went out on the Nisqually and Puyallup rivers south of Seattle, Washington to protest the treatment of Indian fishermen by the departments of Fish and Game of the state of Washington.

Fishing was a way of life for the Indians of the Puget Sound. They had formerly lived along the numerous rivers and streams emptying into the sound. In 1854 and 1855 when the United States was desirous of obtaining a peaceful settlement of the region, Isaac Stevens was sent to the coast to negotiate treaties for land cession. Stevens received title to the entire northern coastal area in a series of six treaties. The small tribes agreed to go to selected reservation areas but they rigorously maintained that they should have the right to hunt and fish in all of their accustomed places since their entire economic structure was built upon the salmon runs of the rivers of the territory.

At first the Indians were left in relative peace and they provided the new population with almost all of its seafood. In fact at one time there was considerable concern that the Indians would not fish and that the territory would be left without adequate food supplies. But as the territory of Washington became a state and more people poured into the land, tensions began to mount. The discovery of efficient methods of canning meant the development of a commercially profitable fishing industry and soon Indians were being pushed aside from their traditional fishing sites by whites.

SOURCE: From *Red Man in the New World Drama*, by Jennings C. Wise, edited and revised by Vine Deloria, Jr. Copyright © 1971 by Vine Deloria, Jr. Reprinted with permission of The Macmillan Company.

During the 1920's, the development of sports fishing and the tremendous state income deriving from the sale of fishing licenses meant virtually the end of Indian fishing. Quickly the state began moving in against the Indians, confining them within the reservation boundaries and often challenging their right to fish, even on the reservations.

Nineteen sixty-four began the modern Indian war in the northwest over Indian fishing rights. The state of Washington, in violation of the edicts of the Supreme Court of the United States and a congressional statute of 1954 specifically exempting Indian fishing rights from the jurisdiction of the states, began a relentless harassment of the Indian fishermen—particularly on the Nisqually, Green, and Puyallup rivers. The state Game Department was particularly oppressive since it represented the sportsmen (being almost entirely financially dependent on the revenue of fishing licenses for its income).

The Fish and Game officers would swoop down on an Indian settlement, break up the Indian boats, cut or confiscate their nets, and after numerous acts of brutality, arrest the Indians for "disturbing the peace," "unlawful assembly," or "inciting to riot," thus effectively preventing the helpless red men from getting the issue of fishing rights into the federal courts where they could receive protection.

By the middle of 1970 the Indians had begun to get sufficient publicity on the struggle so that the public at large was becoming aware of the unequal situation. So the Game Department officers lessened their harassment and gangs of vigilantes, consisting sometimes of their sons and relatives, took to cowardly tactics of ambush and night raids to destroy the Indian fishing gear and to frighten off the Indian fishermen.

Finally the inevitable happened. On January 19, 1971 in the early morning mists, two white vigilantes caught Hank Adams, leader of the Indian fishermen, alone in his car sleeping by the riverbank. They threw open the car door and shot Adams in the stomach. It was a near miss. Fortunately Adams survived the assassination attempt, since the sportsmen were not the best of shots. But the crisis had undoubtedly reached its climax. Later that day in the hospital, police questioned Adams and implied that he had shot himself in an effort to gain publicity for his cause. Neither the police nor the F.B.I., reluctantly called in by the hesitant Nixon administration, which had been elected on a platform of law and order, followed up the assassination attempt very rigorously.

Perhaps the worst part of the fishing rights struggle was the almost complete news blackout in the state of Washington itself. The newspapers were almost unanimously against the Indians, and what stories were published reflected the sportsmen's side of the controversy. In Tacoma, the nearest large city to the Indian settlements, the television stations were controlled by the newspapers—thus effectively blocking out any news whatsoever on the fishing troubles. Numerous Indian leaders across the nation tried to bring the issue to the American public via national television programs, but these programs were never shown in the state of Washington. When it came time to rerun them the stations of the state would substitute other programs. Thus the white population of the state that might have been sympathetic toward the Indians was never allowed to hear the Indian side of the story.

If the fishing rights struggle showed anything, it was that the Indian wars had not ended and that in all probability they would never end so long as there were any Indians on the continent. The spectacle of 200 Indian fishermen constantly harassed by two state departments representing some 3,000,000 whites and aided behind the scenes by federal officials who were sworn to protect the Indians demonstrated the basic inequality of the American way of life more eloquently than had Wounded Knee or Sand Creek. America had not come far in the intervening century.

Tribal councils were rather reluctant to engage in the struggle to protect treaty rights. The National Congress of American Indians came to be dominated by a few larger tribes that lived rather comfortably while their brethren from the smaller tribes were pushed around. But for one period in 1966–67 even these lethargic political leaders saw the danger that was confronting them.

By early 1966 the Poverty program was spending substantial sums in Community Action Programs on the respective reservations. The basic theory of the Office of Economic Opportunity was to involve the poor in all decisions affecting their lives. Thus tribal councils had early become sponsoring agencies for the various Poverty programs operating on the reservations. This development meant that suddenly millions of dollars were being subcontracted to the tribal governments for operation. With funds of their own to operate programs, many tribes began to show remarkable independence from the Bureau of Indian Affairs. And hence the trouble began.

After nearly a century of complete domination of tribal life the career bureaucrats of the Interior Department found themselves in a drastic position. In previous years they had only to submit their budgets, pacify the reservation leaders, listen to the continual complaints of a rural people who had no knowledge of the workings of the government, and await their retirement date. By 1966 these civil servants were extremely nervous and irritable. Congressmen and senators were asking pointed questions about the inability of the Bureau of Indian Affairs to solve basic problems and the efficiency of the Bureau was being unfavorably compared with the apparent success of the Poverty program.

Hence, in April of 1966 there was an effort by the officials of the Interior Department to convince congressmen on the appropriations committee to change the operation of the Poverty program and to give the funds now being diverted to tribal governments directly to the Interior Department for programming. Contending that the Interior Department had extensive experience with Indians and that the reservation people could not operate a large program successfully over a longer period of time, they asked that all funds used in the Poverty program for Indians simply be included in Interior's annual budget.

The impact of this plan would have been to deprive the tribal councils of some $40,000,000 in community action funds which they were then contracting from the Office of Economic Opportunity. The various action projects on reservations were already achieving more true community participation with that small amount than Interior officials had allowed even with their massive budget totaling close to $320,000,000 a year. It was a real crisis for the tribal governing bodies who had tasted their first real freedom since the Great Depression.

In April of 1966 a meeting of the tribes was called to coincide with a meeting of the Bureau of Indian Affairs in Santa Fe, New Mexico. The Bureau meeting was advertised as a means of letting the high Bureau officials gather with Stewart Udall, then Secretary of the Interior, and directly responsible for Indian programs, to decide what was best for reservation development. For three days, two meetings were held simultaneously. The Bureau of Indian Affairs met at a little green Episcopal church in town while the assembled tribes met at the federal building three blocks away.

Sixty-two tribes answered the call for meeting. With their already considerable experience operating the community action programs and sensing a heady success when the bureaucratic front began to melt, the tribal leaders planned out a series of policy resolutions that would come to fruition in later years. The foremost of these was subcontracting of agency functions to the tribal governments along the same guidelines as the Poverty program. An old law, the "Buy Indian Act," allowed the Bureau of Indian Affairs to subcontract services and purchase of materials to any Indian or Indian tribe. Yet this law was rarely used. It was the consensus of the tribes at Santa Fe that the tribes gradually take over the operation of the Bureau of Indian Affairs by subcontracting as many of its functions as possible.

At first the Bureau officials would not allow Indian delegates into their conference. This was particularly galling to the Indian meeting, since representatives of the national churches and a representative of one of the old-line Indian interest groups were attending the meeting. Breaking through this ancient alliance of white friends and career civil servants was not originally a goal of the tribal meeting. But it became apparent to many delegates that they might again be squeezed out of all considerations and the policies of the old alliance would once again be put into effect. It was this coalition that had made the allotment process so destructive and had resulted in the loss of the Indian land base.

The result of the Interior meeting was the announcement that the Secretary of the Interior would consult with the various tribal leaders and, on the basis of this consultation, present to Congress the following year, a massive piece of legislation tentatively entitled the "Omnibus Bill," which would update and solve all the tribal problems. But when the meeting of tribal leaders asked for an advisory committee to the Secretary of the Interior to assist in drawing up the legislation, they were turned down, thus indicating that Interior officials had their own ideas of what was meant by consultation.

By the summer of 1966 it was apparent that there would be no effort to consult with the tribal representatives. Rumors began to float through the various government agencies that legislation was being prepared in spite of the promise by Udall that Indians would share in the creation of the Omnibus Bill. The National Congress of American Indians managed to secure a copy of the proposed legislation and in September of that year passed out copies to every tribe in the land. From that point on, it was downhill for the new program. In a series of meetings covering the major areas of Indian population, the tribes stood firm for the principle of consultation and the legislation, when it was finally introduced, received only perfunctory consideration by congressional committees and then died.

The first meeting of the consultation tour taken by then Commissioner Robert Bennett was indicative of the rising expectations of the Indian people. In Minneapolis when the tribal leaders were called together to discuss the new legislation, a group of Indians living in the Twin Cities demonstrated against the policies of the Bureau in that urban area. Some minor changes in procedure were effected but the success of the demonstration foretold the manner in which techniques were changing. Following the Minneapolis demonstration, the Indians of that city organized the American Indian Movement, an activist group that was prepared to challenge the arbitrary manner in which the Bureau of Indian Affairs administered its program for off-reservation Indian people.

In the years following Minneapolis, the American Indian Movement, nicknamed "A.I.M." expanded its operations over most of the Midwest. It became the most sophisticated Indian activist group, with branches in Milwaukee, Chicago, Denver, Rapid City, South Dakota, Cleveland, and Spokane, Washington. In its home city of Minneapolis, A.I.M. concentrated on eliminating the discriminatory practices of the local city government. The chief practice they opposed was enforcement of city ordinances against the resident Indian population.

For nearly a century the Chippewa living in the northern part of the state had come to the Twin Cities to seek employment. Gradually little Indian neighborhoods formed, usually around certain bars where the men would go at night after work. During this time the practice had grown up of arresting the Indians for drunkenness and disturbing the peace whether they were doing so or not. Technically it could be called "preventive detention." In practical terms it meant that the police could pad their records by inflating them with statistics representing Indians unfairly arrested.

A.I.M. organized an Indian Patrol to conduct surveillance of police activities in areas predominantly Indian. Choosing areas which showed the highest arrest records, A.I.M. relentlessly followed the police and checked every arrest they attempted to make. After nearly a year of surveillance there were no arrests of Indians made. A.I.M. proved beyond a doubt that the police practices had been discriminatory and that once proper procedures were followed in determining arrests that Indians were no more lawbreakers than any other group.

While the American Indian Movement was expanding its influence throughout the Midwest, another movement was beginning on the West Coast. Centered in the San Francisco Bay area were the universities of California and Stanford with their thousands of activist-minded students. The Bay area also contained a substantial number of Indians who had moved to the coast in the last twenty-five years. When the ideologies of the student began to influence the resident Indian population, Indian activism took on a new twist.

Sometimes identifying with the Third World Movement, sometimes as an offshoot of the activism and ideology of Berkeley, small groups of Indian students began to make themselves felt. They began to develop a militancy and a willingness to go farther than any other group of Indians had ever gone to make their point. The problem they faced was that few of them had ever lived on reservations and there was an inability of some to identify with the philosophies of the tribal leaders who controlled the reservations. With this split, based primarily on residency and experience, the urban Indians began to appear as a threat to reservation existence.

In November 1969 a crisis developed in the Bay area that radically changed the nature of the national Indian community. The San Francisco Indian Center which had served the Indians of the Bay area for a number of years burned down following a meeting of Indian centers. With no center to which they could relate, the Indians of the Bay area were cast adrift in confusion. Appeals to the Bureau of Indian Affairs were useless since the Bureau had already determined that urban Indians would not receive services from its regular budget.

In casting about for a new location for an Indian center, eyes began to turn toward a small island in San Francisco Bay—Alcatraz, the abandoned federal prison. The rush was on.

In two different invasions the island was secured and the young Indian activists achieved world-wide attention overnight. Alcatraz was the master stroke of Indian activism. It was a symbol with which anyone in the world could identify. A stark forbidding island topped with a crumbling penitentiary, barren and useless. It was, the invading activists declared, exactly like an Indian reservation. And Americans quickly got the point.

Alcatraz inspired young Indians everywhere and its organization, Indians of All Tribes, was quickly copied all over the country. Almost instantaneously the nation was blanketed by groups calling themselves Indians of All Tribes and they meant business. An activist roll call comparable to the Civil Rights roll call of Selma, Birmingham, and Memphis was quickly made up. "Indianness" was judged on whether or not one was present at Alcatraz, Fort Lawton, Mount Rushmore, Detroit, Sheep Mountain, Plymouth Rock, or Pitt River. The activists took over and controlled the language, the issues, and the attention that other Indians had worked patiently and quietly to build.

By late 1970 the tribal leaders were cringing in fear that the activists would totally control Indian Affairs. Old issues of taxation, treaty rights, tribal sovereignty, land consolidation, and economic development were being completely neglected as the federal government and the American public were responding to the demands of the Indian activists. But it was the tribal leaders' own fault that the activists had parlayed Alcatraz into a national phenomenon. For decades the N.C.A.I. and other national groups had cast aside young people and urban Indians in favor of local reservation politicians. They had no reason to expect that these people, cast aside and unwanted, would suddenly rally to their aid.

The situation was deeper and more serious than that however. Almost every Indian active on the national scene had missed the significance of Alcatraz. They all looked at Alcatraz in terms of land restoration, and when balancing seventeen acres of rock in San Francisco Bay against the possible loss of the Colville Reservation in Washington state which was in danger of being terminated, or against the return of Blue Lake to Taos Pueblo, 44,000 acres of sacred land, no one could see why Alcatraz should have any importance.

If the tribal leaders had rallied to the cause of Alcatraz immediately and used it correctly as a symbol of land restoration legislation that was badly needed by the tribes they could have redoubled the effectiveness of the activism while using the movement to project real needs of reservations into the area of policy consideration. But the tribal leaders' first inclination was to avoid the issue and withhold support and this doomed them thereafter from raising their issues in a context in which they could have gained public support.

Nor did the young activists take the time to examine the issues that affected the reservations. They were centered primarily in the colleges and young working classes. Heirship land problems, taxation of Indian allotments, and economic development had little meaning for them. There was little available literature to inform them had they been interested. And tribal chairmen did nothing to inform or cooperate with the activists to bring them into Indian Affairs as an action arm of national Indian politics.

Thus this unfortunate combination of circumstances resulted in activism for activism's sake and irrational fears on the part of reservation political leaders that their influence was being undermined. Indian Affairs disintegrated into a confused state and no one could conceive of any way to bring the diverse groups into one unified front for any kind of action or program. Conferences split between activists and tribal chairmen, each suspicious of the other and neither willing to grant the validity of the other person's ideas of programs.

The situation was further marred by the appearance of pseudo-organizations of Indians. Charismatic Indians who had a spectacular style of speaking began to make their appearance. By simply publishing a newspaper, claiming an unusually large membership, and appearing at every Indian conference, a number of individuals were able to influence events far beyond their actual individual following, if indeed they had any following. After all, who would check a nonexistent membership list in the middle of a conference to determine if the speaker represented any Indians at all? Once started, the contemporary Indian movement expanded beyond any boundaries ever conceived at the start of the decade by the youth in Chicago in 1961. There were no ground rules and no channels by which ground rules could be constructed.

One thing that the Indian activist movement did prove was that competent leadership existed off the reservations as well as on the tribal councils. People such as Stella Leach of Alcatraz; Bernie White Bear of Fort Lawton; Fred Lane of Seattle; Dennis Banks, Clyde Bellcourt, and Russell Means of A.I.M.; and other activists could easily have chaired the larger tribes with outstanding results. Leadership was not confined to reservation councils. A great deal of it existed in the activist groups.

And conversely the movement showed that some respected tribal leaders could only function in an atmosphere in which there was no competition. If confined only to the internal politics of the National Congress of American Indians or regional groups such as the Northwest Affiliated Tribes these people were adequate. But once faced with a new situation and intelligent young rivals, long-standing Indian leaders were unable to function and resorted to tactics of fear in an effort to buttress their reputations.

When the activist years are considered in a historical perspective the situation has little novelty. The confusion of the present was mirrored in the efforts of Little Turtle, Pontiac, and Tecumseh to create a coalition of tribes and their subsequent failure to maintain a united front in the face of constant opposition by the invading white men. Within the currents of historical movement it has been exceedingly difficult for anyone to properly assess his actual situation in time to respond effectively. Only in those rare moments when religious fervor enables a people to coalesce for action have any significant changes been made.

Insofar as the activist movement had triggered off a return to ancient tribal customs, then, it could be counted as an important development in the red man's historical drama upon this continent. For by returning to Indian religions, by adopting the traditional customs by which tribal members related one to another, by forming useful and efficient alliances with forces in contemporary society, by these means alone could the red men ensure their survival.

The beginnings of such a movement were clearly evident in a meeting of the traditional medicine men of the tribes, which was held on the Crow Reservation in Montana in the summer of 1970. Originally organized by a group of anthropologists from Monteith College in Detroit against the advice of supposedly knowledgeable Indian political leaders, the conference was an unqualified success. After a week's meeting in which ideas and evaluations of the contemporary scene were made, the rapid movement of Indian emotions toward the traditional values was evident to everyone. No one had dreamed that the offshoot of activism had been to revive the inherent strengths of the basic tribal beliefs to the point that they were beginning to dominate every decision made by Indians.

A long time ago Chief Seattle had warned that the white man would never be alone in his civilization and that the Indian dead were not really dead but still roamed and walked the land. Even Wovoka had foreseen the day when the irresistable movement of Indians would reclaim the continent. The meeting at Crow had made clear that this time was approaching. It remained only for the religious leader to arise and integrate all of the diverse strands of political, economic, religious, and social movements into one strong contemporary Indian structure. For the red man, at least, the drama was taking on a special significance.

PART III

JAPANESE AMERICANS: THE "MODEL MINORITY" IN PERSPECTIVE

RUSSELL ENDO

The Japanese Americans are probably among the least understood ethnic groups in America. Prior to World War II they were virtually unknown except in Hawaii and on the Pacific Coast where the group was largely concentrated, and even in those areas they had often been regarded with considerable distrust as an unassimilable alien element. The federal decision during World War II to evacuate West Coast Japanese Americans and place them in concentration camps brought a greater degree of national attention. Their subsequent dispersal into other parts of the country and their dramatic progress during the past three decades have made them more widely known. Nevertheless many Americans remain unaware of the basic experiences of this group.

Compared with other American racial and ethnic groups, the number of Japanese Americans appears relatively small. The 1970 census counted approximately 590,000 Americans of Japanese descent scattered throughout the

NOTE: Several people made comments on an earlier draft of this introduction, and the author would especially like to thank James Morishima, Frank Miyamoto, George Rivera, and Calvin Takagi.

country, although located primarily in Hawaii (217,307), California (213,280), Washington (20,335), Illinois (17,299), New York (20,351), and several additional Western states.[1] Japanese Americans form a majority of the Hawaiian population while elsewhere they are a minority, even in areas of their heaviest concentration around Los Angeles, San Francisco, Seattle, Chicago, New York, and Denver.

Despite their number, the Japanese Americans are a significant ethnic group. The general story of their history, culture, communities, and contributions is itself worthy of attention, but certain features of their experience make them of particular interest. Unlike most other American immigrant groups, the Japanese Americans could be distinguished on the basis of their physical or racial features as well as their cultural differences. This fact made them easily identifiable targets for oppression and presented a major obstacle to their progress in American society. The evacuation and internment during World War II was a unique discriminatory event that created another serious obstacle and raised important moral and legal issues. Yet even with a long history of racial problems, the Japanese Americans have remarkably achieved a middle-class status and earned widespread acceptance and respect. The problems and differences that currently beset the group, however, are an indication that upward mobility may not be a sufficient condition for group success.

HISTORY

Small numbers of Japanese students, laborers, and pioneer settlers journeyed to the United States during the two decades prior to 1885, but it was not until after Japan repealed a restrictive emigration policy in that year that significant numbers of migrants began to leave.[2] The Japan of that era was moving from the feudal system of the Tokugawa rulers into a period of rapid industrialization and urbanization under Emperor Meiji. However, most migrants were attracted by economic opportunities available in America. Others were students, adventurers, or evaders of military conscription. The relative successes of some early migrants and the development of economic and social networks within the immigrant communities undoubtedly encouraged the ensuing migrants. Large numbers first stopped in Hawaii where they provided labor on the sugar plantations. Other migrants made their way directly to the mainland, eventually settling in the West and especially in California. Most of the migrants initially retained their identification with Japan and fully intended to return after a brief stay.

It is important to bear in mind the numbers of Japanese immigrants to the United States in light of later anti-Japanese agitation. During the peak years of 1901–1908, 125,000 entered, and the total number up to the immigration closure of 1924 was 300,000.[3] This migration was miniscule when compared with the millions that arrived on the East Coast during this same period from Eastern and Southern Europe. During the peak years, Japanese comprised only 1.7 per cent of the immigrants to this country.[4] Simultaneously, some were returning to Japan, and therefore the total population was actually less than these statistics indicate. The Japanese in America numbered 72,000 in 1910 and 111,000 in 1920. In 1920, the Japanese made up only 0.1 per cent of the American population and 2.1 per cent of the people in California.[5] Clearly, immigration from Japan did not constitute the inundation by a "yellow tide" that alarmists claimed.

A large majority of the immigrants came from rural farming areas in the southern ken or prefectures of the island of Honshu, and from the island of Kyushu. Most were literate and probably represented an ambitious segment of the Japanese population. Until the second decade of the 1900's, a high proportion of immigrants were young, single men. Early migrants worked as agricultural laborers in Hawaii and provided labor for mainland vegetable and fish canneries, logging and road construction crews, railroads, mines, smelters, and meatpackers. Later, significant numbers went into farm labor. In these early occupations, the Japanese usually proved to be industrious and generally uncomplaining about low wages and poor working conditions. Those characteristics made them valuable to their employers but aroused the animosity of various worker and labor groups.

Japanese tradition has long placed a high value on private enterprise. Motivated by such ambitions, large numbers of Japanese eventually moved from farm labor into farm proprietorship. This brought them into competition with other growers and diminished the size of the permanent farm labor force. While they were often forced to cultivate the least desirable land, Japanese farmers prospered through hard work and the application of intensive and specialized methods of farming. Their successes and the depletion of the farm labor pool resulted in efforts to restrict Japanese farming. In 1913 an Alien Land Act was passed in California that prohibited the ownership of farm land by Japanese aliens. Nevertheless, legal loopholes and the demand for agricultural products generated by World War I continued to stimulate their farming activity. Japanese agriculture reached a peak in California in 1920 with crops valued at $67 million.[6] A 1920 California Land Act and similar bills in other Western states reduced this growth in farming, although Japanese farmers continued to circumvent the intent of these laws. In subsequent years, Japanese farmers perfected the techniques of cultivation necessary to produce truck crops and a number of other vegetables, fruits, and rice. By the beginning of World War II, these farmers were growing between 25 to 90 per cent of the truck crops in California.[7] The Japanese made major contributions to West Coast agriculture through their productiveness, their introduction of new methods and crops, and their reclamation of thousands of acres of once useless lands.

Japanese immigrants settling in urban areas gradually moved into the ownership of small business enterprises such as hotels, stores, cafes, dry goods shops, and restaurants. Often these operations catered mainly to other Japanese. The development of businesses was helped by mutual aid arrangements, the pooling and loaning of capital, and the interpendence of many enterprises. Some

Japanese went into fishing, gardening, and flower growing and over time occupied a variety of sales, service, and eventually professional occupations.

These economic occurrences were paralleled by the growth of Japanese
communities in the cities and smaller towns of the West. Community development was enhanced by the later immigration of large numbers of women
and the establishment of families. In addition, community development was
promoted by residential segregation practices and the desire of the Japanese
to maintain a separate set of institutions with which they could provide
mutual assistance and some degree of protection. Besides small businesses, the
communities soon included economic, social, political, and religious organizations and groups, and less visible but intricate networks of family, friendship,
business, and organizational relationships and ties.[8]

Early in their history it becomes more appropriate to refer to the migrants
as Japanese Americans rather than Japanese, partly because of their gradual
acculturation and partly because most will decide to remain in America.
Japanese-American society has become structured into a number of more or
less age-discrete generational groupings, and these carry distinctive names
which will also now be used. The immigrant or first generation, presently very
elderly, are the *Issei*, and their children, born around World War I and now
well into middle age, are the second generation or *Nisei*. The current teenage
and young adult off-spring of the Nisei, born largely after World War II, are
the third generation or *Sansei*. The still emerging fourth generation are the
Yonsei. Japanese-American generational groupings are seen to differ not only
with respect to age, but also as to their backgrounds, experiences, and characteristic personality types and behaviors. Other important social groupings are
the Nisei educated in Japan (the *Kibei*), the World War II brides of American servicemen, and recent immigrants, businessmen, and students.

The development of economic activities and the growth of Japanese-
American communities did not proceed without serious problems. The Issei,
once welcomed as an important source of labor and a replacement for the now-
excluded Chinese immigrants, found themselves the target of economic and
social discrimination, often by organized anti-Japanese movements. Part of this
treatment can be traced to the persistence or reemergence of the hatred generated against the earlier Chinese immigrants. Because of Chinese economic
competition with white workingmen and their seemingly strange customs and
language, labor-stimulated anti-Chinese movements had previously emerged
on the West Coast, especially in California. These movements had succeeded
in passing numerous restrictive and harassing pieces of legislation culminating
in the Exclusion Act of 1882. They had also created a climate within which
discrimination and violence were condoned and even encouraged.

An anti-Japanese movement, primarily in California, first assumed prominence at the turn of the century. Only its major features are summarized
here.[9] As in the case of the Chinese, much of the impetus came from labor,
farm, and nativist organizations. In 1900 the first large-scale protest took place
in San Francisco. By 1905 the agitation had intensified as the *San Francisco*

Chronicle and other newspapers launched attacks against "the Japanese invasion." The Asiatic Exclusion League, a coalition of nearly seventy organizations, was founded and played a leading role in the agitation. The California Legislature passed unanimously an anti-Japanese resolution calling for an end to immigration; in each session over the next 40 years the Legislature continued to introduce anti-Japanese legislation. In 1906 the San Francisco School Board passed a resolution favoring the restriction of Japanese pupils to a segregated school. Protests by the Japanese government and concern expressed by President Theodore Roosevelt over possible international repercussions focused national attention on this incident. Roosevelt intervened and the order was rescinded.

After extensive negotiations between Japan and the federal government, an understanding was reached in 1908 known as the Gentleman's Agreement whereby the Japanese government voluntarily limited the emigration of laborers to the continental United States. The flow of migrants consequently subsided. But the Agreement did permit the entry of wives and relatives, and the years after 1908 saw a rapid influx of brides and wives. In 1913 the California Legislature passed the Alien Land Act prohibiting the ownership of farm lands by Japanese aliens and restricting farm leases to no more than three years. However many Issei placed their farm ownership in the names of their native-born offspring or white citizen friends and business associates. Angered by evasions of this Act, the continued growth of Japanese farming, and the numbers of immigrant women, the Legislature passed a tougher Land Act in 1920. By this time the anti-Japanese forces had the active support of many labor and nativist groups, politicians, civic leaders, and the sympathy of the general public. Their final triumph came in 1924 when, because of their pressures as well as racist and nativist sentiments throughout the country, the National Origins Act was passed by Congress. This Act assigned an immigration quota to most foreign nations and barred immigration from Japan.

The anti-Japanese legislation of this period did not specifically mention the Japanese Americans but instead "aliens ineligible for citizenship." This phrase was derived from a 1790 naturalization act and later laws. It points out the fact that the Issei were not eligible to become full citizens and were therefore denied the rights and protections guaranteed to most Americans. A 1914 challenge to these laws resulted in a 1922 Supreme Court ruling continuing the denial of citizenship. Not until 1952 were the Issei given the opportunity to become naturalized citizens.

The anti-Japanese laws and policies of this era were accompanied by blatant prejudice and discrimination on other levels. Stereotypes depicted the Japanese Americans as unassimilable, sly, greedy, dishonest, immoral, overly aggressive, and deliberately undercutting labor standards. These characterizations were perpetuated in attacks by the media and politicians. Many occupations outside of the community were closed to members of the group. Residential segregation was practiced, and a wide range of social, welfare, civic, and religious activities were inaccessible. Individual Japanese Americans were sub-

ject to assaults, and their businesses sometimes became targets for damage
or boycotts. In response to these incidents, public authorities usually provided
little sympathy or protection. One effect of this prejudice and discrimination
was to further isolate Japanese-American communities from the mainstream
of American life. The isolation, in turn, contributed to the persistence of
racism by preventing meaningful intergroup contacts. Isolation also hindered
the development of political resources that might have been used to exert
pressures for change.

The late 1920's and the 1930's were a time of slow yet steady economic
progress for the Issei.[10] Both agriculture and the urban businesses experienced
growth, and some Issei began moving into new occupational areas. A few
prospered, and their stories are in the finest "rags to riches" tradition. Much of
the Issei progress can be attributed to their ambition and their adherence
to traditional values, such as hard work, that closely resemble the American
ideals embodied in the Protestant Ethic. Also important was the mutual
support furnished by the community through its business and social networks,
which likewise grew and prospered during these years.

A significant event of this period was the emergence of the Nisei. As in
other immigrant groups, the second generation became much more Americanized than their parents, a situation which led to value conflicts and rejection of the traditional culture. The greater acculturation of the Nisei
resulted in part from their education in American schools. Their excellent
academic performance was due to the heavy community and family emphasis
on education as a means of bettering one's position in society. On the other
hand, Nisei socialization within the family and community also resulted in
the retention of many ethnic values and norms. On the eve of World War II,
Japanese-American society encompassed two generations and had in the
Nisei an acculturated group, the members of which would later use their
education and ambition in an intense drive for middle-class status.

The Japanese attack on Pearl Harbor and the onset of World War II set
the stage for a tragedy of immense proportions.[11] During the first weeks of
the war, an apprehensive Japanese-American population took great pains to
reaffirm their loyalty and support for the United States. Some politicians and
private citizens publically announced their sympathies for the group. Nevertheless curfew regulations were imposed and certain enemy aliens arrested,
including over 2,000 relatively harmless Issei community leaders. Anti-Japanese
sentiment was reawakened in California by nativist and patriotic groups, the
press, and farm and labor organizations that stood to gain by the removal of
Japanese-American competitors. Rumors were spread about Issei and Nisei
disloyalty, their engagement in espionage and sabotage, their treachery at
Pearl Harbor, and their potential for assisting any Japanese invasion of the
U.S. mainland. In a population nervous about the war and indoctrinated with
anti-Japanese sentiment, fear spread rapidly. Popular opinion turned against
the group and large numbers of major Western politicians jumped on the
bandwagon. Pressures mounted for an evacuation of Japanese Americans away

from the Pacific Coast. After a complex chain of events, President Franklin Roosevelt signed Executive Order 9066 in February 1942 authorizing the establishment of strategic military areas and the removal from them of persons viewed as security threats. Congress passed Public Law 503 giving military commanders further authority to carry out the provisions of the Executive Order. General John DeWitt was designated as the military commander assigned to carry out the evacuation. DeWitt set up a military area encompassing the western halves of California, Washington, and Oregon and portions of Arizona from which Japanese Americans were to be removed. A series of exclusion orders were issued, and from March to November 1942, 110,000 Japanese Americans, two-thirds of them American-born citizens, were uprooted to ten hastily constructed relocation centers or concentration camps. Besides the tremendous social and psychological costs, the evacuation was a major economic disaster since many evacuees were given insufficient time to sell or securely store belongings and prevent the eventual loss of the businesses and farms.

The first stop for the evacuees were fifteen assembly centers, often located at racetracks or fairgrounds. From there they were moved to ten relocation centers in desolate areas of the West and the humid bottomlands of Arkansas. The centers or camps consisted mainly of tarpaper barracks surrounded with barbed wire fences and guard towers. The housing lacked privacy and space, and the evacuees had to construct their own furniture from scrap lumber. Weather was usually a problem, being very hot or cold, rainy or humid, depending upon the location and the season. Meals were eaten in common messhalls. The camps became self-contained communities with the evacuees providing the manpower and also organizing social groups and activities. The evacuees were reasonably cooperative, but many were understandably concerned and upset or angry. Intense feelings of hatred and rebellion did develop, particularly among some Issei and Kibei. Outbreaks of violent resistance and civil disobedience occurred in a few assembly centers and most camps. Because of their past or present activities or their responses to controversial "loyalty" questions on a 1943 questionnaire, certain evacuees were considered dangerous and segregated into the camp at Tule Lake, California. This camp was the scene of frequent unrest.[12]

It is difficult to measure the negative aspects of the evacuation, though the breakup of Japanese-American communities, the financial losses, and the psychological blow of continued oppression after two decades of progress were certainly significant. The camp experience itself generated unhealthy group differences and fostered a certain amount of government dependence previously unknown. It also had unsettling effects on family structure. Husbands were no longer major sources of income and hence lost prestige. The communal life and lack of privacy weakened traditional family controls. However the camps did introduce the Japanese Americans to new occupations and to participation in community decision making. And since important positions were held by Nisei, this experience eased their transition into leadership roles.

For many, these years were a time to reconsider personal and group identity, although relatively few asked to be repatriated to Japan.[13]

The Japanese Americans' cooperation with evacuation orders and their relative compliance in the camps was probably the cumulative result of a number of factors, including their fear and apprehensiveness, their lack of political power, and the counseling of cooperation by many young Nisei leaders. Also important were cultural values that stressed obedience to authority and the widespread belief that cooperation would eventually prove group loyalty and lead to the opportunity to make a comeback. Finally, the suddenness and shock of the Pearl Harbor attack, the speed with which ensuing events took place, and the restrictive curfew regulations would have seriously hampered any early efforts at group organization and effective resistance.[14]

A small number of Japanese Americans were in vigorous opposition to the evacuation, and a few, including Gordon Hirabayashi, Fred Korematsu, Minoru Yasui, and Mitsuye Endo, took their protests to the courts in long and lonely attempts to challege its legality. Subsequent Supreme Court rulings declared that the initial curfew was legal, that military necessity could be used to justify exclusion from certain geographical areas, but that it was unlawful to detain loyal Nisei citizens in the camps.[15] By the time of the latter decision in late 1944, increasing sympathies for the Japanese Americans and the declining of the war had already prompted the closure of some camps and the release of a number of Nisei to jobs and colleges in the Midwest and East. The exclusion orders were removed in January 1945 and most Japanese Americans allowed to return home.

Part of the sympathy for the Japanese Americans resulted from the participation of Nisei in the Armed Forces during the conflict. In 1943 two all-Nisei infantry units were formed largely of volunteers from Hawaii and the camps on the mainland. These units, the 100th Battalion and the 442nd Regimental Combat Team, fought with great distinction in Europe and were showered with military honors. Other Nisei language and intelligence specialists performed well against the Japanese in the Pacific. For many Japanese Americans and others, this effort was viewed as proof of the group's loyalty to this country.[16]

The evacuation raises two major questions: why did it occur, and was it justified? An answer to the first question requires a thorough examination of the history of anti-Japanese agitation, the climate of the nation just after Pearl Harbor, and the reasons behind the anti-Japanese sentiments of the press, nativist and patriotic groups, farm and labor organizations, and political leaders. Political events leading up to the evacuation and governmental decision making which determined major policies need to be scrutinized. Finally, an answer must take into consideration the reactions of the Japanese Americans, their lack of political power, their cultural background, and the isolation of their communities.[17]

The answer to the second question is undoubtedly "No, it was not justified." In retrospect it is clear that Japanese Americans posed no threat to the security of the nation. No verified cases of espionage or sabotage were ever recorded. At the time of the removal, the nearest Japanese enemy activity was over 5,000 miles away, and the Army itself felt there was little possibility of a West Coast invasion. Individuals who were considered dangerous, albeit incorrectly, had been arrested, and others could have been screened out without removing the entire group. Any revision of the "no" answer must also explain two anomalies. In Hawaii, the scene of the initial attack and the home of a very large Japanese-American population, no massive evacuation took place. And despite substantial evidence of espionage activity by Germans in this country, no moves were made to indiscriminately round up German or Italian Americans, whether citizens or aliens. It is apparent that the security justification was false, and that the entire episode was a tragic error and a miscarriage of justice.

Some of the evacuees settled in the Midwest or East, but many returned to California and the West. Public opinion had changed, yet pockets of hostility remained and incidents of terrorist activity occurred. An unsympathetic California Legislature allocated funds for the filing of escheat actions, prosecutions of alleged Issei violations of the land laws. In a series of legal tests, the courts eventually ruled the escheat actions and also the land laws unconstitutional. An attempt to amend the California constitution to include the entire 1920 Land Act was defeated in 1946, and other states slowly removed restrictive legislation from their books.[18]

Japanese Americans fought hard for these and other legislative and legal gains. After a difficult political history, the 1952 Walter-McCarran Immigration and Naturalization Act was passed, creating an opportunity for the Issei to become naturalized citizens and eliminating the bar to immigration from Japan and other Asian nations. While Japan was only given a small, token immigration quota, a revised 1965 Immigration Act did away with formal national quotas. However, the memory of evacuation lingered in the Internal Security Act passed during the Joe McCarthy era. In its Title II, the Act authorized the Attorney General, upon Presidential declaration of an "internal security emergency," to apprehend and detain persons if there were reasonable grounds to believe they would engage in espionage or sabotage. An internal security emergency could be created by an invasion, declaration of war, or internal insurrection. Title II allowed for mass detention on mere suspicion as a precautionary measure, and did not provide for normal court and jury trials. Several camps were actually constructed and maintained during the 1950's.[19] Title II gained new meaning with its threatened use against black militants in the late 1960's. After several years of effort led by the Japanese Americans, Title II was repealed by Congress in 1971.

It has been estimated that the evacuation cost the American taxpayer about $248 million and the Japanese Americans $400 million. A 1948 Claims Act was passed to recompense the evacuees, and by the 1950 filing deadline, 23,600 claims had been registered for $132 million, one third of the estimated loss. Most claims were only for household items; 60 per cent were less than $2,500. A large number of families were unable to adequately document losses and therefore could not file. Perhaps predictably, the government was not generous in restitution. Claims were settled slowly, the last being paid in 1965, and many were challenged in court. In the end only $38 million was paid out, less than 10 per cent of the total cost. Even worse, claims had to be made in 1942 dollars yet were paid in the inflated currency of the postwar period.[20]

With little economic or community basis upon which to rebuild, it is a remarkable tribute to the Japanese Americans that since the war they have earned widespread acceptance and moved into the American middle class.[21] The general group strategy has been the continuation of one begun in earlier days, that of accommodation rather than confrontation, of education, hard work, and patience until opportunities became available. The educational attainments of the Nisei have been an important part of the strategy. Education has been viewed in an instrumental sense, as a means of getting a good job. The heavy emphasis on academic achievement is indicated by high grades, by the large proportion going on to college, and by 1940, 1950, and 1960 Census statistics showing Japanese Americans completing more years of school than any other racial or ethnic group, including whites.[22]

These educational attainments have been reflected in occupational mobility and increased levels of income. In 1940, 19 per cent of the urban Japanese Americans were classified as laborers and 5 per cent in professional and technical occupations; in 1960 the respective percentages were 7 per cent and 26 per cent, and 56 per cent were classified as white collar. The percentage of Japanese Americans in farm labor jobs has declined markedly from 1940 to 1960.[23] The 1960 statistics placed the Japanese Americans in a better position than any nonwhite racial or ethnic group, although they were slightly under the occupational levels for whites. Income statistics from 1940 to 1960 showed the same kind of increase and the same general position in 1960 with respect to nonwhite groups and whites.[24] The 1970 figures will probably reveal additional gains but little change in relative positions.

Occupationally, the Nisei have gone into a variety of jobs in education, agriculture, business, and certain of the professions such as engineering, architecture, dentistry, optometry, medicine, accounting, and law. Nisei education and work have been important, though one cannot discount the greater opportunities available in an expanding postwar economy and the changing attitudes toward Japanese Americans.

With mobility along the occupational and income dimensions has come the adoption of the middle-class life style and many of its norms and values. For some this has meant a move to the suburbs. Residential concentrations continue to exist in most Western cities, but they are usually maintained by choice and have mostly moved from the oldest parts of the inner city. The Nisei have used American models in developing their organizations and institutions. And while interest in these remains high, there is also an increasing participation in groups and organizations on the outside and a lessening of dependence upon the community. However primary friendship patterns and marriage choices have generally remained within the group. The Sansei children have been raised in a partly traditional, partly American manner. Their early environment has often been the ethnic community, though one different from that which their Nisei parents knew. Many Sansei have adopted the values and orientations of their parents, such as the emphasis on educational achievement, the drive toward greater mobility and assimilation, and participation both within the Americanized community and on the outside. Other Sansei have been moving in new directions as will be seen below.

One recent source of concern for Japanese Americans has been that large numbers of individuals are not found in certain occupational areas, nor are they often in key upper-level positions for which they are qualified by education and experience. This may be due to the continued existence of subtle discrimination and also the accommodation strategy of the group. The Nisei especially have been reluctant to push for expanded job opportunities and have instead trained themselves (using education in a job-training manner) and waited for opportunities to appear.[25] The net result has been an over-representation in fields such as gardening, technical-scientific occupations, and some businesses, and a relative underrepresentation in artistic-humanistic pursuits, social science occupations, and in politics.[26] In addition, many Nisei are overqualified for their positions, and some are passed over for promotions to higher levels of power, influence, and visibility. This latter problem can be seen in statistics which show that despite the high correlation between education and income, Japanese Americans with higher levels of education than whites achieve lower levels of income.[27]

This characteristic of the economic area is one of several concerns facing the Japanese Americans today. Others include the gradual loss of older community institutions and organizations and the dying of the traditional culture. The existence of subtle and at times overt forms of discrimination and prejudice have become an increasing irritant. Other concerns are the welfare of the aged Issei and increases in delinquency, divorce, crime, and mental illness. Most of these issues have only begun to receive serious recognition and attention in the past several years.

CULTURE AND COMMUNITY

Cultural patterns include many elements, but the most central are norms, values, and beliefs. Norms are rules and procedures that serve as guidelines for appropriate behavior. Values and beliefs are attitudes about those things considered worthwhile. These elements are usually woven in consistent and intricate patterns.

As with any culture, that of the Japanese Americans is complex. It consists of elements from the traditional Japanese and the American middle-class cultures. Here only a few of the more important Japanese-derived elements will be discussed. In a recent study, Mamoru Iga has found the following Japanese values to be more characteristic of Japanese Americans than whites:

conformity and obedience; compromise and yielding (as opposed to aggressiveness); obligation and dependence, especially within the family; and aspiration and competitiveness. Other characteristic values are behavioral discipline
and an emphasis on the importance of group needs over those of the individual.[28] Harry Kitano points out that significant Japanese-derived norms
stress duty and obligation within a well-defined social system. Kitano also
argues that a complex of norms called the *enryo* syndrome explains much
Japanese-American behavior. *Enryo* is a sense of modesty in the presence of
one's superiors and manifests itself in hesitancy and reticence, behavioral
reserve, noncommital answers, and the tendency to play down one's own
characteristics and accomplishments. An important motive behind *enryo* is the
individual's concern with how other people will react to or think about his
behavior.[29] Other important values are *ga-man*, the suppression of anger, and
shikatagani, the acceptance of fate. Such values and norms are apt to produce
individuals who are obedient, quiet, conforming, and highly correct in their
behavior. Kitano notes that these values and norms function well in Japanese
society where everyone understands their use and knows how to play the
game. They have helped the Japanese Americans by making them look good
to others and by being integral parts of the accommodation strategy. However, many feel that they are no longer useful and that Japanese Americans
must cultivate the more aggressive, less conforming and obedient forms of
behavior that exist in American society.[30]

   Several notes of caution are properly in order. Japanese-American culture
includes many more elements than have been described above. The impact
of culture varies by individuals according to their upbringing and experiences.
Major differences are noticeable by generation, with the more acculturated
Nisei and Sansei exhibiting fewer of these characteristics in their behavior.
Finally, variations occur by geographical area, urban-rural residence, and extent
of participation in ethnic communities.

   The concept of community is a more difficult one to define. It includes
notions about areas of residence and of commercial and cultural districts.
Before World War II, Japanese Americans lived in rural areas or near the
central areas of cities and towns on the Pacific Coast. Today urban concentrations still exist, but they are away from the central districts. In addition
there is more dispersion of the population into outlying neighborhoods.
Fewer Japanese Americans live in rural areas, and more can now be found in
the Midwest and on the East Coast. Before the war, many cities and towns
with sizable numbers of Japanese Americans had ethnic centers with businesses, churches, and other buildings. These areas were abandoned with the
evacuation and were never rebuilt on their former scale. Revitalization efforts
are presently under way in a few cities, though some new districts, such as
San Francisco's Japanese Cultural and Trade Center, emphasize tourism.

   The concept of community usually includes the characteristic of a shared
sense of identification and group awareness. This arises out of common cul-

tural patterns and experiences, and from in-group marriages, friendship networks, and organizational participation. For many Japanese Americans, this characteristic of community has endured. However, some Sansei are attempting to redefine its meanings.

Another useful view of community is as a set of distinct institutions. These develop from common cultural patterns and experiences, in-group social relationships, and a sense of group identification. District institutions, in turn, reinforce these same variables.[31] In the Issei-dominated community of the prewar years, the major social and political institutions were the Japanese Associations, the *kenjinkai* or prefectural groups, and the Japanese newspapers and language schools. The Japanese Associations performed a protective function, ironing out individual and community problems, and organized social activities such as youth groups and picnics. *Kenjinkai* provided social services for the Japanese Americans from a particular *ken* or prefecture, sponsoring recreational activities, serving as employment agencies, and furnishing welfare assistance. Ken ties were important in friendships, marriage, and business. Japanese language newspapers were a vehicle of community communication and the only source of news for many Issei. Language schools were established to teach the Nisei Japanese and traditional values and ethics. While few learned the language well, lasting friendships were made at these schools.

In the postwar Nisei community, many of these earlier institutions declined in prominence. The Nisei developed social and political institutions patterned after American counterparts. The most important Nisei organization has been the Japanese-American Citizens League (JACL). The JACL was founded in 1930 from previous Nisei groups which were concerned with combatting discriminatory policies and asserting Nisei rights and responsibilities as American citizens. The JACL continued to emphasize these concerns and was prominent during the evacuation when its leaders counseled cooperation. After the war it was in the forefront of the struggle to recompense the Japanese Americans, eliminate restrictive legislation, and obtain the right of naturalization for the Issei. With a national membership, a Washington lobby, and a widely read newspaper (*The Pacific Citizen*), the JACL continues to be the major organization in the community. Its present activities are split between purely social and recreational pursuits and community concerns and problems—for instance, discrimination and the renewal of cultural centers. Other current Nisei groups are sports clubs, veterans organizations, and Nisei chapters of service clubs such as the Optimists and Lions.

Japanese-American occupations and businesses together with their supporting organizations make up the significant economic institutions in the community. In the early years, supportive organizations were the trade guilds, *kenjinkai*, argricultural groups, and informal associations among businesses. Another important source of support was the *tanomoshi*, a pooling of money with credit and interest. Later supporting groups were the business organizations and Japanese Chambers of Commerce which, in the postwar Nisei-dominated community, closely resembled their American cousins. Some continue to function effectively today. Other current sources of support are large Nisei-controlled businesses and investment capital from Japan.

Religious institutions include the Buddhist and Japanese Christian churches. The Christian churches handled a variety of services for the early immigrants, like job information and language training. Later welfare services, women's clubs, preschools, and kindergarten were provided. The moral and ethical lessons taught by the Christian churches were similar to those of the Buddhist church. The early Buddhist church exerted a conservative influence on the community, being a kind of repository for traditional culture and rituals. Over time, its organization and practices became Americanized and closely resembled those of the Christian church. However, in recent years, both have been seen as important links to the ethnic heritage, and churches help to sponsor language classes, cultural festivals, and similar activities.

Other community institutions, like the family, were initially distinctive and later modified their form as the Japanese Americans became more acculturated. The sole exception, as noted earlier, was the educational institution. Many Japanese Americans did attend special language schools, but they received the bulk of their education in American classrooms.

In summary, it can be seen that the Japanese-American community developed many separate and distinct institutions. In the early community, these institutions made the Japanese Americans somewhat self-sufficient, providing jobs and job training, welfare and social services, and exposure to religious, social, and civic roles and experiences that might otherwise have been unobtainable. These institutions allowed the group to cope with some of its problems. They also perpetuated traditional cultural patterns, making less difficult the social and psychological adjustment to American society and furnishing a basis for positive individual and group identity. In subsequent years, the Nisei changed these institutions, and while they became Americanized, they often remained segregated and had distinct ethnic qualities. At the same time, the Nisei began to participate more widely in the institutions of American society.

The development of separate institutions had negative as well as positive effects. Separate institutions tended to concentrate the Japanese Americans geographically and economically, increasing their visibility to opponents and possibly facilitating exploitation. The tightly knit aspect of the community hindered the use of opportunities on the outside (albeit limited) and prevented the development of needed resources, especially in the political realm. Separate institutions, even when patterned after American models, probably exerted (and continue to exert) a negative influence on greater assimilation through integration. This latter process was once seen as desirable by the vast majority of Japanese Americans, but some are questioning it today.

TODAY AND TOMORROW

Nearly three decades have passed since World War II, and the Japanese Americans have made considerable progress in the face of numerous obstacles. The media, once the nemesis of the group, have recently showered accolades upon it.[32] The picture now presented is one of a success story by a model minority, a group that started at the bottom and moved up through their own efforts and their adherence to values and behaviors that Americans find admirable. Many Japanese Americans accept and promote this picture, and it is certainly to the credit of the group that they have remained strong in the face of oppression and patiently accomplished so much in their brief history.

Yet there are dissenters among the Japanese Americans who take exception to what is rapidly becoming a new stereotype. The dissent has two basic rationales.[33] One is that if in fact the stereotype is valid, there are those who would use it and the Japanese Americans as examples to other racial and ethnic groups, especially the blacks, on how progress should be made in American society. Unfortunately, the effectiveness of the "hard work, patience, and accommodative strategy" was based on group characteristics not necessarily found in others, and upon external historical conditions that no longer exist. Present societal conditions, and the makeup and past experiences of other groups may dictate their use of different strategies.

The second rationale for dissent is probably more significant. It argues that progress has carried with it a heavy price, not only in terms of past suffering and losses, but also in terms of the present decline of the traditional community, the increase in cultural conflicts and consequent rise in mental illness, and the uncritical acceptance of American values and beliefs including prejudices and intolerances. This rationale for dissent also questions the success label itself and the educational, economic, and life-style criteria upon which it is based, noting gaps in areas of occupational attainment and community involvement and the existence of social problems such as delinquency, crime, and poverty among some of the aged Issei. In addition this line of dissent points to the continued existence of prejudice and discrimination as an indication of less-than-complete success and of an opportunity structure that still has limits. It is argued that the new success stereotype shields from the view of both insiders and outsiders the existence of Japanese-American problems and the costs associated with group progress, thereby hampering efforts to alleviate them. Needless to say, all Japanese Americans do not share the same perceptions of their current situation, nor do they all agree with this second rationale for dissent.

The existence of discrimination is one of the major bones of contention between those who accept and those who question the success stereotype. Though difficult to measure and often more subtle than in earlier years, discrimination persists, for instance, in the unavailability of housing in certain neighborhoods, the exclusion policies of private social clubs, the reluctance of some employers to hire or promote Japanese Americans, some evidence of quota systems in education for students and teaching-administrative staffs, the omission of the Japanese-American experience from textbooks and curriculum materials except in cursory or inaccurate treatments, the stereotyping of Asians in films and television programs and commercials, and the less frequent but existing discourtesies, insults, and stereotyping that occur in everyday face-to-face interaction. Particular acts of discrimination are sometimes directed only at Japanese Americans, though more often the same behaviors are exhibited toward all Asian Americans (and Asians), and at times are part of a general discrimination against all racial and ethnic groups. Those who question the success stereotype argue that these examples and others reveal the persistence of at least some degree of racism. Others not in agreement contend that they are isolated incidents that have been blown out of proportion by those trying to generate social activism in the community.

The challenge of the success and model-minority image is just one manifestation of a reawakening interest among Japanese Americans in themselves. The reawakening can be attributed to many sources including the black protest of the 1960's and the emergence of new forms of community and identity among other rocial and ethnic groups. The reawakening has two interrelated features. One is a renewed sense of ethnic consciousness and a consequent reexamination of community, culture, identity, and behavioral patterns. The other feature is a greater amount of community involvement.

Not all Japanese Americans can be identified with this reawakening, and attitudes toward it vary. A number of reasons might explain the lack of sympathy or support by many individuals. Some consider greater assimilation through further integration a more desirable or inevitable goal and see this reawakening as a passing phenomenon or a minor nuisance. Others feel that it may negate the gains made by the group and may even result in fewer opportunities in the future. A few Japanese Americans have concluded that success has been achieved and that no serious issues remain to be considered. Finally, there are those too complacent or too caught up in other activities to give the matter much consideration. While many Japanese Americans are in agreement with some or most aspects of the reawakening, fewer are active supporters. And though the two features of ethnic consciousness and community involvement are interrelated, probably far more people have been affected by or have responded to the former than the latter.

Community involvement has taken several forms, and the individuals or groups working in one area do not always recognize the priorities, strategies, or legitimacy of those in other areas. Community involvement for some means a new interest in Japanese culture, language, and traditions. For others, involvement means renewed participation or continuing service and social activity in existing community organizations and institutions. Some press for changes while others seek to perpetuate what presently exists. Another form of community involvement is the redevelopment of commercial and cultural centers like the planned multimillion-dollar renewal of the Little Tokyo district in central Los Angeles. Finally, for a small but visible and vocal segment of the community, involvement means an attack upon important social problems and the dissemination of accurate information about the group through research, curriculum reforms, ethnic studies, community exhibits, and lecture-discussions. These forms of involvement differ, but a general distinction can be made between the social-problems orientation and the others. And within the problems orientation, something of a cleavage exists between what might be labeled the liberals, both Nisei and Sansei—with their moderate social welfare goals and programs—and the more radical activists, primarily Sansei, who stress the development of new cultural patterns, the establishment of alternative community institutions, and the use of organization and power strategies to effect social change.

Though the Sansei activists are still very Japanese American in their values and behavior, they are engaged in a conscious break with characteristics of the existing culture and community such as the heavy stress on educational and occupational achievement, the emphasis on obedience and conformity, the sometimes closed nature of social activities and friendship-marriage patterns, and what are seen as predominant Nisei desires for assimilation and acceptance of middle-class notions of materialism and security.[34] The breaking process has led to severe criticisms of the Nisei accommodation strategy and their nonresistance to discrimination, particularly during the evacuation period. It has also led to criticisms of conservative Nisei-dominated community institutions and to community involvements that do not lead toward an increasing emphasis on social issues. The breaking process has necessitated the development of new emphases, however diverse or tentative. Among the more apparent are an identification with other Asian groups (including those abroad) and their problems, a concern with community organization and mobilization, criticism of the success stereotype, awareness of problems like discrimination, and attempts to redefine the group's relationship to American society through a reexamination of Asian-American history and elements of traditional Japanese culture. The breaking process has led to the establishment of alternative organizations and groups such as drop-in centers, legal and medical clinics, film making and artistic collectives, newspapers, journals, ethnic studies programs, and community action programs. For some individuals, the process has been accompanied by the creation of new self-identities and more aggressive political and interpersonal forms of behavior.

Beyond this brief description, it is difficult to adequately characterize Sansei activism because of its many variations and changes. For example, Sansei groups engage in activities that range from volunteer community service to militant political action, and group ideologies vary. Some groups are primarily community-based while others operate from college or high school campuses. Groups may be supported by existing organizations such as churches or the JACL, or they might be funded from local or national social service or research grant sources.

Some Sansei activists have been quick to overemphasize their impact and the extent of their support. But given the many tentative steps, variations, and reorientations, some opponents have been just as ready to dismiss this activism as a passing fad, an adolescent attempt to work out identity problems, a bad emulation of black or student protest rhetoric and behavior, the work of a few self-aggrandizing groups of radicals, or a temporary manifestation of the generation gap in the affluent middle class. Whatever one's perceptions, this activism has captured the attention, if not active support, of many (though certainly not all) Sansei. The activism has also created a greater awareness of group problems, and it has been influential in prompting more social involvement among existing organizations such as the JACL. While many Japanese Americans would venture beyond this point in defending or attacking Sansei activism, it is best to reserve judgment until further successes and failures unfold within the next few years.

Sociologically, the Sansei activism is worthy of immediate attention. It represents a first attempt by a portion of the third generation to break away from the domination of the others; it is a challenge to the once predominant strategy of accommodation to achieve assimilation; and it is a somewhat unique movement within a basically middle-class ethnic group. It also serves as a reminder that group progress does not necessarily bring an end to problems or the rapid disappearance of racial and ethnic groups.

The Sansei activism is sometimes taken to be synonymous with the recent political development of the community, especially by activists in other racial and ethnic groups. In actuality, recent political development can be viewed as a separate phenomenon that does not completely coincide with any single aspect of the current Japanese-American ethnic consciousness and community involvement. The term "political development" is appropriate because Japanese Americans do not have an extensive history of political activity. On the Pacific Coast in prewar years, such activity was mainly confined to scattered efforts to combat discrimination. For instance, Japanese Associations filed court actions against Alien Land Laws, and business organizations unified the community against white boycotts designed to drive down the competition of Japanese-American entrepreneurs. Further activity was deterred by the inability of the Issei to vote and their mistrust of a political process that so often was directed against them. The relative isolation of the community prevented the development of resources such as specialized knowledge, access to the mass media, outside connections, and political specialists. Political activity was also inhibited by cultural elements that emphasized obedience to authority, duty, conformity, and accommodation. After the war, some political activity was directed toward legal and legislative efforts to abolish discriminatory policies, win the right of naturalization, and eliminate immigration barriers. However, in Hawaii, where Japanese Americans had been elected to the state legislature in the 1930's, they became very prominent in politics at the state and local levels. Currently, one of the U.S. Senators from Hawaii, Daniel Inouye, is Japanese American (the other is Chinese American), as are both Congressional Representatives, Patsy Mink and Spark Matsunaga.

On the mainland, political development is now in an embryonic stage and is taking many forms. There is a new interest in conventional politics, including the running for state or local political office, and a greater amount of participation in general civic affairs through school boards, human relations councils, etc. There is an increase in political activity by some established community organizations, especially in fighting discrimination. Finally, there is the political activity of the Sansei activists, with its stress on community mobilization and the establishment of programs to aggressively attack social problems. Most efforts by the activists have not been coherent or sustained and, with some exceptions, there has been a relative absence of the militant protest and demonstrations that have characterized many black movements. Sansei political activity has not yet generated widespread community support nor the assistance of outside liberal allies. Consequently, efforts are directed at developing support and forging coalitions with additional Asian American or other racial and ethnic groups. In some locales, the Sansei have also turned to conventional politics, helping candidates for public office and attempting to influence the decisions making of governmental agencies.

As mentioned earlier, recent political development and the new ethnic consciousness and community involvement can be taken as separate though related phenomena. One does not necessarily enhance or contribute to the other. For instance, some who desire further assimilation see forms of political activity as either indicators of or a means to further progress. And, conversely, many who are involved in community work eschew any political activity. Neither is it possible simply to view greater assimilation away from ethnicity as retarding political development. Only with a degree of assimilation have Japanese Americans become fully aware of the benefits and the intricacies of the political process, while the retention of some older cultural values and norms would inhibit such activity. Political activity and the interest in ethnicity and community do coincide in the Sansei activism, but even here the relationship is complex. For example, some activists view greater political activity as flowing from new definitions of ethnicity and community, but others are clearly using such activity as one of several means to arrive at new definitions. For all this diversity, political development takes its place along with the reawakening of ethnic interest as part of the present Japanese-American scene.

While this reawakening of interest in things Japanese American and the features of ethnic consciousness and community involvement exist, there has also been a gradual but continuing trend toward less participation in the ethnic community and more within the institutions of American society. It is difficult to gauge the extent to which this latter trend has occurred, or to say whether it will continue. Ironically, the differences evident within the community between those promoting various forms of involvement may actually promote its demise in an unintended fashion by blurring the meaning of community and culture.

It is unfortunately far easier to think of obstacles that must be overcome by these two trends than to make accurate predictions about the future. Ethnic consciousness and community involvement must overcome differences within the group as well as apathy. They must also make opportunities outside the community compatible with community development. The trend toward greater integration and eventual assimilation must overcome the strong sentiment that an ethnic community should continue to provide a source of friendship-marriage relationships, protection, the means to work out group problems, and a basis for individual identity. In addition, this trend must cope with present and future blocks to opportunity that still persist in a society where racial and ethnic backgrounds are highly significant social characteristics. It may well be that this second trend is the dominant one. Recent studies showing a continuation of group socioeconomic mobility and startlingly high rates of Sansei intermarriage with non-Japanese Americans lend support to this contention.[35]

The future of Japanese Americans may hinge on yet unforeseen events. However the outcome of these two trends will almost certainly be affected by the resolution or nonresolution of community differences, the manner in which the Sansei generation comes to dominance within the community, and the extent to which the highly trained Sansei disperse themselves geographically in pursuit of jobs. Of additional importance may be the political and economic relationship between Japan and the United States, a factor that has always been significant in the past because of the tendency of many Americans to stereotypically identify Japanese Americans with Japan. Finally, the future of the group will be affected by the struggles of other racial and ethnic groups. Some of the basic factors that prevent these groups from full participation in American society may continue to be the source of barriers for the Japanese American.

THE READINGS

This introductory essay supplies the background and context for the selections that follow. The significance of the readings can be evaluated with reference to the introduction and by comparison with one another.

The first four selections provide a more detailed overview of Japanese American history. "The Japanese American Experience: 1890–1940" and "Why It Happened Here," both by Roger Daniels, discuss the prewar and the evacuation periods respectively, especially their political aspects. Roger Daniels is professor of history at State University College of New York (Fredonia) and the author of several works on Japanese Americans, including *The Politics of Prejudice* and *Concentration Camps USA: Japanese Americans and World War II*. "The Great Betrayal" by Audrie Girdner and Anne Loftis is a more detailed view of the first and most drastic removal of Japanese Americans, those in the Terminal Island area of Los Angeles harbor, and also an examination of the relocation camps. Both authors are freelance writers, and these selections are from their more detailed work on the evacuation, *The Great Betrayal*. In "Six Times Down, Seven Times Up," William Petersen recounts some of the postwar problems of the group and then outlines its later progress. William Petersen is professor of sociology at Ohio State University and author of *Japanese Americans*.

The next two selections concern aspects of the Japanese-American community and culture.[36] "The Community" by Harry Kitano discusses two important organizations, the Japanese Association and the JACL, as well as religious institutions and youth activities. Kitano is professor of sociology and social welfare at the University of California, Los Angeles, and the author of numerous publications on Japanese Americans including *Japanese Americans: The Evolution of a Subculture*. "Kenjin and Kinsmen" by Ivan Light provides good insights into the kenjinkai and other supportive economic organizations. Light is assistant professor of sociology at the University of California, Los Angeles, and this selection comes from *Ethnic Enterprise in America*, a comparative study of black, Chinese, and Japanese economic institutions in America.

The final two selections detail some of the present trends and issues covered in the concluding section of the introductory essay. "The Intolerance of Success" by Daniel Okimoto questions the image of Japanese Americans as a success story and makes observations on problems facing this group. Daniel Okimoto is a doctoral candidate in political science at the University of Michigan, and the selection is from his autobiographical *American in Disguise*. In the last article, Harry Kitano comments on Japanese-American success and a variety of other topics including mental illness, alienation, and assimilation. The interview originally appeared in *Roots: An Asian American Reader*, which is a collection of articles that reflect many of the focuses, criticisms, and strategies of Asian-American activists.

It would be incorrect to assume that the introductory essay and the eight selections present more than a brief overview of the Japanese Americans. Readers are encouraged to examine the works listed in the selected bibliography. Further references can be found in the bibliographical sections of these books and in two published bibliographies: *Asian Americans: An Annotated Bibliography* by Harry Kitano et al., and *Asians in America: A Selected Annotated Bibliography* by Isao Fujimoto et al.[37]

NOTES

1. U.S. Department of Commerce, Bureau of the Census, *1970 Census of Population: General Population Characteristics* (Washington, D.C.: U.S. Government Printing Office, 1972).

2. A more detailed discussion of the early history of the immigrants is available in BILL HOSOKAWA, *Nisei: The Quiet Americans* (New York: Morrow, 1969), pp. 19–132; HARRY H. L. KITANO, *Japanese Americans: Evolution of a Subculture* (Englewood Cliffs, N.J.: Prentice-Hall, 1969), pp. 10–29; and WILLIAM PETERSEN, *Japanese Americans* (New York: Random House, 1971), pp. 9–65.

3. ROGER DANIELS, *Concentration Camps USA: Japanese Americans and World War II* (New York: Holt, Rinehart & Winston, 1971), p. 5.

4. PETERSEN, p. 15.

5. DANIELS, p. 6.

6. KITANO, p. 17.

7. MASAKAZU IWATA, "The Japanese Immigrants in California Agriculture," *Agricultural History* 36 (1962), pp. 25–37.

8. See SHOTARO FRANK MIYAMOTO, "Social Solidarity Among the Japanese in Seattle," *University of Washington Publications in the Social Sciences* 2 (December 1939), pp. 57–130.

9. A more detailed discussion can be found in ROGER DANIELS, *The Politics of Prejudice* (Berkeley: University of California Press, 1962).

10. For a more detailed discussion of this period see HOSOKAWA, pp. 133–219.

11. Discussion of the war years and the evacuation can be found in HOSOKAWA, pp. 243–432; KITANO, pp. 30–46; PETERSEN, pp. 66–100; DANIELS, 1971, pp. 26–170, and a number of other sources, including AUDRIE GIRDNER and ANNE LOFTIS, *The Great Betrayal* (New York: Macmillan, 1969).

12. See DANIELS, 1971, pp. 104–129. The amount of cooperation and resistance has been the point of some controversy.

13. KITANO, pp. 34–39.

14. *Ibid.*, pp. 44–46.

15. See, for example, JACOBUS ten BROEK et al., *Prejudice, War and the Constitution* (Berkeley: University of California Press, 1954), pp. 211–321.

16. See HOSOKAWA, pp. 393–422.

17. See KITANO, pp. 42–44; ten BROEK et al., pp. 185–208; and DANIELS, 1971, pp. 26–73.

18. DANIELS, 1971, pp. 157–70; KITANO, pp. 41–42; and HOSOKAWA, pp. 435–50.

19. An unfortunately poorly written discussion of the camps that were available for use under Title II can be found in CHARLES ALLEN, JR., *Concentration Camps USA* (Philadelphia: Robins Distributing Co., 1969).

20. HOSOKAWA, pp. 445–47. Other major claims efforts have involved recovery by Japanese American depositors in U.S. branches of Japanese banks of funds that were seized during the war as enemy property. See, for example, U.S. House of Representa-

tives (Committee on Interstate and Foreign Commerce), *Claims of Yokohama Specie Bank Depositors,* hearing before the Subcommittee on Commerce and Finance, August 4, 1972. Over time, these efforts have resulted in favorable court decisions and legislation such that thousands of depositors have been able to receive compensation for at least part of their accounts. However even today, more than three decades after Pearl Harbor, some individuals are only beginning to recover their money. Most recently Congress enacted a bill in 1972 allowing Japanese nationals interned or paroled during World War II to file for refunds on their accounts in the prewar Yokohama Specie bank.

21. Brief discussions of the postwar era are found in PETERSEN, pp. 108–130; HOSO-KAWA, pp. 457–97; and KITANO, pp. 47–59.
22. CALVIN F. SCHMID and CHARLES E. NOBBE, "Socioeconomic Differentials Among Nonwhite Races," *American Sociological Review* 30 (1965), pp. 910–13.
23. *Ibid.,* pp. 913–18. For some additional data on occupational mobility see BARBARA F. VARON, "The Japanese Americans: Comparative Occupational Status, 1960 and 1950," *Demography* 4 (1967), pp. 809–819.
24. SCHMID and NOBBE, pp. 918–21.
25. KITANO, p. 57.
26. *Ibid.,* pp. 58–59.
27. SCHMID and NOBBE, pp. 910–13, 917–21.
28. MAMORU IGA, "Changes in Value Orientation of Japanese Americans," paper read at the Western Psychological Association Meeting, Long Beach, April 1966. Summarized in KITANO, pp. 107–108.
29. KITANO, pp. 103–105.
30. *Ibid.,* pp. 110–12, 113–15.
31. For a further discussion on this conception of community see RUSSELL ENDO, "Toward a Comprehensive Conceptualization of Ethnic Communities," *Et Al.* (in press). The description of community institutions draws upon MIYAMOTO, pp. 70–122, and KITANO, pp. 79–98.
32. See, for example, WILLIAM PETERSEN, "Success Story, Japanese American Style," *New York Times Magazine,* January 6, 1966; and PAUL BRINKLEY-ROGERS, "Success Story: Outwhiting the Whites," *Newsweek,* July 21, 1971. The article by journalist Brinkley-Rogers was the subject of much controversy within the Japanese-American community. It is actually an abridged version of a longer piece subsequently reprinted in the March 16 to April 1, 1972 editions of the *Rafu Shimpo,* a Los Angeles Japanese newspaper.
33. Some of this dissent is voiced in recent letters to the editor in the *Pacific Citizen* and in several of the articles in AMY TACHIKI et al., *Roots: An Asian American Reader* (Los Angeles: University of California, Los Angeles, Asian American Studies Center, 1971).
34. Some aspects of this activism can be seen in the articles in TACHIKI et al. Also see *Gidra,* a monthly activist Asian American newspaper.
35. See GENE N. LEVINE and DARREL M. MONTERO, "Socioeconomic Mobility Among Three Generations of Japanese Americans," *Journal of Social Issues* 30 (1973), pp. 33–48; AKEMI KIKUMURA and HARRY H. L. KITANO, "Interracial Marriage: A Picture of the Japanese Americans," *Journal of Social Issues* 30 (1973), pp. 67–81; and JOHN N. TINKER, "Intermarriage and Ethnic Boundaries: The Japanese American Case," *Journal of Social Issues* 30 (1973), pp. 49–66.
36. Because of space limitations, additional articles on community and culture could not

be included. Interested readers should examine MIYAMOTO, pp. 57–130; KITANO, pp. 99–115; TACHIKI et al., pp. 1–127, 247–343; and STANFORD LYMAN, "Generation and Character: The Case of the Japanese Americans," pp. 81–97, in STANFORD LYMAN, *The Asian in the West* (Reno: Desert Research Institute, University of Nevada, 1970).

37. These are available respectively from the Asian American Studies Center, 3235 Campbell Hall, University of California, Los Angeles 90024; and the Asian American Studies Division, Department of Applied Behavioral Sciences, University of California, Davis 95616.

BIBLIOGRAPHY

BOSWORTH, ALLAN R. *America's Concentration Camps.* New York: W. W. Norton & Company, 1967.

CONROY, HILARY, and T. SCOTT MIYAKAWA, Eds. *East Across the Pacific: Historical and Sociological Studies of Japanese Immigration and Assimilation.* Santa Barbara: American Bibliographic Center, 1972.

DANIELS, ROGER. *Concentration Camps USA: Japanese Americans and World War II.* New York: Holt, Rinehart & Winston, 1971.

——. *The Politics of Prejudice.* Berkeley: University of California Press, 1962.

Gidra (a monthly Asian American activist newspaper).

GIRDNER, AUDRIE, and ANNE LOFTIS. *The Great Betrayal.* New York: Macmillan, 1969.

HOSOKAWA, BILL. *Nisei: The Quiet Americans.* New York: Morrow, 1969.

Journal of Social Issues 30 (1973), (special issue on Asian Americans).

KITAGAWA, DAISUKE. *Issei and Nisei: The Internment Years.* New York: Seabury Press, 1967.

KITANO, HARRY H. L. *Japanese Americans: Evolution of a Subculture.* Englewood Cliffs, N.J.: Prentice-Hall, 1969.

LIGHT, IVAN H. *Ethnic Enterprise in America.* Berkeley: University of California Press, 1972.

LYMAN, STANFORD M. *The Asian in the West.* Reno: Desert Research Institute, University of Nevada, 1970.

MEYER, DILLON. *Uprooted Americans.* Tucson: University of Arizona Press, 1971.

MIYAMOTO, SHOTARO FRANK. "Social Solidarity Among the Japanese in Seattle," *University of Washington Publications in the Social Sciences* 2 (December 1939), pp. 57–130.

OKIMOTO, DANIEL I. *American in Disguise.* New York: Weatherhill, 1971.

OKUBO, MINE. *Citizen 13660.* New York: Columbia University Press, 1946.

Pacific Citizen (weekly newspaper of the Japanese American Citizens League).

PETERSEN, WILLIAM. *Japanese Americans.* New York: Random House, 1971.

SUE, STANLEY, and NATHANIEL N. WAGNER, Eds. *Asian Americans: Psychological Perspectives.* Ben Lomond: Science and Behavior Books, 1973.

TACHIKI, AMY, et al. *Roots: An Asian American Reader.* Los Angeles: University of

California, Los Angeles, Asian American Studies Center.

ten BROEK, JACOBUS, et al. *Prejudice, War and the Constitution*. Berkeley: University of California Press, 1954.

THOMAS, DOROTHY S., and RICHARD NISHIMOTO. *The Spoilage: Japanese American Evacuation and Resettlement During World War II*. Berkeley: University of Cailifornia Press, 1946.

The Japanese-American Experience: 1890-1940

Roger Daniels

. . . The immigrants from Japan who began to arrive in the United States in significant numbers after 1890 (Japan had legalized emigration only in 1885) already had two strikes against them.[1] The western United States in general and California in particular had learned to despise Orientals before this Japanese migration began. Immigration from China, starting at about the same time as the gold rush of 1849, had created an entirely new strain of American racism, from which the Japanese Americans were to suffer greatly. The anti-Orientalism of California and the West was separate from but certainly related to the general prejudice against colored people—"the lesser breeds without the law" as Kipling put it—which was endemic to white Americans from almost the very beginning of our history. Similar prejudices, usually called nativism, were exhibited even against white people if they happened not to speak English or practiced a non-Protestant variant of Christianity. But even within the general ethnocentric intolerance of American society, anti-Orientalism was something special.

The earliest Chinese immigrants were not particularly mistreated. Their outlandish costumes and unique appearance—apart from "color" most Chinese men wore their hair in a long pigtails, or queues—added merely another exotic note to the polyglot cosmopolitanism of gold rush San Francisco. The fantastic boom then in progress made any addition to the labor force welcome, and these earliest immigrants found a ready-made economic niche. (The Chinese characters for California can also be translated "golden mountain.") This economic attraction—what historians of immigration call "pull" —coupled with the "push" of Chinese peasant poverty and the existence of cheap and frequent trans-Pacific sail and steamship transportation produced a steady stream of Chinese migration to the United States, as the tables show.

Relatively speaking, the Chinese were a large fraction of the population of the West in the years after the Civil War. In 1870 Chinese comprised perhaps 10 per cent of California's population and almost a fourth of the population of its metropolis, San Francisco.[2] The economic impact of the

Immigration of Chinese to the United States

Years	No. of Immigrants
To 1860	41,443
1861–1870	64,301
1871–1880	123,823

Chinese Population, by Census

	United States	Pacific States	California
1860	34,933	—	34,933
1870	63,199	52,841	49,277
1880	104,468	87,828	75,132

Chinese was even greater than their numbers would suggest for almost all of them were adult males who competed with white workingmen for jobs. This competition first asserted itself in the mining districts, but became really acute after the completion of the Union–Central Pacific Railroad in 1869, which had employed some 10,000 Chinese laborers to construct its western leg. From an economic point of view the almost unanimous hostility with which far-western workingmen viewed the Chinese was quite rational. Chinese labor was cheap labor, and far-western labor had been, due to its scarcity, expensive labor. The result of this competition was a popular anti-Chinese movement, led for a while by the immigrant demagogue Dennis Kearney. His rallying cry, "The Chinese Must Go," is a good shorthand description of the whole movement. Originally the sole property of Kearney's third-party movement, the Workingmen's party, a Chinese exclusion policy was soon appropriated by both Democrats and Republicans, first at the state and regional levels, and then nationally.

But the protest was not solely economic. Based upon the legitimate and understandable economic grievances of western workingmen against what they considered unfair competition (one is reminded of present-day California farm workers' resentment of the importation of Mexican nationals on a temporary basis), the movement soon developed an ideology of white supremacy/Oriental inferiority that was wholly compatible with the mainstream of American racism. Not only did "John Chinaman," as he was often called, "work cheap and smell bad," but he was also subhuman.[3] California courts refused to accept his testimony; municipal ordinances were passed to harass him; the state legislature tried to stop his further immigration; and the

California constitution itself, as rewritten in 1879, had an entire anti-Chinese section which, among other things, called upon the legislature to

> . . . prescribe all necessary regulations for the protection of the state, and the counties and towns . . . from the burdens and evils arising from the presence of aliens who are and may become . . . dangerous and detrimental to the well-being or peace of the state, and to impose conditions upon which such persons may reside in the state, and to provide the means and modes of their removal.[4]

Apart from "legal" discrimination, the Chinese suffered greatly from individual and mob violence. Since they lived in isolated mining camps or in segregated urban ghettoes, assaults against Chinese were usually witnessed only by other Chinese, whose testimony was inadmissible in court. In a sense, California courts declared an open season on Chinese, who were subjected to everything from casual assault (cutting off a pigtail was a popular sport) to mass murder. The worst single California atrocity occurred in Los Angeles during a one-night rampage in 1871 in which a white mob shot, hanged, and otherwise murdered some twenty Chinese.[5] Other similar mob violence took place throughout the state, and indeed, throughout the West. Outside California the bloodiest outbreak took place in Rock Springs, Wyoming, in 1885 in a massacre of Chinese, originally employed as strikebreakers in a Union Pacific coal mine; 28 were killed and 15 wounded, and damage to property came to nearly $150,000.[6]

Some employers, outside the West, saw the presence of Chinese as an opportunity. They were brought to New England to break a shoemakers' strike, and some fantastic schemes were hatched to use Chinese as substitutes for newly freed and fractious Negroes on southern cotton plantations and as a solution to the vexatious "servant problem" that troubled the upper middle class in Gilded Age America.[7] But, in essence, the Chinese question was a western question, and largely a California problem at that.

The West, however, could not solve the problem; to put an end to immigration from China, federal power was required, and by the early 1870's western legislatures and western political parties were petitioning Congress to end Chinese immigration and adopting planks calling for Chinese exclusion. An exclusion bill passed both houses of Congress in Rutherford B. Hayes's administration, but received a presidential veto. In 1882, however, Chester Alan Arthur reluctantly bowed to congressional feeling and signed a compromise exclusion bill, barring all Chinese for ten years. The ten-year ban was renewed by Congress in 1892 and then made "permanent" under the progressive administration of Theodore Roosevelt in 1902. A regional problem had required a national solution; that solution was certainly easier to achieve than it might have been for two quite separate reasons. It was easy for most Americans to extend their feelings about the inferiority of the Negro to all "colored races"; in addition, China was a weak, defenseless nation, and the protests of its government did not have to be taken seriously. Chinese exclusion represented the first racist qualification of American immigration policy, although it would not be the last. In addition, the whole anti-Chinese episode in our history served as a kind of prophetic prologue for what would befall immigrants from Japan.

Significant immigration from Japan actually started about 1890. The census of that year enumerated 2039 Japanese in the entire country, more than half of them in California. According to the not always accurate immigration data of the federal government, about 25,000 immigrants came in the 1890's, 125,000 in the peak period of immigration between 1901 and 1908, and then about 10,000 a year until the Immigration Act of 1924 barred further immigration from Japan. During the entire period, fewer than 300,000 Japanese were recorded as entering the United States. In comparison to the total immigration picture—between the end of the Civil War and 1924 some 30 million immigrants came to the United States—this is a very small number indeed. But even the 300,000 figure greatly overstates what some publicists liked to call the "yellow flood." Cheap and rapid trans-Pacific transportation made it possible for a number of individuals to go back and forth many times. Others were students and "birds of passage," that is, sojourners rather than immigrants. A brief population table will put the demographic data into clearer perspective. . . . Yet, as we shall see, this tiny population became the focus of local agitation, national concern, and international negotiation and insult. But before we consider the furor that was raised over them, we ought to look at the immigrants themselves.

	Japanese in U.S.	United States Population	Japanese in California	California Population
1890	2,039	63,000,000	1,147	1,200,000
1900	24,326	76,000,000	10,151	1,500,000
1910	72,157	92,000,000	41,356	2,400,000
1920	111,010	106,000,000	71,952	3,400,000

Immigrants from Japan (hereafter called Issei, from the combination of the Japanese words for "one" and "generation"; their children, the American-born second generation, are Nisei; and the third generation are Sansei) came to the United States for exactly the same kinds of reasons that other immigrants came: for economic opportunity and to escape severe economic and social dislocations at home. The Japan which they left was rapidly undergoing its own industrial revolution. (According to W. W. Rostow, the Japanese economy "took off" between 1878 and 1900.)[8] Unlike many other contemporary immigrant groups however, emigration for the Issei did not mean rejection of the old country. Most of them maintained an interest and a pride in the

accomplishments of Japan, a pride that they publicly exhibited on such traditional occasions as the Emperor's birthday or on the occurrence of special
events like Admiral Togo's victory over the Russian fleet during the Russo-
Japanese War.

For many of the Issei generation, the United States itself was not the first
stop. The first significant trans-Pacific migration of Japanese was to the kingdom of Hawaii, where they provided cheap agricultural labor on the semifeudal
sugar plantations of the American economic elite.[9] During the period of
heaviest immigration (1900–1908) more than 40,000 of the Japanese entering
the United States came via Hawaii. The attraction of the United States
vis-à-vis Hawaii was simple: wages were higher, hours were shorter, and
economic opportunity more abundant. But whether they came by way of
Hawaii or directly from Japan, the Issei generation started at the bottom of
the economic ladder. Few came with any significant amount of capital; the
vast majority were young adult males without family ties. One Issei recently
told an interviewer:

> I grew up in a farm in Japan. My father owned a fairly large piece of land,
> but it was heavily mortgaged. I remember how hard we all had to work, and
> I also remember the hard times. I saw little future in farm work; my older
> brothers would later run the farm, so at my first good chance I went to
> work in Osaka. Later I came to California and worked as a laborer in all
> kinds of jobs. However, for the first five years I had to work in the farms,
> picking fruit, vegetables, and I saved some money. Then I came to live in
> the city permanently.[10]

This immigrant's experience was, if not typical, common. Most of the Issei
came from the Japanese countryside rather than the city; most seem to have
come from somewhere above the lowest socioeconomic strata of the population; and most exhibited that combination of energy and ambition which has
made the Japanese Americans the most upwardly mobile nonwhite minority
in the United States.[11] (If the Japanese had been white Protestants, the
tendency would be to attribute their success to what Max Weber and others
have called "the Protestant Ethic." That is, that the "Puritan traits" of
honesty, industry, zeal, punctuality, frugality, and regularity advanced the
growth of capitalism by promoting rational, systematic economic conduct.
Apart from the Japanese, the American ethnic group that best exemplifies
these traits are the Jews.) Whatever its cause, the spectacular economic
achievement of the Issei generation—especially within agriculture—was an
important causal component of the animosity it engendered.

This achievement can be best seen in California, where the bulk of the
Issei settled. By 1919 about half of the state's 70,000 Japanese were engaged
in agriculture. They controlled over 450,000 acres of agricultural land, some
of it among the most fruitful in the state. Although this amounted to only
1 per cent of the state's land under cultivation, the labor-intensive agricultural
techniques which the Issei brought from Japan produced about 10 per cent of

the dollar volume of the state's crops. The historian of Japanese-American agriculture, Masakazu Iwata, has ably summarized the contribution the Issei made.

> [First] they filled the farm labor vacuum and thus prevented a ruinous slump. . . . [Then] as independent farm operators, the Japanese with their skill and energy helped to reclaim and improve thousands of acres of worthless lands throughout the state, lands which the white man abhorred, and made them fertile and immensely productive. They pioneered the rice industry, and planted the first citrus orchards in the hog wallow lands in the San Joaquin Valley. They played a vital part in establishing the present system of marketing fruits and vegetables, especially in Los Angeles County, and dominated in the field of commercial truck crops. From the perspective of history, it is evident that the contributions of the Issei. . . were undeniably a significant factor in making California one of the greatest farming states in the nation.[12]

Most of the Issei farmers achieved a steady but unspectacular prosperity; one Japanese immigrant, however, had a career that reads like a Horatio Alger story. George Shima (he Americanized his name) came to the United States directly from Japan in 1889 at the age of 26 with less than $1,000 in capital. The son of a relatively prosperous Japanese farm owner, he worked first as a common laborer and then rather quickly became a labor contractor who specialized in marketing the services of his countrymen to white agriculturalists. He invested his profits in hitherto unused land, starting with a leasehold on 15 acres. Working in partnership with other Issei, Shima created his own agricultural empire, specializing in potatoes, then a new crop in California. By 1909 the press was referring to him as the "Potato King" of California. By 1913, when a Japanese graduate student surveyed his holdings, Shima controlled nearly 30,000 acres directly, and, through marketing agreements, handled the produce raised by many of his compatriots. By 1920 it was estimated that he controlled 85 per cent of California's potato crop, valued at over $18 million that year. He employed over 500 persons in a multiracial labor force that included Caucasians. When he died, in 1926, the press estimated his estate at $15 million; his pallbearers included such dignitaries as James Rolph, Jr., the mayor of San Francisco, and David Starr Jordan, the chancellor of Stanford University. In 1909 he bought a house in one of the better residential sections of Berkeley, California, close to the university. A protest movement, led by a professor of classics, demanded that he move to an Oriental neighborhood. Shima held his ground, although he did erect a large redwood fence around the property, as he told the press, "to keep the other children from playing with his." Even an Issei millionaire could not escape the sting of discrimination.[13]

Most of the Issei, whether they lived in the city or the country, did not offend the housing mores of the majority; they lived the segregated life typical of American minority groups. Those who did not go directly into agriculture usually started out as common laborers or domestic servants. Like their rural

fellow immigrants, they too demonstrated upward social and economic mobility. Starting with almost token wages—in 1900, $1.50 a week plus board
was standard—these immigrants quickly learned English and the "ropes,"
and moved into better-paying jobs, although several thousand remained
domestic servants. Since California trade unions almost universally barred
Orientals from membership, work in manufacturing, the building trades, and
many other occupations was closed to them. The typical pattern for urban
Issei was to establish a small business—a laundry, a restaurant, a curio shop—
or to go to work for an Issei businessman who was already established. A
great many of these businesses catered to the immigrant community; others
provided specialized services to whites (for example, contract gardening) or
served as retail marketing outlets for Japanese agriculturalists, usually specializ-
ing in produce or flowers. A smaller group—and one that was to arouse special
concern after Pearl Harbor—went into commercial fishing; more than any
other group of Issei entrepreneurs the fishermen were in direct economic
competition with white businessmen. Most other Issei formed a complementary rather than a competing economy. Their businesses employed almost exclusively members of their own ethnic community at lower wages and
longer hours than generally prevailed.

If Californians and other westerners had been the rational "economic men"
of nineteenth-century classical economic theory, there would have been no
anti-Japanese movement. The Issei subeconomy neither lowered wages nor
put white men out of work. Its major effect, in fact, was a lowering of the
cost of fresh fruit and vegetables for the general population, and Issei agriculture was one of the bases which allowed California's population to expand as
rapidly as it did, from less than 1.5 million in 1900 to almost 7 million in 1940.
But race prejudice, of course, is not a rational phenomenon, even though in
some instances, as in the anti-Chinese movement, it does have a certain
economic rationale.[14] Nothing more clearly indicates the nonrational, inherited
nature of California's anti-Japanese movement than the fact that it started
when there were fewer than a thousand Japanese in the entire state.

The anti-Japanese war cry was first raised by elements of the San Francisco
labor movement in 1888, and for the first two decades of agitation labor took
the lead, as it had done against the Chinese.[15] In 1892 the demagogue Dennis
Kearney returned to the hustings and unsuccessfully tried to base a political
comeback on the slogan "The Japs Must Go!" and in the same year a San
Francisco newspaper launched a self-styled journalistic "crusade" against the
menace of Japanese immigration. These first moves were abortive: in 1892
probably not one Californian in ten had even seen a Japanese. But they were
indicative of things to come. Just eight years later the real anti-Japanese movement began. At a meeting sponsored by organized labor, the Democratic mayor
of San Francisco, James Duval Phelan, effectively linked the anti-Chinese
and anti-Japanese movements. The major purpose of the meeting was to
pressure Congress to renew Chinese exclusion, but Phelan pointed out a new
danger:

> The Japanese are starting the same tide of immigration which we thought we had checked twenty years ago. . . . The Chinese and Japanese are not bona fide citizens. They are not the stuff of which American citizens can be made.

Another speaker at the same meeting was the distinguished sociologist Edward Alysworth Ross, then teaching at Stanford University. Ross rang some changes on Phelan's remarks and made a common analogy with the protective tariff: If we keep out pauper-made goods, he asked, why don't we keep out the pauper? In those years few academics championed the cause of labor (Ross would soon lose his job at Stanford because of his economic views), but most of those who did were opposed to immigrants in general and Oriental immigrants in particular. Although their grounds for this objection were ostensibly economic, most flavored their arguments with racist appeals. The same could be said for most American socialists in the years before 1920. From staid Victor Berger of Milwaukee to flamboyant Jack London of California, socialists insisted that the United States must be kept a white man's country.

These arguments of the left quickly found echoes in the more traditional segments of the political spectrum. During the summer of 1900 all three major political parties—Republicans, Democrats, and Populists—took stands against "Asiatic" immigrants, and at the end of the year the national convention of the American Federation of Labor asked Congress to exclude not only Chinese, but all "Mongolians."

Agitation of this sort continued sporadically until 1905; in that year the anti-Japanese movement escalated significantly. The reasons for the escalation are to be sought both inside and outside the United States. On the world scene, the startling triumph of Japan over czarist Russia in both land and naval battles effectively challenged, for the first time, white military supremacy in Asia and raised the specter of the yellow peril. At home, heightened immigration of Japanese—45,000 came between 1903 and 1905—made the "threat" of Japanese immigration much more real than it had been five years before. In February the San Francisco *Chronicle*, a conservative Republican paper and probably the most influential on the Pacific Coast, began a concerted and deliberate anti-Japanese campaign. The first front-page streamer, THE JAPANESE INVASION, THE PROBLEM OF THE HOUR, set the tone for the whole campaign. In addition to the usual economic and racial arguments, arguments that stressed a lowering of the standard of living and the impossibility of assimilation, the *Chronicle* injected two new and ugly elements into the agitation: sex and war. The paper insisted that Japanese were a menace to American women and that "every one of these immigrants . . . is a Japanese spy."

A little more than a week after the *Chronicle*'s campaign started, both houses of the California legislature unanimously passed a resolution asking Congress to limit the further immigration of Japanese. Included in a long bill of particulars were statements that

> Japanese laborers, by reason of race habits, mode of living, disposition and general characteristics, are undesirable. . . . Japanese . . . do not buy land [or] build or buy houses. . . . They contribute nothing to the growth of the state. They add nothing to its wealth, and they are a blight on the prosperity of it, and a great and impending danger to its welfare.

The legislature was obviously reacting in a sort of racist conditioned reflex, a reflex conditioned by decades of anti-Chinese rhetoric. Within a few years the tune of the anti-Japanese song would change: the new refrain would stress not Japanese pauperism but Japanese landholding. The 1905 legislature had one other distinction: it limited itself to an anti-Japanese resolution. For the next forty years, every session of the California legislature would attempt to pass at least one piece of anti-Japanese legislation.

A major factor in the introduction of these bills was the existence of anti-Japanese organizations and pressure groups which sprang up throughout the state from 1905 on. In May of that year the first of these organizations, the Asiatic Exclusion League, was set up. In effect, the League and its immediate successors were appendages of the powerful San Francisco labor movement. But the anti-Japanese movement appealed to more than labor; in December 1905, two California Republican congressmen, using League arguments, introduced similar Japanese exclusion bills into Congress. Although these bills never got out of committee, they produced one significant reaction: a leading southern politician, Oscar W. Underwood of Alabama, pledged that on this race question the South would support the Pacific Coast.

Despite this momentary national attention, the anti-Japanese movement failed to attract any publicity outside the Pacific Coast in 1905. When national and international notoriety did come, in the very next year, it was not immigration but school segregation that drew the spotlight. In May 1905, in response perhaps to the *Chronicle's* continuing crusade, the San Francisco School Board announced that it intended sometime in the future to order Japanese pupils—native and foreign-born—removed from the regular schools and placed in the already existing school for Chinese. The stated reason was so that "our children should not be placed in any position where their youthful impressions may be affected by association with the Mongolian race." (The use of the term "Mongolian" was dictated by an old California school law which permitted exclusion of children of "filthy or vicious habits," or "suffering from contagious diseases," and segregation in separate schools of American Indian children and those of "Chinese or Mongolian descent." The law made no provision for Negro children.) But like so many pro-integration statements of intent today, these segregationist sentiments were left purely verbal, and no national or international notice was taken of them.

A year and a half later, the school board acted, and ordered the segregation to take place. In the meantime the famous San Francisco earthquake and fire of April 18, 1906, had taken place, and, in the chaotic conditions that followed, the anti-Japanese movement changed from peaceful if bigoted protest to direct action. Japanese restaurants, laundries, and other business establishments were picketed and boycotted, and in many instances businessmen, employees, and even white customers, were physically abused. By the fall of 1906 assaults upon individual Japanese were too frequent to have been accidental. Most of those who suffered were humble immigrants, but a distinguished party of visiting Japanese seismologists was stoned and otherwise attacked in various parts of northern California. More typical was the complaint of a laundry proprietor, as put forth in the stilted English of an employee of the Japanese consulate:

> I am proprietor of Sunset City Laundry. Soon after the earthquake the persecutions became intolerable. My drivers [of slow, horse-drawn laundry wagons] were constantly attacked on the highway, my place of business defiled by rotten eggs and fruit; windows were smashed several times. . . . The miscreants are generally young men, 17 or 18 years old. Whenever the newspapers attack the Japanese these roughs renew their misdeeds with redoubled energy.

Apparently there were never any convictions of whites for assault on Japanese during this period, although several Japanese were punished when they tried to defend themselves. It was in this atmosphere that the San Francisco School Board promulgated its segregation order on October 11, 1906. It was apparently unnoticed in the rest of the United States, and even the San Francisco papers gave it very little space. But nine days later the segregation order was front-page news in the Tokyo newspapers, and from that moment on the anti-Japanese movement was both a national and an international problem.

The Japanese government, always solicitous about the welfare of its citizens abroad, naturally protested. (Hilary Conroy has pointed out that the chief motivation for this solicitude "was the protection of her own prestige as a nation.") [16] These protests, raising as they did the question of American-Japanese friendship, naturally disturbed many Americans, but few were disturbed as mightily as President Theodore Roosevelt. Roosevelt had been aware of the growing anti-Japanese agitation on the West Coast and as early as 1905 had privately expressed his disgust with the "idiots" of the California legislature. In response to the Japanese protests of October 1906, he dispatched a Cabinet member to investigate the school situation in San Francisco and privately assured the Japanese government of American friendship. But even before the report was in, Roosevelt publicly denounced the San Francisco proposal. In his annual message of December 2, 1906, the President asserted, falsely, that Japanese were treated, in most of the United States, just as most Europeans were treated. He went on to denounce the action of the school board as a "wicked absurdity" and then proposed that the naturalization laws—which provided for the naturalization of "free white persons and persons of African descent"—be amended to permit the naturalization of Japanese.

Roosevelt thus differentiated sharply between Chinese and Japanese. As we have seen, he signed the Chinese Exclusion Act of 1902, and strongly reiterated

his opposition to Chinese immigrants in 1905. The reason Roosevelt discriminated between Orientals was because of the different relative military
strengths of China and Japan. As he himself put it in his 1906 message, "the
mob of a single city may at any time commit acts of lawless violence that
may plunge us into war." Japan was strong, so its immigrants must be treated
with respect; China was weak, so its immigrants could be treated as the mob
desired. But, it should be noted, Roosevelt quickly retreated from his advanced position on Japanese naturalization; he soon discovered that Congress
would not permit it, and he never again publicly proposed it.

Shortly after his annual message, Roosevelt received and published the report on San Francisco schools from his Secretary of Commerce and Labor
Victor H. Metcalf. It was something of an anticlimax for most of the nation
to discover that the whole furor had been raised over a grand total of 93
Japanese students distributed among the 23 public schools of San Francisco.
Twenty-five of these students had been born on American soil, and since
they were American citizens, the federal government could do nothing for
them. Separate but equal facilities had been condoned by the United States
Supreme Court in Plessy v. Ferguson (1896), so segregation of American
citizens was perfectly legal. But for the 68 school children who were subjects
of the empire of Japan, the government could do something. They were protected by a stronger shield than the Constitution: the 1894 treaty between
Japan and the United States, which guaranteed reciprocal "most favored
nation" residential rights to nationals of both countries. Secretary of State
Elihu Root himself, working with Department of Justice lawyers, prepared
a federal desegregation suit directed against the San Francisco School Board.

At the same time, however, the federal authorities entered into discussions
with the Japanese government designed to alleviate what they considered the
real problem—continued immigration from Japan. In a complicated series of
maneuvers Roosevelt, at a personal interview at the White House, persuaded
the San Francisco School Board to revoke the offending order, managed to
restrain the California legislature from passing anti-Japanese legislation relating to schools and other matters, and began an exchange of notes with Japan
which collectively became known as the Gentlemen's Agreement of 1907–
1908. The Japanese government agreed to stop issuing to laborers passports
that would be good in the continental United States (Japanese labor was still
wanted on Hawaiian sugar plantations), but it was agreed that passports could
be issued to laborers who had already been to the United States and, most
significantly, "to the parents, wives and children of laborers already there."

Roosevelt and his subordinates apparently failed to realize that under the
provisions of the Gentlemen's Agreement thousands of Japanese men resident
in the United States would send for wives, and that these newly married
couples would increase and multiply. They presented the Gentlemen's Agreement to the hostile California public as exclusion. When, under its terms,
the Japanese population of California continued to grow, first largely from the
immigration of women and then from natural increase, Californians and

others concerned about the Japanese problem insisted that they had been betrayed by their government in Washington. Instead of easing racial tension in California, the Roosevelt administration, in the final analysis, exacerbated it." [17] The subsequent sessions of the California legislature, in 1909 and 1911, witnessed persistent attempts, usually led by Democrats, to pass anti-Japanese legislation. The measures were defeated, one way or another, by Republican majorities in both houses under pressure from national Republican administrations concerned about the possible effects of this legislation on relations between Japan and the United States. In 1913, however, a different situation prevailed. Republicans still controlled the California government, but the Democratic administration of Woodrow Wilson was in charge nationally. California Republicans, who during three elections had suffered Democrats' slurs about their national party's position on the Japanese question—in the 1908 election one Democratic slogan was "Labor's choice [is] Bryan—Jap's choice [is] Taft"—now saw a chance to make political capital and embarrass their opponents. In this whipsaw of the politics of prejudice the Japanese issue once again became an international affair.

By 1913 California politics had become dominated by progressive Republicans, and one of the chief architects of progressivism, Hiram W. Johnson, sat in the governor's chair. Two years previously, cooperating with a national administration of his own party, he had "sat upon the lid" and prevented passage of significant anti-Japanese measures. With a Democratic administration, Johnson quite early foresaw, as he wrote his most trusted adviser, a "unique and interesting" situation and "one out of which we can get a good deal of satisfaction." What the wily Johnson foresaw came about. A popular antialien land bill, designed to forbid "aliens ineligible to citizenship" (that is, Asians) from purchasing land, moved rapidly through the California legislature, with Johnson doing some behind-the-scenes stage-managing. Johnson arranged a public hearing in the spacious Assembly chamber in Sacramento, and seems also to have planned a "spontaneous" demonstration by farmers. The leading "farmer" was, in fact, a former Congregational clergyman, Ralph Newman, who made an appeal that ended:

> Near my home is an eighty-acre tract of as fine land as there is in California. On that tract lives a Japanese. With that Japanese lives a white woman. In that woman's arms is a baby. What is that baby? It isn't a Japanese. It isn't white. It is a germ of the mightiest problem that ever faced this state; a problem that will make the black problem of the South look white.

The specter of interracial marriage or sex, although often raised by extremists, was not really a significant factor; Japanese rarely married or cohabited outside their own ethnic group. What had changed was the perceived nature of the Japanese threat. No longer the pauper immigrant, but an increasingly successful entrepreneur, Newman's image—the Japanese possessing the white woman—could be interpreted as the sexualization of a different kind of usurpation, the yellow man's taking of what the white man conceived to be his rightful place in society. With this kind of send-off, the anti-Japanese land bill seemed assured of passage.

Back in Washington, Woodrow Wilson and his Secretary of State William Jennings Bryan were faced with persistent diplomatic protest in the very first weeks of their administration. They were reluctant to intervene, as both Roosevelt and Taft had, for three reasons. First, they feared, correctly, that the Republican California administration would reject their pleas. Second, each of them had expressed and still held distinct anti-Japanese sentiments. Third, both of them, like most Democrats of their time, held strongly Jeffersonian state's rights views, and were much more reluctant to intervene in the internal affairs of a state than were their Hamiltonian Republican predecessors. But national power brings responsibility, and Wilson and Bryan at least made an effort to moderate the California action. Bryan went all the way to California, addressed the legislature, caucused with followers, all to no avail. The Alien Land Act passed both houses overwhelmingly and was quickly signed by Johnson.

Although passage of the Alien Land Law of 1913 was a great psychic triumph for the Californians—after almost a decade they had finally thwarted Washington—it served very little real purpose, as the more astute California politicians (including Hiram Johnson) knew at the time. Japanese land tenure was not seriously affected by the law; although it prohibited further ownership by Japanese aliens, it did permit leasing. It was quite simple for the attorneys who represented Japanese interests in California to evade the alleged intent of the law in many ways. The simplest was through incorporation so that control was ostensibly held by whites. For the growing number of Issei who had American-born children, things were even easier; they simply transferred the stock or title to their citizen children whose legal guardianship they naturally assumed.

When the truth about the impotence of the bill dawned on many Californians, their bitterness against the Japanese and their own government merely increased. The years that followed, however, were years of war, and during part of that time Japan was on our side, or at least fighting the same enemy, Germany. During those years anti-Japanese activity, organized and spontaneous, was at a minimum. The years after the war, however, saw the anti-Japanese movement go over the top and move from triumph to triumph.

How representative of white California were the exclusionists? The best possible measure of the popularity of the anti-Japanese position came in 1920, when a stronger Alien Land Act, one that prohibited leasing and sharecropping as well as land purchase, was put on the California ballot as an initiative. It passed by a margin of more than 3 to 1. Few of the more than six hundred thousand California citizens who voted for the measure can have been in any way actual or potential competitors with Japanese farmers; the measure carried every county in the state, and did well in both urban and rural areas. The simple fact of the matter was that Californians had come to hate and fear Japanese with a special intensity.

Late in 1919 this hate and fear became focused in one omnibus anti-Japanese organization—the Oriental Exclusion League. Although it had a vast number of cooperating organizations, four of them provided the real clout: the California Federation of Labor, the American Legion, the State Grange, and the Native Sons and Daughters of the Golden West. This curious coalition agreed on little else—the Legion and organized labor were almost always on opposite sides of the fence—but it did formulate an anti-Japanese program about which they could all agree. They had five basic demands, four of which were quickly achieved.

1. Cancellation of the Gentlemen's Agreement.
2. Exclusion of picture brides.
3. Rigorous exclusion of Japanese as immigrants.
4. Maintaining the bar against naturalization of Asians.
5. Amending the federal Constitution to deny citizenship even to native-born Asians.

The picture brides, about whom the nativists were so bitter, need some explanation. Under the Gentlemen's Agreement, as we have seen, Japanese men already in the United States were given the right to bring in wives. The Japanese government was reasonably careful about granting such passports, and usually went far beyond the terms of the agreement. To ensure that these women immigrants would not become public charges, the husband or prospective husband was often required to present evidence to a Japanese consulate in California showing that he could support a wife, before her passport would be issued. In many instances the prospective bridegroom would return to Japan and bring back a bride. In other instances, however, friends and relatives at home would do the selecting for him. A proxy wedding would take place; a picture of the bride would be sent to California, followed, eventually, by the bride herself. As shocking as this seemed to the American ideal of romantic love, marriages arranged in such a manner were quite common in Japan and not infrequent among some European immigrant groups. The matchmakers, or go-betweens, took pride in their work, and, in fact, their reputations depended upon the success of the marriages they arranged. To the Japanese this seemed natural; to most Americans, unnatural; but to many Californians this age-old method of mate selection seemed just another aspect of a massive and diabolical plot to submerge California under a tide of yellow babies.

The California reaction to the picture brides, to the creation of yellow American citizens, can only be described as paranoid. One leading exclusionist, V. S. McClatchy, former publisher of the Sacramento *Bee* and a director of the Associated Press, once assembled "indisputable facts and figures" which demonstrated that America's Japanese population, unless checked, would reach 318,000 in 1923, 2 million in 1963, and 100 million in 2063. One female exclusionist was sure that California was being "Japanized" in the same way as the South was being "Negroized"; she warned her fellow Californians about "Japanese casting furtive glances at our young women." Cora W. Wood-bridge, a state legislator and an officer of the California Federation of Women's Clubs, dismissed the Issei woman as "a beast of burden up to the time of the birth of her child [who], within a day or two at most, resumes her task and continues it from twelve to sixteen hours a day." Even more outrageous to the convinced exclusionists were the white allies of the Japanese, who were called "Jap-lovers" and "white-Japs, who masquerade as Americans, but, in fact, are servants of the mikado." All this emotion, remember, was gen-erated at a time when there were only 70,000 Japanese in the state; they amounted to one Californian in fifty. But Californians were convinced that they were threatened. After passage of the 1920 Alien Land Act, which in-hibited the growth of Issei agriculture but did not cripple it, the state had used all its alternatives. As had been the case with the anti-Chinese movement, the goals of the exclusionists could only be achived with federal power.

California, of course, had allies. Most other western states, but particularly Oregon and Washington, had anti-Japanese movements of their own and passed similar alien land laws. In addition, most southern senators and repre-sentatives stood ready to support their fellow "beleaguered" whites. But a western and southern bloc cannot carry Congress. National support had to be organized. Much of the support came from two of the major California pressure groups. At the national level both the American Legion and the American Federation of Labor worked hard for exclusion. But even more crucial support came, however indirectly, from Japan itself. Sometime be-tween the beginning of the Russo-Japanese War and the end of World War I the Japanese became, in the eyes of most Americans, villains. Aggressive ac-tions by Japan, particularly its demands against China and its conflict with the United States in Siberia during the short-lived occupation of parts of Soviet East Asia, helped cause American public opinion to turn against Japan, thus providing more support for the exclusionist position.

But at least equally important was the growing racist feeling in the United States, a feeling exacerbated by both the postwar retreat from internationalism and the domestic upsurge against "un-American" ideas and individuals. Intel-lectual racists like Lothrop Stoddard and Madison Grant warned of a "rising tide of color" that menaced white civilization; the second Ku Klux Klan, focusing its attack on Catholics, Jews, and foreigners, gained brief power and pseudorespectability in much of the Midwest and some of the East. These two factors, added to the persistent anti-Japanese propaganda and organiza-tional activity of the western exclusionists, eventually created a climate of opinion that made exclusion possible.

Perhaps the key organizational meeting, at the national level, was held in the caucus room of the United States House of Representatives on April 20, 1921. Called by Senator Hiram Johnson and the rest of the California delega-tion, it united one senator and one representative from each of twelve other western states into an informal executive committee to push exclusion through

Congress. The group insisted that the West was being "invaded." Their argument is worth quoting at length.

> The process of invasion has been aptly termed "peaceful penetration." The invasion is by an alien people. They are a people unassimilable by marriage. They are a people who are a race unto themselves, and by virtue of that very fact ever will be a race and a nation unto themselves, it matters not what may be the land of their birth.
>
> Economically we are not able to compete with them and maintain the American standard of living; racially we cannot assimilate them. Hence we must exclude them from our shores as settlers in our midst and prohibit them from owning land. Those already here will be protected in their right to the enjoyment of life, liberty, and legally acquired property. . . .
>
> The alternative [to exclusion] is that the richest section of the United States will gradually come into the complete control of an alien race. . . . A careful study of the subject will convince anyone who will approach it with an open mind that the attitude of California, and other states . . . is not only justifiable but essential to the national welfare.[18]

But before this powerful congressional group could get into action, the Supreme Court of the United States made things a little easier for the exclusionists. As we have seen, Japanese and other Asians were considered aliens ineligible to citizenship. This presumption stemmed, not from any constitutional bar, but from the naturalization statute, which, after the Dred Scott decision of 1857 and the Fourteenth Amendment, had been rewritten to permit naturalization of "white persons" and aliens of African descent. Although in some jurisdictions—most significantly Hawaii—courts had naturalized Japanese and other aliens, prevailing practice had been to bar them. This practice was challenged by Takao Ozawa, born in Japan but educated in the United States. The court conceded that he was "well qualified by character and education for citizenship."

Ozawa's counsel, George W. Wickersham, who had been Attorney General under William Howard Taft, argued that in the absence of any specific congressional provision barring Japanese, they were eligible for citizenship, and he pointed out that the original language, which went back to 1790, had spoken of "free white persons." The original intent of Congress, Wickersham insisted, had not in any way been aimed at Japanese or other Asians. The court unanimously rejected Wickersham's argument, and confirmed the denial of citizenship to Ozawa.[19] The decision meant that congressional exclusionists could now safely use the time-honored "aliens ineligible to citizenship formula" and did not have to resort to a special Japanese exclusion act, as had been the case with the Chinese.

For tactical reasons, the exclusionists bided their time; exclusion of Japanese would come, not through special action, but as a part of the general restriction of immigration which the nativist climate of the 1920's made a foregone conclusion.

What became the National Origins Act of 1924 originated in the House of Representatives in late 1923. After much backing and filling the House Committee on Immigration—under the chairmanship of a West Coast representative, Albert Johnson of Washington—came up with a frankly racist quota system whose basic aims were to reduce greatly the volume of immigration in general and to all but eliminate "non-Anglo-Saxon" immigration from eastern and southern Europe. As reported by the Committee and passed by the House, the bill also contained a section barring all "aliens ineligible to citizenship." (Had the quota system, which was based on the number of individuals from each country reported in the 1890 census, been applied to Japan, the result would have been a maximum of 100 immigrants a year.)

In the Senate, however, exclusionists did not control the Immigration Committee, and the bill reported to that body provided for a Japanese quota. While the debate was in progress Secretary of State Charles Evans Hughes suggested to Japanese Ambassador Masanao Hanihara that a letter from him containing an authoritative description of the Gentlemen's Agreement would be helpful in combating the drive for exclusion, which neither government wanted. Hanihara complied. In the course of the letter to Hughes, which was made public, Hanihara spoke accurately of the possible results of exclusion as opposed to a token quota.

> I have stated or rather repeated all this to you rather candidly and in a most friendly spirit, for I realize, as I believe you do, the grave consequences which the enactment of the measure retaining [the aliens ineligible to citizenship] provision would inevitably bring upon the otherwise happy and mutually advantageous relations between our two countries.

At the time Hanihara's note was made public by Hughes, it seemed possible that the Senate, usually more sensitive to the international implications of its actions, would reject the exclusion provisions of the House bill. But in a shrewd but utterly unprincipled tactical stroke, Senator Henry Cabot Lodge of Massachusetts, seizing upon the phrase "grave consequences," made the language of the Japanese ambassador's friendly note seem to be a "veiled threat." "The United States," he insisted, "cannot legislate by the exercise by any other country of veiled threats." Once the matter had been made a question of national honor, reason flew out the window. Senators who had previously expressed themselves as favorable to a Japanese quota or a continuation of the Gentlemen's Agreement, now, for what they said were patriotic reasons, joined the exclusionist side of the debate. On the key roll call, the Senate vote was 76–2 against the Japanese.

With the passage of the Immigration Act of 1924 all but one of the basic demands of the anti-Japanese movement had been met. Although many individual exclusionists continued to agitate for a constitutional amendment that would deprive Nisei of their citizenship, such an amendment was never seriously considered by Congress. But, after a campaign of nearly a quarter century, exclusion had been achieved, the immigration question had been settled. The exclusionists were exultant: "I am repaid for my efforts," wrote former California Senator James D. Phelan who had been an exclusionist from the beginning; "the Japs are routed."

But left in the wake of the rout was a sizable immigrant community with a growing number of citizen offspring. At the time of the Gentlemen's Agreement male Issei had outnumbered females by better than 7 to 1; the years of largely female immigration after 1908 had somewhat redressed that balance, but many thousands of older Issei were doomed to bachelorhood if they remained in America. Despite the halt in immigration, the Japanese population of the United States continued to rise (the slight drop in total population between 1930 and 1940 would soon be reversed by the births of Sansei, which were just beginning), as the table indicates:

Japanese Population, Continental United States

	Total	Alien	Native	Per Cent Native
1920	111,010	81,383	29,672	26.7
1930	138,834	70,477	68,357	49.2
1940	126,947	47,305	79,642	62.7

The Japanese American community was thus really becoming two communities in the years after 1920: the Issei community, alien and somewhat Japan-centered, and the Nisei community, native and distinctly American-oriented. As the years passed, the first grew steadily older and smaller—absolutely and relatively—while the second matured and saw its influence grow. But during most of these years the overwhelming majority of Nisei were children. In a typical Issei family, children were born in the years 1918–1922 to a 35-year-old father and a 25-year-old mother; this meant that the numerically most significant group of Nisei were coming of age between the years 1939 and 1943. Even without any external crisis, generational conflict surely would have arisen between the Issei and their children. As John Modell has observed:

> [The Nisei] had inherited from his parents a remarkable desire to succeed in the face of hardship, but had also learned the American definition of success, by which standard the accommodation made by his parents could not be considered satisfactory.[20]

The older immigrant generation and their American children had many conflicts, but essentially these conflicts were over life style. The Issei, like many immigrant groups before and since, tried to re-create a Japanese society in America, but the image of Japan which most of them held was static. They remembered, as immigrants usually do, the Japan of their youth, not the emerging, industrializing Japan of the twenties and thirties. Since the United States deliberately tried to keep them separate by both law and custom, the Issei were probably better insulated against Americanization than were contemporary immigrant groups from Europe. Within the Issei community almost all the institutions—the press, the church, and the other associational groups—were Japan- and Japanese-language centered. At the same time, membership in a board spectrum of Americanizing institutions was denied to them. Had the immigrant generation been eligible for naturalization and at least potential voters, certain opportunities would have been open to them.

On the other hand, despite their own cultural isolation, the Issei insisted that their children not only accept education but excel in it. The Nisei thus went to school and were subjected to the most powerful Americanizing influence; fortunately for them, their number in any school was generally so small that the classrooms they attended were truly integrated. Therefore, they participated, from early childhood, in at least a part of American society; despite the general anti-Orientalism of western American society, the schools themselves seem to have been, almost without exception, more than fair to the Nisei children. At least part of the explanation for this was the exceptional behavior and aspiration of the Nisei children; from the very first they charmed their American teachers and ranked quite high in scholastic achievement. That these achievements were not always appreciated by the rest of the society is perhaps best illustrated by the case of John Aiso, now a judge in Los Angeles. He was the Los Angeles winner in the American Legion oratorical contest one year, but the authorities of that organization sent the second place finisher, a Caucasian to represent Los Angeles in the national finals in Washington.

Outside school, however, the Nisei faced a society that rejected them regardless of their accomplishments. Fully credentialed Nisei education majors, for example, were virtually unemployable as teachers in the very schools in which they had excelled. Whatever their skills, most Nisei were forced into the ethnic economic community; their parents expected and accepted this—shouldn't children follow in the footsteps of their parents? —but the Nisei resented and chafed at the low wages, long hours, and lack of status which jobs in the ethnic community entailed. As one Nisei wrote, in 1937:

> I am a fruitstand worker. It is not a very attractive nor distinguished occupation. . . . I would much rather it were doctor or lawyer . . . but my aspiration of developing into such [was] frustrated long ago. . . . I am only what I am, a professional carrot washer.[21]

The almost total lack of economic opportunity outside the ethnic community had closed down the horizons for this young man. He went on to say that the zenith of his aspirations was to save some money and get a business of his own, which would probably be a fruit or vegetable market. Other Nisei were similarly "trapped" in agriculture, gardening, curio shops, and other aspects of the economic ghetto. Despite what Modell calls their

"American definition of success," all but a very few of the maturing Nisei generation found that their "safest recourse" was within the ethnic economic structure.

There was generational political and cultural conflict as well. Most of the Issei identified with Japan. Their organizations—for example, the Japanese Chamber of Commerce of Los Angeles—tended to support or at least find a rationale for Japanese aggression. In a 1931 publication the Chamber complained of "China's oppressive policy toward the Japanese" and insisted that the purpose of Japanese troops in Manchuria was "purely to protect the life and property of our countrymen" and that "we possess no political ambition." Similar treatment was given to what the Japanese liked to call the "China incident" of the mid-1930's.[22]

The Nisei did not share in these sentiments. It was not so much a case of opposing the interests of Japan, although there were a few members of both the immigrant and second generation who participated in such anti-Japanese activities as picketing Japanese ships in the late 1930's. It was simply that the vast majority of the Nisei were almost wholly America-oriented and simply did not concern themselves with things Japanese. As early as the 1920's they began to form their own organizations; there were Japanese-American Young Republicans and Young Democrats and even some all-Japanese American Legion posts. What was to become the most important of the Nisei organizations—the Japanese-American Citizens League (JACL)—formally came into being in 1930 and had arisen out of a number of local and regional organizations of the second generation.

Even if there had been no war crisis, the JACL was on a collision course with the organizations of the older generation. Since it was an organization for citizens, the older generation was barred; since it stressed Americanization and minimized even cultural ties with Japan, its goals were somewhat repugnant to many of the Issei, especially to the community leaders. The JACL creed, written in 1940, perhaps best expresses the orientation of the more articulate Nisei on the eve of World War II, and is worth quoting in full.

> I am proud that I am an American citizen of Japanese ancestry, for my very background makes me appreciate more fully the wonderful advantages of this nation. I believe in her institutions, ideals and traditions; I glory in her heritage; I boast of her history; I trust in her future. She has granted me liberties and opportunities such as no individual enjoys in this world today. She has given me an education befitting kings. She has entrusted me with the responsibilities of the franchise. She has permitted me to build a home, to earn a livelihood, to worship, think, speak and act as I please—as a free man equal to every other man.
>
> Although some individuals may discriminate against me, I shall never become bitter or lose faith, for I know that such persons are not representative of the majority of the American people. True, I shall do all in my power to discourage such practices, but I shall do it in the American way—above board, in the open, through courts of law, by education, by proving myself to be worthy of equal treatment and consideration. I am firm in my

belief that American sportsmanship and attitude of fair play will judge citizenship and patriotism on the basis of action and achievement, and not on the basis of physical characteristics. Because I believe in America, and I trust she believes in me, and because I have received innumerable benefits from her, I pledge myself to do honor to her at all times and all places; to support her constitution; to obey her laws; to respect her flag; to defend her against all enemies, foreign and domestic; to actively assume my duties and obligations as a citizen, cheerfully and without any reservations whatsoever, in the hope that I may become a better American in a greater America.[23]

This hypernationalism, as we have seen, did not spring from the Nisei experience or accurately reflect the current status of the second generation. It was, rather, an expression of expectations, a hopeful vision of what the future would be like. As many historians of immigration have observed, when the second generation becomes patriotic, quite often it tries to become 200 per cent American. A good part of this overreaction is compensation and a conscious rejection of an alien heritage that is seen as retarding the aspirations of the second-generation group concerned. Another factor is surely the belief, conscious or unconscious, that if only it protests its loyalty loudly enough, the majority will come to believe its protestations. In addition, of course, many of the Nisei had become so thoroughly Americanized that they actually believed the creed as written, although one wonders how the "professional carrot washer" with his frustrated ambitions felt about the "wonderful advantages . . . liberties and opportunities such as no inidvidual enjoys in this world today."

But, whatever its basic cause or motivation, the superpatriotism of the JACL availed the Nisei little. They were prepared to defend America "against all her enemies," but when war came America identified them as the enemy. They tried, in many ways with success, to be better Americans than most of their white fellow citizens, but when the chips were down their countrymen saw only the color of their skin and remembered only that their parents had come from the land of the rising sun.

NOTES

1. HARRY H. L. KITANO, *Japanese Americans: The Evolution of a Subculture* (Englewood Cliffs, N.J.: Prentice-Hall, 1969), p. 14.
2. These and other population data from U.S. Census and immigration figures. Some of the nineteenth-century data used later are not wholly accurate.
3. On Chinese, the standard work is ELMER SANDMEYER, *The Anti-Chinese Movement in California* (Urbana, Ill.: University of Illinois Press, 1939); but see also

GUNTHER BARTH, *Bitter Strength: A History of the Chinese in the United States, 1850–1870* (Cambridge, Mass.: Harvard University Press, 1964).

4. California Constitution, 1879, Article XIX.

5. WILLIAM R. LOCKLEAR, "The Celestials and the Angels," *Southern California Quarterly* (September 1960).

6. PAUL CRANE and ALFRED LARSON, "The Chinese Massacre," *Annals of Wyoming*, January–April 1940; and ARLEN RAY WILSON, "The Rock Springs, Wyoming, Chinese Massacre, 1885," M.A. thesis, University of Wyoming, 1967.

7. FREDERICK RUDOLPH, "Chinamen in Yankeedom: Anti-Unionism in Massachusetts in 1870," *American Historical Review* (October 1947).

8. WALT W. ROSTOW, *The Stages of Economic Growth: A Non-Communist Manifesto* (London: Cambridge University Press, 1960).

9. HILARY CONROY, *The Japanese Frontier in Hawaii, 1868–1898* (Berkeley and Los Angeles: University of California Press, 1953).

10. KITANO, p. 16.

11. ROGER DANIELS, "Westerners from the East: Oriental Immigrants Reappraised," *Pacific Historical Review* (November 1966). See also JOHN MODELL, "The Japanese American Family: A Perspective for Future Investigations," *Pacific Historical Review* (February 1968).

12. MASAKAZU IWATA, "The Japanese Immigrants in California Agriculture," *Agricultural History* (1962).

13. This and the subsequent pages on the anti-Japanese movement are condensed from ROGER DANIELS, *The Politics of Prejudice: The Anti-Japanese Movement in California and the Struggle for Japanese Exclusion* (Berkeley and Los Angeles: University of California Press, 1962; paperback edition, New York: Atheneum, 1968).

14. For a discussion of rationality and prejudice, see ISABELLA BLACK, "American Labour and Chinese Immigration," *Past and Present* (July 1963); and my comments in the April 1964, issue.

15. *Coast Seaman's Journal* (San Francisco), July 25, 1888.

16. CONROY, p. 140.

17. Many diplomatic historians take a more favorable view of Roosevelt's efforts. See, for example, RAYMOND A. ESTHUS, *Theodore Roosevelt and Japan* (Seattle: University of Washington Press, 1966).

18. House Document No. 89, 67th Cong., 1st Sess. (1921), p. 4.

19. For an analysis of Ozawa and similar cases, see MILTON R. KONVITZ, *The Alien and the Asiatic in American Law* (Ithaca, N.Y.: Cornell University Press, 1946), pp. 81 ff.

20. JOHN MODELL, "Class or Ethnic Solidarity: The Japanese American Company Union," paper read at the Pacific Coast Branch Meeting, American Historical Association, August 1968.

21. TAISHI MATSUMOTO, "The Protest of a Professional Carrot Washer," *Kashu Mainichi*, April 4, 1937, as cited by MODELL, "Class or Ethnic Solidarity."

22. Japanese Chamber of Commerce, *The Present Situation in Manchuria and Shanghai* (Los Angeles, ca. 1931).

23. Written by MIKE MOSAOKA some time in 1940, it was published in the *Congressional Record* for May 9, 1941, p. A2205.

Why It Happened Here

Roger Daniels

Writing in *Harper's* Magazine in September 1945, constitutional law specialist Eugene V. Rostow unhesitatingly characterized the evacuation and
incarceration of the West Coast Japanese as "our worst wartime mistake."
Two decades of scholarship have merely rung the changes on that indictment.
Professor A. Russell Buchanan writing on World War II in the authoritative
New American Nation Series argued that it was "the most widespread dis-
regard of personal rights since . . . slavery." Most educated persons today
would echo these sentiments; in addition, most Americans seem to have
changed their basic attitudes toward the Japanese. This dramatic change of
image is perhaps best reflected in a pair of Gallup polls which asked a cross-
section of Americans to characterize Japanese. In 1942, the image was negative: the five most frequently mentioned adjectives were "treacherous," "sly,"
"cruel," "warlike," and "hard-working." In 1961 the same question drew a
quite positive set of adjectives: "hard-working" moved to the top, followed by
"artistic," "intelligent," and "progressive," with a residual "sly" ranking fifth.

With this highly favorable image, in part at least a result of the magnifi-
cent and well-publicized performance of Japanese-American troops during
the war plus a reaction against wartime excesses, it is almost impossible
for the generations that have come to maturity since the war to comprehend how it was possible for such an undemocratic act to occur in this
country under the most liberal government it had ever known. When
one tries to explain to students that it was one of the most popular wartime acts, many react with stunned disbelief. This essay has a dual burden:
to tell first of all, what happened here and how it happened, and then
to try to place the wartime evacuation into a more long-range historical
perspective.

First of all I would like to try to convey something of the feeling of
the weeks after Pearl Harbor in Los Angeles: much of the material presented will be drawn from the pages of the Los Angeles *Times*. The result
would be much the same had almost any other California newspaper been

SOURCE: From *Racism in California* by Roger Daniels and Spencer C. Olin, Jr. Copyright ©
1972 by Roger Daniels. Reprinted by permission.

NOTE: This selection, first delivered to a symposium on the twenty-fifth anniversary of
the relocation and sponsored by the Extension Division of the University of California,
Los Angeles, draws heavily on the research findings of Stetson Conn, now the United
States Army's Chief Military Historian. For an expanded treatment see Roger Daniels,
Concentration Camps, USA: Japanese Americans and World War II (New York: Holt,
Rinehart and Winston, 1971).

used: the *Times* was not especially prejudiced against Japanese (by 1941 California standards that is) and was more moderate than many papers. The predominant feeling that one gets from reading the press of that period is one of near hysteria. Hawaii, which had actually been attacked, was relatively calm. California, thousands of miles from the scene of operations, was nervous and trigger happy. The paranoid style in California life is not as recent as some would have us believe. A thousand movies and stories and reminiscences have recorded the solemn mood with which the nation reacted on that "day of infamy" in 1941. Yet, at Gilmore Field, the *Times* informs us

> Eighteen thousand spectators at the Hollywood Bears–Columbus Bulldogs football game . . . jumped to their feet and cheered wildly when the public address system announced that a state of war existed between Japan and the United States.

In its first editorial reaction, the *Times* announced that California was a "zone of danger": and invoked the ancient vigilante tradition of the state by calling for

> . . . alert, keen-eyed civilians [who could be] of yeoman service in cooperating with the military and . . . civilian authorities against spies, saboteurs and fifth columnists. We have thousands of Japanese here. . . . Some, perhaps many, are . . . good Americans. What the rest may be we do not know, nor can we take a chance in the light of yesterday's demonstration that treachery and double-dealing are major Japanese weapons.

Day after day, throughout December, January, February, and March, the *Times* and the rest of the California press spewed forth racial venom against the Japanese. The term "jap," of course, was standard usage. Japanese were also "Nips," "yellow men," "mad dogs," and "yellow vermin," to name only a few of the choicer epithets. Individual columnists and bylined writers in the *Times* added their bit. Ed Ainsworth cautioned his readers

> . . . to be careful to differentiate between races. The Chinese and Koreans both hate the Japs more than we do. . . . Be sure of nationality before you are rude to anybody.

Just after a series of murderous and sometimes fatal attacks on Japanese residents by Filipinos, a *Times* sports page feature was headlined:

FILIPINO BOXERS NOTED FOR COURAGE, VALOR

Columnist Lee Shippey, who often stressed that some Japanese were alright, prophetically suggested, on New Year's Day, that there be established

> . . . a number of big, closely guarded, closely watched truck farms on which Japanese-Americans could earn a living and assure us a steady supply of vegetables.

If a Nazi had suggested doing this with Poles, Shippey undoubtedly would have called it a slave labor camp. But the palm for *shrecklichkeit* must go to Westbrook Pegler, a major outlet of what Oswald Garrison Villard once called "the sewer system of American journalism." Taking time off from his vendettas with Eleanor Roosevelt and the American Labor Movement, Pegler proposed, on December 9, that every time the Axis murdered hostages

> . . . the United States could raise [them] 100 victims selected out of [our] concentration camps [for German Bundists, Italian Fascists and] many alien Japanese.

I shall conclude this brief survey of incitement to racial violence by our supposedly responsible press by quoting a few headlines, none of which had any basis in fact and all of which heightened local hysteria and made people believe that military or paramilitary Japanese activists were all around them:

JAP BOAT FLASHES MESSAGE ASHORE
ENEMY PLANES SIGHTED OVER CALIFORNIA COAST
TWO JAPANESE WITH MAPS AND ALIEN LITERATURE
   SEIZED
JAP AND CAMERA HELD IN BAY CITY
VEGETABLES FOUND FREE OF POISON
FOOD PLOT FEARS SPIKED
CHINESE ABLE TO SPOT JAP
MAP REVEALS JAP MENACE
   Network of Alien Farms Covers
   Strategic Defense Areas Over Southland
JAPS PLAN COAST ATTACK IN APRIL
   WARNS CHIEF OF KOREAN SPY BAND

In short, any reading of the wartime California press—or for that matter viewing the wartime movies that still pollute our television channels—shows clearly that while a distinction was continually being made between "good" and "bad" Germans—a welcome change from World War I—few distinctions were ever made between Japanese. The evil deeds of Nazi Germany were the deeds of bad men: The evil deeds of Tojo's Japan were the deeds of a "bad" race. While the press was throwing fuel on the fires of racial animosity, other faggots were contributed by politicians, federal officials, and, above all, the military. The Governor of California, Culbert L. Olson, a liberal Democrat, had insisted, before Pearl Harbor, that Japanese Americans should enjoy all their rights and privileges even if war with Japan came, and correctly pointed out that equal protection under the law was a "basic tenet" of American government. But Olson's constitutional scruples were a casualty of Pearl Harbor: on December 8, the Governor told the press that he was thinking of ordering all Japanese, alien and citizen, to observe house arrest "to avoid riot and disturbance."

The Federal Department of Justice, working partially through the F.B.I. and calling on local law enforcement officials for assistance, began round-ups of those they considered "dangerous" enemy aliens. Throughout the nation this initial round-up involved about 3,000 persons, half of whom were Japanese, most of them living in California. In other words, the federal authorities responsible for counter-espionage thought that some 1,500 persons of Japanese ancestry or nationality constituted a danger to the nation. This was slightly over 1 per cent of the country's Japanese population. It might be useful to give the 1940 census figures. There were, in the continental United States about 127,000 Japanese, fewer than one-tenth of 1 per cent of the total population; 113,000 of these (almost 90 per cent) lived in the three Pacific states and Arizona, while 94,000 (almost 75 per cent) lived in California. Almost two-thirds of the total were native-born citizens. The nearly 1,500 who were initially rounded up were almost universally of the Issei or immigrant generation—and thus enemy aliens—and usually community or organizational leaders. The government, acting as it so often does on guilt by association, automatically pulled in the officers and leading lights of a number of Japanese organizations and religious groups. Many of these were perhaps "rooting" for the emperor rather than the president and thus technically subversive, but most of them were rather elderly and inoffensive gentlemen and not a threat to anything. This limited internment, however, was a not too discreditable performance for a wartime government security agency, but it must be noted that even at this restrained level the government acted much more harshly, in terms of the numbers interned, toward Japanese nationals than toward German nationals, and more harshly toward Germans than Italians. It should also be noted, however, that more than a few young Nisei leaders applauded this early round-up and contrasted their own native-son loyalty to the presumed disloyalty of many of the leaders of the Issei or immigrant generation.

In addition to the selective round-up of enemy aliens, the Justice Department also announced the sealing off of the Mexican and Canadian borders to "all persons of Japanese ancestry, whether citizen or alien." Thus by December 8, 1941, that branch of the federal government particularly charged with protecting the rights of our citizens was willing to single out one ethnic group for invidious treatment. Other national civilian officials discriminated in other ways: even Fiorello La Guardia, who was for a time director of the Office of Civilian Defense as well as Mayor of New York, pointedly omitted mention of the Japanese in two public statements calling for decent treatment of enemy aliens and suggesting presumptive loyalty for Germans and Italians. Seventeen years earlier La Guardia had been one of three congressmen to speak openly in favor of continued Japanese immigration, but in December 1941, he could find nothing good to say about the Japanese.

Even more damaging were the mendacious statements of Frank Knox, Roosevelt's Secretary of the Navy. On December 15, in a story that made front pages all over the country, Secretary Knox, returning from a quick inspection of the damage at Pearl Harbor, spoke of "treachery" there and insisted that much of the disaster was caused by "the most effective fifth column work that's come out of this war, except in Norway." The disaster at Pearl Harbor, as is now generally acknowledged, was caused largely by the unpreparedness and incompetence of the local military commanders, as Knox already knew. But the secretary probably didn't want the people to lose faith in their Navy, so the Japanese population of Hawaii—and indirectly all Japanese Americans—was made the scapegoat on which to hang the big lie. (Knox, it should be remarked, as a Chicago newspaper publisher in private life had a professional understanding of these matters.)

But the truly crucial role was played by the other service, the United States Army. The key individual, initially at least, was John L. De Witt, in 1941 a Lieutenant General and Commander of both the Western Defense Command and 4th Army, with headquarters at San Francisco's Presidio. Despite these warlike titles De Witt was essentially an administrator in uniform, a staff officer who had specialized in supply and had practically nothing to do with combat during his entire Army career. Serving under him, in December 1941, as a Corps Commander and in charge of the defense of Southern California was a real fighting man, the then Major General Joseph W. Stilwell, the famed "Vinegar Joe" of the heartbreaking Burma campaigns. His diary of those hectic days gives an accurate and pungent picture of the hysteria and indecisiveness that prevailed at De Witt's headquarters.

> Dec. 8—Sunday night "air raid" at San Francisco. . . . Fourth Army kind of jittery.
>
> Dec. 9— . . . Fleet of thirty-four [Japanese] ships between San Francisco and Los Angeles. Later—not authentic. . . .
>
> Dec. 11 [Phone call from 4th Army] "The main Japanese battle fleet is 164 miles off San Francisco." I believed it, like a damn fool. . . .
>
>   Of course [the 4th Army] passed the buck on this report. They had it from a "usually reliable source," but they should never have put it out without check.
>
> Dec. 13—Not content with the above blah, [the 4th] Army pulled another at ten-thirty today. "Reliable information that attack on Los Angeles is imminent. A general alarm being considered." . . . What jackass would sound a general alarm [which would have meant warning all civilians to leave the area] under the circumstances? The [4th] Army G-2 is just another amateur, like all the rest of the staff. Rule: the higher the headquarters, the more important is *calm*.
>
> Dec. 18 [An unidentified subordinate commander in the Long Beach-Torrance area wanted Stilwell to evacuate all Japanese from Terminal Island and to take other measures against the civilian population] "We talked to midnight," Stilwell wrote, "by which time he was pretty well calmed down."
>
> Dec. 19 [Stilwell tries to soothe the fears of an Air Corps Lt. Col. in charge of a bombing range in the Mohave Desert] ". . . he was fearful of a parachute attack that would come in off carriers or from a secret base in

Lower California, and murder them all. Or Japs from Los Angeles could sneak up and sabotage everything. . . . (P.S. The colonel has seen some suspicious signaling with flashlights)
This situation has produced some strange cases of jitters. Common sense is thrown to the winds and any absurdity is believed.
The wild, farcical and fantastic stuff that G-2 Fourth Army pushes out!

Just before Christmas Stilwell was transferred to Washington; shortly after his arrival there he noted that Lieutenant General Lesley J. McNair, Deputy Commander, Army Ground Forces had told him that "De Witt has gone crazy and requires ten refusals before he realizes it is 'No.' "

It was in this panic-ridden, amateurish Western Defense Command atmosphere that some of the most crucial decisions about the evacuation were made. Before discussing them, I should point out that the nearest Japanese aircraft during most of December were attacking Wake Island, more than 5,000 miles west of San Francisco, and any major Japanese surface vessels or troops were even farther away. In fact, elements of the Luftwaffe over the North Atlantic were actually closer to California than any Imperial Japanese planes. But despite the patent absurdity of these fears, it is axiomatic that misconceptions, when acted upon, may become more significant than the reality that they distort.

The official Army history of the evacuation—written by Stetson Conn, a perceptive civilian historian in the office of the Chief of Military History —gives us additional insights into General De Witt's confusion. On December 19, De Witt formally proposed to the War Department that alien Japanese 14 years of age and older be removed from the West Coast and that these individuals "be held under restraint after removal . . . in order to preclude their surreptitious return." De Witt felt that these 40,000 persons constituted an immediate and potential menace to vital measures of defense. (De Witt's language in this message was enemy aliens, Germans, Italians, and Japanese; the number he proposed evacuating however, was the number of alien Japanese.)

A week later, the Provost Marshal General of the War Department, Major General Allen W. Gullion, the Army's top cop, a service intellectual who had once read a paper to an International Congress of Judicial Experts on the "present state of international law regarding the protection of civilians from the new war technics," telephoned De Witt and told him that he (Gullion) had just been visited in Washington by a representative of the Los Angeles Chamber of Commerce who asked that all Japanese in the Los Angeles area be rounded up. De Witt was opposed to this and told General Gullion that:

I'm very doubtful that it would be common sense procedure to try and intern 117,000 Japanese in this theater. . . . An American citizen, after all, is an American citizen. And while they all may not be loyal, I think we can weed the disloyal out of the loyal and lock them up if necessary.

At about the same time De Witt opposed a pet Army project—to have control over enemy aliens transferred from the Justice Department to the War Department. This was apparently instigated in the Provost Marshal General's office by an empire-building lawyer in uniform, Major Karl R. Bendetsen. He and his chief, General Gullion, continually pushed General De Witt to adopt their point of view. Engaged in a bureaucratic battle with Attorney General Francis Biddle to transfer the enemy aliens from civilian to military control, from due process to martial law, they apparently felt they could win only if a field commander declared that such a transfer was a military necessity.

General De Witt, not a strong character, as we have seen, soon got the message. By mid-January he was telling the War Department that any raid on the West Coast would be accompanied by "a violent outburst of coordinated and controlled sabotage." On January 24 he told General Gullion that:

> The fact that nothing has happened so far is more or less ominous in that I feel that in view of the fact that we have had no sporadic attempts at sabotage there is control being exercised and when we have it it will be on a mass basis.

The next day the "quickie" investigation of Pearl Harbor conducted by the Roberts Commission was released. One of its erroneous conclusions was that there had been widespread espionage by Japanese residents in the Islands. On January 27 De Witt met with Governor Olson of California and told Washington afterwards that "the best people in California" wanted all the Japanese out. Two days later De Witt saw California Attorney General Earl Warren, a Republican who was then preparing his campaign that would defeat Olson in November. Warren, the General told Washington, was in thorough agreement with the Governor that the Japanese population should be removed from the coastal areas. In this same conversation, De Witt for the first time joined the growing consensus for a mass evacuation of aliens and citizens, and came around to the Provost Marshal's view that the military should have charge of enemy aliens, at least within the Western Defense Command. In the same conversation, Bendetsen told De Witt that, without authorization from his civilian chiefs, he was meeting with California and other Western congressmen and reporting De Witt's new views to them. The legislators were organizing under the aegis of Hiram W. Johnson, California's senior Senator who organized a similar ad hoc steering committee in the 1920's to get Japanese exclusion. What Bendetsen was actually doing was telling the Western congressmen that the way to get what both he and they wanted—the removal of all Japanese from the West Coast—was to undercut the Attorney General Francis Biddle, a civil libertarian but not, in this instance, a fighter. Biddle was also being undercut by one of his own subordinates, Tom C. Clark, a future justice of he Supreme Court, who was the Justice Department's coordinator for enemy aliens on the West Coast.

In early February, De Witt told Washington that what the California authorities really wanted was to move the Japanese to interior agricultural areas of the state to avoid the possible influx of Mexicans and Negroes to replace them if they were completely removed. De Witt thought that this proposal was consistent with "military necessity" as he understood it. By this time the Provost Marshal's proposal had drifted up the chain of command to the civilian leadership of the department—Secretary of War Henry L. Stimson and his Assistant Secretary, John J. McCloy. Both of these men were Eastern Establishment Republicans brought into the administration as a unity move. On February 3, the civilians, in the words of General Mark Clark, were "pretty much against" the mass evacuation of the Japanese "and they are also pretty much against interfering with citizens unless it can be done legally." Despite the apparent disavowal by their civilian chiefs, Gullion and Bendetsen continued to assume, correctly as it turned out, that they would get their way in the end.

On February 6, Gullion and Bendetsen rejected De Witt's California-oriented suggestions about resettlement within the state—in the words of the key Provost Marshal memorandum on the subject because it contained "too much of the spirit of Rotary" and ignored "the necessary cold-bloodedness of war." Instead Gullion and Bendetsen formally recommended to the civilian Assistant Secretary McCloy that all alien Japanese be interned east of the Sierra Nevadas with as many citizen members of their families as would voluntarily accompany them, and the exclusion of the remaining citizen Japanese from precisely those areas of the West Coast where most of them lived. The next day, February 7, Stimson and McCloy who only four days previously were "pretty much against it," had somehow become converted to the Bendetsen-Gullion view. Perhaps they had become convinced that it was "pretty much legal." At any rate, by February 7 McCloy had decided to send Lieutenant Colonel Bendetsen (he had just been promoted) to the West Coast "to confer with General De Witt in connection with the mass evacuation of all Japanese." Three days later, Attorney General Biddle, who made a poor fight in a good cause, indicated that he was ready to throw in the sponge, but insisted that the Army would have to do its own dirty work.

The conflict at the Cabinet level necessitated an appeal to the Commander-in-Chief, whose final approval would have been needed in any event. On Wednesday, February 11, 1942—the real day of infamy as far as the Constitution was concerned—Stimson and McCloy sent Franklin D. Roosevelt a brief memorandum that listed four alternatives and is worth quoting in full:

1. Is the President willing to authorize us to move Japanese citizens as well as aliens from restricted areas?

2. Should we undertake withdrawal from the entire strip De Witt originally recommended, which involves a number of over 100,000 people, if we included both aliens and Japanese citizens?

3. Should we undertake the intermediate step involving, say 70,000,

which includes large communities such as Los Angeles, San Diego, and Seattle?

4. Should we take any lesser step such as the establishment of restricted areas around airplane plants and critical installations, even though General De Witt states that in several, at least, of the large communities this would be wasteful, involve difficult administration problems, and might be a source of more continuous irritation and trouble than 100 per cent withdrawal from the area?

President Roosevelt refused to choose. After a brief telephone call the decision-making power was passed to two men who had never been elected to any office. "We have *carte blanche* to do what we want as far as the President is concerned," McCloy telephoned Bendetsen at the Presidio. According to the Assistant Secretary, Roosevelt's only qualification was "Be as reasonable as you can."

Why did Roosevelt do it? No historian can ever answer, definitively, this kind of question, but every historian worth his salt must at least try. Nothing anyone can say in explanation, however, can expiate; no doctrine of historical relativism can absolve Franklin Roosevelt. But the student of history must also try to understand the forces that were at work. February 1942 was not a good time for the United States. The Japanese had landed on the island of Singapore on February 8, on New Britain on February 9, and were advancing rapidly in Burma. Roosevelt was concerned, first of all, with winning the war, and secondly with unity at home, so that he, unlike Wilson, could win the peace with the advice and consent of the Senate. He could read the congressional signs well and knew that cracking down on the Japanese Americans would be popular both on Capitol Hill and with the nation at large. And the last thing he wanted was a rift with establishment Republicans such as Stimson and McCloy. So do what you think you have to do to win the war, he told the civilian spokesmen for the military. And one can imagine him on the phone in the great Oval office where so much of our history has been made, that leonine head lifting up and with the politician's charm and equivocation, saying "Be as reasonable as you can." Thus do great and good men do evil acts in the name of good. The closest historical analogy that comes to mind is Lincoln's amoral insistence, at the start of the Civil War, that preservation of the union was central and slavery peripheral to the nation's war aims. But the very centrality of slavery slowly but surely asserted itself despite the politicians and the war for the union did become in Mrs. Howe's prophetic words, a "fight to make men free."

But the 110,000 Japanese who were eventually sent to ten God-forsaken camps in the name of a fictitious military necessity remained merely an incident of global war. Outside the West Coast the internment received very little notice and I suspect that during the war years most Americans east of the Rockies were only vaguely aware of it. The Japanese went quietly and voluntarily, as they had been counseled to do by most of their leaders. Schedules were posted and published, and they went, in the same quiet law-abiding manner in which they had lived their lives up to then. But were they being law-abiding? Was the evacuation, necessary or not, legal? Stimson and McCloy had been satisfied that it was "pretty much legal," the President signed the executive orders, Congress had passed ratifying legislation and appropriated money, but what would the Supreme Court say? In the months ahead the Court had three separate chances to strike down the legality of the evacuation, but instead the Court merely "struck out" as far as civil liberties were concerned.

The first case, *Hirabayashi*, involved curfew violation. Gordon Hirabayashi, a native-born American, was arrested and convicted for refusing to obey a curfew order by General De Witt. In a decision handed down on June 21, 1943—North Africa had been liberated but we were still fighting in the Solomons—the court upheld the general rather than the citizen. Chief Justice Harlan Fiske Stone, speaking for a nondissenting but uneasy Court, argued that:

> We cannot close our eyes to the fact demonstrated by experience, that in time of war residents having ethnic affiliations with an invading enemy may be a greater source of danger than those of a different ancestry.

The second and third cases—*Korematsu* and *Endo*—were handed down during Christmas week of 1944, when final victory in the war seemed assured. Fred Korematsu had simply refused to report to a designated point for evacuation, and so was arrested. The Court refused to judge. Justice Hugo Black, writing for the majority, insisted that:

> Korematsu was not excluded from the Military area because of hostility to him or his race. He was excluded because we are at war with the Japanese Empire, because the properly constitued military authorities feared an invasion of our West Coast and felt constrained to take proper security measures, because they decided that the military urgency of the situation demanded that all citizens of Japanese ancestry be segregated from the West Coast temporarily and finally, because Congress, reposing its confidence in this time of war in our military leaders—as inevitably it must—determined that they should have the power to do just this. There was evidence of disloyalty on the part of some, the military authorities considered that the need for action was great, and time was short. We cannot—by availing ourselves of the calm perspective of hindsight—now say that these actions were unjustified.

In a pithier concurrence, Justice William O. Douglas simply stated:

> We cannot sit in judgment on the military requirements of that hour.

Three justices, however, did so sit and found the judgment bad. Owen J. Roberts, Frank Murphy, and Robert L. Jackson all dissented sharply with their brethren. Justice Murphy, probably stated it best when he simply and bluntly characterized Black's majority decision as a "legalization of racism."

The third case involved Mitsuye Endo, a 22-year-old native daughter of undisputed loyalty with a brother in the United States armed forces. She went off to camp, as ordered, but on July 13, 1942, she filed for a writ of *habeas corpus*. Two years and four months later—she was still in camp—the Court ordered her release but refused to inquire into the constitutional question of how she got there, much to the disgust of Justices Murphy and Roberts. Thus, if anyone asks you about the legal status of concentration camps requested by the military, established by executive order, and eventually sanctioned by Congress, tell him simply to go quietly and file for a writ of *habeas corpus* upon his arrival—but warn him that he may have to wait a long time on the docket.

The Supreme Court thus made obeisance to the doctrine of "military necessity," itself a dubious extra-legal criterion, but there was no "military necessity." As we now know, our top military planners did not fear an invasion of the West Coast in 1942, and the Japanese high command never even contemplated one. Is this just the exercise of what Justice Black called the "calm perspective of hindsight?" No, it is not; there was ample evidence available at the time, most glaringly in the differential treatment given Hawaii and the West Coast. The West Coast was a war zone only by virtue of proclamation; Hawaii had been struck by war, and would certainly have been occupied as a necessary prelude to any invasion of the continental United States. In Hawaii persons of Japanese ancestry constituted roughly one-third of the population; yet there was no military necessity to round them up. Without the crutch of "military necessity," the shaky legal underpinnings of the evacuation collapsed completely, and we are left with Justice Murphy's bitter analysis—racism legalized.

This, then, is how it happened here; but there remains the even bigger question of why it happened. The real answer to that question, far beyond the scope of this essay, must be sought in both the American racist tradition, in which, in the words of Chief Justice of the United States Roger B. Taney in 1857, nonwhites "had no rights which the white man was bound to respect," and in the special California racist tradition, which nearly exterminated the Indians, systematically despoiled Spanish-speaking Californians after the American conquest, and, shortly after the beginnings of immigration from China during the Gold Rush, began nearly a century of consistent anti-Oriental behavior. By the 1920's the chief enemy was the Japanese. One dedicated opponent of the Japanese could argue:

> The Japanese are less assimilable and more dangerous as residents in this country than any other people. . . . With great pride of race, they have no idea of assimilating in the sense of amalgamation. They do not come here with any desire or any intent to lose their racial or national identity. They come here specifically and professedly for the purpose of colonizing and establishing here permanently the proud Yamato race. They never cease being Japanese. . . . In pursuit of their intent to colonize this country with that race they seek to secure land and to establish large families. . . . They

have greater energy and greater determination, and greater ambition than the other yellow and brown races. . . . California regards herself as a frontier state. She has been making for 20 years the fight of the nation against the incoming of alien races whose peaceful penetration must in time with absolute certainty drive the white race to the wall, and prior to that time inevitably provoke international trouble across the Pacific.

Added to these fears about Japanese immigrants, there was that phenomenon known as the "yellow peril"—the fear of invasion by armed Oriental hordes. This started out as almost pure fantasy: the first yellow peril books in the 1870's and 1880's feared China, in the nineteenth century a victim rather than a predator. After 1895 it was clear to most that Japan was the real power in the Far East, and when, in 1905, with shots that were truly heard around the world Japan defeated a European power, Czarist Russia, the yellow peril literature began to proliferate. Literally hundreds of books, most of them utterly devoid of any literary or intellectual merit, were written on this theme; there were also movies, articles, and even whole pulp magazines devoted to imaginary invasions. In the popular press, particularly the papers of William Randolph Hearst, the shrill warnings about the menace of Japan became an integral part of editorial policy. By the end of World War I, the threat of a coming Pacific War, a war of the races, was part of the conscious intellectual equipment of almost all Americans. When, in the 1930's Japan began the truly atrocious phase of her imperial expansion into East Asia, the fantasy image seemed to merge with the historical reality.

In short, as the winter of 1941 approached, the American mind was ready to believe anything—literally anything—about Japan and her people. Fear and contempt, as we have seen, were strangely mixed. When, after a stunning and unfair blow, Japan scored success after success, it is not at all surprising that men were able to convince themselves that the evacuation was necessary. Naturally, the overwhelming majority of Americans who were aware of it, approved it, and would have approved worse. It has even been argued that the evacuation was a good thing, because it prevented the mass violence against Japanese Americans that many feel would surely have come. Perhaps. It seems to me, however, that using our prejudice to distort due process was, in some ways at least, worse than the mob violence that might have occurred but didn't. The evacuation did more than commit a legal atrocity against 110,000 innocent people; measured against the total human cost of World War II that wasn't so very much. As the late Morton Grodzins put it, the evacuation gave "precedent and constitutional sanctity for a policy of mass incarceration under military auspices. . . . That . . . betrayed all Americans."

Who was responsible for this betrayal? The question of responsibility has been argued back and forth, and will be again. California pressure groups—the American Legion, the Native Sons and Daughters of the Golden West, the State Grange, the state Federation of Labor, all played their role, as did politicians. General De Witt, the Army, Secretary Stimson, and President Roosevelt have all been blamed. It can also be argued that history itself was really responsible. But men make history, and surely the names of all the leading culprits have been mentioned in this essay. But nearly unnoticed in all this has been the rather Prussian tradition in America that in wartime generals should become the arbiters of all things. The great French war leader, Georges Clemenceau, once said that "War is too important to be left to the generals." No American war leader could say such a thing publicly. But for this particular military atrocity, however, I would amend the statement to read: "Wartime decisions of military necessity are too important to be formulated by second rank bureaucrats." Clearly Bendetsen and his chief Gullion shaped policy and set the stage for the betrayal that was executed by their superiors. Bendetsen, who received the Distinguished Service Medal from a grateful nation for efficiently incarcerating his fellow Americans, admitted (perhaps the right word is boasted) that he "conceived method, formulated details and directed" the mass evacuation of the West Coast Japanese. America has so far been spared from the man on horseback; perhaps what it really has to fear is the middle-echelon manipulator behind a desk.

The Great Betrayal

Audrie Girdner and Anne Loftis

. . . While the Tolan Committee was holding hearings in Portland there took place the first mass evacuation of a Japanese group, both citizens and aliens. One of the committee members referring to the shock that accompanied it, called the removal of the Japanese families from Terminal Island on forty-eight hours' notice a minor Pearl Harbor. It was the first episode in which citizens were involved and the first evacuation ordered by the military. Though only a few hundred people were affected, it is also remembered as the harshest and most arbitrary action taken against the West Coast Japanese during the war.

The fishing colony on Terminal Island, within rifle shot of a great naval base, had been a source of concern to military authorities even before December 7. There were originally about two thousand Japanese on the island, of whom eight hundred were aliens. Five hundred of the group were fishermen and many of their wives worked in the ten canneries on the island until war regulations prevented Issei from doing either. They were situated in a sensitive military zone because it was convenient for fishing and the canneries rented them houses in order to have their labor easily available on short notice.

The houses were really shacks with jagged shingle roofs and no yards. Five rooms rented for $15 a month. "The houses were awful" in the word of Virginia Yamamoto, then Virginia Swanson, who worked as a Baptist missionary on the island for five years before the war. "The Baptist Church was the one beautiful building on the Island, a symbol of hope for the people." There was also a Shinto shrine. The Terminal Islanders were unsophisticated people who worked hard and had little contact with the world on the mainland except for the high-school-age children who crossed by ferry to San Pedro daily to attend classes. The events of the war frightened them all the more because they had led such isolated lives.

Spies on Terminal Island figured importantly in the Dies Committee's "Yellow Book" which was by coincidence released to the press on February 27, the final date for the evacuation of the Island. The committee published the testimony of a Los Angeles police officer assigned to patrol Fish Harbor, who revealed his prejudice when describing a cafe which catered to a "class of trade which would be called 'low' such as Mexicans, Filipinos, and Japanese." He claimed that before the war when Japanese ships

SOURCE: From *The Great Betrayal*, by Audrie Girdner and Anne Loftis. Copyright © 1969 by Audrie Girdner and Anne Loftis. Reprinted with permission of The Macmillan Company.

docked at San Pedro, the crews went to homes on Terminal Island where they "spent many hours in deep conversation pertaining to the American fleet anchored in the harbors of San Pedro and Long Beach respectively." [1] He cited illegal gambling in pool halls, propagandistic Japanese movies, a pay-off man who rewarded spies, and a cafe proprietor who got American soldiers and sailors drunk in order to elicit information from them.

Another witness was a Yugoslavian fisherman who was asked, "Is it not a fact that these Japanese fishing boats, by employing Japanese crews, keep good American citizens from obtaining employment . . . ?" He answered, "Oh, yes; absolutely— The Japanese work cheaper and the canneries like to employ them in preference to us." [2] The fisherman answered affirmatively the question, "Therefore, you believe, do you not, that the concentration of a Japanese alien population in such close proximity to the national defense area and the principal fleet base of the United States is a definite menace?" [3] One of the witnesses, an attorney, Benjamin Harrison, though not indifferent to the possible danger said, "Personally, I am unable to testify to any acts of espionage nor do I know of any sabotage which has been committed by the group of aliens operating our fishing fleet. . . ." [4]

Carey McWilliams wrote in March 1942, "Despite the fact that most of the residents are either loyal or quite harmless, nevertheless the colony provided a convenient screen for possible subversive activities. That Japanese spies were working among the fishermen was, in fact, pointed out years ago by some of the Japanese themselves." [5] He has since clarified this statement, "As to the Terminal Island incident, it is true that at one time individual Japanese officers tried to pick up whatever information might be available and may have used the Japanese-American communities as cover for their own activities, but I am sure that there was very little of this and that the resident communities themselves were not involved." [6]

In any case, most of the alien Japanese men on Terminal Island were apprehended by the FBI, some on December 7 and the rest in a mass raid on February 1. They had been under constant suspicion since the outbreak of the war. When an Issei fisherman on the Island, speaking in Japanese tried to warn a friend who had moved for safety to the mainland that he would probably be arrested by the FBI in a roundup of noncitizen Islanders, the telephone operator interrupted, saying, "You cannot continue this conversation."

The sea log of another Island fisherman, with routine notations about the weather, tides, and channels, written in Japanese, was confiscated by a reporter for a magazine and photographed as a Japanese spy's diary. Virginia Swanson remembers that as the FBI swept onto the Island and took away the Issei men, the families huddled together sorrowing and weeping. The movie men were all set with cameras outside the cottages, hoping to catch a picture of a struggling Japanese. But people also remembered the bus driver who dropped his cap and picked it up slowly to give the women and children time to say goodbye to their men.

The total evacuation of the Japanese population on Terminal Island was expected, but it was assumed the residents would have at least a week's notice. About half the families had left in January or February to stay with relatives or friends. Most of the rest literally had no place to go. On February 14, anticipating a crisis, Virginia Swanson wrote a letter, copies of which she sent to the Tolan Committee, still in Washington, D.C., at that time, to Francis Biddle, Mrs. Roosevelt, Tom Clark, and various West Coast military men. In it she outlined the plight of the families who might be forced within thirty days to find homes in communities hostile to Japanese. Would the government help? She asked, "Could you work to find a place where they could move? Can you be sure families won't be broken up?" No one answered her letter.

The evacuation notices were served on the Islanders around noon on February 25. Miss Swanson phoned the Navy to try to get the deadline extended, but without success. She and Dr. Ralph Mayberry of the Baptist Mission Board, Esther Rhoads and Herbert Nicholson of the American Friends Service Committee, Allan Hunter, a Congregational minister, and some JACL members decided they would have to move the families themselves in the absence of any help from the government. They had located hostels. Some were former Japanese Language Schools, which they cleaned up and prepared as best they could. They managed to recruit volunteers with trucks to transport the Islanders and some of their possessions to the hostels. Joe Moody, the owner of a mattress company, who had had a Nisei roommate in college, donated mattresses and quilts and sent six of his trucks over to help with the moving.

On February 26 the narrow streets between the little shacks were jammed with trucks and milling women and children. Secondhand dealers, "descending like wolves to prey on the helpless," flocked in to take off the things people could not carry with them. They were reported to be giving a nickel on the dollar. A Nisei volunteer wrote later, "The women cried awful. . . . Some of them smashed their stuff, broke it up, right before the buyers' eyes because they offered such ridiculous prices."[7] Virginia Swanson remembers the beautiful wedding tea sets, saved for better homes, lying smashed to pieces on the floors of cottages.

She said, "The volunteers with trucks worked all night. The people had to go, ready or not. Some had to be pulled forcibly from their homes. They were afraid they were going to be handed over to a firing squad. Why should they have believed me, telling them to get into trucks with strangers?" The weeks of suspense with husbands gone, amid conflicting rumors and the badgering of profiteers, had frightened the women badly. The only representatives of the government they saw were the FBI agents who took away their menfolk and an officer from the State Board of Equalization who came to make sure the store proprietors paid their sales taxes before they left. He attached the property of a frantic widow who ran a beer parlor.

The refugees were thrust into hostels, only one out of seven prepared for them. Some people were dropped after midnight with no lights, nothing set up, no one to meet them. Esther Rhoads, in a letter to a friend, described the scene at the Forsyth School where she marked off floor space for families with chalk. "All afternoon trucks and Japanese kept coming. They were tired and dazed as a result of the sudden exodus. . . . We have old men over seventy—retired fishermen whom the FBI considered ineffective, and we have little children—one baby a year old . . . practically no men between thirty-five and sixty-five, as they all are interned either in Montana or South Dakota. . . . I feel especially sorry for the old men. They seem so lost in the high-ceilinged rooms of the Forsyth School. I think they long for the low ceilings and the cozy feel of their little homes back on Terminal Island." She asks, "Where are these people to go? There are many Japanese with young leaders able to face pioneer life, but those who have come to our hostels represent a group too old or too young to stand the rigors of beginning all over again." [8]

The refugees stayed on in the hostels or moved to temporary quarters, exhausting their meager resources, for in most cases their income had been cut off since the beginning of the war. They were among the first to go to the Manzanar assembly center. Back on the Island the looting of their homes began almost before they were out of them. Eventually the homes and shops were razed by the Navy. Bloom and Riemer wrote that the "Terminal Island Japanese Americans probably suffered more heavily in the Evacuation than any other occupational or locality group." [9] They had to abandon business property and expensive fishing equipment. The nets, even when safely stored, deteriorated without care and use. Many of the boats that were not owned outright had to be relinquished to the canneries.

After the Japanese left, it was reported that their places in the canneries would be taken by Filipinos, Yugoslavians, and Portuguese. Naval shore patrols stood watch on Fish Harbor. Virginia Swanson returned to the Island, where she had got permission to salvage a few personal possessions of the families, to find combat cars driving up and down the narrow alleys. As she entered the empty, silent church, she remembered the last communion service when people in the congregation had broken into sobs. On her way out she left the key on the table and the door open—for the Navy. . . .

*   *   *

The total list of these more permanent, prison-like camps was ten: Manzanar and Tule Lake in California, Poston and Gila River, both on Indian reservations in Arizona, Topaz, which was sometimes called Central Utah, Amache in Colorado, Heart Mountain in Wyoming, Minidoka in Idaho, and two camps in Arkansas—Rohwer and Jerome. Plans for an eleventh, Otwell, also in Arkansas, were dropped. Construction on Heart Mountain and Amache did not begin until the end of July. Topaz, Jerome, and Rohwer were finished even later, with residents streaming in heavily in the autumn.

The ten had been culled from a possible three hundred sites by a number of cooperating government agencies, including the relocation authorities, the office of Indian Affairs, the Soil Conservation Service, the Bureau of Reclamation, the Bureau of Agricultural Economics, the Farm Security Administration, the Forest Service, the Public Health Service, and others. The sites had to be remote from military zones but accessible to railyards or highways, had to have adequate water and power and at least 7,500 acres of land with agricultural possibilities. The land had to be government owned or controlled, and the projects were not to displace white settlers. As a result the tracts selected were places where no one else would choose to live.

Physically and psychologically, the camps were much alike in their isolation, in the ruggedness and primitive character of the terrain, in their confinement and almost total lack of conveniences at the start. Topaz, with a population of 8,000, was perhaps the most barren of all the camps in appearance. The terrain was absolutely flat, and residents, looking in one direction, could see apparently forever into the horizon. Looking the other way they could see a mountain range, very small and far away. There was nothing but sagebrush for vegetation; there were no trees at all until later a few were planted around the hospital and the administration buildings along with some sunflowers. After that it was not quite so dusty. There were twisters or whirlwinds and heat in the summer and snow in the winter, but the spring was fairly nice, at which time the sagebrush appeared to be a little greener than in the winter. Topaz was near the towns of Abraham and Delta in Utah's Millard County. It was 140 miles south of Salt Lake City. Most of the San Francisco Bay Area people had been transferred there from Tanforan. Like city real estate developments named after imaginary lakeviews, the streets running north to south at this center were a study in overcompensation: Ponderosa, Locust, Cottonwood, Greasewood and Elm, Tamarisk, Willow, and Juniper, named for the trees indigenous to the area but actually too far off from the camp to be seen. The soil was too alkaline even for greasewood. The area in the environs of Topaz was rich in gems and minerals, however, as the camp name itself and its streets running east and west attested—Alexander, Malachite, Jasper, and Obsidian. Climatically speaking, Topaz was improved by its 4,561-foot altitude.

The camp itself was crowded into a typical square-mile barbed wire enclosure. The barracks were the familiar black tarpaper; there were 42 blocks, 12 barracks per block, here and there a recreation hall—the usual picture. But to one of the residents who had come from Santa Anita, even as she slept in an unfinished room with the rain showering upon her bed, Topaz represented comparative freedom: to her it was "a haven of peacefulness." [10] Despite crowded conditions, she commented that at Topaz there was at least no everlasting emphasis on "cooperation," a word of which all had become very tired. But a Topaz bachelor did not find much comfort in his unfinished room with its open roof: he was badly burned when hot roof tar fell on him.

The desert camp at Gila River was physically better appearing than Poston or Topaz. Teiko Wada, who had believed they were all being sent away to die, perhaps of starvation, found the camp at Gila was not so bad as she had anticipated. The buildings were whitewashed and, like those at Manzanar, they all had red roofs, not black. The soil was good enough for residents to achieve favorable results from their gardening efforts. The Superstition Mountains rose in the distance, and the hardier residents scaled them for exercise, though the rocks broke off in their hands as they climbed.

Yuri Katai recalls watching outside movies at Gila River. "We would all sit on a hill on an army blanket. A big cactus was sometimes in our way when we tried to see the screen. Once in a rain storm the lightning hit this cactus and smashed it to smitherines."

Amache near Granada in Colorado with its sagebrush and cactus, its cottonwood trees, its rattlers and prairie dogs, was arid and dusty like the others, but the camp was on a little hill surrounded by flatland at a 3,500-foot elevation. The heat, while considerable, was not quite so intense as at Poston. In October the snows began. Amache was located in Prowers County in the Arkansas River Valley, 130 miles east of Pueblo. The nearby town was Lamar where "Japs Not Wanted Here" signs were posted.

Melons and fruit grew on nearby farms. Half of Amache's 10,000 acres were under cultivation when the center opened, the land being reasonably fertile, though sandy. Water came from wells which had a pumping capacity of 1,000 gallons a minute.

To the north of these centers, Camp Minidoka in Idaho was a crescent-shaped site 15 miles across set in an area described optimistically as "virgin desert sageland." The 68,000-acre tract was broken up by huge outcroppings of lava. Well guarded and drab, it housed approximately 9,000 evacuees. From extreme heat in the summer, temperatures dropped to 25° below zero in winter. Minidoka was later called Hunt after the town that supplied its postmark which was named for the first white man to explore the Snake River.

Because of the name, Tule Lake, George Shimada, on being evacuated from Burlington, Washington, had visualized a pretty spot in the woods. Located on a 26,000-acre tract of land in California's Modoc County owned by the Federal Bureau of Reclamation, Tule Lake, 35 miles south of Klamath Falls was actually a hot and dusty desert-type area covered by a sparse growth of tule and grasses. "All I saw for trees," he reports, "were watchtowers and chimneys sticking up out of the barracks." There was no lake, only a reclaimed lake bottom 4,000 feet above sea level. While the winters were long and cold, with temperatures that fell to 29° below zero, from the point of view of climate, Tule Lake was probably the most pleasant of the ten relocation centers. The temperature never reached unbearable degrees in summer, and the air was dry. The black barracks-covered land stretched out for miles with two "mountains," Castle Rock and Horse Collar, in the distance, one shaped like an abalone shell, neither larger than a hill. But in appearance, according to Irene Takemoto, Tule Lake was "a pretty sad place."

A sense of isolation, a feeling of being forsaken pervaded all the camps.

At Jerome and Rohwer, which were located in the swampy lowlands of. Arkansas where there were trees and lush vegetation, the Caucasians who lived nearby, the hill people, were not themselves in the mainstream of American life. Internees in Arkansas were often better informed about the world and the war through their camp papers and radios than many of these natives. Jerome was near the town of Dermott, which was put off-limits after a visiting Japanese-American soldier was shot at by a local person. Rohwer was near McGehee in Desha County in the Mississippi River Delta of southeast Arkansas. The town of Little Rock was about 150 miles from Rohwer, but the evacuees never went there.

Clearing away the forest and brush was one of the first objectives at Rohwer, and the administration began sending evacuee surveyors to the wooded areas outside the camp. One such engineering party, working in the forest, was suddenly shocked to see shotguns pointing in their direction from out of the trees. The bearers of the guns stepped forth. They were local people, apparently unaware of the existence of the relocation camp close by. They thought the members of the surveying party were Japanese paratroopers who had been dropped onto their countryside, and they marched them into town, and down the street, to the city jail. There was no reasoning with them. The project director was forced to go down and get his evacuee surveyors out of jail.

As at the other centers, advance medical groups had come in early before there were even floors in the barracks. Camp Rohwer experienced the usual outbreaks of measles and mumps and some food poisonings. Epidemics though greatly feared did not occur but some former swampland internees, presently afflicted with arthritis, feel their disability began at Rohwer because of the unaccustomed heavy work and the sultry climate.

Jerome, in the low delta country, was likewise beautiful and damp. The heat and the penetrating "damp cold" were felt more. Rains were frequent with the result that most of the inhabitants were struck by the tropical beauty about them. Barrack gardens were rewarding, and great blossoms showed through their windows. "Between the barracks," according to Sada Murayama, "there was a trellis with morning glories, forming a tunnel of flowers. One block in particular was a showplace. Any outside visitors were taken there."

There was no need for guards in the towers at Jerome, and the fences were not high. The camp was surrounded by swamps infested with water moccasins. Four of the most deadly snakes in America were indigenous to the area. There was continuous danger of malaria, even though the Army had sprayed the swamps with DDT. Evacuees sometimes got permission to go beyond the fences to pick up wood or to gather mushrooms. But there was no telling what they might encounter when reaching for the mushrooms. A cartoon in "Lil Dan'l," a mimeographed booklet covering one year at Rohwer, showed frightened residents with rattlers all around them, and a little boy holding up a small snake. The boy was saying, "What are you afraid of? It's only anopheodrys aestivus." [11] Despite the beauty of the surroundings and displays of humor and fortitude, it has been noted that there was a low state of morale in the Arkansas camps.

While living facilities presented essentially the same picture as in the assembly centers, they sometimes varied in one place or another in certain details. Poston rooms were slightly larger than those at Heart Mountain. Generally of cheap, single-wall construction, some camp barracks had double walls, ceilings and closets, celotex, even occasionally linoleum. Other camps had none of these things. When floors were finally laid in Arkansas, they were of hardwood—made from native red oak cut from the surrounding forests. Floors at Amache were lined with brick, and the rooms had set-in heaters.

The problem of privacy remained. When families consisted of fewer than five persons, they had to be prepared for others to move in with them. Two small rooms on the ends of the barracks were reserved for couples. Walls were not built to the ceiling, but sick persons or parents worrying about their children overhearing people next door sometimes obtained special permission to put on their own sheet rock and to close up the openings between the rooms.

Again, as before, necessities were provided, but living was Spartan. Changes in regulations under the WRA allowed a certain amount of equipment and personal belongings to be shipped in at no extra cost from government storehouses—chairs, tables, sewing machines, but only occasionally refrigerators or stoves. A certain number of nonperishable foods were also allowed. Family washes were done on scrub boards, although Heart Mountain possessed a very few plunger-type machines. To do their washing or to take showers, internees might have to walk a mile in rain, snow, or dust, and "by the time you walk back you need another shower."[12]

A government information circular put out during this period implied the evacuees were fortunate. "Had canvas for great tent cities been available it would have been used. Tents would have been pitched and evacuees would then have gone to work building their new wartime homes. . . . The houses [as actually built] might be called 'basic' structures; they are soundly constructed and provide the essentials for decent living. They are not fancy, but they are good. . . ." [13]

Facilities were much improved by 1943. Nevertheless, a great many people were anxious about the cheap structures. If the barracks stood up for the duration of the war, they felt they would be lucky. The outbreak of fire in these flimsy buildings jammed close with people was an ever-present concern. In a fire the shacklike structures of tar paper, celotex, and pinewood would burn to the ground within six or ten minutes. A strong wind at such a time might mean a major catastrophe. Fire hazards were numerous. At Topaz, stoves were close to the walls, and difficult disposal of hot ashes compounded the danger. People shoveled ashes out to the bare ground and wetted them down with water supplied by three deep wells. Personnel and evacuees there as elsewhere carried on extensive fire prevention programs. Posters and bulletins were displayed throughout the camp; warning articles appeared in the papers.

Until people learned to run the stoves inside their rooms at Heart Mountain properly there were a number of fires, none of them serious. A stray spark from burning rubbish at Manzanar ignited a brush fire which swept 200 feet before 20 workers working frantically to clear a firebreak in front of the advancing flames got it under control. . . .

NOTES

1. *Hearings Before a Special Committee on Un-American Activities*, House of Representatives, 77th Congress, 1st Session, Appendix VI (Washington, D.C.: U.S. Government Printing Office, 1942), p. 1839.
2. *Ibid.*, pp. 1825–1826.
3. *Ibid.*, p. 1826.
4. *Ibid.*, p. 1830.
5. CAREY McWILLIAMS, "California and the Japanese," *The New Republic* (March 2, 1942).
6. Letter to the authors, January 23, 1967.
7. CAREY McWILLIAMS, *Prejudice* (Boston: Little, Brown, 1944), p. 196.
8. Letter in the Conard-Duveneck Collection, Hoover Institution on War, Revolution, and Peace, Stanford University, Stanford, Calif.
9. LEONARD BLOOM and RUTH RIEMER, *Removal and Return* (Berkeley and Los Angeles: University of California Press, 1949), p. 163.
10. Letter to Galen Fisher, October 17, 1942, Galen Fisher Collection, Bancroft Library, University of California, Berkeley, California.
11. "Lil Dan'l—One Year in a Relocation Center," undated, Bancroft Library, University of California, Berkeley, California.
12. Letter, undated, Grace Nichols Pearson Collection, Hoover Institution on War, Revolution, and Peace, Stanford University, Stanford, California.
13. *The War Relocation Work Corps—A Circular of Information for Enlistees and Their Families* (Washington, D.C.: War Relocation Authority, 1942), p. 7.

Six Times Down, Seven Times Up

William Petersen

"Military necessity" as the justification for the camps linked the Japanese subnation with America's enemy, and by the end of the war people throughout the country not only deprecated a group of whom most had had no personal knowledge, but based their hostility on gross misinformation. Only 32 per cent of a national sample believed that Japanese Americans had not "destroyed any American war materials"; only 13 per cent that they had not done "any spying for the Japanese government." Asked about "the average Japanese person who lives in this country," 50 per cent characterized him as "loyal" and 25 per cent as "disloyal," with the remaining 25 per cent admitting that they did not know (National Opinion Research Center, 1946).

To most of these questions, the responses from the West Coast were close to the national average. In California, opposition to anti-Japanese policies remained as anomalous as before the war. The same small groups that had tried to secure the release of college students from the camps, or to mitigate the life there for the others, now undertook to facilitate the evacuees' return. Most of these activists were thoroughly respectable citizens, with hardly a political radical among them. Pasadena, the patrician suburb of Los Angeles, continued to stand out as a center of moral concern about the Japanese. In that city and similar enclaves along the Pacific, men who described themselves as "hard-headed believers in the virtues of the American form of government" organized Fair Play Committees to spread this sentiment among the general public [Modell, 1969a: chap. 11].

It was uphill work. Competitors of prewar Japanese produce wholesalers had founded an American League of California, which "sincerely" urged Japanese Americans to demonstrate their patriotism by "remaining away from the Pacific Coast." A newly organized California Citizens Council agitated for a law excluding Japanese. A post of the Veterans of Foreign Wars distributed bumper stickers proclaiming, NO JAPS WANTED IN CALIFORNIA. John Lechner, who had become one of the most active of anti-Japanese spokesmen, became obsessed during the war years, when internment whetted his appetite for more decisive measures. Fletcher Bowron, the liberal mayor of Los Angeles, warned that "the people here are thoroughly aroused, and it would be very unsafe for the Japanese themselves" if they tried to return. Three times in 1943 and 1944 a polling organization surveyed public opinion

SOURCE: From *Japanese Americans* by William Petersen. Copyright © 1971 by Random House, Inc. Reprinted by permission.

in Los Angeles County, and on each occasion about two-thirds of the respondents advocated a constitutional amendment to deport all Japanese from the United States [Modell, 1969a].

The crucial difference from 1942 was the official position of the government. Once the Supreme Court had declared detention in camps to be unconstitutional, the WRA started to issue propaganda pamphlets denouncing the whole of the policy it had been administering. Statements by U.S. servicemen on "what we're fighting for" began with a quotation from a veteran of Guadalcanal: "Our American citizens of Japanese ancestry are being persecuted as though Adolf Hitler himself were in charge" [U.S. Dept. of the Interior, 1945b]. Another pamphlet, designed to dispel "common misconceptions" about Japanese Americans, refuted point by point the official rationalization of the evacuation—dual citizenship, Shinto, Japanese-language schools, concentration in strategic areas, not to mention the "honesty of the Japanese as a race" and their "soil-conservation practices" [U.S. Dept. of the Interior, 1945a]. The War Relocation Authority, with its name changed to the War Agency Liquidation Unit, tried in various ways to hasten the evacuees' readaptation to a civilian environment [U.S. Dept. of the Interior, 1947].

> [During the] battle of words, ideas, and efforts to manipulate the thinking of those who differed, the social climate was . . . emotional and threatening to state and community solidarity. The extremists on both sides, for or against the return, lined up in bitter verbal attacks in forums, sermons, discussions, letters to the editor, and mimeographed resolutions. . . . [But those favoring the return of the Japanese] happened also to be on the side of the Army, the Supreme Court, the Constitution, and the governor. [Luomala, 1946].[1]

Some of the hatred of "Japs" was deflected to the "Jap-lovers." In particular, the WRA became a target of abuse, for it had allegedly "engineered" the rescission of the evacuation order [Loumala, 1946].

The long-feared homecoming began in Los Angeles late in 1944 and proceeded slowly, gradually, over the following months. The carefully prepared hostility caused only a few incidents. Until the end of 1945, the Teamsters Union boycotted Japanese produce. The California Board of Equalization issued no commercial licenses to Japanese until the WRA threatened to bring suit. Early in 1946, California's Attorney General Robert W. Kenny charged one sheriff with malfeasance for his acts against evacuees. And this firm stand by a few official agencies helped bring about a general change of attitude. In the 1946 election, when the California ballot included a proposition to make the Alien Land Law part of the state constitution, it was defeated by 56 to 44 per cent.

This does not mean, of course, that the Japanese were generally welcomed back into their old neighborhoods. According to a WRA report:

> The whole occupational picture is characterized by a degrading of skilled personnel, loss of seniority and civil service status, the exploitation [as] domestic

help of the families of hired agricultural workers, and the great difficulty of finding leases for farm land. [quoted in Modell, 1969a: chap. 11].

The elderly in particular were beaten down and afraid. Lacking the strength to start a new fight, they settled down in trailer camps that the WRA established in out-of-the-way spots and recalled with pitiful nostalgia the relative comfort and certitude of the recent past.

The whole West Coast had been swollen by the wartime influx of workers to new industries, and in most cities a residence was all but unobtainable. Evacuees who had laboriously constructed furniture out of scrap lumber were forced to leave the camps as they had entered them, with no more than the baggage they could carry. For more than a decade, Japanese Americans found housing to be "the single most important area of discrimination," worse in the Los Angeles area than around San Francisco, but serious everywhere [Kitano, 1960].

GOVERNMENT ASSISTANCE

The fact that, somewhat belatedly, a few official agencies declared themselves in support of the Constitution has been extrapolated into the pleasant myth that most public authorities, having recognized the grave inequity suffered by Japanese Americans, did their best to make amends. According to the *Washington Post* of October 9, 1965:

> The injustice done to the Japanese Americans will remain forever a stain on American history. There is some comfort, however, in the general acknowledgement of this injustice and in the conscientious effort that has been made to provide restitution for the property losses suffered by the evacuated citizens. [quoted in Bosworth, 1967: 235]

Whether "conscientious effort" is the appropriate phrase to describe any element of the government's postwar aid program can be doubted. It is certainly not an apt designation of the decades-long litigation briefly described in the last chapter. Nor does it truly characterize the sometimes helpful activities of the WRA and its successor, whose employees "wished desperately to be rid of this bothersome group" [Modell, 1969a: chap. 11]. What then of the restitution of property losses?

Immediately after the war, the JACL memorialized Congress to authorize adequate compensation for the losses incurred because of the forced evacuation. A draft of a bill was written by the WRA staff, and Dillon Myer, its director, guessed that the total payments would "probably not exceed $10,000,000," or about $91 per capita.[2] This modest estimate was based not on an approximation of the losses, but on the amount that would have to be reimbursed to evacuees who "thought they had sufficient proof to support their claims" [Bloom and Riemer, 1949: 200]. The losses actually incurred can be suggested by a few examples. Robert Asazawa, who had left his 18-acre fruit farm in charge of a tenant, came home to find the tenant gone and most of the trees dead. Yoshimi Shibata found his home and his 125,000 square feet of nurseries in ruins. The Nichiren Temple in Los Angeles, where 600 families had stored their household goods, had been ransacked. George Yanagimachi found that his oyster beds had been systematically pirated, with a loss of nearly $100,000 [Hosokawa, 1969: 437].

The law as passed on July 2, 1948 (that is, some three and a half years after the dissolution of the camps started) followed Myer's logic. No payments were authorized for "death or personal injury, personal inconvenience, physical hardship, or mental suffering"; nor was any compensation made for losses in earned income and earning power, which for most families were greater than the only type of claim that could be filed, real and personal property lost as "a reasonable and natural consequence of the evacuation." Almost 24,000 claims were filed within the 18-month period stipulated in the law; 60 per cent were for less than $2,500, 73 per cent for less than $5,000. During all of 1950 the Department of Justice heard 211 claims and agreed to pay 137 of them. The average payment to the claimant was $450; the average cost of adjudicating the case was $1,400 [Hosokawa, 1969: 445–446].

After some undignified haggling, the government permitted two extensions of the deadline and reduced the red tape involved in settlements. The cases adjudicated from January 3, 1950, to June 30, 1956, have been collected in a book [Banse, 1956], whose dry legalese highlights the cold, official pettiness in reaction to one instance after another of guiltless suffering.

> Shigeru Henry Nakagawa sold some of his household goods for $300; he was allowed $460 to make up the difference between that amount and their "fair and reasonable value." Some Japanese books, valued at $10, for which he received no allowance, "he destroyed . . . voluntarily, and his alleged motive for doing so, the fear that he might be punished, has no relation to the evacuation but springs from the general hysteria." He withdrew his claim for stored goods that had been stolen, since an investigation might reveal the thief and he did not want "to cause embarrassment to any person." [Banse, 1956: 93–95]

> Yasuhei Nagashima received $308.75 for goods stored with the WRA and erroneously sold at public auction. However, a claim for a loss of $499 incurred in the sale of his truck was not allowed; the claimant, in ignorance of the law, had not originally included this item, and an amendment to his claim that introduced new subject matter constituted "an insurmountable bar" to settlement. [Banse, 1956: 135–139]

> Kihei Hashioka claimed $220 as the loss incurred in the sale of various goods, including, however, a short-wave radio that he should have deposited with the local police. Since the $80 he received included an unknown proportion for the radio, it was deemed necessary to adjust his claim downward. "A fair method of computing such price would be to allocate this unknown [amount] to $65, which represents the true value of the radio, in the same proportion as the $80 received for all the property bears to the $166 which has been found to be its true value. Thus: $(80/166) =$

(x/65), or $31.33. This $31.33, the sale price of the radio, deducted from the $80, total sales price, leaves $48.67, the sale price of the remaining property, . . . leaving claimant with a compensable loss of $52.33." [Banse, 1956: 176–177]

The last settlement was made in late 1965 to the Koda family for 5,000 acres of fertile rice land 50 miles northwest of Fresno and a large rice mill, valued at $1,210,000. When he was sent off to camp, Keisaburo Koda had left his property in charge of a white attorney and others, who proceeded to swindle him of virtually everything. During the 15 years it took to settle the case, the original claimant died, as well as one of his two sons, two lawyers and an accountant who worked on the case, and the men most involved in the fraud (who thus avoided criminal prosecution). The settlement was for $362,500, or slightly more than the cost of the litigation.

From the first payment made—$303.36 to Tokuji Tokimasa on December 16, 1949, for books and office equipment he was forced to abandon when he evacuated his Los Angeles real-estate office—to the settlement with the Koda family, a total of about $38 million was paid out to approximately 26,500 claimants. At the time of the evacuation, the Federal Reserve Bank estimated the property losses incurred by Japanese Americans at $400 million, or slightly more than the total requested—but not paid. The payments averaged 10 cents per dollar claimed, less 10 per cent in attorney's fees. The claims were at 1942 dollar values, with no allowance for the considerable postwar inflation, and no interest was paid. A year and a half after the last property settlement, in the spring of 1967, the Supreme Court released to the last individual depositors about $4 million that had been confiscated from American branches of Japanese banks. Presiding over the Court was Chief Justice Earl Warren (Justice Tom Clark abstained). Once again, grudging justice was so long delayed that many of the claimants were dead.

One of the complicating facts in the Koda case was that during the war California had filed an escheat action to seize the property because the "real owner," Keisaburo Koda, was an alien. Early in February 1942, Attorney General Warren had recommended a tightening up of the lax enforcement of the Alien Land Law as one step in the displacement of Japanese Americans [Grodzins, 1949: 277]. Of the 79 escheat proceedings taken under the law, 59 were started under Warren's prodding. One of these involved the 8 acres of farmland that Kajiro Oyama, an Issei, had bought for his Nisei son, Fred. According to a unanimous decision of the California Supreme Court, the statute prohibiting an alien ineligible for citizenship from acquiring land was improperly evaded when that alien purchased land for a citizen. It seemed, thus, that the property losses suffered in the forced evacuation would be compounded after the internees' return by the confiscation of land owned by Nisei. On appeal, the JACL took the case to the U.S. Supreme Court, which in a majority opinion reversed the decision concerning escheatage without commenting on the prohibition itself. In *Takahashi v. Fish and Game Commission*, similarly, the Court found unconstitutional a California wartime statute that excluded aliens ineligible for citizenship from commercial fishing in coastal waters. In these two cases, "the Supreme Court, as if in penance, struck down a racial classification involving the Japanese on what was virtually a presumption of its unconstitutionality, without applying the normal and less stringent rules of equal protection of the laws" [tenBroek, 1968: 304–310].

The most important victory of the JACL was to get a revision of the Immigration and Naturalization Act. A bill to relax the restrictions that Congressman Walter H. Judd introduced in 1950 almost passed, but was defeated for reasons irrelevant to the JACL's campaign. Two years later, as part of a general revision of American immigration law sponsored by Congressman Francis E. Walter and Senator Pat McCarran, Japan was given a token quota and race was eliminated as a bar to naturalization.[3]

> Issei . . . by the hundreds enrolled in citizenship courses sponsored by churches, JACL chapters, and other organizations. . . . In time, . . . men and women in their sixties and seventies and eighties . . . stood before federal judges and took the oath of allegiance as America's newest citizens. It was a privilege and an honor that had been a long time coming. [Hosokawa, 1969: 455]

*   *   *

UPWARD MOBILITY

The main key to material success in the United States for anyone is education. Since 1940, Japanese have had more schooling than any other race in the American population, including whites. In Figure 1, note the position of "nonwhites"—virtually the same as that of Negroes, but a gross distortion of the level of other subnations included in that artificial category. Note also that among other racial minorities (Filipinos, Chinese, and to a lesser degree Negroes) females acquired more education than males, but that Japanese of both sexes ranked highest. By 1960, almost 7 out of every 10 Japanese of either sex had at least a high school diploma [Schmid and Nobbe, 1965], and a high proportion of these went on to college.

Adding to these census data is difficult, for most other statistical series are not broken down by race. Detailed knowledge can be based on only a few scattered studies, but in general their findings reinforce one another.

In the 1930's, many Nisei children had a poor command of English, as a consequence of both their home environment . . . and, sometimes, the more or less segregated schools they attended [Hormann, 1957; R. Bell, 1935: 7–8]. In any scholastic or "intelligence" test based on language ability, therefore, their performance was often mediocre, but they did so well in such other elementary subjects as arithmetic and spelling that they typically placed at the top of their class [Strong and Bell, 1933: chap. 3]. In later grades, however, as less qualified whites dropped out of school while a much higher proportion of Nisei remained, the competition became keener, so that in high school whites and Nisei ranked about equal [Bell, 1935: 61].

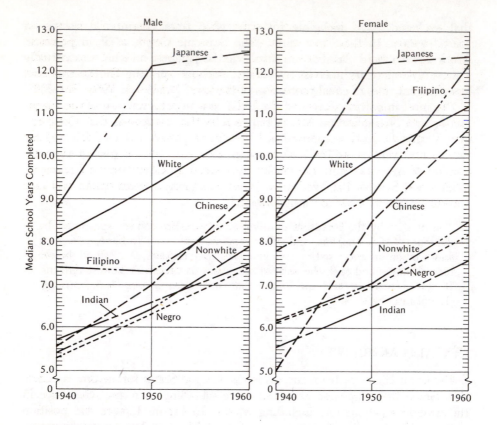

FIGURE 1.   Median School Years Completed, Persons 25 Years and Over
by Sex and Race, United States, 1940–1960.

SOURCE: After census data as compiled in Calvin F. Schmid and Charles E. Nobbe, "Socioeconomic Differentials among Nonwhite Races," *American Sociological Review* 30 (1965),
909–922.

According to a number of postwar studies in Hawaii, the "cultural traditions of national-ethnic groups" are important in determining both whether
students go on to college and, if so, what they study there [Dole, 1961; Dole
and Sherman, 1962]. In 1959, when entering freshmen at the University of
Hawaii were surveyed, 57.5 per cent were Japanese and 16.9 per cent Caucasian, with the remaining 25.6 per cent scattered among six other racial categories. In a survey of seniors the following year, the percentages were,
respectively, 64.6, 13.8, and 21.6 [Dole and Iwakami, 1960a; 1960b]. Since no
other table in these two studies is classified by race, they tell us nothing about
Japanese students except that proportionately many start and even more
finish.[4] According to the indications from two minor studies, the scholastic
performance of Sansei has remained high in Hawaii [Arkoff and Leton, 1966],
but may have fallen somewhat on the mainland [Kitano, 1962].
    From the files of the University of California placement bureau, I was able

to derive a composite impression of the Japanese who had attended the Berkeley campus during the late 1950's and early 1960's. Their marks were good to excellent, but apart from a few outstanding individuals, this was not a group that would succeed solely because of extraordinary academic achievement. The extracurricular activities they listed were prosaic—the Nisei Student Club,[5] various fraternities, field sports. Their education had been conducted like a military campaign against a hostile world, with intelligent planning and tenacity. Their heavy dependence on the broader Japanese community was suggested in a number of ways. The personal references students listed were often from Japanese professors in totally unrelated fields, and the part-time jobs they held (almost all had had to work their way through college) were typically in plant nurseries or other Japanese business establishments. Their degrees, almost never in liberal arts, were in business administration, optometry, engineering, or some other middle-level profession. For them, education was obviously a means of acquiring a salable skill that could be used either in the general commercial world or, if that remained closed, in a small personal enterprise. Asked to designate the beginning salary they wanted, the applicants' guesses ranged between precisely the one they got in their first professional job and something under that.

In a word, these young men and women were squares. Any doubts they may have had about the transcendental values of the American middle-class life did not reduce their determination to achieve at least that level of security and comfort.

For years after World War II, no firm in San Francisco's financial district would hire a Japanese American, and nothing the Berkeley placement bureau did could break this ban. Finally, the director herself went to the president of one of the largest and most prestigious companies, offered to pay out of her own pocket a Nisei applicant's salary during a trial period, and thus shamed the corporation into hiring the young man. The personnel officer soon became enthusiastic about not only him but any of his race. Some months later, when the same company called the placement bureau specifically requesting more Nisei, the director gently reminded her client that it was against state law to discriminate on the basis of race.

It is difficult to find data on discrimination more broadly based than such personal anecdotes. In a 1947 survey in Seattle, Frank Miyamoto and Robert O'Brien asked their Japanese respondents to compare job discrimination then with that just before the war. The distribution of the answers was:

	Per Cent Nisei	Per Cent Issei
Less	28	20
Same	56	68
More	16	12

What these replies signify is hard to tell, for before the war many Issei had been so thoroughly embedded in the Japanese community that they never in fact tested the tolerance of the whole city. "There was generally a tendency to regard conditions as better than expected" [U.S. Dept. of the Interior, 1947: 132]. In the early 1950's Alan Jacobson and Lee Rainwater conducted a study of how 79 firms evaluated their Japanese employees. In spite of the probable race prejudice of some respondents, undoubtedly reinforced in some cases by surviving wartime hostility, an extraordinarily high proportion of the white employers expressed satisfaction.[6] More than two-thirds were "very positive," and the occasional negative remark was typically that Japanese are "too ambitious and want to move on to a better job too quickly" [Caudill and DeVos, 1956].

In Hawaii, there was a long tradition that Japanese were most suitably employed at a menial level. For males, as we have seen, the route out of field work was usually into either small business or a skilled craft; for females, it was generally into domestic service. From the beginning of the century to after World War II, well over half the servants in Hawaii's private households were Japanese [Lind, 1951]. In the mid-1930's, according to the employment secretary of the Honolulu YWCA, persons seeking employees "generally express[ed] a racial preference," and for household work the principal demand was for Japanese women, especially Issei. A Japanese girl who worked as a waitress or salesgirl was routinely paid less than a Caucasian or Portuguese [Dranga, 1936]. Some worked as barbers, getting an average weekly wage of $12, compared with $15 for a Japanese male performing the same service [Kimura, 1939].

Whether any anti-Japanese discrimination exists in postwar Hawaii is hard to determine. In 1964, a fair-employment practices law went into effect, but its enforcement has not been very stringent. During the first four and a half years, only 40 complaints were investigated, of which 11 were found to be well based. Only 2 complaints involved a Japanese, both filed by the same woman, who charged discrimination on the basis of her age.[7] The Fair Practices Training Council, a private firm operating under a federal grant to train unemployed persons, put a total of about 1,100 persons through its program. Though no statistics on race were kept, the director estimated that 90 per cent were "non-Caucasians," including a small number of Japanese.

Whatever discrimination remained after the war, both in Hawaii and on the mainland large numbers of Japanese succeeded in moving up to middle-class positions. As with every nationality, the first data available were about outstanding individuals who were the first to achieve some post or honor. Takeshi Yoshida was the first Nisei admitted to Annapolis; Minoru Yamazaki became a world-famous architect; Stephen C. Tamura became superior judge of Orange County, California [Morita, 1967: chap. 6]. The Nisei honored by the JACL at one of its postwar conventions included—in addition to those distinguished for their services specifically to the civil rights of Japanese Americans—Tomi Kanazawa, the first Nisei given a leading role with the Metropolitan Opera Company; Ford Hiroshi Konno, "America's greatest swimmer"; John F. Aiso, a justice of the California Court of Appeals; Jack Murata, an agricultural chemist with the U.S. Department of the Interior; and Kijo Tomiyasu, technical director of General Electric's laser laboratory [Hosokawa, 1969: chap. 27]. According to the Japanese American Research Project currently under way at UCLA, Naoki Kikuchi, a watch repairman in Seattle, had ten children, of whom two died. One daughter is married to a pharmacist; the other is president of a women's college. His sons are a professor of physics, a printing technician, an artist, a research physicist, an architect, and an electrical engineer.

Such individual cases, once a sufficient number accumulates, are significant in themselves, but they merely suggest the social mobility of the subnation as a whole. Another kind of data is needed to give a broader indication of the movement of Japanese into the upper middle class—for example, the membership lists of various professional associations in Hawaii. Japanese were identified as such by their names, which for this nationality are an excellent index. At the specified dates, the numbers in the more important professions were as follows:

Civil Engineers: In 1951, 18 of the professional association's total membership of 124 (14.5 per cent) were Japanese Americans; in 1968, 167 of 350 (48 per cent). At the latter date, 4 of the 6 officers plus 6 of the 17 committee chairmen were Japanese.[8]

Professional Engineers: Of the 92 resident engineers registered in Hawaii in 1928, only 6 (or 6 per cent) were Japanese. In 1967 the comparable figures were 331 of a total of 795 (42 per cent).

Architects: None of the resident architects registered in Hawaii in 1928 was Japanese. In 1967 there were 50 of a total of 196 (25 per cent).

Surveyors: Of the 61 resident surveyors registered in 1928, only 7 (11 per cent) had Japanese names. Of the 151 registered in 1967, 69 (46 per cent) were Japanese.[9]

Physicians: The Japanese among residents licensed to practice medicine constituted 95 out of 346 (27 per cent) in 1940, 176 out of 600 (29 per cent) in 1959, and 223 out of 978 (only 23 per cent) in 1968.[10] Why in this case there was a relative decline is not known.

Lawyers: In 1959, 119 out of the total of 416 who had been admitted to the bar (28 per cent) were Japanese, compared with 168 out of 603 (again, 28 per cent) in 1968. Though there was no change over this period in the proportion among all lawyers, a far larger number moved up within the profession. Of the 48 members of legal firms in 1959, only 2 (Shiro and Genro Kashiwara, members of their own firm) were of Japanese origin. In 1968, 32 out of 150 (thus, 21 as compared with 4 per cent) were Japanese; and of these, 12 were in firms that included non-Orientals as members.[11]

The information on lawyers can be supplemented by a survey of 75 Japanese practicing in Honolulu in 1959 [Yamamoto, 1968]. Almost all had moved up from their fathers' occupations, which in the main were either blue-collar (26 per cent) or small retail proprietor or farmer (27 per cent). Three-fifths had been able to attend law school only with veterans' benefits. After they were admitted to the bar, more than one in four worked for a government agency. Though all had received their degrees from distinguished law schools, as of that date none had become a partner in any of the large firms, in part because the Japanese lawyers preferred the greater independence of a small establishment. There was then a marked division of labor between the two types of firms, with the first concentrating on the commercial counseling of large corporations, the second on general practice.

On a national scale, the great shift in occupational status took place during the 1950's (Figure 2). From findings of this type, one analyst [Varon, 1967] concluded that Japanese Americans no longer constitute a "minority," since (by Louis Wirth's definition) "minority status carries with it the exclusion from full participation in the life of the society." If the Japanese have moved to or beyond parity with the whites in their education and occupational status, Varon hypothesized, then by other criteria their social status must also be rising almost as fast. Even if we do not quite accept this prognosis, it is significant that anyone could make it from a conscientious study of a colored minority in the United States.

In spite of their advances in education and occupational status, mainland Japanese had not achieved parity with the income of whites by 1959 (Table 1). Japanese males earned more in California than elsewhere, but the discrepancy was also greater there. If the age structures of the two races had been the same, the differences in the median incomes would be still larger. At least as of that date, a considerable discrimination persisted, since a group with qualifications that should have commanded larger salaries in fact earned less on the average.

TABLE 1. Median Personal Income, White and Japanese Males Aged 14 and Over, Mainland United States and California, 1959

	White	Japanese			
		Census	I.D.*	Stand-ardized †	I.D.*
Mainland					
United States	$4,339	$4,305	2	$4,064	3
California	5,109	4,385	10	4,149	13

* The "index of dissimilarity"—that is, the percentage of Japanese which would have to change to another income category in order to make the two distributions identical.

† Standardized to the age distribution of the white population.

SOURCE: Census data as reported in Monica Boyd, "The Japanese Americans: A Study in Socio-Economic Integration," paper presented at the meeting of the Southern Sociological Society, Atlanta, Georgia, 1968.

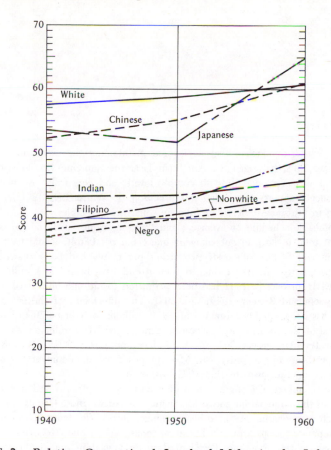

FIGURE 2. Relative Occupational Level of Males in the Labor Force, by Race, United States, 1940–1960.

* The scores were computed essentially by the method described in Charles B. Nam, *Methodology and Scores of Socio-economic Status*, Working Paper No. 15 (Washington, D.C.: U.S. Bureau of the Census, 1963). The scores represent weighted averages, which in the Schmid-Nobbe paper are combined with education and income scores to derive a graphic profile for each race.

SOURCE: After Calvin F. Schmid and Charles E. Nobbe, "Socio-economic Differentials among Nonwhite Races," *American Sociological Review* 30 (1965), pp. 909–922.

NOTES

1. Governor Warren announced that he favored maintaining the evacuation until after the war's end, but that since the Army (in fact, the Supreme Court) had decided otherwise, it was everyone's duty to comply loyally and cheerfully [Luomala, 1946]. This statement supports the earlier interpretation of Warren as a politician mainly responding to pressures rather than following his own principles.

2. With a probable schedule of average claims ranging from $250 to a maximum of $2,500, the total to be paid out, allowing one claim per family, would have been not $10 million, but $52.6 million. If two claims per family had been allowed under a community-property rule, the estimated total would have been $79.3 million; if each person aged 18 or over in 1942 had been permitted to file, it would have been $90.1 million [Bloom and Riemer, 1949: 202–203]. The direct cost of the evacuation and detention has been roughly estimated at $350 million, including $70 million for the construction of the assembly and relocation centers and $150 million for maintenance of the inmates [Arrington, 1962: 6; cf. Girdner and Loftis, 1969: 480–481]. Given a total expenditure of this order, Mr. Myer proposed an addendum of less than 3 per cent to make up the losses to the evacuees.

3. These three members of Congress, each of whom was deeply involved in the effort to permit again the immigration and naturalization of Asians, most liberals would classify as thorough reactionaries. As in other instances, justice for Japanese Americans was never incorporated as part of the liberal program. When the McCarran-Walter Act passed Congress the first time, President Truman vetoed it—mainly because it continued the national-quota system. And when Congress passed it over his veto, he appointed a President's Commission on Immigration and Naturalization, which submitted a report analyzing all the new law's faults and limitations. [*Whom We Shall Welcome* (Washington, D.C.: U.S. Government Printing Office, 1953)]. The section on Japanese immigration reads: "That racial and national discrimination is the essence of the Immigration and Nationality Act of 1952 is shown . . . [for example, by] the fact that although the law repeals the Japanese Exclusion Act and sets up a minimum quota for Japanese, it establishes a racial quota under which Orientals are to be charged to the 'Asia-Pacific Triangle' on the basis not of place of birth—as is true in all other cases—but of their own racial background" (p. 90). The discussion of citizenship (chap. 16) does not mention the fact that under the new law foreign-born Asians became eligible for naturalization.

4. Although the question on race was specified as optional in both these surveys, less than 0.5 per cent of the respondents chose not to answer it. Even so, the administration of the university has become absurdly touchy on this matter. Not only are no data compiled by race (or so I was told), but several administrators refused point-blank to permit me to use lists of students in order to compare Japanese (identifiable by their names) and non-Japanese as groups. This resistance was in contrast to the cordial cooperation given me in every other facet of my research.

5. The University of Hawaii has no counterpart to the Nisei Student Club typical on West Coast campuses. In the 1967/68 academic year, the Honolulu campus had a total of 96 officially recognized student organizations, variously based on professional interest, residence hall, social or cultural activities, and religion. Two presumably were predominantly Japanese—a Young Buddhist Association and a society to enhance members' knowledge of Japanese culture. Among the others, 38 had presidents with Japanese names.

6. But the reason—according to this interpretation—did not suggest that the Nisei deserved any commendation. "Because of the compatibility between Japanese and American middle-class cultures, individual Nisei probably have a better chance of succeeding than individuals from other ethnic groups where the underlying cultural patterns are less in harmony with those of the American middle class" [Caudill and DeVos, 1956]. In other words, it was pure coincidence that American employers preferred promptness, accuracy, diligence, cleanliness, neatness, and so on; and these traits, of no particular relevance to the conduct of their business, just happened to be characteristic of their Nisei employees.

7. Interview with K. Tanimoto, a specialist in fair employment, State Employment Relations Board, Honolulu, August 1968. Of the 15 complaints during the first three and a half years based on alleged discrimination by race, religion, color or ancestry, 8 were filed by Caucasians, 5 by Negroes, 1 by a Cambodian, and 1 by a Hawaiian-Portuguese.

8. *Directory of the American Society of Civil Engineers, Hawaii Section,* various dates, supplemented by an interview with Mr. Ben Taguchi, secretary of the section in 1968.

9. *Roster of the State Board of Registration of Professional Engineers, Architects and Land Surveyors, State of Hawaii,* various dates.

10. *Roster of Physicians Licensed in the State* (or *Territory*) *of Hawaii,* various dates.

11. *Martindale-Hubbell Law Directory, Hawaii,* various dates.

BIBLIOGRAPHY

ARKOFF, ABE, and DONALD A. LENTON. 1966. "Ethnic and Personality Patterns in College Entrance." *Journal of Experimental Education* 35: 79–83.

ARRINGTON, LEONARD J. 1962. *The Price of Prejudice: The Japanese-American Relocation Center in Utah During World War II.* Logan, Utah: Utah State University.

BANSE, WALTER F., Ed. 1956. *Adjudications of the Attorney General of the United States.* Vol. I: *Precedent Decisions under the Japanese-American Evacuation Claims Act, 1950–1956.* Washington, D.C.: U.S. Government Printing Office.

BELL, REGINALD. 1935. *Public School Education of Second-Generation Japanese in California.* Stanford: Stanford University Press.

BLOOM, LEONARD, and RUTH RIEMER. 1949. *Removal and Return: The Socioeconomic Effects of the War on Japanese Americans.* Berkeley: University of California Press.

BOSWORTH, ALLAN R. 1967. *America's Concentration Camps.* New York: Norton.

CAUDILL, WILLIAM, and GEORGE DeVOS. 1956. "Achievement, Culture and Personality: The Case of the Japanese Americans." *American Anthropologist* 58. 1102–1126.

DOLE, ARTHUR A. 1961. *A Study of Values as Determinants of Educational-Vocational Choices in Hawaii*. Honolulu: Hawaii Department of Education.

———, and EILEEN E. IWAKAMI. 1960a. "Statistical Profile of a Freshman Class: A Survey of University of Hawaii 1959 Freshmen." Honolulu: Bureau of Testing and Guidance, University of Hawaii.

———, and RUTH SHERMAN. 1962. "Determinants of the Choice of a Science Program by Ninth-Grade Males." Honolulu: Psychological Research Center, University of Hawaii.

DRANGA, JANE. 1936. "Racial Factors in the Employment of Women." *Social Process in Hawaii* 2: 11–14.

GIRDNER, AUDRIE, and ANNE LOFTIS. 1969. *The Great Betrayal: The Evacuation of the Japanese-Americans During World War II*. New York: Macmillan.

GRODZINS, MORTON. 1959. *Americans Betrayed: Politics and the Japanese Evacuation*. Chicago: University of Chicago Press.

HORMANN, BERNHARD L. 1957. "Integration in Hawaii's Schools." *Social Process in Hawaii* 21: 5–14.

HOSOKAWA, BILL. 1969. *Nisei: The Quiet Americans*. New York: Morrow.

KIMURA, YUKIKO. 1939. "Honolulu Barber Girls—A Study of Culture Conflict." *Social Process in Hawaii* 5: 22–29.

KITANO, HARRY H. L. 1960. "Housing of Japanese-Americans in the San Francisco Bay Area." In Nathan Glazer and Davis McEntire, Eds. *Studies in Housing and Minority Groups*. Berkeley: University of California Press, pp. 178–97.

———. 1962. "Changing Achievement Patterns of the Japanese in the United States." *Journal of Social Psychology* 58: 257–64.

LIND, ANDREW W. 1951. "The Changing Position of Domestic Service in Hawaii." *Social Process in Hawaii* 15: 71–87.

LUOMALA, KATHARINE. 1946. "California Takes Back Its Japanese Evacuees: The Readjustment of California to the Return of the Japanese Evacuees." *Applied Anthropology* 5: 25–39.

MODELL, JOHN. 1969a. "The Japanese of Los Angeles: A Study in Growth and Accommodation, 1900–1946." Doctoral dissertation, Columbia University.

MORITA, YUKIO. 1967. "The Japanese Americans in the United States Between 1945 and 1965. Master's essay, Ohio State University.

National Opinion Research Center. 1946. *Attitudes Toward "The Japanese in Our Midst."* Report No. 33. Denver: University of Denver.

SCHMID, CALVIN F., and CHARLES E. NOBBE. 1965. "Socio-economic Differentials Among Nonwhite Races." *American Sociological Review* 30: 909–22.

STRONG, EDWARD K., JR., and REGINALD BELL. 1933. *Vocational Aptitudes of Second-Generation Japanese in the United States*. Stanford: Stanford University Press.

ten BROEK, JACOBUS, EDWARD N. BARNHART, and FLOYD W. MATSON, 1968. *Prejudice, War and the Constitution*. Berkeley: University of California Press.

U.S. Department of the Interior, War Relocation Authority. 1945a. *Myths and Facts about the Japanese Americans: Answering Common Misconceptions Regarding Americans of Japanese Ancestry*. Washington, D.C.: U.S. Government Printing Office.

———, ———. 1945b. *"What We're Fighting For": Statements by United States Servicemen About Americans of Japanese Descent*. Washington, D.C.: U.S. Government Printing Office.

———, War Agency Liquidation Unit. 1947. *People in Motion: The Postwar Adjustment* of the *Evacuated Japanese Americans*. Washington, D.C.: U.S. Government Printing Office.

VARON, BARBARA F. 1967. "The Japanese Americans: Comparative Occupational Status, 1960 and 1950." *Demography* 4: 809–19.

YAMAMOTO, GEORGE K. 1968. "The Ethnic Lawyer and Social Structure: The Japanese Attorney in Honolulu." Unpublished manuscript.

The Community

Harry H. L. Kitano

JAPANESE COMMUNITY INSTITUTIONS

. . . Perhaps closer analysis of several other Japanese community organizations will best illustrate the action of the community and the changes in community expectations from generation to generation. The Japanese Association is illustrative of an influential Issei organization, and the Japanese-American Citizen's League (JACL) of a Nisei-Sansei group. We will also examine the influences of acculturation upon religious institutions, and of the community opportunity structure upon Japanese youth programs.

The Japanese Association

The Japanese Association was the most important Issei group. Every community having a Japanese population would have a Japanese Association, so that a Japanese in Pocatello, Idaho, would be under the same kind of ethnic protection as a Japanese in San Francisco or Los Angeles.[1] Most of the associations were founded within a few years after Issei immigration; therefore they date well back to the start of the century. Although there was a loose coordinating structure, each of the associations operated somewhat independently.

A major portion of the activities of a Japanese Association was devoted to intracommunity affairs. It established and maintained graveyards, provided translators, placed people in contact with legal and other necessary services, and policed the activities of the Japanese community. For instance, the Japanese Association would try to curtail prostitution, gambling, and other activities which might "give a bad name" to the Japanese. They also sponsored picnics and gave backing to youth groups and youth services. But these organizations had few contacts with the majority community, and those few contacts were limited to formal business or ritualistic occasions involving the leaders only. The Japanese Association might participate with the larger community to the extent of sponsoring a float in a local parade or helping to collect for the Community Chest.

The principal function of the Japanese Association, at least in the minds of its members, was protective. The following anecdote is illustrative. Mr. H. Takata, an Issei living in San Francisco stated:

SOURCE: From Harry H. L. Kitano, *Japanese Americans: The Evolution of a Subculture,* copyright © 1969. Reprinted by permission of Prentice-Hall, Inc.

> I am a lodging house keeper. On August 28, 1906, about 9:00 P.M., my window was smashed by a person or persons unknown. Again on August 30, about 11:00 P.M., someone broke my large front window. I reported the incidents to the Japanese Association, but not to the police.[2]

The Japanese Association would then attempt to contact the police; they might also contact the Japanese consul and even if there was very little that could be done formally, the Japanese individual felt somewhat better because he felt that his problems were being handled by people with his interests at heart.

Part of the protective power of the Japanese Association lay in its relationship with the Japanese consulate. The Issei were technically citizens of Japan, so that cases of discriminatory or wrongful treatment were often brought to the attention of the Japanese government rather than local officials. It was felt that most local police officers would ignore individual complaints by Japanese but might listen to the requests of the Japanese Association and the consulate.

Not surprisingly, the Japanese Associations played a conservative role in regard to acculturation. These organizations, modeled after Japanese groups had in their prime (1920–1941) an important voice in keeping the ethnic community "Japanese." Many young Nisei groups chafed against the power of the elder statesmen of the Japanese Association, which reinforced the Issei motto, "don't become too American too quickly."

The associations have gradually lost their former positions of power. The advanced age of the Issei, their loss of economic control, and the changing needs of the community have encouraged the development of differently oriented organizations in their stead.

The Japanese-American Citizen's League (JACL)

The JACL can be thought of as a second-generation counterpart to the Japanese Associations. It, too, developed in response to the special problems and interests of the Japanese, but primarily of the Nisei. Although its initial function was protective, it served, in a way that the Japanese Associations did not, to accelerate acculturation. It was first begun in the early 1920's by young Nisei, who felt that their interests were not served by the Japanese Association, and who therefore established local Nisei groups, called by various names such as Loyalty League, or Citizen's League. By 1930, these local groups had consolidated into a national organization (JACL), supported by local chapters that cut across religious, ken, political, and special-interest ties. The special plight of the Nisei was more than sufficient to override these previously divisive factors. There were problems of citizenship for their Issei parents, of the continuing discrimination and prejudice with which they themselves were faced, and their own problems in the larger society. In addition, the Nisei group was relatively homogenous in age, interest, and goals, so that, as is often the case with groups formed in response to special social crises, the JACL developed quickly into an effective organization.

The gravest crisis with which the JACL had to deal was World War II and the evacuation. Because it was the only national Japanese-American organization, many Japanese looked to it for leadership. It decided to cooperate fully with evacuation orders. In this decision it actually had little choice, because there were few alternatives; the community was disorganized, many Issei leaders had been arrested by the FBI, and all ethnic organizations had been disbanded. Many Issei and Nisei had lost their jobs, and small businesses were in precarious condition. The might of the American government was paramount. For these reasons, it is not likely that JACL could have effected any other course. And it is probable that, whatever the JACL might have decided, the Japanese community would have cooperated with evacuation procedures as it did anyway.

However, because they had declared themselves willing to cooperate, many JACL leaders became scapegoats for feelings of resentment that later developed. Some had extremely harrowing experiences at the hands of fellow Japanese in the relocation camps, and the JACL is to this day resented by some for its cooperation during the World War II crisis.

The primary importance of the JACL remains its role in the acculturation of the Nisei. It accelerated this process in two ways: First, it broke away from the Issei community, and, secondly, it was modeled after American groups. The early conventions, planned and financed by Nisei, concentrated on Nisei problems exclusively, but the debates and procedures followed American patterns. Most importantly, exposure to local and national issues widened the horizons of the Nisei. A possible measure of the general success and affluence of this group is perhaps provided by the sites of its present meetings. Early gatherings were held in local community halls or churches. Today they are held in expensive resorts, with all the external trappings of any middle-class American convention.

Membership in JACL remains high, with more than 20,000 paid-up members in the mid-1960's. The *Pacific Citizen*, its weekly paper, has an estimated readership of over 60,000. The group retains an able professional lobbyist in Washington to represent the interests of the Japanese in the United States as a whole.

With acculturation, increased affluence, and diminishing hostility from the larger community, the JACL finds itself forced to redefine its functions and goals. Many of the unifying issues, such as payment of wartime evacuation claims, and citizenship for Issei, have been resolved, and the attention of the group has turned to problems that are not specifically Japanese. This has introduced new divisive factors. For instance, some JACL members are interested in the problem of *bracero* labor in California, that is, the importation of Mexican agricultural labor. The majority tend to favor a liberal position, which supports the interests of the Mexicans, but other members reflect the attitudes of agricultural employers, so that any JACL stand cannot be unanimously endorsed. Many members expect the JACL to take an active stand on various social problems, but others prefer an organization that emphasizes social functions within the community. The JACL is accused by some of being too liberal and by others of being too conservative. This dissension is probably a reflection of the general acculturation of the Japanese, of the fact that they have moved from problems of a strictly Japanese nature to those of general community interest.

The JACL can be compared to organizations representing other minority groups, such as the Anti-Defamation League, and appears especially similar to the National Association for the Advancement of Colored People (NAACP).[3] For example, both organizations maintain lobbies in Washington; both lodge legal protests against discriminatory practices and both stand ready to protect and aid their respective ethnic groups.[4] Both organizations rely on a predominantly accommodative strategy so that the value of maintaining their tax-free status often takes precedence over stands on other issues. Finally, both organizations have achieved an aura of respectable middle-professional and upper-classness.

It will be interesting to observe the relation of the JACL to the third and fourth generation of Japanese. The Nisei were able to break away from the paternalistic control of the Issei and to develop their own organizations based on their own perception of needs. The barriers of communication, generation, and culture functioned to the advantage of the Nisei in this respect, since ready-made Issei structures and organizations were not handed down to them. There is, however, a strong tendency on the part of the Nisei to provide such organizations for the newer generations (e.g., a junior JACL), with subsequent problems of goals, purposes, control, policy, and membership that might not develop if the Sansei were permitted to evolve their own groups out of their own needs.

RELIGION

Religion, in the American sense of Sunday School attendance, belief in a single faith, and relative intolerance of other faiths, is alien to the Japanese. In general they are tolerant of all theologies and have not institutionalized religion to the extent that most Americans have. This was true in Japan at the time the Issei were growing up there, and appears to be true in Japan today. For example, while in Japan recently, we saw a pilgrim on his way to a Shinto shrine, carrying a Protestant bible and wearing a Catholic crucifix. We were told that this was not uncommon, and that many people like to feel they were "touching all bases." The Issei brought with them to America a similarly flexible approach to religion. Most had gone through no baptismal or confirmation ritual, and were not churchgoers, although most came from a broadly Buddhist background that influenced the ceremonial aspects of birth, weddings, and deaths. Otherwise, the focus of any religious training was ethical behavior—how one acted toward parents, friends, and strangers.

It is therefore not surprising to find certain discrepancies and inconsistencies in religious censuses even today. Many Japanese claim a Buddhist background but may attend an all-Japanese Christian church. A religious survey by Miyamoto of the Japanese in Seattle in 1936 showed that most were Protestants.[5] Data gathered at the time of the wartime evacuation show the same thing. Data gathered among Japanese in Brazil found most of them to be Catholic, suggesting that Japanese tend to adopt the religion of the country in which they find themselves.[6]

Initially, it was believed that religious preference was a good predictor of acculturation. Miyamoto indicated that the Buddhists were much more conservative and more "Japanese" than the members of Christian churches. But this point of view, though historically correct, probably ignores the religious flexibility of the Japanese and of the Buddhist church itself in adapting to changing religious conditions.

Early Christianity

Although early attempts to introduce Christianity into Japan were not successful, Japanese immigrants in the United States provided a fruitful missionary field. Their adoption of the Christian faith was strongly reinforced by practical considerations, because Christian churches had much to offer the new immigrant in the way of employment and Americanization. Many found employment through their church, particularly as house boys. In fact, this was so common that at one time the Japanese house boy was referred to as a "mission boy." The churches also provided an opportunity to learn to speak and behave like Americans, and had therefore an important acculturative function. Several other factors contributed to the development of Christianity among the Japanese. The social welfare functions of the church were congruent with Issei experience, and church attitudes of benevolence and helpfulness toward others were sympathically received. Where the new immigrant was without family, the church served in a family role, supplying the feeling of group participation which the family had provided in Japan. Christianity was also less complicated and expensive than Buddhism when it came to such practical matters as weddings or funerals. Churches often provided mission schools, preschools, and kindergartens. The Christian concepts of ethical and moral training were congruent with those of Buddhism, and, finally, the churches played a strong part in defending the Japanese from legislative and political attacks.

Church activities were particularly important in the acculturation of Japanese women. Women's clubs provided for many a first exposure to American ways—food and fashions, democratic group procedures such as voting, and an opportunity to serve in positions of leadership. Many Nisei remember the unexpected results of mother attending a cooking class—spaghetti, whipped cream desserts, Chinese chow mein, and Italian veal cutlets.

These early church activities were usually presided over, in a missionary spirit, by Caucasian ministers and interested congregations. However, as time went on, the Japanese tended to form all-Japanese congregations. This has by now produced an interesting reversal, in which the educational activities of the church provide, not lessons in Americanization but lessons in Japanese culture—flower arranging and sukiyaki—and are for many Nisei and Sansei the sole contact with their Japanese heritage.

There was one potential source of conflict between Christianity and the Japanese culture. This was the Christian emphasis on individualism, which, on the surface of things, would seem to be incongruent with the group emphasis of Japanese social principles. But because, within the cohesive Japanese community lay an inherent competitiveness, the apparent philosophical incongruence provided no real practical difficulties.

Although theoretical differences in the roles played by Buddhist and Christian churches in acculturation can be hypothesized, actual differences are hard to detect. Buddhist children sing "Buddha loves me, this I know," to the tune that Christian children sing "Jesus loves me." Both churches have Sunday school, Sunday services, and bazaars, social services, women's and youth programs. Buddhist weddings have been shortened and thereby resemble Christian ceremonies. Both churches provide services in English for Nisei and Sansei, and in Japanese for Issei. The ministers of both churches are usually Japanese, and both congregations are mostly segregated. In general, although there may have been initial differences in the direction of acculturation, both institutions, but particularly the Buddhist, have themselves changed to the point that they are remarkably similar and remarkably American. And Japanese parents of either religion usually agree that "it doesn't matter what church you go to, so long as you go to church."

Present Religious Problems

An interview with the minister of a large Japanese Christian church emphasizes the current similarity of the Japanese and other populations.[7] Interests and problems reflect age and generation rather than ethnicity. The concerns of the Issei are appropriate to the aged, and those of the Sansei are those of a young, but not necessarily Japanese, group. For example, the Issei, whose average age is now in the middle 70's, attend both Buddhist and Christian churches in large numbers, and appear to be seeking reassurance in the face of aging and death. Prayer and study groups are well attended. Many regret the spiritual poverty of their pasts, and feel that their previous concern with work and advancement left them unprepared for the philosophical considerations of later life.

Some Issei have turned to the Sokka-Gakkai, a fast-growing religious movement from Japan that combines nationalism and simplistic solutions to metaphysical anxiety. The ultimate importance of this religion is difficult to predict at present, but it seems mainly to involve new immigrants and older Issei.

The Nisei, on the other hand, have different concerns. Most are in comfortable positions economically, and many appear to be more interested in social status than in the welfare of their souls. It seems likely that many tend to think of religion primarily in these terms. Some regard the ethnic church as conferring less status than that conferred by attendance at an all-white church in Brentwood, Bel-Air or other high-status suburban areas. However, for a gardener, no matter what the income, Bel-Air is not a comfortable place. Many resolve this conflict by dropping church attendance altogether, or by remaining inactive in the ethnic church. The social status of the occupation is likely to influence church-going patterns in this way. There have not yet developed sharp social class differences between Japanese churches.

Religious integration is showing another interesting trend. The Japanese churches reflect the financial solidarity of their memberships, and are therefore likely to have new and attractive buildings and impressive social programs. Many have therefore begun to attract non-Japanese. Of the 34 active churches comprising the Southern California Ministerial Fellowship (a Japanese Protestant body), over half report Caucasians among their congregations. Interaction with Negro and Mexican populations remains minimal.

The Sansei generation is not especially active in any church. Many have dutifully gone to Sunday school and have been baptized, but few commit themselves to serious churchgoing. Many "shop around" and join either Christian or Buddhist churches that have good social or athletic programs. In general, they appear no more, and no less, religious than the youth of the larger community. But they may become active when they are older and have families.

In general terms, it is possible to say that while Japanese churches have played important roles in acculturation and in the development of community solidarity and cohesion, they have retained their pluralistic structure, so that while members of a given faith participate in the matters affecting that denomination throughout the country, they remain surrounded by members of their own ethnic group. In this, the Japanese churches have followed a pattern similar to that of other Japanese institutions.

OTHER COMMUNITY ORGANIZATIONS

It would be difficult to overlook the vast network of services and opportunities available to the Japanese youth. Some are by definition acculturative —the Boy and Girl Scouts, the YM and YWCA's, and the Campfire Girls. Others, such as Judo or Kendo groups, are more ethnically enclosed, but all serve to function as agents of socialization and social control.[8]

Probably best known to the Nisei and least known to outsiders were the ambitious all-Japanese athletic leagues. These tended to concentrate on basketball, a sport that did not require expensive uniforms and facilities, and because of considerations such as physical size, limited competition with non-Japanese groups. The all-Japanese leagues were organized into divisions according to age and locality, and held regional and statewide playoffs. At one time there was a national Oriental championship. The golden age of Nisei basketball was in the late 1930's and again in the late 1940's and early 1950's. It offered the usual advantages of participation in a group activity—team and group identification, travel, competition, and rewards. Ironically, the Nisei basketball team was often the only group through which a youngster identified with his high school. For example, one Nisei relates:

> I used to wait for the All-Hi Tournaments. It was the time when all Nisei going to different high schools in San Francisco would get together and compete. We'd have rooting sections, championship playoffs, all-star teams, medals and trophies, and then a big victory dance.[9]

After the tournament, a Nisei, who might have been named the "most valuable player," and have been much-praised in the ethnic newspaper, would resume his anonymous role among the larger student body of his Caucasian high school.

The Nisei learned far more from these teams than the skills of athletic competition. It was an experience of independence, travel, social interaction and role-playing. Here a boy could be a "big fish in a little pond"; his brothers, sisters, and girl friends would come to see him play; there would be dances, bazaars, and other fund-raising and supportive activities. The basketball teams therefore became primary reference groups for many, and a Nisei would often introduce himself by saying "I'm from the Cardinals," which meant that he was from Los Angeles, or as being from the Zebras of San Jose, or from the Greyhounds—a YMCA group in San Francisco.

The basketball teams served as vehicles for acculturation. The Issei remained aloof from them, and considered them rather frivolous, so that the Nisei were free to develop in the American pattern. The play, the rules, the goals and values, were all American; only the players were Japanese. In spite of this, any integration attempts were firmly resisted. Big fights were apt to occur if a non-Japanese or part-Japanese played with one of the teams. In the 30's, a great crisis developed when a group called the San Francisco Mikados —perennial champions—left the league to play in a larger community league. "Do they think they're too good for us now?" stormed the other players, ethnic newspapers, and community sponsors. The offending group came back to play in the ethnic league again the following year.

The years have produced some changes in the Japanese athletic teams. Now the squads are much smaller and tend to be limited to those people with athletic ability. The play is probably better today, but its popularity has waned. Increased opportunities in other areas for individual and group participation and identification are reflected in a general lack of interest and support of these ethnic leagues.

The Little League has to some extent replaced basketball as the most important social-athletic institution in the ethnic community. The Japanese baseball Little Leagues in Los Angeles are extremely well organized and efficiently run, and serve large numbers of Sansei. They still are predominantly all-Japanese, and there have been cases of reverse discrimination, in which Caucasian youngsters have been excluded when they have tried to join the impressive, well-run Sansei clubs. In the Little League, unlike the prewar basketball teams, there is a significant degree of father-son interaction, which may be a mixed blessing.

The Japanese continue to be interested in athletics. It is therefore somewhat curious that few Nisei have become professional athletes; this is an avenue often used by lower-class groups to earn money and status. It is partly accountable to the fact that the Nisei were apt to be physically smaller than other groups. Also important, perhaps, was their emphasis on team sports or on events such as weight-lifting, gymnastics, and swimming. Sports such as tennis or boxing, through which some might have won recognition, have never been popular among the Japanese, although even this pattern is changing. Whatever the reason, the Japanese have never had the athletic heroes available to other groups—no Joe DiMaggio, no Hank Greenberg, no Joe Louis. . . .

NOTES

1. KIYO MORIMOTO, "A Developmental Analysis of the Japanese Community in Pocatello, Idaho," unpublished term paper, May 25, 1956. Harry H. L. Kitano, private collection.
2. HERBERT B. JOHNSON, *Discrimination Against Japanese in California* (Berkeley, Calif.: The Courier Publishing Co., 1907).
3. LOUIS E. LOMAX, *The Negro Revolt* (New York: Signet Books, 1963).
4. The term "Jap" is an especially sensitive one for the Japanese, and JACL chapters are constantly fighting the use of this term.
5. FRANK S. MIYAMOTO, "Social Solidarity Among the Japanese in Seattle," *University of Washington Publications in Social Sciences* 11:2 (December 1939), pp. 99–104.
6. "Japanese Immigrants in Brazil," *Population Index* 35:2 (April 1965) (Princeton, N.J.: Princeton University Press, Office of Population Research), p. 136.
7. KITANO, private collection.
8. The popularity of the "martial arts" has spread to some non-Japanese. Aikido and karate clubs are examples where non-Japanese individuals can be seen in ever greater numbers. Many adherents feel that the discipline and training of these "arts" help to develop character.
9. KITANO, private collection.

Kenjin and Kinsmen

Ivan H. Light

Among the Japanese settlers in America the decisive community ties were those created by *ken* affiliations. The *kenjinkai* were social organizations based on the provincial origins of immigrants. Immigrants from Hiroshima prefecture in Japan affiliated with the Hiroshima kenjinkai, and so forth. Since 89 per cent of Japanese emigrated from 11 southern prefectures, virtually all Japanese settlers were eligible for membership in some ken organization.[1] People from the same ken referred to one another as *kenjin* ("fellow ken people") even when not active members in a prefectural club. Kenjin were said to differ in respect to basic personality traits. Ken endogamy was preferred. Dialectal differences also distinguished the different ken groups. Ken-consciousness was, however, characteristic only of overseas Japanese. In Japan, ken ties had not counted for much in daily life.[2]

The manifest purposes of the kenjinkai were social and benevolent. The prefectural clubs sponsored festival occasions when the membership came together for fellowship and recreation. Observance of Japanese and American holidays was normally in the province of the prefectural clubs, and kenjin made a point of attending these occasions: "We have a store which is run by my family. We are poor, busy, and have many children. We cannot go out like other families. But we have never missed a kenjinkai picnic; it is the only occasion when we can meet many friends. . . . We eat, drink, and chat in our native dialect."[3] In addition to these recreational functions the kenjinkai also played a leading role in overseeing the social and economic welfare of the immigrants. The kenjinkai published newspapers, offered legal advice to members, sponsored the tanomoshi, and served as employment agencies.[4] Prefectural contacts were critical sources of influence in business and politics. Kenjinkai provided direct welfare assistance to destitute or needy members, buried the indigent, and paid medical bills. Because of these varied prefectural services, Japanese thought that membership in a large *kai* was a distinct advantage. Some unfortunates were from kens that did not have many eligible members in a locality; thus they lacked the services a large prefectural club could provide.

The private welfare activities of kenjinkai were extensive. They tended, therefore, to preempt public relief services so that, as a result, few Japanese became public welfare clients. For example, the kenjinkai helped organize

SOURCE: From *Ethnic Enterprise in America* by Ivan H. Light. Originally published by the University of California Press. Copyright © 1972 by The University of California Press. Reprinted by permission of The Regents of the University of California.

massive relief for the 10,000 Japanese made homeless by the San Francisco earthquake and fire of 1906. Because of this private assistance, virtually no Japanese applied to public authorities for disaster relief and rehabilitation.[5] In the middle of the Great Depression a Japanese spokesman in Los Angeles noted that "the number of destitute is increasing; and usually they are assisted by *kenjinkai*." Thanks to this assistance, hardly any Japanese were to be found on the rolls of public unemployment relief.[6] Of course, the language barrier and resulting ignorance of welfare rights played a part in curtailing the number of Japanese applicants for public welfare relief of various sorts. But these inhibitions might more quickly have disappeared had the kenjinkai not busied themselves in finding jobs for the unemployed and relieving the destitute.

AVOIDING DISGRACE

Although stressed in public pronouncements, the welfare activities of the prefectural clubs were in practice restricted in scope by the social disgrace attendant upon accepting this relief. As a relief organization, the prefectural club stood at the apex of a pyramid of community agencies expected to aid needy Japanese. Those who obtained relief from the prefectural club did so only *in extremis* and testified thereby to a disgraceful lack of intimate social affiliations. The close family was conventionally expected to constitute the lowest level relief agency. Appeals for aid beyond this circle were then to be directed to extended relatives, friends, and so forth up the ladder of informal agencies, until finally the needy person lacking other resources might petition his prefectural club. "In actual practice the [indigent] family is cared for by the village or town, because it is considered a disgrace when a community cannot care for its own indigents."[7] The kenjinkai did not formally restrict their beneficence to Japanese who were participating members of their club, although they did, of course, draw the line at Japanese who were from another ken. But the direct relief of ken people in difficulty was, at best, an obligation grudgingly fulfilled by the kenjinkai. The following comments of the secretaries of some kenjinkai suggest the attitude of the prefectural organizations to indigent Japanese who had no other source of relief or assistance:

> [Indigents] were the ones who never joined any organizations, such as the Japanese Association, *kenjinkai*, trade associations, or social club. They were not members of any religious organizations. They were transients who . . . spent money for their own pleasures. They never helped anybody when they were young and able; they were so selfish that they could not make any friends in their lives. . . .

> It seems to be that [indigents] are the people who have the wrong attitudes toward life and society. . . .

> Always [indigents] were people who despised the works of the association and laughed at those who are members. . . .

> Yes, members [of the ken organization] help one another as far as they can. But it is strange enough that members never get in financial trouble.[8]

The striking feature of the prefectural clubs' attitude toward their own destitute was the condemnation of the poor for excessive individualism. This attitude contrasts starkly with middle-class views of the poor in which the moral fault of the indigent is located in a lack of self-reliance.[9] Japanese kenjinkai, however, viewed extreme self-reliance and individualism as tokens of characterological depravity. Moreover, such individualism was conventionally taken to explain the predicament of the poor in an altogether logical and unemotional sense:

> Repeatedly the [prefectural] secretaries stressed the point that those who are assisted and cared for by *kenjinkai* are usually nonmembers who have no families, relatives, or friends. The absence of application for aid on the part of members is due to the fact that mutual aid is practiced in a direct, personal manner among members, before the need of a family is known to *kenjinkai*. . . . Very naturally, cases brought to the attention of the *kenjinkai* are those in desperate condition, where there are no relatives or friends able to assist.[10]

Only those Japanese who lacked more intimate social ties made their way to the prefectural club in search of assistance. Joining and participating in community organizations were characteristics of those Japanese who never found it necessary to request aid from their prefectural club. Under these circumstances, the Japanese naturally interpreted the predicament of the indigent as tokens of a dissolute individualism and isolation from community life.

To be sure, the Japanese did not lightly undertake the support of the needy nor view without some disdain those who found it necessary to request charity. In this sense the kenjinkai encouraged individuals to be industrious, thrifty, and so forth, and so to make provision for hard times on their own. But, however grudgingly, applicants for relief were provisioned from the community storehouse rather than turned away to perish. Such relief was counted a moral obligation. The mendicant poor were upbraided for cutting themselves off from the community and encouraged to develop the lower level social connections which would relieve kenjin of the necessity for supporting them. Prefecturalism thus played the most important role in producing the Japanese-Americans' astounding prewar record of virtually complete absence from public welfare rolls.[11]

ECONOMIC IMPORTANCE OF PREFECTURAL TIES

The attitude of the Japanese toward the friendless destitute is illuminated when the occupational and economic aspects of the kenjinkai are examined. Regional loyalties embodied in the kenjinkai carried over to the sphere of strictly economic relations. The prefectural clubs functioned as employment agencies for members. Members in need of work were able to secure an introduction to other members in need of help through the intervention of the club's secretary and social activities. The Japanese gave preference in hiring to persons from the same prefecture, and Japanese employers were expected to make hiring opportunities known to their kenjinkai.[12] In the early days of Japanese settlement in America, especially before the establishment of formal kenjinkai, Japanese boardinghouse keepers and hotel managers doubled as employment agents for Japanese roomers. The hotels and boardinghouses attracted a clientele from the ken of the owner-proprietor, and naturally the owner-proprietor became the employment agent of kenjin residing with him. In this manner ken affiliations soon became connected with the employment prospects of a Japanese looking for work. Understanding this connection, many Japanese considered participation in prefectural activities a wise policy.

Ken participation was further strengthened by the closure of alternatives. In the general labor market the employment opportunities of Japanese were limited by discrimination to menial positions. In the Japanese economy, employment opportunities were further limited by the preference of other Japanese for members of their own kenjinkai. Ultimately, employment opportunities outside of domestic service were limited to those which employers from one's own prefecture were able to supply; and insofar as prefectural clubs provided a pipeline into the domestic service occupations, the kenjinkai were able virtually to monopolize the allocation of employment to Japanese.

Regional loyalties also affected areas of settlement in the United States. Thus, the Japanese in a given Pacific region tended to be from the same ken; for example, the San Francisco and East Bay Japanese were from the Hiroshima ken. People from the same ken also tended to concentrate in the same lines of work as well as in the same Pacific locale:

> The barbers in Seattle tended to be people from the Yamaguchi-*ken*, for Mr. I. came first and established himself in that line, and then helped his friends from Japan to get started. Then again, in the restaurant business, the majority . . . are Ehine-*ken*, for men like Mr. K. first got into this, and then aided his *ken* friends to follow in the same field. Homes like those of Mr. I. were places of congregation for young men who were eager to learn things . . . and in the course of their association learned such trades as their friends knew.[13]

The tendency of ken fellows to congregate in the same lines of trade was furthered by the prevailing paternalism in employment relations. An important aspect of this paternalism was the social obligation of the employer to enable a diligent employee to open a business of his own. Said a Japanese employer of this obligation: "There's a custom in Japan which you won't find in America: that a man who has worked for another for a long time will eventually be financed by his employer in starting a branch office of his own. In other words, it's natural that everyone should own his individual shop."[14] The bare sequence thus suggested was not, of course, a sequence limited only to Japanese. The notion of career movement from wage employment to self-employment to employership is what Abraham Lincoln referred to as the "natural course of labor." In the American tradition the natural course of labor has provided a cornerstone of the ideology of entrepreneurial individualism. But Lincoln did not expect an employer to finance his apprentice. In his version, the financing of such an enterprise depended on the apprentice's thrift; moreover, the apprentice's new business opened as a competitor rather than "branch office" of his former boss. Of course, the Japanese custom is more comprehensible in light of the prefectural ties in which master and apprentice were involved. These reciprocal social obligations of a quasi-primary sort intervened between Japanese employer and employee, thereby weakening the purely contractual elements in their relationship.

The tendency of kenjin to prefer each other in hiring and to pile up in the same trades naturally produced problems of internal competition. Traditional guild organizations recommended themselves in this connection. Guild organization of their trades enabled Japanese to regulate internal competition by discussion and collective decision making, rather than by individualistic competition in a devil-take-the-hindmost scramble for survival. In every trade in which Japanese were extensively employed, they organized guilds. Naturally, the membership of the guild or trade association tended extensively to overlap with memberships in the kenjinkai, as well as with family and neighborhood groupings. Like the kenjinkai, the trade guilds combined benevolent, social, economic, and welfare functions. In this combination, the trade guilds went considerably beyond the normal range of activities of a Western trade association.

JAPANESE TRADE GUILDS

The operation of the Japanese trade guilds is illustrated by the Kako Domei Kwai, the Japanese Shoemakers Guild. The organization and operation of the Kako Domei Kwai were typical of most urban Japanese trade guilds such as restaurants, boardinghouses and hotels, expressmen, dry cleaners, tailors, domestics, curio art goods, grocery stores, and so on. The Kako Domei Kwai was founded in 1893 by Japanese shoe repairmen who had been brought to San Francisco by a Western capitalist, a Mr. Cheese. For a while the Japanese worked in Mr. Cheese's shoe factory on Ecker Street in San Francisco; but the Shoemakers' Union (white) of San Francisco, learning of their presence, forced Mr. Cheese to close his factory. The discharged Japanese shoe repairmen began to open their own shoe repairing establishments and formed the Kako Domei Kwai for their mutual benefit and protection. The Japanese repairmen did a good business, largely with a white clientele, despite the vigorous, sometimes violent opposition of the white Shoemakers' Union. After nine years of struggle, the white shoemakers recognized the permanency of the Japanese competition, and in 1904 struck a bargain with the Kako Domei Kwai concerning hours of labor, prices, and the business districts in which the Japanese would operate.

The internal organization of the Kako Domei Kwai followed the lines of traditional guild organization. The guild made every effort to control the market. According to the U.S. Immigration Committee, the Kako Domei Kwai

> not only fixes a scale of prices to be charged . . . but controls the location of shops and protects and furthers the interests of its members in various ways. In opening shops, no two may be located within 1,000 feet of each other. A member of the union operating a shop in a locality where no Japanese shop is in existence may be assisted by a loan of money from the organization. . . . The Union also maintains a supply house in San Francisco and several thousand dollars of the "business fund" accumulated from dues paid are invested in the stock of goods carried. . . . Finally, this organization controls apprenticeship to the trade, and maintains a system of fraternal benefits. . . . The advantages in competition derived from the organization are apparent.[15]

The fraternal benefits involved in the Japanese trade guilds were of many sorts. When a member of the guild was ill and unable to work, the trade guild requested other members to send their assistants to the shop of the sick man. Until the individual recovered, the assistants operated his store—normally for free. The assistants were paid by their own masters, and all of the cash they took in on behalf of the ill member was received by his family. When a member of the guild died, the trade guild paid his survivors a lump sum of money. When someone in a member's family died, the trade guild paid the survivors a smaller sum as koden, or funeral money. At the height of the Great Depression, a member of the Japanese Hotel Association remarked that, "until a few years ago, the Association had a special provision for . . . mutual aid to the members. But now we do not have any. However, mutual aid is extended to members of the Association individually, as the members know each other very well." [16]

Reinforced by the overlapping solidarities of kenjinkai, family, and neighborhood, the Japanese guilds provided the membership with a critical organizational instrument for survival in business. A preliminary task of Japanese trade guilds was the rebuff of white competitors' efforts to expel them from the market. Particularly in the early period of Japanese settlement, before a modus vivendi with white tradesmen was achieved, the creation of Japanese business establishments unavoidably entailed the initiation of competition with white tradesmen already employed in the line. Threatened by Japanese competition, white tradesmen responded with "Swat the Jap" campaigns intended to stir up racial animosity against Japanese business establishments and to enlist the race solidarity of the "white" caste in the pecuniary interest of white tradesmen.[17] Such campaigns took the form of boycotts, picketing, mob violence, arson, and threats of reprisal directed against Japanese businesses, white patrons of Japanese establishments, and white suppliers of these establishments. Since organized labor was waging its own crusade against Japanese immigration under the banner of the Asiatic Exclusion League, white tradesmen had no difficulty in recruiting thugs for their "Americanism" campaigns of intimidation or in appealing to the racial "idealism" of many poor whites.[18]

In San Francisco, grass roots campaigns against Japanese business and the reign of terror employed to implement them reached a peak between 1905 and 1908. Police rarely interfered. Similar campaigns went on in Los Angeles until the 1920's.[19] So long as such campaigns confined themselves to the marketplace, however, the Japanese were normally able to survive in business. The solidarity of the Japanese community and of the different trade guilds permitted the Japanese to carry on a successful defensive struggle in the market place. Faced with boycotts by white suppliers, the Japanese responded—as an organized group—in kind and took reprisals against the boycotters. "It was never impossible to find the weakest link in the line of boycotters and every effort to drive them [Japanese] out failed." [20] Thugs employed by the white merchants to terrorize Japanese businessmen were bought off through funds subscribed by the membership of the Japanese trade guilds. Sometimes the trade guilds employed private police to guard the premises of threatened Japanese against arsonists or strong-arm men. As for their white clientele, for every customer lost through the racial appeals of threatened white merchants, the Japanese were able to find another by providing better service and lower prices than their white competitors.

When, however, anti-Japanese campaigns moved into the political arena, the Japanese were largely unable to resist. Since foreign-born Japanese were aliens and ineligible for citizenship, the immigrant residents of California had not even the feeble voice of the minority vote to protect their interests. In both agriculture and city trade, political authorities, on the motion of various commercial interests, restricted Japanese competition. In the laundry trade, for example, the Anti-Jap Laundry League was formed in 1908 by white proprietors of steam laundries, the Laundry-Drivers Union, French laundry operators, and white laundry workers. The league conducted a two-pronged campaign against Japanese laundries. First, it attempted to reduce the business volume of the Japanese laundries by boycott, personal solicitation of white patrons, and anti-Japanese billboard advertising. Second, it put pressure on San Francisco politicians to refuse city permits to Japanese laundries. In this political campaign, the league was partially successful in that city authorities denied Japanese applicants the permits necessary to conduct the new-fangled steam laundry. When in 1919 a Mr. Tsukamoto opened a steam laundry without a permit in defiance of the authorities, his laundry was closed by police. Mr. Tsukamoto's subsequent suit against the city of San Francisco in the Supreme Court of the United States was defeated.[21]

JAPANESE AGRICULTURE

The most striking legal disabilities imposed on the Japanese were the various alien land laws enacted by the state of California in 1913 and thereafter. From the point of view of the white ranchers, the Japanese had been altogether too successful in agriculture. Primarily from farming backgrounds, the Japanese immigrants had naturally gravitated to agricultural pursuits in California. In the early period of Japanese immigration, growers welcomed the Japanese migrants who provided an inexpensive supply of harvest laborers, a task for which the resident Chinese population had grown too old because of legislated Chinese exclusion. However, the Japanese farm laborers began to work and lease land as contract, share, and tenant farmers, and ultimately began to purchase substantial amounts of land outright. In this progression, the Japanese were exceptionally advantaged by their acquaintance with traditional Japanese methods of intensive cultivation. The poor Issei farm laborers had little money and could rent or purchase little land; but from small plots of land they were able to generate extraordinarily large harvests because of their knowledge of methods of intensive cultivation.[22] They introduced new crops, notably rice, in the cultivation of which by dint of enormous effort they were able to make use of the most barren wastelands. Thus, the Japanese began to branch out of agricultural wage labor by purchasing small tracts of barren land at very low prices. Since they were able to cultivate this land more successfully than others had anticipated, they began to make money in agriculture.[23]

The Issei shift from farm labor to independent and contract farming proved an embarrassment to large California agricultural concerns for two reasons. Of these two the direct competition of Japanese in the produce market was probably the less important. The Japanese system of intensive cultivation was successful only with particular crops, notably truck vegetables, berries, and flowers. To a considerable degree, white growers were uninterested in these specialties "because of the backbreaking labor involved." [24] Moreover, Japanese competition in agricultural products was limited to specific California markets, especially Los Angeles and San Francisco. Japanese agriculture was an insignificant competitor on the national market toward which California growers oriented their enterprise. However, the Japanese withdrawal from farm labor disconcerted California growers who relied on Japanese labor to harvest their crops. This refusal to serve as a permanent harvest labor force probably inflamed California growers more than did the direct competition of Japanese in the produce market.[25]

Through the Alien Land Law of 1913, California growers hoped to force the Japanese out of agricultural self-employment and into the position of agricultural laborers. The law drastically restricted the right of aliens ineligible for citizenship to own, rent, or lease agricultural land. However, the Japanese found loopholes in the law and were thereby able to progress in California agriculture until 1920. An important means of circumventing the law was to buy or lease land in the name of the native-born children of the Issei farmers. As citizens, the Nisei infants were exempt from the provisions of the law debarring landholding by aliens. In response to this successful evasion, California enacted a strengthened land law in 1920. This law was effectively administered and plugged up the loopholes previously permitting the Japanese to flourish in agriculture. As a result, Japanese agricultural holdings declined from 458,026 acres in 1920 to 330,053 in 1923 and 304,966 in 1925.[26] But, although the California growers were successful in restricting Japanese agriculture, they were not successful in forcing the Japanese population to serve as agricultural laborers. Banished from the soil, the Japanese moved to the cities. Although this tendency doubtless reflected the general rural-urban migration and its impersonal causes, the Japanese migration to the cities began in 1920—reflecting the precipitating effect of the stringent land law.[27]

In the early transition from agricultural labor to independent farming, the social organization of Japanese farm laborers played an important role. The Japanese boardinghouse keepers with their ken affiliations doubled as employment agents for their roomers. The boardinghouse keepers maintained connections with Japanese agricultural "bosses." The bosses recruited agricultural work crews and negotiated directly with the California farmers for the employment of their crews.[28] The system was quite popular with the growers, for it enabled them to secure labor through contact with appropriate bosses who took the entire responsibility of recruiting, transporting, and paying the crew. Rancher and farm laborer confronted one another only through the mediation of the boss. Unlike a labor contractor, a Japanese boss was an agent of his crew rather than a solo entrepreneur. In their contractual relationships with the growers, agricultural bosses were outspokenly mercenary on behalf of their crews. They negotiated with the employers concerning the wage rate and unhesitatingly allocated their crew to whichever rancher offered the men the best terms. The bosses were also quite prepared to take their crew out of any farmer's field the instant a competitor offered a higher rate. Indeed, this propensity of the Japanese agricultural boss sometimes involved the violation of contractual agreements.[29]

The Japanese boss system in agricultural labor constituted an embryonic form of trade unionism. Insofar as the kenjinkai were able to monopolize the supply of Japanese agricultural labor, the Japanese boss was perforce dependent on the kenjinkai (through the boardinghouses) for his agricultural crew. Moreover, boss and crew typically shared a loyalty to a ken, dialect, religious sect, and circle of friends. Under these circumstances, relationships between boss and crew could not be entirely commercial. The boss was thus inhibited in the tendency to define himself as a profit-maximizing entrepreneur of agricultural labor and induced to take on the role of representative of his crew. The counterpart of the fraternal social ties uniting boss and crew was the strictly mercenary relationship between boss and employer. The contract labor system became "the central instrument" of the Japanese rise from agricultural day labor to independent farming.[30] Prefectural control of the labor supply and of the contractor enabled Japanese farm hands to extract maximally favorable terms from white ranchers and so expedited the development of widespread proprietary status.

In independent farming, the Japanese made similar use of thorough organization and cooperation. According to the California Board of Control, in 1920 there were 19 local affiliates of the Japanese Agricultural Association of Southern California and 36 associations in northern and central California affiliated with the Japanese Agricultural Association and the California Farmers Cooperative Association.[31] Almost every Japanese farmer belonged to some Japanese agricultural organization. These associations were organized along the familiar lines of the trade guild, taking as their purpose the marketing of members' produce, control of prices and wages, regulation of labor disputes and of internal competition, protection of farmers' interests, and guardianship of the social welfare of members' families.[32]

The most striking feature of the pre-World War II Japanese economy in California was the liaison between Japanese farmers and urban Japanese wholesalers and retailers of farm produce. Japanese sellers specialized in crops that were largely monopolized by Japanese growers. Since the bulk of Japanese trade with whites was in agricultural products, the rural-urban liaison provided the critical prop to the Japanese-American economy.[33] Marketing arrangements were complex. In southern California, the Japanese farmers' associations of Guadalupe, San Luis Obispo, Pismo Beach, and Lompoc, in conjunction with the Japanese Produce Merchants' Association of Los Angeles, formed the Japanese Cooperative Farm Industry (JCFI) of Southern California in 1929. Jointly maintained by the farmers and the merchants, this association controlled Japanese agriculture in Southern California. The Japanese Cooperative Farm Industry took charge of produce distribution through Japanese-owned outlets such as the Southern California Flower Market and the City Market of Los Angeles.[34] The white-owned Wholesale Terminal Market in Los Angeles posed a special problem for Japanese farmers. To deal with it they founded the Nippon-California Farmers Association in 1909. This body represented the interests of Japanese growers in negotiations with the market.[35]

The JCFI studied the produce market continuously in order to determine the amount of produce which could be marketed while maintaining the price. It also coordinated the activities of farmers and merchants for their mutual benefit. A special fund reimbursed farmers whose produce had been dumped by the JCFI in order to maintain the price. The JCFI collected the daily proceeds from the purchasers, forwarded them to the local Japanese farmers' associations which then issued checks to the individual farmers, so that farmers never confronted the market as individuals. Like other Japanese associations, the Cooperative Farm Industry held in reserve a welfare fund for the benefit of members. Of the income of the association, 40 per cent went for operating costs and 60 per cent for welfare and relief of needy members.[36]

Japanese cooperation in agriculture was, however, primarily informal. Japanese farmers spontaneously organized systems of mutual aid at the local level.[37] The Great Depression stimulated the JCFI to develop formal controls to supplement mutual aid on the local level. The Japanese experienced some strain in attempting to operate large secondary associations, because parochial and personalistic social connections constantly influenced operating patterns.[38] One way of circumventing this problem was to create larger structures by piling up primary grouplets. Most of the larger Japanese farms in California were amalgams of the holdings of several smaller families. The families operated the joint acreage as a sort of cooperative.[39]

The Japanese farmer involved in cooperative relationships with his Japanese neighbors could not operate his farm as a solo entrepreneur. Since others had connected their interest with his in meaningful ways, others had a legitimate interest in how an individual managed his enterprise. If a Japanese farmer were tempted to lease more land than he was able to manage, neighboring farmers would warn him against overextension. Should a farmer neglect his land, thereby jeopardizing those who had countersigned his notes, the neighborhood undertook a sterner warning. Where a farmer was in danger of economic collapse, Japanese neighbors would descend upon the farm and by mutual effort bring the land "up to proper condition as speedily as possible." A persistent individualism manifesting itself in an unwillingness to manage the farm as others thought it ought to be managed involved, in the extreme case, the denial of cooperation—and subsequent banishment of the individualist from the Japanese economic structure.[40]

JAPANESE FISHERMEN

Cooperative practices also prevailed among Japanese fishermen in California. Japanese fishermen tended to settle in communities populated by persons from their own ken. The important fishing community of Terminal Island, East San Pedro, for example, was settled originally by Japanese fishermen from the village of Taiji. These fishermen organized the Japanese Fishermen's Association of San Pedro in 1907. The association took charge of Japanese fishing activities—overseeing prices, working conditions, apprenticeship, welfare, and politicoeconomic representation of Japanese fishing interests. The association organized strikes against the canneries on behalf of higher prices for raw fish. The fishermen were convinced of the economic value of cooperation through the association:

> This association has . . . forced the price of fish up. When the price has fallen, the fall has not been to the low point that occurred before the rise began. . . .
> I have no hesitation in saying that wherever we find association principles ignored, a low rate of prices prevails, and the reverse is true where organization is perfected. The most approved remedy for low prices is cooperation.[41]

Shortly after its founding, the association erected the Fisherman Hall Community Center. This center busied itself with the extensive social, fraternal, and welfare activities of the trade guild.

INDUSTRIAL PATERNALISM

In view of the racial discrimination experienced by Japanese in the general labor market, the characteristic paternalism of pre-World War II Japanese business is the more understandable. Since Japanese employees had little opportunity to secure employment in the general economy other than in menial positions, the Japanese-American economy was perforce their only alternative. In the Japanese economy, work was largely available only through the mediation of kin and kenjin. To receive a job in the Japanese-American economy was to become the recipient of a benevolence bestowed upon one by virtue of social connections. Typically, the relevant social connections were those linking the Issei so that Nisei workers secured employment on the basis of their parents' social connections.

By virtue of the intrusion of fraternal ties into the economy, matters of wages and hours were largely removed from the direction of the market and hinged on normative conventions, custom, and social obligation. Under this control, the inhibition on the exploitation of Japanese workers by their employers was the very social obligation by which an employee had managed to secure a job in the first place. An unjust or exploitative employer could be curbed only through social pressures. Such pressures constituted the only legitimated defense of the Japanese worker. Traditionalism and paternalism in employment relations imposed on the employer the duty of fair treatment for his employees in return for the employees' loyalty and submission. Complaining, striking, and quitting—the defense of the Western worker against exploitation—were denied to the Japanese employee of a Japanese-owned firm.[42] The Americanized Nisei experienced especial difficulty in conforming to the normative requirements of traditional Japanese paternalism:

> We had to put up with this sort of thing because jobs were so scarce and there were family obligations. My employer was a fellow church member and a friend of the family so he took advantage of me and honestly felt that he was my benefactor. The Japanese employers figured that the Nisei workers were part of a family system and that is why they took advantage. It may have been the system in Japan, but I could not take it. . . .
>
> [The Issei employers] expected us to put in this overtime because it was supposed to be our duty to the store. Their idea was that it was the employee's responsibility to come to the aid of the company when it was busy. They certainly had funny ideas about a worker's duty to the company.[43]

The employers took the view that in hiring this or that individual they had bestowed a benevolence that obligated the favorite to the employer and justified very long hours, low pay, and hard work.[44] This aspect of the relationship was peculiarly American in that it stemmed, ultimately, from the shortage of work caused by Japanese exclusion from the general economy. But, of course, Japanese culture contributed to this result too.

Low pay, hard work, and long hours were the normal lot of the Japanese worker. But it is difficult to lay categorically the entire blame for such exploitation on the Japanese employer. After all, the small Japanese firms survived only on the basis of hard work and long hours. Certainly the Nisei were very naive about the Japanese situation in California and heaped onto their employers frustrations which might more properly have been directed to the system of racial discrimination which barred them from all but menial positions in the general economy. Ultimately, this system was responsible for the economic plight of the Japanese worker. Then, too, the Americanization of the Nisei caused them to perceive as exploitative economic relationships which were customary among the Issei.[45]

NOTES

1. STANFORD M. LYMAN, "The Structure of Chinese Society in Nineteenth-Century America," (Ph.D. diss., University of California, Berkeley, 1961), pp. 48–71; YASA-BURO YOSHIDA, "Sources and Causes of Japanese Emigration," *Annals* 34 (September 1909): 377–87. Also see HARRY H. L. KITANO, *Japanese Americans*, (Englewood Cliffs, N.J.: Prentice-Hall, 1969), p. 10.
2. SHOTARO FRANK MIYAMOTO, "Social Solidarity Among the Japanese in Seattle," *University of Washington Publications in the Social Sciences* 2 (December 1939), pp. 117–18; cf. YUKIKO KIMURA, "Locality Clubs as Basic Units of the Social Organization of the Okinawans in Hawaii," *Phylon* 29 (Winter 1968), pp. 333–35.
3. FUMIKO FUKUOKA, "Mutual Life and Aid Among the Japanese in Southern California," (M.A. thesis, University of Southern California, 1937), p. 17.
4. JOHN MODELL, "The Japanese of Los Angeles," (Ph.D. diss., Columbia University, 1969), pp. 133–34.
5. RUSSELL SAGE FOUNDATION, *San Francisco Relief Survey* (New York, 1913), pp. 94–95; HERBERT B. JOHNSON, *Discrimination Against Japanese in California* (Berkeley: Courier Publishing, 1907), p. 67.
6. FUKUOKA, "Mutual Life," p. 19; MODELL, "Japanese of Los Angeles," pp. 161, 261.
7. FUKUOKA, "Mutual Life," p. 15. See also KITANO, *Japanese Americans*, p. 73; FORREST E. LA VIOLETTE, *Americans of Japanese Ancestry* (Toronto: Canadian Institute of International Affairs, 1946), p. 90.
8. FUKUOKA, "Mutual Life," pp. 50–53.
9. See REINHARD BENDIX, *Work and Authority in Industry*, (New York: John Wiley, 1956), pp. 86–99.
10. FUKUOKA, "Mutual Life," pp. 51–52. See also STUART ALFRED QUEEN, *Social Work in the Light of History* (Philadelphia: J. B. Lippincott, 1922), pp. 275–276.
11. FUKUOKA, "Mutual Life," p. 86; MIYAMOTO, *Social Solidarity*, p. 58; KITANO, *Japanese Americans*, p. 76; KIMURA, "Locality Clubs," pp. 335–36; LEONARD BLOOM and RUTH RIEMER, *Removal and Return* (Berkeley and Los Angeles: University of California Press, 1949), pp. 63–64.
12. MODELL, "Japanese of Los Angeles," pp. 133–34; FUKUOKA, "Mutual Life," pp. 17, 51–53, 57; MIYAMOTO, *Social Solidarity*, pp. 74–75.
13. MIYAMOTO, *Social Solidarity*, p. 75; also see ISAMU NODERA, "A Survey of the Vocational Activities of the Japanese in the City of Los Angeles," (M.A. thesis, University of Southern California, 1936), p. 8.

14. MIYAMOTO, *Social Solidarity*, p. 7. The "branch office endowment was common among late Tokugawa merchants." See TAKEO YAZAKI, *Social Change and the City in Japan* (Tokyo: Japan Publications, 1968), pp. 214–15.

15. United States Senate, Sixty-First Congress, 2d Session, *Immigrants in Industries*, pt. 25, *Japanese and Other Immigrant Races in the Pacific Coast and Rocky Mountain States*, vol. 1, *Japanese and East Indians*, p. 206. Also see SCHICHIRO MATSUI, "Economic Aspects of the Japanese Situation," (M.A. thesis, University of Southern California, 1922), pp. 66, 75.

16. FUKUOKA, "Mutual Life," p. 30; MIYAMOTO, *Social Solidarity*, p. 98. See also QUEEN, *Social Work*, p. 282.

17. GLADYS HENNIG WALDRON, "Anti-Foreign Movements in California, 1919–1929" (Ph.D. diss., University of California, Berkeley, 1956), pp. 252–53, 265.

18. ROGER DANIELS, *The Politics of Prejudice*, (Berkeley: University of California Press, 1962), pp. 16–30, 97; KAINICHI KAWASAKI, "The Japanese Community of East San Pedro, Terminal Island, California" (M.A. thesis, University of Southern California, 1931), p. 164; United States Senate, Sixty-First Congress, *Immigrants in Industry*, p. 170.

19. JOHNSON, *Discrimination Against Japanese*, p. 99; CAREY McWILLIAMS, *Prejudice* (Boston: Little, Brown, 1944), p. 26; WALDRON, "Anti-Foreign Movements," pp. 252 ff.

20. MIYAMOTO, *Social Solidarity*, p. 76.

21. MATSUI, "Economic Aspects," pp. 59 ff.; United States Senate, Sixty-First Congress, *Immigrants in Industry*, pp. 189–90.

22. JEAN PAJUS, *The Real Japanese California* (Berkeley: James J. Gillick, 1937), p. 79; DANIELS, *Politics of Prejudice*, p. 87.

23. YAMATO ICHIHASHI, *Japanese in the United States*, (Stanford: Stanford University Press, 1932), pp. 178–206; T. IYENAGA and KENOSKE SATO, *Japan and the California Problem* (New York: G. P. Putnam's Sons, 1921), p. 132.

24. BRADFORD SMITH, *Americans from Japan* (Philadelphia: J. B. Lippincott, 1948), p. 237.

25. State Board of Control of California, *California and the Oriental*, (Sacramento, 1920), p. 101; DANIELS, *Politics of Prejudice*, p. 89.

26. ICHIHASHI, *Japanese*, p. 196; MODELL, "Japanese of Los Angeles," p. 35; DANIELS, *Politics of Prejudice*, p. 88.

27. ICHIHASHI, *Japanese*, p. 101; NODERA, "Survey of Vocational Activities," pp. 8–9.

28. United States Senate, Sixty-First Congress, *Immigrants in Industry*, pp. 45–50, 62; MODELL, "Japanese of Los Angeles," pp. 56–57.

29. MATSUI, "Economic Aspects," p. 72; IYENAGA and SATO, *Japan and the California Problem*, p. 127; ROBERT E. PARK and HERBERT A. MILLER, *Old World Traits Transplanted* (New York: Harper & Brothers, 1921), pp. 177–78.

30. MASAKAZU IWATA, "The Japanese Immigrants in California Agriculture," *Agricultural History* 36 (January 1962), p. 28; LLOYD H. FISHER, *The Harvest Labor Market in California* (Cambridge: Harvard University Press, 1953), p. 25.

31. State Board of Control, *California and the Oriental*, p. 104.

32. IWATA, "Japanese Immigrants," p. 33; FUKUOKA, "Mutual Life," p. 27.

33. BLOOM and RIEMER, *Removal*, pp. 82–83; R. D. McKENZIE, "The Oriental Finds a Job," *Survey* 56 (May 1, 1926), p. 218; DAVIS McENTIRE, "An Economic and Social Study of Population Movements in California, 1850–1944" (Ph.Dd. diss., Harvard University, 1947), p. 292.

34. FUKUOKA, "Mutual Life," pp. 10, 28; IWATA, "Japanese Immigrants," p. 34.
35. NODERA, "Survey of Vocational Activities," p. 108.
36. FUKUOKA, "Mutual Life," pp. 28, 37 ff.; MATSUI, "Economic Aspects," pp. 79–80.
37. State Board of Control, *California and the Oriental*, p. 82; J. MERLE DAVIS, "The Orientals," in *Immigrant Backgrounds*, Henry Pratt Fairchild, Ed. (New York: Wiley, 1927), p. 189.
38. FUKUOKA, "Mutual Life," p. 70; MIYAMOTO, *Social Solidarity*, p. 78.
39. National Labor Relations Board, "Los Angeles County Vegetable Growers Survey" (typewritten; Los Angeles: National Labor Relations Board, March 6, 1937), p. 5.
40. State Board of Control, *California and the Oriental*, p. 82.
41. KAWASAKI, "Japanese Community," p. 132.
42. T. SHIBUTANI, "Memorandum on a Comparative Study of the Resettlement Program in Chicago and St. Louis" (typewritten; Chicago: Evacuation and Resettlement Study, 1943). Also see LA VIOLETTE, *Americans of Japanese Ancestry*, pp. 56–57, 91; KITANO, *Japanese Americans*, p. 20.
43. CHARLES KIKUCHI, "The Social Adjustment Process of the Japanese-American Resettlers to Chicago During the Wartime Years" (M.A. thesis, Columbia University, 1947), p. 48; R. NISHIMOTO, "Japanese in Personal Service and Urban Trade" (typewritten, n.d.), p. 44, See also LEONARD BROOM and JOHN I. KITSUSE, *The Managed Casualty* (Berkeley and Los Angeles: University of California Press, 1956), p. 10.
44. LA VIOLETTE, *Americans of Japanese Ancestry*, pp. 81–82.
45. JITSUICHI MASUOKA, "Changing Moral Bases of the Japanese Family in Hawaii," *Sociology and Social Research* 21 (November-December 1936): 163–66; MATSUKICHI AMANO, "A Study of Employment Patterns and a Measure of Employee Attitudes in Japanese Firms at Los Angeles" (Ph.D. diss., University of California, Los Angeles, 1966), pp. 14–38. Cf. JAMES C. ABEGGLEN, *The Japanese Factory* (Glencoe, Ill.: Free Press, 1958), p. 99; ROBERT EVANS, JR., "Evolution of the Japanese System of Employer-Employee Relations, 1868–1945," *Business History Review* 44 (spring 1970), pp. 110–25.

The Intolerance of Success

Daniel Okimoto

Despite the outpouring of praise from the white community, my own reactions to the celebrated success story of the Japanese minority are not quite so effusive or onesided. While the many achievements of this minority should be acknowledged, it must also be pointed out that much of the praise that is showered upon us springs from a fountainhead of middle-class assumptions, some of questionable value, and that these neglect to mention the reverse side of success: the sacrifices that had to be made, the shortcomings that are all but overlooked in our pilgrimage into the Land of Milk and Honey. Since to dwell exclusively on our accomplishments is to present an incomplete picture, some of the less attractive aspects of the Japanese-American pattern of acculturation need to be discussed. Of greatest importance, perhaps, are the costs at which our social advancement has been won.

In adapting to American society, we have had to face the persistent and perplexing problem of how to look upon our dual heritage. The difficulty of reconciling these twin aspects of our lives is often revealed in that moment of hesitation many experience when asked, "What are you?" In my own life there have been times when I have been frankly at a loss how to reply. Depending on my mood and the circumstances, my answers have vacillated between "American," "Japanese," and "Japanese American." Whatever the response, it usually felt somehow unnatural. I never considered myself 100-per cent American because of obvious physical differences. Nor did I think of myself as Japanese. The social opprobrium associated with being a member of a minority also made me slightly uncomfortable about declaring myself a Japanese American.

Perhaps this question would not pose such problems if an atmosphere of greater tolerance existed in America. Certainly if the United States were a harmonious melting pot in which all races are accepted equally—as myths would have one believe—there would not be any need to feel hesitant about identifying with a minority, particularly one as successful as the Japanese. But in the face of prejudice it is often hard indeed to resolve the Japanese and American elements.

Like a number of others, I passed through a period when I almost always responded to questions about my nationality with "American." The mere fact of being questioned made me bristle with indignation at the ignorance of

298

those who felt the need to inquire. At the bottom of my eagerness to be recognized as an American, was a deep-seated discomfort about my Asian past. Even at those times when I referred to myself in jest as a "Buddha-head" there was probably some degree of self-derogation.

Unfortunately, as a consequence of this state of mind, we Nisei all too frequently attempt to jettison the Asian aspects of our personalities. In our eagerness to scramble to the top of American society, many of us have paid the costly price of abandoning the "baggage" of our cultural heritage, the finest features of which have contributed to the competitive position we now hold. Although Japanese Americans still stick together in closed groups, the substance of our subculture has lost much of its "Japaneseness." Certain old-country stresses, such as that placed on education, survive today, but gradually these have come to be associated less with Japanese-American values than with middle-class American norms.

As any casual conversation will reveal, Japanese Americans are on the whole no better informed about their ancestral homeland than non-Japanese. Few are willing to make an effort to learn anything about it. Although this disinterest may perhaps be inevitable as the struggle to establish an American identity goes on, it is nevertheless a loss to lament, particularly in view of the richness of Japanese culture. Japanese concepts of aesthetics as expressed in such art forms as ink painting, woodblock prints, folkcrafts, traditional gardens, and architecture stand up well in comparison with the world's great artistic achievements. The same can be said of Japanese literature, cinema, martial arts, flower arrangement, tea ceremony, Noh, Kabuki and Bunraku drama, and Zen Buddhism. How unfortunate that so few Japanese Americans consciously seek to keep alive this cultural heritage.

Interestingly, there is a movement taking shape now among the postwar generation to reevaluate the problem of identity and the significance of their ethnicity. No longer apologetic about being members of a minority nor eager to discard their past, many college-age Nisei today are rebelling against remnants of racism and old Oriental stereotypes, and are aggressively raising a cry for Yellow Power. Like Afro-American groups, Asian-American organizations are appearing on campuses throughout the country, their members demanding courses that can help them recover a sense of their historical roots. They are redefining their role and place in society and, from a newly delineated perspective, participating in the momentous issues confronting the nation.

The new ethnic consciousness and defiance against racial prejudice owes much to the Black Power movement which, by boldly challenging the status quo, brought vividly to light conditions of injustice that confront all minorities, leading the way for other races to join in the long-delayed fight against discrimination. Borrowing the insights and even some of the rhetoric of the blacks, the Asian-American movement represents a sharp divergence from the old pattern of silence and passivity. While Yellow Power may never become the rallying cry for Orientals in the same way that Black Power has for Negroes, the affirmation of racial ancestry is the kind of major shift in attitude that could have far-reaching implications for Asian subcultures in the United States.

Even though the term "Nisei" applies to Japanese in both North and South America, the two groups are quite different in their identification with their Japanese past. Nisei in Latin America appear on the whole to have come under less compulsion to shed their Asian identity than those in North America. Not only do they tend to speak better Japanese, retain more Oriental customs, and maintain closer ties with relatives in Japan, but they also hold their ancestral culture in higher esteem than their counterparts in the States. This may be the result of timing; large-scale immigration to South America took place more recently than that to the United States. But it is probably more directly related to differences in the areas into which Japanese culture was carried. Location helps explain why Japanese Americans on the mainland and in Hawaii are not the same. In the presence of more Japanese and perhaps less anti-Japanese prejudice, Hawaiian Nisei seem to retain more of their racial identity, maintain a larger and more cohesive ethnic community, and in general appear less frantic about Americanizing than those on the continent.[1]

The successes of the Japanese in mainland America have been predicated on a thoroughgoing accommodation to white middle-class norms. The high degree of conformity is evident in the general behavioral patterns of Nisei students: in the classroom they are extremely well-behaved, seldom make noise, never talk back to teachers, faithfully finish their school assignments on time. Neatly dressed, cleanly scrubbed, polite and deferential, Nisei on the whole would be among the last to join hippie communes or participate in avant garde movements. Although some postwar youths are beginning to defy traditional modes, the majority of Japanese are still the epitome of the clean-cut all-American prototype in all but physical appearance.

Quiet conformity has no doubt helped to minimize social deviation and outbreaks of crime; in this sense it has functioned positively in gaining Japanese Americans admission into American society. However, from quite another perspective, the unquestioning, almost mindless acceptance of middle-class standards has given rise to an insensate conservatism that has all but deadened impulses toward individualism and creativity. It is rare to find among the Japanese community individualists who not only think heretically but dare to court strong social disapproval by disregarding convention. Accolades from the Caucasian community, inadvertently perhaps, have reinforced this timidity by convincing Japanese Americans that it is better to be safe than conspicuous. As a result, Nisei are proud of their upstanding reputation and are reluctant to risk damaging it with unorthodox activity. Told what exemplary citizens we are, we have responded gratefully by continuing to embrace the order and norms of the white mainstream. How dull the United States would be, I have thought at times, if it were populated only by those of Japanese ancestry.

Given this social orientation it is hardly surprising that artistic creativity, except perhaps in certain fields of the visual arts, is not an attribute for which Japanese Americans are noted. Strict conformity to established norms will probably insure continued prominence in traditional middle-class occupations. Successful Nisei dentists, pharmacists, engineers, and businessmen there will always be in great abundance. But the odds are stacked against writers of originality or poets of genius. So long as Nisei swallow set standards of social propriety so unquestioningly, so long as they are intent on following the well-worn paths to middle-class success, they will probably lack the raw material of experience, the social relevance, individual perception, and artistic vision, to say nothing of the personal daring needed to assume the high risk of failure, that are basic ingredients for genuine creative expression. Though of course the possibility cannot be ruled out, it appears unlikely that literary figures of comparable stature to those of minorities like the Jews and blacks will emerge to articulate the Nisei soul. Japanese Americans will be forced to borrow the voices of James Michener, Jerome Charyn, and other sympathetic novelists to distill their own experience. Even if a Nisei of Bernard Malamud's or James Baldwin's talents did appear, he would no doubt have little to say that John O'Hara has not already said.

The drive to adapt to white standards of success has recently prompted some postwar Nisei to make the charge that behind our conformity and ambition lies a strong desire to become white. Once securely ensconced in high social positions, some Japanese Americans have become yellow Uncle Toms, or in the lively jargon of the militant young, "bananas"—yellow on the outside, white inside. Currently ranking as Top Banana is S. I. Hayakawa, who was appointed president of San Francisco State College during its bitter strike. Although Dr. Hayakawa became the darling of the silent white majority in California by ripping out wires from student microphones and by following a get-tough policy against recalcitrant blacks, he hardly endeared himself to many postwar Nisei who felt he had sold out completely to the white Establishment. To them it was unforgivable that he had callously misused his ethnicity to thwart the aspirations of another minority. They pronounced him guilty of willingly becoming the flunky of reactionary white politicians in need of a Japanese lackey to lead the "holy alliance" against the "lawless" insurrection of the blacks.

Nor is Hayakawa the only banana. Combined with their apolitical bent, the conformity of the Japanese Americans has prevented many from involving themselves in the great social issues facing the nation today. The Nisei in southern California seem at times as allergic to liberal causes, such as fair housing and civil rights, as other residents in the area whose reactionary political views are notorious throughout the country. The aversion to participate in just causes is puzzling in light of the historical suffering of the community; but it is yet another aspect of our adaptation that has been largely overlooked.

There are happily some signs of change, at least insofar as self-interests are at stake. The dismissal of Dr. Thomas Noguchi as Los Angeles County Coroner is a case in point. When complaints against the alleged sadism and morbid personality of Dr. Noguchi were made public, many of the good citizens of L.A. screamed for the "Jap's" removal from office. Whether such a hue would have been raised against a white or whether such charges would have been so readily believed is doubtful. Operating on the assumption that a minority suspect is guilty unless proven innocent, the County Board of Supervisors acceded to pressures by dismissing the doctor without investigating carefully the facts of the matter or granting him the right of a public hearing. Although some influential Japanese typically recommended that he accept the dismissal without a fight, thousands of others grouped together in an ad hoc organization called JUST—Japanese United in Search of Truth—which collected over 10,000 signatures of protest, raised large sums of money, took the case to court, proved Noguchi's innocence, and won his reinstatement as County Coroner.

However, the Nisei community is in little danger of winning medals for social crusading on the behalf of those outside its own circle. Sociopolitical apathy continues to be one of our most debilitating defects. Lack of concern for fellow humans is graphically captured in the statement I have heard expressed much too often: "We've made it. We've overcome the barriers of racial prejudice without help from anyone else. Why can't the others?" S. I. Hayakawa embodied this hardhearted outlook in its extreme when he simplistically suggested that Negroes emulate Nisei in their struggle to find a place in society.

Such attitudes raise the question of whether an ethnic minority such as ours can really be considered successful. True, Japanese Americans have succeeded in securing a comfortable bourgeois life, an accomplishment for which we have earned the rousing commendation of the white majority. But this praise, it must be realized, has been based on value judgments that ultimately serve the purposes of the established social order. Professor Harry Kitano, in his informative book, correctly points out that "the judgment of Japanese Americans as the 'model American minority' is made from a strictly majority point of view. Japanese Americans are good because they conform—they don't make waves—they work hard and are quiet and docile." [2] When this lauded minority sits back indifferently and says, "We made it, why can't they?" I doubt whether we have succeeded in any but the narrowest materialistic definition of the word. For in a broader spiritual and humanistic sense we have failed abysmally, not only as a minority group but as compassionate human beings.

The spiritual dimension of the Nisei success story is obviously as important as the material, yet this aspect is often overlooked by those whose eyes catch only the glitter of our position and possessions. Failure of the human spirit does not register in sociological studies—intangibles of the heart are not amenable to points on a graph or lines on a chart. Ours is not a failure of wrong action; rather it is one of omission, which is no less reprehensible because it involves doing nothing at all. Indeed, passivity in the face of injustice is particularly insidious because it often goes unnoticed or is subject to deceptive rationalization.

Perhaps my reaction to the conservatism and political lethargy of the ethnic community may strike some delicate Japanese Americans, particularly those incorrigible optimists who insist America is indeed the Promised Land, as excessively harsh. But "don't rock the boat," "let them work for it" attitudes strike me as basically immoral. Perhaps this is because my family, having lived in the ghetto after the war, takes the civil rights movement very personally and has become involved in it in one way or another. My brother, Joe, has in effect dedicated his life to working with the poor and oppressed.

After graduating from Harvard Medical School, Joe was moving safely along the established tracks toward the security of a job as a surgeon, a most prestigious and lucrative profession. During his residency, however, he began to feel deeply uneasy about the disconnection between the wonders of modern medicine and the world of human misery inhabited by blacks and other minority groups. Health care seemed to be largely a middle-class luxury, out of the reach of those poverty-stricken people who most needed it. Unhappy with the elitist orientation of the career he was headed for, Joe quit surgery to devote himself to that area of medicine—public health and social medicine—where he believed he could best help the minority races and the poor.

Joe's decision to throw away assured wealth and status was perlexing for many of his colleagues and friends, who could only conclude that he was hopelessly confused. Within their hierarchy of values, he indeed will never reach the pinnacle of success epitomized by a surgical career; nor will he boost statistics about the Nisei success story. For Joe, who lived in the slums of San Diego, it is back to the "ghettos, Indian reservations, and other areas of poverty," as he put it in his letter of resignation. This move may be both foolish and foreign to some Nisei, particularly those whose prime ambition is to set up practice on East First Street of Little Tokyo, an area about as remote in spirit from the ghettos, Indian reservations, and other areas of poverty as the Japanese Americans are from the struggles of those minorities. But regardless of what others think of him or his decision, he will have the satisfaction of knowing he acted as his heart and conscience dictated.

It is unfortunate that so many Nisei, climbing up the social ladder, have given primacy to material over humanistic values. Gradually, many have assumed some of the less desirable features of their newly acquired status. Preoccupied with materialism as are the majority of Americans, many are deeply committed to the stylish life. Comfortable houses, sleek cars, and fashionable clothes are the accouterments of the middle-class success they have pursued so single-mindedly. Conversations with some Nisei friends have left me wondering at times whether any values supersede material accumulation in their view.

With the passage of time the Japanese in America have also begun to display more of the patterns of delinquency and crime found in other American groups. Acculturation has resulted in the erosion of some of the principle qualities that set Japanese apart as a particularly law-abiding minority. While crime statistics still fall substantially below other groups', violence and other forms of destructive behavior have become increasingly prevalent. Unthinkable in the past, crime rates and juvenile delinquency have risen to such a point that it is no longer rare to witness gangs of Japanese youngsters marauding through the streets of Los Angeles, fighting with knives and guns, and aimlessly destroying property.

In taking an overview of the Japanese-American road to success it might seem that the pattern of adaptation through passive conformity to the structure and norms of society points beyond the simple abandonment of ethnic legacy and the assumption of certain middle-class values ultimately toward total assimilation. Although there may be a long-term trend in this direction, powerful currents are moving counter to the drift toward assimilation, as shown by the resistance of the subculture to diffusion within the larger framework of society. It is true that the postwar generation of Japanese Americans, unlike the prewar breed, no longer need to band together defensively in the face of such blatant discrimination as existed before the war, yet social barriers continue to exist, and today's generation seems to prefer the company of its kind. Quite apart from the question of whether this is desirable or not, the presently visible evidence indicates that it is premature to forecast dissolution of the Japanese subculture.

The matter of marriage, the key to final assimilation, is a complicated question for which no clear tendencies are discernible. There appears to be a growing open-mindedness about marrying into other racial groups, which is nevertheless offset to a certain extent by definite preferences, even among many of the postwar set, to find spouses within the ethnic community. The whole marriage issue has been, and still is, overladen with all sorts of volatile emotions and stubborn prejudices. Even when young Japanese Americans choose marital partners from the subculture, as many prefer to do, difficult problems can still arise. The Issei did not come to America wholly unfettered by social biases; even today Issei grandparents occasionally object to marriages involving partners whose ancestry can be traced back to "undesirable" social origins: those from Okinawa or worse, eta (outcast class in Japan), are anathema to many Issei, who might try to prohibit marriages despite the freedom of the youngsters from such biases.

The situation becomes even more complex when hakujin (whites) or kokujin (blacks), enter the picture. This is partly because some Japanese Americans continue to harbor a distrustful attitude toward non-Japanese. This defensive suspicion is unlikely to disappear so long as the remnants of anti-Japanese hostility are not erased. The arsenal of arguments against interracial marriage from the standpoint of Japanese Americans is frequently well stocked with racial and social myths, some of which are quite farfetched, concerning the physical incompatibility of races, the alleged ease with which whites divorce, unresolvable differences of background, and social difficulties for mixed children. It is my impression that many Nisei parents will try just as hard as, if not more so than, non-Japanese families, to dissuade their children from marrying out of their race. My parents as ministers have frequently been called upon by desperate parents to discourage Nisei-white, Nisei-Mexican, Nisei-Chinese, and sometimes Nisei-Negro couples from intermarrying. The tranquility of a number of households has been shattered by the eruption of emotions over prospective non-Japanese in-laws. If persuasion fails, some parents as a last resort will threaten to disown the children. But the passage of time, particularly if a grandchild has been born, generally restores harmony within the family.

The issues of intermarriage and ultimate assimilation, like a host of other complex questions, await answers from future generations of Japanese Americans, beginning with the postwar group now reaching adulthood. The Nisei community has come to a new, and in some ways decisive, turning point in its comparatively short history in the United States. The questions that face my generation will undoubtedly require new answers and call for fresh modes of action in determining our future role in American society from those that have brought us to our present position.

The imminent danger that confronts us now is not so much the obstacle of social oppression or the threat of another bitter internment experience or the looming specter of potential failure. Unlike our prewar predecessors we face comfort not hardship, security not uncertainty, and general tolerance not discrimination. Our challenge stems, paradoxically, from an excess of success. The question that will concern us is not whether we can make it in American society, but whether the price of achieving social success is too high. Concretely, this means: Can we receive praise without losing perspective? Can we adjust to middle-class living without necessarily accepting wholesale the inbuilt prejudices and undesirable characteristics? Can we relish our newly won social status and material affluence without forgetting the misfortunes of those who are still seeking them? Can we enjoy our freedom without forgetting the oppression other minorities suffer?

These challenges demand no less determination or courage, because they arise from the very successes that have been passed on to us, than did the imposing barriers that pushed the Issei and older-generation Nisei to the limits of their abilities. Indeed they are perhaps in the long run even more demanding and difficult, because they represent internal challenges, not external obstructions, involving the human spirit and heart. Whether we possess that extra measure of inner strength and spiritual greatness to rise up to these subtle but stern tests is a matter only the future will tell. Our present response to them, however, will determine whether the much-publicized Japanese-American experience is really a success story.

NOTES

1. Some of the differences between Hawaiian and mainland Japanese are significant enough to merit mention that this discussion of Japanese Americans is based upon the pattern on the mainland, specifically in California. Many of the generalized comments, however, do hold true for both mainland and Hawaiian groups.
2. HARRY KITANO, *Japanese Americans: The Evolution of a Subculture* (Englewood Cliffs, N.J.: Prentice-Hall, 1969), p. 146.

An Interview with Harry Kitano

Amy Tachiki, Eddie Wong, and Franklin Odo

Question: How valid a description do you think the success image of the Japanese Americans and other Asian Americans is?

Kitano: When you define success, you have to define it along different parameters. If you use education as one criterion, they come out (the Asians) reasonably well. For occupations and income and jobs, there is some evidence that they don't get paid as much for the same amount of work as the average white person, so on that level, they are less successful. If you come to behavior such as crime, delinquency, mental illness—in those the Japanese and Chinese come out relatively good, at least in terms of official hospitalized rates. But if you analyze areas like creativity or personality development, I think that you can start seeing how racism can affect a "very successful" minority group. It means that, generally for the Asians, they don't have the full range of possibilities offered to the white person, given a similar status and background or whatever else. The greatest disservice is to take just one or two of those dimensions like occupation and income and then indicate that this is an overall successful group, because success is made up not only of different criteria, but also what you value as successful. For some people being conforming and quiet and being accepted gets to be a very high value; if you equate that with success, you come out differently than if you value something else.

The fundamental problem of a small, powerless minority group (and I think we can use the Asians in this whole context) really does raise a whole series of questions that very few of us are even aware of. One of the problems of a small group such as ours, especially if there are two other dominant groups, the whites and the blacks, is that probably the most difficult position, sociologically anyway, would be that of a permanent middleman minority. Just

SOURCE: From *Roots: An Asian American Reader* by Amy Tachiki, Eddie Wong, and Franklin Odo, with Buck Wong. Reprinted by permission of the Asian American Studies Center, University of California, Los Angeles.

by that description, I think you can get a pretty clear implication that if you are in the middle between two opposing forces, in one way you can first never achieve what you want because you are being determined by two other large groups, or the middleman obviously sometimes becomes the scapegoat of all the ills of that kind of social system and that kind of society. I think we have some evidence that the whites use us and the blacks may use us; the question that people in the middle should think about is "Where does the middleman minority go? Does it try to become a majority; does it try to join the subordinated minorities; does it try to remain somewhat aloof?" It might be very wise to stop and think because even in terms of color, we are in the middle, and that until we first come to some sort of agreement among ourselves of "What is the best way?", then we end up in a sense fighting each other, which we do. Right now we are fighting between the Hayakawas and the non-Hayakawas, but I don't think that we have really addressed ourselves to the major questions yet. As far as I know, historically no middleman minority has ever handled this position quite well, because the final power may lie outside the group, but still, if we think that we have some choice, we may be able to decide some of the consequences of the ways that we might be going.

Question: Do you see any division between the class aspect or caste aspect of being yellow? Would that be a factor in deciding which way the Asians might go?

Kitano: One of the solutions for the middleman minority is to try to emphasize other modes of stratification such as class, which means that instead of color being the most dominant criterion—occupation, income, and position are, and that's certainly been the answer of many Asians. Historically, many have tried to deny and hide the fact that yellow was an important variable and it was hard work and achievement that lead to economic success. At least that's the way that a large number of the middleman group have tried to answer the question—maybe not consciously but this is the way they have behaved. Now the problem with that approach is that it will serve those who have, if you want to call it, the mobility and drive, but it certainly doesn't answer the question of what happens to those yellow people of less motivation or capabilities. Again, I think this is why we are seeing certain problems within our own ethnic community. Those who have become successful on the social class level almost deny the importance of color and yet when you see large proportions of our group now not making it (at least in the traditional sense) then it raises another spectra of an unresolved issue. I think that's essentially where the problem lies.

Question: Is there a tendency among Japanese Americans to believe in the success story about themselves too much? Is there a danger in that?

Kitano: The danger with the Japanese Americans is that there is enough empirical evidence to indicate that they have become relatively successful in this narrow fashion; and they forget that they may have paid an extremely high price for it. I think that we have some evidence that the most successful Japanese, at least according to the stereotype, are those who really paid for it psychologically; if you look at things like stomach cancer, ulcers, and other internalized modes of adaptation, that is one price. But I think the other price that comes out so clearly is that we have developed either a servant or a second-class mentality. Our drive for acceptance has really been to follow the cues of the dominant white society, and they have told us that to be successful you have to be quiet and humble and those other characteristics. If we really believe that that's the way we can become successful, then one can become rather pessimistic about the future of our group because that means that we have been "conned" or that we have "conned" ourselves almost completely into taking a second-class role.

Question: It's always been an interesting point in your book that it's not so much that Japanese cultural values are the same as American middle-class cultural values, but that Japanese have one value of adapting or accommodating to a situation. There is a functional compatibility when American cultural values dictate that minorities should be quiet and work hard, even though for Americans, being quiet is not highly emphasized. How does that carry out with the younger generation when that cultural value is no longer followed to the same degree?

Kitano: The validity of one set of prescriptions for one generation may not hold for another because of the changes in not only time and place but situation. I still think the adaptation syndrome that was a part of not only the first but also the second generation has been instilled to a large degree in the third, current generation. And like all role prescriptions that are put forth, it does have validity if it works—it's like any other kind of tool; if you do certain things and it works out for you, then you continue in this fashion. Part of it may be simple generational reaction. So even if it does work, a lot of the Sansei may very well take an opposite tact, which is not too unusual in all groups and is labelled adolescent rebellion. At this stage one would almost predict two levels: they will try newer ways of adapting and they will hold and maintain that kind of adaptation that they feel gets them closer to what they want.

Question: You have done a lot of research on mental illness of Japanese

Americans. Why is there relatively low incidence of mental illness among Japanese Americans?

Kitano: It's both intriguing and very tricky to interpret this question because in all of these areas there is what we call official rate: in crime and delinquency—that's what appears on the police records and the FBI records; in mental illness—the number in mental hospitals, and things like that. But I think the true incidence is generally hidden, and a lot depends on how the culture defines it. If Japanese Americans thought that exposing mental illness to the larger culture was the source of either embarrassment or shame or at least a negative characteristic, then I think that in many ways they would try to hide this; I think there is some evidence that this is what they do. The shame on the family and the shame on the ethnic group would mean that even if you had a "mentally ill" person, and that again is a debatable term, the average Japanese might deny that he has a mentally ill person and not send the person in for treatment. He would most likely try to handle the mentally ill person within his own ethnic group, community or family. Therefore, this person never shows up in a mental hospital. There are other factors that go with that too. Economic independence often leads to taking care of one's own. Japanese sometimes have a pride in that. Another one which is a sheer functional kind of thing is that if the average Japanese, especially of another generation, went into a mental hospital and all he spoke was Japanese, the chances are very good that he will never get well, because who is going to know that he is getting better? You can probably come out with a reasonable generalization that the Japanese are not superior or inferior, if you want to use those terms, to other groups in terms of mental illness; the rates are probably very similar. But the second part of that generalization is that they don't show up in mental hospitals or those facilities at the same rate as most of the other groups.

Question: Can we pursue alienation as a source of the identity crisis? Let's take the family as a contributor to the Asian identity crisis. How does the Japanese-American family contribute to that problem?

Kitano: From my point of view, you have to answer it from a relative sense. If you compare it with different families, then I see the alienation of the Japanese much less than the average white families, the average black families, and perhaps most similar to the Jewish families. Although it is changing, the Japanese family still retains sort of a unit and a function that is still qualitatively different from the average American family. You can even use simple statistics such as separation and divorce as one example. Another one might be mobility. Chances are good for many white families that they might have moved five or six times within a lifetime, and the moves may have been from New York to Miami. So when you follow that kind of pattern and think that the family can contribute to alienation by not providing either a consistent background or in some degree of stability through an intact family and all the amenities that go with that, then I think the Japanese and Chinese families are much more cohesive. For all of us who live in Asian families, that cohesion as told to us by the white man is really a myth—the white man really thinks that the families think together, do things together, and everyone obeys, etc. But I think there is still enough truth in a relative sense in that compared to the average white family, we do come up as a less alienated group. Now the other question which is interesting is alienation in the Jewish family. In some ways it may almost be a reaction to the over-closeness and over-dependency that sometimes appears to be a stereotype of a Jewish family; you look for ways of breaking away from that kind of interdependency.

Question: The Portnoy syndrome.

Kitano: Look at the Asian family—there are enough parallels. I think that some of the chuckles and insights when we discuss Portnoy point up the similarities.

Question: Do you feel that if the family stays together as a unit, it leads to conservatism among its members?

Kitano: That may very well be. Family units generally are much more conservative, especially if you get input from different generations. The grandmothers and grandfathers have lived or experienced a more conservative era, so the risk that you pay obviously is much more conservatism.

Question: Has the family prompted the "quiet American" stereotype?

Kitano: I think the average Japanese-American family usually has his own home, has a late model car, is given all the material things, and thinks that the one way he achieved this is through his quiet demeanor. Many feel the maintenance of this kind of posture may be very important in getting even a greater proportion of the goods of the society.

Question: A lot of parents will encourage quiet behavior and say it's because they brought it over from Japan. Isn't it more of a response to succeeding in *this* society?

Kitano: I would say that generally, if you are from lower classes or less powerful groups of any immigrant population, the chances are high that you had to adapt to the system in Asia, and that if you didn't adapt, than you paid some kind of price. It's this kind of psychological orientation that many Asians might have brought over here. It was a translation of one group in power to another; it was not that difficult. That's what I mean by the congruence. But to mistake that as part of the Japanese culture . . . I think this is the error that many Americans make. White Americans start saying, "That's the culture." But they forget that depending upon your class and your position in Japan, you will behave appropriately; if you came from the upper class or the middle class, then you can be arrogant or loud, depending on the time, place, and situation. The mistranslation of the characteristics of a small social class group over here and saying that it's part of Japanese culture is a misperception.

Question: How does the relocation experience fit into this model of quiet Americans?

Kitano: I think that the evacuation has now become the Japanese-American Rorschach test, which I think is quite appropriate. It means that now we can go back to a concrete event, but interpret it in a way that we think appropriate. The facts themselves are not really as important as the interpretation and its symbolic meaning. Again, as in any event like this, you can line up the positive and the negative and then remake your analysis from there. I think that if I had to interpret the event, it becomes the symbol of a racist, oppressive society that does this thing to one ethnic group. The problem with getting too hung up with that approach is that one may forget what it did to an essentially conservative community. I am for family interaction, but not for that oppressive kind of family interaction that was characteristic of many Japanese families right up and through that World War II era. Your father almost determined your occupation, who you were going to marry, where you were going to live, and because most Japanese were poor and dependent, you had to follow through on what your parents told you to do because there were no alternatives. A cohesive family really is good if it's somewhat voluntarily entered into. But if a cohesive family was forced upon you because there was no other choice, then I suspect that it could become very restrictive. It would deny opportunities. It can give you a rigid way of looking at the world. But you still can't over-react to the racism and that's the one thing. The other thing about the evacuation was that it forced young Japanese, especially, to go to live in Chicago and New York and other places where they experienced different kinds of input—we saw how white families lived, we saw upper classes, middle classes, lower classes—and that kind of exposure is quite necessary so that you can get some newer perspectives. Now whether it should be forced on one through something like the evacuation obviously is unfair.

Question: Looking back at recent history, how do you reevaluate the assimilation process in America?

Kitano: I think inevitably, in the long run, when you have different racial groups, especially so visible as in our culture, there are two main choices: One is to go completely pluralistic so that each visible ethnic group develops its own culture, language, styles, institutions, and organizations. So you have within that one system a whole series of different cultures living side by side with almost minimal interaction with each other. The ultimate would be perhaps several states set aside. I don't think that that will ever come about, because I guess it's so impractical. The other way would be complete integration, some sort of assimilation so that out of this melange comes a new kind of American—maybe some part Asian blood, some part black blood, and Indian, and whatever else. That too, I suspect would be an almost impossible reality at the [current] time. I think where we're at now—is where the white man is still on top and all the other groups are fighting for the scraps and trying to become something. The direction towards pluralism may be one feasible direction for the ethnic groups. As ethnic groups develop their own identities and skills, they will develop a social class system within their own ethnic group. The minute you develop a social class or other kind of stratification within your own ethnic group, the probabilities are very, very high that if you are say, upper-class, middle-class, or lower-class Japanese, that you will be much more similar to the white and the black and the Chicano across that line rather than within your own ethnic group. As they develop their own stratification systems, then that stratification would no doubt lead to cross-ethnic kinds of interaction. I think the obvious example (it's almost becoming a cliche) is that one may then ask "Is he a doctor?" rather than "Is he Japanese?" And if your beloved daughter brings home a Jewish doctor or a black doctor, eventually that may be more salient in terms of what you want than, "Is he Japanese?" I see the stage of ethnic puralism as almost a pre-stage for some kind of integration on a different level.

Question: In your position as a researcher, what do you feel should be your relationship to the Asian-American Community?

Kitano: I don't know. That's a question most researchers never face. I think there is a dimension of ethnic responsibility and that you try very hard to do research on several levels, and what comes out is a value choice. Anything that I think will be extremely damaging to the

Asian Community, I would probably not research; and if I did find something at a period that in my judgment might be misused grossly, I would probably not publish. One tries to report back to the ethnic community in those areas where one thinks, at least from my point of view, they could stand some sort of improvement. But with sound empirical data. If I think that there's a high degree of discrimination going on by Asian groups, then at least among Asian groups I try to point this out as gently as I can. But if I had to make a blatant remark saying, "The Asians are as racist as anybody else," I probably would not say that because obviously that could not only be used, but misused. And the empirical evidence will be mixed on that score. This is why if it comes out that Japanese are less criminal, less delinquent or whatever, I find that it's something I will publish without any difficulty, at least in the scholarly journals. But always in the interpretations, I try to indicate that there are other features of the culture that should also be assessed; and the second thing is not to compare the Japanese with any other groups with the implication that we're good and the others are bad.

Question: Hayakawa said during the San Francisco State Strike that there is no such thing as an innocent bystander. You're either there or not. His warning was to go watch the demonstrations on T. V. So that's what really concerns me about being a middleman minority, it's not your choice to be a middleman minority. It's decided for you. How is that going to work when Sanseis say that they have a Third World perspective because they see the future not with white people and that their values lie with the struggles of Third World peoples?

Kitano: Except that the Third World concept is a nebulous one too. And so I don't know what any of these systems has to offer to people in the middle. Previous generations tried to join the White World and, depending on your definition, were successful in certain areas and not successful in others. I think a lot of the younger generation feel that joining the Third World is a possible solution. And I don't doubt at all that many Asians have joined the White World, others the Third World, and if they've achieved a degree of identity and comfort, I say, "Good, join those." But that still leaves a large group of people in the middle who aren't too sure which to join, and I think that's why the middleman thing is of such a personal interest to me. I don't want to join the White World wholeheartedly; I don't think the Third World makes more than a certain degree of sense. If the blacks took complete power of the United States and the whites were at the bottom, we would still be in the middle. The middleman by definition will fare no better or worse at the top or the bottom—you're the middle of that sandwich whether the wheat bread goes on top or the white bread goes on top. So in some ways a permanent middleman position is maybe what the Asian in the United States has to look forward to. Then you start thinking, "What does that mean?"

Question: I don't see much optimism in your conclusion that we're going to be a middleman minority no matter who's on top in America. Do you feel you have a responsibility to find alternate models?

Kitano: Yes and no. I think for me, the best solution is to achieve a sense of reality. Whether what I see is a good world or a bad world, that's the next question; but as long as I know what the realities are, then I think I can make my own choices. But if I don't know what the realities are, if people give me myths and dreams and illusions and lies and falsehoods, then I would be in bad shape. So I don't use the term pessimism or optimism although eventually I'll have to, but the first stage is that once any human being knows the realities of the world and the realities of his choices, then hopefully he can make whatever choices he thinks are appropriate. This is why I think I'm wiser now knowing that I live in a racist state as a member of a middleman minority group than when I was younger, when I felt that I lived in an open democracy and I could do exactly what I wanted; I was really living in a dream world.

It's really a cliche, "Know yourself"—know yourself, your world, your enemy, and your friends.

I think that once you are reasonably clear as to where the problem lies, then a search for newer and perhaps more creative models will be in order. But if you are not clear and have an illusory grasp of the world, then there may never be a creative next step.

PART IV

MEXICAN AMERICANS: FROM INTERNAL COLONIALISM TO THE CHICANO MOVEMENT

RUDOLPH GOMEZ

The term "Mexican American" refers to a heterogeneous grouping of people living in the United States who share either an ethnic link to Mexico or to the Spanish settlement of what is today the "American" Southwest. The term insinuates a homogeneity which simply does not exist. Nonetheless we use it here because we believe it has wider acceptance than such alternative terms as Chicano, latino, hispano, and Spanish surname.

DEMOGRAPHY

The 1970 census of "Spanish origin and/or language" Americans in the Southwest was 6,172,000.[1] However, "in preparation for one court case, Public Advocates, Inc. analyzed population data and concluded that Mexican Americans were undercounted in the 1970 census by at least 15 per cent."[2] The highest concentration of this population is found in the five states of

NOTE: Several scholars have commented on earlier drafts of this introduction. I am indebted to each for their very helpful remarks. I would especially like to thank my colleague Dr. Rudolph de la Garza.

Arizona, California, Colorado, New Mexico, and Texas. Table 1 contains the latest figures.

TABLE 1.   Population Breakdown of Five Southwestern States, 1970

State	Total Population	Spanish Origin * and/or Language	Per Cent Spanish Origin and/or Language
Arizona	1,771,000	333,000	19
California	19,957,000	3,101,000	16
Colorado	2,207,000	283,000	13
New Mexico	1,016,000	407,000	40
Texas	11,195,000	2,048,000	18
Southwest	36,146,000	6,172,000	17

* This heading was used by the U.S. Census Bureau in the 1970 count.

source: Richard I. Ferrin et al., *Access to College for Mexican Americans in the Southwest* (Austin, Texas: Southwestern Regional Office, College Entrance Examination Board, 1972), p. 18.

Like other ethnic groups the Mexican American has found itself lagging behind the general population of the United States in achieving the advantages which permit the full utilization of opportunity. The most recent census data reveal Mexican Americans as a group to be less educated,[3] more unemployed,[4] less white-collared,[5] and earning less income [6] than the general population. The Census Bureau found that the total number of persons of "Low Income Status" living in the United States in 1972 was 25,559,000, or 12.5 per cent of the total population; 1,520,000 of these were of Mexican origin and comprised 28.9 per cent of the total Mexican-American population.[7] In the five Southwestern states of Arizona, California, Colorado, New Mexico, and Texas, 12.8 per cent of the total population had "Low Income Status," while 30.5 per cent of the Mexican-American population fell in this category.[8] Obviously, Mexican Americans have not received an equitable share of the resources available to the general population.

The relatively poor position occupied by Mexican Americans vis-à-vis education, employment, and income can hardly be due to their unwillingness to work, inasmuch as the percentage of Mexican-American males in the labor force is higher than that for the total population (see Table 2).

MEXICAN-AMERICAN DEPRIVATION

How, then, do we account for the present relatively deprived status of Mexican Americans? For the chain-linked series of "reasons why" we must reach back into history for several hundred years. Many Mexican Americans are descended from families who had lived in parts of the present-day

TABLE 2. Labor Force Participation of Persons 16 to 64 Years Old, by Age, Sex, and Ethnic Origin: March 1972

| Male | Total Population | Spanish Origin | | Puerto Rican |
		Total	Mexican	
Number in Labor Force				
Total, 16 to 64 years old	52,900,000	2,039,000	1,175,000	295,000
16 to 24 years old	11,938,000	439,000	296,000	60,000
25 to 44 years old	23,267,000	1,108,000	612,000	182,000
45 to 64 years old	17,695,000	492,000	267,000	53,000
Per Cent in Labor Force				
Total, 16 to 64 years old	86.0	85.0	86.5	76.6
16 to 24 years old	68.7	64.7	70.1	53.1
25 to 44 years old	96.1	95.4	96.5	88.3
45 to 64 years old	88.2	88.0	88.1	Base less than 75,000

SOURCE: U.S. Department of Commerce, Social and Economic Statistics Administraton, Bureau of the Census, *Current Population Reports: Population Characteristics*, "Selected Characteristics of Persons and Families of Mexican, Puerto Rican, and Other Spanish Origin: March 1972" (Washington, D.C.: U.S. Government Printing Office, 1972), Table 5, p. 6.

Southwest long before the region was annexed by the United States—this was their region. But, adding insult to injury, the invading newcomers—the Anglos who in time became the dominant majority—have not always regarded these "annexed" residents or their descendents as full-fledged citizens of the United States.

The unique legal position of the Mexicans living in the territories ceded by Mexico to the United States in the Treaty of Guadalupe Hidalgo was clearly recognized by Article IX which states:

> The Mexicans who, in the territories aforesaid [comprising present-day Texas, Arizona, New Mexico, Utah, Nevada, and part of Colorado] shall not preserve the character of citizens of the Mexican Republic, . . . shall be incorporated into the Union of the United States and be admitted, at the proper time (to be judged by the Congress of the United States) to the enjoyment of all the rights of citizens of the United States according to the principles of the Constitution; and in the mean time shall be maintained and protected in the free enjoyment of their liberty and property, and secured in the free exercise of their religion without restriction.[9]

The terms of the Treaty of Guadalupe Hidalgo have been more breached than honored. In March 1970, the United States Commission on Civil Rights published a study on the administration of justice in the Southwest in which it was found that "Although Mexicans were not considered in as low a category as Negroes, they were regarded as racially inferior to Anglo-Americans." [10] The Mexicans' rights to their property guaranteed by Article IX was ignored by "Anglo-Saxon banking, land and business practices which . . . all but stripped the original Californians of their lands. . . [so that,] with the decline of economic influence, Mexican American political power waned." [11] But the Treaty terms that were breached went beyond property to life itself. In Texas, for example, "Violence against Mexican citizens and Mexican Americans became so widespread that, in 1922, the Secretary of State warned the Governor of Texas that action would have to be taken to protect Mexicans." [12]

INTERNAL COLONIALISM

Mexican Americans claim, with considerable justification, that state and federal governments, following a policy of "internal colonialism," have treated them as a captive people. The historian Rodolfo Acuña enumerates the conditions that define a policy of internal colonialism:

1. The land of one people is invaded by people from another country, who later use military force to gain and maintain control.

2. The original inhabitants become subjects of the conquerors involuntarily.

3. The conquered have an alien culture and government imposed upon them.

4. The conquered become the victims of racism and cultural genocide and are relegated to a submerged status.

5. The conquered are rendered politically and economically powerless.

6. The conquerors feel they have a "mission" in occupying the area in question and believe that they have undeniable privileges by virtue of their conquest.[13]

Dr. Acuña's internal-colonialism thesis will undoubtedly be challenged by many; yet there is abundant evidence to support his argument. For example, the physical subjugation of Mexican Americans was more or less systematically practiced in Texas. The late Dr. Walter Prescott Webb of the University of Texas at Austin and one-time president of the American Historians' Association, estimated that "anywhere from 500 to 5,000 Mexicans were killed by Texans in the Rio Grande valley" between the years 1908 to 1925.[14] Stan Steiner notes the execution of 100 to 300 Mexican residents in the 1920's, and the lynching of 114 "Mexican citizens" by mistake.[15]

The subjugation of Mexican Americans has not been restricted solely to the state of Texas. Nor has it ended. The United States Commission on Civil Rights found in 1970 that:

> In the five Southwestern states which were the subject of . . . study, the Commission heard frequent allegations that law enforcement officers discriminated against Mexican Americans. Such discrimination includes more frequent use of excessive force against Mexican Americans than against Anglos, discriminatory treatment of juveniles, and harassment and discourteous treatment toward Mexican Americans in general. . . .[16]

The allegation, in support of the internal-colonialism thesis, that an "alien culture" has been imposed on Mexican Americans, stems from the policy of local school boards to declare English as the "official" language of public schools attended by sizeable numbers of Mexican Americans and to prohibit the use of Spanish on school grounds. Thomas Carter in his book *Mexican Americans in School: A History of Educational Neglect* lists the institutional arguments in favor of this "no Spanish rule" thusly:

1. English is the national language and must be learned; the best way is to prohibit Spanish.
2. Bilingualism is mentally confusing.
3. The Spanish spoken in the Southwest is a substandard dialect.
4. Teachers don't understand Spanish.[17]

Carter suspects that the real reason for the "no Spanish rule" is that it is "an extreme threat to authority: those in power don't know what the Mexican Americans are saying. . . . The enemy is seen to be using undecipherable code and thus violating the established conventions of war (school regulations)."[18]

Another argument relating to an "imposed alien culture" is that until very recently no public schools offered courses that contained Mexican history, art, culture, literature, and so on. Nor were courses taught regarding the historical experience of Mexican Americans in the United States. The failure of public schools in the Southwest to help the Mexican American locate himself within his country is an indictment of the workings of local school boards as well as state departments of education. The fact that schools all over the Southwest are currently revising curricula to include Mexican-American related courses [19] attests to the shortcomings of the earlier school programs.

RACIAL DISCRIMINATION

Another in the chain of reasons explaining the relatively low status of Mexican Americans in the United States today is the presence of institutional racial discrimination. By discrimination is meant the practice of distinguishing categorically rather than individually. This means that relationships among or between groups, individuals, or institutions are created on the basis of a class or category, Mexican American, for example, as opposed to individuals, Juan Peón, for example. Discrimination against Mexican Americans has been documented in a number of areas in addition to those already mentioned in the discussion of internal colonialism.

Joan W. Moore and Frank G. Mittelbach investigated the subject of housing segregation in the Southwest. The authors found that there were two kinds of discrimination in housing—one against blacks and the other against Mexican Americans.[20] The authors of the study in question were able to establish patterns of discrimination in housing in 26 of the 35 cities they studied in the Southwest.[21] They found that "segregation scores for the three principal types of segregation were found to rank as follows: the highest is that of Negroes' segregation from Anglos; the second highest is that of Mexican Americans from Negroes; and the lowest score is that of Mexican Americans from Anglos." [22] For 9 of the 35 cities studied the researchers discovered that "The two minorities—Negroes and Mexican Americans—are both relatively highly segregated from the dominant Anglos, but not from each other." [23]

Racial discrimination against Mexican Americans is also observable in the area of employment. The 1972 employment figures published by the Bureau of Census reveal that Mexican Americans are below the national average in white-collar employment and above the national average in blue-collar employment (see Table 3). Conscious discrimination against Mexican Americans in the employment market, as pointed out by numerous authors,[24] certainly accounts in large part for the fact that Mexican Americans are underemployed in the white-collar ranks and overemployed in the laborer ranks.

Discrimination can also be detected in public education. Use of the public school system as an instrument for the socialization of Mexican-American children not only has resulted in inculcating Anglo values and norms but has also served to reject non-Anglo values. Surely denial of a minority culture by the institutions of the majority is discriminatory. But the practice of discrimination in public education is visible in other ways. In Texas, for example, the U.S. Commission on Civil Rights found "the amount of money spent for the education of many Chicano students is three-fifths that spent to edu-

TABLE 3.   Employed Men 16 Years Old and Over, by Major Occupation
Group and Ethnic Origin: March 1972

| Occupation | Total Population | Spanish Origin | | |
		Total	Mexican	Puerto Rican
Total employed	49,401,000	1,890,000	1,088,000	262,000
Per Cent	100.00	100.00	100.00	100.00
White-collar workers	40.4	23.2	17.5	21.5
Professional and technical	14.1	6.9	4.8	2.7
Mgrs., adminis., exc.	13.2	6.5	5.6	6.7
Sales workers	6.3	2.9	2.6	2.2
Clerical workers	6.9	6.9	4.5	9.9
Blue-collar workers	46.7	58.4	62.4	59.1
Craftsmen and kindred	20.7	19.7	20.9	15.1
Operatives, including transportation	18.7	27.2	27.2	36.8
Laborers, exc. farm	7.2	11.5	14.3	7.2

SOURCE: U.S. Department of Commerce, Social and Economic Statistics Administration, Bureau of the Budget, *Current Population Reports: Population Characteristics,* "Selected Characteristics of Persons and Families of Mexican, Puerto Rican, and Other Spanish Origin: March, 1972," Table 7, p. 7.

cate Anglo children." [25] And, in a series of reports published between 1971 and 1972, the Commission found that:

Mexican Americans constitute 17 per cent of pupils in the public elementary and secondary schools but only 4 per cent of the teachers.

In 15 per cent of the elementary schools of the Southwest, the use of Spanish is still discouraged on the school grounds.

Of 100 Mexican-American students entering grade one, it is estimated that 23 enter college and 5 complete college. Among Anglo students the corresponding figures are 49 per cent and 24 per cent.

Nearly half of Mexican-American elementary and secondary students in the Southwest attend schools that are predominantly Mexican American in their ethnic composition. . . .

. . . the underrepresentation of Mexican Americans in higher education is well known. Using 1970 enrollment figures, . . . [it was] estimated that Mexican-American enrollment would have to be increased 330 per cent in order to secure proportional representation for Spanish-speaking persons in higher education.[26]

Politics, also, reflect discrimination against Mexican Americans. Stan Steiner, writing in 1970, noted that according to his analysis of Mexican-American population figures there should have been fifteen Mexican Americans serving in the U.S. House of Representatives—there were three serving at the time he wrote.[27] There are no Mexican-American governors in any of the states containing sizeable numbers of Mexican Americans. There is no major city in the Southwest with a Mexican-American mayor. Nor do state legislatures contain a fair proportion of Mexican Americans. According to the 1970 Census, 17 per cent of the total population in the Southwest was Mexican American. Yet, only in New Mexico was there more than token representation by Spanish-surnamed senators and representatives. Political gerrymandering, which is discriminatory, is as responsible as voter apathy for this state of affairs.

Racial discrimination is discernible throughout the web of American life. Armando J. Sanchez, for example, argues: "It is my hypothesis that the welfare dollar sustains and enlarges the economic and political power of a few in the community. The corollary is that the welfare dollar does not contribute to the economic and social development of low-income communities." [28] And Guadalupe Salinas, using court cases alleging discrimination against Mexican Americans as basic data, establishes the existence of discrimination in public accommodations, jury duty, law enforcement, employment, and education.[29]

POLITICAL ACTIVITY

Racial discrimination and internal colonialism both appear to be on the decline or are at least becoming less blatant. This is due, in part, to a spate of civil rights legislation, enacted by the national government in the 1960's, which sensitized the public to minority problems. The coming of age of Mexican-American political participation has also been instrumental in the gradual elimination of these twin problems of American life. We speak of the "coming of age" to indicate the historical dimension of this participation; for Mexican Americans have been politically *active* since the very beginning. They are only now becoming politically *effective*. In our judgment it is this *effective political participation* that is responsible for the development of national programs designed to protect the rights of the heretofore marginal ethnic Americans.

The Mexican-Americans' fight to secure their rights as Americans has been a long one. Octavio Romano writes that Mexican Americans do "not view themselves as traditionally unchanging social vegetables . . . but as creators of systems in their own right, for they have created cooperatives, mutualist societies, political blocks, international networks of communications, and social networks. . . ."[30] He argues that Mexican Americans have continuously engaged in "social issues"; that they helped pioneer the labor movement in the West; and that they engaged in political activities, as demonstrated by their newspaper publishing activities between 1848 and 1950.[31] Rodolfo Acuña dates Mexican-American political activity to the late 1850's when Juan Cortina waged open warfare with Texas authorities who had defaulted on their obligations as imposed by the Treaty of Guadalupe Hidalgo.[32] The El Paso Salt War of 1878 is cited by the same author as an example of "a people's revolt—against the foreign occupier's domination."[33]

In the early twentieth century Mexican-American political activity took the form of *mutualista* organizations. "These organizations sponsored social halls, where members congregated and talked about common problems . . . they planned ways of improving their lives or of protecting themselves against police or governmental malfeasance."[34] The most famous of the early organizations was the *Alianza Hispano Americana*, formed in Tucson, Arizona, in 1894. It grew to include 275 lodges and in the 1960 presidential campaign was active in sponsoring many *Viva Kennedy* clubs.[35]

In 1928 in Harlingen, Texas, the League of United Latin American Citizens (LULAC) was founded. The association was comprised of middle-class Mexican Americans. Its stated purpose was "to develop within the members of our race the best, purest, and most perfect type of a true and loyal citizen of the United States."[36] LULAC councils eventually spread to 21 states. LULAC was instrumental in keeping alive issues of importance to the Mexican Americans at a time when the environment was patently hostile to them.

During World War II, thousands of Mexican Americans served in the armed services of the United States. "They thought they had [thereby] earned their rights as U.S. citizens. . . . But the continued discrimination and exclusion—racism, denial of political participation, economic oppression— shattered the illusions of many of the returning veterans. . . ."[37] As a consequence of post-World War II disillusionment, many Mexican Americans began to organize and to agitate more vigorously to secure their rights as American citizens.

The Community Service Organization (CSO), founded in Southern California in 1947, was instrumental in securing the election of Edward Roybal to the Los Angeles City Council in 1949.[38] The American G.I. Forum, founded in Corpus Christi, Texas, in 1948, is a nonpartisan social organization interested in securing political and social reforms for Mexican Americans. Today forums are found in 23 states. Other postwar organizations included the Political Association of Spanish Organizations (PASO) in Texas and the Mexican American Political Association (MAPA) in California. Each of these organizations has contributed something to the successes garnered thus far by Mexican Americans. Each has labored within the institutional framework provided by "the system" to better the lot of their particular interests.

Yet the fact that they chose to work for change within the system imposed limits upon what they could achieve. The system is premised upon compromise and give and take—which is satisfactory if parties to the system enjoy equal status. But if one or more of the parties do not enjoy equal status then the ones lacking that status will always lag behind in the game of compromise and give and take. This was the situation Mexican Americans found themselves in at the dawn of the 1960's decade. They had made progress toward equal status, but it had been painfully slow. Something was needed to break the grip of "the system's" compromise politics. That "something" happened without any one single person or group really intending for it to happen. That "something" was "the Chicano Movement."

THE CHICANO MOVEMENT

The Chicano Movement emerged in the mid-1960's, and is based on the desire of Mexican Americans to participate in determining their own future. The self-applied name "Chicano" symbolizes a declaration of independence from the stereotypes developed for Mexican Americans by the dominant culture in which they have lived. Eliu Carranza distinguishes between Mexican American and Chicano thusly:

> . . . for generation after generation Mexican Americans have been driven according to the horse's conception of driving. They have been governed, trained, and educated according to the Anglo-white's conception of what it is to be a man. . . but [this] is no longer true of the Chicano. And this is the essence of the Chicano Cultural Revolution. A confrontation and a realization of worth and value through a brutally honest self-examination has occurred and has revealed to Chicanos a link with the past and a leap into the future, a future which Chicanos are fashioning, a future that has validity for Chicanos because Chicanos are the agents, i.e., the creators and builders of their destiny. This is called Self-Determination; its implementation—The Movement; Chicano determination—la Causa; the benefactors— la Raza; and the agents—Chicano Militants. . . . the Chicano has shown his face at last! He has shed the "servant mentality. . . .[39]

Chicanos are trying to formulate their own futures by participating in a wide range of activities. On university campuses, for example, student organizations have been involved in protest activities designed to make their education more relevant to their interests. Three of the better known organizations are the United Mexican American Students (UMAS), the Moviemiento Estudientil Chicano de Aztlán (MECHA), and the Mexican American Student Association (MASA). The specific reforms these groups seek are delineated in the *Plan de Santa Barbara*, which was formulated by Chicano faculty, students, and administrators in the summer of 1968 at the University of California at Santa Barbara. The *Plan de Santa Barbara* is premised on the notion that "we do not come to work for the university, but to demand that the university work for our people."[40] The programs demanded in the plan include:

"1. Admission and recruitment of Chicano students, faculty, administrators, and staff.

2. A curriculum . . . and . . . academic major relevant to the Chicano cultural and historical experience.

3. Support and tutorial programs.

4. Research programs.

5. Publications programs.

6. Community cultural and social action centers." [41]

The Chicano Movement has also sponsored an active cultural and intellectual life. There are Chicano theater groups in each of the large cities (often known as the *teatro urbano*) and one nationally known group from Delano, California (*El teatro campesino*).[42] Chicano poets, intellectuals, and writers are being published in Chicano journals, newspapers, and in the conventional presses as well. The latest edition of Stanford University's annotated bibliography on Mexican Americans lists 64 Chicano periodicals currently published in the United States.[43] An interesting sidelight of the publishing activity is that it self-consciously seeks to reach the entire community. According to Ysidro Ramon Macias, the Chicano press tries to reach even the less reputable members of the Mexican-American population. He writes: "It has endeavored to reach all levels of the community, including the non-English speaking, the *pintos* (convicts or ex-cons), *tecatos* (drug-users, usually of hard drugs), and the *Vatos locos* (street persons)." [44]

If the Chicano Movement accomplishes no more than it has already done intellectually it can be adjudged a success. Thanks to the movement, Mexican-American students will possess a knowledge of their background that heretofore was only within the purview of a cognoscenti. Additionally, that generation of students will contribute to the movement and thus ensure its future. So it may be that the Chicano Movement is well on the way to becoming an institution. And as an institution it can count on an existence independent of individuals, groups, and events.

Chicano political activity ranges from conventional forms of participation (campaigning for public office, voting, etc.) to more militant forms of confrontation. Much has been written in the popular press about ethnic militancy so we will not dwell on that type of activity here. Our primary focus will be on more conventional forms of political activity. We would like to emphasize that, while critics of the Chicano Movement stress its radical and militant orientation, much of what it seeks is sought within the framework of conventional, traditional forms of partisan political activity. Thus we have a situation in which a group that avowedly seeks substantial systemic changes is seeking them through procedures created by that system for that purpose. One could paraphrase Rap Brown and say that "politicking" is as American as apple pie and therefore what Chicanos seek through conventional political activity is as American as apple pie.

The political party founded by leaders of the Chicano Movement is called *La Raza Unida*. A literal translation of the title would be "the united race" or "the united people." There is no clear founding date for the party since it sprang up independently in several states in the late 1960's and early 1970's. In Colorado, for example, the party ran a full slate of candidates for state and national office in the 1970 general election.[45] In Texas the party has won local elections and ran a candidate for governor in the 1972 election.[46]

One of the founders of *La Raza Unida* in Texas, José Angel Gutierrez, gave the reason for its founding when he explained that "in the state of Texas there is no democracy for the Mexican American, black, poor, or Liberals. There is a one-party system and it is controlled by industries and special interests. . . . If you want to implement and see democracy . . . you can do it through a Chicano Party." [47] A rough index of the support the party enjoys in Texas is provided by the vote its gubernatorial candidate, Ramsey Muniz, received in the 1972 general election: 6 per cent statewide and as high as 12 and 13 per cent in areas containing sizeable populations of Mexican Americans.[48] In Colorado, in the 1970 general election the party's slate of candidates received a percentage of the vote ranging from a low 1.8 per cent cast for the gubernatorial candidate, Gurule, to a high of 16 per cent cast for a senatorial candidate running from the third district (Pueblo).[49] These data indicate that while the *La Raza Unida*'s electoral support is not as large as its leaders would like to see, it is large enough to hypothesize that it would gain in importance in a close election. And it could, in time, become sizeable enough to affect the pattern of party activity in a state. That is to say that in a one-party state or district the size of voter support for *La Raza Unida* could presage the advent of a two-party system, and in a two-party area such support could mean the emergence of multiparty activity. The point is that such electoral support can affect the political party patterns in a constituency if it becomes a pattern itself.

The program of *La Raza Unida* party hews to the reform tradition of American political parties of the past. For example, of the major planks of the party's 1972 platform in Texas are grouped around the domestic problems of education, public welfare, the economy, and crime. Although each of these problems can be related to the entire population of the United States they are of particular interest to Chicano political leaders.

PROGRAM OF *LA RAZA UNIDA* POLITICAL PARTY IN TEXAS, 1972

Education

The thrust of the proposals relating to education are compensatory in nature. They are designed to eliminate or reform educational policies that have ill served Mexican-American students in the past. Thus the program suggests:

1. That the educational process of Texas include multilingual and multicultural programs at all levels—preschool through college.

2. That all levels of school personnel, including administration, be propor-

tionatcly representative of the people of the community in which the school is located.

3. That school funds be allocated to all students on an equal basis.

4. That poorer schools be given priorities over more adequately equipped and funded schools by relevant funding agencies.

5. That preschool training and education be provided for all children at public expense.

6. That learning be a shared experience and not one imposed from above upon a captive audience.

Public Welfare

The aim of *La Raza Unida's* welfare proposals is to provide more financial assistance to needy recipients and to eliminate the degrading aspects of the current state welfare program. Accordingly the platform calls for:

1. The installation of a cash assistance grant program for welfare recipients in the state of Texas.

2. The elimination of the present legislative ceiling upon welfare expenditures.

3. The reform of public attitudes toward welfare.

The Economy

La Raza Unida party believes that the economic system in Texas and in the United States serves to perpetuate and preserve an inequitable system of distribution and therefore the party seeks to:

1. Reduce the economic advantages enjoyed by the very rich by ending the regressive system of taxation.

2. Restore competition to the economic system by pursuing a vigorous antitrust policy and by supporting needed community services.

3. Increase transfer payments to the poor in order to bring about a more equitable distribution of wealth in the United States.

Crime

The elimination of a double standard of justice in Texas and the United States is sought by the 1972 *La Raza Unida* party's platform. To ensure that equal protection under the law obtains for all, the party resolves:

1. That civilian review boards act upon complaints directed to law enforcement agencies at all levels of government.

2. That the Texas Rangers be abolished.

3. That the present bail bond system be studied and reformed.

4. That civil and criminal juries be selected from the community's total population—including the ethnic and poor portions.

5. That free legal services be provided for the indigent in Texas.

6. That cruel and unusual punishment be abolished since it serves no rehabilitative purpose.

It would be deceptive to claim that the goals of *La Raza Unida* party's 1972 program are on the verge of being fulfilled. But it would be equally deceptive to claim that the program is of no utility. It not only serves to list the grievances of Chicano leaders and electorate but it also serves as a rallying point around which to group for future political activity. And it may be that if Mexican Americans are serious about becoming a political force in the United States it will be behind the banner of *La Raza Unida* party.

SUMMARY

The term "Mexican American" is used in reference to the largest ethnic minority group living in the United States Southwest. Although early members of this group were resident in the Southwest long before it became part of the United States, Mexican Americans have never enjoyed equal civil, social, economic, or political status with the newer white, *anglo*, population, which now constitutes the majority group throughout the United States. For more than a hundred years, Mexican Americans have struggled to release the chains of subservience placed on them by conscious and unconscious attitudes of "internal colonialism" and racial discrimination. They actively supported the early labor movement in the West, and in the late nineteenth century, they formed *mutualista* associations to provide basic social services. From the 1920's through the 1950's Mexican Americans created organizations through which to achieve their social, economic, and political goals. Although success did not always accompany these early efforts, they did establish a tradition and furnished a model for subsequent organization and activities.

The mid-1960's saw a coalescence of Mexican-American participation in public affairs and it became possible to speak of the emergence of a "movement," subsequently labeled the "Chicano Movement." The Chicano Movement seeks to place Mexican Americans in the mainstream of American public life by guaranteeing their participation in every area of importance: economic activity, cultural activity, governmental activity, political activity. Already, the Chicano Movement has called forth an extremely active and rich cultural and intellectual outpouring which is of importance not only for Mexican Americans but for all Americans.

The reforms sought by the movement's party, *La Raza Unida*, indicate not only what needs to be done but by whom; and the Chicano Movement has already affected the conduct of government and politics in the Southwest. It is not too soon to speak of its success in the light of increasing evidence to suggest that Mexican-American participation in public life and community affairs has become an indispensable ingredient for a final solution to the domestic problems of modern life in the Southwest.

THE READINGS

The readings which follow were selected carefully so that the reader could get as comprehensive an understanding of the Mexican-American "problem" as could be presented in the limited space available in this book.

In the first selection, Lawrence B. Glick examines a number of relationships between Mexican Americans and the United States national, state, and local political systems. His conclusion is that Mexican Americans have lived in a "heritage of civil inequality and social prejudice that are, in large part, the basis for present economic deprivation."

Glick notes that Mexican Americans, unlike blacks in the United States, have never had their status "fixed by statute and ordinance" and to that extent have suffered racial discrimination less than the blacks. However, the fact remains that Mexican Americans have suffered from "unwritten laws" which "established a degrading system of segregation and social inferiority that insured a subservient status for them" in the American Southwest.

Glick has uncovered an important distinction between the legal treatment accorded blacks and Mexican Americans in the United States—namely that blacks had their inferior status confirmed by written laws while Mexican Americans had theirs validated by unwritten customs and local practices. The consequence of this distinction has been that black leaders have had overt, clearly discernible targets against which to mobilize support—both from the national government and from the black masses themselves. The absence of similar targets has inhibited the mobilization of·support—both governmental and popular—that Mexican Americans need to become as politically effective as their black counterparts.

The greater part of Glick's article details the local and individual practices occurring in much of the Southwest that have served to impose an inferior status upon Mexican Americans. Mr. Glick offers abundant evidence to establish that in virtually every aspect of life devoted to self-improvement—education, employment, housing—Mexican Americans have suffered discrimination. Discriminatory treatment against them has also been established in certain state policies, in law enforcement, and in jury service. The inescapable conclusion to be drawn from the evidence offered by Glick is that most Mexican Americans in the Southwest, as well as in other parts of the country where they can be perceived as constituting an identifiable "racial" group, have found themselves victimized and stymied by racial prejudice and discrimination.

Mr. Lawrence B. Glick is a lawyer who has been associated with the U.S. Commission on Civil Rights since 1962. He is currently the Deputy General Counsel of that Commission. In 1970 he was the Project Director of a study published by the Commission titled: *Mexican Americans and the Administration of Justice in the Southwest.*

Alfredo Cuellar's concern in the second reading is the political development of Mexican Americans in the United States. His data reveal four stages of political participation experienced by Mexican Americans: an apolitical stage; a conventional politics stage; a politics of accommodation stage; and, finally, the radicalization of politics stage.

The two independent variables that have shaped these four political stages have been the Anglo and Mexican-American actors engaged in allocating the values of society, in the Southwest primarily, but also in other parts of the United States where sizeable numbers of Mexican Americans can be found. The inability of Anglo majorities to accept the human equality of Mexican Americans has given politics in the Southwest racial overtones that have always worked against the interests of the Mexican Americans.

Cuellar's description of the political development of Mexican Americans indicates that even when the Mexican Americans adopted conventional political procedures—voting for Democratic and Republican candidates for public office, for example—or when they abased and devalued their cultural heritage by trying to assimilate into the "melting pot" of Anglo America they remained, for the most part, second-class citizens.

Notable successes in self-determination did not occur until the middle-to-late 1960's when Mexican Americans began to radicalize their political behavior. The significance of the Chicano Movement lies in that it has succeeded in awakening in Mexican Americans a realization of the need for an attitudinal change. Specifically, what Chicano elites are trying to sell is the notion that conventional political activity has paid off quite modestly to date; therefore they argue it is time to change the style and substance of Mexican-American political behavior in order to succeed.

Alfredo Cuellar is a doctoral student in political science at the University of California at Los Angeles. He took his master of art's degree at North Texas State University in 1969 where his thesis title was "A Social and Political History of the Mexican-American Population of Texas: 1929–1963."

Rodolfo Acuña's article on internal colonialism argues that Mexican Americans have been treated as a conquered people by Anglo majorities. Acuña supports his contention by developing an outline of the conditions found in colonialized societies. His book *Occupied America*, for which the article presented here is the introduction, contains abundant evidence in support of his thesis.

Dr. Acuña received his Ph.D. from the University of Southern California in 1967 in Latin American history. Presently he is a member of the Chicano Studies Department at California State University at Northridge.

Joan W. Moore of the University of California, Riverside, is concerned with adapting the concept of "colonialism" for use in the social sciences. In this article Professor Moore argues that different colonial patterns emerge in the American Southwest: "classic colonialism" in New Mexico, "conflict colonialism" in Texas, and "economic colonialism" in California. These are useful distinctions to bear in mind since they reveal that racial oppression can take many forms.

Joan W. Moore has written widely on the subject of Mexican Americans.

She is a co-author of the monumental study *The Mexican-American People: The Nation's Second Largest Minority*. She is also the author of *Mexican Americans* from which the article titled "Perspective on Politics," appearing below, was taken.

The "Four Declarations of Independence" list some of the specific goals sought by different Mexican-American organizations. Collectively they reveal the ideology that is the rallying point for the emerging Mexican-American political mobilization.

The Four Declarations were compiled by Armando Rendon and placed in an appendix in his most recently published book: *Chicano Manifesto*. Rendon is a journalist who has published numerous articles dealing with Mexican Americans. His *Chicano Manifesto* is probably the best one-volume revelation of the attitudes being adopted by increasing numbers of younger Mexican Americans today.

The final reading spells out in abundant detail how Anglos and Mexican Americans in the Southwest are joined together in one community composed of persons who are united by one or more values—including language, purposes, ideas, and interests. In a most insightful article Carey McWilliams argues that the Spanish-speaking people of the Southwest are not an immigrant group in the U.S. but are "an integral part of a much larger population unit [Mexico] to which it is bound by geographic and historical ties."

McWilliams develops his one-community theme by illustrating some of the surface aspects of that community, noting that the daily language contains words and phrases of both Spanish and English; that Spanish place names are used to identify and locate natural landmarks, towns, streets and places; and that the architecture, the culture, the arts all reflect a fusion of the Spanish, Anglo, and Indian cultures.

The immediate task confronting members of this single community is to use these shared communal areas as foundations upon which to construct cohesive educational, economic, and political communities. Success in this endeavor would probably terminate the need for a Chicano Movement—it might well mean the end of ethnic politics. No one at this time, probably, entertains the notion that such an end is in sight.

Carey McWilliams wrote *North from Mexico*, from which the article "One and Together" was taken, in 1948. The book was reprinted in its entirety in 1968. Mr. McWilliams has published at least five books on ethnic groups and migrant laborers in the United States and is currently the editor of *The Nation*.

NOTES

1. RICHARD I. FERRIN, RICHARD W. JANSEN, and CESAR M. TRIMBLE, *Access to College for Mexican Americans in the Southwest: Higher Education Surveys Report No. 6* (Austin, Texas: Southwestern Regional Office, College Entrance Examination Board, 1972), p. 18.
2. *Ibid.*, p. 7.
3. U.S. DEPARTMENT of COMMERCE, SOCIAL and ECONOMIC STATISTICS ADMINISTRATION, Bureau of the Census, *Selected Characteristics of Persons and Families of Mexican, Puerto Rican, and Other Spanish Origin: March 1972* (Washington, D.C.: U.S. Government Printing Office, 1972), Table 4, p. 5.
4. *Ibid.*, Table 6, p. 7.
5. *Ibid.*, Table 7.
6. *Ibid.*, Tables 8 and 9, p. 8.
7. *Ibid.*, Table 10, p. 9.
8. *Ibid.*
9. WAYNE MOQUIN with CHARLES VAN DOREN, Eds., *A Documentary History of the Mexican Americans* (New York: Praeger Publishers, Bantam Books, 1972), p. 247.
10. U.S. COMMISSION on CIVIL RIGHTS, *Mexican Americans and the Administration of Justice in the Southwest* (Washington, D.C.: U.S. Government Printing Office, March 1972), p. xii.
11. *Ibid.*
12. *Ibid.*
13. RODOLFO ACUÑA, *Occupied America: The Chicano's Struggle Toward Liberation* (San Francisco: Canfield Press, 1972), p. 3.
14. As cited in STAN STEINER, *La Raza: The Mexican Americans* (New York: Harper & Row, Colophon Edition, 1970), p. 360.
15. *Ibid.*
16. U.S. COMMISSION on CIVIL RIGHTS, *op. cit.*, p. 13.
17. THOMAS P. CARTER, *Mexican Americans in School: A History of Educational Neglect* (New York: College Entrance Examination Board, 1970), p. 97.
18. *Ibid.*
19. *Ibid.*, pp. 187–98.
20. RUDOLPH GOMEZ, Ed., *The Changing Mexican American* (Boulder, Colorado: Pruett Press, 1972), pp. 80–89.
21. *Ibid.*
22. *Ibid.*
23. *Ibid.*
24. See, for example, PAUL BULLOCK, "Employment Problems of the Mexican American," *Industrial Relations* 3:3 (May 1964), pp. 37–50; and DONALD JANSON, "Many Farm Labor Offices Favor Growers," *The New York Times*, October 3, 1971.

25. U.S. COMMISSION on CIVIL RIGHTS, *Mexican American Education in Texas: A Function of Wealth* (Washington, D.C.: U.S. Government Printing Office, 1972), p. 27.

26. FERRIN *et al.*, *op. cit.*, p. 4.

27. STEINER, *op. cit.*, p. 188.

28. ARMAND J. SANCHEZ, "Affluence Amid Poverty," *El Grito* 3:4 (Summer 1970), p. 81.

29. GUADALUPE SALINAS, "Mexican-Americans and the Desegregation of Schools in the Southwest," *El Grito* 4:4 (Summer 1971), pp. 40–43.

30. OCTAVIO IGNACIO ROMANO-V, "Social Science, Objectivity, and the Chicano," *El Grito* 4:1 (Fall 1970), p. 13.

31. *Ibid.*

32. ACUÑA, *op. cit.*, pp. 46–50.

33. *Ibid*, p. 50.

34. *Ibid.*, p. 188.

35. *Ibid.*, p. 189.

36. *Ibid.*

37. *Ibid.*, p. 199.

38. *Ibid.*, p. 209. Roybal is currently a member of the U.S. House of Representatives.

39. ELIU CARRANZA, "The Mexican American and the Chicano"; ANTONIA CASTANEDA SHULAR, TOMAS YBARRA-FRAUSTO, and JOSEPH SOMMERS, Eds., *Literatura Chicana: Texto Y Contexto* (Englewood Cliffs, New Jersey: Prentice-Hall, 1972), pp. 39, 41.

40. *Ibid.*, p. 86.

41. *Ibid.*

42. ALFREDO CUELLAR, "Perspective on Politics," in Joan W. Moore with Alfredo Cuellar, *Mexican Americans* (Englewood Cliffs, New Jersey: Prentice-Hall, 1970), p. 153.

43. LUIS G. NOGALES, Ed., *The Mexican American: A Selected and Annotated Bibliography*, rev. ed. (Stanford, California: The Center for Latin American Studies, 1971), pp. 156–62.

44. YSIDRO RAMON MACIAS, "The Chicano Movement" in Wayne Moquin with Charles Van Doren, Eds., *op. cit.*, p. 505.

45. RUDOLPH GOMEZ and ROBERT ECKELBERRY, "The 1970 Election in Colorado," *Western Political Quarterly* 24:2 (June 1971), p. 279, Table 6.

46. The information for this section was taken from unpublished research papers prepared for Dr. Rodolfo de la Garza's Chicano Politics course offered at the University of Texas at El Paso during the 1972 fall semester. The authors and the titles of their papers were: NORMA NUNEZ, "La Raza Unida: Structure of Interest Articulation and Interest Aggregation"; and JOSE A. RAMIREZ, "Three Political Platforms: An Evaluation."

47. *Ibid.*, NUNEZ, p. 3.

48. Unofficial figures published in *Nosotros* 2:9, p. 3.

49. GOMEZ and ECKELBERRY, *op. cit.*, p. 279.

BIBLIOGRAPHY

ACUÑA, RODOLFO. *Occupied America: The Chicano's Struggle Toward Liberation*. San Francisco: Canfield Press, 1972.

BEAN, WALTON. *California: An Interpretative History*. New York: McGraw-Hill, 1968.

BECK, WARREN A. *New Mexico: A History of Four Centuries*. Norman: University of Oklahoma Press, 1962.

BURMA, JOHN A. *Mexican Americans in the United States: A Reader*. New York: Harper & Row, 1970.

GALARZA, ERNESTO. *Spiders in the House and Workers in the Field*. Notre Dame: University of Notre Dame Press, 1970.

———, HERMAN GALEGAS, and JULIAN SAMORA. *Mexican-Americans in The Southwest*. Santa Barbara: McNally and Loftin, 1969.

GAMIO, MANUEL. *Mexican Immigration to the United States*. Chicago: University of Chicago Press, 1930.

GOMEZ, RUDOLPH, Ed. *The Changing Mexican-American*. Boulder, Colorado: Pruett Press, 1972.

GREBLER, LEO, JOAN W. MOORE, and RALPH C. GUZMAN. *The Mexican-American People: The Nation's Second Largest Minority*. New York: Free Press, 1970.

HOLMES, JACK E. *Politics in New Mexico*. Albuquerque: University of New Mexico Press, 1967.

MADSEN, WILLIAM. *Mexican-Americans of South Texas*. San Francisco: Holt, Rinehart & Winston, 1964.

MANUEL HERSCHEL T. *Spanish-Speaking Children of the Southwest*. Austin: University of Texas Press, 1965.

MATTHIESSEN, PETER. *Sal Si Puedes*. New York: Random House, 1969.

McWILLIAMS, CAREY. *North from Mexico*. New York: Greenwood Press, 1968.

MOORE, JOAN W., with ALFREDO CUELLAR. *Mexican Americans*. Englewood Cliffs, New Jersey: Prentice-Hall, 1970.

NABOKOV, PETER. *Tijerina and the Courthouse Raid*. Albuquerque: University of New Mexico Press, 1969.

PAZ, OCTAVIO. *The Labyrinth of Solitude: Life and Thought in Mexico*. New York: Grove Press, 1961.

RAMOS, SAMUEL. *Profile of Man and Culture in Mexico*. Austin: University of Texas Press, 1962.

RENDON, ARMANDO. *Chicano Manifesto*. New York: Macmillan, 1971.

SANCHEZ, GEORGE I. *Forgotten People: A Study of New Mexicans*. Albuquerque: University of New Mexico Press, 1940.

SAMORA, JULIAN, Ed. *La Raza: Forgotten Americans*. Notre Dame: University of Notre Dame Press, 1966.

STEINER, STAN. *La Raza: Forgotten Americans*. New York: Harper & Row, Colophon Books, 1970.

The Right to Equal Opportunity

Lawrence B. Glick

Two ethnic, or racial, groups in the United States are currently distinguished by their inferior economic status as compared with the nation as a whole. These are the Negroes and the Spanish-speaking. It is not surprising that these two groups, however dissimilar, have in common histories unlike those of any other groups in the nation. The Negroes have endured slavery in the United States, and the Spanish-speaking have suffered defeat in battle with the United States.

From these histories comes the heritage of civil inequality and social prejudice that are, in large part, the basis for present economic deprivation. The struggle for Negro civil rights has focused attention on a past in which such rights have been denied. Little attention has been given to the history of the Spanish-speaking, and their civil rights have largely been ignored.

The status of the Spanish-speaking has never been rigidly fixed by statute and ordinance as was that of Negroes in the states of the South. Nevertheless, the unwritten laws of many communities in Arizona, California, Texas, New Mexico, and Colorado established a degrading system of segregation and social inferiority that insured a subservient status for them. Many communities, with at least the tacit approval of local government, enforced the segregation of this group in schools and in housing, restricted their level of employment, and prohibited their participation in public affairs such as service on juries and police forces. Moreover, in many communities the police have failed to provide protection for them or, in fact, have singled them out for harassment.

The object of this paper is to indicate briefly the historical basis for the status of the Spanish-speaking group, the current situation, the programs in progress to improve the situation, and some views of the prospect for the future.

EDUCATION

In the school segregation cases of 1954, *Brown v. Board of Education* (347 U. S. 483), the United States Supreme Court held that the segregation by race of children in public schools is a deprivation of their basic right to equal educational opportunity. To what extent Spanish-speaking children have been

SOURCE: From Julian Samora, Ed., *La Raza: Forgotten Americans.* Copyright © 1966 by the University of Notre Dame Press. Reprinted by permission of the author and the Notre Dame Press.

denied this right through the process of enforced segregation is difficult to estimate. However, that such segregation existed is clearly shown by suits as early as 1930 and as recently as 1957 to require school officials to cease the practice of segregating Spanish-speaking children solely on the basis of their ethnic origin.

In *Independent School District v. Salvatierra* (Texas Civ. App. 33 S.W. 2nd 790, 1930), it was alleged that Spanish-speaking children were denied equal protection of the laws under the Constitution because a separate school was maintained for Spanish-speaking, mostly migrant children. The court held the maintenance of separate facilities to be constitutional if the good faith purpose was to solve the children's language and educational retardation problems. It was held to be unlawful discrimination to the extent that it applied only to Mexicans and without any consideration of each child's abilities. Thus it is clear that there is no legal basis for the segregation of Spanish-speaking pupils in Texas, unless for the legitimate purposes of special education reasonably designed to overcome educational deficiencies, particularly those of language.[1]

Apparently the Salvatierra case did not end the practice of segregation in Texas. In 1957, three years after the school segregation cases, another suit was brought in behalf of Spanish-speaking children to achieve their admission to school on a nonsegregated basis. In this case, *Hernandez v. Driscoll* (Civ. No. 1384, U.S.D.C. So. Dist., Tex., Jan. 11, 1957, 2 Race Rel. L. Rep. 329), the plaintiff contended that the Driscoll school district deprived Spanish-speaking children of equal protection of the laws under the 14th amendment by maintaining separate classes and an educational system that required a majority of the children to remain in the first two grades for three years. The court found that it was reasonable to group "in good faith" children with language deficiencies for the first year but only after examination by school authorities. The practice of segregating Spanish-speaking children for any other reason was held to be contrary to the 14th amendment. Suits brought on similar grounds and with similar results in Arizona, *Gonzales v. Sheely* (96 F. Supp. 1004, D.Ariz. 1951) and California, *Mendez v. Westminster* (64 F. Supp. 544, aff'd, 161 F.2d 774, 9th Cir. 1946) are recorded testimony of the extent to which segregation of Spanish-speaking children has been commonplace in the schools of the Southwest.

Physical segregation, however damaging it may be, is not the only impediment to a child's success in the American scheme of education. When cultural and linguistic differences exist (ignored by the school systems) as well as segregation, the result is a basic inequality of educational opportunity.

Studies of the culture of the Spanish-speaking emphasize the significance of loyalty to the Spanish language as the mother tongue and the resistance to the use of English. Furthermore, residential segregation of this group, whether voluntary or not, reinforces their commitment to Spanish as the primary and favored language. In such a community, a child can and frequently does reach school age knowing only Spanish and having had no contact with what is to him the foreign world of the Anglos.

For many children entrance into the public school brings the first confrontation with the English language.[2] The inability of the non-English-speaking pupil to understand or respond in the language of instruction results in academic failure and an accompanying diminished self-image.[3]

As may be expected, Spanish-speaking children communicate with each other in Spanish. In the attempt to force the children to learn English, the schools usually prohibit the use of Spanish in the classroom or on the school grounds.[4] When Spanish is suppressed and its use is treated as misconduct subject to punishment and as a mark of inferiority, it becomes identified as the language of the conquered, the poor, and the ignorant.[5]

Early in his school experience the non-English-speaking pupil is confronted by testing and classification procedures that play a large role in his school career. Such procedures are designed for the English-speaking child, who is not inhibited by language difficulties from scoring at his highest potential level. The Spanish-speaking child facing tests given in what is to him a foreign language can hardly be expected to score well, regardless of his innate intelligence and ability.

At a congressional hearing held in Los Angeles in 1963, there was testimony that because of the language barrier, testing procedures used by the schools are inherently discriminatory against Spanish-speaking children.[6] An elementary school teacher of many years' experience stated:

> Sometimes these children—and many of them were in the primary grades—were placed in lower achievement groups. Sometimes they were tested and found to be retarded. Sometimes they were passed along to the next grade with barely passing grades.[7]

The results of such testing procedures for Spanish-speaking children was described as follows:

> . . . Once the child has been classified as below a certain IQ level or mentally retarded, the schools then set the schedule to service this type of student, and the schedule will usually encompass vocational or industrial arts training, so that in fact they are segregating this particular ethnic group of Mexican-Americans into an economic group which is in fact a vocational type of worker-laborer who is not afforded the opportunities of higher education.[8]

In a report submitted at this same congressional hearing it was alleged that some counselors tend to guide Spanish-speaking children into vocational study, believing this to be a "realistic" course of action.[9] Similarly, in a survey of the Denver public schools, it was reported that counselors assume all too frequently that Spanish-speaking pupils will probably not go to college and therefore provide a minimum of guidance.[10]

A factor influencing education of these children is the cultural distance between the Spanish-speaking and Anglo communities. This has been described as a function of de facto residential segregation. Little positive contact exists between the schools and the parents in the Spanish-speaking community. The parents want the best education for their children but feel that the school is not part of the community.[11] Observers in Los Angeles have stated that school principals and their staff run the PTA meetings, are patronizing with the parents, and communicate the feeling that the Spanish-speaking community, not the school, is at fault for "not wanting to better itself." [12]

Although gerrymandering of school districts to create or maintain educational segregation is no longer common, the residential concentrations of Spanish-speaking have served to return these pupils to the depressed economic milieu from which they came. Culturally and linguistically handicapped, these children are tested and classified by Anglo standards, shunted into the non-academic vocational school environment, and, at best, face a limited economic future.

But if the educational picture for urban children is bleak, it is vastly better than that for the children of migrant farm workers. Migration to the northern states begins in the spring, before the school term ends, and return to the Southwest is not until months after school has reopened in the fall.[13] The migrant child may move every few days or weeks.[14] It has been said that the schools in some Texas counties are so overcrowded by the influx of migrant children that some are denied admission.[15] Other schools have refused to accept these children on the ground that they were nonresidents of the state and not entitled to its educational facilities.[16]

Even when a child is permitted to enroll in school in each district to which migration takes him, he may be handicapped by difficulty in transferring records, differences in the methods and level of instruction, lack of proper food and clothing,[17] age-grade retardation, and economic pressure to take field jobs as they become available.[18] It has been estimated that more than 50 per cent of the 100,000 school-age migrants in the nation are from one to four years behind in school by the time they reach the age of fourteen.[19] Seventy-five per cent of the 3,800 school-age migrants in Colorado each farm season are Spanish-speaking; [20] 67 per cent or more are retarded in age-grade status; [21] 95 per cent are socially retarded; [22] and 90 per cent of them need to make up school work.[23] Almost three-fourths of these children speak Spanish as the chief language in the home,[24] and 14 per cent do not speak English at all.[25] In Texas approximately 80 to 90 per cent of the migrant children know little English.[26]

Although late in season, there is a growing realization among educators and legislators in the Southwest that the special needs of these children of school age have not been met. In California, Texas, and Colorado special programs for Spanish-speaking pupils and migrant children are underway. To what extent these programs will repair a hundred years of neglect is difficult to estimate. However, it may be projected with reasonable certainty that if these programs and those supported by the federal government prove to be inadequate, the endless cycle of poverty among the Spanish-speaking cannot be broken. What this cycle means in terms of the employment levels of the Spanish-speaking is the theme of the next section of this paper.

EMPLOYMENT

In proportion to their populations, four times as many Anglos are found in professional and technical occupations as Spanish-speaking. One-third of the Spanish-speaking men are engaged as laborers or farm workers. Only 7 per cent of Anglo men are so employed.[27] Of nearly 450,000 federal employees in the five-state area in 1964, 8 per cent were Spanish-speaking, and they were concentrated in the lower-paying jobs.[28] The same pattern prevails in employment by federal contractors,[29] and state employment follows a similar course.

Of all workers, Spanish-speaking farm workers occupy the lowest rung on the employment ladder in the five states. Nationally, 586,000 Spanish-speaking Americans were listed as part of the civilian labor force in 1960.[30] Nearly half were engaged in agricultural labor. More than 80 per cent of this farm group was located in the five southwestern states.[31]

Spanish-speaking work more days for less pay and have a higher rate of unemployment than other farm workers. In 1960 the average income of a Spanish-speaking farm worker in the Southwest was $1,256 for 183 days of work. In an area designated as the "Southern region" by the United States Department of Agriculture—mainly Texas—farm workers worked only 115 days and earned an average of $656.[32]

There is evidence suggesting that discrimination because of ethnic origin plays a part in their employment plight, but the degree is difficult to fix. It cannot be said that any governmental agency maintains an official and avowed policy of discrimination. The relative status of the Spanish-speaking, while generally low, varies without predictable pattern from area to area in the Southwest. One Texas congressman has stated that "racial discrimination in job opportunities and wages is not unusual." But, he added, "education is a substantial part" of the problem.[33]

Federal Employment

Spanish-speaking are under-represented on federal employment rolls in California, Arizona, and New Mexico in terms of their percentage of the total population in those states. In Texas and Colorado the proportion who are federal employees is about equal to their share of the population. In all five states, the greatest percentage of Spanish-speaking in federal employment hold blue-collar jobs paying $5,000 a year or less.

The figures showing the quantitative percentages vary widely from state to state. In California, Spanish-speaking hold 3.8 per cent of the federal jobs but represent 9.1 per cent of the total population. The comparable percentages for Arizona are 7.6 and 14.9; for New Mexico, 21.1 and 28.3; for Texas, 14.8 and 15.2; and for Colorado, 9.0 and 8.9.[34]

Overall, 41.8 per cent of the Spanish-speaking federal employees make $5,000 or less per year.[35]

Similar patterns were found in a study of federal employment in four southwestern communities. Spanish-speaking constitute 3.4 per cent of the federal employees and 9.3 per cent of the total population in Los Angeles. Spanish-speaking comprised 4.6 per cent of those who inquired about and 5.4 per cent of those who competed in federal employment examinations, as compared with 45.8 and 39.2 per cent, respectively, for Negroes. Negroes represent only 13.5 per cent of the population.[36]

The U.S. Civil Service Commission reported that several leaders of the Spanish-speaking community offered as reasons for the seeming disinterest in government employment "a cultural aversion to having more contact with government than is necessary," a generally low level of education, language difficulties on written examinations, a lack of interest in office work of the women, and the belief, widely held among well-educated Spanish-speaking, that they have a greater potential in private than in public employment.[37] What might be added is the reluctance of proud people to subject themselves to a possible rejection because of prejudice or discrimination.

In San Antonio Spanish-speaking represent 36.2 per cent of the federal employees and 37.4 per cent of the total population.[38] The federal government is a major employer of the civilian labor force of the city. As an equal opportunity employer, it is ranked ahead of the city government and private business.[39]

United States Senator Joseph Montoya of New Mexico has related to U.S. Commission on Civil Rights investigators that Roswell, New Mexico, is the one city in the state that has traditionally discriminated against Spanish-speaking.[40] Nearby Walker Air Force Base has followed Roswell's example, the Senator said; Walker has 420 civilian workers, 80 of whom are Spanish-speaking. Only 27 of the 80 are in white-collar classifications, and only four of these earn more than $6,000 a year.[41]

The federal government is one of Denver's largest employers. There, Spanish-speaking constitute 4.8 per cent of federal employment and 6.5 per cent of the population. The majority of these employees are at the lower wage board and classified levels.[42]

Despite various programs for minority recruitment, firm nondiscrimination policies, and a rise during 1962–63 of 2.8 per cent in total federal employment throughout the Southwest, employment of Spanish-speaking by the federal government increased by only 1 per cent. However, when in 1963–64, the number of federal jobs in the five-state area declined 2.8 per cent, those held by Spanish-speaking rose 8.3 per cent.[43] The programs apparently have borne some fruit, although the percentages are less impressive than the total number of jobs gained for Spanish-speaking—1,945 in 1963–64.[44]

State Policies and Actions

Four of the five southwestern states have adopted legislation to eliminate job discrimination, including the establishment of machinery for hearing and handling specific complaints. The laws of California, Colorado, and New Mexico cover both private and public employment. Arizona covers only public employment. Texas has enacted no laws in either area.[45]

Relatively few Spanish-speaking have filed complaints of discrimination.[46] Language problems, ignorance of the statutes, distances between their residence and government offices, a tendency to avoid and distrust Anglo government, and an unwillingness to equate their problems with those of Negroes— all these have been cited for the relatively low incidence of complaints from the Spanish-speaking.[47]

An official state document of California says that:

> If you are a California Negro, you are almost twice as likely to lose your job as a white person—and if a Mexican-American nearly half again as likely to became unemployed as other whites.

The same document attributes this situation to lack of education and job skills, language handicaps, seasonal employment, and "out and out racial discrimination."[48] The California State Employment Service has set up a minority group program to seek out "qualified minority applicants for . . . employers who are actively trying to integrate their work forces."[49] Yet Spanish-speaking, who represent 8.3 per cent of the insured labor force, filed 12 per cent of all new unemployment claims during the last half of 1963.[50]

During 1963 the state conducted an ethnic survey of its more than 100,000 employees. It showed that the state employed 89,904 "Caucasians," 5,467 Negroes, 3,190 Orientals, 2,409 Mexican-Americans, and 720 "other non-whites." Significant findings of the survey were:

1. The high concentration of minorities in the urban area limits the types and salaries of state jobs available to minority-group applicants.

2. Urban minority concentrations also influence the choice of occupations.

3. Mexican-Americans and Negroes dominate the low-skill jobs; relatively few occupied the crafts, trades, or professional jobs.

4. Minority representation in law enforcement is low.

5. Better representation of minorities in policy and management levels would make state government better able to deal ". . . with many of the cultural, economic and educational problems peculiar to minority persons."[51]

In California, as well as in other states, citizenship requirements tend to exclude otherwise qualified Spanish-speaking from public employment. Inadequate state support for adult education classes inhibits the ability of resident aliens to prepare themselves to meet the literary and other requirements of citizenship.[52] However, it has been said that the most significant factor in greater Spanish-speaking representation in public employment at the policy level would be to create a better image and inspiration for young members of the community.[53]

A survey by the Los Angeles County Commission on Human Relations has shown that of 42,583 county employees, 1,973 are Spanish-speaking, 10,807 are Negro, and 28,584 are Anglo. The remainder is divided among Orientals and "other nonwhite." In every job level, Negroes far outnumber the Spanish-speaking.[54]

From the high percentage of Negro employment, particularly in professional and secretarial work, it would appear that racial or ethnic discrimination is not an inhibiting factor in employment. The Los Angeles Commission on Human Relations has not, however, offered any analysis of the relatively low numbers of Spanish-speaking employees. Yet this agency has stated that there is a lack of reliable statistics defining their problems in the Los Angeles area.[55]

Other California counties and cities have been surveyed either by other governmental agencies or U.S. Commission on Civil Rights staff. Available data do not show discriminatory hiring practices. Studies in the City of Los Angeles by the Civil Service Department revealed no evidence of discrimination. However, the Department resisted requests by the California FEPC to make a "head count." [56]

U.S. Commission on Civil Rights investigators found significant numbers of Spanish-speaking employed by the California cities of Montebello, Santa Fe Springs, El Centro, Monterey Park, and Pico Rivera.[57] The California FEPC reported that hiring practices in San Diego are not inherently discriminatory, but nevertheless the city had not projected a strong image of equal employment opportunity.[58]

Few Spanish-speaking are found in law enforcement work, although most of the cities surveyed by the Commission had some Spanish-speaking police officers. In Los Angeles City there are 180 such officers in the police department, which numbers 4700.

San Diego employs a police force of 833, of whom 27 are Spanish-speaking. According to the chief of police of this city, the high entrance requirements weed out approximately 92 per cent of all applicants. He also stated that newspaper advertisments were being used to seek out applicants to fill what he considered a need for more Spanish-speaking on the force.[59]

In other states of the Southwest, municipal employment patterns appear to be determined by factors unique to each area. In Texas employment opportunities are greater in the larger cities where the size of the Spanish-speaking population is substantial. An exception is Austin, where only 6.5 per cent of city employees are Spanish-speaking.[60] In Corpus Christi, Laredo, Edinburg, Crystal City, and San Antonio, representation in municipal employment is more closely related to their percentage of the population.[61] The director of personnel for El Paso, Texas, pointed out that 62.8 per cent of the municipal employees were Spanish-speaking compared with 35.1 per cent

Anglo. Although the majority of the former are in custodial or other low level jobs, a substantial number occupy senior positions in professional and supervisory capacities.[62]

Allegations have been made that the Texas Highway Patrol and the Texas Rangers practice employment discrimination against Spanish-speaking.[63] Whether or not this is true is difficult to determine. However, it is clear that few Spanish-speaking are employed by state law enforcement agencies. Of a total force of 1,119 Highway Patrol officers, eight are Spanish-speaking, while none are employed by the Texas Rangers among the 62 officers.[64]

No allegations of discrimination against persons of Latin heritage have been made with respect to public employment in New Mexico. A prominent leader in the Latin community of New Mexico indicated that the only discrimination that may exist would be in private employment and in a subtle way that would make it difficult to prove.[65]

The city manager of Las Cruces, New Mexico, has stated that in his opinion discrimination is very limited if it exists at all. Indeed, the municipal government is dominated by Latin-American personnel from supervisory to custodial. The city has had an antidiscrimination ordinance for about three years, but there have been no tests of the law to date. Las Cruces is said to be not unusual among New Mexico municipalities.[66]

Public employment opportunities have apparently improved for Spanish-speaking in Denver, Colorado. Currently the director of the City Welfare Department and the deputy undersheriff are Spanish-speaking. Public and private employment opportunities are said to be much more restricted in Colorado Springs, Colorado. Of a total 1,200 persons employed by the city, only 107 are Spanish-speaking. The police and fire departments have employed no Spanish-speaking, the explanation being that few apply and that those who do have difficulty meeting minimum height qualifications! None are employed in the City Hall and few are employed in other white-collar or administrative jobs.[67]

Colorado counties outside Denver and Colorado Springs apparently have few job opportunities for Spanish-speaking except in farm work or menial labor. It is reported that in some counties (Adams, Bent, Boulder, Otero, Rio Grande, and Weld) unemployment is a serious and chronic problem for Spanish-speaking.[68]

Although Spanish-speaking workers in urban areas of the Southwest generally occupy a low economic status, the status of agricultural workers is almost invariably lower. Agricultural workers generally earn less than any other group and experience a high rate of unemployment. Many farm workers occupy housing without electricity, heat, running water, or sanitary facilities. Agriculture ranks third among occupations in the number of accidental deaths.[69] Nearly 400,000 children of agricultural workers in the United States work in the fields with their families.[70] Farm laborers are generally exempt from federal legislation providing for minimum wages, unemployment insurance, and workmen's compensation.

HOUSING

In housing, as in education and employment, the Spanish-speaking have had a different experience from that of the majority of the community. In many parts of the Southwest, housing for this minority has traditionally been restricted to well-defined sections of city or town. Historically, almost all the towns of the lower Rio Grande Valley in Texas were divided by the Missouri Pacific Railroad tracks into Anglo and other sections. In some of these cities, in Colorado and California, the railroad tracks remain the physical dividing line between Anglo and Spanish-speaking. In large urban centers of the Southwest there is a marked degree of housing concentration. More than one-half of the approximately 700,000 Spanish-speaking residents of Los Angeles are concentrated in the central portion of the city. In San Antonio, Spanish-speaking, comprising almost 40 per cent of the city's population, are largely concentrated on the west side of the city. In Phoenix, more than half the Spanish-speaking people are located in a single section called the "inner city."

Housing segregation of this population is not a declining phenomenon. In 1964 the executive director of the Los Angeles County Commission on Human Relations testified that "the City of Los Angeles in particular is becoming a much more highly segregated community than it has ever been before." [71]

Today more than 80 per cent of the Spanish-speaking inhabitants of the Southwest live in urban areas. Although poor housing is a natural consequence of their low income status, in many areas residential restriction has also been a direct cause of poor housing. Confinement to a specific residential zone results in ever-increasing demand on a limited housing supply. As a result, the housing dollar of Spanish-speaking buys less than the housing dollar of other whites. In California, they pay more and live in lower quality housing than other whites.[72] In Texas and California these families occupy worse housing than any other ethnic group,[73] and the housing situation of the Spanish-speaking population of Texas is the worst in the Southwest. In 1950 more than four-fifths of the Spanish-speaking families of Texas were housed in substandard dwellings.[74] In 1960 in some major Texas metropolitan areas, six times as many dwellings of Spanish-speaking as other whites were overcrowded, and from 19 to 39 per cent were deteriorating.[75] In other southwestern cities, including Phoenix, Tucson, Albuquerque, Denver, and Los Angeles, deterioration, dilapidation, and overcrowding are common characteristics of the homes of Spanish-speaking.[76]

Not infrequently Mexican-American residential areas in the Southwest have been excluded from the usual municipal services. Commission staff investigation has found a number of instances in which local governments have failed to provide Mexican-American sections with the municipal services provided for the predominantly Anglo sections. In Weslaco, Texas, the Spanish-speaking residential area north of the railroad tracks has almost no paved streets, sidewalks, or curbing.[77] A similar situation prevails in Crystal City, Texas,[78] and in Cotulla, located in the Upper Rio Grande Valley.[79]

In South Tucson, Arizona, where there is a 60 to 70 per cent Spanish-speaking population, it is reported that the city sanitation codes are not enforced and that little police protection is provided in their section of the city. Moreover, it has been alleged that refuse collection is regular on the north side, but rare on the south side.[80]

It cannot be denied that the residential segregation of Spanish-speaking in the Southwest is to a certain extent self-imposed and the existence of "barrios" is in part a matter of choice. Such clustering of ethnic group members in particular parts of urban areas is found throughout the country. In many cities of the Southwest there are no artificial limitations on the sections in which Spanish-speaking with adequate financial resources find housing. However, there is evidence that neither choice nor economic inadequacy is solely responsible for the inability of this group to find adequate housing. In the past restrictive covenants were used to bar this group from Anglo neighborhoods. An officer of the Los Angeles chapter of the National Association for the Advancement of Colored People has commented, "Nowhere in the Nation were there as many of these restrictive covenants which included Negroes, Orientals, and Mexicans, as in California." [81] Even after the 1948 United States Supreme Court decision holding that restrictive housing covenants excluding persons because of race are unenforceable, these covenants were applied to Spanish-speaking.[82] Housing officials in Phoenix have reported that restrictive covenants were used to bar Spanish-speaking as recently as 1954.[83]

Real estate brokers in the Southwest have played a role in restricting the housing available to Spanish-speaking. Article 5 of the Code of Ethics of the National Association of Real Estate Boards states: "A realtor should not be instrumental in introducing into a neighborhood a character of property or use which will clearly be detrimental to property values in that neighborhood." Although this article contains no reference to race or ethnic group, it is commonly interpreted by local boards of realtors to prohibit the introduction of persons into areas in which their race or ethnic group is not traditionally housed. Brokers' application of this exclusionary policy to Spanish-speaking is reportedly still common in Los Angeles, San Diego, Denver, Austin, and a number of small Texas cities.[84]

Real estate brokers in Denver allegedly hang up the telephone on callers who speak with a Spanish accent. For those who have no accent but whose name is typically Spanish, the brokers make appointments that are never kept. It is alleged that such practices are common enough to be a factor in maintaining definite "Mexican areas in Denver." [85]

Correspondence received by the U.S. Commission on Civil Rights from a member of the state legislature of Texas from San Antonio enclosed a complaint from a Spanish-speaking constituent who alleged that a broker had refused to rent an apartment in Austin to her son because of his ethnic background. The representative stated that he had received "many similar complaints." [86] In Weslaco, Texas a Spanish-speaking physician who tried to purchase a home in an Anglo section in 1961 was informed by a real estate broker that he could not do so because the area was "restricted." [87]

It has been charged that financing institutions such as banks and loan associations also play a part in restricting the housing market for this group. In 1964 a Spanish-speaking realtor in Los Angeles stated before the California Advisory Committee to the U.S. Commission on Civil Rights that it was difficult to place loans for Spanish-speaking who wished to buy homes in certain areas.

One factor playing a generally unspoken but significant role in housing discrimination against Spanish-speaking is skin color. Those who are *trigueño* —"dark" in skin color—are more apt to meet discrimination than those who are more fair-skinned.[88] Such discrimination has been reported in Oakland, California [89] and in some areas of Colorado and Texas.[90]

It was reported that in 1960 a light-skinned Spanish-speaking who purchased a home in an Anglo neighborhood in Harlingen, Texas, referred another darker-skinned acquaintance to the same broker, who told him, "I'm sorry, you can't buy that house; the neighborhood is restricted to Anglos." [91] A Spanish-speaking woman with an Anglo name who resides in Los Angeles stated that she received a cordial reception from realtors on the telephone and an invariably unfavorable reaction to her obviously Latin appearance upon meeting them in person.[92] In late 1964 a biweekly English-language Los Angeles newspaper that is directed to the Spanish-speaking community charged that the president of a realty board had instructed members not to sell to dark-skinned Spanish-speaking, and that a prospective buyer had recently been told by a broker over the telephone, "If you are light-skinned, we have several homes available, but if you are dark-skinned, don't waste my time." [93]

LAW ENFORCEMENT

No discussion of the Spanish-speaking of the Southwest in a civil rights context would be complete without reference to law enforcement and the relationships of police and this minority. Although it is dangerous to generalize from the experience of only two urban areas, it is clear that if Los Angeles and Denver are typical, this minority and the police are at arms length. Undoubtedly, the poor are more subject to harassment by law enforcement officers than others, and it becomes difficult to separate poverty from ethnic origin as a basis for the unsatisfactory relationship of this group with the police. If the now well-known remarks of Chief William Parker of Los Angeles are indicative of a general attitude, it is obvious that the ethnic factor is germane. At a hearing held by the U.S. Commission on Civil Rights in Los Angeles in 1960, Chief Parker stated:

> So we keep the record straight, the Latin population that came in here before us and presented a great problem because I worked over on the East Side, when men had to work in pairs . . . and it's because of some of those people being not too far removed from the wild tribes of the district of the inner mountains of Mexico. I don't think you can throw the genes out of the question when you discuss behavior patterns of people.

An assistant to Governor Edmund Brown has stated that much of the unrest and racial problems complicating police-community relations in Los Angeles are the result of police attitudes typified by Chief Parker. He also claimed personal knowledge of arrests, both of individuals and groups of youths on their way to perfectly legal activity at their neighborhood youth center. These arrests were alleged to be without proper cause and the juveniles were later released without prosecution.[94]

Harassment of Spanish-speaking, particularly young persons, by police rather than physical brutality is the major source of conflict in Los Angeles. Although cases in which physical brutality is involved do occur, these are difficult to prove and the Spanish-speaking victims are usually unwilling to compound their difficulties by seeking redress through legal processes. A particular problem confronting these youths in Los Angeles is the police practice of arrest on suspicion. This has been described as arresting everyone in sight or in reach when a crime has been committed. The result of this is that many young men accumulate long arrest records without even being tried or convicted of a crime. An arrest record, with or without convictions, is difficult to overcome in future educational or employment opportunities.

In Denver, as in Los Angeles, there are unsatisfactory relationships between the Spanish-speaking community and the police. Here the view of the minority would appear to be that the police have little concern for the right of citizens to be free from assault under the guise of official conduct. The attitudes of both police and members of minority groups in Denver are well illustrated by the Salazar case in 1964, which also may serve as an illustration of why members of the Spanish-speaking community tend to distrust officialdom.

On March 10, 1964 a 19-year-old youth named Alfred Salazar died of a brain injury caused by a skull fracture.[95] A policeman had struck him on the head while breaking up a fight.[96]

On March 12 the American GI Forum and *Los Voluntarios*, both organizations of Spanish-speaking, joined the family in demanding a full investigation by the mayor into the death of the youth.[97] A police investigation produced no evidence of police brutality. The Congress of Racial Equality asked for a public hearing into the circumstances of the death of Salazar.[98]

On March 23, 1964 the district attorney announced that there would be a grand jury investigation of the death of Salazar.[99] The district attorney said that conflicting statements by witnesses to the fight were contained in the report prepared by the police. He said the "grand jury should review the entire matter to determine who has told the truth." [100]

On March 30, 1964 the Colorado Committee Against Police Brutality branded the grand jury investigation as "an attempt to silence widespread public criticism and still do nothing." [101]

On April 16, 1964 civil rights organizations sent a letter to Governor Love calling on him "to take aggressive and constructive steps to stop what can now only be interpreted as retaliation against Spanish and Mexican-Americans by the Denver Police Force." [102] The Governor said he would defer to the Denver grand jury in its investigation of the alleged police brutality.[103]

Officials of CORE, *Los Voluntarios*, GI Forum, and the United Mothers Club asked the president of the city council to introduce an ordinance to set up a 12-member commission to investigate complaints of police brutality. The draft of the ordinance was referred to the judiciary committee of the city council. The president of the city council said that the Police Internal Bureau and the Mayor's Commission on Community Relations were adequate to take care of any disciplinary action in the police department.[104]

On May 11, 1964 the grand jury filed its report on the Salazar case and on other allegations concerning the police department. It was found that Salazar was struck at least twice in the fight, once by a participant and once by a policeman. The grand jury found that he complained that his head hurt, but refused medical attention; that when it was recognized that medical aid was necessary, it was provided; but that "due to the abnormal thinness of his skull, no medical treatment could have offset the effects of the fatal blow"; and that no evidence of the use of excessive force on the part of police officers was found.[105] The grand jury recommended that police training be improved to include: training in public relations in the understanding and handling of minority groups; that the Internal Affairs Bureau of the Police Department be abolished; that no citizens' complaints should be handled by any department of the police concerning allegations of police brutality or improper treatment; [106] and that a citizens' board be established by a charter amendment with its members to be appointed by the mayor.[107]

By the time the grand jury handed down its report, the Colorado Anti-Discrimination Commission had begun special hearings on equal enforcement of the law in Denver. There were six sworn charges of brutality to Spanish-speaking made against the police department.

The safety manager and the city attorney advised 29 Denver policemen under investigation not to appear at a Commission hearing on May 16, 1964. The mayor reiterated his position that the Colorado Anti-Discrimination Commission had no legal responsibility for looking into accusations against the police department of Denver.[108]

This tangled story of charges and denials is difficult to evaluate, but it is clear that there are serious and continuing problems between the Spanish-speaking and the police in Denver and that cases such as that of Alfred Salazar are not unique.

JURY SERVICE

Of particular concern throughout Colorado is the issue of jury service. In recent years Spanish-speaking have served on the juries of six Colorado counties (Adams, Bent, Boulder, Otero, Rio Grande, and Weld) very infrequently. The United States Supreme Court in *Hernandez v. Texas* [109] held that Spanish-speaking people may not be systematically excluded from jury duty. Later, in a Colorado case,[110] the Supreme Court of Colorado held that these people had been systematically excluded from the juries of Logan County, Colorado. It was proved that although there were persons with Spanish surnames on the tax rolls of the county who were qualified to serve, no Spanish-surname person had appeared on the jury lists in eight years. According to the arguments in the Montoya case, a finding of systematic exclusion requires that a substantial segment of the population, some of whose members are eligible to serve as jurors, must be absent from juries for a substantial period of time. By these criteria, the Colorado counties have not engaged in systematic jury exclusion because a few Spanish-surname persons have appeared on juries in all of the counties for most of the years surveyed. However, the number of Spanish-surname persons serving has been extremely small and has not been in proportion to the numerical strength of the Spanish-speaking people in these counties.[111]

In all six Colorado counties the proportion of Spanish-speaking appearing on jury lists was much smaller than their proportion of the total population. In Bent County, where the Spanish-speaking constitute more than 25 per cent of the population, less than 9 per cent of this group appeared on the 1964 jury list. Over a five-year period from 1959 to 1963, only 17 of the county's more than 1,500 Spanish-speaking residents served on juries. In 1961 there were no such persons on the juries of Bent County. Rio Grande County has a Spanish-speaking population of more than 34 per cent. Between 1959 and 1963, only 3 to 8 per cent of the persons on the final jury list were from this population.

Over 20 per cent of the population of Otero County is Spanish-speaking. Between 1959 and 1964 Spanish-speaking persons on the jury lists ranged between 4 and 9 per cent, and only 2 and 6 per cent of these were summoned. In 1959 and 1961 no Spanish-speaking person served on juries in Otero County. For the rest of the years examined, approximately one-half to one per cent of the jurors were Spanish-speaking (with the exception of 1960, when the percentage was 4). In five years, the total days served on Otero County juries by this group was about 36.

In Boulder and Adams Counties Spanish-speaking have appeared on juries. The Spanish-speaking population of Boulder is about 4 per cent, in excess of 2 per cent of which have appeared on the jury list during the past five years. Adams County, with less than 10 per cent Spanish-speaking, had substantial numbers of these on the jury list.

There are almost 9,000 Spanish-speaking persons in Weld County, approximately one-ninth of the population. In five years, about 50 such persons were summoned for jury service. Only 16 of them actually served. Eleven of those served in a single year, 1963. According to a local official, in that year, an attempt was made to include as many Spanish-speaking names as possible on the jury list. One-thirtieth of those summoned were Spanish-speaking.

The relatively small number of Spanish-speaking people appearing on juries, particularly in Bent, Rio Grande, and Otero Counties, may be influenced by the means of jury selection in these areas. In Bent, Rio Grande, and

Otero, prospective jurors are taken from the county tax lists. Colorado law permits counties to compile jury lists from tax rolls and other documents that may provide the names of persons eligible to serve. Spanish-speaking people are property owners less often than other whites and so are less likely to appear on the county tax rolls. In Otero County a questionnaire is sent to the prospective juror to establish eligibility to serve. This questionnaire poses a question which could be used to disqualify a Spanish-speaking juror: #22. "Can you read, write, and understand English?" It is important to note that Colorado law does *not* require a juror to *read and write* English. It states only that he may be challenged for cause if he cannot *speak or understand* the English language.[112] In Rio Grande the list goes to the county commissioners, who present the court with a final list of "chosen jurors." Colorado law provides that the jurors shall be summoned by chance, drawing from box of statutory specifications.

Boulder and Adams Counties, with relatively larger numbers of Spanish-speaking persons on their jury lists, take the names from voter registration lists (Adams) and election records (Boulder), send out a questionnaire to establish eligibility, and then summon eligible jurors by drawing their names from a wheel. A Boulder County judge admits that the county has been under close scrutiny in its jury selection practices for several years (probably since the Montoya case) and that attorneys keep a sharp eye on procedures. The Boulder, Adams, and Weld Counties' questionnaire ask the prospective juror whether he owns real estate in the county. The relevance of the question is not apparent.

In conclusion, to discuss the Spanish-speaking in the context of equal protection under the laws as we speak about Negroes is to put the discussion in an improper context. In the Southwest there have never been especially established mechanisms, operated through state agencies (from the governor to the highway patrol), *based in law* that have established the Spanish-speaking as an inferior group such as was true of the Negroes in the South. To be sure, as has been pointed out throughout, there have been many instances of prejudice and discrimination directed at the Spanish-speaking and involving education, employment, housing, police brutality, public accommodations and jury service. These, however, have been instances of individual prejudice or of local practice and not denials of equal protection under the laws. It is this point that is important to bear in mind, and which is devastating to deliberate discriminatory practices.

NOTES

1. The current policy of the State of Texas Educational Agency (T.E.A.) is cited in the *Handbook for Local School Officials*, T.E.A. Revised, Nov. 1963, p. 131: "The intent of state law is that the public schools of Texas be operated in such a way that equal educational opportunity is provided for all children. The separation of children of Latin-American descent from children of Anglo-American descent in the public schools is contrary to law."

2. MILDRED BOYER, "Texas Squanders Non-English Resources," in the *Bulletin of the Texas Foreign Language Association* 5:3 (October 1963), 1. Similarly, a teacher of the Anaheim (California) city schools has commented that ". . . [t]he Spanish-speaking child may never have heard English spoken or have spoken it himself until he enters school. [He] often comes to the first grade knowing little or no English. He is given a directive to forget his Spanish and to learn how to understand, speak, read, and write English, which to him is a foreign language. The irony is further heightened by the fact that the reading-readiness program has been planned for English-speaking children." Remarks of Miss Delia Gomez, quoted in California State Department of Education, Bureau of Elementary Education, *Report of the Orange County Conference on the Education of Spanish-speaking Children and Youth*, Garden Grove, Calif., February 14–15, 1964.

3. Victor Sumner, Research Director, Texas Education Agency, quoted in the *Bulletin TFLA* 5:3, 4.

4. An interesting example of Mexican-American children's attitude toward Spanish is an essay written by a seventh grade pupil in San Antonio (sent to Dr. Bruce Gaarder, U.S. Office of Education under cover of a letter from Mr. Alonso M. Perales, San Antonio, dated October 13, 1964).

"When I entered Elementary school we weren't allowed to speak Spanish, sometimes I got mad and said inside myself 'why shouldn't we speak Spanish?' it's our language. In the second, third, and fourth grades we talked Spanish without teachers getting mad at us. Since the first grade, I can remember her getting after us. I was moved twice in the first grade to other first grade rooms; and in each we couldn't talk Spanish. In the fifth grade while playing outside we were talking Spanish, and a teacher heard us from inside, and said if we kept on talking Spanish we would [go] down to the office, several times it happened. Our real teacher though, didn't think that at all. She said that while we were outside, we could talk any language, except bad words. In the sixth grade the teacher always got mad[e], because she said if we didn't stop talking she wouldn't let us have the special privileges other had. But everything that has been told to me has gone into one ear and out the other, I guess, because I still like to talk Spanish everywhere."

5. For a full discussion of the educational implications of the suppression of Spanish, see *Language Loyalty in the United States*, Office of Education, U.S. Dept. of Health, Education and Welfare, Vol. III, 1963.

6. Hearings Before the Select Subcommittee on Education of the Committee on Educa-

tion and Labor, U.S. House of Representatives, 88th Cong. 1st Sess., Los Angeles, August 12, 1963.

7. Statement of Mrs. Ninfa Nieto, Hearings, August 12, 1963, p. 26.
8. Statement of Rudolph Rivas, Hearings, August 12, 1963, p. 14.
9. Hearings, August 12, 1963, p. 65.
10. *Report and Recommendation to the Board of Education, School District Number One,* Denver, Colorado (A Special Study Committee on Equality of Educational Opportunity in the Denver Public Schools), March 1, 1964, C-34.
11. Statement of Lillian Aceves, Higher Horizons Program, August 12, 1963, p. 14.
12. Hearings, August 12, 1963, p. 25.
13. METZLER and SARGENT, "Income of Migratory Agricultural Workers," *Texas Agricultural Experiment Station* 6 (March 1960).
14. POTTS, "Roadside School Bells Are Your Challenge," *Proceedings of Western Interstate Conference on Migratory Labor,* Phoenix, Ariz., April 10–13, 1960, p. 17. One-third of a group of Colorado families travelled to one work area during the season, one-half to two places, and the rest to three or more locations. POTTS, "Providing Education for Migrant Children," Colo. State Dept. of Education, Denver, 1961, p. 2.
15. TEXAS COUNCIL on MIGRANT LABOR, "Texas Migrant Workers 1963, Summary of Data, March 1964, p. 2.
16. POTTS, note 15, p. 51. Colorado law permits school boards to deny educational facilties to nonresidents. Colo. Rev. Stat. 123-10-22 (1953), 123-21-2 (1953).
17. Calif. Senate Fact-Finding Committee on Labor and Welfare, *supra* note 79 at 48.
18. POTTS, note 15, p. 63.
19. SENATOR WILLIAMS, "For A National Task—A National Program," *Proceedings of Western Interstate Conference on Migratory Labor,* p. 10.
20. POTTS, note 15, p. 53.
21. POTTS, p. 1.
22. POTTS, p. 35.
23. POTTS, p. 37. Almost three-fourths of the parents of these children did not go beyond grade school; p. 62. Almost one-third of the mothers and about one-fifth of the fathers speak only Spanish; p. 60.
24. POTTS, p. 61.
25. POTTS, p. 60.
26. TEXAS EDUCATION AGENCY, *Proposed Curriculum Program for Texas Migratory Children,* 1963, 3.
27. *U.S. Census of Population 1960: Persons of Spanish Surname,* Final Report PC(2)-1B.
28. President's Committee on Equal Employment Opportunity, *Report to the President,* 1964.
29. "Total and Spanish-American White Collar and Blue Collar Employment by Government Contractors in Five Selected States," July 1, 1964. Source: Standard Form 40, Prepared by: LR, 10/7/64. Letter from N. Thompson Powers, Executive Assistant to Secretary, U.S. Department of Labor to the U.S. Commission on Civil Rights, October 15, 1964.
30. U.S. DEPARTMENT of LABOR, *Manpower Report of the President and a Report on Manpower Requirements, Resources, Utilization and Training,* March 1964, p. 120.
31. U.S. DEPARTMENT of AGRICULTURE, *Economic, Social and Demographic Characteristics of Spanish-American Wage Workers on U.S. Farms,* 1963, p. 5.

32. *Ibid.,* pp. 5, 11.
33. Statement of Representative Henry B. Gonzales, *Hearings Before Subcommittee on Employment and Manpower, Relating to the Training and Utilization of the Manpower Resources of the Nation,* U.S. Senate Committee on Labor and Public Welfare, 88th Cong., 1st Sess. Prt. 4, 1963, pp. 1250–1254.
34. Source: President's Committee on Equal Employment Opportunity: *Minority, Employment Survey 1964,* and *U.S. Census of Population 1960: Persons of Spanish Surnames,* Final Report PC(2)-1B.
35. PRESIDENT'S COMMITTEE on EQUAL EMPLOYMENT OPPORTUNITY: *Minority Employment Survey,* 1964.
36. U.S. CIVIL SERVICE COMMISSION: *Los Angeles Community Review,* 1964.
37. *Ibid.*
38. Source: President's Committee on Equal Employment Opportunity and U.S. Census of Population, *supra,* note 10.
39. U.S. CIVIL SERVICE COMMISSION, *San Antonio Community Review,* 1934.
40. Interview with Senator Joseph Montoya, *Investigation Report No. 64-01-77,* July 22, 1964. N.B. The author has examined the files of the U.S. Commission on Civil Rights. All references to interviews refer to material in the files of this federal agency.
41. Interview with C. C. Robinson, Director of Civilian Personnel, Walker Air Force Base, Roswell, New Mexico, *Investigation Report No. 64-01-98,* September 11, 1964.
42. Source: President's Committee on Equal Employment Opportunity and U.S. Census of Population, *supra,* note 10. See also U.S. Civil Service Commission, *Denver Community Review 1963.*
43. PRESIDENT'S COMMITTEE on EQUAL EMPLOYMENT OPPORTUNITY *Minority Employment Surveys,* 1963 and 1964.
44. *Ibid.*
45. Arizona Revised Statutes, Title 23, 373-375, *Equal Public Employees Opportunities Act,* 1955; 44 Ann. Calif. Code, sec. 1735 and 1410–1435, *The California Fair Employment Practices Act.* Colorado Revised Statutes, 80-21-1,2, *Colorado Labor on Public Works;* Colorado Revised Statutes, 81-19-1, 18-19-8, *The Colorado Anti-discrimination Act of 1951.* New Mexico Statutes Ann. 59-4-1, 59-4-14 (1949), *Equal Employment Opportunities Act.*
46. Letter held in U.S. Commission on Civil Rights files from John Hope II, Director, Federal Employment Program, President's Committee on Equal Employment Opportunity, September 2, 1964. See also State of California FEPC, *Discrimination Complaints by Persons of Spanish Surname,* September 18, 1959–June 30, 1964.

    Mexican-American leaders are reported as saying that the California FEPC was doing a "dismal" job for their people in California and demanded representation on the State Personnel Board, programs to train or retrain Mexican Americans in rural areas, and that Mexican Americans be hired for positions which deal with the Spanish-speaking public (Los Angeles *Times,* November 11, 1964, p. 28). Nevertheless, between September 1959 through June 1964, the California FEPC received only 200 employment complaints from Mexican Americans. Of these, 111 showed either no discriminaton or insufficient evidence; 26 were satisfactorily adjusted; the remainder were either dropped, discontinued, or did not fall within FEPC jurisdiction.
47. E.g., letter from staff member, California FEPC to the Commission, August 4, 1964.
48. California Department of State, Document DE-NR-366, February 5, 1964.
49. WOODS, "Employment Problems of the Mexican-Americans," *Assembly by Sub-*

committee *on Special Employment Problems at East Los Angeles College*, January 10, 1964.

50. CALIFORNIA DEPARTMENT of EMPLOYMENT, "Racial Characteristics of New Claimants of Unemployment Benefits in California, July–December, 1963."

51. *Press Release–LH #838*, Governor Edmund G. Brown, November 27, 1963.

   Governor Brown directed appropriate department heads to make a detailed analysis of the census, "the first step towards meeting our objective of complete equality of opportunity. . . ." Other steps promised by the governor were: (1) a conference of educators to study educational practices as they pertain to state and private employment, with special reference to counseling practices, curricula, and educational policy to determine if we are properly meeting our obligations . . . especially (to) members of minority groups—for employment; (2) a complete study of all state job applications to determine whether minorities are applying for state jobs; and (3) a request to the State Personnel Board to recommend new education and in-service training programs specifically tailored to the needs of minority groups.

   Attachments to Press Release 838, Report to Governor Edmund G. Brown from FRANK A. MESPLE's *Ethnic Survey of Employment in State Government*, p. 3. Frank A. Mesple is Secretary to the Governor's cabinet.

52. Remarks of Herman Gallegos before the California Senate Fact-Finding Subcommittee on Race Relations and Urban Problems, San Francisco, Calif., October 2, 1963, p. 2.

53. U.S. Commission on Civil Rights interview with Judge Legsoldo Sanchez, Los Angeles, May 15, 1964.

54. U.S. Commission on Civil Rights interview with John Buggs, Chairman, Los Angeles County Commission on Human Relations, Los Angeles, Calif., July 22, 1964.

55. *Ibid.*

56. U.S. Commission on Civil Rights interview with Joseph Hawthorne, General Manager, Civil Service Dept., Los Angeles, Calif., July 27, 1964. Memorandum to the city administrative officer from the General Manager, Civil Service Dept. Subject: Survey of city's employment practices, dated October 8, 1962.

57. U.S. Commission on Civil Rights interviews with: Mr. Malcolm C. Gerschler, city planner, Montebello, July 15, 1964; Robert T. Wilson, City Manager, Santa Fe Springs, August 19, 1964; Mr. Leonard E. McClintock, El Centro, August 5, 1964; Mr. Samuel R. Norris, Finance Director, Monterey Park, July 15, 1964; Mr. Jerrold Gonce, Administrative Assistant, Pico Rivera, July 15, 1964.

58. California FEPC, "Employment Practices, City of San Diego," June 23, 1964, pp. 1, 2.

59. U.S. Commission on Civil Rights interview with Wesley S. Sharp, Chief of Police, August 5, 1964.

60. U.S. Commission on Civil Rights interview with James G. Wilson, Assistant City Manager, Austin, Texas, April 22, 1964. The vast majority of Mexican Americans are employed in park or custodial jobs. Of a police force of 299, seven are Mexican American; of 282 in the fire department, two are Mexican American. Mr. Wilson noted, however, that recently of 500 applicants for the fire department, four were Mexican American.

61. U.S. Commission on Civil Rights interviews with Benjamin Franklin, Personnel Director, Corpus Christi, April 27, 1964 (of a 1680 total employed by the city of Corpus Christi, 793 are Mexican American. In police and fire departments, Mexican Americans number 108 of a total of 325. Most are employed in custodial work in the departments. The population is almost 55 per cent Mexican American.); Judge E. D.

Salinar, Laredo, June 17, 1964; Alfonso R. Ramires, Mayor of Edinburg, June 16, 1964; George Ozuna, Jr., City Manager, Crystal City, June 10, 1964; Frank Valdez, April 3, 1964, *Field Investigation Report No. 64-01-07* (May 18, 1964). Mr. Valdez, a professional architect stated that there were few, if any, issues of discrimination in San Antonio. On the other hand, in an interview with John C. Alaniz, April 13, 1964, Mr. Alaniz, an attorney and state legislator, alleged that discriminatory hiring and promotion practices were evident in the city-owned gas and utility company. He stated that only menial jobs are available for the Mexican American. Commission investigation (interview with J. T. Duly, Assistant General Manager, and John M. Costello, Personnel Director, Public Service Board, April 20, 1964, revealed that Mexican Americans make up 95 per cent of the unskilled; of the office force—630 total—12 were Mexican American; of the skilled workers—1125 total—two were Mexican-American).

62. *Ibid.*
63. U.S. Commission on Civil Rights interview with John Alaniz, Attorney and Representative to State Legislature, San Antonio, Texas, April 13, 1964.
64. U.S. Commission on Civil Rights interview with Homer Garrison, Jr., Director, Texas Department of Public Safety, Austin, Texas, June 3, 1964.
65. U.S. Commission on Civil Rights interview with Luis Tellez, Chairman, G. I. Forum, Albuquerque, N. Mex., September 1, 1964.
66. U.S. Commission on Civil Rights interview with Fred Alvarez, City Manager, Las Cruces, N. Mex., September 1, 1964.
67. U.S. Commission on Civil Rights interview with Mrs. Pauline Knopp and Mr. John M. Biery, City Manager, Colorado Springs, Colo., May 15, 1964.
68. U.S. Commission on Civil Rights Field Investigation Report by George Roybal, Special Field Consultant, August, 1964.
69. Sixty-five deaths per 100,000 workers, National Safety Council, *Accident Facts* 85 (1964). California reports 56.5 disabling injuries per 1,000 agricultural workers compared with 31.9 injuries per 1,000 workers in the all-industrial average. This rate was exceeded only in construction and mining in California. California Senate Fact-Finding Committee on Labor and Welfare, *California's Farm Labor Problems*, Pt. II, 1963, p. 37.

    Between 1951 and 1960 there were more than 3,000 farm workers in the nation poisoned by sprays. During this time, 22 adults and 63 children died from the effects of the sprays. Bennett, "Still the Harvest of Shame," *Commonweal*, April 10, 1964, p. 85.

    Transportation accidents are common hazards for migrants. In 1956 the Interstate Commerce Act was amended to permit the Interstate Commerce Commission to establish safety and comfort regulations for trips exceeding 75 miles and crossing a State line. Pt. II of the Interstate Commerce Act 70 Stat. 958 (1956), 49 U.S.C. Sec. 304 (3a) (1958).
70. In 1961 there were more than 350,000 children between the ages of 10 and 13 who work in the fields of the nation, U.S. Dept. of Agriculture, *The Hired Farm Working Force of 1961*, 18 (1963) note 47, p. 85. No data available for children of a lower age. State and federal laws permit children to work after school and during vacation. On the federal level the child labor provision of the Fair Labor Standards Act permits children under age 16 to work in agriculture outside of school hours. Fair Labor Standards Act of 1938, 52 Stat. 1060, 29 U.S.C. (1938), 29 U.S.C. sec 203(e), 212, 213(c) 1958. Child Labor Regulation, Orders and Statements of Interpretation, 29,

CFR 1500, 123 (1951). Laws in the southwestern states limit ages and conditions of the employment of minors in agriculture but do not prohibit it. Texas Penal Code Ann. (Vernon's) Art. 1577, 1578a (1964 Supp.); Calif. Labor Code, sec. 1394; Colo. Rev. Stat. 80-8-1 (1953); N.M. Rev. Stat. Ann. 59-6-2, 59-6-3, 59-6-8 (Supp. 1963); Ariz. Const. Art. 18, sec. 2, Ariz. Rev. Stat. Ann. secs. 23-231 to 23-248 (1956).

71. Proceedings in re California Advisory Committee to the U.S. Commission on Civil Rights (Los Angeles), January 13, pp. 56–57/79, January 13–14, 1964 (unpublished document in the Commission Library). Hearings Before the U.S. Commission on Civil Rights, Los Angeles, Calif., January 25–26, 1960.

72. U.S. COMMISSION on CIVIL RIGHTS, *op. cit., supra* note 81 at 142 and Governor's Advisory Commission on Housing Problems, *Housing in California*—Appendix 129, April 1962.

73. McENTIRE, *Residence and Race* (1964), pp. 126 and 131; Governor's Advisory Commission on Housing Problems, *op. cit.*, note 82, pp. 129 and 141.

74. McENTIRE, note 83, p. 125.

75. U.S. CENSUS of POPULATION: 1960, Final Reports PHC (1) Series; U.S. Census of Housing: 1960 Final Reports PHC (1) Series.

76. *Ibid.*

77. U.S. Commission on Civil Rights Interview with Armando Cuellar, M.D., Weslaco, Texas, May 19, 1964.

78. U.S. Commission on Civil Rights interview with George Ozuna, City Manager, Crystal City, Texas, May 19–20, 1964. Crystal City is only 20 per cent Anglo. The Mexican-American section of town has long needed paved streets, street lamps, sewage service, and running water. According to Mr. Ozuna, Zavala County originally contributed $60,000 to a joint local-federal project to construct new municipal buildings, including a jail and fire station. After a completely Mexican-American city administration was elected in April 1963, the county government withdrew this support, on the basis that it lacked confidence in the municipal administration.

79. U.S. Commission on Civil Rights interview with William Balbour, Esq., City Secretary, Cotulla, Texas, May 25, 1964. In Cotulla, inspection by a member of the Commission staff revealed lack of paved streets and interior plumbing in the Mexican-American section east and south of the railroad tracks, and poor street lighting. Until recently, there was no trash collection. The Anglo section was generally paved and had some sidewalks. The city secretary stated that city improvements, planned to be carried out with the aid of federal funds, will concentrate on Mexican-American sections. It is expected that these funds will be used for a sewage system for the Mexican-American part of town.

80. U.S. Commission on Civil Rights interview with Luis Martinez, Tucson, Ariz., August 5, 1964.

81. Hearings Before the U.S. Commission on Civil Rights, Los Angeles, Calif., January 25–26, 1960.

82. *Shelley v. Kraemer*, 334 U.S. 1 (1948). In 1948 a California district court in the San Francisco Bay region, in compliance with the Supreme Court ruling, held a covenant barring sale to "persons of the Mexican race" unenforceable. *Matthews v. Andrade*, Civ. No. 13775, Dist. Ct. of Appeals, 1st Dist., Div. 1, Calif. (October 13, 1948).

83. U.S. Commission on Civil Rights interview with Roy B. Yanez, Exec. Director, Phoenix Housing Authority, and Fred S. Piper, Asst. Dir., July 28, 1964.

84. Information derived from numerous U.S. Commission on Civil Rights interviews in these cities.

85. U.S. Commission on Civil Rights interview with Roger Cisneros, Esq., Denver, Colo., April 5, 1964.

86. Letter from John Alaniz, Esq., September 18, 1964.

87. Interview, *supra* note 88.

88. U.S. Commission on Civil Rights interview with Mrs. Grace Davis, Los Angeles, Calif., April 8, 1964.

89. Transcript of Proceedings Before the California State Advisory Committee to the U.S. Commission on Civil Rights, Oakland, California, May 12, 1964, p. 154.

90. U.S. Commission on Civil Rights interviews.

91. U.S. Commission on Civil Rights interview with Raul Garza, Harlingen, Texas, May 26, 1964.

92. Davis interview, *supra* note 91.

93. Carta editorial, Los Angeles, Calif., Vol. II, No. 5, pp. 1 and 2 (August 1, 1964).

94. U.S. Commission on Civil Rights interview with William Becker, Special Asst. for Human Rights, Sacramento, Calif., April 1964.

95. Denver *Post*, March 10, 1964, p. 3.

96. *Rocky Mountain News*, March 11, 1964, p. 5.

97. Denver *Post*, March 24, 1964, p. 11.

98. Denver *Post*, March 20, 1964, p. 1.

99. Denver *Post*, March 24, 1964, p. 1.

100. *Rocky Mountain News*, March 25, 1964, p. 54.

101. Denver *Post*, March 30, 1964.

102. *Rocky Mountain News*, April 17, 1964.

103. Denver *Post*, April 17, 1964.

104. Denver *Post*, April 18, 1964.

105. Report of the Grand Jury. Second Judicial District, No. 57775, June 11, 1964, p. 2.

106. *Ibid.*, p. 4.

107. *Ibid.*, p. 5.

108. Denver *Post*, May 18, 1964.

109. 347 U.S. 475 (1954).

110. *Montoya v. People*, 345, P.2d 1062 (1959).

111. The source for the following material on jury service in Colorado is (except where otherwise noted) from reports in the files of the U.S. Commission on Civil Rights submitted to George Roybal, special consultant to the Commission.

112. Colo. Rev. Stat. 78-2-1, 78-3-3, 78-4-3, 78-4-4 (1953).

Perspective on Politics

Alfredo Cuellar

The political development of Mexican Americans can be traced through roughly four periods of political activity that begin with the American conquest of the Southwest.

Such a survey must begin with conflict. Though the first three generations of American rule (from the late 1840's until about 1920, the first phase of political development for Mexican Americans) can be termed "apolitical," it is a period that covers widely disparate activities. Through the first generation (until perhaps the mid-1870's) there was widespread violence and disorder accompanying the consolidation of the conquest. In the following 50 years throughout most of the Southwest Mexican Americans were politically submerged. Neither the violence of the first generation nor the quiescence of the second and third can be considered "normal" American political participation. Force and its aftermath of suppression were the rule.

There were two exceptions to the dominant apolitical pattern. Organized political activity was very much present in New Mexico. Here the political system, even during the long period of territorial government, reflected the demographic and social weight of a large Spanish-speaking population. In southern California, moreover, a wealthy land-owning group of Mexicans retained substantial, although declining, political power until the late 1880's and the coming of the railroads.

In the second period, what may be considered conventional political activity began, born in a context of violence and suppression. This period (beginning roughly in the 1920's) was a time of adaptation and accommodation, reflecting the changing position of Mexican Americans in the social structure of communities in the Southwest. A small Mexican-American middle class began to gain some strength and tried to come to terms politically with a still hostile and still threatening social environment.

This period of accommodation was typified by the efforts of the new Mexican-American groups to prepare and to "guide" the lower-class and newly arrived immigrant Mexican Americans to "become Americans." Notably, they did *not* press for full political participation. As we shall see, it was also during this period that at least some of the negative ideological assumptions about Mexicans held by the majority were reflected in their political activity.

The third period, beginning in the 1940's, saw increased political activity.

SOURCE: From Alfredo Cuellar, "Perspective on Politics," in Joan W. Moore with Alfredo Cuellar, *Mexican Americans*. Copyright © 1970. Reprinted by permission of Prentice-Hall, Inc.

Although the results fell far short of full participation in American political life, this period was characterized by a more aggressive style and more organization. During this time, so to speak, the Mexican Americans began to "play the game" according to Anglo political rules. The new idea of progress became associated with exercising the franchise and attempting to gain both elective and appointive office. The political achievements of Mexican Americans in New Mexico exemplified political progress. There, they had kept a political voice through the change from Mexican to U.S. rule: there were Mexicans in the state legislature and in Congress. Most areas, however, fell short of the accomplishment in New Mexico, especially south Texas, where political exclusion and manipulation were the heritage of violence and suppression. This exclusion and manipulation continued in many communities to be enforced by the local Anglo power structure.

The new aggressiveness that appeared after World War II was largely a phenomenon of urban life and reflected again the changing situation of Mexican Americans. They were becoming more urbanized, and more were middle class; they were increasingly American-born. World War II itself was one of the most important forces for change: hundreds of thousands of Mexican Americans served in the armed forces and gained radically new experiences, being sent outside their five-state *barrio* and given opportunities to develop a drastically changed view of American society.

In recent years a fourth type of political activity is becoming important. For convenience, it may be called the radicalization of Mexican-American political activity. This new style is exemplified in the growth of the *Chicano* movement. Although this movement assumes different forms in various parts of the Southwest and although its acceptance is far from uniform, it is a very different concept of political activity. It questions and challenges not only the assumptions of other generations of Mexican-American political leaders but some of the most basic assumptions of American politics as well.

These four phases are roughly sequential, as noted in this outline, but they also overlap a good deal. Violence continues to suppress Mexican-American political activity in many communities and to foster an apolitical attitude. In other areas there is a tentative and fearful kind of accommodation politics. Conventional political activity is slowly bringing a quite new political visibility to the Mexican Americans, which is particularly evdent in Washington with the recent creation of the Interagency Committee on Mexican American Affairs. Radical politics is also becoming institutionalized in some parts of the Southwest. Despite this confusing and complex overlapping and coexistence, we will discuss each type of political activity separately.

CONFLICT AND APOLITICS

Conflict between Mexicans and Anglo Americans characterized the American Southwest for the better part of the nineteenth century.[1] Let us recall some of the history of the region with specific reference to its political consequences. . . . The first sizeable number of Anglos who entered this region settled in Texas in 1821 under the leadership of Stephen Austin. Alarmed by their rapid increase in numbers and their failure to accept Mexican law and custom, the Mexican government shut off further Anglo immigration in 1830. The end result was the Texas Revolution of 1835–1836, just 15 years after the first legal immigration began. In spite of the Texas declaration of independence from Mexico, there were then 10 years of sporadic warfare, culminating in open warfare between the United States and Mexico in 1846 after the annexation of Texas by the United States.

The Treaty of Guadalupe Hidalgo ended the declared war, but it did not end the fighting between Mexicans and Anglos. Even in New Mexico, acquired "bloodlessly," an abortive rebellion followed the American occupation. In Texas, the next generation lived through an almost endless series of clashes, which reached the status of international warfare again in the late 1850's. Mexico's defeat and the humiliating invasion she suffered cost her nearly a third of her territory. For years afterward elements in Mexico dreamed of reconquest. On the American side the new territories were vast and remote from the central forces of government. The feeble hold that the United States had on the Southwest, the recurrent fears of Indian rebellion, and the divisive forces unleashed by the Civil War were all reflected in American fears of reconquest. Today, with the United States stretching from sea to sea, we rarely question the inevitability of this pattern. But a hundred-odd years ago, this "Manifest Destiny" had something of the character of a crusade, a national mission to be accomplished despite the acknowledged existence of great obstacles. In this climate of opinion, defeating Mexico was a very special victory, and holding these territories a special cause.

Anglos used force to gain control, and Mexicans retaliated with force. Texas, the scene of virtually all of this activity and the home of most Mexicans resident in the United States, saw hostilities between substantial armies and a nearly constant state of guerilla warfare. Many Mexicans, perhaps the most dissident, chose to return to Mexico. From the Texas point of view, many of those who remained were ready as always to join any successful marauder from across the border.

Of these, the most successful was Juan Cortina, who first invaded Texas in 1859 in a series of skirmishes known now as the Cortina Wars. These long "wars" illustrate many of the important themes in Texas-Mexican-American history, showing the comparative lack of distinction between "Mexican" and "Mexican American." They illustrate the racial nature of the conflicts, and they also show that these early decades of conflict were inextricably linked with some larger American problems, most notably the Civil War.

. . . It should be reiterated that the shift in land use entailed a shift in ownership. Often, political promises were made and broken; legal contracts were made and broken; legal protection for Mexicans—landowners and others—was promised and withheld. As Webb concludes in his history of the Texas Rangers, "The humble Mexicans doubted a government that would not protect their person and the higher classes distrusted one that would not safeguard their property. Here, indeed, was the rich soil in which to plant the seed of revolution and race war." [2]

Juan Cortina's expeditions began as a personal vendetta in Brownsville, Texas against an Anglo sheriff who used unnecessary force in arresting one of Cortina's former ranchhands. Cortina soon extended his campaign to a call for the general emancipation of Mexicans from American rule. He exhorted Mexicans to rise against their oppressors, to claim their lands and to drive out the *gringos*. Mexicans on both sides of the Rio Grande flocked to his camp. His army engaged troops in Texas in numerous battles, although eventually he and his army were forced to retreat into Mexico.

A few years later, after the Civil War, Cortina "helped" U.S. federal troops in the skirmishes and military occupation that preceded Reconstruction, an act that confirmed his unpopularity among Texas Anglos. Cortina went on to become brigadier general in the Mexican army and later, governor of the border state of Tamaulipas in northern Mexico. But as late as the middle of the 1870's he was still leading raids into Texas.

Hundreds of other leaders led groups ranging from the pseudo-military to the simple bandit (though Mexicans often viewed such bandits as *guerilleros* fighting for their people). In California, "outlaws" such as Tiburcio Vásquez and Joaquín Murieta (the latter so romanticized that it is difficult to separate fact from fantasy) and in Texas, Juan Flores Salinas, were variously remembered by Anglos anxious for law and order and by Mexicans unwilling to recognize the legitimacy of the American regime. A monument to Salinas was erected in 1875 and carries the inscription: *que combatiendo murió por su patria* ("who died fighting for his country").

The end of the Civil War, however, released troops for the "pacification" of the southwestern Indians, and the railroads could bring in hordes of Easterners looking for land and a new frontier. The era of overt violence between Anglo and Mexican American came to an end and was followed by a long period of quiet. With the beginning of revolution in Mexico in 1910 came the beginning of large-scale immigration. This process rekindled the historical distrust of Mexican Americans, especially now that their numbers were being rapidly increased by refugees from Mexico. It was therefore not surprising that this process would have a depressive effect on political participation among Mexican Americans at this time.

There seemed always to be incidents to keep the Americans fearful. In 1915, for example, a Mexican agent was arrested in a Texas border city with a detailed "Plan de San Diego, Texas," for an insurrection in the Southwest in which "all Anglos over the age of 16 would be put to death." Bandit activities in Texas were being carried out to finance the revolutionary plans of the Flores Magon brothers, who were then operating out of Los Angeles in an effort to begin yet another revolution in Mexico. I.W.W. and anarchist activities among the Mexicans added to the anxiety. Then, in 1916 General Pancho Villa climaxed a number of border raids with an attack on Columbus, New Mexico. The United States retaliated with the Punitive Expedition of

General John Pershing into northern Mexico. This comic-opera rerun of the tragic war with Mexico 70 years earlier increased distrust and resentment toward the Mexican-American population. Then came the famous Zimmerman Note of 1917, which appeared to confirm all suspicions: the Germans offered to unite Mexico and Japan with Germany for a war against the United States to restore the Southwest to Mexico and give the Far West to Japan. Mexico showed no interest in the scheme, but it touched a sensitive nerve in the United States. As usual, the Mexican Americans in the Southwest were caught in the middle.

Given the background of distrust and violent suppression it is not surprising that the style of the first important Mexican-American political groups should have been very circumspect. They could not have been anything but accommodationist.

THE POLITICS OF ADAPTATION

The politics of accommodation can be traced from the 1920's with the appearance of several new political organizations. A good example was the *Orden Hijos de America* (Order of the Sons of America), founded in San Antonio in 1921.[3] The founding members came almost entirely from the newly emerging middle class. Apparently, though, a few refugees from the Mexican Revolution were also involved. More important, both the social and the economic position of these founding members were precarious, and one can note in their announced objectives important concessions of the Anglo definition of the proper role for Mexicans in politics. For example, the goals of the OSA did *not* include demands for equality, either between Mexican Americans themselves or in terms of the dominant majority. Thus, only "citizens of the U.S. of Mexican or Spanish extraction, either native or naturalized" were eligible to join.[4] This exclusion by citizenship was meant— and acted—as an exclusionary mechanism. The implication was that Mexican Americans were more trustworthy to Anglos than Mexican nationals, and also more deserving of the benefits of American life.

This can be understood partly as a reaction to the Anglo conception of Mexicans as an undifferentiated group of low status, regardless of social achievement or citizenship. Hence, all were equally to be distrusted. As an organization of upwardly mobile individuals (albeit of modest achievements) OSA was concerned to show the dominant Anglo majority that they were different from other, "trouble-making" Mexicans. Of course citizenship would have been functionally useful if the *Orden* had been a truly political group, but the symbolic meaning of the requirement is indicated by another regulation. The organization declared itself "to assume no partisan stand, but rather to confine itself to training members for citizenship."

Obviously, "training members for citizenship" is not a strong political position, although presumably this included some activities aimed at increasing political participation, such as by voting. In general, though, this adaptive position could be interpreted as a reflection of the great social and economic vulnerability of Mexican Americans during the 1920's. Validation and recognition meant being as noncontroversial as possible—and preferably with declarations of loyalty to the United States of America.

OSA functioned for nearly ten years. By that time some splintering had begun to occur in the group and its chapters, and on February 17, 1929, several Mexican-American groups, among them the OSA itself, the Order of Knights of America, and the League of Latin-American Citizens, met in Corpus Christi, Texas. Out of this meeting a new organization emerged to meet the need for harmony and to present a unified front to the Anglo-American community. The theme of unity was embodied in the name of the new organization: the League of United Latin-American Citizens, or LULAC. Once again, membership was restricted to citizens of Mexican or Spanish extraction, one of the group's aims being "to develop within the members of our race the best, purest and most perfect type of a true and loyal citizen of the United States of America." [5]

This obvious sensitivity to Anglo opinion was intensified by the debate in Congress and in the press at the time concerning the rising tide of Mexican immigration. This affirmation of loyalty and citizenship may therefore be interpreted as one further example of a protective device used by middle-class Mexican Americans vis-a-vis the Anglo society.

Thus in 1929, to protect themselves from social and economic sanctions, the willingness of Mexican Americans to assert even minimum political demands was tempered at all times and in all expressions by a desire to reaffirm citizenship and loyalty to the United States. It is not surprising that there was at this time no pressure for Mexican civil rights, particularly if it might have involved any kind of open demonstrations. (As a matter of fact, Article 1 of the LULAC's by-laws contains one item that states, "We shall oppose any radical and violent demonstration which may tend to create conflicts and disturb the peace and tranquility of our country.") Once again, a statement designed to appease, to reassure those Anglos who feared the worst. And it also served as a warning to Mexicans who might conceivably entertain such radical notions.

Notable by its omission among 25 articles is any demand for any form of cultural pluralism, despite the willingness of some members to preserve a semblance of their ethnic identity.

Throughout, the aims and purposes of the new organization reflected its middle-class orientation, a conformity to the standards of Texas Anglo society, and above all, an emphasis on adapting to American society, instead of emphasis on aggressive political participation, and much less on any kind of political participation based on a separate ethnic identity.

Such circumspection must, as we have noted earlier, be judged in the context of the political milieu of Texas in the 1920's. Both Mexicans and Negroes "knew their place." Although Mexicans did vote in Texas, in some counties the votes were under the control of an Anglo political boss.[6] In other counties

Mexicans seldom voted because of the poll tax and other such limitations. The influence of the Anglo *patrón* may be seen in the following letter written by one such boss, who felt it necessary to scold his "Mexican-Texas friends" for forming such a group as LULAC:

> I have been and still consider myself as your Leader or Superior Chief . . . I have always sheltered in my soul the most pure tenderness for the Mexican-Texas race and have watched over your interests to the best of my ability and knowledge. . . . Therefore I disapprove the political activity of groups which have no other object than to organize Mexican-Texas voters into political groups for guidance by other leaders. . . . I have been able to maintain the Democratic Party in power with the aid of my Mexican-Texas friends, and in all the time that has passed we have had no need for clubs or political organizations.[7]

Between hostility and economic vulnerability Mexican Americans were making the best of a difficult situation, which was very slow to change. LULAC gained power among the middle class and ultimately became a spokesman for those Mexican Americans who had achieved a measure of economic and social advancement. In Texas it is still an important political group. Other organizations (as well as branch chapters of LULAC) appeared throughout the Southwest, and many were modeled after LULAC. All of them skirted the question of aggressive political action with considerable skill. Accommodation was the style in the 1920's and 1930's; it may very well have been the only possible style. Since World War II LULAC has taken a much more aggressive stance, a change preceded by a number of changes in the structure of the Mexican-American population.

THE POLITICIZATION OF MEXICAN AMERICANS

The politicization of Mexican-American communities in the Southwest dates only from the years following World War II. For the most part politicization was prefaced by deep social changes among the Mexican-American population, discussed elsewhere in this book. In sum, they brought Mexicans into new and partly unforeseen contact with American society, particularly in urban areas. The word "urbanization" hardly conveys their impact. A demand for labor brought hundreds of thousands of Mexicans into cities from rural areas, and at the same time many hundreds of thousands of young Mexican-American men found themselves in uniform—and racially invisible to Anglos from other areas of the United States and to other peoples in foreign lands. At the same time, however, their families began to find that the urban areas of the Southwest, like rural ones, were highly discriminatory (this was the time of the "zoot suit riots" in Los Angeles and San Diego, California[8]). (In the rural areas, however, the social fabric that supported and justified discrimination was hardly changed.)

In the cities the urban migrants could find only poor housing, the lowest unskilled employment, and restricted access to schools and other public facilities. As before, few Mexican Americans took part in political activity, although the tradition of political accommodation now seemed outmoded. So did the political organizations built to formalize this relationship to the larger community. A middle class had begun to increase rather rapidly as a result of wartime prosperity, and it was increasingly dissatisfied. Against this background a group of articulate former servicemen (helped substantially by the educational and training benefits of the G.I. Bill of Rights) began to press for changes in the community. In Los Angeles a more open environment facilitated a new alliance with labor elements, Anglo civil leaders, and religious leaders.

One outcome of this alliance was the California-based Community Service Organization (CSO). In Los Angeles the CSO tried to develop indigenous leaders to organize community activity around local issues, using the techniques of larger-scale grassroots community organization. In this manner the Community Service Organization mobilized large segments of the Mexican-American community into activities directed against restricted housing, police brutality, segregated schools, inequitable justice, and discriminatory employment, all problems endemic in the Mexican-American areas of southern California as much as in other parts of the Southwest. In this process CSO became an important and meaningful post-World War II political phenomenon in the Mexican-American community.

In general CSO pressed for full and equal rights for Mexican Americans. The new emphasis was the extra appeal for active and increased participation by as many elements of the community as possible. Therefore, in contrast to previous organizations, CSO tended to be more egalitarian. Under the influence of an outside catalyst (Saul Alinsky's Industrial Areas Foundation) it became a group that no longer served as the vehicle of a relatively few and successful Mexican Americans. Although the leadership tended to be new middle class, on the whole it made an effort to recruit members of the working class and other lower-class elements, including new arrivals from Mexico. CSO also had some non-Mexican members, although they were comparatively few.

This idea of an alliance of equals from various strata of Mexican-American society became important. In contrast to the paternalism of previous organizations such as LULAC, there was little concern with the assimilation of lower-class elements into the mainstream of American life. Nor, for that matter, did CSO show any interest in "Mexican culture." The guiding idea of CSO was to cope with concrete and immediate social, economic, and political problems.

The founders of CSO assumed that American institutions were basically responsive to the needs and demands of the Mexican-American population. There were no questions about the legitimacy of these institutions; it was always assumed that proper community organization and action would force Anglo institutions to respond to the needs of Mexican Americans. Accordingly, getting Mexicans to exercise the right to vote became a prime CSO objective. Members organized large-scale nonpartisan community drives to register voters. In Los Angeles these registration drives rather significantly increased the number of Spanish-surname voters. The immediate results were electoral victories by Mexican-American candidates, there and in nearby communities. Furthermore, CSO pressure on public housing authorities, on the Fair Employment Practices Commission (FEPC), and against police brutality also yielded results. Housing authorities eased discriminatory practices, Mexican-American representation was included in the FEPC, and the police department agreed "to go easy on Mexicans" on the Los Angeles East Side.

At the time members considered CSO tactics radical and militant, and throughout the 1950's the CSO remained a politically powerful organization that emphasized direct, grassroots community action. Numerous CSO chapters were organized throughout the state of California, each duplicating the Alinsky approach to community organization.

In recent years CSO has declined as a potent community organization, in part because of the withdrawal of financial support from the Industrial Areas Foundation, and in part because it lost some of its most energetic members. For example, the single most well-known former member of CSO, César Chávez, split with the urban-centered CSO to organize a union of farm workers. Also contributing to the decline of CSO was the rise of competing organizations of Mexican Americans.

Other organizations in the Southwest reflect the aggressive political style growing after World War II. In Texas, there is the important American G.I. Forum. The G.I. Forum was founded by a south Texas physician, Dr. Hector Garcia; the immediate cause of its formation was the refusal of a funeral home in Three Rivers, Texas, to bury a Mexican-American war veteran in 1948. The incident attracted national attention, and the idea of the G.I. Forum spread rapidly not only in Texas but also throughout the Southwest, to several midwestern states, and to Washington, D.C. Although the Forum is concerned with nonpartisan civic action, it has moved increasingly toward more direct and aggressive political activities. In Texas, where its main strength lies, the G.I. Forum launched intensive "Get out the vote" and "Pay your poll tax" drives in the 1950's. Subsequently, it has continued voter registration drives since the repeal of the Texas poll tax. On a number of other issues, the Forum continues to act as a spokesman against the problems that beset the Mexican-American community in Texas.

If the CSO and the American G.I. Forum reflect the goals of the immediate postwar years, two political groups founded in the late 1950's show a shift in both the political goals and the resources available in the community. In California the Mexican American Political Association (MAPA), founded in 1958, and in Texas the Political Association of Spanish-Speaking Organizations (PASSO) were organized essentially as groups pressuring the political system at the party level. These were not primarily attempts to organize the Mexican American poor to register and vote; they were efforts to use growing middle-class strength to win concessions for Mexican Americans from the Anglo-dominated political parties. Essentially the goal of both associations was simply to get Mexican Americans into political office, either as nominees for elective office in the regular parties or as appointees of elected Anglo officials. Thus the best-publicized effort of either group was the successful deposition of the Anglo political structure in Crystal City, Texas, in the early 1960's. In this venture, PASSO joined with some non-Mexican groups, notably the Teamsters and the Catholic Bishops' Committee for the Spanish Speaking. (Although the victory in Crystal City was short-lived, it was as significant to Texas Mexicans as the more recent victory of a Negro mayor in Mississippi was to the black community.)

Both MAPA and PASSO gain strength by virtue of their statewide connections, which are particularly important in the outlying rural areas where repression has been a norm. Statewide ties give courage and support to local efforts. (At this writing one of the strongest MAPA chapters in California is the chapter in the Coachella valley, a citrus- and date-growing area not far from Palm Springs. The local chairman, a vociferous spokesman for Mexican-American laborers, is constantly subject to harassment. He is also constantly in demand outside the immediate area. The intervention of outside elements in a local and rather repressive situation has reduced isolation and repression. As in Crystal City, one of MAPA's victories has been the election of Mexican-American officials in the grower-dominated town of Coachella.)

Although both MAPA and PASSO are still largely confined to California and Texas, respectively, there are branches and organizational efforts in other states. The two associations once considered amalgamation into a regional group; but, incredibly, the effort failed because the two groups could not agree on a common name. Texas Mexicans could not afford the then too overt ethnic pride suggested by "Mexican American;" and the California group would not accept the euphemism "Spanish-speaking." At these discussions, one disgusted delegate finally proposed "CACA" (a Spanish equivalent of the English "doo-doo") to represent the "Confederated Alliance of *Chicano* Associations." Interestingly, only in such an intensely in-group situation could the name *Chicano* be suggested. At the time this word could not be used for a serious political discussion.

THE CHICANO MOVEMENT

Throughout this chapter we have suggested that Mexican-American political activity has often been related to social structural factors. Because much of this political activity was possible only after certain structural changes in Mexican-American life, there were seldom any real alternatives beyond simple reaction to Anglo pressure. The importance of the *Chicano* movement as an alternative to pressures from the majority society can hardly be overemphasized. It is a distinctively novel development in the Mexican-American community. The *Chicano* movement developed in southern California no earlier than 1966, and it is already a sharp new force in the political expression of Mexican Americans throughout the Southwest.

The *Chicano* ideology includes a broad definition of political activity. Ironically, such thinking was possible only for a new generation of urbanized and "Anglicized" (that is, assimilated) young Mexican Americans, who were much less burdened by social and class restrictions than their elders were and whose education had exposed them to new ideas.

The exact beginnings of the movement are obscure. There is some evidence that the *Chicano* movement grew out of a group of conferences held at Loyola University in Los Angeles in the summer of 1966. As originally conceived by its Catholic sponsors, the conferences were to create a fairly innocuous youth organization for the middle-class Mexican students attending various colleges throughout California. Very quickly the movement grew beyond the intent or control of its sponsors (Loyola has never been very noted for its interest in Mexican-American education) and it drew in yet others, not students and not middle class, who were attracted by the ideology of *chicanismo*. Thus it cannot be understood as a movement limited to the young, to students, or even to urban areas. It must also be understood as including the followers of Reies Tijerina in northern New Mexico and César Chávez' embattled union of striking farm workers in central California. In 1969 Rodolfo (Corky) González was the principal leader and inspiration of the *Chicano* movement in Denver although his interests were mainly in urban civic action. Moreover, "Corky" has organized regional youth conferences and his influence spreads far beyond the local area. No one leader has yet emerged in southern California or in Texas.

As this wide range of activity shows, the *Chicano* movement is extremely heterogenous, and its elements have different aims and purposes. In this way the movement cuts across social class, regional, and generational lines. Its aims range from traditional forms of social protest to increasingly more radical goals that appear as a sign of an emerging nationalism. It is a social movement, in that it can be described as "pluralistic behavior functioning as an organized mass effort directed toward a change of established folkways or institutions." [9] The dynamic force of the movement is its ideology—*chicanismo*.

The new ideology is advanced as a challenge to the dominant Anglo beliefs concerning Mexicans as well as to the beliefs of Mexican Americans themselves. Although we have emphasized that students are by no means the only element of the *Chicano* movement, we will reconstruct *chicanismo* primarily as it has been developed among students. Actually, this is only one of several ideological strands but it is the most consistently developed, thus the best illustration of the change from protest to nationalism and a synthesis of the ideology of *chicanismo*.

The first student form of the *Chicano* movement coincided with the development of new student organizations in California universities and colleges in 1966 and 1967. Some of these groups were the United Mexican-American Students (UMAS), the Mexican-American Student Association (MASA),

Mexican-American Student Confederation (MASC), and Movimiento Estu-
diantil Chicano de Aztlán (MECHA). More recently the Mexican-American
Youth Organization (MAYO) has appeared, with particular strength in Texas.
(MAYO is also the name adopted by the new organizations of *Chicanos* in
California prisons.) These student groups were at first concerned with a rather
narrow range of problems in the field of education, particularly those concerned with increasing the number of Mexican-American students in college.
To the extent that these student groups were active in the Mexican-American
community, they were involved with various forms of protest against specific
and longstanding grievances, such as police brutality and inferior educational
facilities, although other forms of community activity also involved political
campaigns.

Chicano student groups thus have never repudiated ordinary forms of political activity, although for them such forms as voting constitute only one
political alternative. Actually, given the wide range of problems facing the
Mexican-American community, *Chicanos* view conventional forms of political
activity as perhaps the least effective. Instead, they favor forms of confrontation as the most effective means to gain access for the traditionally excluded
Chicano, even though it has, on occasion, led to violence. In general, this
conception of politics contrasts sharply with the ideas of more conservative
Mexican-American leaders, most of whom adhere to very limited and "safe"
politics with an emphasis on voting and "working within the system" to gain
political leverage. This is not to say that *Chicanos* reject working for social
change within the system; as a matter of fact, much recent activity has fo-
cussed on bringing about change in the universities and colleges as well as in
the public school systems. Nevertheless, whereas the moderates seek to bring
major change in American society through nonviolent means, the more militant speak of the need for "revolutionary activity," though they often leave
the details and direction of this revolution unspecified. While they admire
the life style and aspirations of revolutionary leaders like Ché Guevara, they
have thus far made no systematic theoretical connection between the *Chicano*
movement and the general literature on revolution. The theoretical underpinnings of the *Chicano* movement thus often lack a strong direction.

And yet, the advent of the *Chicano* movement does represent a revolutionary phenomenon among Mexican Americans. As we shall see, most of the
change from traditional forms lies in (or is reflected in) the ideology of *chicanismo*. Basically eclectic, *chicanismo* draws inspiration from outside the
United States and outside the Mexican-American experience. The Cuban Revolution, for example, exerts some influence, as do the career and ideals of Ché
Guevara. For instance, the Brown Berets (a *Chicano* youth group) affect the
life style of this revolutionary. Black Power also offers something of a model.
Most recently, *Chicanos* have resurrected the Mexican revolutionary tradition.

Basically, however, *chicanismo* focuses on the life experience of the Mexican
in the United States. It challenges the belief system of the majority society
at the same time that it attempts to reconstruct a new image for Mexican

Americans themselves. *Chicanos* assume that along with American Indians and black Americans, Mexicans live in the United States as a conquered people. This idea allows *chicanismo* to explain the evolution of the *Chicano* as essentially conflictful (sic). In each conflictual relationship with Anglos, the Mexicans lost out and were thus forced to live in the poverty and degradation attendant upon those with the status of a conquered people. This is no better illustrated than by the Mexicans' loss of communal and private property. As a result, they had no choice but to work the land for a *patrón* (usually an Anglo, but sometimes a Mexican, who exploited his own people). When the Mexican was thrown off the land, he was forced to become an unattached wage earner, often a migrant farm worker; or he might migrate to a city, where the exploitation continued. In any event, *chicanismo* emphasizes that the Mexican was transformed into a rootless economic commodity, forced either to depend on migrant farm work or to sell his labor in the urban centers, where his fate depended upon the vicissitudes of the economy. Ironically, indispensable as Mexican labor was for the economic development of the Southwest, the Mexican got little recognition for his contribution and even less benefit from it.

Chicanos therefore see the economic expansion of the Southwest as essentially a dehumanizing process. They also point out that during periods of economic depression in the United States, when the Mexican became "superfluous" and "expensive," Anglo society had no qualms about attempting to eliminate Mexicans from the United States, as in the repatriations of the 1930's. The repatriations are viewed as a conscious attempt to eliminate the *Chicano* from American society.

The thrust of *chicanismo* is not only economic, but also cultural. In many ways, the exploitation and suppression of his culture is what most angers the *Chicano*, who views the attempt to deracinate Mexican culture in the Southwest as the reason why Mexican Americans are disoriented about their culture and often attempt to deny it. The *Chicano* points out that the Anglo himself often views Mexicans with a great degree of ambivalence. Anglos oftentimes take over aspects of "Spanish" (which is really Mexican) culture and at the same time deny it to the Mexican himself. In this fashion Mexicans were denied the development of a more autonomous cultural life, especially as it touches upon Spanish language use, the arts, and so on. (This was done in spite of the agreements made in the signing of the Treaty of Guadalupe Hidalgo. Early drafts of the treaty contained Mexican government efforts to make formal recognition of language rights for Mexicans who chose to remain in the United States after the Mexican War. These provisions were not approved by the U.S. Senate.)

Worse yet, the ideology goes on, the cultural suppression continues to the present day, reinforced by Anglo institutions, particularly the schools. The extreme position (although by no means infrequent) is represented by the fact that Mexican-American students in the public schools are corporally punished for using Spanish, their native language. Under these circumstances, it is understandable that the Mexican-American student remains ignorant and often ashamed of his past. When the Mexican is mentioned in textbooks, it is in a romanticized and stereotypically Anglicized version of "Spanish culture" that may be congenial to Anglos but is remote and irrelevant to the Mexican American. The *Chicano* considers this type of whitewashed "Spanish" culture particularly galling because he feels that while Anglos may selectively choose certain motifs from Mexican culture, the person behind the culture, the Mexican himself, is given neither recognition nor respect.

Chicanismo also focuses on race, and in some ways this emphasis constitutes one of the most controversial aspects of *chicanismo*. It is argued that Anglo racism denies the Mexican his ethnicity by making him ashamed of his "Mexican-ness." Mexican ancestry, instead of being a source of pride, becomes a symbol of shame and inferiority. As a consequence, Mexicans spend their lives apologizing or denying their ancestry, to the point that many dislike and resent being called "Mexican," preferring "Spanish American," "Latin," "Latin American," and similar euphemisms. For these reasons, the term "*Chicano*" is now insisted upon by activists as a symbol of the new assertiveness.

Advocates of *chicanismo* therefore hope to reconstruct the Mexican Americans' concept of themselves by appeals to pride of a common history, culture and "race." *Chicanismo* attempts to redefine the Mexicans' identity on the basis not of class, generation, or area of residence but on a unique and shared experience in the United States. This means that appeals for political action, economic progress, and reorientation of cultural identity are cast in terms of the common history, culture, and ethnic background of *la raza*.

Chicano ideologues insist that social advance based on material achievement is, in the final analysis, less important than social advance based on *la raza*; they reject what they call the myth of American individualism. The *Chicano* movement feels that it cannot afford the luxury of individualism; if Mexicans are to confront the problems of their group realistically they must begin to act along collective lines. Hence, the stirrings of a new spirit of what *chicanismo* terms "cultural nationalism" among the Mexican Americans of the Southwest.

Chicanismo has led not only to increased participation in community activities, but also to a heightened and often intense interest in cultural life. *Chicano* poets, playwrights, journalists, and writers of all varieties have suddenly appeared. There are *Chicano* theater groups in several large cities (often known as the *teatro urbano*) and one nationally known and well-travelled group from Delano, California (*El teatro campesino*), which tells the story not only of the striking California farm workers but of *Chicanos* in general. Newspapers and magazines also reflect this desire to disseminate the idea of *chicanismo*. Throughout the Southwest numerous *Chicano* "underground" newspapers and magazines publishing literary materials have emerged. There is even a *Chicano* Press Association, a regional association representing *Chicano* publications from Texas to California. Furthermore, because of the strong base in colleges and universities, a serious and generally successful drive to develop "ethnic studies" programs has appeared, especially in California. As part of the drive to spread the idea of *chicanismo* in education, *Chicanos* place an emphasis on Mexican contributions to American society, thus giving *Chicano* college students a new conception of their past and present.

Chicano student groups share an orientation similar to that of black students, and on occasion they cooperate and support each other on similar demands. (There is more mutual support between black and brown students than between their counterparts at the community level.) The alliance between black and brown students, however, has not been close, harmonious, or continuous. *Chicano* student organizations have not yet been significantly involved with Anglo radical student groups, although these groups sometimes claim their support or claim that they are working for the benefit of *Chicanos*.

THE ECHO OF CHICANISMO

How much has this student manifestation of the *Chicano* movement affected the larger Mexican community? At this writing the ideological reverberations have been considerable, particularly among the young people of college age and including also those in the secondary schools. We must not forget that the Mexican-American population is very young. Some counterparts of *Chicano* college militancy have appeared throughout the Southwest in high schools as, for example, among students in Denver, Los Angeles, San Francisco, and many smaller cities.

The demands have often been modest, in most instances no more than for increased counselling services for Mexican-American students and other changes in the methods and content of instruction. In some Texas cities and in Denver, Colorado, the student militants further demanded the end of punishment for using Spanish on the school grounds. In most cases the school boards have acceded to this particular demand. But the reaction of the Anglo community has often been fierce. In Los Angeles a school "walk-out" by Mexican-American students in 1968 resulted in the arrest of 13 alleged leaders for criminal conspiracy. In Denver a sharp reaction by the police resulted in the injury of 17 persons and the arrest of 40. In other areas in the Southwest there have been similar, if less publicized, responses to *Chicano* militancy.

Neither the Anglo reaction nor the rapid spread of *chicanismo* should be taken to mean that a full-blown social movement is in progress among Mexican Americans. In many areas, on the contrary, established Mexican-American leaders have dissociated themselves from the *Chicanos*. For instance, a school walkout by Mexican students in Kingsville, Texas brought an angry denunciation from a Mexican-American Congressman from Texas and other community leaders. At the same time, the *Chicano* movement poses a very difficult dilemma for most older Mexican Americans. They sympathize with the goals of *chicanismo*, yet they fear that the radical means used to pursue these ends will undermine their own hard-earned social and economic gains. The Anglo community expects a denunciation of what it considers to be irresponsible acts of these young people. But for the older leaders to oppose the *Chicano* protest might be a slow form of personal political suicide as well as acting to exacerbate divisiveness in the Mexican-American community.

In California, *Chicano* student groups have grown rapidly; they have acquired the power to pass on Mexican-American faculty appointments in many high schools and colleges. Typically such faculty members are avidly sought to assist with the new ethnic studies programs and centers. Ultimately, though, *Chicano* students are faced by responsibility to the community. These students are aware that the popularity of *chicanismo* among Mexican-American students means a major opportunity for the development of an entire new generation of young professionals to carry these ideas back to the Mexican-American community.

Beyond the universities there have been other sources of support, some of them quite substantial. Grants and direct organizing assistance have come from American Protestant denominations, notably the National Council of Churches. In 1968 a substantial ($630,000) grant from the Ford Foundation to the Southwest Council of La Raza (headquarters in Phoenix) helped the organization of a number of militant *Chicano* groups. The Southwest Council of La Raza considers itself permanent and accepts money for "barrio development" from not only the Ford Foundation but churches, labor groups, and other interested organizations. Both the announced ideals of the council and its membership assure commitment to the ideals of *chicanismo*.

The *Chicano* movement began as a protest. Only later did its dynamics carry it toward an increasing cultural nationalism. The first steps toward social change did not go beyond demands for equality of opportunity for Mexican Americans, which are still being made (by the less militant in the movement). Until recently no Mexican American had tried to define the problems of the community in any terms except those of assimilation. It is precisely these ideas of assimilation and social "adjustment" that the *Chicano* militant rejects. As a new alternative, *chicanismo* represents a conception of an autonomous and self-determining social life for Mexican Americans.

It is interesting that it was not until the 1960's that the *Chicano* leaders emerged to question some of the oldest and most fundamental assumptions of Mexicans in American society. This protest probably would not have been possible in a period of general social calm and stability. That the *Chicano* protest emerged when it did is perhaps due in large part to the emergence of other social groups that also began to question basic notions about American society. But if these other groups feel a sense of alienation in American society, the *Chicano*'s alienation is doubly acute. It is not only from American society that he feels alienated; he also feels left out of the mainstream of Mexican history and, simultaneously, he feels a sense of guilt for having "deserted" the homeland. It is this sense of being in two cultures yet belonging to neither (*ni aquí ni allá*) that is the source of his most profound alienation and now, anger. It is against this background that the *Chicano* is attempting with a deep sense of urgency to reconstruct his history, his culture, his sense of identity.

In practical terms the result is increasing radicalization, with which comes a new set of problems. Cultural nationalism has emerged, bringing with it questions that must be answered if the *Chicano* movement is to become a potent force for all Mexican Americans in their diverse circumstances throughout the Southwest and other parts of the United States.

NOTES

1. The historical material in this chapter is drawn heavily from the historical source material cited in . . . WALTER PRESCOTT WEBB, *The Texas Rangers: A Century of Frontier Defense* (Boston: Houghton Mifflin, 1935), and . . . RALPH GUZMÁN, "The Political Socialization of the Mexican American People" (unpublished manuscript, 1967).
2. WEBB, *Texas Rangers*, p. 176.
3. This section draws heavily on GUZMÁN, "Political Socialization." See also MIGUEL D. TIRADO, "Mexican American Community Political Organization" (unpublished manuscript in files of Ralph Guzmán, University of California Santa Cruz, 1969), and ROBERT A. CUÉLLAR, "A Social and Political History of the Mexican-American Population of Texas, 1929–1963" (unpublished Master's thesis, North Texas State University, Denton, Texas, 1969).
4. Article III, constitution of OSA, cited by O. DOUGLAS WEEKS, "The League of United Latin-American Citizens," *The Southwestern Political and Social Science Quarterly*, X (December 1929), p. 260, cited in TIRADO, "Mexican American Political Organization," p. 5.
5. WEEKS, "League," p. 260, cited in GUZMÁN, "Political Socialization," p. 355.
6. Mexican American voting was "managed," in V. O. Key's term. For a specific discussion of Texas-Mexican-American politics see his *Southern Politics* (New York: Vintage edition, Alfred A. Knopf, 1949), pp. 271–76. Key also puts the Texas pattern into the general Southern political context.
7. Letter published in the *Hidalgo County Independent*, Edinburg, Texas, March 8, 1929, cited in WEEKS, "League," pp. 275–76, cited in GUZMÁN, "Political Socialization," p. 160.
8. The zoot suit riots were a series of racial incidents in Los Angeles during the summer of 1943—later called "race riots"—between U.S. servicemen and Mexican-American youth (also called "pachuco riots"). These battles, the humiliation of Mexican Americans, ensuing mass arrests of Mexicans (not of the servicemen who were later shown to have provoked them) had a deep impact on the Mexican-American community. It resulted immediately in a sharp increase in Anglo discrimination of all kinds against Mexicans and laid the ground for a deep anger and bitterness among the Mexican-American community which had been largely impotent to deal with the situation. McWilliams gives an account of the riots in *North from Mexico*.
9. As defined by ABEL, in *Why Hitler Came to Power*, as cited in MARTIN OPPENHEIMER, *The Urban Guerilla* (Chicago: Quadrangle Books, 1969), p. 19.

"Introduction" from Occupied America

Rodolfo Acuña

History can either oppress or liberate a people. Generalizations and stereotypes about the Mexican have been circulated in the United States for over 124 years. Adjectives such as "treacherous," "lazy," "adulterous," and terms such as "meskin," or "greaser," have become synonymous with "Mexican" in the minds of many Anglo-Americans. Little has been done to expose the false premises on which such cultural and racial slurs have been based. Incomplete or biased analyses by historians have perpetuated factual errors and created myths. The Anglo-American public has believed and encouraged the historian's and social commentator's portrayal of the Mexican as "the enemy." The tragedy is that the myths have degraded the Mexican people—not only in the eyes of those who feel superior, but also in their own eyes.

Many of these myths have their foundation in the nineteenth century, when Anglo-Americans began infiltrating into the Mexican territory of Texas. They were nurtured by the accounts these Anglos gave of their Mexican neighbors, by the clash between Anglos and Mexicans in the Texas revolt of 1836, and by the Mexican-American War that erupted in 1846. Anglo-American historians glorified and justified the deeds of the "heroic" men who "won the West"—at the expense of the Mexicans, who were fighting to preserve their homeland. The Mexican became the outsider, and his subordinate status in the United States after 1848 was explained as the inevitable result of a clash between dynamic, industrious Anglo-Americans and apathetic, culturally deprived Mexicans.

These are myths that must be challenged—not only for the sake of historical accuracy, but for another, and even more crucial, reason. Mexicans—Chicanos—in the United States today are an oppressed people. They are citizens, but their citizenship is second class at best. They are exploited and manipulated by those with more power. And, sadly, many believe that the only way to get along in Anglo-America is to become "Americanized" themselves. Awareness of their history—of their contributions and struggles, of the fact that they were not the "treacherous enemy" that Anglo-American histories have said they were—can restore pride and a sense of heritage to a people who have been oppressed for so long. In short, awareness can help them to liberate themselves.

It would be impossible in the space of one volume to refute the assumptions and historical inaccuracies of 124 years of Southwest history. This text, then, is not an attempt at a definitive history of the Chicano and his struggle toward liberation. Rather, I have attempted to underscore my thesis that Chicanos are a colonized people in the United States through the use of both public records and secondary sources. The result, I hope, is a clear alternative to traditional explanations offered by historians. But even more, I hope that the story of occupied America, and its thematic approach to Anglo imperialism, will spur Third World historians to take on the monumental task of primary research that still needs to be done in relation to the Southwest and the Chicano. Then, and perhaps much more effectively than I have done, they can challenge the conclusions of other historians.

Before focusing on my thesis of the colonization of the Chicano, I would like to clarify several points. *First*, the title of this monograph might appear to be a misnomer. Many readers will argue that *Occupied Mexico* would have been more appropriate since the monograph is about the occupation of an area formerly belonging to Mexico. While this argument is valid, I feel that *Occupied America* is more precise, for "America" is the identification that Europeans gave to two continents. When the name was later appropriated by thirteen colonies, the designation "America" was deemed the exclusive province of the new nation, and United States citizens considered themselves the "Americans." Chicanos, as well as other peoples, however, refute this exclusivity and correctly maintain that all inhabitants—on both north and south continents—are Americans and that the whole hemisphere is indeed America. Thus, I hold that Anglo control of Mexico's northwest territory is an occupation of a part of the American hemisphere.

Although some readers might consider it a trivial matter, I feel compelled to distinguish between United States Americans and other Americans. Thus, in referring to people of the United States, I have used the term Anglo-American, or simply Anglo (derived from Anglo-Saxon), to underline the distinction. Similarly, I refer to U.S. settlers in Texas as Anglo-*Tejanos* (Anglo-Texans) in contrast to the native Texan population, which was Indian and Mexican.

Second, some U.S. citizens of Mexican extraction might object to the identification of "Chicano" in the title, for many call themselves simply *Mexicanos* or Mexicans. Moreover, a minority refer to themselves as Spanish-Americans or Latin Americans. Recently, the label Mexican-American has become popular, following the hyphenization tradition of other ethnic groups. Anglo-Americans have promoted the use of this label, and for a time it seemed as if it would be universally accepted. But within the last four years, activists have begun to question this identification. At first, some just dropped the hyphen and symbolically broke with the Americanization tradition. Others sought to identify themselves with a name of their own choice. They selected the term Chicano, which had often been used to designate lower-class Mexicans. Even though it had negative connotations for the middle class, activists considered that it was a symbol of resistance as well as a demand for self-determination. Such self-identification is, I believe, a necessary step in the process of awareness by which Chicanos can liberate themselves collectively.

In this work, I often use the terms Mexican and Chicano interchangeably. Mexican is used more in the first part of the book in recognition of the fact that nineteenth-century Mexicans were a conquered people. In the second part, which deals with the twentieth century and the changing situation in the United States, Chicano is used to distinguish Mexicans living north of the border from those residing in Mexico.

Central to the thesis of this monograph is my contention that the conquest of the Southwest created a colonial situation in the traditional sense—with the Mexican land and population being controlled by an imperialistic United States. Further, I contend that this colonization—with variations—is still with us today. Thus, I refer to the colony, initially, in the traditional definition of the term, and later (taking into account the variations) as an internal colony.

From the Chicano perspective, it is obvious that these two types of colonies are a reality. In discussions with non-Chicano friends, however, I have encountered considerable resistance. In fact, even colleagues sympathetic to the Chicano cause vehemently deny that Chicanos are—or have been—colonized. They admit the exploitation and discrimination, but they add that this has been the experience of most "Americans"—especially European and Asian immigrants and black Americans. While I agree that exploitation and racism have victimized most out-groups in the United States, this does not preclude the reality of the colonial relationship between the Anglo-American privileged and the Chicano.

I feel that the parallels between the Chicanos' experience in the United States and the colonization of other Third World peoples are too similar to dismiss. Attendant to the definition of colonization are the following conditions:

1. The land of one people is invaded by people from another country, who later use military force to gain and maintain control.

2. The original inhabitants become subjects of the conquerors involuntarily.

3. The conquered have an alien culture and government imposed upon them.

4. The conquered become the victims of racism and cultural genocide and are relegated to a submerged status.

5. The conquered are rendered politically and economically powerless.

6. The conquerors feel they have a "mission" in occupying the area in question and believe that they have undeniable privileges by virtue of their conquest.

These points also apply to the relationship between Chicanos and Anglos in Mexico's northwest territory.

In the traditional historian's viewpoint, however, there are two differences that impede universal acceptance of the reality of Anglo-American colonialism in this area.

1. Geographically the land taken from Mexico bordered the United States rather than being an area distant from the "mother country."

Too many historians have accepted—subconsciously, if not conveniently—the myth that the area was always intended to be an integral part of the United States. Instead of conceptualizing the conquered territory as northern Mexico, they perceive it in terms of the "American" Southwest. Further, the stereotype of the colonialist pictures him wearing Wellington boots and carrying a swagger stick, and that stereotype is usually associated with overseas situations—certainly not in territory contiguous to an "expanding" country.

2. Historians also believe that the Southwest was won in fair and just warfare, as opposed to unjust imperialism.

The rationale has been that the land came to the United States as the result of competition, and in winning the game, the country was generous in paying for its prize. In the case of Texas, they believe Mexico attacked the "freedom-loving" Anglo-Americans. It is difficult for citizens of the United States to accept the fact that their nation has been and is imperialistic. Imperialism, to them, is an affliction of other countries.

While I acknowledge the geographical proximity of the area—and the fact that this is a modification of the strict definition of colonialism—I refute the conclusion that the Texan and Mexican-American wars were just or that Mexico provoked them. Further, I illustrate in this monograph that the conditions attendant to colonialism, listed above, accompanied the U.S. take-over of the Southwest. For these reasons, I maintain that colonialism in the traditional sense did exist in the Southwest, and that the conquerors dominated and exploited the conquered.

The colonization still exists today, but as I mentioned before, there are variations. Anglo-Americans still exploit and manipulate Mexicans and still relegate them to a submerged caste. Mexicans are still denied political and economic determination and are still the victims of racial stereotypes and racial slurs promulgated by those who feel they are superior. Thus, I contend that Mexicans in the United States are still a colonized people, but now the colonization is *internal*—it is occurring *within* the country rather than being imposed by an external power. The territories of the Southwest are states within the United States, and theoretically permanent residents of Mexican extraction are U.S. citizens. Yet the rights of citizenship are too often circumvented or denied outright.

In reality, there is little difference between the Chicano's status in the *traditional colony* of the nineteenth century and in the *internal colony* of the twentieth century. The relationship between Anglos and Chicanos remains the same—that of master-servant. The principal difference is that Mexicans in the traditional colony were indigenous to the conquered land. Now, while some are descendants of Mexicans living in the area before the conquest, large numbers are technically descendants of immigrants. After 1910, in fact, almost one-eighth of Mexico's population migrated to the United States, largely as a result of the push-and-pull of economic necessity. Southwest agribusinessmen "imported" Mexican workers to fill the need for cheap labor, and this influx signaled the beginning of even greater Anglo manipulation of Mexican settlements or colonias.

The original colonias expanded in size with the increased immigration and new settlements sprang up. They became nations within a nation, in effect, for psychologically, socially, and culturally they remained Mexican. But the colonias had little or no control over their political, economic, or educational destinies. In almost every case, they remained separate and unequal to Anglo-American communities. The elected representatives within the colonias were usually Anglo-Americans or Mexicans under their control, and they established a bureaucracy to control the political life of the Mexican settlements—for the benefit of the Anglo privileged.

Further, Anglos controlled the educational system—they administered the schools and taught in the classrooms, and designed the curriculum not to meet the needs of Chicano students but to Americanize them. The police patrolling the colonia lived, for the most part, outside the area. Their main purpose was to protect Anglo property. Anglos owned the business and industry in the colonias, and capital that could have been used to improve the economic situation within the colonias was taken into Anglo-American sectors, in much the same way that capital is drained from underdeveloped countries by foreign economic imperialists. In addition, the colonias became employment centers for industrialists, who were assured of a ready supply of cheap labor.

This pattern is one that emerged in most Chicano communities, and one that contradicts the belief in Anglo-American equality. In sum, even though the 1960 census documented that 85 per cent of Chicanos are native-born U.S. citizens, most Anglo-Americans still considered them Mexicans and outsiders.

In discussing the traditional and internal colonization of the Chicano, it is not my intention to rekindle hatreds, nor to condemn all Anglo-Americans collectively for the ignominies that the Mexican in the United States has suffered. Rather, my purpose is to bring about an awareness—among both Anglo-Americans and Chicanos—of the forces that control and manipulate seven million people in this country and keep them colonized. If Chicanos can become aware of why they are oppressed and how the exploitation is perpetuated, they can work more effectively toward ending their colonization.

I realize that the initial stages of such awareness might result in intolerance among some Chicanos. However, I caution the reader that this work does not create a rationale for brown power just because it condemns the injustices of Anglo power. Extended visits in Mexico have taught me that Chicano power is no better than any other power. Those who seek power are deprived of their humanity to the point that they themselves become the oppressors. Paulo Freire has written:

The great humanistic and historical task of the oppressed [is]: to liberate themselves and their oppressors as well. The oppressors, who oppress, exploit, and rape by virtue of their power, cannot find in this power the strength to liberate either the oppressed or themselves. Only the power that springs from the weakness of the oppressed will be sufficiently strong to free you.*

It is my hope that *Occupied America* can help us perceive the social, political, and economic contradictions of the power that has enabled Anglo-American colonizers to dominate Chicanos—and that has too often made Chicanos accept and, in some instances, support the domination. Awareness will help us take action against the forces that oppress not only Chicanos but the oppressor himself.

* Paulo Freire, *Pedagogy of the Oppressed* (New York: Herder and Herder, 1972), p. 28.

Colonialism: The Case of the Mexican Americans

Joan W. Moore

American social scientists should have realized long ago that American minorities are far from being passive objects of study. They are, on the contrary, quite capable of defining themselves. A clear demonstration of this rather embarrassing lag in conceptualization is the current reassessment of sociological thought. It is now plain that the concepts of "acculturation," of "assimilation," and similar paradigms are inappropriate for groups who entered American society not as volunteer immigrants but through some form of involuntary relationship.[1]

The change in thinking has not come because of changes within sociology itself. Quite the contrary. It has come because the minorities have begun to reject certain academic concepts. The new conceptual structure is not given by any academic establishment but comes within a conceptual structure derived from the situation of the African countries. In the colonial situation, rather than either the conquest or the slave situation, the new generation of black intellectuals is finding parallels to their own reactions to American society.

This exploration of colonialism by minority intellectuals has met a varied reaction, to say the least, but there have been some interesting attempts to translate these new and socially meaningful categories into proper academic sociologese. Blauner's (1969) article in this journal is one of the more ambitious attempts to relate the concept of "colonialism" as developed by Kenneth Clark, Stokely Carmichael, and Eldridge Cleaver to sociological analysis. In the process, one kind of blurring is obvious even if not explicit: that is, that "colonialism" was far from uniform in the nineteenth century, even in Africa.[2] In addition, Blauner (1969) makes explicit the adaptations he feels are necessary before the concept of colonialism can be meaningfully applied to the American scene. Common to both American internal colonialism of the blacks and European imperial expansion, Blauner argues, were the involuntary nature of the relationship between the two groups, the transformation or destruction of indigenous values, and, finally, racism. But Blauner warns that the situations are really different: "the . . . culture . . . of the

NOTE: I would like to thank Carlos Cortes for his very helpful comments on an earlier draft of this paper.

SOURCE: From *Social Problems*, Vol. 17, No. 4, pp. 463–72. Copyright by The Society for the Study of Social Problems. Reprinted with the permission of the author and the publisher.

[American black] colonized . . . is less developed; it is also less autonomous. In addition, the colonized are a numerical minority, and furthermore, they are ghettoized more totally and are more dispersed than people under classic colonialism."

But such adaptations are not needed in order to apply the concept fruitfully to America's second largest minority—the Mexican Americans.[3] Here the colonial concept need not be analogized and, in fact, it describes and categorizes so accurately that one suspects that earlier "discovery" by sociologists of the Mexican Americans, particularly in New Mexico, might have discouraged uncritical application of the classic paradigms to all minorities. The initial Mexican contact with American society came by conquest, not by choice. Mexican American culture was well developed; it was autonomous; the colonized were a numerical majority. Further, they were—and are—less ghettoized and more dispersed than the American blacks. In fact, their patterns of residence (especially those existing at the turn of the century) are exactly those of "classic colonialism." And they were indigenous to the region and not "imported."[4]

In at least the one state of New Mexico, there was a situation of comparatively "pure" colonialism. Outside of New Mexico, the original conquest colonialism was overlaid, particularly in the twentieth century, with a grossly manipulated voluntary immigration. But throughout the American Southwest where the approximately five million Mexican Americans are now concentrated, understanding the Mexican minority requires understanding both conquest colonialism and "voluntary" immigration. It also requires understanding the interaction between colonialism and voluntarism.

In this paper I shall discuss a "culture trait" that is attributed to Mexican Americans both by popular stereotype and by social scientists—that is, a comparatively low degree of formal voluntary organization and hence of organized participation in political life. This is the academic form of the popular question: "What's wrong with the Mexicans? Why can't they organize for political activity?" In fact, as commonly asked both by social scientist and popular stereotype, the question begs the question. There is a great deal of variation in three widely different culture areas in the Southwest. And these culture areas differ most importantly in the particular variety of colonialism to which they were subjected. In the "classically" colonial situation, New Mexico, there has been in fact a relatively high order of political participation, especially by comparison with Texas, which we shall term "conflict colonialism," and California, which we shall term "economic colonialism."[5]

NEW MEXICO

An area that is now northern New Mexico and parts of southern Colorado was the most successful of the original Spanish colonies. At the beginning of the war between the United States and Mexico, there were more than 50,000 settlers, scattered in villages and cities with a strong upper class as well as a peasantry. There were frontier versions of Spanish colonial institutions that had been developing since 1600. The conquest of New Mexico by the United States was nearly bloodless and thus allowed, as a consequence, an extraordinary continuity between the Mexican period and the United States period.[6] The area became a territory of the United States and statehood was granted in 1912.

Throughout these changes political participation can be followed among the elite and among the masses of people. It can be analyzed in both its traditional manifestations and in contemporary patterns. In all respects it differs greatly in both level and quality from political participation outside this area. The heritage of colonialism helps explain these differences.

On the elite level, Spanish or Mexican leadership remained largely intact through the conquest and was shared with Anglo leadership after the termination of military rule in 1851. The indigenous elite retained considerable strength both in the dominant Republican party and in the state legislature. They were strong enough to ensure a bilingual provision in the 1912 Constitution (the only provision in the region that guarantees Spanish speakers the right to vote and hold office). Sessions of the legislature were—by law—conducted in both languages. Again, this is an extraordinary feature in any part of the continental United States. Just as in many Asian nations controlled by the British in the nineteenth century, the elite suffered little—either economically or politically.

On the lower-class level, in the villages, there was comparatively little articulation of New Mexican villages with the developing urban centers. What there was, however, was usually channeled through a recognized local authority, a *patrón*. Like the class structure, the *patrón* and the network of relations that sustained him were a normal part of the established local social system and not an ad hoc or temporary recognition of an individual's power. Thus political participation on both the elite and the lower-class levels were outgrowths of the existing social system.

Political participation of the elite and the *patrón* system was clearly a colonial phenomenon. An intact society, rather than a structureless mass of individuals, was taken into a territory of the United States with almost no violence. This truly colonial situation involves a totally different process of relationship between subordinate and superordinate from either the voluntary or the forced immigration of the subordinate—that is, totally different from either the "typical" American immigrant on the eastern seaboard or the slave imported from Africa.

A final point remains to be made not about political participation but about proto-political organization in the past. The villages of New Mexico had strong internal organizations not only of the informal, kinship variety but of the formal variety. These were the *penitente* sects and also the cooperative associations, such as those controlling the use of water and the grazing of livestock.[7] That such organizations were mobilized by New Mexican villagers is evidenced by the existence of terrorist groups operating against both Anglo and Spanish landowners. González (1967) mentions two: one functioning in the 1890's and one in the 1920's. Such groups could also act as local police forces.

Let us turn to the present. Political participation of the conventional variety is very high compared to that of Mexican Americans in other states of the Southwest. Presently there is a Spanish American in the United States Senate (Montoya, an "old" name), following the tradition of Dennis Chavez (another "old" name). The state legislature in 1967 was almost one-third Mexican American. (There were no Mexican American legislators in California and no more than six per cent in the legislature of any other southwest state.) This, of course, reflects the fact that it is only in very recent years that Mexican Americans have become a numerical minority in New Mexico, but it also reflects the fact that organized political participation has remained high.

Finally, New Mexico is the locus of the only mass movement among Mexican Americans—the *Alianza Federal de Mercedes*, headed by Reies Tijerina. In theme, the *Alianza*, which attracted tens of thousands of members, relates specifically to the colonial past, protesting the loss of land and its usurpation by Anglo interests (including, most insultingly, those of the United States Forest Service). It is this loss of land which has ultimately been responsible for the destruction of village (Spanish) culture and the large-scale migration to the cities.[8] In the light of the importance of the traditional village as a base for political mobilization, it is not really surprising that the *Alianza* should have appeared where it did. In content the movement continues local terrorism (haystack-burning) but has now extended beyond the local protest as its members have moved to the cities. Rather than being directed against specific Anglo or Spanish land-grabbers, it has lately been challenging the legality of the Treaty of Guadalupe Hidalgo. The broadening of the *Alianza's* base beyond specific local areas probably required the pooled discontent of those immigrants from many villages, many original land grants. It is an ironic feature of the *Alianza* that the generalization of its objectives and of its appeal should be possible only long after most of the alleged land-grabbing had been accomplished.

TEXAS

Mexican Americans in Texas had a sharply contrasting historical experience. The Mexican government in Texas was replaced by a revolution of the American settlers. Violence between Anglo-American settlers and Mexican residents continued in south Texas for generations after the annexation of Texas by the United States and the consequent full-scale war. Violence continued in organized fashion well into the twentieth century with armed clashes involving the northern Mexican *guerilleros* and the U.S. Army.

This violence meant a total destruction of Mexican elite political participation by conquest, while such forces as the Texas Rangers were used to suppress

Mexican-American participation on the lower status or village levels. The ecology of settlement in south Texas remains somewhat reminiscent of that in northern New Mexico: there are many areas that are predominantly Mexican, and even some towns that are still controlled by Mexicans. But there is far more complete Anglo economic and political dominance on the local level. Perhaps most important, Anglo-Americans outnumbered Mexicans by five to one even before the American conquest. By contrast, Mexicans in New Mexico remained the numerical majority for more than a hundred years after conquest.

Texas state politics reflect the past just as in New Mexico. Mexican Americans hold some slight representation in the U.S. Congress. There are two Mexican-American Congressmen, one from San Antonio and one from Brownsville (at the mouth of the Rio Grande river), one of whom is a political conservative. A minor representation far below the numerical proportion of Mexican Americans is maintained in the Texas legislature.

It is on the local level that the continued suppression is most apparent. As long ago as 1965 Mexican Americans in the small town of Crystal City won political control in a municipal election that electrified all Mexican Americans in Texas and stirred national attention. But this victory was possible only with statewide help from Mexican-American organizations and some powerful union groups. Shortly afterward (after some intimidation from the Texas Rangers) the town returned to Anglo control. Some other small towns (Del Rio, Kingsville, Alice) have recently had demonstrations in protest against local suppressions. Small and insignificant as they were, the demonstrations once again would not have been possible without outside support, primarily from San Antonio. (The most significant of these San Antonio groups have been aided by the Ford Foundation. The repercussions in Congress were considerable and may threaten the future of the Ford Foundation as well as the Mexican Americans in Texas.)

More general Mexican-American political organizations in Texas have a history that is strikingly reminiscent of Negro political organization. (There is one continuous difference: whites participated in most Negro organizations at the outset. It is only very recently that Anglos have been involved with Mexicans in such a fashion. In the past, Mexicans were almost entirely on their own.) Political organization has been middle class, highly oriented toward traditional expressions of "Americanism," and accommodationist. In fact, the first Mexican-American political association refused to call itself a political association for fear that it might be too provocative to the Anglo power structure; it was known as a "civic" organization when it was formed in Texas in the late 1920's. Even the name of this group (LULAC or the League of United Latin American Citizens) evokes an atmosphere of middle-class gentility. The second major group, the American G.I. Forum, was formed in an atmosphere of greater protest, after a Texas town had refused burial to a Mexican-American soldier. In recent years, increasing politicization has been manifested by the formation of such a group as PASSO (Political

Association of Spanish-Speaking Organizations). But in Texas, throughout the modern period the very act of *ethnic* politics has been controversial, even among Mexican Americans.[9]

CALIFORNIA

The California transition between Mexican and American settlement falls midway between the Texas pattern of violence and the relatively smooth change in New Mexico. In northern California the discovery of gold in 1849 almost immediately swamped a sparse Mexican population in a flood of Anglo-American settlers. Prior to this time an orderly transition was in progress. Thus the effect was very much that of violence in Texas: the indigenous Mexican elite was almost totally excluded from political participation. A generation later when the opening of the railroads repeated this demographic discontinuity in southern California the Mexicans suffered the same effect. They again were almost totally excluded from political participation. The New Mexico pattern of social organization on a village level had almost no counterpart in California. Here the Mexican settlements and the economy were built around very large land holdings rather than around villages. This meant, in essence, that even the settlements that survived the American takeover relatively intact tended to lack internal social organization. Villages (as in the Bandini rancho which became the modern city of Riverside) were more likely to be clusters of ranch employees than an independent, internally coherent community.

In more recent times the peculiar organization of California politics has tended to work against Mexican-American participation from the middle- and upper-status levels. California was quick to adopt the ideas of "direct democracy" of the Progressive era. These tend somewhat to work against ethnic minorities.[10] But this effect is accidental and can hardly be called "internal colonialism," coupled as it was with the anti-establishment ideals of the Progressive era. The concept of "colonialism," in fact, appears most useful with reference to the extreme manipulation of Mexican immigration in the twentieth century. Attracted to the United States by the hundreds of thousands in the 1920's, Mexicans and many of their U.S.-born children were deported ("repatriated") by welfare agencies during the Depression, most notably from California. (Texas had almost no welfare provisions; hence no repatriation.) The economic expansion in World War II required so much labor that Mexican immigration was supplemented by a contract labor arrangement. But, as in the Depression, "too many" were attracted and came to work in the United States without legal status. Again, in 1954, massive sweeps of deportations got rid of Mexicans by the hundreds of thousands in "Operation Wetback." New Mexico was largely spared both waves of deportation; Texas was involved primarily in Operation Wetback rather than in the welfare repatriations. California was deeply involved in both.

This economic manipulation of the nearly bottomless pool of Mexican labor has been quite conscious and enormously useful to the development of California extractive and agricultural enterprises. Only in recent years with increasing—and now overwhelming—proportions of native-born Mexican Americans in the population has the United States been "stuck" with the Mexicans. As one consequence, the naturalization rate of Mexican immigrants has been very low. After all, why relinquish even the partial protection of Mexican citizenship? Furthermore the treatment of Mexicans as economic commodities has greatly reduced both their motivation and their effectiveness as political participants. The motivations that sent Mexican Americans to the United States appear to have been similar to those that sent immigrants from Europe. But the conscious dehumanization of Mexicans in the service of the railroad and citrus industries in California and elsewhere meant an asymmetry in relationship between "host" and immigrant that is less apparent in the European patterns of immigration. Whatever resentment that might have found political voice in the past had no middle-class organizational patterns. California was structurally unreceptive and attitudinally hostile.

Thus in California the degree of Mexican political participation remains low. The electoral consequences are even more glaringly below proportional representation than in Texas. There is only one national representative (Congressman Roybal from Los Angeles) and only one in the state legislature. Los Angeles County (with nearly a million Mexican Americans) has no Supervisor of Mexican descent and the city has no Councilman of Mexican descent. Otherwise, the development of political associations has followed the Texas pattern, although later, with meaningful political organization a post-World War II phenomenon. The G.I. Forum has formed chapters in California. In addition, the Community Service Organization, oriented to local community political mobilization, and the Mexican-American Political Association, oriented to state-wide political targets, have repeated the themes of Texas' voluntary association on the level of the growing middle class.

How useful, then, is the concept of colonialism when it is applied to these three culture areas? We argue here that both the nature and extent of political participation in the state of New Mexico can be understood with reference to the "classical" colonial past. We noted that a continuity of elite participation in New Mexico from the period of Mexican rule to the period of American rule paved the way for a high level of conventional political participation. The fact that village social structure remained largely intact is in some measure responsible for the appearance of the only mass movement of Mexicans in the Southwest today—the *Alianza*. But even this movement is an outcome of colonialism; the expropriation of the land by large-scale developers and by federal conservation interests led ultimately to the destruction of the village economic base—and to the movement of the dispossessed into the cities. Once living in the cities in a much closer environment than that of the scattered small villages, they could "get together" and respond to the anti-colonialist protests of a charismatic leader.

Again following this idea, we might categorize the Texas experience as "conflict colonialism." This would reflect the violent discontinuity between the Mexican and the American periods of elite participation and the current struggle for the legitimation of ethnic politics on all levels. In this latter aspect, the "conflict colonialism" of Texas is reminiscent of black politics in the Deep South, although it comes from different origins.

To apply the colonial concept to Mexicans in California, we might usefully use the idea of "economic colonialism." The destruction of elite political strength by massive immigration and the comparative absence of local political organization meant a political vacuum for Mexican Americans. Extreme economic manipulation inhibited any attachment to the reality or the ideals of American society and indirectly allowed as much intimidation as was accomplished by the overt repression of such groups as the Texas Rangers.

To return to Blauner's use of the concept of "internal colonialism:" in the case of the Mexicans in the United States, a major segment of this group who live in New Mexico require no significant conceptual adaptation of the classic analyses of European overseas colonialism. Less adaptation is required in fact than in applying the concepts to such countries as Kenya, Burma, Algeria, and Indonesia. Not only was the relationship between the Mexican and the Anglo-American "involuntary," involving "racism" and the "transformation . . . of indigenous values," but the culture of the Spanish American was well developed, autonomous, a majority numerically, and contained a full social system with an upper and middle as well as lower class. The comparatively nonviolent conquest was really almost a postcript to nearly a decade of violence between the United States and Mexico which began in Texas.

The Texas pattern, although markedly different, can still be fitted under a colonialist rubric, with a continuous thread of violence, suppression, and adaptations to both in recent political affairs.

The Mexican experience in California is much more complicated. Mexicans lost nearly all trace of participation in California politics. Hence, there was no political tradition of any kind, even the purely negative experience in Texas. Then, too, the relationship between imported labor and employer was "voluntary," at least on the immigrants' side. The relationships were much more asymmetrical than in the "classic colonial" case.

If any further proof of the applicability of the idea of "colonialism" were needed, we have the developing ideology of the new *chicano* militants themselves. Like the black ideologies, *chicanismo* emphasizes colonialism, but in a manner to transcend the enormous disparities in Mexican-American experience. Thus one of the latest versions of the ideology reaches out to a time *before* even Spanish colonialism to describe the Southwestern United States as "Aztlán"—an Aztec term. "Aztlán" is a generality so sweeping that it can include all Mexican Americans. Mexican Americans are the products of layer upon layer of colonialism and the overlay of American influence is only the most recent. That the young ideologues or the "cultural nationalists" (as they call themselves) should utilize the symbols of the first of these colonists, the Aztecs (along with Emiliano Zapata, the most "Indian" of Mexican revolutionaries from the past), is unquestionably of great symbolic significance to the participants themselves. But perhaps of more sociological significance (and far more controversial among the participants) is the attempt to legitimate *chicano* culture. This culture comes from the habits, ideas, and speech of the most despised lower-class Mexican American as he has been forced to live in a quasi-legal ghetto culture in large Southwestern cities. These symbols are all indigenous to the United States and are neither Mexican, nor Spanish, nor even Aztec. But they *do* offer symbols to all Mexican Americans, after a widely varying experience with Americans in which, perhaps, the ideologues can agree only that it was "colonialist."

NOTES

1. Oddly enough it now appears that the nature of the introduction into American society matters even more than race, though the two interact. I think this statement can be defended empirically, notwithstanding the emergence of, for example, Japanese-American *sansei* militancy, with its strong race consciousness (see KITANO, 1968).
2. For a good analysis of the variation, and of today's consequences, see the collection of papers in KUPER and SMITH (1969).
3. Mexican-American intellectuals themselves have persistently analyzed the group in the conquest frame of reference. For a significant example, see SANCHEZ (1940).
4. "Indigenous" by comparison with the American blacks. Spanish America itself was a colonial system, in which Indians were exploited. See OLGUIN, (1967), for an angry statement to this effect.
5. Of course, we are not arguing that colonialist domination—or for that matter the peculiar pattern of voluntary immigration—offers a full explanation of this complex population, or even of the three culture areas which are the focus of this paper. Mexican Americans and the history of the region are far too complexly interwoven to pretend that any analytic thread can unravel the full tapestry. For other theses, see the analyses developed in GREBLER ET AL, (1970).
6. This account draws on GONZALEZ (1967); LAMAR (1966); HOLMES (1964); and DONNELLY (1947). Paul Fisher prepared a valuable analytic abstract of all but the first of these sources while a research assistant. I have used his document extensively here.
7. GONZALEZ (1967:64) concludes that *moradas*, or *penitente* organizations, "were found in most, if not all, of the northern Spanish settlements during the last half of the 19th Century and the first part of the 20th."
8. GONZALEZ (1967:75) analyzes the *Alianza* as a "nativist" movement, and suggests that its source is partly in the fact that "for the first time many elements of Spanish-American culture are in danger of disappearing" (emphasis added).
9. This discussion draws on GUZMAN (1967) and CUÉLLAR (1970).
10. FOGELSON (1967) gives a good picture of political practices which had the latent consequence of excluding Mexicans from Los Angeles politics—a fact of great importance given the very large concentrations of Mexican Americans in that city. Political impotence in Los Angeles has affected a very significant fraction of California's Mexican Americans. HARVEY (1966) gives a broader picture of California politics.

BIBLIOGRAPHY

BLAUNER, ROBERT (1969). "Internal colonialism and ghetto revolt." *Social Problems* 16 (Spring 1969), pp. 393–408.

CUÉLLAR, ALFREDO (1970). "Perspective on politics." In Joan W. Moore with Alfredo Cuéllar. *Mexican Americans.* Englewood Cliffs, N.J.: Prentice-Hall.

DONNELLY, THOMAS C. (1947). *The Government of New Mexico.* Albuquerque: The University of New Mexico Press.

FOGELSON, ROBERT M. (1967). *The Fragmented Metropolis: Los Angeles, 1850–1960.* Cambridge, Mass.: Harvard University Press.

GONZALEZ, NANCIE L. (1967). *The Spanish Americans of New Mexico: A Distinctive Heritage.* Advance Report 9. Los Angeles: University of California, Mexican American Study Project.

GREBLER, LEO, et al. (1970). *The Mexican American People.* New York: Free Press.

GUZMAN, RALPH (1967). "Political socialization." Unpublished manuscript.

HARVEY, RICHARD B. (1966). "California politics: Historical profile." In R. B. Dvorin and D. Misner, Eds. *California Politics and Policies.* Reading, Mass.: Addison-Wesley.

HOLMES, JACK E. (1964). *Party, Legislature and Governor in the Politics of New Mexico, 1911–1963.* Ph.D. Dissertation, Chicago: University of Chicago.

KITANO, HARRY H. L. (1968). *The Japanese Americans.* Englewood Cliffs, N.J.: Prentice-Hall.

KUPER, LEO, and M. G. SMITH, Eds. (1969). *Pluralism in Africa.* Berkeley and Los Angeles: University of California Press.

LAMAR, HOWARD ROBERTS (1966). *The Far Southwest, 1845–1912: A Territorial History.* New Haven: Yale University Press.

OLGUÍN, JOHN PHILLIP (1967). "Where does the 'justified' resentment begin?" New Mexico Business offprint, July 1967.

SANCHEZ, GEORGE I. (1940). *Forgotten People.* Albuquerque: University of New Mexico Press.

Four Declarations of Independence

Armando B. Rendon

These are four plans, or manifestos, which have been written by Chicanos and which evolved out of specific and significant events in the past five years.

EL PLAN DE DELANO

Plan for the liberation of the Farm Workers associated with the Delano Grape Strike in the State of California, seeking social justice in farm labor with those reforms that they believe necessary for their well-being as workers in these United States.

We, the undersigned, gathered in Pilgrimage to the capital of the State in Sacramento, in penance for all the failings of Farm Workers as free and sovereign men, do solemnly declare before the civilized world which judges our actions, and before the nation to which we belong, the propositions we have formulated to end the injustice that oppresses us.

We are conscious of the historical significance of our Pilgrimage. It is clearly evident that our path travels through a valley well known to all Mexican farm workers. We know all of these towns of Delano, Fresno, Madera, Modesto, Stockton, and Sacramento, because along this very same road, in this very same valley the Mexican race has sacrificed itself for the last hundred years. Our sweat and our blood have fallen on this land to make other men rich. Our wages and working conditions have been determined from above, because irresponsible legislators who could have helped us have supported the rancher's argument that the plight of the farm worker was a "special case." They saw the obvious effects of an unjust system, starvation wages, contractors, day hauls, forced migration, sickness, and subhuman conditions.

The farm worker has been abandoned to his own fate—without representation, without power—subject to the mercy and caprice of the rancher.

We are suffering. We have suffered unnumbered ills and crimes in the name of the Law of the land. Our men, women and children have suffered not only the basic brutality of stoop labor, and the most obvious injustices of the system; they have also suffered the desperation of knowing that that system caters to the greed of callous men and not to our needs.

Now we will suffer for the purpose of ending the poverty, the misery, and the injustice, with the hope that our children will not be exploited as we have been. They have imposed hungers on us, and now we hunger for justice. We draw strength from the very despair in which we have been forced to live. WE SHALL ENDURE!

This Pilgrimage is a witness to the suffering we have seen for generations. The penance we accept symbolizes the suffering we shall have in order to bring justice to these same towns, to this same valley. This is the beginning of a social movement in fact and not in pronouncements.

We seek our basic God-given rights as human beings. Because we have suffered—and are not afraid to suffer—in order to survive, we are ready to give up everything, even our lives, in our fight for social justice. We shall do it without violence because that is our destiny.

To the ranchers and to all those who oppose us we say, in the words of Benito Juarez, "Respect for another's rights is the meaning of Peace."

We seek the support of all political groups, and the protection of the government, which is also our government. But we are tired of words, of betrayals, of indifference. To the politicians we say that the years are gone when the farm worker said nothing and did nothing to help himself. From this movement shall spring leaders who shall understand us, lead us, be faithful to us, and we shall elect them to represent us. We shall be heard!

We seek, and have, the support of the Church in what we do. At the head of the Pilgrimage we carry the Virgin of Guadalupe because she is ours, all ours, Patroness of the Mexican people. We also carry the Sacred Cross and the Star of David because we are not sectarians, and because we ask the help and prayers of all religions. All men are brothers, sons of the same God; that is why we say to all men of good will, in the words of Pope Leo XIII, "Everyone's first duty is to protect the workers from the greed of speculators who use human beings as instruments to provide themselves with money. It is neither just nor human to oppress with excessive work to the point where their minds become enfeebled and their bodies worn out." God shall not abandon us!

We shall unite. We have learned the meaning of unity. We know why these United States are just that—united. The strength of the poor is also in union. We know that the poverty of the Mexican or Filipino worker in California is the same as that of all farm workers across the country, the Negroes and poor whites, the Puerto Ricans, Japanese and Arabians; in short, all of the races that comprise the oppressed minorities of the United States. The majority of the people on our Pilgrimage are of Mexican descent, but the triumph of our race depends on a national association of farm workers. We must get together and bargain collectively. We must use the only strength that we have, the force of our numbers; the ranchers are few, we are many. United we shall stand!

We shall pursue the Revolution we have proposed. We are sons of the Mexican Revolution, a revolution of the poor seeking bread and justice. Our revolution shall not be an armed one, but we want the order which now exists to be undone, and that a new social order replace it.

We are poor, we are humble, and our only choice is to Strike in those ranches where we are not treated with the respect we deserve as working men, where our rights as free and sovereign men are not recognized. We do not want the paternalism of the ranchers; we do not want the contractor; we do not want charity at the price of our dignity. We want to be equal with all the working men in the nation; we want a just wage, better working conditions, a decent future for our children. To those who oppose us, be they ranchers, police, politicians, or speculators, we say that we are going to continue fighting until we die, or we win. We shall overcome!

Across the San Joaquin Valley, across California, across the entire Southwest of the United States, wherever there are Mexican people, wherever there are farm workers, our movement is spreading like flames across a dry plain. Our Pilgrimage is the match that will light our cause for all farm workers to see what is happening here, so that they may do as we have done.

The time has come for the liberation of the poor farm worker. History is on our side. May the Strike go on! Viva la causa!

March 1966

PLAN DE LA RAZA UNIDA PREAMBLE

On this historic day, October 28, 1967, La Raza Unida organized in El Paso, Texas, proclaims the time of subjugation, exploitation and abuse of human rights of La Raza in the United States is hereby ended forever.

La Raza Unida affirms the magnificence of La Raza, the greatness of our heritage, our history, our language, our traditions, our contributions to humanity, and our culture. We have demonstrated and proven and again affirm our loyalty to the Constitutional Democracy of the United States of America and to the religious and cultural traditions we all share.

We accept the framework of constitutional democracy and freedom within which to establish our own independent organizations among our own people in pursuit of justice and equality and redress of grievances. La Raza Unida pledges to join with all our courageous people organizing in the fields and in the barrios. We commit ourselves to La Raza, at whatever cost.

With this commitment we pledge our support in:

1. The right to organize community and labor groups in our own style.

2. The guarantee of training and placement in employment in all levels.

3. The guarantee of special emphasis on education at all levels geared to our people with strong financial grants to individuals.

4. The guarantee of decent, safe, and sanitary housing without relocation from one's community.

5. We demand equal representation at all levels of appointive boards and agencies, and the end to exploitative gerrymandering.

6. We demand the strong enforcement of all sections of the Treaty of Guadalupe Hidalgo particularly the sections dealing with land grants, and bilingual guarantees.

7. We are outraged by and demand an end to police harassment, discrimination and brutality inflicted on La Raza, and an end to the kangaroo court system known as juvenile hall. We demand constitutional protection and guarantees in all courts of the United States.

8. We reaffirm a dedication to our heritage, a bilingual culture and assert our right to be members of La Raza Unida anywhere, anytime and in any job.

THE DEL RIO MEXICAN AMERICAN MANIFESTO TO THE NATION

(Original Version as Read to an Audience of More than Two Thousand)

On this historic day, March 30, 1969, the Mexican-American community of the United States of America stands in solidarity with the Mexican-American poor of Del Rio, Texas. The infamy recently perpetrated upon them by local and state authorities has exhausted our patience. From throughout the country and all walks of life, we have come to join our voices with theirs in denouncing the forces that oppress them and us, and in demanding redress of their grievances and ours. We believe that both our denunciation and our demand are firmly in keeping with a country made up of minorities and committed to abide by democratic ideals.

Recent events in this city have made it amply clear that our minority continues to be oppressed by men and institutions using the language of democracy while resorting to totalitarian methods. A highly regarded OEO project of self-determination, the Val Verde County VISTA Minority Mobilization program, has been arbitrarily cancelled by Governor Preston Smith at the request of three Anglo county commissioners representing less than 5 per cent of the population. The fourth commissioner, a Mexican American representing the rest of the citizens, while originally abstaining, joined his vote to that of the other three following the Governor's decree. The charges were pathetic—a reflection of nervous power-wielders who saw the growing assertiveness of the poor served by VISTA Mexican Americans as a threat to their traditional supremacy. A collusion was alleged between the VISTA volunteers and the Mexican American Youth Organization (MAYO), a local group of youngsters, mostly high schoolers, who frequently assail the injustices of what they call the "gringo system." Without bothering to consult with the local Community Action Program Board, or the Austin Regional OEO office, both of which continue to endorse the Del Rio VISTAs, the Governor sent wires to the National VISTA office and to all Texas judges in whose counties other VISTA programs are operating, informing them of the cancellation of the Val Verde County program, and adding, "the abdication of respect for law and order, disruption of the democratic process, and provocation of disunity among our citizens shall not be tolerated by this office."

A dispassionate analysis of this appalling misuse of power by both the Val Verde Commissioners and the Governor reveals it is they, not the poor, the VISTAs, or MAYOs who are guilty of "abdication of respect for law and order, disruption of the democratic process, and provocation of disunity among our citizens." Del Rio was no paradise of unity, before VISTAs and MAYOs arrived. Except for minor differences of detail, the list of local grievances they have dramatized parallel the experience of countless other communities where Mexican Americans are still treated as conquered people. We see our own conditions elsewhere as we review the sorry catalogue that our destitute Del Rio brothers have shared with us in describing the Anglo-controlled establishment:

1. It is they who built a multi-million dollar school for their chidren, then built barracks for ours.

2. It is they who stole our land, then sold it back to us, bit by bit, crumb by crumb.

3. It is they who speak one language and resent us for speaking two.

4. It is they who preach brotherhood and practice racism.

5. It is they who make ado about equal opportunity but reserve it to themselves or their replicas.

6. It is they who proclaim concern for the poor through a welfare system calculated to keep our people in perpetual dependency.

7. It is their police system that harasses and overpolices our sons and daughters.

8. It is their educational system that violates the innocence of our children with required literature like *The Texas Story*, a book that caricatures our ancestors.

9. It is their double standard of justice—minimum penalty for gringo and maximum for Chicano—that makes criminals of our young men.

10. It is they who denounce our militancy but think nothing of the legal violence they inflict on us mentally, culturally, spiritually, and physically.

There must be something invincible in our people that has kept alive our humanity in spite of a system bent on suppressing our difference and rewarding our conformity. It is such an experience of cultural survival that has led us to the recovery of the magnificence of LA RAZA. However we define it, it is a treasure house of spirituality, decency, and sanity. LA RAZA is the affirmation of the most basic ingredient of our personality, the brownhood of our Indian ancestors wedded to all the other skin colors of mankind. Brown is the common denominator of the largest number among us—a glorious reminder of our Aztec and Mayan heritage. But in a color-mad

society, the sin of our coloration can be expiated only by exceptional achievement and successful imitation of the white man who controls every institution of society. LA RAZA condemns such a system as racist, pagan, and
ultimately self-destructive. We can neither tolerate it nor be a part of it. As
children of LA RAZA, we are heirs of a spiritual and biological miracle where
in one family blood ties unite the darkest and the fairest. It is no accident
that the objects of our veneration include the black Peruvian Saint Martin
de Porres, the brown Indian Virgin of Guadalupe, the blond European
madonnas, and a Jewish Christ of Indian and Spanish features.

We cannot explain our survival and our strength apart from this heritage—
a heritage inseparably linked to Spanish, the soul language of LA RAZA. On
this day we serve notice on Del Rio and the nation that for their sake and
ours we are willing to lay down our lives to preserve the culture and language
of our ancestors, to blend them with that which is best in these United
States of America, our beloved country. Let no one forget that thousands of
our Mexican-American brothers have gallantly fought and died in defense of
American freedoms enjoyed by us more in hope than reality. We shall
escalate the defense of such freedoms here at home to honor those who fell
for them yesterday, and to sustain those who live for their fulfillment to-
morrow. We are committed to nonviolence, even while living in the midst
of officially tolerated violence. We are prepared, however, to be as aggressive
as it may be necessary, until every one of our Mexican-American brothers
enjoys the liberty of shaping his own future.

We feel compelled to warn the Val Verde Commissioners and Governor
Preston Smith that they are inviting serious social unrest if they do not immediately rescind their VISTA cancellation action. Likewise, we feel compelled to warn the United States Congress that unless legislation is enacted
to protect the VISTA principle of self-determination from arbitrary termination by local and state officials, the entire concept of volunteer service,
whether at home or abroad, will be prostituted in the eyes of those idealistic
fellow-Americans who participate in it. Lastly, we feel compelled to warn the
whole nation that unless the ideal of self-determination is upheld with our
poor at home, the entire world will judge us hypocritical in our attempt to
assist the poor abroad.

On this day, Mexican Americans commit themselves to struggle ceaselessly
until the promise of this country is realized for us and our fellow-Americans:
one nation, under God, *indivisible*, with liberty and justice for *all*.

THE SPIRITUAL PLAN OF AZTLÁN

(Crusade for Justice Youth Conference, Denver, Colorado)

In the spirit of a new people that is conscious not only of its proud
heritage, but also of the brutal "gringo" invasion of our territories, we, the
Chicano, inhabitants and civilizers of the northern land of Aztlán, from
whence came our forefathers, reclaiming the land of their birth and consecrat-

ing the determination of our people of the sun, *declare* that the call of our blood is our power, our responsibility, and our inevitable destiny.

We are free and sovereign to determine those tasks which are justly called for by our house, our land, the sweat of our brows, and by our hearts. Aztlán belongs to those that plant the seeds, water the fields, and gather the crops, and not to the foreign Europeans. We do not recognize capricious frontiers on the Bronze Continent.

Brotherhood unites us, love for our brothers makes us a people whose time has come and who struggles against the foreigner "gabacho" who exploits our riches and destroys our culture. With our heart in our hand and our hands in the soil, we declare the independence of our mestizo Nation. We are a bronze people with a bronze culture. Before the world, before all of North America, before all our brothers in the Bronze Continent, we are a Nation. We are a union of free pueblos. We are *Aztlán*.

To hell with the nothing race.

All power for our people.
March 31, 1969

One and Together

Carey McWilliams

"No one who has grown up in California," wrote Josiah Royce, "can be under an illusion as to the small extent to which the American character, as here exemplified, has been really altered by foreign intercourse, large as the foreign population has always remained. The foreign influence has never been for the American community at large, in California, more than skin-deep. One has assumed a very few and unimportant California ways, one has freely used or abused the few (Spanish) words and phrases, one has grown well accustomed to the sight of foreigners and to business relations with them, and one's natural innocence about foreign matters has in California given place, even more frequently than elsewhere in our country, to a superficial familiarity with the appearance and the manners of numerous foreign communities. But all this in no wise renders the American life in California less distinctly native in tone. . . . You cannot call a community of Americans foreign in disposition merely because its amusements have a foreign look." [1]

To Royce—the most perceptive and sensitive of California historians—this summation seemed quite clear and obvious in 1886. But it was not quite accurate, even then, to say that "the California ways" which had survived were "few and unimportant." More deeply than Royce imagined, the customs, the laws, and the economic practices and institutions of the native Californians had exerted a definite influence on the culture which began to emerge after the American conquest. However, it did appear in 1886 that the native Californians had suffered an irreparable defeat and that the initial contact between the two cultures had resulted in the eclipse of the one without any substantial modification in the basic pattern of the other.

But today the ineluctable facts of geography and history dictate a somewhat different conclusion. Mexico is not France or Italy or Poland: it is geographically a part of the Southwest. Residing in the Mexican states immediately south of the border are approximately 2,900,000 Spanish-speaking people; in the American border states approximately the same number of Spanish-speaking reside. Essentially these are one people, occupying a single cultural province, for the Spanish-speaking minority north of the border (a majority in some areas) has always drawn, and will continue to draw, support, sustenance, and reenforcements from south of the border. Our Spanish-speaking minority is not, therefore, a detached fragment but an integral part of a much larger population unit to which it is bound by close geographic and

SOURCE: From "One and Together" from *North from Mexico* by Carey McWilliams. Copyright © 1968 by Carey McWilliams. Reprinted with permission of the author and Greenwood Press, Publishers.

historical ties. Furthermore, Hispanic influences in the United States have a strong anchor in New Mexico where these influences are actually older, and perhaps more deeply rooted, than in the Mexican border states.

The Spanish-speaking and the Indians of the Southwest have the highest birth rates of any ethnic groups in the region. Infant mortality rates are declining, for both groups, throughout the borderlands: between 1929 and 1944 the rate decreased in New Mexico from 145.5 infant deaths per 1,000 live births to 89.1. With high birth rates and rapidly declining infant mortality rates, the Spanish-speaking element will retain its position relative to Anglo-Americans for many years to come, barring unforeseeable contingencies.

These facts alone would indicate that the Hispanic minority cannot be regarded as merely another immigrant group in the United States destined for ultimate absorption. In this instance, however, demographical considerations are fortified by the facts of geography and the implications of history. While Spanish cultural influences have retreated in portions of the Southwest, they have never been eclipsed. "Whether they will or not," wrote J. P. Widney in the 1880's, "their future [that is, the future of Anglos and Hispanos] is one and together, and I think neither type of race will destroy the other. They will merge." With the Spanish-speaking element having been reenforced by a million or more immigrants in the last forty years, virtually all of whom have remained in the Southwest, some type of cultural fusion or merger must result. In fact, a surprising degree of fusion has already taken place.

BY ANY OTHER NAME

The development of speech and language patterns not only mirrors the relationships between Anglos and Hispanos in the Southwest but is the best gauge of the degree of cultural fusion that has occurred. Needless to say, I discuss this highly complex subject not as a linguist; nor in terms of its linguistic interest; but rather to indicate what has actually happened to the two cultures in the region and to trace a relationship. For the attitude of a minority toward language and speech has an important bearing on the direction that the process of acculturation is likely to take.

The language pattern in the Southwest has, of course, a number of variable factors. It varies in relation to the numerical proportion between the two groups in any one place; the age of the community; whether it is rural or urban; the degree of isolation; the history of social relations in the community; and many other factors. Quite apart from these variations, however, there is a larger aspect to the language pattern which can be considered from three points of view: Spanish borrowings from American-English speech; Anglo-American borrowings from the Spanish; and the development in both groups of a kind of jargon which is more "Southwestern" than Spanish or English.

In 1917 Dr. Aurelion M. Espiñosa listed some three hundred words of Anglo-American origin which have been incorporated into the Spanish language as spoken in New Mexico after first being Hispanized. Most of these words had been borrowed from necessity rather than choice, for they related, in the main, to commodities, practices, things, and concepts for which there was no Spanish equivalent (at least not in the Spanish spoken in New Mexico). Many of them had to do with commercial, industrial, and political practices unknown to the Spanish population prior to the American conquest as shown by the fact that more than 50 per cent of the terms had been incorporated after 1880. In large measure the adopted words had to do with "work terms" related to the new jobs which New Mexicans had acquired; others related to slang expressions used in American sports. Obviously most of this borrowing was based on strictly utilitarian considerations.[2]

In another study of word-borrowing, Dr. Manuel Gamio listed the following among many terms that had been hispanicized: picnic, laundry, ties (railroad ties), matches, stockyards (estoque yardas), groceries, lunch, tickets, depot, time-check, truck, truck-driver, biscuit, omelette, bootlegger, taxes, ice cream, board and boarder, boss, automobile, sweater, jumper, sheriff, etc. In still another list, Dr. Harold W. Bentley added: home run (jonronero); scraper (escrepa); plug (ploga); puncture (ponchar); jack (llaqui); and such expressions as "vamos flat"—to have a flat tire (literally, "we go flat"). Generally, the Spanish-speaking people have borrowed from necessity rather than choice and have shown either resistance or indifference to other types of borrowings. Still the number of such borrowings, from necessity or otherwise, has been substantial and would probably be much greater today than when these studies were made.

According to Alfred Bruce Gaarder, there are four types of Spanish spoken in the Southwest: the Spanish spoken by the "old folks," particularly in New Mexico, which contains many archaic forms known only to the sixteenth century; the language of the "middle generation" which keeps some of the archaic and obsolete forms but adds a large vocabularly of Anglicisms developed to meet the needs of trade or business; the speech of the "youngest group" which increases the confusion by the use of slang expressions current among their schoolmates; and, lastly, the jargon of the city gangs, identical with the third grouping above, except that expressions of a shady, sinister, or double meaning have been added; often this jargon is used as a secret language.[3]

It is in the speech of the city gangs, "the pachuco patois," that the attempt to fuse the two languages is most clearly apparent. For these youngsters play wonderful variations on both languages, Anglicizing Spanish and Hispanicizing English as it suits their purpose and often coining an expression of their own. Opposite are some of their inventions or fusion as reported by Dr. Gaarder. Other pachuismos are: anteojos, front window; bote, jail; chante, house (probably from shanty); choque, chalk; chillar, to cry; escamado, frightened; jefa, mother; jefe, father; lira, guitar; tambo, jail; tambique, jail; tramo, suit.

The second generation uses many slang expressions also found in the talk of the pachucos: aleluyas, converts to Protestantism; birria, beer; bolillo, an American; bolucha, or bolita, picking oranges; brecas, brakes; chapos, Japanese; cho, a movie; chutear, to shoot; cuivo, hello; datil, a date; diez y penny, a five-

Pachuco	Spanish	English
bolar	dólar	dollar
borlo	baile	dance
calco	zapato	shoe
caldiarre	enojarse	to be angry
canton	casa	house
carlo	caló	cant
carnal	hermano	brother
carnala	hermana	sister
carrucha	automóvil	automobile
chero	policía	police
duro	dólar	dollar
frajo	cigarro	cigar–cigarette
grena	pelo	hair
greta	marihuana	marihuana
huisa	muchacha	girl
jando	dinero	money
jetiar	dormir	sleep
jura	policía	police
mostacho	bigote	mustache
pildora	policía	police
rolante	automóvil	automobile
simon	sí	yes
tonda	sombrero	hat
vesca	marihuana	marihuana

and-ten store; engascado, in love; esa, hello (to a girl); ficha, money; fila, or filero, a razor; gavacho, an American; ginar, to commit robbery; gua he, a guitar; guayn, wine; jalar, to work; lorcha, a match; lucas, crazy; manil, money; mono, a movie; nagualones, imported worker from Mexico; pistiar, to drink liquor; rolar, to sleep; ser maleta, to see a movie; sut, suit; tintos, Negroes; and trola, a match.[4]

WORDS THAT FIT

Anglo-American borrowings from Spanish have also been dictated by necessity, in many cases, but from other motives as well. One important grouping of borrowed words has to do with things and practices for which there was no English equivalent, as in the cattle industry, the mining industry, and in the pack-train business. . . . But, in addition to these borrowings-by-necessity, there is a long list of Spanish words which have apparently been taken over for local color, humorous effect, and, above all, for their appropriateness in an arid environment. In his *Dictionary of Spanish Terms in English* (1932), Dr. Bentley lists some four hundred words which have been incorporated in the English spoken in the Southwest. Actually the list is much longer than linguists such as H. L. Mencken and George Philip Krapp have indicated, for they have not been looking in the right quarter, namely, the Southwest.

Considering that we had just fought a war against Mexico, it is indeed remarkable that so few Spanish place-names were changed after 1846. In addition to the names of rivers and mountains, Dr. Bentley states that there are two thousand or more cities and towns in the United States with Spanish names: four hundred or more in California; two hundred and fifty in Texas and New Mexico; and a hundred or more in both Colorado and Arizona. In Colorado the name of the state and the names of nineteen countries are Spanish. Spanish place-names also appear, with less frequency, in such states as Nevada, Wyoming, Utah, Oregon, Montana and Idaho; in fact, they appear in every state in the union. Ofter the original Spanish has been Anglicized, as in Waco, California (originally Hueco); and, in many cases, Spanish and English terms have combined, as in Buena Park, Altaville, and Minaview. There are eight "Mesas," four "Bonanzas" and thirteen "El Dorados" in the United States. Many of the Spanish place-names outside the Southwest refer to the names of battles or of events related to the Mexican-American War.

In the Southwest most of the Spanish place-names were preserved—in my opinion—because of their extraordinary appropriateness and beauty. The Spanish named places with the uncannily descriptive accuracy of poets. For example, who could improve on "Sangre de Cristo" for the name of the great range of mountains in northern New Mexico? The very persistence with which resident Spanish-speaking people kept calling mountains, rivers, and towns by their Spanish names must, also, have been a factor. In Southern California, virtually all the Spanish place-names were retained; but many of the street names, in places such as Santa Barbara, San Diego, and Los Angeles, were changed or Anglicized after 1846.

Long familiar with an arid environment, the Spanish gave vivid and accurate names to the novel features of the Southwestern landscape. "The *acequia madre* ('mother ditch') of every village," writes T. M. Pearce, "has almost a personality of its own. It becomes the most intimate friend of every inhabitant of the place. With dancing and ceremony, the *acequias* are opened in the spring . . . with scrupulous care the *acequias* are scraped and strengthened in the villages and towns." To call these life-giving main canals "ditches" would have been to minimize their importance in this environment.

And so it is with many similar expressions, relating to the natural environment of the Southwest, which were retained and incorporated into Anglo-American speech. The list is a long one indeed and includes such words as: *malpaís, mesa, vega, cumbre, bosque, sierra, pozo, hondo, loma, bajada, ciénaga, piloncillo, potrero, arroyo, laguna, barranca, cañon, llano, brasada, chaparral, canada,* and many others. "The Southwest," writes Pearce, "with its peculiar brilliance of day and quick shadows of nightfall, with its hard-baked earth and sudden water gushes, with its thirsty sands at the very edge of soggy river bottoms, cannot be described in terms of Shakespeare's Stratford." For example, an *arroyo* is *not* a gully. As Pearce points out, "it is a bare rent in the side of Mother Earth where only yellow jaws yawn until a cloudburst in the mountains miles away sends the lashing torrents hurtling through it to crush and engulf everything caught in its maw." The word *malpaís* means more than "badlands"; it refers to the lava ridges or serrated volcanic ash "dumps" to be found in the Southwest. It is quite impossible to convey the peculiar significance of *ciénaga*, as used in the Southwest, by some such expression as "marshy place," for the latter does not carry the connotation of an encompassing aridity. Thus *vega* is not just "meadow"; *bosque* is more than "a clump or grove"; and *sierra* carries overtones of meaning not suggested by "saw-toothed range."

It is not by chance, furthermore, that so many Spanish names for trees, plants, and shrubs have been borrowed in the Southwest. Many of these items have never had a name other than that given them by the Spaniards: *grama, sacaton, aparejo, alfilaria* (grasses); *mesquite, chaparral, chamiso, sahuardo, palo verde, huisache, mogote, maguey, manzanito, bellotas, álamo, tule, amole, capulin, plumajillo,* and *piñones* (for trees, shrubs, and plants). Similarly, the Anglo-Americans borrowed many terms related to the type of architecture they found in the Southwest: *portal, corbel, adobe, fogón* (three-cornered fireplace), *ramada* (shaded arbor), *azotea* (the flat, platform-like roof), *cabana, casa grande, hammock, presidio, hacienda, jacal, patio, placeta, plaza, viga, palacio, zaguán* (open passage way), *cañales* (roof gutters), *trostera* (large cupboard), and many others. Many animals and insects—*tecolote* (owl), *coyote, cucaracha* (cockroach), *javalina, mosquito, cougar, labos, jaguars, conejos* (rabbits), *venalos* [sic] (deer), are Spanish in origin or, in the Southwest, are known by their Spanish names. Names for items of dress have likewise been appropriated: *sombrero, tilma, rebozo, manta,* and *sarape.* From the Spanish-American War, came *rurale, machete, ley fuga, mañana,* hoosegow (*juzgado*), and a number of other words and expressions.

From the contact between the British and Spanish navies came such words as armada, cask, cork, and cargo. And then there is, of course, a long list of words, Spanish in origin, which have become fully "naturalized": vigilante, filibuster, avocado, barbecue, cockroach, corral, creole, tobacco, cannibal, vanilla, hammock, tornado, alfalfa, canary, cigar, maroon, Negro, palaver, paragon, parasol, sherry, soda, canoe, banana, alligator, cocoa, sassafras; as well as many words that came by way of South America: alpaca, armadillo, chinchilla, cocaine, condor, cougar, jaguar, llama, and tapioca.

Spanish borrowings from American speech have naturally been most numerous in the speech area along the Rio Grande and immediately south of the border; while American borrowings have been most common throughout the old Spanish borderlands area. Many southwestern words and idioms are Spanish in origin: jerky, hackamore, buckaroo, mustang, stampede, lariat, fandango, hoosegow, wrangler, desperado, vamoose, hombre, adios, agua, bandido. In this area, the corruption of Spanish has been paralleled by the cultivation of what J. Frank Dobie calls "sagebrush" or "bull-pen" Spanish. Most of the borrowings, on both sides, have been by ear for neither group has been a serious student of the language of the other. In the isolation of the region, each group borrowed from the other so that today part of the vocabulary of the Southwest is bilingual in origin. A kind of Spanish is still spoken in the range country along the border where, according to Doris K. Seibold, fully half the cowmen are bilingual.[5] Most of the Mexicans born in the region since 1900 are, of course, bilingual. Cowboy talk is so thoroughly bilingual that, in a single issue of *Lariat*, a popular "western" or "cowboy" magazine, Dr. Bentley found 376 Spanish words or words of Spanish origin.[6] Most authors who have written about the Southwest have felt compelled to include a glossary of Spanish terms in common use.[7]

NEIGHBORS IN ISOLATION

Considering the degree of hostility which has prevailed between Anglos and Hispanos in the Southwest, the extent of cultural fusion which has already occurred is most surprising. The isolation of both groups has been a prime reason for this mutual borrowing and adaptation. In the absence of deeply rooted educational institutions, the borrowing has been unconscious, careless, and natural—a product of intimacy in isolation. However antagonistically each group may have regarded the other, the plain fact is that they have been in continuous, direct, and often intimate contact in the Southwest for over a century. There was a period, in all the borderland states, when the two groups existed, side by side, in the friendliest intimacy with mixed marriages being quite common. Dr. Espiñosa, and many other observers, have commented upon the fact that this intimacy was "much more frequent in the first years of the American occupation." Since most of the mixed marriages of this earlier period involved Anglo-American husbands and Spanish-speaking wives, it is impossible to estimate the degree of intermixture which has taken place but it is much greater than most people imagine.

This initial *rapprochement* came to an end when the railroads penetrated the Southwest. With the appearance of the railroads, wrote Dr. Espiñosa, "there has come a check in the race fusion and the mutual contact and good feeling between the two peoples." Obviously it was the sequence of economic changes which the railroads initiated, not the railroads per se, which produced this effect. Previously the motive for dominance was largely lacking, for, in the absence of markets, a barter rather than a profit economy prevailed. In the isolation of the frontier both groups felt compelled to seek a degree of cooperation to mitigate the rigors of a harsh and unfriendly environment; on the frontier, as someone has said, "all churches look alike." While this earlier intimacy came to an end, the relationships which came out of it could never be effaced. Thus there exists in the Southwest an antecedent pattern of fusion and merger which continues to exert an influence, however imperceptible, upon present-day relationships.

It must also be remembered that the process of acculturation is somewhat different in the Southwest than elsewhere in the United States. Here we adopted the Spanish-speaking minority; they did not adopt us. It is this difference which accounts for the tenacity with which the Spanish-speaking have clung to certain aspects of their native culture. As late as 1917, Dr. Espiñosa estimated that there was not one Spanish-American family out of a hundred in

New Mexico that had entirely abandoned Spanish as the language of the home. Nowadays nine out of ten of the native-born New Mexicans speak English but Spanish is still the mother tongue for most of them. The persistence of Spanish speech, however, is due to many factors: the prevailing isolation; constant discrimination; the lack of educational facilities; the existence of segregated schools; the migratory pattern of employment, and so forth. Whatever the reasons may be, the point is that this persistence in Spanish speech has been most influential in forcing a degree of cultural fusion. To appreciate the importance of this factor all one has to do is to compare the rapidity with which the *Nisei* or native-born Japanese have abandoned or lost all familiarity with the Japanese language. Regardless of length of residence, only a small proportion of Mexicans in the United States have lost all knowledge of Spanish or have abandoned its use in the home, no matter how meager their training in the language may have been or how imperfectly they may speak it.

While Mencken and others have suggested that Southwestern Spanish is doomed to vanish, sooner or later, the facts would seem to cast grave doubts on this conclusion. This becomes more apparent when one considers the thorny issue of language instruction in the schools.

WHO IS BEING STUBBORN?

In the bundle of issues that is called "the Mexican Problem" none has occasioned more discussion and controversy than the language issue in the schools. Both the history and latter-day ramifications of this issue are most complex. Prior to 1846 the borderlands were without schools, public or private; illiteracy was the rule, literacy the exception. The first school systems were dominated, in administration and personnel, by Anglo-Americans who knew little or no Spanish. While official concessions were made to Spanish speech in New Mexico, school officials in the Southwest have always insisted upon English as the language of instruction. They still invest their position, on this issue, with an emotional halo of moral and patriotic self-righteousness. To a generation of American teachers trained in the normal schools of the period from 1890 to 1910, it seemed both heretical and disloyal, despite the guarantees of the Treaty of Guadalupe Hidalgo, to tolerate any form of bilingualism. In some areas, the issue has even been colored by religious prejudices of one kind or another. According to Dr. Ortega, Anglo teachers have actually changed the names of Spanish students, on the first day of school, to some English equivalent by way of emphasizing the "terrible handicap" that Spanish speech is supposed to be. In other cases, Hispano teachers in rural schools made up of Spanish-speaking children have used Spanish surreptitiously for fear of being called on the carpet by some irate Anglo administrator.

The natural consequence of this official attitude has been to foster a generation illiterate in both languages, for the teaching of Spanish has been as systematically neglected as instruction in English has been systematically stressed. Spanish-speaking children often come to the schools without a word of English and without the environmental experience upon which school life is based. In many cases, they are not even familiar with the concepts for which they are supposed to learn English names. The use of standard curricula, books, and instruction materials in such schools has been ludicrously inept.

Once Anglo-American teachers had "retarded" Spanish-speaking students, they sought to rationalize their incompetence as teachers by insisting on segregated schools which only aggravated the problem. Notoriously bad linguists, Anglo-American teachers have been known to show an unreasoning irritation over the mere sound of a Spanish word or phrase spoken in their presence. This irritation is often reflected in a hostile attitude toward Spanish-speaking students. Over a period of many years, I have heard Anglo-American teachers in the Southwest complain bitterly about the "stubbornness" of Mexican-American youngsters who just *will* persist in speaking Spanish on the playgrounds, etc.

Actually the language issue in the Southwest is part and parcel of a much larger set of socioeconomic issues from which it cannot be separated. It is most absurd, therefore, to attempt to isolate this issue and to regard it as a special problem which might be solved, apart from the larger issues, by the development of special teaching techniques and especially trained personnel (important as these items would be). Obviously the issue is related to bad housing, lack of nutrition, migratoriness, social disorganization, segregation, dominant group hostility, and a dozen other factors. The language problem, in short, is a community problem; a problem involving the relationship of the school to the community and of the community to the school. Today the issue is widely recognized as the major educational problem in the Southwest. Furthermore, the conclusions now being drawn are indirectly premised on the assumption that a type of cultural fusion actually exists. "The intermingling of different home languages in the Southwest," to quote from one report, "*is a relatively permanent* condition, for here the waters from two great reservoirs of language flow together, constantly renewed from sources back from the border".[8] (Emphasis added.)

In other words, the borderlands have consistently remained the borderland of the two cultures; neither has prevailed in toto and neither is likely to win a complete victory over the other. Each group has gained recruits; the number of bilinguals is steadily increasing; and the area of fusion is expanding south and, to some extent, north of the border. Dynamic factors are involved in the extension of the borderlands for experience has shown that Mexican immigrants cannot be kept out of this area. We stopped Mexican immigration but imported 180,000 Mexican workers in wartime; workers are still crossing the border illegally, as they have for years, and the number of "wetbacks" is currently estimated at around 80,000. Regardless of how it changes, the Southwest is "an ever-normal granary" so far as Mexicans are concerned.

Emphasis on the language issue as "relatively permanent" merely reveals the true cultural background of the region. There are more persons of Italian than of Mexican descent in the United States but no one has suggested that bilingual instruction is a major problem in the education of Italian-Americans.

By insisting on regarding "the Mexican Problem" as part of a familiar Americanization process, identical with European immigration, we have consistently missed the point. Failing to recognize the degree of cultural fusion which has actually occurred, we have steadily belabored the Mexican for his "stubbornness" in adhering to a culture which prevails in the very areas of the United States in which he resides. It is as though we were to accuse the Eskimos of Alaska for their "stubborn" adherence to the only culture they have ever known. In this instance, the "stubbornness" is ours in not recognizing the real character of the culture which prevails in the borderlands. . . .

"Once I had a dream," writes Dr. Ortega, "that there was in Latin America a republic in the midst of which lived an English-speaking population just as a Spanish-speaking population lives in the midst of New Mexico. If that could be made a reality, we would have the right Pan-American setup for two complementary links, and then, perhaps, the delicate problems of adjustment might be solved with a measure of equity and mutual understanding. As it is today, the Spanish-speaking population of the Southwest represents a living example of disorientation, of American political and social failure as a colonizing metropolis. . . . How are we going to bid friendship to the Latin Americans, with what face are we to talk of democracy and equality to them, what are our titles, besides those of purely material power, to aspire to be the big brothers in the Pan-American empire, if we have made within our borders a mess of the relatively simple problem of dealing with an Hispanic group? How dare we, in all fairness, to call backward the Latin American republics and blame their lot on misgovernment, when we here have not managed in nearly a century to do a better job with the same human material?" [9]

THE INDELIBLE IMPRINT

Throughout the Southwest the imprint of Spain and Mexico is indelible; not as Spanish or Mexican influence per se but as modified by contact with Indian and Anglo-American culture. The three influences are woven into nearly every aspect of the economy, the speech, the architecture, the institutions, and the customs of the people. For the people of the Southwest share a mixed cultural heritage in which the mixtures, rather than the pure strains, have survived. In a Navajo rug, an adobe house, or an irrigated farm, one may find elements of the three cultures inextricably interwoven and fused. The rug may be of Indian design, woven by Indian hands, and colored by native dyes; but the loom may be Spanish or Mexican and the wool probably came from some New Mexican's herd or it may have been purchased from an American mail-order catalogue. The rug, however, is most likely to be owned by an Anglo-American. The irrigated farm may lie within a district irrigated by water from some huge dam or reservoir built by American engineers, but the fields will be tilled by Mexicans, using a knowledge of irrigation which, in part, was acquired from Indians.

"Three types of domestic architecture," writes Ruth Laughlin, "have come down to us in their chronological order—the Pueblo, the Mexican, and the American-Spanish. They are seldom found absolutely true to type for the needs of men have overlapped since the days of the first Americans. In each we find resemblances to the others, like the faces of mothers and daughters." Where these elements have been mixed, as in the domestic architecture of New Mexico, they have attained the most enduring expression. Where the Indian element has been lacking, as in the so-called "Spanish-Colonial" architecture seen in Florida and Southern California, the fusion has been least successful. Even the public buildings of the Southwest tend more and more to derive from Indian and Spanish-Mexican sources with the Anglo-Americans showing great ingenuity in adapting these forms to modern uses. In short, this mixed heritage belongs to all the people of the Southwest; not to any one group or to the combination of any two.

Of paramount importance to the future of this culture is the role that the coming generation of Mexican Americans will play. The region has yet to experience the impact of the first articulate generation of persons of Mexican descent. In another generation, Mexican Americans will be found in all walks of life—in the arts, the professions, in the colleges and universities—and in significant numbers. In the past, Mexicans have been a more or less anonymous, voiceless, expressionless minority. There has yet to be written, for example, a novel of Southwestern experience by an American-born person of Mexican descent or a significant autobiography by a native-born Mexican. The moment the group begins to achieve this type of expression, a new chapter will be written in the history of the Southwest. For as the Spanish-speaking attain cultural maturity, as they achieve real self-expression, they will exert a profound influence on the culture of the region and Spanish-Mexican influences that have remained dormant these many years will be revived and infused with new meaning and vigor.

It is the borderlands, not the border, that is important in the Southwest. For the borderlands unite the Anglo-American and the Hispano-American worlds and the area in which this mixed culture exists is expanding north and south. As the possibilities of the Good Neighbor Policy are realized, the border will have even less meaning than it has had in the past. By simply exploring the neighboring state of Sonora, Arizona businessmen have been able to increase the total traffic through the port of Nogales from $50,000,000 in 1945–1946 to $76,000,000 in 1946–1947. Incredible as it may seem, these same Arizona businessmen had for years assumed that merchandise destined for Sonora had to be shipped to Mexico City and then rerouted north to Sonora. By investigating the situation at first hand, they discovered that trucks could transport merchandise from Arizona to any point in the province, just as the pack-trains had done two hundred years ago.

Today machinery, wire, pipe, cement, steel, farm implements, glass, crockery, paint, and plumbing fixtures are moving south across the border and Mexican minerals, shoes, fish, flax, bamboo, guano, tomatoes, chickpeas and other products are moving north. Furthermore the imbalance between imports and exports changed from $7,000,000 in favor of the United States to somewhat less than $1,000,000 in the space of one year and even this margin may soon disappear.[10]

Just as Arizona is discovering that Nogales is the logical gateway to the west coast of Mexico, so Texas is discovering that its border towns are the logical gateways to eastern Mexico. Over how large an area, therefore, is the cultural fusion of the borderlands likely to expand in the next quarter-century? As the borderlands expand, both the Anglo and the Hispano elements will receive numerical reenforcements, so that the process of cultural fusion will be repeated; in fact, it is already apparent that this process is a constant factor in the life of the borderlands. Hence it is extremely difficult to imagine any working-out of this process that would involve the complete absorption of one culture by the other.

In a sense the settlement of the United States has always moved against the grain of geography, for the east-to-west movement of the American people has been *against* the flow, the natural movement, of the landscape. In moving westward, the American people have crossed mountain ranges, crossed the plains, crossed the rivers, crossed the deserts. Yet the geographical flow of the continent is not from east to west but from north to south; our major mountain ranges run along north-south lines as do most of our great river systems. Unwittingly we have been bucking geography, not cooperating with it. With the lodestar being ever in the West, we have simply failed to change our vision and to note the natural contours of the country.

Prior to the settlement of the eastern seaboard by European colonists, the continent was orientated on a north–south, rather than an east–west, axis and it may yet be orientated in this fashion. Since the westward movement of the American people "leapfrogged" over the intermountain states to the West Coast, we have failed to let our eyes follow the natural lines and contours which run in the opposite direction. Hence it involved an abrupt turnabout when the New Mexican frontier, with its face turned anxiously east, became a part of the last American frontier, with its face turned eagerly west. Not only is the movement "North from Mexico" older in point of time than the westward movement, but it has remained constant through the years; it is continuing now and is likely to continue indefinitely.

"THE SUN HAS EXPLODED"

On July 16, 1945, a rancher went to visit his sheep camp in the San Andres Mountains in New Mexico. "As usual his sheepherders," writes Ruth Laughlin, "had started out before dawn that morning in spite of a mountain rain storm. They had not gone far when they saw a terrific flash at the other side of the eighty-mile sweep of prairie. They ran back to the sheep camp, shaken and terrified, and cried to their *patrón*, 'The sun has exploded, señor. We saw it. It was so bright that we fell on our knees and our sheep stampeded. Take us back to our families and let us go into the church. It is the end of the world.' "

When the great mushroom-like cloud of smoke and dust cleared away from the testing ground beyond Almogordo—in this first release of atomic power in world history—the isolation of New Mexico—the isolation of all men everywhere—ended once and forever. Today New Mexico is the center of American research and experimentation in the use of atomic power and the corner where the states of New Mexico, Arizona, Colorado, and Utah meet is reported to be one of the richest centers of fissionable materials in the United States. Over the radio, as I write these lines, comes word of still another mysterious plant in New Mexico which is now employing sixty-five thousand people.

The explosion at Almogordo unlocked the latent richness of the mineral resources of the Southwest. What Emerson said many years ago has now come true: "To science there is no poison; to botany no weed; to chemistry no dirt." The science that released atomic power in the Southwest can now find new uses for resources long regarded as worthless and can reclaim large portions of its arid wastes. Here, in the heart of the old Spanish borderlands, the oldest settled portion of the United States, a new world has been born and the isolation of the region has been forever destroyed. Like the peoples of the world, the peoples of the borderlands will either face the future "one and together" or they are likely to find themselves siftings on siftings in oblivion.

NOTES

1. *California*, by JOSIAH ROYCE (1897), p. 226.
2. *The Pacific Ocean in History* (1917), the chapter on "Speech Mixture in New Mexico," by AURELIO M. ESPIÑOSA.
3. *Hispania*, vol. 28, pp. 505–507.
4. From a list given me by Ruth D. Tuck; see also "The Pachuco Patois," by BEATRICE GRIFFITH, *Common Ground* (Summer 1947), pp. 77–84.
5. *Arizona Quarterly* (Summer 1946), p. 24.
6. See also, *The Story of the Cowboy*, by EMERSON HOUGH, p. 26; *Cowboy Lingo* by RAMÓN F. ADAMS, 1936.
7. *Starry Adventure*, by MARY AUSTIN, p. 62; *Coronado's Children*, by J. FRANK DOBIE, pp. 361–367; *Caballeros*, by RUTH LAUGHLIN, pp. 403–410.
8. Papers, Conference on Educational Problems in the Southwest, Santa Fe, August 19–24, 1943.
9. *The Compulsory Teaching of Spanish in the Grade Schools of New Mexico*, by JOAQUÍN ORTEGA (University of New Mexico Press, 1941), p. 9.
10. *New York Times*, August 10, 1947, article by GLADWIN HILL.

1 2 3 4 5 6 7 8 9 10